Encyclopedia of
United States
Stamps
and Stamp
Collecting

Encyclopedia of
United States
Stamps
and Stamp
Collecting

Rodney A. Juell & Steven J. Rod, Editors
United States Stamp Society

Kirk House Publishers
Minneapolis, Minnesota

Encyclopedia of United States Stamps And Stamp Collecting
Rodney A Juell & Steven J. Rod, Editors
United States Stamp Society

Library of Congress Cataloging-in-Publication data

Encyclopedia of United States stamps and stamp collecting / Rodney A. Juell & Steven J. Rod, editors.
    p. cm.
  Includes bibliographical references.
  ISBN-13: 978-1-886513-98-3
  ISBN-10: 1-886513-98-8
  1. Postage stamps--United States--Encyclopedias. 2. Stamp collecting--United States--Encyclopedias. I. Juell, Rodney A., 1948- II. Rod, Steven J., 1945- III. United States Stamp Society.
  HE6185.U5.E53 2006
  769.56973--dc22
                        2005036450

Kirk House Publishes, PO Box 390759, Minneapolis, Minnesota
Printed in China

Table of Contents

Foreword 7
Acknowledgements 9

Stamps of the United States

1. Stampless Covers 12
2. Postmasters' Provisionals 21
3. Series of 1847 27
4. Series of 1851 and 1857 34
5. Series of 1861 and 1869 Pictorials 44
6. Bank Notes of 1870-1894 57
7. Series of 1894 67
8. Series of 1902 75
9. Washington-Franklin Series 86
10. Series of 1922 98
11. Presidential Series 109
12. Liberty Series 119
13. Prominent Americans Issue 128
14. Americana Issue 140
15. Great Americans Issue 147
16. Transportation Coils 158
17. Late Twentieth Century Definitives 169
18. Nineteenth Century Commemoratives 180
19. Twentieth Century Commemoratives, 1901-1933 . . . 191
20. Twentieth Century Commemoratives, 1933-1971 . . . 203
21. Twentieth Century Commemoratives, 1971-2000 . . . 217
22. Twenty-first Century Stamps 230
23. Air Mail Stamps 238
24. Special Usage Stamps 250
25. Federal Revenue Stamps 263
26. State Revenues 279
27. U.S. Possessions, Usages Abroad, and Occupied Areas 284
28. Postal Stationery 296
29. Precancels and Perfins 308
30. Carriers' and Locals 322
31. Confederate States of America 331

History, Production, and Technology

32. United States Post Office Department 340
33. United States Postal Service 351
34. Bureau of Engraving and Printing 361
35. Stamp Production – The Flat Plate Press 371
36. Stamp Production – The Stickney Rotary Press 377
37. Stamp Production – Modern Presses 383
38. Stamp Production – Modern Private Printers 396
39. Stamp Separation, 1857-1980 405
40. Stamp Separation, Since 1980 415
41. Self-Adhesive Stamps 422
42. Watermarks 431
43. Plate Construction and Layout 436
44. Plate Numbers 445
45. Marginal Markings 457
46. Plate Varieties 477
47. Stamps in Booklets, 1900-1977 485
48. Stamps in Booklets, Since 1977 497
49. Stamps in Coil Rolls, 1907-1980 509
50. Stamps in Coil Rolls, Post 1980 521
51. Inks, Colors, Papers, and Gums 530
52. Errors, Freaks, and Oddities 543
53. Essays and Proofs 553
54. Luminescence 564
55. Test Stamps 572

Expanding the Collector's Scope

56. United States Stamp Society 582
57. United States Stamp Research 588
58. Postal History – Markings 596
59. Rates and Classifications 608
60. First Day Covers 624
61. Meters and Machine Generated Postage 636
62. Philately Never Ends 648

Appendices

Appendix A – Glossary 656
Appendix B – Print Resources 709
Appendix C – Internet Resources 727
Appendix D – Benefactors 728

Foreword

Welcome to a book dedicated to all who enjoy collecting United States (U.S.) stamps and designed for all who want to explore this wonderful hobby.

In 1847 the United States Post Office issued its first postage stamps to facilitate the prepayment of postage. Almost from the beginning citizens everywhere found these attractive little pieces of paper to be wonderful collectibles, and a new hobby was born. Men, women, and children in every ensuing generation have found pleasure in collecting and studying U.S. stamps.

There is a superb body of highly specialized literature available on various aspects of stamp colleting. There is no resource, however, that encompasses all of the many facets of U.S. stamp collecting. This book fills that void.

Collecting U.S. stamps involves one in history, politics, production and technology, design, searches and detective work, and discovery. The collector learns about culture and institutions, geography and the arts, and many people whose visions shaped our country. As you look at the Table of Contents you will see the broad range of U.S. stamps covered in this book. You will also note chapters devoted to history, production, technology, and research that will help make you a more informed collector.

Each chapter employs a similar format, beginning with an introductory text providing an overview. Stamps and covers may be illustrated in other than actual size. Occasional "side-bars", in tan shaded boxes, explore some aspect of the story. The introductory text is followed by "Notes on Collecting" which contains advice on collecting the stamps or subject matter under consideration. Next is the "Almanac" which provides a chronological reference for the topic. Following this is "What Others Have Said", which presents the topic the way others have seen and understood it in the past, while also providing a sampling of the vast array of literature available to the serious U.S. stamp collector. Attribution of these quotes is abbreviated. The full reference for each is found in Appendix B – Print Resources. Next will generally be provided some examples of typical usage of this material. The majority of items illustrated are easily obtainable from a stamp dealer or local *bourse*. Finally, "Where to Find More Information" suggests resources for further study. Full citations for these sources appear in Appendix B – Print Resources. Many of these are available from dealers in philatelic literature. All should be available at a good philatelic library, of which the leading one is the American Philatelic Research Library (APRL) in Bellefonte, Pennsylvania (www.stamplibrary.org/thelibrary/lib_abouttheaprl.htm). APRL offers a photocopy service.

For collectors new to the hobby, this book is an introduction to the many aspects of U.S. stamp collecting. For the experienced collector, many of the chapters may incite curiosity about a previously unexplored facet of the hobby. For all readers, we trust this book will educate, entertain, and inspire you as a U.S. *philatelist*.

One of the great joys of collecting stamps is that there is no "right" or "wrong". Everyone has the freedom to collect what they want and in the manner they choose. Enjoy yourself! However most collectors would agree that the hobby is most fully appreciated by those who participate at some level in organized philately. Join a local stamp club. Attend shows, locally, regionally, or even nationally. Join the American Philatelic Society (www.stamps.org) and those societies that focus on your area of interest. We particularly recommend membership in the United States Stamp Society (www.usstamps.org), under whose auspices this book is published. Society membership will help sustain your enjoyment of our hobby and offer you the opportunity to be on the cutting edge of U.S. stamp collecting.

NOTES:

There are several valuable resources for U.S. stamp collectors that relate to most chapters in this book, and are recommended for the library of every collector. Rather than identify them repeatedly throughout the book, they are listed here:

- *Scott Specialized Catalogue of United States Stamps & Covers.*
- *Durland Standard Plate Number Catalog.*
- *U.S. Domestic Postal Rates, 1872–1999* and *U.S. International Postal Rates, 1872-1996*, both by Henry W. Beecher and Anthony S. Wawrukiewicz. Updates to these books are available at www.spiritone.com/~tonywaw/Updated_Rates.html.
- *Linn's World Stamp Almanac*, while not limited to U.S. stamps, contains extensive information on U.S. stamps, stamp production, postal rates, and other topics of interest to the U.S. collector.
- *Fundamentals of Philately*, by L.N. Williams, while not limited to U.S. stamps, supplements much of the information on production and technology that is presented in this book.

Appendix A, a glossary, defines terms with which the reader may not be familiar. Selected terms throughout this work appear in **this typeface**, indicating they appear in the glossary.

Unless otherwise indicated, all numbers in parentheses are references to the numbers used in the *Scott Specialized Catalogue of United States Stamps & Covers*. For the sake of brevity, all references to this *Catalogue* will simply be *Scott*. Since *Scott* numbers occasionally change on the basis of new information, it is suggested that the reader refer to the latest edition.

Rodney A. Juell
Steven J. Rod
May 27, 2006
Washington, D.C.

Acknowledgements

This book exists because of the contributions of many people, including some of the most knowledgeable and respected philatelists on the contemporary American scene.

The Recruiting Committee of the United States Stamp Society recognized the need for this work and the Board of Governors of the United States Stamp Society encouraged and supported its publication. Co-editors Rodney A. Juell and Steven J. Rod brought their diverse gifts and perspectives to the work and in the process became close friends and trusted colleagues.

No chapter in this book is the exclusive work of any one individual. Most have involved six or more people in various ways. Nevertheless, while the editors take full and sole responsibility for any errors, most chapters have one or two primary contributors. They are: Lynn Batdorf (Twentieth Century Commemoratives, 1933-71; Twentieth Century Commemoratives, 1971-2000; and Twenty-first Century Stamps), Steven Belasco (Stamps in Coil Rolls, 1907-1980), Roger Brody (Series of 1902; Prominent Americans; and Precancels and Perfins), Rick Burdsall (Plate Numbers), Paul Bourke (Washington-Franklins), Wallace Cleland (Special Usage Stamps), Doug D'Avino (Late Twentieth Century Definitives; and Marginal Markings), David Eeles (Stamp Production – Modern Presses; and Stamp Production – Modern Private Printers), E.J. Guerrant (United States Stamp Research), Bob Hohertz (Federal Revenue Stamps), John Hotchner (Stamp Separation, 1857-1980; and Errors, Freaks, and Oddities), Rodney A. Juell (Postmasters' Provisionals; Series of 1922; Twentieth Century Commemoratives, 1901-1933; U.S. Possessions, Usages Abroad, and Occupied Areas; Confederate States of America; United States Postal Service; Bureau of Engraving and Printing; and Plate Varieties), Eliot Landau (Series of 1861 and 1869 Pictorials; Bank Notes of 1870-1894; and Inks, Colors, Papers and Gum), Nicholas Lombardi (Self-Adhesive Stamps), Peter Martin (The United States Stamp Society), Jim Milgram (Stampless Covers), Harvey Mirsky (Series of 1847), Thomas Myers (Transportation Coils), Ralph Nafziger (First Day Covers), Gerald Nylander (Stamp Production – The Flat Plate Press), Gene Paquette (Luminescence), James Patterson (Essays and Proofs), Michael Perry (Stamps in Booklets, 1900-1977; and Stamps in Booklets, Since 1977), Stephen Reinhard (Air Mail Stamps), Louis Repeta (Stamp Production – The Stickney Rotary Press; and Watermarks), Steven J. Rod (Liberty Series; Nineteenth Century Commemoratives; United States Post Office Department; and Meters and Machine Generated Postage), Jeff Shapiro (Presidential Series; and Americana Issue), Rick Smith (Plate Construction and Layout), Thomas Stillman (Carriers' and Locals), Jay Stotts (Great Americans Issue; and Rates and Classifications),

Bob Trachimowicz (Postal History – Markings), Herb Trenchard (Philately Never Ends), Gene Trinks (Stamps in Coil Rolls, Post 1980), Dan Undersander (Postal Stationery; and Test Stamps), Albert Valente (Series of 1851 and 1857), Kent Wilson (Series of 1894), and Wayne Youngblood (Stamp Separation, Since 1980; and Stamps in Coil Rolls, 1907-1980). Many of these primary contributors also served as consultants and reviewers for chapters other than their own.

In addition to those primary contributors to various chapters, a number of individuals have served important secondary roles critiquing various chapters, answering editors' questions and supplying illustrations: Peter H. Adams, Nicholas Baker, Larry Ballantyne, Jay Bigalke, Ronald Blanks, John D. Bowman, Jim Callis, John Denune, Jr., Joseph Dow, Thomas Glavin, Chip Gliedman, Ken Hall, Eric Jackson, Kim Johnson, Joann Lenz, James Lee, Larry Lyons, Tom Mazza, R.C. de Mordaigle, Joe Napp, Gerry Nylander, Stanley Piller, Charles Posner, Dilmond Postlewait, Bob Rabinowitz, Robert G. Rose, Jack Schiff, Arnold Selengut, K. David Steidley, Bob Szymanski, Donald Thompson, Alan Thomson, Don Tocher, Ed Waterous, and Larry Weiss. Illustrations have been supplied by the family of siderographer Andrew Black, the National Postal Museum, the Department of the Treasury, Bureau of Engraving and Printing, and Bill McAllister of Linn's Stamp News.

To Lynn Batdorf goes a special word of thanks for his superb and meticulous proofreading and compilation of the Print Resources. Doug D'Avino has assisted with additional critical proofreading and with successful fund raising. Both Lynn and Doug are to be thanked for all their efforts, including joining the editors at a memorable, four-day long, cover-to-cover review of the final manuscript. Max Zollner helped verify the accuracy of *Scott* numbers.

All of the above named individuals served without compensation, for the good of the hobby.

To Leonard Flachman of Kirk House Publishers in Minneapolis goes a word of thanks for his wise and patient counsel in producing this book.

Finally the editors wish to thank their wives, Diane Juell and Fran Rod, for their extraordinary patience the past four years while countless hours, often at their expense, have been devoted to this book.

Stamps of the United States

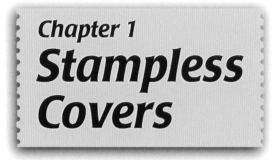

Chapter 1
Stampless Covers

Long before there were U.S. postage stamps, letters were carried via the mail system. Since colonial times, covers have legitimately moved through the mails without bearing stamps. Such "stampless" covers, as they are called, fall into three broad categories.

The first is covers from the time before the introduction of postage stamps on July 1, 1847 (fig. 1). The second is covers from the period during which postage stamps were available, but their use was not obligatory, July 1, 1847 to January 1, 1856. The third is stampless covers from later time periods, legitimately not bearing stamps, even though postage stamps were required on most contemporaneous mail. Stampless covers are collected for their fascinating and diverse array of *postal markings*, and as artifacts of postal, and sometimes political and cultural history.

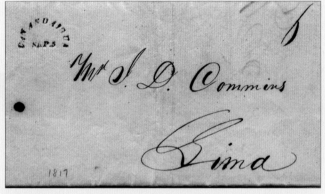

Figure 1

This unpaid 1817 cover bears a handstamped "Canandaigua (New York) Sep. 5" postmark and a manuscript rate of "6," indicating that the letter was carried only a short distance.

Stampless Covers prior to July 1, 1847

Before the introduction of envelopes in the 1840s, a typical letter writer would use one or two sheets of paper, generally smaller than the standard 8½ x 11 inch paper of today. The letter was folded in such a way as to conceal the writing, while leaving an exposed surface blank. After the name and town of the addressee were written on the exposed surface, the letter was sealed closed with a wax wafer or drop of wax from a stick of sealing wax. Most paper was cream in color. Shades of blue were also common, particularly in the first half of the nineteenth century. White paper was unusual.

During colonial times mail moved regularly across the Atlantic Ocean between the various colonies and Great Britain. Ship captains carried much of it privately. Lesser amounts of mail moved between and within the colonies. Many letters were carried by hand and show no postal markings because they never entered a postal service. There were also official dispatches carried by paid express riders. In the late seventeenth century a postal system gradually evolved which placed various postal markings on letters (ch. 58). Formal contracts were given to carry the mail on a regular schedule and a series of **post roads** was designated for mail carriers.

Letters to be mailed were taken to a post office. There were no post boxes on the corner. Also, the vast majority of letters had to be picked up at the post office. Except for the few times and places where **carrier** service was available for an extra fee, there was no home delivery. Post offices were often located in buildings that housed other businesses that were the primary source of income for the postmaster. Only in the largest cities were special post office buildings erected.

Several markings could be placed on a letter. One was the postal rate. The earliest ones were hand written in manuscript. Then, **handstamp** and inkpad came into use by 1789. Handstamped rate markings came into widespread use by the 1830s. Postal rates were determined both by the distance a letter was carried and by the number of sheets of paper. For example, a single sheet letter mailed from Boston to New York in 1710 was rated at 1 shilling. The postage rate on a similar letter from Boston to Connecticut, a lesser distance, was 9 pence. If the letter contained two sheets of paper, the rate doubled.

Another marking, **PAID**, was applied if postage was prepaid – an unusual occurrence. Both manuscript and handstamped paid markings were used. The first known paid handstamp occurred in 1673. While strange to a postal patron today, the vast majority of letters were sent postage due, not prepaid. Postal rates were high and mail service was uncertain. Therefore most people did not want to pay for a postal service until it had been completed.

Another marking indicated the site of origin of the letter. Known as **postmarks**, the earliest ones were handwritten (manuscript). Later the use of a handstamp became more common, especially in larger towns. A New York town handstamp, used in 1710, is the earliest known. Special dating handstamps, which did not include the year, were used in a few locations.

During the Revolutionary War, British forces controlled a number of major American cities. Letters were postmarked similar to the early colonial period whether a post office was in the hands of loyalists or patriots. Ratings in pennyweights (0.05 troy ounce) of silver, hard currency, and paper equivalents were frequently written on letters. The lack of hard currency during the war usually meant that the postal charges were paid in paper money. The period of the American Revolution and the subsequent years under the Articles of Confederation were characterized by complex and frequently changing postal rates. There were short periods with very high rates due to inflation. In 1788 Congress attempted to stabilize a series of lower rates by calculating all rates in pennyweights and grains of silver. Handstamped postmarks were often used in the larger post offices and manuscript postmarks in smaller ones. Handstamped postmarking devices with the town of origin are divided into four categories, based on the configuration of the lettering. The four categories are: Straight lines, Arcs, Ovals, and **Circular Date Stamp**.

Collectors categorize handstamp markings by type fonts, punctuation marking, number of lines of type, special decorations in the letterings or between letters, and by any type of frame around the entire marking, such as a rectangular frame for a straight line marking.

The U.S. Constitution was ratified in 1787, initiating what has been called the "statehood" period of stampless covers. The Act of February 20, 1792, effective June 1, 1792, established nine separate rates for single-page letters, based on the distance carried. These rates ranged from 6¢ for not over 30 miles, up to 25¢ for over 450 miles. Newspapers paid a lower rate, but few showing postal rates have survived. In 1794 a special rate for a **drop letter** was enacted. **Ship letters** were charged a fee in addition to the regular postage.

Rates changed in 1799, but were still based on distance and the number of sheets of paper. Rates were increased by 50% in 1815, following the War of 1812. Those increases were repealed in 1816. The rates set in 1816 were very similar to the rates of 1799, and continued in effect, essentially unchanged, until the postal reform of 1845.

Proponents of lower postage rates within the United States were victorious in 1845 when rates were simplified and reduced. Half-ounce letters carried less than 300 miles were charged 5¢, and those carried over 300 miles were charged 10¢. There was a 2¢ rate for drop letters and single sheet circulars (printed matter). Over the next several years some other rates were established, such as a 40¢ rate to the Pacific Coast. However, with fewer rates in effect, more and more postmasters obtained and used handstamps to indicate a letter's rate.

One effect of reduced postage rates in 1845 was the widespread use of envelopes. Prior to July 1, 1845 an envelope had counted as a sheet of paper, dramatically increasing the cost of sending a letter.

July 1, 1847 to December 31, 1855 – Stampless Covers of the Transitional Period

The United States Post Office began selling stamps on July 1, 1847. However their use was not required for the prepayment of postage until January 1, 1856. Many postal patrons did not use stamps during this "transitional" period, preferring to send their mail in the traditional "postage due" manner (fig. 2). Postage due mail was labor intensive for the Post Office. To encourage prepayment, rates on prepaid mail were reduced on July 1, 1851 to 3¢ for letters carried up to 3,000 miles, and to 6¢ for letters going over 3,000 miles. The rates on letters not prepaid were 5¢ for up to 3,000 miles and 10¢ for over 3,000 miles. However, even when mail was prepaid, it was not necessarily prepaid with stamps! There are many stampless covers bearing "PAID 3" handstamps from the transitional period, suggesting that while stamps were used on some paid mail, much of it was still stampless. Finally, on April 1, 1855, late in the transitional period, the Post Office required the prepayment of postage, although the use of stamps for prepayment was still optional.

Figure 2

Stamps were available, but their use was not required, when this unpaid cover was used during the transitional period. With a "5" rate marking, and handstamped "CHESTERVIL-LAGE MS. 17 JUNE" (1851), it traveled under 300 miles, and 5¢ was collected from the recipient.

The reduction in postage rates for prepaid letters, and the subsequent requirement for prepayment of postage, were incentives to the public to use stamps. Another incentive was the availability of postal boxes, into which letters prepaid by stamps could be dropped, avoiding the use of the post office window. These boxes came into use during the transitional period. However, after the end of 1855 postal patrons no longer had a choice. Beginning January 1, 1856, the use of stamps became obligatory, ending the transitional period of stampless covers.

As the United States expanded westward, new lands were organized as territories prior to their admission as states. The earliest markings were often in manuscript, or some other primitive style, using local printer's typeface. Postal rates in effect in the territories were the same as those used in established states.

Stampless Covers from Latter Time Periods

There are several sub-categories of stampless covers from 1856 into the twenty-first century. One is the *free frank* letter, sent with a signature rather than postage (fig. 3). The American Continental Congress adopted the practice in 1775 and the First Congress wrote it into law in 1789. Over the years the privilege of sending mail free of postage has been extended to, and withdrawn from, various individuals including government officials and military personnel. Occasionally the free franking privilege even applied to mail sent to the qualified person. A qualified person generally exercised the free franking privilege by signing his or her name, generally in the upper right corner of the envelope or folded letter.

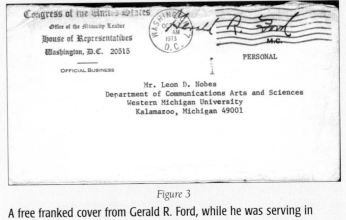

Figure 3

A free franked cover from Gerald R. Ford, while he was serving in Congress, before he became president.

A significant amount of mail that was not official business of the government was sent in free franked letters. Some postmasters were notorious abusers of their free frank, some even applying their frank to the correspondence of other individuals. After the Civil War this abuse was largely corrected and the use of the free frank was restricted to official business. One of the most challenging and exciting free frank collections is that of Presidential free franks – covers signed by U.S. Presidents.

Another sub-category is soldiers' mail (fig. 4). During the Civil War, Congress allowed soldiers' mail, with certification on the face of the envelope by an officer, to be sent postage due. During subsequent wars, through to the twenty-first century, soldiers on active duty have sent mail without postage by writing either "Soldiers' Mail" or "*Free*" in the top right corner. One of the many valuable accomplishments of the **Universal Postal Union** was the unobstructed passage of such mail between combatants, though the implementation of this system has not always worked smoothly.

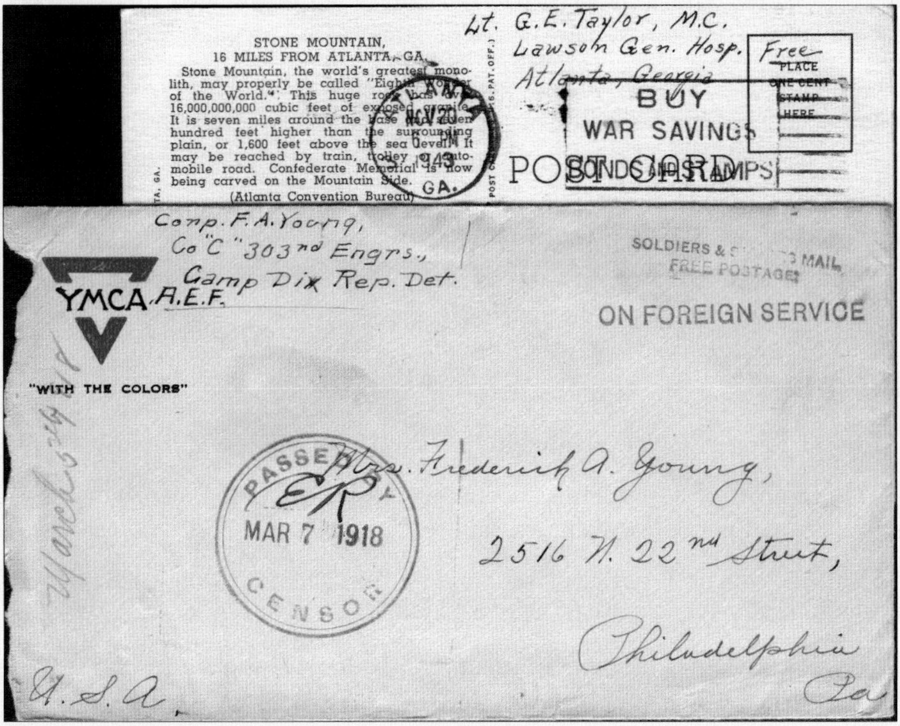

Figure 4

A free franked World War II postcard mailed in 1943 by a Marine Corp lieutenant (note "Free" written where the stamp would normally be placed, and the machine cancellation, "BUY WAR SAVINGS BONDS AND STAMPS"), behind a 1918 letter from a member of the American Expeditionary Force. Note the YMCA supplied envelope, and the markings, "SOLDIERS & SAILORS MAIL / FREE POSTAGE" and "ON FOREIGN SERVICE".

A large number of stampless covers originated in the Confederate States of America (ch. 31). Handstamped paid markings were used in many Confederate cities and towns when no Confederate stamps were available.

Notes on Collecting

The many varieties of stampless covers from the American colonial period are listed with great care in the *American Stampless Cover Catalog*. While many of these covers are expensive, it is possible to acquire other covers, and to build an attractive collection, at a reasonable price.

The unpaid rate (postage due) for up to 3,000 miles was 5¢, effective July 1, 1851. However, unless the year date of a cover can be established, it is not always possible to differentiate between a letter send unpaid after July 1, 1851, and ones sent prior to that date, when the rate was 5¢, prepaid or postage due.

There are thousands of Presidential and Congressional free franks to be collected. Some Presidential free franks are out of reach of most collectors, but the vast majority of free franks of other government officials are obtainable at modest cost.

Free franks from World War I are both difficult to find, and vary in value. World War II and subsequent war zone free frankings are commonly available. Covers with an unusual destination or usage, unusual postal markings, or a famous sender or addressee are more valuable.

Almanac

1673 – The first known postal marking is applied to a letter on January 22.

1847 – The first postage stamps are issued on July 1, marking the beginning of the transitional period for stampless letters.

1855 – Prepayment of postage is required on April 1, though not necessarily with stamps.

1856 – Use of stamps becomes obligatory on January 1, and the transitional period ends.

What Others Have Said

The First Postmarks
"What we call postmarks were invented by Henry Bishop, an Englishman, who headed the London General Post Office in 1660....there were no town names in the markings, merely a small circle divided into two compartments with a diameter line, in the upper part which was the abbreviated month and below the date of the month. When Benjamin Franklin became the American Colonial Postmaster for the English Crown, he adopted the prevailing English type of markings, but omitted the dividing line between the month and the date."

—*Harry M. Konwiser, "'Way' Postal Markings," The United States Specialist, 1935.*

The transition period provides many opportunities
"The Act of March 3, 1855 (effective April 1, 1855) made prepayment of most domestic postage compulsory, and the following rates were established per $\frac{1}{2}$ ounce: Not over 3,000 mile, 3¢; over 3,000 miles, 10¢. The same Act contained the following provision: 'From and after January 1, 1856, the Postmaster General may require postmasters to place postage stamps upon all prepaid letters upon which stamps may not have been placed by the writers.' It might be thought

that this provision would mark the end of stampless covers....but it should be remembered that compulsory prepayment by means of postage stamps did not then apply to local drop letters, circulars or foreign mail generally."

—*Clarence Hennan, "Stampless Covers of Chicago,"* Stamps Magazine, 1943.

Stampless covers with the word "Railroad" written on them

"The first railway transportation of mail occurred in 1834 when the stage contractor for the New York to Albany mail subcontracted mail to the Camden and Amboy R.R....On July 7, 1838, Congress designated every railroad then existing and also those to be constructed as postal routes... The earliest postmarks were both manuscript and handstamped 'Railroad' in several styles. Fortunately for collectors, many of these are fairly common, and thus these very historical postmarks are quite inexpensive."

—*James W. Milgram, "Early Railway Postmarks,"* The United States Specialist, 1972.

The origins of Congressional and Presidential Free Franks

"On December 28, 1779, Congress extended [free] franking [privileges] to the Commander-in-Chief and other army personnel and to the Departments of War, Finance and Foreign Affairs. On March 11, 1782, an ordinance repealed all franking except for those Members of Congress in attendance [many stayed away], the Commander-in-Chief, commanders of separate armies, but only for official mail on public service. The October 18, 1782 Act set the norm for distinguishing between legislative mail, unhindered as to content, concerned only with weight...and Executive Department franks, mail that must be official, not personal in nature."

—*Tom Clarke, "Free Franks and Official Mail,"* La Posta: A Journal of American Postal History, 1996.

Free Mailing Privilege for Operation Desert Shield

"...free mailing privileges have been extended to all military personnel on active duty assigned to Operation Desert Shield....Military personnel authorized this privilege may use it to mail only letters, postcards, and video and sound recordings, having the character of personal correspondence to delivery addresses served by United States post offices....The address side of the mailpiece must have the word Free written in the handwriting of the sender in the upper right corner, and the sender's name, grade and complete military address in the upper left corner. Free mail sent under this privilege will be treated as First-Class matter for purposes of processing..."

—*"Free Mail Privilege for Operation Desert Shield,"* United States Postal Service Postal Bulletin, 1990.

Examples of Postal Usage

Figure 5

A Colonial era stampless cover with manuscript markings. The marking in the lower left indicates Captain Hulme QDC (whom God may preserve) carried the letter from London on the tenth of Nov. 1767. Upon arrival in Boston he carried the letter to the post office were it was marked "Bostn 2:16," which is both a town marking and postal rate in silver. Note that, as customary, the address only gives the town of destination, not a street address.

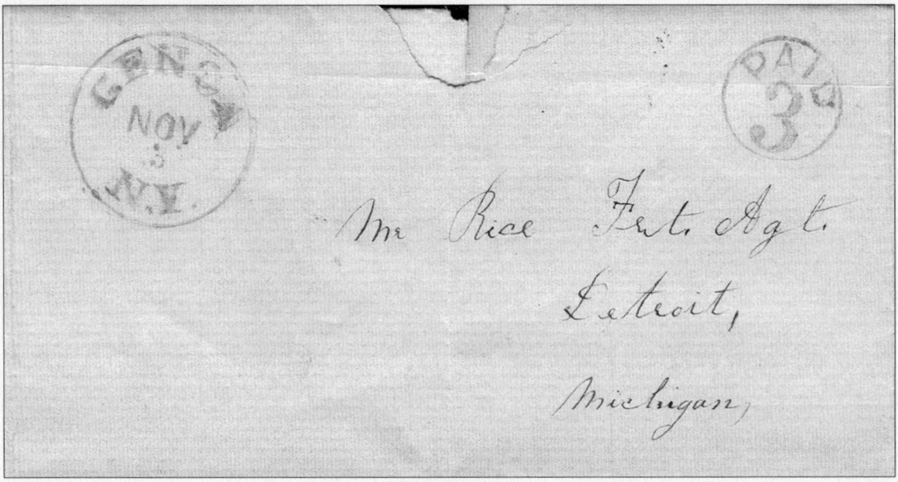

Figure 6

The sender of this 1851 cover paid the 3¢ postage in cash, as evidenced by the circular "PAID/3" handstamp. Had this letter been sent unpaid, the postage due would have been 5¢.

Where to Find More Information

- *The American Stampless Cover Catalog* is the essential reference for stampless covers. It consists of three volumes, though Volume I, edited by David G. Phillips, will meet the needs of all but highly specialized collectors.

- *History of the "Free Franking" of Mail in the United States* by Edward Stern treats stampless covers sent postage free.

Chapter 2
Postmasters' Provisionals

A "provisional" is a stamp produced as an interim (temporary) measure to meet an immediate need. For a brief period in the 1840s the postmasters in some cities and towns felt an "immediate need." As a result of that need they issued the stamps and stamped envelopes known today as "Postmasters' Provisionals." These provisionals constitute the very first listing in *Scott*, where they are listed with an "X" (for the stamps) or a "XU" (for the envelopes) prefix in their catalogue number. Provisionals were also issued in the Confederacy during the Civil War (ch. 31).

The "immediate need" felt by at least eleven postmasters resulted from the Congressional Act of March 3, 1845. This Act both reduced and simplified the postage rates that had previously been in effect. Beginning July 1, 1845, a letter could be mailed up to 300 miles for 5¢ per half ounce. For distances over 300 miles the rate was 10¢ per half ounce.

It would not be until two years later, on July 1, 1847, that the first regular postage stamps would be issued by the U.S. Post Office. During this two-year window of opportunity, provisionals were issued by the postmasters of Alexandria, Va., Annapolis, Md., Baltimore, Md., Boscawen, N.H., Brattleboro, Vt., Lockport, N.Y., Millbury, Mass., New Haven, Conn., New York, N.Y., Providence, R.I., and St. Louis, Mo. Although the provisionals were intended only for use in the cities where issued, we know that the postmaster of New York sent some of his provisional stamps to other post offices, and that some were used on letters sent to New York City.

The list of cities issuing Postmasters' Provisionals is striking in at least two ways. Only one city on the list (St. Louis) was not in an eastern state, and the issuing postmasters came both from large cities and small towns. These postmasters went

Figure 1

This New York City provisional (9X1) carries the manuscript initials "ACM". Initials were placed on stamps in New York as a control mark before being sold to the public or passing through the mails.

to the effort of issuing provisionals in part because they expedited mail handling, but also because prepaid mail increased the revenue of a post office, which had a direct and positive impact on the postmaster's salary!

Two of the postmasters (Annapolis and New Haven) issued only stamped envelopes. The postmaster at New Haven, Edward A. Mitchell, signed each of the envelopes sold there. The postmaster at Baltimore issued both envelopes and stamps. This Baltimore postmaster, James M. Buchanan (not to be confused with the then Secretary of State and future president), earned himself name recognition among future philatelists by conspicuously placing his signature on the stamps and envelopes he issued.

Postmasters in the remaining cities issued only stamps

All of the cities that issued provisional stamps issued a 5¢ denomination. Baltimore, Providence and St. Louis issued 10¢ provisionals as well. St. Louis alone issued 20¢ provisionals. Since most of the mail leaving St. Louis went to destinations further than 300 miles away, St. Louis no doubt had a greater need for 10¢ and 20¢ stamps than the other cities ever experienced.

Designs on provisionals vary greatly. Postmaster Buchanan in Baltimore used his signature. The Brattleboro postmaster, Frederick N. Palmer, used his initials. A portrait of George Washington appears on the provisionals from New York (fig. 1) and Millbury. The striking St. Louis provisionals depict the Missouri Coat of Arms. The two bears in that coat of arms gave rise to the nickname "Bears" for these provisionals.

Figure 2

A sheet of 12 Providence provisionals. A number of these sheets were discovered in Providence some years after they became invalid for use. An unused Providence provisional (10X1), is the most affordable of the Postmasters' Provisionals.

Some of the provisional stamps were produced from printing plates. The largest plate, with forty subjects, was used by the firm of Rawdon, Wright and Hatch to print the New York stamps for Postmaster Robert H. Morris. (This was the same firm that would print the first regular postage stamps of 1847.) Other cities used smaller plates. The Providence provisional stamps came from a plate of 12 subjects that would print eleven 5¢ stamps and one 10¢ stamp (fig. 2). Baltimore also used a single plate of 12 subjects to print its two different denominations. The three denominations of the Saint Louis provisionals were also all printed from a single plate, a plate with six subjects, but the quantity of each denomination on the plate was changed several times in order to meet real or anticipated needs. Brattleboro printed from a plate of ten subjects. Stamps from Boscawen, Lockport, and Millbury seem to have been printed one at a time. Since there are two known varieties of the Alexandria provisional, they may have been printed two at a time.

Postmaster Morris personally initialed some of the first stamps from his New York office, but soon turned that responsibility over to his clerks, who initialed most of the remaining stamps with their own initials.

Provisional stamps and envelopes became invalid on July 1, 1847; their retirement brought about by the issuance of the first regular U.S. postage stamps (ch.3).

Notes on Collecting

As a group, provisionals are among the rarest and most valuable stamps listed in *Scott*. Listings begin at a few hundred dollars, rising to hundreds of thousands of dollars.

Since few collectors can afford to collect Postmasters' Provisionals, a less expensive alternative is to collect stampless covers (ch. 1) postmarked from these cities during the two-year peri-od 1845-1847 that provi-sionals were doing their postal duty (fig. 3). It is at least possible to obtain some of the same post-marks used on provision-als, if not the provisionals themselves!

The New York provision-als offer the most material to the postal historian. Most existing covers come from New York, and there are more recorded covers to Europe from New York than from all the other cities combined.

Figure 3

Here is a "poor-man's" alternative to the very rare Alexandria provisional. This modestly priced folded letter was postmarked from Alexandria while the provisionals were current, on April 19, 1847. It has "10" and "PAID" markings. Notice the "DC" in the circular date stamp. Alexandria was a part of the District of Columbia in 1847, and only later transferred to Virginia.

Some Postmasters' Provisionals, or "primitives" as they are sometimes called, were unknown to stamp collectors until some years after they were issued. For example, the Alexandria provisional went unrecognized among stamp collectors until 1872 when John K. Tiffany, a prominent collector, found one.

Paper varieties are known on the provisional stamps of Alexandria, Baltimore, New York and St. Louis. The provisional envelopes from Baltimore exist on various papers, causing some to suggest that customers furnished their own envelopes, which were stamped with the requested rate by the postal clerk.

Unused provisionals are rarely found except from Providence. A number of remainder sheets of Providence provisionals were found in the 1850s, and probably most unused provisionals in existence today come from this supply.

The devices from which provisionals were made were sometimes placed to questionable use in the years after 1847. Cut square reprints of the New Haven provisional were made on several occasions, the original die having remained in the possession of Postmaster Mitchell and his family. The last New Haven reprint was made in 1932, at which time the plate was defaced to prevent further reprints. Reprints of the New York provisional were made, around 1862, under obscure and contrived circumstances. They will not bear a set of initials – unless forged. Providence provisionals were reprinted in 1898, but can be distinguished from the originals by the letters printed on their backs.

Almanac

1845 – The March 3 establishment of uniform postage rates, to become effective on July 1, opens the opportunity for local postmasters to issue their own provisional stamps.

1845 – U.S. domestic postage rates are reduced on July 1 to 5¢ per ½ ounce for letters traveling up to 300 miles; 10¢ per ½ ounce for letters traveling beyond 300 miles.

1847 – Postmasters' Provisionals become obsolete on July 1 when the first regular postage stamps are issued.

What Others Have Said

Postmasters' Provisionals seen as a "test"
"The government did not issue stamps until 1847, but the Postmaster-General, and the department, are said to have observed this operation with keen interest, as an experiment to test the practicability of the use of postage stamps throughout the United States. There is little doubt that the issue of this New York

stamp, and its successful use, greatly influenced the subsequent issue of adhesive stamps by the Post Office Department."

—*George B. Sloane, "New York Postmaster's Stamp Used from Washington,"* Sloane's Column, 1945.

The Day of Philatelic Finds is Not Over

"…a find made recently at Ogdensburg, N.Y. – a dozen, including a block of nine, of the 5¢ New York Postmaster's stamp. The block, according to Gordon Harmer, of Harmer, Rooke and Company, New York…is the largest used multiple piece of the 5¢ New York known to experts. The cover was found in a correspondence that also included three other covers, each bearing a pair of the 5¢ New York. The stamps bear the magenta "ACM" initials of Alonzo Castle Monson, and are also pen-cancelled. Postal markings are a curved red "PAID" a circular red "NEW YORK" dated town mark and a manuscript "60"."

—*"The Day of Philatelic 'Finds' is Not Over,"* The American Philatelist, 1952.

The Fear of Counterfeiting

"Postmaster Morris…shared the general fear of counterfeiting that helped delete authorization of postage stamps from the Act of March 3, 1845, which reduced postal rates to a basic 5¢. This is shown in his July 14 New York Express advertisement announcing his having caused the stamp to be prepared, viz: 'To prevent counterfeits they will be sold only at this office and the branch office." And after the stamps were printed they were sold after being initialed in red ink as a further effort to avoid counterfeiting."

—*Clarence W. Brazer, "New York Postmaster's Miniature Plate of Nine,"* Twentieth American Philatelic Congress Book, 1954.

New York's Postmaster Robert Morris takes the lead

"The Postmaster General initially considered issuing adhesives on his own authority but decided against it. Meanwhile, Robert Morris, Postmaster of New York City decided to issue his own adhesives….Morris' decision to issue his own adhesives was a definite gamble, but a worthwhile one. The new postal law took effect on July 1, 1845. It was Morris' intention to issue his stamps concurrently with this date but their appearance was delayed. Some accounts place the issuance of Morris' stamp on July 14 but the best available information appears to indicate July 15 was the first day of issue. With little fanfare the stamp was put on public sale. Its appearance marked another milestone for adherents of postal reform and foreshadowed a new era to come."

—*Steven Rosen, "The Events Leading Up to the Postmaster Provisionals,"* The United States Specialist, 1979.

Collectors Bullish on St. Louis Bears

"The Matthew Bennett International auction of the Margie Faiman collection of St. Louis Bears postmaster's provisional stamps realized a remarkable 30 percent more than presale estimates. The…sale featured 102 lots of the postmaster's provisional stamps known to collectors as the St. Louis Bears….The stamps get their name from the design chosen by St. Louis Postmaster John H. Wimer that shows the Great Seal of the State of Missouri flanked by two bears. The highlight of the auction was the triple-rate folded letter sent to Charnley & Whelen of Philadelphia, and bearing the unique se-tenant pair of the 20¢ and 10¢ stamps, Scott 11X6 and 11X5…hammered down for $176,000."

—*Rick Miller, "Collectors Bullish on Faiman's St. Louis Bears; Many Lots Hit Record Multiples of Catalog Value," Linn's Stamp News, 2003.*

Example of Postal Usage

Figure 4

This 1845 folded letter to Lyon, France has its New York provisional canceled with a manuscript (pen) mark. It also exhibits several interesting postal markings, including an Oct. 15 New York circular date stamp (CDS), a "PAID" marking and transit and arrival markings. These markings add to the interest, and value, of the cover.

Where to Find More Information

- John N. Luff's *Postmasters' Provisional Stamps.*

The following sources deal with the stamps of specific cities:

- *The 'Charnley and Whelen' Find of the United States Postmaster Stamps of St. Louis, Missouri,* H.R. Harmer Sale, December 12-13, 1948, Sale #503.

- "1845 Provisional Postage Stamps of James M. Buchanan," by Muriel Bemis Hayes.

- *The New York Postmaster's Provisional* by Stanley M. Piller.

- *The Stamps of the Providence R.I. Postmaster* (1846-1847) by A.B. Slater.

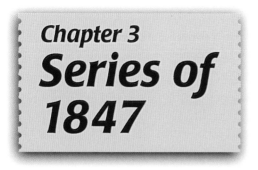

Chapter 3
Series of 1847

The stamps of 1847, a 5¢ Benjamin Franklin and a 10¢ George Washington, were the first general issue adhesive postage stamps issued by the United States Post Office (*Scott* 1 and 2, fig. 1). Issued on July 1, 1847, they remained valid for use until June 30, 1851. New York City was the first to receive the new stamps, and has the **earliest documented uses** (EDU) – July 7 for the 5¢ stamp, and July 2 for the 10¢ stamp.

The 1847 stamps represent an innovation that the Post Office had previously resisted – providing a convenient method for the public to prepay the postage on their letters. While an obvious idea today, it was, at the time, considered radical by many.

Effective July 1, 1845 postage was reduced. After this reduction in 1845 the next step of postal reform was the issuance of postage stamps in 1847. Although their use was optional, it was anticipated that the availability and convenience of the new stamps would encourage the public to use them for the prepayment of postage.

Figure 1

The two 1847 stamps, with a common red grid cancellation on the 5¢ and a pen cancellation on the 10¢.

Despite the added cost of printing these stamps, they still promised a less expensive and more efficient way for the Post Office to conduct business.

The concept of purchasing adhesive stamps prior to, or at the time of, mailing and then applying them on letters to pay the postage was developed in Great Britain in 1840. In the U.S., private **carriers** used adhesive stamps as early as 1842 (ch. 30) and in 1845 local postmasters in several cities issued provisional stamps under Post Office authority (ch. 2). The two stamps of the 1847 issue were the first ones issued and distributed by the Post Office for use throughout the country.

There were many advantages to the new stamps. They paid the new 5¢ and 10¢ rates and they could be purchased in advance, thus eliminating the need to stand in line at the post office to mail a letter. They were easy to apply (they had gum on the back) and they provided extra convenience as businesses or individuals could affix a stamp to a letter. They could be dropped in the post office receiving slot, not only during regular office hours, but at anytime.

Adhesive postage stamps were more convenient for the public and efficient for the Post Office. However there was also an implicit hope in their introduction, that if this method of prepaying postage was accepted by the public, it would be possible to require the use of stamps on all letters carried by the Post Office. This new system would virtually eliminate the costly and inefficient postage due system. The stamps were used in every part of the country and by all segments of society. There were no social, commercial, or logistical problems associated with their use, and when postage rates were lowered again in 1851, with a preferential rate for prepaid mail, the popularity of adhesive postage stamps soared. Effective January 1, 1856 the Post Office was able to require that all domestic postage be prepaid by the use of stamps or stamped envelopes. Stampless letters, even when the sender wanted to prepay postage in cash, were no longer permitted.

The firm of **Rawdon, Wright, Hatch, & Edson**, a well-known producer of bank notes, was selected to design and print the stamps. Their initials "RWH&E" appear in small letters at the bottom of each stamp — the only time a printer's name or initials were shown within the frame of a postage stamp. The stamps were printed using the *flat plate press*, line engraved method, a process used to print all subsequent stamps in the nineteenth century. Rawdon, Wright, Hatch, and Edson was the same firm which in 1842 produced the first adhesive stamp used in the U.S., the 3¢ black on grayish paper stamp issued by the City Despatch Post, a local carrier in New York City. They also produced the 5¢ New York Postmaster Provisional in 1845.

The **vignettes** used on the 1847 stamps were from stock dies which the engraving firm possessed and had previously used on banknotes. The dies were based on James Longacre's painting of Franklin, and a Gilbert Stuart painting of Washington. Asher Durand, an American artist who went on to be a founder of the Hudson River School of painting, did the engravings.

The portraits of Franklin and Washington appear in ovals on their respective stamps, with foliate embellishments between the ovals and the frame lines. The style of lettering is the same on both stamps; one has "FIVE CENTS" beneath the portrait, and the other has "TEN CENTS." It is an interesting curiosity that the Arabic numeral "5" is used on the Franklin stamp, while the Roman numeral "X" is used for the Washington stamp. Only a few other U.S. stamps have used Roman numerals.

The 1847s were printed in sheets of two side-by-side panes of 100 stamps each, for a total of 200 stamps per sheet. The 10¢ Washington has been **plated**. That means, by examining the imprint characteristics of any 10¢ Washington stamp, the specific sheet position from which it originated can be identified. Plating was first accomplished by Elliott Perry in 1923.

Two types of cancels appear on the 1847s – those that were authorized and those that were not. Recognizing the need for canceling the new stamps, the Post Office distributed canceling devices to some of the largest post offices in the country. The device was a **handstamp** that imparted a circular, 7-bar enclosed grid when struck.

The Postal Regulations of 1847 discussed the use of the new postage stamps and specified how the stamps were to be cancelled:

> Stamps so affixed are to be immediately cancelled in the office in which the letter or packet may be deposited, with an instrument to be furnished to certain of the post offices for that purpose [i.e., the 7-bar grid]. In post offices not so furnished, the stamps must be cancelled by marking a cross X on each with a pen.

Some postmasters did not follow these regulations and apparently used whatever means was at hand to cancel a stamp. Frequently they employed a handstamp originally designed for use on stampless covers. Thus there are examples of the 1847 issue cancelled by town marks (**circular date stamp**), rating numerals (both open or enclosed in a box or circle), railroad Route Agent date stamps, straight-line markings such as, "**PAID**," "**WAY**," "**FREE**," "STEAM" (or "STEAM/SHIP" in two lines), and even the name of a specific vessel. Straight-line Philadelphia Railroad and Baltimore Railroad markings are also seen as cancels on the 1847 issue.

Some local postmasters ordered or made their own distinctive handstamps for canceling the new adhesives. Many of these were variations of the government-issued 7-bar grid. Usually, these custom-made handstamps had fewer lines (bars) in the grid than the government issue handstamp, but in some instances the grids were larger and contained more than 7 lines. Other postmasters ordered or made their own distinctive handstamps for canceling the new adhesives. Some of these are referred to as **fancy cancels**. Examples include the "scarab" cancel of St. Johnsbury, Vermont; the "herringbone" of Binghamton, New York; and the 13-bar grid cancel of Brattleboro, Vermont.

Postal regulations did not require that a specific color ink be used when applying the handstamp cancel, but the most commonly used color was red. Blue ink was also used frequently while black ink was less common. Still less common was the use of magenta, green, orange, or violet.

There are approximately 100 examples of bisected (*fractional usage*) 10¢ stamps used on cover in existence. Although the Post Office did not specifically sanction their use, they were accepted by the Post Office as payment for 5¢ postage. The greatest number of these bisects was used in May and June of 1851, apparently in an attempt to use up the remaining 1847 stamps prior to their demonetization on July 1. One theory explaining the *demonetization* is that the stamps were made invalid for postage because the Post Office did not control the dies and plates used to produce them, and thus sought to avoid unauthorized printings from being circulated and used.

In 1875, two stamps (3 and 4) printed by the Bureau of Engraving and Printing were official imitations of the two 1847 stamps. Because new dies and plates were made for these stamps, there are subtle differences between the originals and the reproductions. The reproductions were sold to collectors at face value, but were not valid for postage. The occasion for these official reproductions was the 1876 Centennial Exposition in Philadelphia.

Notes on Collecting

The stamps of 1847 are not inexpensive, but once the decision is made to collect one or more of these stamps, other decisions must then be made. Since they are *imperforate* and were sometimes not cut apart with great care, not all copies have four equal margins. Copies with four equal margins will command a premium over examples with less than four margins. Stamps that were separated by cutting into the design will sell at a discount. The cancellation also affects the value and price of a stamp. *Manuscript* (pen) canceled stamps are generally the most affordable.

The same designs of the 1847 stamps were reproduced in distinctive colors on *souvenir sheets* in 1947 (948) while similar designs appeared on souvenir sheets in 1997 (3139 and 3140).

Almanac

1847 – Postage stamps are introduced on July 1, in 5¢ and 10¢ denominations, intended to pay the postage rates established July 1, 1845 as well as the new 40¢ west coast rate.

1849 – Domestic postage on foreign-bound mail is standardized on March 3 at 5¢ per ½ ounce, regardless of distance traveled from point of origin to port of departure, except mail sent to or from California or Oregon.

1851 – Postal Treaty with Canada on April 6 establishes 10¢ per ½ ounce (or 6 pence Canadian), to or from any place in the U.S., and to or from anyplace in

Canada, except to or from the West Coast of the U.S., the rate for that service being 15¢, or 9 pence Canadian.

1851 – June 30 is the last day of valid use for 1847 issue.

1851 – On July 1 new lower postage rates are introduced (including preferential rate for prepaid mail); new stamps are issued to pay the new rates.

What Others Have Said

A contract to print the first stamps
"The contract for the 1847 issue was made between the Postmaster General, Cave Johnson, and the firm of Rawdon, Wright, Hatch and Edson of New York City.... This was the same firm that had made the New York Postmaster's Provisionals. As far as can be determined no details of this contract have ever been found.... This firm probably obtained the contract because of their prominence and their excellent work in printing bank notes and similar examples of engraving."

—*Carroll Chase, "The United States 1847 Issue," The Philatelic Gazette, 1916. This is from the first of nine monthly installments in* The Philatelic Gazette *which Chase had intended be published as a separate booklet. It was not.*

New Collectors should work toward buying 5¢ Franklin
"One of the first things I tell newcomers who ask my advice on collecting U.S. is to consider starting at the beginning and to buy a copy of Scott #1, the 5¢ stamp of 1847. This is not an inexpensive stamp, but the hobbyist who takes up skiing, sailing, or tropical fish is likely to spend much more on the entry level. Scott #1 is listed at $525 for a used copy in very fine condition. But a copy with a pen or manuscript cancellation is priced at $275. This is one of the first lessons that this stamp teaches the collector. The price varies depending on the cancellation [and] on condition.... For all these reasons, a collector who buys a copy of this stamp generally will not be making his or her purchase without some research.... another lesson that his stamp teaches: shop carefully, and buy each stamp with planning and care."

—*Gary Griffith, "Solid Beginning Helps Lead to Success," Stamp Collector, 1996.*

Many shades of 5¢ Franklin exist
"At the time of the 1847s, color mixing was still an art. Periodically, a new ink formulation would have to be made and checked. A new batch might be made up weekly or daily. Even when the ink was the same it needed stirring and occasional additional thinner. Consequently there could be substantial variation even within the same day....The rare...shades...probably came from

testings made at the beginning of a day, a new batch of ink or from the tail end of a batch."

—*Calvet M. Hahn, "Reexaming the 1847 Colors,"* The Collectors Club Philatelist, *1986.*

The 1847 reprints precede the Philatelic Agency by 46 years!

"Upon orders from the Post Office Department, the Bureau of Engraving and Printing in 1875 made and used its first plates prepared with the design of a postage stamp, the 5c and 10c of 1847. We have carefully worded this statement because the circumstances are peculiar....We do not call them postage stamps as that was not their intent, and we mean by that that apparently the sole purpose of their manufacture was to supply specimens imitating our first stamps in the absence of being able to supply examples of the original engraving to those wanting same. They were not available for postage legally as the original issue had been demonetized at the close of business June 30, 1851. And these reproductions were freely available to those who knew of their existence – at the values printed thereon. Making them available was an early example of a Philatelic Agency type of operation, the first in this country."

—*George W. Brett, "The U.S. Postage Stamp Plates of the Banknote Companies,"* The Bureau Specialist, *1964.*

Examples of Postal Usage

Figure 2

Folded letter using a 5¢ Franklin, addressed to Philadelphia, postmarked from Baltimore, Md. on April 27, 1851.

Figure 3

Double weight letter franked with a 10¢ Washington, addressed to the same recipient as the letter in figure 2. It is postmarked Baltimore, Md. October 5, 1851. It was registered on receipt in Philadelphia, as indicated by the "R" marking.

Where to Find More Information

- An in depth and masterful study of the 1847s is George Brett's "Updating the U.S. 1847's on Their 150th Anniversary: Beginning, Production, Ending".

- "The United States 1847 Issue" by Carroll Chase provides numerous ideas on how the general collector should approach the 1847 Issue.

- Volume I of *The Postage Stamps of the 19th Century*, by Lester Brookman.

- "The 5¢ and 10¢ General Issue of 1847" by Wayne E. Saadi updates Brookman's work.

- "Reexamining the 1847 Colors" by Calvet M Hahn provides the definitive study of the 5¢ shade variations.

- "Plating the 10¢ 1847" by Elliot Perry is a series of nine illustrated articles on the plating of the 10¢ stamp.

- *U.S. Stamp Facts – 19th Century*, edited by Eliot Landau et al., provides information on topics including designers, engravers, plate arrangements, quantities issued, and most typical usage.

- *United States 1847 Issue Cover Census* by Thomas J. Alexander.

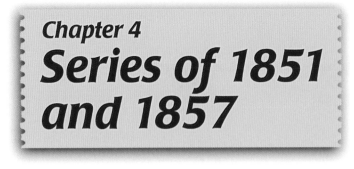

Chapter 4
Series of 1851 and 1857

The 1851 Series

A bill passed by Congress in March 1851, dramatically reduced postage rates. Effective July 1, a mailer prepaying domestic postage (as opposed to sending mail collect), could send a letter up to 3,000 miles for only 3¢, and could send one over 3,000 miles for only 6¢. The cost of mailing printed matter was also dramatically reduced. In anticipation of these new lower rates, Postmaster General Nathan Hall signed a contract on June 10, 1851 with the firm of **Toppan, Carpenter, and Casilear** to produce the needed postage stamps. The firm set up a printing shop in Philadelphia for that purpose. Production of the old 5¢ and 10¢ stamps of 1847 (ch. 3) ceased, and they were **demonetized** on July 1, 1851. New 1¢, 3¢, and 12¢ stamps appeared in July and August of 1851 while new 5¢ and 10¢ stamps were issued in 1856 and 1855 respectively. Since no perforating machine was available, all the stamps were **imperforate**. Due to the unusual and improvisational way that printing plates were made, and because of variations in ink colors, these five basic stamps exist in many varieties, with *Scott* numbers from 5 through 17 (fig. 1).

Figure 1
The five basic imperforate stamps of the Series of 1851.

The 1851 issues were printed on sheets of handmade paper a few inches smaller than the machine-made paper used later in the century. This created a real challenge for the **siderographer** to fit everything onto the printing plate (ch. 43). The standard **plate layout** was 200 stamps per sheet, divided into two panes of 100 each (10 rows by 10 columns). The stamps with rectangular frame lines (3¢ and 12¢) did not pose a great problem, but 1¢ and 10¢ stamps, with their larger and more elaborate scrollwork were difficult to fit onto the plate. In order to fit all the needed subjects on the plate, parts of designs were occasionally cut away from the **transfer rolls**. **Type numbers** were assigned to stamps by collectors, based on the nature of the trimming on the transfer roll, and on the basis of subsequent **recutting** of lines on plates. Only the 5¢ and 12¢ imperforate stamps do not have "types" based on these characteristics. Each "type" of each stamp is assigned a separate *Scott* number, which is why there are more than five *Scott* numbers representing the five basic stamp designs! Different types exist on stamps that originate from the same plates, adding to the challenge and pleasure of collecting these stamps.

The design of the 1¢ stamps of 1851 features a bust of Franklin sculpted by Jean Jacques Cafferi (5, 5A, 6, 7, 8, 8A, and 9). The blue 1¢ Franklin made its first appearance on July 1, 1851. Early printings are a pale blue, which was followed by a rich deep blue. Dirty plates apparently plagued stamp production in 1854, resulting in poor color quality. A new supervisor, Charles Steel, was assigned in 1855, and print quality was significantly improved thereafter. The 1¢ Franklin stamp was primarily used to pay the rate on unsealed circulars.

The size of the design of the 1¢ stamp presented a particular problem for plate makers. Two hundred complete designs simply would not fit on a plate! To make a plate of 200 subjects, most designs had to be less then complete. Type I (5) is the most complete – and a great rarity, found only in one position, known as 7R1E. ("7R1E" identifies it as originating from the seventh position on the right side of plate 1 in its early state.) Other types of this stamp, Ia, Ib, II, III, IIIa, and V, all lack some portion of the design. The first plate used to print the 1¢ stamp suffered from significant plate wear. This plate underwent deep **reentry** and recutting of 199 of its 200 positions, before returning to service in 1852. The recutting was primarily to the top and/or bottom frame and label lines, creating a variety called Type IV (9). In 1916 Dr. Caroll Chase discovered the two states of this plate, which he called "early" and "late". A total of four physical plates were used for this imperforate stamp, however collectors recognize the early and late states of plate 1 as separate plates.

The 3¢ orange-brown (10) with the left-facing bust of Washington by Hudon appeared on July 1, 1851, and was printed from plates numbered 0, 1E, 1I (intermediate), 2E, and 5E. This stamp was issued for the single weight (½ oz.) first class rate for up to 3,000 miles. In pairs it paid the 6¢ rate to and from the West coast. Original printings were in a pale orange brown turning to a rich orange brown shortly thereafter. Stamp production began slowly, then a sudden demand quickly outstripped the supply. In September of 1851, as the pace of manufacturing picked up significantly, the rich orange brown inks gave way to variations of a dull red (11). The orange-brown and dull red stamps are so significantly different that *Scott* classifies them as two different stamps, with two different catalogue numbers, 10 and 11. A total of nine physical plates were used to print the imperforate 3¢ stamp, although collectors recognize the early and late states of some of them as separate plates. For example, there is a **triple transfer** at 92L2L (position 92 from the left side of plate 2, late state).

The four outer frame lines were recut on almost every 3¢ stamp. The weak inner frame lines were also recut on many stamps, as were various other portions of the design. Such time consuming recutting was sharply curtailed after 1853. Many early stamp collectors found the hundreds of re-cut designs both confusing and interesting. Prominent collector Dr. Caroll Chase, working from strips, pairs, and blocks, managed to make sense of the situation, reconstructing plates in much the same way that a jig-saw puzzle is assembled. The publication of Chase's plate reconstruction notes launched an era of unparalleled popularity for this stamp.

The 5¢ red brown stamp (12), printed from a single plate, issued in 1856, features a portrait of Thomas Jefferson by Stuart. This stamp was used to pay the British Open Mail rate to foreign destinations. Thus the 5¢ stamp paid the U.S. domestic (inland) postage, while the ocean and transit postage was collected from the recipient in the country of destination. The 5¢ Jefferson is commonly found used in strips of three on covers addressed to France.

For some time it was believed the 5¢ stamp was issued to pay the registry fee. In 1856 a registry fee of 5¢ was paid in cash, and domestic money letters, those containing valuables, were marked with the letter "R". The international community was moving towards a serialized tracking system on such parcels and letters, and in 1856 registry stamps had begun to appear in several other countries. A serialized system was adopted in the U.S. in July 1857, but Congress had yet to approve any change in the law regarding cash payment. So, despite the purpose for which it was apparently intended, the 5¢ Jefferson was never officially used for registry services.

Issued in May 1855, the 10¢ green Washington (13, 14, 15, and 16) printed from a single plate, saw extensive use on transcontinental and Central American mail lines to California. The rate to and from California (over 3,000 miles) had been increased to 10¢ on April 1 of that year, in part due the cost of developing railroads and ports in Panama, and the maintenance of staging posts across the vast frontier.

The black 12¢ (17), printed from a single plate, features a left facing portrait of Washington by Stuart, the same portrait that appears on the 10¢ stamp. Recutting of the weak rectangular frame lines is exhibited on many stamps. The

12¢ was primarily used in pairs to pay the 24¢ rate to England. This combination was also used to pay four times the first class rate on domestic mail. This stamp was legally bisected to pay the 6¢ rate to and from the West coast (17a).

The 1857 Series

The public responded so well to the reduced postal rates of 1851 that the use of postage stamps grew ten fold that year. Use increased another ten fold between 1852 and 1858. Originally, stamps were distributed to post offices from the Third Assistant Postmaster General's office in Washington, D.C. However by 1855, large quantities of stamps could no longer safely travel by train from the printer in Philadelphia, so the office of U.S. *stamp agent* was established in Philadelphia, and distribution to post offices across the country came directly from the manufacturer under his supervision. About this time the first perforated postage stamps appeared in England, and the Post Office subsequently asked Samuel Carpenter, vice-president in charge of stamp manufacture, to bring this innovation to America.

Figure 2
The eight basic stamps of the perforated Series of 1857

The stamps of 1857, printed by the renamed firm of Toppan, Carpenter & Company, consist of perforated versions of the same stamps issued in the Series of 1851, plus three new stamps whose designs had not been a part of the 1851 Series (fig. 2). Plates created to print the Series of 1851 that were still serviceable were used for the Series of 1857. In addition, other plates were created to

How Foreign Mail Traveled between 1840 and 1875

Prior to the establishment of the Universal Postal Union in 1875, mail was transmitted to foreign destinations in several ways:

"Direct Mail" traveled directly from a port in the country of origin to another port on a ship's route. An example is the Pacific Direct Mail from San Francisco, California to Shanghai, China.

"Closed Mail" moved by ship in sealed bags from a U.S. exchange office to a foreign exchange office. An example would be Prussian Closed Mail by German ship from New York City to Bremen, Prussia (Germany) for delivery to the Prussian Post Office. Many other countries had closed mail service, such as, Austria, Britain, France, and Italy.

"Open Mail" could include mail for many different destinations, sent by ship from a U.S. exchange office to a foreign exchange office for sorting and verifying or re-rating of postage before being sent on to other exchange offices in other countries. An example is the British Open Mail by British ship from Boston, Massachusetts, to Portsmouth, England, thence to Marseille, France and thence via Alexandria, Egypt to Madagascar. The sorting and postage verification at each stop increased chances of misdirection, calculation errors, and delay of mail.

"Overland Mail" traveled across the United States. It includes mail to Canada or Mexico going by a land route.

satisfy production demands. Series 1857 stamps have *Scott* numbers from 18 through 39. Producing perforated stamps created challenges for the manufacturer. Stamp subjects on the plates were very close together, leaving very little room between stamps for the placement of perforations.

The 1¢ Franklin stamps of the 1857 Series were printed from the same plates, though not the early states of those plates, used to print the imperforate varieties, plus nine newly made plates. The perforated stamp exists in all of the types found on the imperforate except for type Ib, but also exists in a type not found on the imperforate, type V (24). Type V is the most common variety of 1¢ stamp, being found on five of the new plates. Type V stamps originate from a **die** that was trimmed on all four sides to make room for perforations. Type I stamps come from newly made plates 11 and 12.

The 3¢ perforated Washington was printed from late states of seven of the nine plates used for the imperforate stamps (25), plus a number of newly made plates (26 and 26a). Stamps printed from the original plate are known as type I (25) and are characterized by complete frame lines. Types II (26) and IIa (26a) from the newly created plate had eliminated distinctive portions of the design and recuts of the frame lines. Again, the goal was to provide more room for the perforations. The 3¢ perforated Washington stamps were printed in a wide variety of color shades.

The perforated 5¢ Jefferson was printed from two plates, the one used for the imperforate stamps (27, 28, 28A, and 29) and a new one made from a die with part of the design cut away at the top and bottom (30 and 30A). There are multiple *Scott* numbers for 5¢ stamps printed from the same plate, based in this case on differences of color, not design. The colors in which the perforated 5¢ Jefferson are printed are known as brick red (27), red brown (28), Indian red (28A), and brown (29 and 30A).

The perforated 10¢ Washington was printed from the same plate used for the imperforate variety, so it also exists with the same four types, I, II, III, and IV (31, 32, 33, and 34 respectively). However, it was also printed from a newly created plate, which was made from a die that had been trimmed at both the right and left sides. This resulted in a type V (35) stamp that appeared in 1859. It was a stamp widely used on mail to Cuba, the Caribbean, Mexico, and Canada.

The perforated 12¢ Washington stamp was printed both from an old plate (36), and from a newly made plate (36b). Since the frame line was not recut on the new plate as it had been on the old one, stamps from the new plate have one or more breaks in the frame lines. The 12¢ stamp was often used in combination with a 3¢ stamp to pay the 15¢ rate to France.

A perforated 24¢ stamp featuring the likeness of George Washington (37) was added to the series in 1860, issued in a gray lilac, but also exists in gray (37a). The 24¢ stamps were all printed from the same plate.

An orange 30¢ stamp (38), printed from a single plate, often used to pay the double rate to France, was also added to the series in 1860. It features the same *vignette* of Franklin used on a short-lived **carrier stamp** in 1851 (L01). Earnest R. Ackerman reported in 1926 that a block of 56 of the 30¢ stamp in his collection paid the postage on a bag of San Francisco gold dust. The $18.00 postage on that shipment is the highest known postage paid on a single mailed item between 1847 and 1870.

The blue 90¢ stamp (39), printed from a single plate, also was issued in 1860. It features a portrait of Washington painted by Trumbull, depicting the general on the eve of the battle of Princeton in 1776.

The stamps of 1851 and 1857 were demonetized in stages by the Postmaster General in the fall of 1861. This prevented the possibility of their sale furnishing funds to the Confederate States.

In 1875 *special printings* were made of the stamps of 1857 (40-47). Printed in connection with the 1876 Centennial Exposition in Philadelphia, they were not valid for postal use.

Notes on Collecting

A general U.S. collection might include one of each of the five basic imperforate designs, and one of each of the eight basic perforate stamps. Depending on one's budget and level of interest, these stamps can be pursued in their various varieties. A basic reference explaining the various types will be necessary, such as the *Scott Specialized Catalogue*. These stamps have been popularized through the works of Dr. Caroll Chase, Stanley Ashbrook, Lester Brookman, Elliot Perry, and Mortimer Ninekin.

Some varieties of these stamps are great rarities and very valuable. The most reasonably priced stamps are the type II of the 3¢ perforated Washington (26). Imperforate pairs are generally 5 to 10 times rarer than large margin singles.

Catalog makers historically combined the imperforate 1851 stamps with the perforated 1857 stamps. However the eight stamp 1857 Series was the first to be designed for perforation and should be collected as an independent set solely on that basis. The typical stamp has good to very good centering, and high denominations are more readily obtainable in unused condition.

Almanac

1851 – Contract for new postage stamps is signed on June 10 with Toppan, Carpenter, Casilear & Co.

1851 – First Class postage rates are reduced and new 1¢ and 3¢ stamps are issued on July 1. The 1847 Series is demonetized.

1855 – Pre-payment of postage becomes mandatory April 1. Letter rate to and from California is increased to 10¢.

1856 – Use of stamps to prepay postage becomes mandatory January 1.

1857 – Post Office experiments with production of perforated stamps in February.

What Others Have Said

A Matter of Reputation
"Mr. Waller has...delivered...the stamps yesterday received by him at Philadelphia. I regret exceedingly that you have not been able to furnish a larger supply...I trust you will at once increase your force and extend your means of multiplying stamps so as to meet the demand as this is very important to our reputation and your own."

—*Postmaster General Nathan K. Hall, from a July 10, 1851 letter to Toppan Carpenter, Casilear & Co.*

The Dropped Relief Myth
"For many years it was...accepted...[the] Plate 2...'big crack'...was caused by a sudden dropping of the roller to the surface of the plate...It must be remembered that the roller with its reliefs were locked in one position and it was the plate on its sliding bed that was raised to come in contact with the roller."

—*Mortimer L. Neinken*, The United States One Cent Stamp of 1851 and 1857, *1972.*

Positional Plating Made Easy
"No other plate from...any United States Stamps presents the field for...easy reconstruction as this One Cent Plate 1L."

—*Stanley B. Ashbrook, "An Analysis of the Types of the U.S. One Cent 1851 and 1857,"* American Philatelist, *1922.*

The Despised 3¢ Stamp
"There are many more interesting points connected with this rather despised stamp, but perhaps enough has been said to show the possibilities that lie in its study."

—*Carroll Chase*, The Hobbyist, *1909.*

The 1861 Series at Less Than Face
"Some years later...stamp dealers obtained a supply of unused remainders of the 1857...series, including the 30¢ and 90¢....For many years these unused stamps were quite common and at times were sold at less than face value,...one dollar per set of eight..."

—*Elliot Perry*, Mekeel's Weekly, *1919.*

Examples of Postal Usage

Figure 3

Pair of imperforate 3¢ Washingtons (11) on a double weight 1856 cover, postmarked with a circular date handstamp from "Chicago, Ill."

Figure 4

Perforated 3¢ Washington type II (26), used on an 1858 cover from "Savannah, Ga.", postmarked with an obsolete "Paid" handstamp.

Where to Find More Information

- Volume I of Lester Brookman's *The United States Postage Stamps of the 19th Century*.

- John L. Luff's *The Postage Stamps of the United States*.

- *U.S. Stamp Facts – 19th Century*, edited by Eliot Landau et al., provides information on topics including designers, engravers, plate arrangements, quantities issued, and most typical usage.

- *The Mircarelli Identification Guide to U.S. Stamps*.

- The imperforate stamps are treated in Jon Rose's *Classic United States Imperforate Stamps*.

Several exhaustive studies treat individual stamps, including:

- *The 3¢ Stamp of the United States 1851-1857 Issue* by Caroll Chase.

- *The 1851-57 Twelve Cent Stamp* by Mortimer L. Neinken.

- Stanley Ashbrook's, *The United States One Cent Stamp of 1851-1857*.

Chapter 5

Series of 1861 and 1869 Pictorials

During the 1860s, the decade of the Civil War and Reconstruction, the Post Office Department (POD) introduced two series of postage stamps, the Civil War inspired Series of 1861, and the short-lived Pictorial Series of 1869. A process known as **grilling** was developed for security purposes during this decade, and was employed on both series of stamps, creating many different varieties.

The Series of 1861 – The Ungrilled Stamps

At the outbreak of the Civil War many U.S. postage stamps and **stamped envelopes** remained in the hands of postmasters in the states that seceded from the Union. It was feared that those stamps might be used to help finance the rebel cause. There was no assurance that southern postmasters would account to the POD for the value of stamps and stamped envelopes in their possession. Ultimately, virtually every cent of postage was accounted for, but that could not have been anticipated in the Spring of 1861. Therefore the POD issued new stamps, and **demonetized** the old stamps.

The contract for the printing of postage stamps was set to expire on June 10, 1861. In order to compete for, and ultimately win a new contract, the National Bank Note Company (National) assembled an outstanding team of engravers. From its shop in New York, National printed sample stamps in July 1861, with full production beginning in August, and stamps reaching local post offices by mid-August. Early versions of the 1861s exist, known **August Issues** or "**Premiers Gravures**", which are actually **essays**. Some 3¢ values inadvertently saw postal use and are highly prized. In each case, the designs on these essays are incomplete versions of the finally issued stamps.

The stamps printed by National (*Scott* 62B, 63–72, and 75–78) were issued in the same denominations, in approximately the same colors, with the same subjects, and sometimes even with the same **vignettes** as the stamps they replaced (ch. 4). The **frames**, however, are considerably different between the two sets.

Figure 1
Ungrilled 1¢ Franklin (63), dot in "U" variety. A small dot is near the top of the left side of the U in the lower left corner of the stamp.

Figure 2
Ungrilled 3¢ Washington (64).

The 1¢ stamp featuring a bust of Franklin (fig. 1) was printed from five plates and exists in a wide range of shades, from dark indigo to blue, ultramarine, and pale or milky blue. It was widely used on circulars, **drop** letters, and **carrier** covers. Like most of the Series of 1861 stamps, it was first available in post offices in mid August 1861.

The 3¢ George Washington stamp (fig. 2) was used to pay the domestic first class letter rate. Twenty-four different plates were required to print all of the stamps that were needed! As was the case with all the plates used to print 1861 stamps, the 3¢ Washington plates printed sheets of 200 subjects which were cut vertically into panes of 100 for distribution to post offices. The stamp exists in a variety of shades of pink (64) and rose (65).

The 5¢ Thomas Jefferson stamp was printed from a single plate and exists in shades of buff or brown. It was most typically used in combination with another stamp on letters to foreign destinations.

The 10¢ George Washington green stamp exists as two types. The "first design" was printed from a single plate (62B), while a "second design" (68) was printed from two plates. This stamp was used to pay the transcontinental rate to or from California until that rate was abolished on July 1, 1863. It was also used on mail to most destinations in North America and the Caribbean.

The 12¢ George Washington was printed in black ink from a single plate. It was typically used on letters to England. It was also used in combination with a 3¢ stamp on letters to France.

The 24¢ Washington (fig. 3) exists in shades that *Scott* describes as red lilac, brown lilac, steel blue, violet, and pale gray violet. The existence of so many shades on this and other stamps of the Series of 1861 demonstrates the variability in stamp production of the time, and the difficulty in maintaining a consistent

Figure 3

An ungrilled 24¢ Washington (70), with a Philadelphia cancel.

Figure 4

The 2¢ Andrew Jackson (73), issued in 1863, is known as the "Black Jack."

ink color. The 24¢ Washington was printed from a single plate and was typically used on double weight letters to England.

National's 30¢ Benjamin Franklin stamp, in yellow-orange, was printed from a single plate. The stamp was typically used on double weight letters to France.

The 90¢ blue Washington was also printed from a single plate. This stamp, and all of those in this series, are perforated 12. Very few 90¢ stamps survive on cover, but examples are known used on cover addressed to China.

On July 1, 1863 the drop rate was increased to 2¢ as part of a rate-restructuring package. A new 2¢ stamp depicting Andrew Jackson (73, fig. 4) was added to the 1861 Series for use on drop letters and on circulars. National printed this stamp in black because it was the most inexpensive ink. Since there was concern that black canceling ink might go unnoticed on a black stamp, a design was created with an exceptionally large vignette that could be readily defaced by canceling ink of any color. This stamp is commonly referred to as the "Black Jack."

On April 14, 1866, another stamp was added to the series, a 15¢ black stamp with a portrait of Abraham Lincoln (77, fig. 5). It was used to pay the *treaty rate* to France and to countries served by the North German Union Confederation.

Some collectors consider the Lincoln stamp, issued on the last day of the official year of mourning, to be the first U.S. commemorative.

Since there was some delay in having the Series of 1861 stamps distributed to postmasters in the Union states, the planned demonetization of the Series of 1851 and 1857 was not fully implemented until January 1862. However, even after that date, some demonetized stamps continued to be used. Some particularly desirable covers exist with the stamps crossed out, and marked postage "due" or "old stamps" or "OLD STAMPS NOT RECOGNIZED" (a Philadelphia marking) and the new 3¢ 1861 used alongside to actually pay postage.

There are a number of **plate varieties** including **double transfers**, also known as double entries. The 10¢ Washington has a doubled "TAG" variety in POSTAGE. The 15¢ Lincoln is known for double entries at the top. It is also known with a spectacular plate crack from the middle left side all the way into Lincoln's cheek. The 1¢ Franklin exists with a dot in the "U" of U.S. caused by a defective **transfer roll** used on the first plate. The 3¢ is known with a missing ball ornament in the lower left corner. Research has shown that small plate scratches can be found on the black and brown stamps caused when small iron particles in the inks, and also from unhardened plates, were trapped on the hog bristle brushes used to clean the printing plates, thereby scratching the plates.

Figure 5

The 15¢ Lincoln (77), issued in 1866, is considered by some to be the first commemorative stamp.

Because these stamps were in use during the Civil War, many of them can be found used on patriotic covers. Occasionally these stamps may be found on registered covers before their use to pay the registry fee was first required in 1867.

The Grilled Stamps

The second part of the story of the Series of 1861 begins in 1867. After National had been producing stamps for about six years, Charles Steel of National convinced the POD to produce stamps impressed with his newly patented grill system. This system used a grilling press with raised pyramid points (like the points of a meat tenderizer or the squared shapes of a waffle iron) on one side, and a receiving plate with indentations that matched the points of the grill. It pressed pyramid shapes into the stamp paper after all other parts of production had been completed. The object of grilling was revenue protection. Grilling made it easier for cancellation ink to penetrate into the stamp paper fibers. It also weakened the paper so that an attempt to wash a cancel out would likely shred the stamp. Grilling therefore made the fraudulent reuse of a stamp less likely.

Grills exist in different sizes. Each of the stamps previously issued in ungrilled condition now appeared with grills of one or more sizes. Each of these created a new major variety with a unique *Scott* number. The first grill covered the entire stamp, is arbitrarily designated the "A" grill, and was used on the 3¢, 5¢, and 30¢ stamps (79–81). Another large grill, measuring 18mm by 15mm is called the "B" grill, and was used on the 3¢ stamp (82). These large grills were eventually rejected because they weakened the paper so much that stamps tended to tear through their middles rather than at the perforations. The "C" grill (13mm by 16mm) was briefly used in regular production on the 3¢ stamp (83), as was the still smaller "D" grill (12mm by 14mm), which was used on the 2¢ and 3¢ stamps (84 and 85). Stamps with any of these four grills are quite scarce. The changes from one grill size to another were done by grinding away some of the pointed pyramids, thus creating larger and larger open spaces between the areas containing the pyramids that remained. All of these grills were made with the grill points going from the face of the stamp down towards the back, an arrangement known as "points up." When stamps are turned over, in oblique light (the stamp being held at a sharp angle so the light can make shadows on the back of the paper), the pyramids show little horizontal ridges.

The "Z" grill, (11mm by 14mm), was used on the 1¢, 2¢, 3¢, 10¢, 12¢, and 15¢ stamps (85A to 85F). It is the only grill that was impressed in the other direction, that is, with the points going up from the back of the stamp toward the face. This is known as "points down," and results in the small "pock marks"

usually seen on the face of the grilled stamp being found on the back instead. The "Z" grill was used only briefly for most values. Only two 1¢ stamps with "Z" grills are known to have survived!

The "E" grill, approximately 13mm by 11mm (fig. 6), was put into production in late 1867 and was used on the 1¢, 2¢, 3¢, 10¢, 12¢, and 15¢ stamps (86 to 91), and all of its examples are on what is referred to as normal or medium hard stamp paper. The same paper was initially used a few months later to produce the "F" grills (approximately 13mm by 9mm) on all ten denominations (92 to 101). However, National began using paper that was thinner, but heavily starched. This had the effect of making the grills stand out much

more sharply. It saved some production time by permitting the grilling of two or perhaps three sheets of stamps at a time. This was not a violation of their contract because investigation has shown that the weight of the thin starched paper equaled the weight of paper used in prior regular production.

Occasionally a sheet (or pane) was shifted during the grilling process, resulting in a portion of a grill appearing on the left side of a stamp and a portion of another grill appearing on the right. These are known as split grills. Double grills occurred when a stamp that may not have had a sharp impression was put back through the grilling rollers and had another grill impressed on it. Sometimes one of the impressions will be complete and another will be split. A very rare occurrence is the quadruple split grill in which the grilling impression falls over the perforation intersections, leaving portions of grills in each corner of each stamp.

The Pictorial Series of 1869

Until 1869, all U.S. stamps featured only portraits in their designs. When the PMG decided to alter the appearance of the nation's postage stamps, the result was the 1869 Pictorial Issue (112–122), which is the shortest-lived definitive series in U.S. history. The stamps went on sale in late March 1869 and were withdrawn in February 1870. The 1¢ through 12¢ stamps were printed from plates of 300 subjects, with sheets divided into panes of 150. The higher values, 15¢ through 90¢, were printed in sheets of 100. These higher values were printed in two colors, and the smaller sized sheets simplified the printer's task. The stamps were grilled. The contract to print them was awarded to National, after a competitive bidding process. The Pictorials, a series of eleven stamps with ten denominations, were significantly different from all prior U.S. definitives in shape, size, and subject matter. Three of the stamps featured methods of mail transportation: post horse and rider, locomotive, and ship. Two stamps used an eagle atop a shield theme, while stamps portraying the landing of Columbus and the signing of the Declaration of Independence were the nation's first to depict historical events. All were approximately square in shape.

Figure 7

The 2¢ Pictorial of 1869 (113) depicts a post rider on his horse and was typically used on drop letter and circulars.

Figure 8

The 3¢ Pictorial (114) depicts a locomotive and was typically used on First Class letters.

Figure 9

The 12¢ Pictorial (117) depicts the S.S. Adriatic and was typically used on letters to Great Britain.

Figure 10

Type I of the 15¢ Pictorial (118) depicts the Landing of Columbus and was typically used on letters to France.

The denominations remained mostly the same as on the 1861s, the one exception being the 6¢ stamp, which could pay the double weight letter rate, replaced the earlier 5¢ stamp.

A round portrait of Franklin appeared on the 1¢ in golden yellow. The 2¢ post rider was printed in a rich red brown (fig. 7). The ultramarine 3¢ featured the railroad engine (fig. 8) while the 6¢ had a portrait of Washington, surrounded by an unprecedented geometrical frame. The 10¢ featured an eagle upon a shield in orange yellow shades. The 12¢ green showed the ocean steamer S.S. Adriatic (fig. 9), a ship built in 1857 that sank off the coast of Africa in 1885. All were single color stamps.

Higher values were two-color stamps. The vignette, in one color, was printed first, followed by the frame which was printed in a different color. The alignment of vignette and frame was not always precise. This was partially caused by the moistening of the paper before the first printing, to better receive the ink. The subsequent uneven shrinkage of the paper made it difficult to properly align the frame when the sheet went to the press its second time. The two step printing process used on the bi-colored stamps created the potential for a sheet to be turned around on its second trip to the press, resulting in an **invert**. This is exactly what happened, with some 15¢, 24¢, and 30¢ stamps becoming the country's first inverts.

The 15¢ stamp has a blue vignette of Columbus landing in America, the same design that would be used in 1893 on the 2¢ **Columbian**, and a brown frame. There are two types of this stamp, based on slightly different frame designs, known as Type I (118, fig. 10) and Type II (119).

The 24¢ is similar in style to the 15¢, with a round cornered rectangular vignette depicting the signing of the Declaration of Independence in violet, with a green frame. The 30¢ is similar to the 10¢, depicting an eagle and shield, with American flags at the sides of the shield. It is printed in ultramarine and carmine.

The 90¢ stamp features Lincoln, using the same vignette, slightly reduced, that was used on the 15¢ in 1866. The 90¢ Lincoln pictorial uses a black vignette with a carmine frame. Some classic collectors consider this stamp to be the most beautiful stamp ever issued.

Some people liked the 1869 designs and colors but the appreciation soon faded. The public complained that it was not easy to handle the smaller-sized stamps. The almost square dimensions were not appreciated. There were occasional complaints that the stamps were too easily torn in the grilled areas rather than along the perforations. This complaint was especially common in the South, and during the summer when more humid air made the problem worse. For all of these reasons, the POD announced in October 1869 that they would be replaced by a new series of stamps. When the new stamps went into use in February 1870, the 1869 Pictorials were withdrawn.

Notes for Collectors

Perhaps the best way to become familiar with grills is to obtain, study, and experiment with inexpensive copies of the 3¢ F grill (94) or the 2¢ or 3¢ cent 1869 Pictorials. One should be able to see places on the face of a grilled stamp where some of the canceling ink did not penetrate because the little pits created on the face were below the surface where the canceller struck. Of course this only works when a cancel is lightly to medium-inked and not if heavily inked.

While collecting every major *Scott* listed variety of these stamps is a virtual impossibility, it is possible to acquire one face-different example of each stamp. This means, for example, acquiring only one example of each of the 1861s, ignoring the grills. Some collect colors and shades, especially of the 1¢ and 3¢ 1861s, and the 3¢ 1869 Locomotive.

The stamps of 1861 and 1869 reappeared as **special printings**, without grills, (102–111 and 123–132) in 1875 in conjunction with the 1876 Centennial Exposition held in Philadelphia. They were valid for postal use, but only a few were so used. The 1869 90¢ Lincoln was reproduced in 1989 on a souvenir sheet (2433, fig. 6, ch. 21), along with three **trial color proofs** of that stamp.

Almanac

1861 – On April 13 Confederate States PMG John Reagan orders all postmasters from seceded states to account, to the POD in Washington by April 31, for all U.S. stamps and stamped envelopes in their possession.

1861 – Distribution of the 1¢ through 30¢ 1861 stamps begins on August 15, followed by the 90¢.

1862 – Following a phased in demonetization, on January 1 Series 1851 and 1857 stamps are no longer valid anywhere in the U.S.

1863 – Free city delivery is instituted July 1; 2¢ Andrew Jackson ("Black Jack") is issued for drop rate; basic nationwide domestic letter rate is set at 3¢.

1866 – The 15¢ black Abraham Lincoln Memorial stamp is issued on April 14.

1867 – Earliest documented use of a stamp with an "A" grill is August 13.

1867 – U.S. Patent No. 70147 is issued to Charles F. Steel on October 22 for his stamp grilling process.

1868 – Prepayment of registry fees by stamps is required beginning June 1.

1869 – Postmaster General lowers registry fee from 20¢ to 15¢ on January 1.

1869 – The 1869 Pictorials are issued on March 19.

1869 – The EDU of the 2¢ Pictorial is March 20. Other denominations have EDUs as late as May 22.

What Others Have Said

Regarding the switch to the National Bank Note Company in 1861
"The contract for the manufacturer of postage stamps having expired on the 10th of June, 1861, a new one was entered into with the NBNC of New York upon terms very advantageous to the Department from which there will result an annual saving of more than 30 percent in the cost of the stamps."

—*Report of the Postmaster General for the Year Ending June 30, 1861.*

Benjamin Franklin appears on many of our early stamps
"It is difficult to understand the reasons for Post Office Department policy in the selection and identification of the busts and portraits of Franklin used on our postage stamps....The Department attributes the ...[1861–1869] designs to the bust by Jean Antoine Houdon, with the exception of the 1c and 30c denomina-

tions of the 1851-60 issues for which no identification of design source is recorded. However...Minkus...ascribes these to Houdon....Luff, in his 1902 work assigns the source of the portrait to a bust after Cerrachi. It is to be hoped that these conflicting statements may be officially resolved."

—*Henry F. Davis, "The Stamp of Approval," The United States Specialist, 1967.*

Explanation of grilling (embossing) process

"The object of my invention is to produce a stamp which shall stick better than usual and which it shall be fraudulently impossible to move and use again...a part of my invention consists in embossing or partially breaking the paper, so as to open the texture of the paper along certain lines without removing any part thereof. This... allows the oil of the cancelling ink, when such is used, to strike in very deeply."

—*Charles F. Steel, U.S. Patent No. 70147, approved October 22, 1867.*

Difficulty in the designs of the 1869 Issue

"Every one of the originally submitted designs was eventually rejected...and altered or eliminated before the stamps were issued. It was found that the 5 cent denomination was unnecessary but that a 6 cent denomination...was needed to take care of double weight letters. The head of Lincoln was removed from the 10 cent and replaced with a shield and eagle while Lincoln was switched to the 90 cent stamp..., the size of the numerals was increased on all denominations."

—*Lester G. Brookman, The United States Postage Stamps of the Nineteenth Century, 1966.*

Withdrawal of 1869 Issue

"In consequence of the National dissatisfaction with the new postage stamps, orders have been given to prepare designs to be issued in place of the present designs... Many protests were received by the Post Office Department and it is our understanding that by October, 1869, requests had been sent out by the Department for the Postmasters to return the supplies of this issue that they had on hand and they were in turn supplied with stamps of the preceding issues, either from remainders on hand or from new stamps printed from the plates."

—*"Boston Herald", 1869.*

Examples of Postal Usage

Figure 11

Strip of three 1¢ Franklins on a Baltimore 1862(?) patriotic cover.

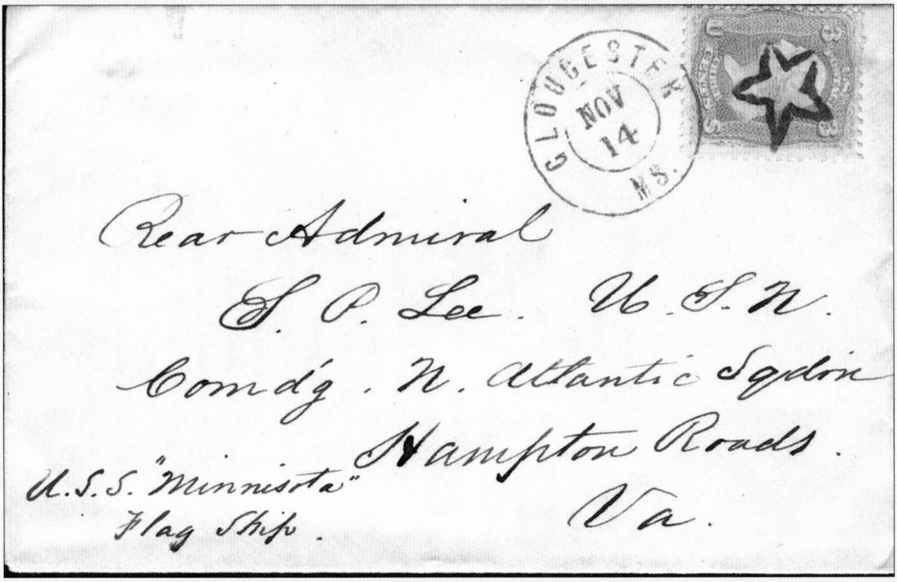

Figure 12

A common 3¢ Washington on cover from Gloucester, Mass., addressed to Union Admiral Samuel P. Lee, a cousin of Robert E. Lee.

Figure 13

That this 2¢ Jackson pays the circular rate, and not the drop rate, is evidenced by the unsealed flap on the reverse.

Figure 14

A 3¢ locomotive pictorial on a cover to New York City, mailed from Salem, Mass. on December 15, 1869. The year is not included in the postmark, but is confirmed by the docketing.

Where to Find More Information

- *The United States Postage Stamps of the 19th Century* by Lester Brookman, Volume II.

- *The United States 1¢ Franklin 1861 – 67* by Don L. Evans, while focusing on the 1¢ stamp, provides a comprehensive introduction to the postal history of the period.

- *United States Postage Stamps of 1869* by Jon Rose is a comprehensive introduction to the 1869s, including the printing history of each stamp and its uses.

- *U.S. Stamp Facts – 19th Century*, edited by Eliot Landau et al., provides information on topics including designers, engravers, plate arrangements, quantities issued, and most typical usage.

- *The Micarelli Identification Guide to U.S. Stamps.*

- *United States Letter Rates to Foreign Destinations, 1847 to 1876 GPU – UPU*, by Charles J. Starnes describes complex postage rates, and Postal Laws and Regulations.

- The U.S. Philatelic Classics Society is a group for collectors interested in the postal issues and postal history from the stampless era up to the Series of 1894. The society publishes "The Chronicle of the U. S. Classic Postal Issues", a quarterly journal containing a variety of articles on nineteenth century stamps. Their website, www.uspcs.org/ has many useful resources.

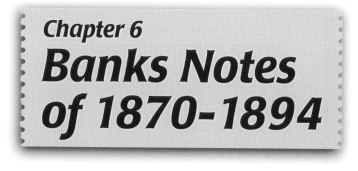

Chapter 6
Banks Notes of 1870-1894

During the years from 1870 until 1894 the nation's postage stamps were printed in succession by three private companies: National Bank Note Company (National), Continental Bank Note Company (Continental), and American Bank Note Company (American). Collectors refer to the definitive stamps from this period, of almost a quarter of a century, as the Bank Notes. Reflecting their physical size, the stamps from the earlier part of the period (1870–1890) are known as Large Bank Notes, while the stamps from the later part of this period (1890–1894) are known as Small Bank Notes.

Large Bank Notes

In 1870 the contract for printing stamps, held by National, came up for renewal. There was intense competition for the contract by National, Continental, and Philadelphia Bank Note Company. Each company prepared a number of *essays* for the Postmaster General's approval. The contract was awarded to National.

In 1870 the Post Office acted to replace the widely criticized 1869 pictorial stamps. On their new series of stamps (*Scott* 134–155), National resumed the practice of depicting American leaders in oval **vignettes**, but with simpler **frames** than those of the pre-1869 issues.

Figure 1

An ungrilled 3¢ Washington (147) printed by National.

Each stamp printed by National was in a single color, although many shades of those colors exist. The colors and subjects were: 1¢ cent ultramarine Franklin, 2¢ red brown Jackson, 3¢ green Washington (fig. 1), 6¢ carmine Lincoln, 10¢ brown Jefferson, 12¢ dull violet Henry Clay, 15¢ orange Daniel Webster, 24¢ purple Winfield Scott, 30¢ black Alexander Hamilton, and 90¢ carmine Oliver Hazard Perry. In 1871, because of a new German treaty rate, a 7¢ vermilion/red orange (138 and 149) was added, with a portrait of the recently deceased Civil War era Secretary of War, Edwin M. Stanton (fig. 2). The stamps were all printed on hard white paper (ch. 51).

Figure 2

A grilled 7¢ Stanton (138) printed by National.

When new stamps were issued in 1870 the POD had a stock of stamps on hand from the Series of 1861 and 1869, which it wanted to use. Because these stamps remained on sale, covers can be found with **mixed frankings**, especially of the higher values.

All of the stamps issued under this contract were to have had **grills**. However only about five to ten percent of them were actually grilled. Ungrilled stamps were produced in all three years of the contract. Grilled stamps (134–144) are most common from spring 1870, when the issues first appeared, through mid-1871. Thereafter, until mid-1872, most stamps were ungrilled (145–155). National resumed grilling again in mid-1872 in order to appear in compliance with the terms of its contract, which was coming up for renewal in the spring of 1873.

National's remedial efforts however, were not enough and their pricing was not competitive. Thus the contract for 1873 to 1876 was awarded to Continental. Because the POD wanted the designs to remain unchanged, National was required to turn its **dies** over to Continental. Before doing so, National placed certain marks on each of them, thus "canceling" the dies. These marks, which are known to collectors as "secret marks," are small, minor, design changes. These secret marks of course appear on stamps subsequently made from these dies by Continental, and still later, by American.

Stamps printed by Continental (156–181) are not grilled, as this was not required in the 1873 POD contract. Initially Continental used the same hard paper previously used by National; however, after Continental's contract was renewed in 1876, they experimented with a number of different papers. By the late summer of 1878 Continental introduced what are known as "soft papers."

During the period of the Continental contract a significant simplification of international postal agreements took place. In 1875 a merger of postal unions and bilateral treaty organization countries created the General Postal Union, later renamed the Universal Postal Union (UPU), to supervise the exchange of mails between member countries. Uniform rates were set and stabilized. For most of the member countries and colonies of the UPU, a rate equivalent to 5¢ per half ounce was created. This rate remained in effect until 1907 when it became 5¢ per one ounce.

United States membership in the UPU resulted in two significant changes in the stamp program. Because the color of the 2¢ Jackson (156) printed by Continental was more often brown, rather than the red brown of the National stamp, there was potential to confuse it with the 10¢ Hamilton (161). Therefore the color of the stamp was changed to a bright orange red called vermillion (178). Continental discontinued production of the 7¢ red orange Stanton when it was no longer needed to meet international **treaty rates**. Instead a 5¢ blue General Zachary Taylor (179, fig. 3) was issued to pay the UPU rate. Both the 2¢ vermillion Jackson and 5¢ blue Taylor stamps were issued on June 21, 1875.

Figure 3

Continental printed a 5¢ Zachary Taylor (179) in 1875 to meet the new UPU rate.

The period of the Continental contract was an era of consolidation in the bank note industry. The American Bank Note Company (American) was formed through a merger. On February 4, 1879 American acquired Continental, taking over its Post Office contract, all of its dies, transfer rolls, plates, paper and ink supplies, most of its workers, all stamps still in production and those waiting delivery to the **stamp agent**.

Scott lists the American printed stamps as 182 to 218. Since no abrupt production changes characterized the transition from Continental to American, it is often impossible to determine if a stamp produced before the summer of 1879 is a product of Continental or American. Stamps formerly printed by Continental continued to be printed by American mostly in the same colors. Only if a new American plate imprint is present or there is a distinctive shade can it be determined if a stamp is American's product. All stamps cancelled or dated on cover before February 5, 1879 were produced by Continental. Production continued on the soft paper, introduced at the end of summer 1878, until changed in the summer 1879 to a very soft unbleached paper similar to newsprint.

Many changes occurred to America's stamps in 1881 and 1882. The 1¢, 3¢, 6¢, and 10¢ stamp designs originally issued in 1873 were re-engraved (206–209). The 1¢ had additional lines placed throughout the curlicues in the upper part of the frame giving it a darker appearance along with its gray blue color. The 3¢ had an obvious line added under the TS of "CENTS." The background of the 6¢ and the underneath ribbon were rendered in solid color in a rose brown shade later changed to red brown and, in an 1888 printing, to brown. The 10¢ was

Figure 4

American introduced a new 2¢ Washington (210) to pay the reduced letter rate that when into effect October 1, 1883.

darkened similarly to the 6¢ and printed in full brown and another variety in a black brown. In February 1882, a new 5¢ stamp was issued picturing the recently assassinated President James A. Garfield in a brown oval portrait with a simple frame (205). While issued in brown instead of black, it is considered a mourning stamp for the late president, and was used to pay the UPU rate.

On October 1, 1883, the postage rate was lowered to 2¢ for domestic letters and a red-brown stamp was issued for this rate. George Washington was portrayed in an oval with a very simple frame (210, fig. 4). It was the first stamp printed on the new steam powered *flat plate presses*. The 2¢ Jackson was discontinued and Jackson reappeared on a new 4¢ stamp for double weight letters (211). The new 2¢ and 4¢ stamps were both issued on the first day of the newly reduced rate.

More changes were made to the series in 1887. A new simplified frame was issued for the 1¢ stamp, though the stamp continued to be printed in blue, and retained the same bust of Franklin for its vignette (212). The red 2¢ Washington, originally issued in brown in 1882, was changed to green (213), while the 3¢ green, which had appeared in 1881, was changed to vermillion (214).

The year 1888 brought still more changes. The 4¢ Jackson was reissued in deep carmine (215), while the 5¢ Garfield was changed to a very dark blue/indigo (216). The 30¢ Alexander Hamilton was shifted from black and gray black to a much better looking orange brown (217) and the 90¢ Perry in carmine was changed to purple (218). The issuance of these stamps brought the "Large Bank Note" era to an end.

Figure 5

The Small Bank Notes, printed by American, all have identical frame designs except for the ribbon or tablet (as shown here) with the denomination. There are eleven values of Small Bank Notes. The illustration is enlarged to 150% of actual size.

Small Bank Notes

The so-called Small Bank Notes (219–229) were printed by American and were issued beginning on February 22, 1890, with the last value appearing on March 21, 1893. The POD returned to issuing smaller sized definitives. Because they were just slightly taller than wide, they also had a more square appearance than the large Bank Notes. Their smaller size also resulted in lower production costs. The designs featured oval vignettes of eleven American leaders inside a frame with the value shown on a tablet or ribbon below the oval (fig. 5). Except for the manner in which the value is depicted, the frame is identical for all stamps in the set. They are the first set of definitive stamps characterized by common frames.

The 1¢ Franklin is ultramarine in color. The 2¢ Washington was originally printed in lake, a very dark red (219D), but the color was soon changed to carmine (220) which, in varying shades, remained the color for the domestic letter rate until the 3¢ deep violet Washington (720) was issued for the new First-Class postage rate effective on July 6, 1932. The 3¢ Jackson was issued in purple and the 4¢ Lincoln in dark brown. Former general and president, Ulysses S. Grant, made his first stamp appearance on the 5¢ orange brown stamp, while President Garfield was on the 6¢ in claret. The 8¢ dark brown showing General William T. Sherman was not issued until 1893 to pay the newly lowered *registry rate*. The 10¢ green featured Daniel Webster while his frequent opponent in most of the famous Senate debates and compromises of the 1840s and 1850s, Henry Clay, was portrayed on the 15¢ indigo (227, fig. 6). Thomas Jefferson was on the 30¢ black, while Commodore Perry stayed on the 90¢ orange. All the Small Bank Notes were printed on soft mildly bleached newsprint paper, and like all the Bank Notes, were unwatermarked and perforated 12.

Figure 6

Henry Clay is on the 15¢ American printed Small Bank Note (227). The denomination is in a ribbon below the oval.

Notes on Collecting

Detailed descriptions of the secrets marks are found in *Scott* and *The Micarelli Identification Guide to U.S. Stamps*. They can sometimes be recognized, even when a heavy cancel is present, because engraving ink is thicker than canceling ink, and will stand up from the surface of the paper, while canceling ink is absorbed into the paper. By using a magnifying glass, and holding a stamp at a sharp angle to a light source, the engraving ink can be seen above the cancel.

Many interesting covers are affordable, especially for the three lowest value stamps: 1¢, 2¢, and 3¢. Many less expensive covers from small towns are often essential to forming interesting collections of county and state post offices. They also help to trace the growth of different methods of transportation across states and the country.

Figure 7

Fancy cancels are common from the Bank Note period, such as this geometric cancel used on foreign mail in New York.

Figure 8

A "CHICAGO, ILL." cancel on a 3¢ vermillion Washington (214).

Many of the higher values range from medium priced to very highly priced, both on and off cover. The lower values are often very modestly priced and provide collecting opportunities for those who wish to specialize.

Some collectors specialize in one particular stamp. Almost every stamp or issue in this period has been the subject of specialized collecting. For example, from the 1870–1889 Large Bank Note era, there have been major exhibits of the 2¢ Jacksons, 6¢ Lincolns, and 1882 2¢ Washingtons, among others. A single stamp can be used to study different rates, changes in service and destinations, at minimal expense.

Because these stamps were issued during the era of fancy cancellations, many collectors seek a variety of cancels on otherwise inexpensive stamps (figs. 7 and 8). Others enjoy collecting different colors and shades, especially on the lower-denomination Bank Notes.

Special printings (167–177 and 180–181) were made of the Bank Notes in 1875 by Continental in conjunction with the 1876 Centennial Exposition in Philadelphia. They were printed on a hard paper somewhat whiter than paper used for normal stamp production. All are rare. In 1880 American produced special printings (192–204) of the 1879 stamps in conjunction with the 1881 Atlanta Cotton Exposition. These are also rare. Between 1880 and 1895 American made special printings (205C, 211B, and 211D) on its own authority, mostly related to experiments with steam-powered presses.

The Bank Notes have **proofs** which are more affordable than the stamps themselves. Proofs have the attraction of clear sharp impressions that highlight the beauty of these engraved (intaglio) stamps.

There are two especially interesting plate varieties on the 2¢ Washington Small Bank Note. The "2"s appear to have "caps", caused by a breakdown of the transfer roll (220a and 220c). Finally, some collect **EFO**s, such as misperforations, ink smears, offsets, broken or **cracked plates**, and unprinted areas caused by **preprinting creases** and **foldovers**.

Almanac

1870 – *Earliest documented use* (EDU) of National's 3¢ ungrilled Large Bank Note (147) is March 1.

1870 – EDU of National's 3¢ grilled Large Bank Note (136) is March 24.

1875 – General Convention on Posts (later, UPU) is formed on July 1. Rate is set at 5¢ per half ounce for foreign mails to most nations.

1876 – Continental Bank Note Company starts stamp paper experiments during the summer.

1879 – American acquires Continental on February 4, with printing plates, paper, gum, perforators, most employees, and all unreleased stamps.

1879 – Introduction of soft unbleached newsprint paper for stamp production begins mid-year.

1881 – Earliest documented use of re-engraved American stamps of 1881 – **1882** is August 7.

1883 – First Class domestic rate is lowered to 2¢ per half ounce on October 1. New 2¢ and 4¢ stamps are issued (210 and 211).

1890 – Earliest documented use of Small Bank Notes stamps is February 22.

1893 – Registry fee is lowered from 10¢ to 8¢ on January 1. New 8¢ stamp (225) to meet this fee is issued March 21.

1893 – BEP files claim on November 29 for the right to compete for the work of postage stamp production and submits bid.

1894 – Agreement between the BEP and POD on June 9 results in the transfer of the production of postage stamps to the BEP, ending the Bank Note period.

What Others Have Said

On the reasons for the Large Bank Note issue in 1870
"The adhesive postage stamps adopted by my predecessor in 1869, having failed to give satisfaction to the public, on account of their small size, their unshapely form, the inappropriateness of their designs, the difficulty of canceling them effectually, and the inferior quality of gum used in their manufacture, I found it necessary in April last, to issue new stamps of larger size, superior quality of gum and new designs... I decided to substitute an entire new series, one-third larger in size, and to adopt for designs the heads, in profile, of distinguished deceased Americans."

—Report of the Postmaster General for the Year Ending June 30, 1870.

At one point, Bank Note plate proofs had little, or no, monetary value!
"Five times between 1875 and 1893 the Post Office Department issued 500 lots of plate proofs on card, in normal colors, of current and obsolete U.S. postage stamps. These lots were made up of imperforate singles and they were distributed by Congressmen much as ballpoint pens are given away today. It is known that others were privately distributed, as the Earl of Crawford had uncut sheets of all of them in 1910."

—Ed Denson, "The 2¢ Plate Proofs on Card: Distinguishing the Emissions," The United States Specialist, 1970.

The Government tells the new printer to keep the former printer's stamp designs
"We know that upon the expiration of the contract with the National Bank Note Company, bids were called for on the manufacture of postage stamps. We know that the low bid was made by the Continental Bank Note Company, and that the contract was awarded to them to supply postage stamps beginning from May 1, 1873. The Government specified that the designs of the 1870 issue, prepared by the National Bank Note Co. be continued in use."

—H.D.S. Haverbeck, "The Grill and other Patents of Charles F. Steele Relating to Postage Stamp Production, 1867-1875," Collectors Club Philatelist, 1956.

The Bank Note period offers collectors lots of secret marks and some unsolvable mysteries
"If you are one of the thousands of collectors who still are hoping to fill the space provided you in a printed album for the 24¢ Continental (banknote) stamp, here is bad news for you. It seems almost certain that the Continental Bank Note Company never manufactured any 24¢ stamps from a plate containing secret marks, nor even made such a plate. To be sure, it did add a secret mark to the 24¢, 30¢ and 90¢ dies previously engraved by the National Bank Note Company. From these modified dies Continental struck proofs which still exist, but apparently never made new plates from the secret mark dies of the high denominations....And because the papers and inks used in producing the 24¢ Bank Notes have thus far

Secret Marks

Secret marks placed on dies by National Bank Note Company went unrecognized until they were discovered by prominent collector John Luff in the 1890s. Some are easier to see than others as, for example, the little crescent in the pearl to the left of the "1" on the 1¢ Franklin and the strengthened vertical shading in the lower left ribbon of the 6¢ Lincoln.

successfully resisted efforts of philatelic researchers to distinguish the one company's product from the other's, it seems reasonable to predict that the mystery of the Continental 24¢ may never be solved."

—Morrison Waud, "Problems of Continental Secret Marks," Chronicle of the U.S. Classic Postal Issues, 1973. Note: For many years, Scott noted: "It is generally accepted as fact that the Continental Bank Note Co, produced and delivered a quantity of 24¢ stamps. They are impossible to distinguish from those printed by the National Bank Note Co." Then in the 1990 Scott, this sentence was added: "The Philatelic Foundation has certified as genuine a 24¢ on horizontally ribbed paper. Specialists believe that only Continental used ribbed paper." Starting with the 1992 Scott this stamp is referred to as 164.

Examples of Postal Usage

A Continental printed 2¢ Jackson (178) on a drop rate cover from Utica, New York, on February 15 in 1876 or 1877. While the cover never left Utica, the negative "E" killer shows the postal clerk was using a canceling hammer preparing mail for the eastbound train out of Utica. Each direction had its own letter (N,S,E,W) for railroad usage.

Figure 9

A cover to Austria using a 15¢ American printed Daniel Webster (189) to pay the 5¢ UPU foreign rate and 10¢ registry rate, with a fancy geared oval cancel from Louisville, Ky., February 2, 1886. It was sent via New York City where a foreign mail registry label with its big "R" and serial number was applied.

Figure 10

Figure 11

An Aug. 8, 1890 Jersey City, N.J. cover bearing an American printed 2¢ Washington in the original lake color (219D).

Where to Find More Information

- *The United States Postage Stamps of the 19th Century* by Lester Brookman, volumes II and III.

- Lester Brookman's *The Bank Note Issues of United States Stamps, 1870-1893*.

- *Cancellations and Killers of the Banknote Era 1870-1894* by James M. Cole contains useful information on cancels and postmarks of the Bank Note era.

- *The United States Two Cent Red Brown of 1883-1887* by Edward L. Willard is a classic text containing general information on nineteenth century stamps, histories, production designs, errors, varieties and much more.

- *U.S. Stamp Facts – 19th Century*, edited by Eliot Landau et al., provides information on topics including designers, engravers, plate arrangements, quantities issued, and most typical usage.

- *The Micarelli Identification Guide to U.S. Stamps.*

- Complex foreign mail rates that existed before the GPU/UPU are explained in Charles J. Starnes' *United States Letter Rates to Foreign Destinations, 1847-1876*.

Chapter 7
Series of 1894

First Bureau Issue

The Series of 1894 holds a unique position in U.S. stamp collecting. Although their designs are a legacy from the American Bank Note Company (American), they were printed by the Bureau of Engraving and Printing (BEP), and have been known to generations of collectors as the First Bureau Issue. Until they were issued, beginning in July 1894, almost all postage stamps had been printed by private printing companies for the Post Office Department (POD). Series of 1894 stamps are categorized into three groups, based primarily on whether or not **watermarked** paper was used, and on their color. The series includes 13 denominations, ranging from 1¢ to $5, with *Scott* numbers from 246 to 284.

On October 16, 1893 the POD began advertising for bids to replace the then current regular issues, printed by American. Bids were due on November 15, 1893 for a four-year contract that would begin on July 1, 1894.

Three bids were received from private printing companies. As soon as the bids were known, a dispute erupted between the low bidder and the second lowest bidder. While the dispute continued, the BEP on November 29 submitted a bid of its own that was lower than any of the private firms. Although this was two weeks after the deadline for the submission of bids, the POD announced its decision on February 21, 1894 to award the contract to the BEP. Under this contract, stamps cost the POD 5¢ per thousand, a savings of 2.47¢ from the previous contract. This contract was the beginning of a new relationship between the BEP and the Post Office that would continue, in various forms, until 2005.

All the incidental supplies, stamps, ***dies***, ***transfer rolls***, and plates in the possession of American related to the 1890 issue were transferred from its New York offices in the late spring of 1894 to the BEP in Washington, D.C. The decision was made to continue using most of the designs previously used by American, including the dies for the 1¢ Franklin, 2¢ Washington, 3¢ Jackson, 4¢ Lincoln, 5¢ Grant, 6¢ Garfield, 8¢ Sherman, 10¢ Webster, and 15¢ Clay. The 30¢ Jefferson was changed to a 50¢ value and the 90¢ Perry was changed to a $1 value. In order to distinguish stamps printed by the BEP from the stamps previously printed by American, the BEP added triangles to the upper right and left hand corners of the American produced dies. These triangles are the chief identifying feature of these stamps. It was also decided to add two additional

Figure 1

The 6¢ Garfield (256) was the first of the Series of 1894 to be issued. Notice the rough perforations, which are characteristic of the early printings of this series.

stamps, a $2 Madison, and a $5 John Marshall. All of the stamps in the Series of 1894 are perf. 12.

The first denomination issued was the 6¢ Garfield (256, fig. 1) possibly on July 18, 1894. Most of the other stamps were issued in the fall of 1894, though the 8¢ Sherman (257) was not issued until March 1895. All stamps in this first group were issued on unwatermarked paper, just as the earlier American printings had been.

There are three varieties of the triangles on the 2¢ stamps (fig. 2). These three triangle types, combined with the use of three slightly different colors, result in five different Scott numbers (248–252) being assigned to the unwatermarked 2¢ stamps. The 2¢ stamp paid the postage on a First Class letter at the time this series was current, thus it was produced in massive quantities. *Plate varieties* of many values exist.

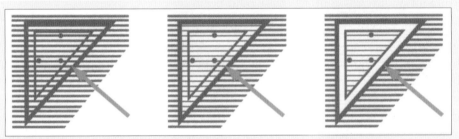

Figure 2

Triangles in the upper right and left corners are the primary distinguishing characteristic of the Series of 1894. Triangles A, B, and C, respectively, from left to right, were used on 2¢ Washington stamps. Scott does not identify triangle varieties on other denominations.

The unwatermarked $1 Perry has two varieties (261 and 261A) because two different dies were used (fig. 3). On one die the circular lines enclosing the "$1" are broken, on the other they are not.

In 1895 a decision was made to print stamps on watermarked paper (ch. 42). Series of 1894 stamps that had only recently appeared on unwatermarked paper now appeared again on paper with a double line USPS watermark (264–278). They are the first postage stamps printed on watermarked paper and constitute the second group of stamps in the First Bureau Issue. The 6¢ and 8¢ stamps have been found printed in error on paper watermarked USIR (271a and 272a).

The third group in the First Bureau Issue (279–284) includes stamps whose colors were changed to conform to **Universal Postal Union** regulations. The 1¢ Franklin was changed from blue to green and the 5¢ Grant from chocolate to blue. In order to avoid confusing postal clerks and the public, the 10¢ Webster, previously printed in green, was reissued in brown (282C) and orange brown (283) and the 15¢ Clay, previously printed in blue, was reissued in olive green. Incidental color changes in this group are the 4¢ Lincoln in shades of brown and the 6¢ Garfield which was changed to lake. The 2¢ Washington is represented by *Scott* 279B and related sub-numbers. As 2¢ plates were produced or repaired, and as dies were repaired, a new type came into existence. Known as "Type IV" it exists only with "Type III" triangle and is found in shades of red (fig. 4).

Figure 3

All of the $1 stamps were printed from one plate of 200 subjects, which was created with two different dies. This combination pair shows type I on the left and type II on the right, with a BEP imprint in the margin.

More *essay* material from the Series of 1894 exists in collector hands than for most other issues printed by the BEP (fig.5). **Large die proofs**, **small dies proofs**, and **plate proofs** also exist in collector hands, as do **color trial proofs** (ch. 53). All of the stamps in this series also exist as imperforate plate proofs printed on stamp paper.

The BEP's first 1894 printings used poor quality paper, which had a "rough" and matte-like finish. This caused the printing inks to bleed easily, sometimes lightly blurring the impression. This paper did not shrink consistently after

Figure 4

Type IV 2¢ Washington (279B) plate number single. Plate 1076 was one of the many plates made using the type IV die, so the presence of this plate number is an easy and foolproof confirmation of its identify as a type IV.

Figure 5

This essay (247-E2) contains two impressions of the 1890 1¢ Franklin die. The right hand impression has a triangle similar to the Type I design in the upper right corner.

printing and produced many slight size variations. It was also very difficult to perforate, resulting in ragged looking perforations. Later printings used a better quality, but still inexpensive, rag paper. This whiter paper also has a smoother finish. Impressions were better and perforations crisper.

The BEP produced a formulation of gum made of dextrin and glucose called "hard" gum that was applied to the stamp sheets before perforation. To prevent stamps from curling, cracking, and detaching during the cold and dry winter season, the BEP altered the formulation to produce a "soft" adhesive "Winter Gum." Post offices receiving stamps with Winter Gum were advised to set them aside when warmer weather set in.

The 2¢ Washington was issued as a booklet pane (279Be) on April 18, 1900. This was the first booklet pane ever issued for a U.S. stamp.

The unwatermarked 2¢ exists imperforate vertically and horizontally (248a, 250d, 252b, and 252c). The 5¢ and 6¢ stamps are known imperforate horizontally (255c and 256a). A number of **EFO**s exist for many 1894 stamps.

Notes on Collecting

The unwatermarked stamps are more valuable than their watermarked counterparts. Since the only difference between two identical looking *Scott*-listed stamps is the presence of a watermark, great care must be taken when purchasing these stamps to be certain that no portion of a watermark is present.

The POD ordered that Series of 1894 stamps not be placed on sale in local post offices until existing stocks of American stamps were depleted. Thus it is uncertain when the BEP printed stamps were actually first used. In 2005 the *earliest documented use* of a Series of 1894 stamp (256) was August 11, 1894. There may well be earlier usages waiting to be discovered.

The 3¢ and 6¢ stamps did not fill any obvious postal need. Three cent and 6¢ stamps were produced by American in 1890, apparently in anticipation of an increase in the first class rate, which never occurred. These stamps are usually seen only in mixed-franking use. The dollar value stamps, which were not available at all post offices, were most likely used as payment receipts. Their use on non-philatelic mail is extremely rare.

First Bureaus exist in many shades. They offer the collector a wonderful challenge to build a collection of shade varieties.

Almanac

1893 – POD begins advertising on October 16 for bidders for a new series of stamps.

1893 – Deadline for the submission of bids is November 15.

1893 – Bureau of Engraving and Printing submits a bid on November 29.

1894 – POD announces on February 21 that a contract will be awarded to BEP.

1894 – BEP assumes contract for printing postage stamps on July 1.

1894 – The first stamp in this series (256) is placed on sale about July 18.

1895 – BEP switches to watermarked paper for postage stamps, creating new varieties.

1900 – The 2¢ Washington is issued as the first U.S. booklet pane (279Be) on April 18.

What Others Have Said

There are gaps in what we know about the First Bureau Issue…
"When the Bureau of Engraving and Printing took over the production of postage stamps in 1894, they assigned the plates they made to a new series, starting with No. 1. We have a complete set of dates on which the plates were assigned, manufactured, certified after manufacture, hardened to extend plate life, and later destroyed after they were cancelled. Except for some information that appeared in the philatelic press at the time, and some dates from other sources, however, we do not have the dates on which the plates were at press prior to September 1898….Nevertheless, we can deduce quite a bit about the printing history of the plates by careful analysis of the dates we do have."

—Wallace Cleland, "Plate Manufacture and Printing by the Bureau," The United States Specialist, 1995.

…but we also have a great deal of detailed information on the series.
"The design of this stamp, bearing the portrait of Commodore Oliver H. Perry, was inherited from the 90-cent value of the 1890-93 issue produced by the American Bank Note Company….In order to save time, the Bureau decided to

use the current designs but with the addition of triangles in the upper corners to distinguish them from the former Bank Note issue. The former 30-cent value was changed to 50-cents and the 90 cents value was raised to $1."

—*Norton D. York, "The Reason for the Two Types of the $1 Stamp,"* American Philatelist, *1965.*

A collector interested in colors and shades is in heaven with the First Bureaus...

"The Post Office Department had agreed to conform to the color scheme adopted by the Universal Postal Union which was to become effective sometime before January 1, 1899. In order to comply with such an arrangement it was only necessary to change the color of two stamps; the one cent blue, to green and the five cent brown, to blue. The other changes were brought about by the Bureau endeavoring to straighten out the color arrangement of the low values of this issue (1895) which had always caused more or less confusion and which were now more likely to do so because of this color change of the one cent and five cent stamps. The new 1c green conflicted with the 10c green, so the ten cent stamp was changed to brown. The 10c brown now conflicted with the 4c brown....The new 5c blue conflicted with the 15c cent blue...The 1898 issue contains some very interesting colors and shades and I am listing each and endeavoring to show just what they are in more detail."

—*Lewis A. Miers, "Shades of the Regular Issue of 1898,"* The Bureau Specialist, *1961.*

...as were the counterfeiters who were happy to note the arrival of the First Bureaus.

"Counterfeiters are quick to take advantage every time the Government lets down on the standard of its product... In 1894, the Bureau of Engraving and Printing was awarded the contract for printing the postage stamps of the United States, but prior to that time the work had always been given out to private contractors. As the Bureau was unaccustomed to the business of printing stamps, the work at first did not come up to the high quality of their predecessors. For a time the two-cent stamps, especially, were in a very light shade, poorly perforated, and on the whole, of a very inferior appearance. Accordingly, it was not long before a counterfeit was being circulated [which were discovered by ads] running in various Chicago newspapers offering $115 worth of current two-cent stamps for $100."

—*George B. Sloane, "Topical Notes on United States Stamps,"* Collectors Club Philatelist, *1922.*

Examples of Postal Usage

Figure6
An early use of the pink 2¢ Washington (248).

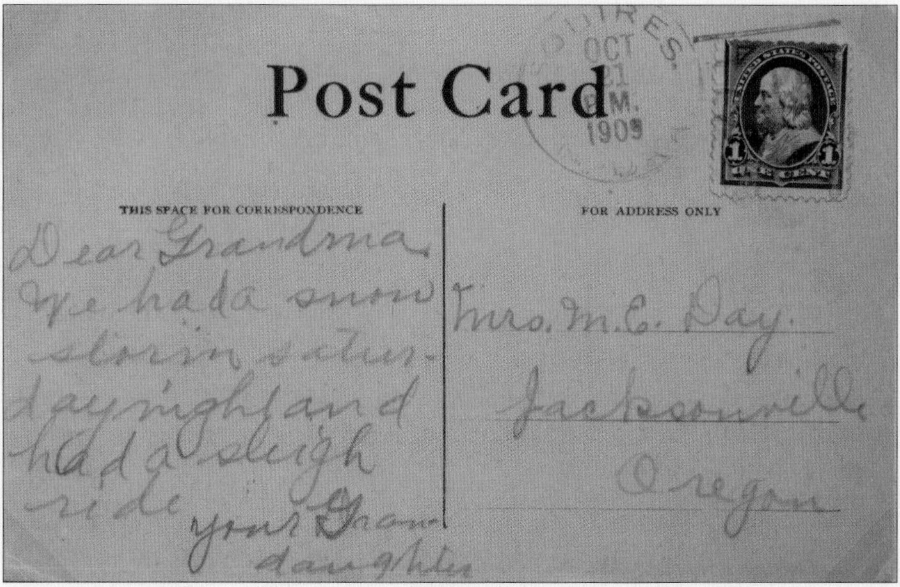

Figure 7
Late usage of a watermarked 1¢ Franklin (264) on a postcard to "grandma".

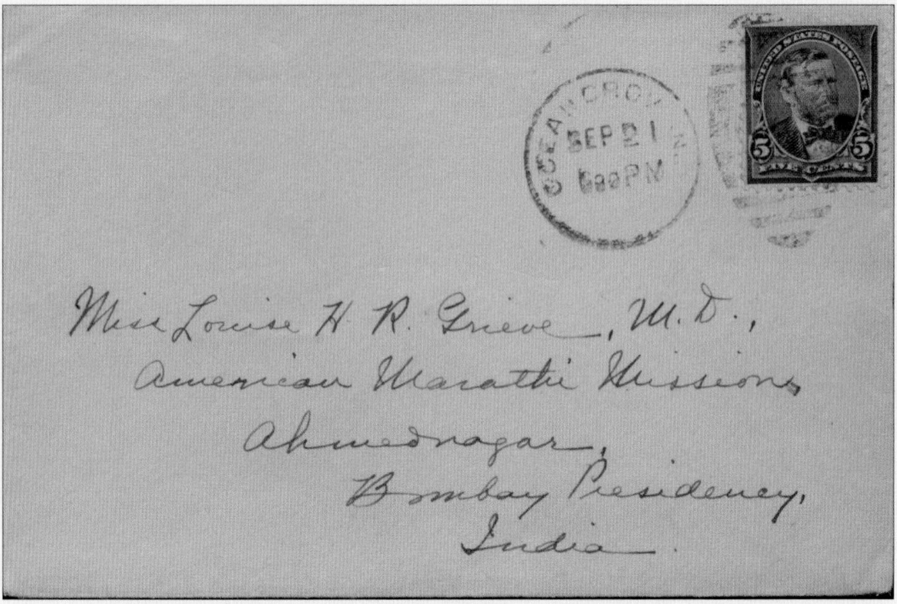

Figure 8

A blue 5¢ Grant (281) used on a missionary letter to India. The color of the 5¢ stamp, which paid the basic foreign rate, was changed from brown to blue in 1898 to conform to Universal Postal Union requirements.

Where to Find More Information

- Volume III of Brookman's *The United States Postage Stamps of the 19th Century*.

- George Brett's "The Two-Cent 1894 Type IV: An Uncatalogued Major Variety" discusses the series and contends that *Scott* may sometimes not be as complete as some scholars would like it to be.

- "The 2¢ Stamps of the First Bureau Issue, Series of 1894-1898" by Kenneth Diehl.

- *U.S. Stamp Facts – 19th Century*, edited by Eliot Landau et al., provides information on topics including designers, engravers, plate arrangements, quantities issued, and most typical usage.

- *The Micarelli Identification Guide to U.S. Stamps*.

- *Encyclopedia of Plate Varieties on U.S. Bureau-Printed Stamps* by Loran C. French provides detailed information on many plate varieties.

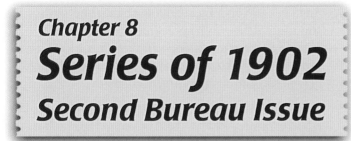

Chapter 8
Series of 1902
Second Bureau Issue

In the final months of 1902, a new set of stamps, the Series 1902, sometimes called the Second Bureau Issue, was introduced. It was the first regular issue of definitive stamps completely designed and produced for the Post Office Department (POD) by the craftsmen of the BEP, unlike the first definitive stamps that were produced by the BEP from the reworked *dies* received from the **American Bank Note Company** (ch. 7). Series of 1902 stamps were released in sheet, coil, and booklet pane formats. They were printed on double-line **watermarked** paper and gauge 12 perforation was used.

The task of designing the Series of 1902 was given to the BEP's chief designer, Raymond Ostrander Smith, who previously had designed both the popular 1898 Trans-Mississippi (*Scott* 285–293) and 1901 Pan-American (294–299) Exposition Issues. There are sixteen designs in the series, including a Special Delivery design, and a replacement for the original 2¢ design. All the stamps produced with these designs (except for the 2¢ replacement) were in general use from their date of issue through 1909. However stamps with the $2 and $5 designs were produced until 1918 and the Special Delivery design continued on stamps until 1922.

Design Features

The Series of 1902 marks the first time that a stamp's design included the name of the person portrayed, as well as year dates of birth and death. Two historical events gave impetus to the inclusion of these features. The 1898 Spanish-American War significantly increased both the country's global territory, and the number of people served by the U.S. postal system. Between 1890 and 1910, 16 million immigrants landed on both shores of the continental United States. By 1902 almost one third of the country's population consisted of immigrants or first generation Americans. Most spoke little or no English. The portraits on these stamps provide one of the few exposures many of them had to some of the great historical figures of

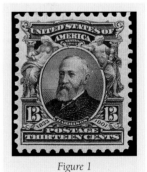

Figure 1

The first stamp issued in the Series of 1902 was the 13¢ stamp honoring President Benjamin Harrison (308).

Figure 2

The 8¢ Martha Washington stamp (306) was often used to pay the fee for registered mail.

American history. By including names, and birth and death dates on these definitive stamps, it was hoped to increase awareness of these historical figures. This in turn would help assimilate all these new postal patrons into American culture.

Only three of the Series of 1902 stamps were actually released during 1902. The 13¢ stamp (fig. 1), honoring the recently deceased Benjamin Harrison (308) was issued in November. It was the first U.S. 13¢ stamp, and was intended to pay the 8¢ registry fee plus 5¢ foreign letter rate. The 8¢ Martha Washington (306, fig. 2) and 10¢ Special Delivery (E6, fig. 3) were issued in December. The remaining stamps of the series, according to the Post Office's plan, were released within the first few months of 1903.

Nine stamps in the Series of 1902 portray the same individuals, using the same denominations, as appeared on the **Series of 1894**. However, William Tecumseh Sherman, who appeared on the 8¢ stamp in the earlier series, was replaced by Martha Washington on the new series. The wife of the first President was the first American woman depicted on a U.S. stamp. This 8¢ stamp was primarily used to pay the 8¢ Registry fee. Commodore Oliver Hazard Perry, Naval hero of the War of 1812, was replaced on the new $1 stamp by Civil War Admiral and Union naval hero David Glasgow Farragut. Former General and U.S. President Ulysses S. Grant went from the 5¢ stamp to the 4¢ denomination. His Commander in Chief, President Abraham Lincoln, was promoted from the 4¢

Figure 3

The "Messenger on Bicycle" design was used on five Special Delivery Stamps, distinguishable on the basis of watermark and perforation gauge.

value to the 5¢, the value used primarily to pay the **Universal Postal Union** (UPU) foreign single letter rate. Lincoln was deemed a better image for a world audience.

Another feature of the series was the inclusion of the words "Series 1902" on each stamp. In 1898 the BEP initiated a policy of printing the "series year" on the revenue stamps issued to pay for the Spanish-American War. This policy was first applied to postage stamps with the 1901 commemorative Pan-American issue. This feature was continued on postage stamps after the Series of 1902, including the five stamp 1904 Louisiana Purchase and three stamp 1907 Jamestown commemorative series, but was discontinued with the introduction of the Washington-Franklin Series (Third Bureau Issue) in 1908.

An unusual aspect of the series was the replacement of the original 2¢ design within the first ten months of its issue (fig 4). The 2¢ three-quarter profile portrait of George Washington with the "flag" frame (301) was beautifully designed. Unfortunately, the stamps produced frequently gave an impression of a "red-faced," and perhaps inebriated, founding father of his country. The criticism of the "flag" design did not

Figure 4

The original 2¢ stamp issued (left, 301) was replaced after a brief period by one that received greater public acceptance (right, 319).

let up, and on September 23, 1903 a replacement, the Washington "shield" design (319) was approved. The first stamps were made available in November. Though often referred to as the Washington Shield stamp of 1903, the stamp was clearly created to replace the original stamp, and is engraved "Series 1902."

The $2 and $5 (fig. 5) values were used well past the introduction of the Washington-Franklin Head Series of 1908–1921 (ch. 9). In fact both of these values were reprinted in 1917, though in the then current unwatermarked, perf. 10 format (479 and 480). These stamps met the demand for postage for foreign mail parcels to Europe and Russia as that continent was engulfed in war. The longest lasting design of the series was the "Messenger on

Figure 5

The $2 and $5 stamps were originally issued perf. 12 on double-line watermarked paper (312 and 313). In 1917 they were reprinted on unwatermarked paper and perforated 10 (479 and 480)

Bicycle," used on five different Special Delivery stamps (E6, E8–11) before it was replaced in 1922.

Producing the Stamps

Like all previous U.S. stamps, the Series of 1902 was **intaglio** printed. The designs were engraved on steel dies. The die imprints were then transferred to rolls for impression of 400 and 200 subjects on the flat steel plates from which the stamps were printed. All Series 1902 stamps were printed on the BEP's four-position flat bed steam presses (ch. 35).

Figure 6

The prominent "gash" plate variety on the 2¢ "shield" Washington stamp appears on both perforated (319f) and imperforate (320a) stamps.

As in all flat press printing, **plate varieties** (ch. 46) were produced. Shifts and **double transfers**, plate cracks, and transfer **relief breaks** are known on several values of the series. One of the most dramatic plate varieties on the 2¢ Washington "Shield" stamp is the "Gash on face" which is known on both perforate and **imperforate** stamps (fig. 6). This gash damage to the printing plate occurred before the plate went to press and is located on position 226 on the 400 subject Plate No. 4671. The position is referred to as 4671 LL 16.

When placed on the press the sheet paper had to be sufficiently water moistened so the ink would adhere. The manual printing process produced many different missing ink varieties resulting from paper folds and paper creases. These oddities are known on most of the values.

When the printed sheets were dry they were pressed (stacked with weights) to be made ready for the gumming process. The method employed to gum the sheets was a process combining both gumming and drying. Operators placed the printed and pressed sheets face down on conveyors that ran the length of the BEP's gumming room. The backs of the sheets were mechanically gummed and carried through heated boxes to dry the gum.

The printed and gummed sheets were then perforated by operators who inserted the 400 subject sheets into a belt-driven pedal activated perforating machine. Circular wheels with perforation pins set 12 per 20 millimeters perforated the sheet in the "insert" direction and a center cutting wheel severed the sheet into 200 subject vertically perforated half-sheets. The half-sheets were turned 90 degrees and inserted into the perforator producing the perpendicular perforations while slicing the sheets into two 100 subject panes.

Horizontal and vertical **guide lines** were printed on the sheets to assist the operators during the perforating process. The sheets were often misaligned producing poorly perforated stamps. There are many examples of sheets fed more than once into the perforator. Other perforation varieties were produced when the sheet paper folded while being fed into the rotating perforator. These are usually found on corners or leading edges.

Important perforation errors exist on the 2¢ Washington Shield stamp. There are "imperforate between" (319e), "rouletted imperforate between" (319e rouletted), and "imperforate horizontal" (319d) errors, all recognized by separate listings in the catalogue.

Production Formats and Innovation

The 1¢ through 15¢ values were printed on 400 subject sheets. The 50¢ and dollar values were printed on 200 subject sheets, as was an initial quantity of the 15¢ value. All of these sheets were cut into the panes of 100 stamps that were sold at post offices. The Special Delivery stamps were printed on 200 subject sheets and cut and sold in panes of 50 stamps.

Booklet stamps had been introduced in 1900 with the 2¢ design of the Series of 1894. The concept was popular and both of the 2¢ designs of the 1902 Series were offered in booklets of 12, 24, and 48 stamps (fig. 7). Booklets contained panes of six stamps. While 2¢ stamps were required for letter postage, 1¢ stamps were required for **post cards**. The 1¢ Franklin design of the Series 1902 was the first 1¢ stamp offered in booklet form. Issued in March 1907, the 1¢ booklet, containing 24 stamps (four panes of six) was created for customer convenience amidst the worldwide picture post card craze of the day.

Figure 7

Booklet panes like this one were assembled into convenient booklets, which were popular with the public.

Additionally, imperforate sheets were made available for the first time in fifty years. Imperforate sheets of 400 of the 1¢, 2¢, and 5¢ values (314, 320, and 315) were made available beginning in late 1906. One shipment of 4¢ stamps (314A) appeared in 1908. These imperforate sheets were made available as an accommodation to the manufacturers of stamp vending and affixing machines. The manufacturers of these machines applied their own unique **Vending and Affixing Machine** Perforations, also known as private perforations, used to mechanically feed the stamps through their machines. The perforated sheet stamps produced by the BEP tore easily and could not successfully be made into coils to work in these vending and affixing machines. Commercial vending and affixing machine manufacturers had asked the Post Office to provide coils with individualized perforations for their machines, but the Post Office would have no part in that idea. The imperforate sheets were offered as a compromise, allowing the private companies to apply their own perforations. Many collectors find the fascinating variety of private perforations a desirable area to collect (ch. 49). These stamps are listed in *Scott* as "Vending and affixing machine perforations."

Introduction of Coil Stamps

The Series of 1902 saw the introduction of the first U.S. coil stamps. The POD recognized the problems vending and affixing machine manufacturers experienced trying to make coils from sheet stamps. The BEP was asked create a limited number of straight edge strips of stamps, manually pasted end to end and rolled into coils. The first of these experimental coil stamp rolls was introduced in February 1908 starting with 1¢, 2¢, and 5¢ vertical coil stamps perforated 12 horizontally (316, 321, and 317). In July of 1908 experimental 1¢ and 2¢ horizontal stamp coils rolls perforated 12 vertically were also made available in limited quantities (318 and 322). These experimental coil stamp rolls were only offered to the machine manufacturers and were not for sale to general public. The experiment lasted for less than a year and only a very limited quantity was distributed.

These experimental coils were initially shunned by collectors. The double straight edges were considered unattractive and collectors believed that they could be easily made by cutting the perforations off sheet stamps. As a result, these first government coil stamps are today great rarities of U.S. philately.

Around the time the experimental perforated horizontal coil rolls were issued in July 1908, the POD also had the BEP produce a very limited quantity of **endwise** and **sidewise** imperforate coils for vending and affixing machine companies. Some of these experimental imperforate coils are actually rarer than their perforated coil counterparts. *Scott* assigns these imperforate coils the same catalogue number assigned to the imperforate sheet stamps from which they were made, but adds an H or a V to the number to indicate that the stamps are coiled horizontally (side by side) or vertically (end to end).

Overprinted Stamps

For a brief period the United States produced overprinted regular issue stamps for use in the Canal Zone and Philippines, a possession acquired from Spain after the 1898 war (ch. 27). Five denominations, the 1¢, 2¢, 5¢, 8¢, and 10¢

stamps were overprinted for use in the Canal Zone. They were used only from July to December of 1904 when special Canal Zone stamps were provided.

All of the denominations, including the 2¢ Shield booklet, were overprinted "Philippines" for use only in the Philippine Islands. They were used from 1903 until they became obsolete in September of 1906. One pane of 100 of the Special Delivery stamp was overprinted as a special favor for the Bureau of Insular Affairs to meet requests for specimens. These Series 1902 Special Delivery stamps, however, never saw service in the Philippine Islands.

Notes on Collecting

Values below one dollar in used condition are readily obtainable at a modest cost. The dollar values present a greater financial challenge. On cover usage of both the sheet and booklet stamps can be obtained at reasonable cost and presents a fascinating variety of postal markings of the period.

Collecting interest can expand to the Canal Zone and Philippine overprinted stamps. **Precancel** and **perfin** collectors (ch. 29) will find a rich variety of examples in what would be considered the classic period for these collectables. As mentioned earlier, the series offers a rich selection of private perforation varieties. Many off cover used examples, while not very expensive, are surprisingly difficult to find. Those wishing to expand in a more specialized way can consider acquiring some production material available in the form of **essays** drawings and **proofs** (ch. 53), and **specimen** stamps. Collectors who have recently won the lottery might consider adding the experimental coils to their shopping list. Since the imperforate coils can easily be faked from imperforate sheet stamps, obtaining an expertizing certificate is essential.

Almanac

1902 – On February 7 Edwin C. Madden, Third Assistant Postmaster General, requests the Treasury Secretary to create a new series of ordinary postage stamps.

1902 – The 13¢ Benjamin Harrison stamp is issued on November 18 as the first in this new series.

1903 – The 2¢ shield stamp is issued to replace the original 2¢ stamp on November 12.

1906 – The 1¢ and 2¢ values are offered in imperforate sheets of 400 beginning October 2.

1907 – The 1¢ Franklin stamps are offered in booklets of 24 stamps beginning March 6.

1908 – The 1¢ and 2¢ values experimental coil stamps are offered beginning February 18 to vending and affixing machine makers.

1908 – The 5¢ value is offered in imperforate sheets of 400 beginning May 12.

1917 – The $2 and $5 values are reprinted March 17 and issued five days later on March 22.

1922 – The 10¢ Special Delivery "Messenger on Bicycle" design is replaced on July 12.

What Others Have Said

A New Series is Requested
"The Third Assistant Postmaster General has asked the Bureau of Engraving and Printing to prepare designs for a new postal issue. The Bureau was asked to supply better photographs (if possible) and to employ special pains in designing a series particularly attractive and distinctive, and fully as creditable as the Pan-American."

—Mekeel's Weekly, 1902.

The only Picture of the First Lady
"The drawing for the eight cents denomination, portrait of Martha Washington, has progressed so far that probably this week the model will be submitted to the stamp division of Department for inspection and suggestions….the portrait of Martha is the one with which everyone is familiar, in fact it is the only picture known to exist of the first 'first lady of the land'."

—J. Walter Scott, "Washington Notes," The Metropolitan Philatelist, 1902. Scott chronicled breaking news of the new Series of 1902 almost every week in this column over a two year period.

For the Benefit of Foreigners
"The new stamp has been made especially for the benefit of those foreigners who know not our history, for do we not perceive under the engraving the name, noble and honored, of Washington? And is there not also the dates showing his time of office [sic]? This is history – and for 2 cents!"

—Frederic D. Pangborn, a letter to the editor of the New York Times, about the new 2¢ Washington Flag stamp, February 9, 1903.

Selection of Subjects for Series of 1902 stamps
"R. Ostrander Smith was called upon to draw up a series that would do justice to the abilities of the department, and we would say that he amply succeeded.

In several ways the issue was to set a precedent. The 8¢ bearing a portrait of Martha Washington was our first stamp to so honor our first lady. The 13¢ was the inaugural use of this denomination and also to honor the twenty-third President. Farragut on the $1 received his first postal recognition."

—*Clifford C. Cole, "United States Gossip – 20th Century – The Issue of 1902-03,"* Weekly Philatelic Gossip, 1947.

Leftover $1 and $5 stamps

"When the new series of 1908 first came out the highest denomination provided was a $1.00 stamp. At that particular time there were in the vaults of the Bureau a fairly large quantity of $2.00 and $5.00 stamps left over from the previous issue of 1902-03 and no doubt this was considered sufficient to take care of the small demands for these high values for some time to come, consequently the issuing of a $2.00 and $5.00 stamp for the new series (1908) was postponed."

—*Lewis A. Miers, "The Two and Five Dollar Stamps of the Bureau Issues,"* The United States Specialist, 1964.

Examples of Postal Usage

Figure 8

Millions of 1¢ Franklins (300) were used on post cards, which were very popular in the early twentieth century. This 1¢ Franklin is on a postcard with an exposition station cancel from the 1909 Alaska-Yukon-Pacific Exposition. Note the partial BEP imprint on the margin attached to the bottom of the stamp.

Figure 9

The 2¢ "shield" Washington (319) on this first class cover replaced the earlier and unpopular 2¢ "flag" Washington (301). The cover was originally mailed October 14, 1905 in Fredonia, Kans. without a stamp. It received an auxiliary marking, "HELD FOR POSTAGE." When the 2¢ "shield" stamp was supplied the cover was postmarked Oct. 16, with a duplex handstamp and sent on its way. The Oct 18 date stamp was applied by the addressee.

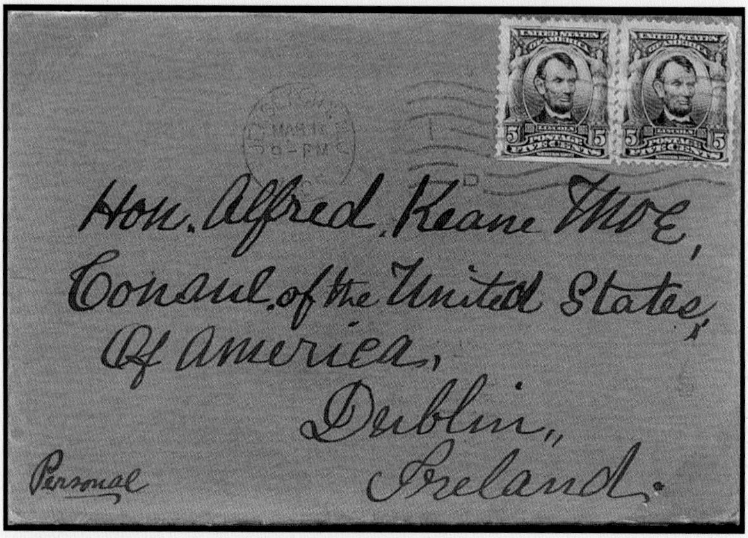

Figure 10

The Universal Postal Union rate for single weight foreign covers was 5¢. The two 5¢ Lincolns (304) indicate this cover to Ireland was double weight. It has a typical International machine wavy line cancel.

Figure 11

This 1903 registered cover to Japan bears a 13¢ Harrison (308), which paid the single weight foreign postage of 5¢, plus the 8¢ registration fee. Note the San Francisco exchange label and several numbers used to track and account for registered mail.

Where to Find More Information

- *The United States Postage Stamps of the Twentieth Century*, by Beverly S. King and Max G. Johl.

- Max Johl's update to the above book, *United States Postage Stamps 1902–1935*.

- *Encyclopedia of Plate Varieties on U.S. Bureau-Printed Stamps* by Loran C. French provides detailed information on many plate varieties.

Chapter 9

Washingon-Franklin Series

Third Bureau Issue

A new series of stamps, commonly known as the Washington-Franklin Head Issue, or simply the Washington-Franklins, appeared in late 1908 (fig. 1). Before the last of these stamps were issued in early 1922 (*Scott* 497, fig. 2), approximately 250 different stamps were issued, all bearing the likeness of either George Washington, the first president, or Benjamin Franklin, the first Postmaster General – hence the name, "Washington-Franklins." Just five *Scott* illustration numbers are needed for all these different stamps. To the casual observer many of these stamps may look identical; however, the subtle differences among them make the series the most challenging definitives to collect. Also known as the "Third Bureau Issue," these Washington-Franklin stamps have *Scott* numbers from 331 to 547.

Figure 1

The first two sheet stamps in the Washington-Franklin Series (331–332), issued in 1908, were perforated 12 and had double line watermarks. The vignettes of Washington and Franklin were used throughout the series, and give the series its name. Note the denomination on these early Washington-Franklin stamps is in words instead of numerals.

In late 1908 the Post Office Department (POD) announced that the then-current ordinary stamps, the Series of 1902 (ch. 8), would be replaced. An October 23 bulletin from the Office of the Third Assistant Postmaster General provided information regarding the new stamps, which included denominations, designs, and some relatively curious information including a specific date for the issuance of a 2¢ booklet (November 16, 1908), and a promise that the 2¢ sheet stamps, and other stamps, would follow thereafter. The bulletin mandated that existing stocks of the old style stamps be sold by local post offices until the supply was exhausted and also informed local postmasters that the Department reserved the right to deliver the old style stamps if demand for the new ones outpaced the supply. As a result of this policy, Washington-Franklin stamps did not enjoy widespread use until the

Figure 2

The rotary press printed 10¢ orange yellow coil (497) was the last Washington-Franklin issued. The vertical joint line between the two stamps was produced on the web at the point where two printing plates met.

first quarter of 1909. Accordingly, usages in 1908 of the 1¢ and 2¢ stamps are scarce and 1908 usages of other denominations are rare. By 1909 however, Washington-Franklin stamps were commonly used, and would remain so into the early 1920s.

These stamps were all designed by Clair Aubrey Huston of the Bureau of Engraving and Printing (BEP). All were printed on the flat plat press with the exception of several coil stamps and experimental sheet stamps printed on the ***rotary press*** late in the life of the series and several sheet stamps produced by ***offset printing*** from 1918 to 1920. The single most notable feature of this series is the use of only two images, those of Washington and Franklin, a radical departure from the trend to expand the number of individuals on stamps. Not since the first two postage stamps of 1847 had only Washington and Franklin appeared on the nation's stamps.

For many years, many collectors found the Washington-Franklins very confusing and had difficulty distinguishing them because of their similarity. As a result many ignored them. Although all these stamps feature Washington or Franklin, using the same two ***vignettes***, the series did experience a number of design and production changes over the years. In 1991 Larry Weiss introduced a way of categorizing the Washington-Franklin ***flat plate intaglio*** printed sheet stamps, based on those design and production changes. His schema of "six major sets", which is presented below, makes the series more intelligible and the stamps easier to identify.

The New Series and its Design Error – First Major Set (331–342)

The designer and postal officials seemed unaware of agreements within the **Universal Postal Union** (UPU) requiring Arabic numerals on all stamps. As a result the words ONE CENT and TWO CENTS appear on the two lowest values as originally issued (fig. 1). The various denominations, all perf. 12 on double-line **watermarked** paper were tied to exact rates of postage and certain postal fees. For example, 1¢ for post cards and printed matter, 2¢ for first class, 5¢ for foreign mail, 8¢ to cover the registry fee, and 10¢ to pay for special delivery. Other stamps paid for multiples of rates, for example, the 4¢ stamp for a 2 ounce letter.

Figure 3

In 1912 a new frame was designed for use on stamps with a denomination of 8¢ through $1. Shown here is a 12¢ claret brown (417), perf. 12 with single-line watermarked.

Changing the Watermark – Second Major Set (374–382)

When originally issued, the stamps were printed on paper with the double line watermarks that the BEP had been using on stamps since 1895 (see ch. 42 - Watermarks). The watermark design was changed to a single line in 1910 in the hope that this would strengthen the paper. This change of watermarks is the distinguishing characteristic of the second major set, with all other characteristics remaining the same as the first set. But this new watermark did not have the intended result of solving the problem of uneven shrinkage of printed sheets of stamps. As a result, perforations frequently continued to cut into designs, and truly well centered stamps may be hard to find.

Fixing the Design Error and Effects of the Parcel Post System - Third Major Set (405–407, 414–423)

In 1912, the 1¢ and 2¢ Washington-Franklin stamps were made to conform to the UPU protocol by identifying their values in Arabic numerals instead of words.

Stamps in additional and seemingly unusual denominations were added to the series to accommodate the demands of the **Parcel Post** system, which was introduced for domestic mail in 1913. Parcel Post rates were based on the weight of an item and the distance it had to travel. Additional stamps were issued to help make up the many different rates that were possible.

When the series was first issued, Franklin appeared on only the 1¢ stamp and Washington on all the others. However, beginning in 1912, the Washington vignette was used on all stamps from 1¢ through 7¢, and the Franklin vignette on 8¢ and above. Additionally, the *frame* for the Franklin stamps (those with a value over 7¢) was changed (fig. 3). It was explained that new values were needed because of the introduction of the Parcel Post system, and since some of those new stamps were in colors similar to existing denominations, a change was necessary in order to reduce confusion among the public and among postal clerks who had to handle and account for these stamps. For example, a 5¢ blue Washington was more readily distinguishable from a 20¢ blue Franklin with a different frame than would have been the case if the same vignette and frame appeared on both values.

Changes in Perforation to Avoid Premature Separation – Fourth Major Set (424–440, 460)

When first issued in 1908, the Washington-Franklin stamps were perforated 12, which was standard at the time. Unfortunately, these perforations were very fine and caused panes and smaller multiples of the stamps to separate prematurely. The size perforation for sheet stamps was changed to 10 in 1914. This new gauge perforation is the defining characteristic of the fourth major set. But this size proved too coarse resulting in stamps that were difficult to separate!

Eliminating the Watermark – Fifth Major Set (462–466, 468–478)

The single line watermarked paper provided only portions of small letters on most stamps. This was barely useful as a security measure and the watermark was still thought to be a source of uneven shrinkage of the paper. Considering these factors, but probably more as an economy measure, a change was made to unwatermarked paper in 1916. This change, unnoticeable to the public, created a fifth major set of sheet stamps for collectors. All values were printed on this unwatermarked paper.

Figure 4

The $2 and $5 Washington-Franklins appeared in a horizontal format and shared a single vignette plate. The $5 stamp shown here (524) was issued in 1918.

The Change to Perforation 11 – Sixth Major Set (498–499, 501–518, and 523–524)

In 1917 the perforation gauge was changed to 11, the defining characteristic of the sixth major set. This size perforation was retained for all flat plate printed sheet stamps for the balance of the issue's lifetime. In 1918 $2 and $5 (524, fig. 4) stamps were added to the series, with the $2 stamp being reissued in a different color in 1920. Printed on unwatermarked paper, these stamps were phased out during 1922–1923.

Other Washington-Franklins

Not all sheet stamps were perforated. A number of Washington-Franklins were issued without any perforations at all and are not included in any of the major sets listed above. Imperforate sheets were manufactured for the benefit of companies who privately perforated them for use in **vending and affixing machines** (ch. 49).

While most of the Washington Franklin stamps were produced by the line-engraved intaglio method of printing, a temporary switch was made to the off-set printing process in 1918 (fig. 5). This was an emergency measure brought about by the U.S. entry into World War I and the resultant shortage of high quality ink. Denominations of 1¢, 2¢, and 3¢ (525–536) were produced in this manner until 1920, when the use of offset printing ceased.

Figure 5

Stamps of the Washington-Franklin series were printed using three types of presses. Illustrated here are examples from the flat plate press (left), offset press (center) and rotary press (right). The flat plate printed imperforate stamp on the left (408) has an "A" marginal marking indicating uniform vertical spacing between columns of stamps. The offset printed stamp (525) has a plate number altered by hand. The pair of rotary press printed stamps on the right (538) is coil waste, sheet stamps created from leftover pieces intended to be made into coil stamps. The "S30" marginal marking indicates the plate was made from a die with an experimental variation in the depth of the frame line. Note the design of the rotary printed stamp is slightly taller than the others due to the nature of rotary printing.

An early attempt at solving the problem of uneven paper shrinkage was the experimental use of so-called **Blue Paper** in 1909 (357–366). This paper contained a substantial amount of rag content, but it did not solve the shrinkage problem. Another attempt to solve the problem was increasing the space between subjects on printing plates, but it met with only limited success. In fact, the paper shrinkage problem, and the resulting problem of poorly centered stamps, was destined to go unsolved throughout the Washington-Franklin era.

Stamp formats continued to evolve during the Washington-Franklin era. The first booklet pane and coil stamps had appeared with the Series of 1902. But it was only during the Washington-Franklin years that these formats came into widespread use. In fact coil stamps became so popular that the BEP could not keep up with demand because coil stamps were printed on the flat plate press and manufactured into rolls by a very labor-intensive process (ch. 49). To help meet the demand for coil stamps, a rotary press (ch. 36) was developed which began producing coil stamps in 1914. This printing method made it possible for coils to be produced "by the mile," and was a tremendous innovation. Having successfully produced coil stamps, the rotary press was adapted to sheet production in 1920 to produce the 1¢ stamp (542 and 543). However the use of the rotary press to print sheet stamps was not fully successful and the stamps produced were not fully satisfactory due to the tendency of panes to curl. Washington-Franklin coils stamps, like their sheet stamp cousins, saw a number of changes in perforations. Coils were first perforated 12, then 8½, followed by 10, and then 11.

Booklet panes of six stamps were popular during these years and were produced perf. 10, 11, and 12. Like the sheet stamps, booklets are also found with double-line watermarks, single-line watermarks, and no watermarks. Booklets with ten panes of 30 stamps each (498f and 499f) were produced for use by the American Expeditionary Forces (AEF) during World War I. Stamps were manufactured in this unusual sized format to facilitate transport of stamps to military post offices abroad, not with the expectation that a soldier would buy a book of 300 stamps!

Some stamps exist with two different perforation sizes on the same stamp. These are known as **compound perforations**. Compound perforations were applied to some of the 1¢ stamps printed on the rotary press (542). Compound perforations were also applied to **coil waste** stamps. A very rare compound perforation came into existence when a perforating wheel of one size was replaced with a perforating wheel of a different size. The resulting stamps (423A–423E) have one size perforation on three sides, and a different size perforation on the fourth side.

Several Washington-Franklin stamps are noteworthy due to special circumstances. There exist three significant *errors* (467, 485, and 505) caused by a *re-entry* (ch. 46). An experimental use of perf. 11 on a 2¢ single line watermarked Washington resulted in a scarce issue (461). Finally, the application of gauge 11 perforations to a small quantity of obsolete 2¢ Washingtons also resulted in a new and scarce variety (519).

Notes on Collecting

The Post Office needed many millions of 2¢ and 3¢ stamps. In an effort to increase production, the BEP resorted to some production techniques that resulted in printed stamps with very minor design differences. Their "type" identifies these slightly different 2¢ and 3¢ stamps, each with its own catalogue number. There are four types of engraved 2¢ stamps and five types of the offset. There are two types of engraved 3¢ stamps and two of the offset. Most of these stamps are not very expensive, but require time and patience to properly identify. The charts in *Micarelli* as well as the listings in *Scott* are very useful in helping to achieve proper identification.

One way to collect the Washington-Franklins is to attempt to build a comprehensive collection of the entire series in mint and used condition. With more than 250 different stamps, many of them stamps that look alike to the naked eye, such a collection will bring great satisfaction. However, the existence of several rare stamps makes attainment of this goal very challenging.

Building a Washington-Franklin cover collection provides many opportunities to search for "cheap covers" which may have substantial value if you are familiar with the various dates and rates involved. For example, to help finance World War I, postage rates were increased from November 2, 1917 until June 30, 1919, when they returned to pre-war levels. During this period of almost two years, mailing a letter cost 3¢ while a post card cost 2¢. Building a cover collection and finding covers, of different usages with these exact dates, and surrounding dates, can be used to tell an important Washington-Franklin story. A cover collection which shows the various denominations in *solo* and multiple stamp use can be developed by consulting the two rate books by Beecher and Wawrukiewicz.

Some Washington-Franklin stamps are commonly faked by the addition of phony perforations and should not be purchased without an expert certificate.

It is advisable to collect Washington-Franklin coils in pairs whenever possible since it to more difficult for pairs to be faked. *Scott* provides a note following the listing of stamps that are commonly faked.

Almanac

1908 – The Third Assistant Postmaster General announces the Washington-Franklin Series on October 23.

1910 – Use of single line watermarked paper begins at BEP.

1914 – First coil stamps are printed by rotary press.

1916 – Use of unwatermarked paper begins at the BEP.

1917 – War rates go into effect on November 17, including the letter rate which rose from 2¢ to 3¢.

1918 – Stamps are first printed by offset press.

1920 – First sheet stamps produced on the rotary press.

1922 – The 10¢ coil (497) is the last Washington-Franklin issued, on January 22.

What Others Have Said

Explanation for the design changes of 1912
"The postage stamps of the 1908 issue, while possessing high artistic merit, had given considerable trouble to the public and to the Postal service on account of the similarity of designs of the different denominations. All of the twelve stamps were of the identical design, except the one-cent denomination that bears the portrait of Franklin, while the others bear the portrait of Washington…. In the rapid handling of mail matter one denomination was very apt to be mistaken for another…. To give more marked contrast [for denominations over 7¢] a change was made in the border design. With these changes the stamps…will [present] the head of the first President on the first six denominations and that of the first Postmaster General, with a different border design…"

—*Post Office press release, July 18, 1911.*

A simple announcement about a Postmaster's decision and his reasoning
"The postmaster general has decided to add the following new values to our stock of stamps, viz., 7c, 9c, 12c, 20c and 30c. The object being to enable any letter postage up to 60c to be prepaid with not more than two stamps."

—*"Chronicle – United States,"* The Metropolitan Philatelist, *1913.*

A Printing Method that generated a huge number of unplanned varieties

"The Offset Printing issue came into being as a direct result of the unusual conditions prevailing prior to this country's entrance into World War I. Shortages, both in the number of available skilled workers and in the proper materials for making stamps from engraved steel plates, resulted in the use of a method hitherto untried in the United States for postage stamp production – the photolithographic or offset printing process. Shortly after the cessation of hostilities, the United States reverted to the engraving method....The Offset Printing issue was the only series for which engraving was not employed by our Government in the manufacture of its postage stamps..... The Offset Printing issue, because of certain innate qualities, abounds in variations from the normal...The unusual is to be expected with the stamps of the 1918 Offset Printing issue. The inclusion of any markings on our postage stamps (other than the plate numbers, and the guide lines and arrows) was contrary to regulations then in effect."

—*David M. Bennett, "Unique Marginal Markings on the U.S. Offset Printing Issue of 1918-20,"* The 1965 Congress Book, *1965.*

The War Tax creates a need for new stamps highlighted by the 13¢ apple green Franklin

"On April 6, 1917, both the United States Senate and House of Representatives passed a resolution of war with Germany....To help finance the war effort, a tax was imposed for certain items mailed in the United States. To postal patrons, this had the net effect of increasing postage rates. In fact, the Act of October 3, 1917, referred to this as a rate change, with Postmaster General liable to the general fund of the Treasury for a monthly amount equal to the estimate of the increase... The existence of the war tax caused the government to release several stamps that had not been previously issued. One of the more notable items was the 13-cent apple green Franklin issue (*Scott* #513) of 1919. It met the new rate for letter plus special delivery, and letter plus registration fees....With the end of the war in 1919, the war tax became a thing of the past. Effective July 1, 1919, letter rates became 2 cents per ounce and the penny postcard returned."

—*Jay B. Stotts, "The Postal War Tax Rates of 1917-1919,"* The United States Specialist, *1993.*

Examples of Postal Usage

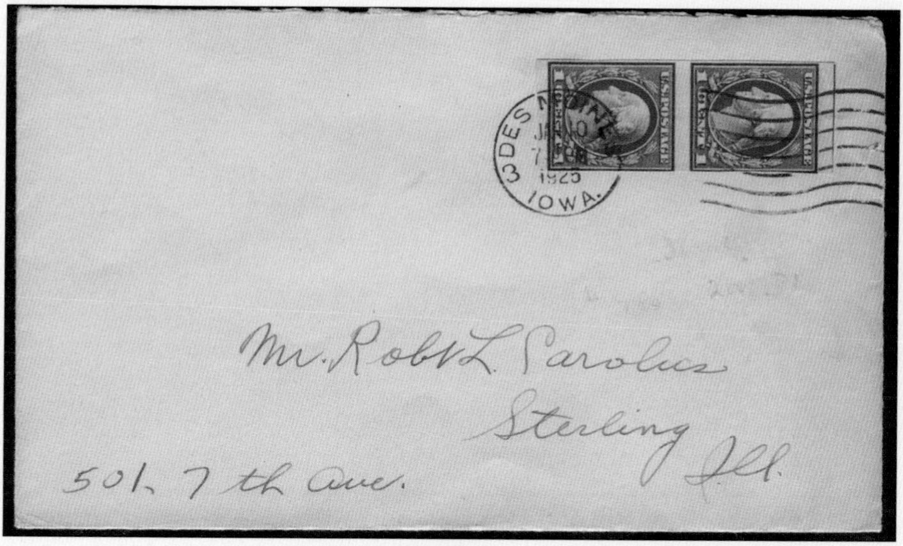

Figure 6

An imperforate pair is used to frank a First Class cover. The stamps are probably unwatermarked (481), but cannot be verified without removing the stamps from the cover to examine them for the presence of a watermark.

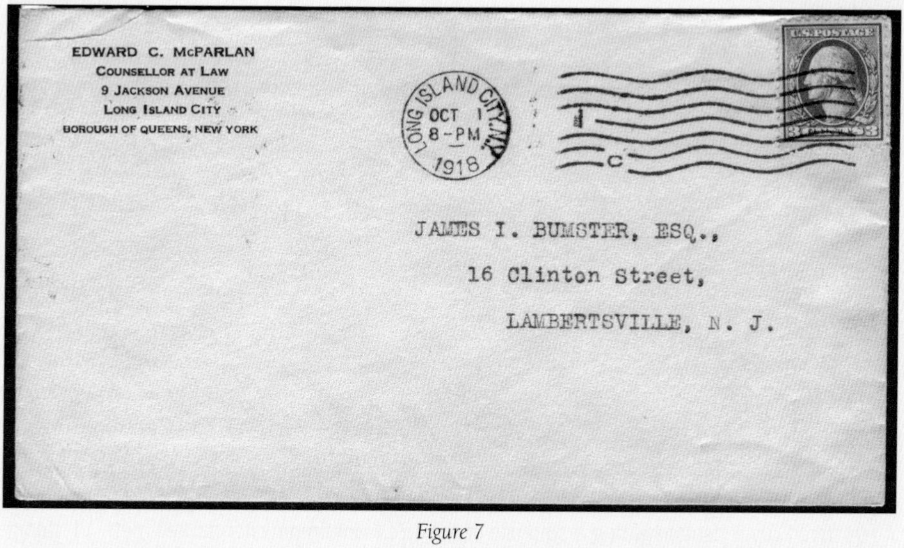
EDWARD C. McPARLAN
COUNSELLOR AT LAW
9 JACKSON AVENUE
LONG ISLAND CITY
BOROUGH OF QUEENS, NEW YORK
LONG ISLAND CITY, N.Y.
OCT 1
8-PM
1918
JAMES I. BUMSTER, ESQ.,
16 Clinton Street,
LAMBERTSVILLE, N. J.

Figure 7

This First Class cover cost 3¢ to mail in 1918. First Class rates were increased by 1¢ from November 2, 1917, until June 30, 1919, to help fund World War I. The stamp is offset printed (529, type III).

Figure 8

A perf. 10 single line watermarked 5¢ Washington (428) on cover addressed to Norway. The identification of this stamp can be verified by noting the unwatermarked stamp was not issued until 1917, and the cover is postmarked 1915.

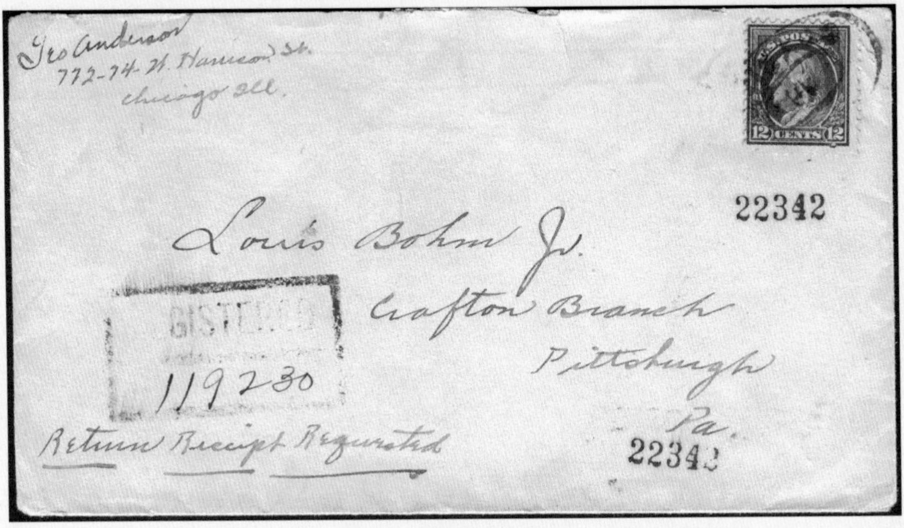

Figure 9

A registered cover demonstrating a solo use of the 12¢ Franklin unwatermarked, perf. 11 stamp (512) used to pay the 2¢ First Class rate and 10¢ Registry fee. The sender requested a return receipt, which was provided without charge in 1923 when the cover was mailed.

Where to Find More Information

- The best over-all description of the Washington-Franklin issues is Larry Weiss' *The Washington-Franklin Heads: Simplified!*

- Martin A. Armstrong's *United States Coil Issues 1906-38* covers the history and characteristics of all the Washington-Franklin coil stamps; and his *Washington Franklins 1908-21* separates the Washington-Franklins into nine groups, or series, and covers their history and characteristics.

- The classic text on these stamps is Max Johl's *United States Postage Stamps 1902-1935.*

- Larry Weiss' "Designing and Engraving the Washington-Franklin Series" presents the history of the conception and design, artwork, engraving, symbolism, and controversy over the choice of subjects.

- *The Micarelli Identification Guide to U.S. Stamps* groups the Washington-Franklins by denomination and provides concise charts and procedures for the identification of the many varieties.

- Paul W. Schmid's *The Expert's Book* provides detailed coverage of the Washington Franklins most commonly faked, identifies the issue(s) that can be altered to fake them and procedures for detecting the fake.

- Two excellent web sites assist in the identification of Washington-Franklin stamps, providing step-by-step instructions:

- "Exploring the Washington-Franklin Era," by Paul Bourke.

- For a helpful website that deals with plate finisher and siderographer initials found on Washington-Franklins, see http://home.earthlink.net/~davinod/Initials.htm.

- *Encyclopedia of Plate Varieties on U.S. Bureau-Printed Stamps* by Loran C. French provides detailed information on many plate varieties.

Chapter 10
Series of 1922
Fourth Bureau Issue

On April 17, 1922 the Third Assistant Postmaster General, W. Irving Glover, wrote to the director of the Bureau of Engraving and Printing (BEP), requesting a new series of ordinary (definitive) postage stamps. These stamps, which would become known as the "Series of 1922", were to replace the Washington-Franklin Series which had been in service since 1908. Some have suggested that Glover, representing the still new postal administration of President Warren G. Harding, wanted new stamps with a "Republican" character to them. The publicly stated reason for a new series of stamps, however, was that postal workers were having a hard time distinguishing among the different face-same Washington-Franklin stamps.

The Series of 1922, also known as the Fourth Bureau Issue, consists of sheet stamps, coil stamps, and booklet stamps, printed on both the *flat plate press* and the *rotary press*. In addition, several different perforation sizes were utilized. These variables resulted in the following *Scott* listed stamps: 551–606, 622–623, 631–642, 653, 684–687, 692–701, and 723. Some collectors also consider the Harding Memorial Issue (610-613), stamps overprinted for commemorative and security reasons (646-48, 658-679), as well as stamps overprinted for use in the Canal Zone, as part of the Series of 1922.

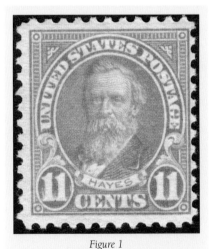

Figure 1

The 11¢ Hayes flat plate stamp (563) was the first stamp in the Fourth Bureau Series to be issued.

Series of 1922 stamps had frames designed by veteran BEP designer Clair Aubrey Huston, whose career at the BEP lasted from 1902 until 1933. The *vignettes* featured on these stamps are attributed to several different artists and designers.

About six months after Glover's request for a new series of stamps, and after much discussion about the appropriate subjects to be included on these stamps, the first stamp in the series, an 11¢ sheet stamp honoring Rutherford B. Hayes (563) was issued on October 4, 1922, the one hundredth anniversary of Hayes' birth (fig. 1). One of the aspects of this stamp worth noting is that it was issued both in Washington, D.C. and in Hayes' hometown of Fremont, Ohio. Thus began the practice of issuing a new stamp on a specific day in a specific city. Many collectors regard **First Day Covers** (ch. 60) of the Hayes stamp as the beginning of modern First Day Cover collecting.

The commencement of printing of a new stamp was sometimes the occasion for great fanfare, attended by postal dignitaries. Often the first few sheets printed were autographed by those dignitaries (fig. 2).

This series is traditional in that portraits of Franklin and Washington continued to be used for the vignettes on the most commonly used stamps, Franklin on the 1¢ and Washington on the 2¢. In fact, the same vignettes used for these two stamps had previously been used on the Washington-Franklin Issue. Vignettes of some other stamps in the series had also seen previous use on stamps. But these stamps were also boldly innovative. Subjects included such icons of American culture as an American Indian, the Statue of Liberty, California's Golden Gate (before the bridge), Niagara Falls, a buffalo, the then newly dedicated Arlington Amphitheater and Lincoln Memorial, the U.S. Capitol, and the head of the Statue of "Armed Freedom" atop the Capitol Dome (mistakenly called "America" on the stamp). This last subject appears on the $5 stamp (fig. 3), and is also incorporated into the seal of the United States Stamp Society, which is printed on the cover of every issue of *The United States Specialist*. The values ½¢ through 15¢ have a vertical orientation, while values from 17¢ through $5 have a horizontal orientation.

The Series of 1922 demonstrates how printing technology was changing in the 1920s. The flat plate press (ch. 35) printed sheet stamps appeared first, and were issued both perforated 11 and

Figure 2

A plate block of the 8¢ flat plate stamp (560) from the first printing of that stamp, signed by (top to bottom) W. Irving Glover, Third Asst. Postmaster General; Harry S. New, Postmaster General; and Louis A. Hill, Director of the BEP.

imperforate. The perf. 11 flat plate stamps are represented in the catalogue by numbers 551–573. The flat plate imperforates are 575–577. These imperforate sheet stamps, while available for purchase by collectors, were primarily intended for sale to private companies, which processed them into coil stamps for use in affixing and vending machines. The practice of providing imperforate stamps for use by private vendors, which originated early in the twentieth century, came to an end by the mid-1920s.

Figure 3
The $5 flat plate stamp (573) is the highest denomination in the series.

The rotary press (ch. 36), which had come into limited use at the BEP during the Washington-Franklin era, came to dominate stamp production during the 1920s. All of the coil stamps of this series (597–606, 686–687, and 723) were produced on this press, also known as the **Stickney press**, after its inventor and the BEP's mechanical expert, Benjamin Stickney. The coil stamps are all perf. 10.

Series of 1922 rotary press sheet stamps began appearing in 1923. They were perforated 10, and values 1¢ through 10¢ (581–591) were issued in this format. Perf. 10 was used for these sheet stamps because the finer perf. 11 would tear too easily during the printing process. While the rotary press produced high quality coil stamps, the sheet stamps were more problematic. The public complained that these perf. 10 stamps were hard to separate, so Benjamin Stickney made modifications to his press that allowed him to change the perforation gauge to 11 x 10½, and the 1¢ through 10¢ rotary press sheet stamps made their appearance in this new gauge (632–642) beginning late in 1926. Later, beginning in 1931, the 11¢ through 50¢ values were also produced on the rotary press, and were perforated 11 x 10½ for the vertically oriented stamps and 10½ x 11 for the horizontally oriented stamps. The dollar values of this series were produced only on the flat plate press.

The 1¢ and 2¢ values were also issued in booklets, produced both on the flat plate and rotary presses. Booklet panes of these stamps are identified by *Scott* as 552a, 554c, 583a, 632a, and 634d. Each booklet pane contains six stamps. The panes were assembled into booklets stapled between cardboard covers. *Scott* recognizes 18 different booklets, based on the number of panes in the booklet, the denominations of the stamps, and the design of the cover. Three of these 18 booklets are combination booklets that contain both 1¢ and 2¢ stamps. One other **combination booklet**, not counted in the above totals, contains four panes of the Series of 1922 flat plate 2¢ stamps, and four panes of 1¢ flat plate Washington-Franklin stamps (BK57).

Another effort to improve the quality of rotary press stamps was the mechanical "breaking" of the gum on finished stamps, and the application of gum to stamps in the form of "ridges". These two processes were developed to reduce the tendency of rotary press sheet stamps to curl.

Effective April 15, 1925 some postage rates were raised in order to fund a pay raise for postal workers. The basic rate for a piece of **Third Class** mail was raised from 1¢ to 1½¢. This necessitated the first 1½¢ stamp in U.S. history, and it featured a portrait of the then recently deceased President Harding. The 1½¢ Hardings were issued initially with Harding shown in profile. Later a full-face portrait was substituted for the profile. The 1½¢ Hardings were produced in both flat plate and rotary sheet format and in coil format. The same increase in postage rates that necessitated a 1½¢ stamp also necessitated a ½¢ stamp. It featured Nathan Hale and was issued in both flat plate and rotary versions.

The Harding and Hale stamps were not the only additions to the Series of 1922 as originally conceived. Over the years Benjamin Harrison appeared on 13¢ sheet stamps printed from both the flat plate and rotary presses, as did Woodrow Wilson on a 17¢ stamp. The 4¢ William Howard Taft stamps appeared in both sheet and coil format. The 4¢ Taft stamps were issued to honor the former President and Supreme Court Chief Justice shortly after his death. In order to honor Taft, Martha Washington was removed from the series.

A few very unusual stamps appeared during these years as the result of attempts to economize. Among them are some of the rarest of twentieth century U.S. stamps. As the rotary press produced stamps intended to become coil stamps it produced some sections of printed web that were not long enough to be made into coils. Instead of being discarded, some of these sections were made into sheets of stamps known as **coil waste** (578, 579, 594, and 595). A similar situation occurred when some short sections of the rotary printed web intended to become sheet stamps were salvaged and perforated with the gauge 11 perforation that was intended only for use on flat plate stamps. These **sheet-waste** stamps (596 and 613) are exceedingly rare.

The USPS issued a souvenir sheet in conjunction with **Washington 2006** which features the dollar values of the Series of 1922. According to the USPS press release, the three stamps were, "produced from the original 1923 dies created by the Bureau of Engraving and Printing and issued in their original denominations."

Notes on Collecting

While *Scott* lists stamps in an order that makes an attractive album page, it does not list them in chronological order. For example, the first Series of 1922 stamp listed in the catalogue, #551, is the 1/2¢ flat plate Nathan Hale, which was not issued until 1925, three years after the series debuted.

For reasons not fully known, a die for the 2¢ Washington stamp was retouched and used to produce both sheet and coil stamps. Stamp collectors did not realize this had happened until 1936! The stamps produced from this retouched die are known as type II and are characterized primarily by a strengthened hair on Washington's head. The type II stamps (599A and 634A) command a premium in the stamp market.

Coil stamps produced on the rotary press were issued wrapped around a paper core and had a paper leader attached at the outside end of the roll. Some collectors collect the coil stamps with these cores or leaders attached.

While the Post Office did not consider a change in a stamp's perforation or its production on a different type of press to result in a new stamp, such changes result in the new stamp being assigned a separate *Scott* number. As a result, some stamps that were classified as "new" only by collectors were distributed with little or no advance notice, making First Day Covers for some stamps either scarce or even non-existent.

Stamps produced on the rotary press are slightly taller or wider than their counterparts produced on the flat plate press. This occurred because the necessary curving of the plate, to make it fit the rotary press, stretched the image of the stamp.

There is just one rotary press imperforate stamp in this series (631). It came into existence when the Post Office accidentally supplied them to a private Chicago company instead of the flat plate imperforate sheets, which should have been supplied.

Most flat-plate sheet stamps were printed on paper with the grain running vertically, while booklet stamps were printed on "special paper" of the same size, but with a horizontal grain. Since paper shrinks and expands mostly across the grain, flat-plate booklet stamps are more nearly square than sheet stamps. When the BEP moved all booklet production to the rotary press, it used the leftover "special paper" to print a quantity of the 11¢, 12¢, 15¢, 20¢, 25¢, and 30¢ definitives. These stamps from the "special paper printings" of 1928 are squarer than the others. This paper was also used for some 15¢ Special Deliveries (E13) and Beacon airmail stamps (C11).

Almanac

1922 – The 11¢ Hayes, the first stamp of the series to debut, is issued on October 4 in Washington, D.C. and Fremont, Ohio. Post Office Department Superintendent of Stamps Michael L. Eidsness presides at a simple ceremony in Fremont, which includes the presentation of a die proof of the stamp to the son of the former president.

1923 – The first coil stamp of the series, the rotary press 2¢ sidewise George Washington (fig. 4) is issue January 15.

1923 – The 1¢ stamp is issued in **precancel** form April 21, the first Series of 1922 stamp to appear in Bureau precanceled form.

1923 – The so-called "Black Harding" flat plate stamp is issued September 1, less than one month after Harding's death. This stamp is similar to Series of 1922 stamps and is considered by some to be part of the series (fig. 5). It is the first U.S. stamp issued for which cacheted envelopes were prepared in advance for obtaining a first day cancellation.

1929 – Stamps are put on sale on May 1 at the Philatelic Agency in Washington, D.C. with "Kans." and "Nebr." overprints, two weeks after

Figure 4

The first coil stamp of the series, the 2¢ sidewise (599).

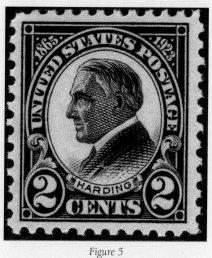

Figure 5

The flat plate Harding Memorial Issue (610).

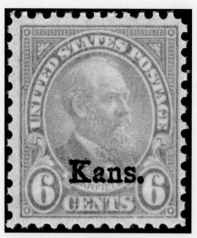

Figure 6

Some stamps of this series were overprinted "Kans." or "Nebr." Illustrated here is a "Kans." overprint (664).

going on sale at some post offices in those states. This is an experimental effort to increase security at post offices in those states (fig. 6). The idea is to discourage post office robberies by making stolen stamps more difficult to "fence" out of state.

1932 – The basic first class letter rate is increased from 2¢ to 3¢ on July 6. Except for a brief period during World War I, the 2¢ rate had lasted almost 50 years!

1934 – The 3¢ Lincoln rotary press printed stamp is reissued on February 7 in connection with the 125th anniversary of Lincoln's birth (635a). New plates were made for this printing and the reissue can be positively identified only by the plate number (fig. 7).

1938 – The $1 Lincoln Memorial stamp, issued February 12, 1923, is withdrawn from sale at the Philatelic Sales Agency (PSA) in Washington, D.C. on September 14, just 15 days after the new $1 stamp of the *Presidential issue* was issued. Most of the Series of 1922 stamps remained on sale at the PSA for longer periods of time after their "replacement" had been issued.

Figure 7

A plate block from the reissued 3¢ Lincoln rotary stamp (635a).

What Others Have Said

A rationale for the Series of 1922

"In response to appeals of the Postmaster General for suggestions for the betterment of the postal service, thousands of letters suggesting a new issue have been received from employees of the postal service, who pointed out the advisability of a more distinct variation in designs for postage stamps as well as colors that do not possess striking similarity. The department knows that thousands of dollars in revenue are lost yearly in the postal service due to the striking similarity in stamps…which prevents employees from detecting short paid matter."

—*3rd Assistant Postmaster General W. Irving Glover.*

An explanation for the denominations chosen for the Series of 1922

"The department encourages the use of a single stamp whenever possible to prepay the required postage as a matter of economy in manufacture costs and to expedite the handling of the mail."

—*Report of the Postmaster General for 1922.*

The first stamp in the Series of 1922 is announced

"The first issue of the new 11-cent stamp will be place on sale October 4, 1922, at Fremont, Ohio, in connection with the celebration of the one hundredth anniversary of the former president's birth. They will also be placed on sale October 4, 1922, at the philatelic sales agency, Division of Stamps, Post Office Department, for the benefit of stamp collectors and dealers."

—*From the Post Office Department announcement of the Hayes stamp.*

Discovery of the Type II was a slow process

"When first discovered, Type II of the 2¢ 1922-1935 issue was not thought to be enough of a change to warrant catalog listing. Opinions subsequently changed, and it now is recognized as a scarce variety of the sidewise coil and rotary press perf. stamp of that design…. First printings of the Type II stamps were made in December, 1928, so any 2¢ stamps with earlier postmarks are automatically excluded from your search for these stamps. The reason the stamp is catalogued less in coil form is that nine plates (19582-83-84-85-86, 19748-49-50-51) were made and these also used, but since coil stamps have a tendency to lay around in post offices, more were found when the search for Type II's began."

—*"U.S. Notes," Linn's Weekly Stamp News, September 24, 1938.*

Examples of Postal Usage

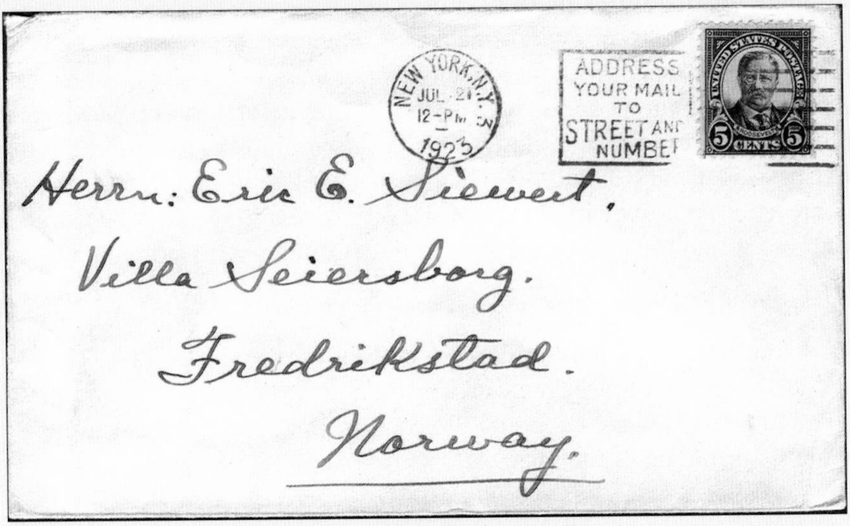

Figure 8

The foreign surface rate was 5¢/oz. throughout the time of the Series of 1922, as illustrated by this 1923 cover to Norway. All 5¢ stamps at the time were blue, including this 5¢ Roosevelt (557), making them readily identifiable to postal workers of all nations.

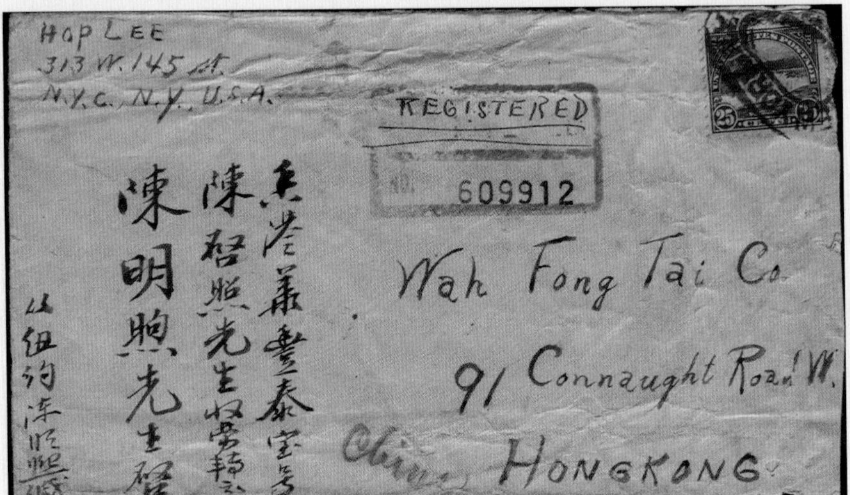

Figure 9

The 25¢ Niagara Falls stamp (568) on this registered cover from New York City to Hong Kong paid the 5¢ foreign rate, 15¢ for registry, and 5¢ for return receipt. Note the faint "AR" handstamp, indicating "avis de reception" or "return receipt."

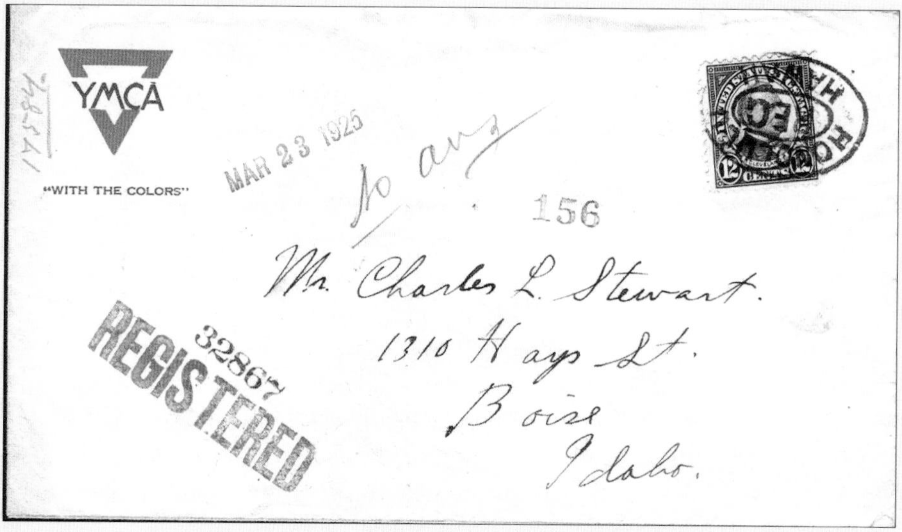

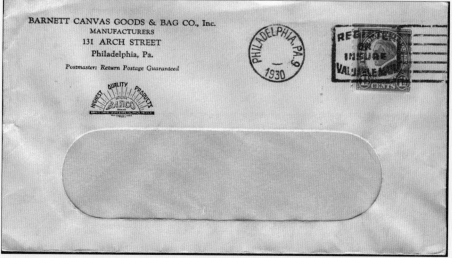

Figure 10

The 12¢ Cleveland (564) on this 1925 domestic cover paid 2¢ first class postage plus 10¢ registration. Note that in accordance with postal policy there is no dated cancellation on the front of the cover.

Figure 11

This piece of third class mail is franked with a 1½¢ Harding (598). Notice that the dial omits the date and time of mailing. While third class postmarks were required to show the post office name (i.e., city and state), the date was not required, and was usually omitted.

Where to Find More Information

- Two essential books by Gary Griffith describe these stamps within the historical context of their times: *United States Stamps 1922–26* and *United States Stamps 1927–32*.

- Max G. Johl studied these stamps as a contemporary. Though some of his findings are now obsolete, his work, *United States Postage Stamps 1902–1935*, remains a classic.

- Jack V. Harvey provides an introduction to modern First Day Cover collecting in his *First Day Covers of the Regular Issue of 1922–1935*.

- The printing history of these stamps can be found in the following Research Papers by the United States Stamp Society: #8 – Printing History of Booklet Pane Plates, 1900–1954; #13 – Printing History of Rotary Sheet Plates, Series of 1922; #14 – Printing History of Coil Plates, Series of 1922; #15 – Printing History of Series of 1922 Flat Plates used for Sheet Stamps (except the 2¢ value); #18 – Printing History of Series 1922 Flat Plates used for 2¢ Washington and Harding Memorial sheet stamps.

- The pages of The United States Specialist contain numerous articles about the Series of 1922. Of special interest is Jay Stotts' "Rate Usages of the Fourth Bureau Issue" and Rodney Juell's "Gum Ridges and Gum Breakers on Rotary Press Sheet Stamps of the Fourth Bureau Issue".

- *The Micarelli Identification Guide to U.S. Stamps.*

- *Encyclopedia of Plate Varieties on U.S. Bureau-Printed Stamps* by Loran C. French provides detailed information on many plate varieties.

Chapter 11
Presidential Series
The Prexies

In early 1934, President Franklin D. Roosevelt suggested that a new series of stamps depicting deceased Presidents be issued. At first, they were to be commemoratives, but it was decided that the proposed stamps would be definitives, replacing the Series of 1922, in use for the past twelve years. It was not until early 1937 an announcement was made of a national competition to design the first stamp in a new series of definitive stamps to be known as the Presidential Series. The competition ended on September 15 and the winner was Elaine Rawlinson of New York City. Her design was used on the 1¢ George Washington stamp (fig. 1), which became the basis of the designs for the rest of the 1938 Presidential Series, also affectionately known as the Prexies or the Fifth Bureau Issue. Each design includes a bust profile of the president, and the dates of his term(s) as president. They were in use for over eighteen years, from 1938 into the mid-1950s. The Prexie stamps depict all twenty-nine presidents who had died before 1938, including many who had never before appeared on a postage stamp. Only then sitting President Franklin D. Roosevelt, and his then living predecessor, Herbert Hoover, do not appear in the series.

The Prexies provide a chronological overview of the American presidency. Studying a set could help a school child memorize the presidents in order. From George Washington on the 1¢ stamp, to Calvin Coolidge on the $5 value, the presidents appeared in order of their presidencies. On stamps from 1¢ through 22¢, each stamp's denomination corresponds to the sequence of each man's presidency, Washington, the first president, on the 1¢, Adams, the second president, on the 2¢, etc. Grover Cleveland, the 22nd president, appears on the 22¢ stamp. However, since Cleveland served two non-consecutive terms, this pattern stops at that point. There is no 23¢ stamp in the series. Benjamin Harrison appears next, on the 24¢ stamp. William

Figure 1

The 1¢ George Washington (804) was designed by Elaine Rawlinson, and became the basis for all other stamps in the Presidential Series.

McKinley, the 25th president appears on the 25¢ stamp. From that point on any attempt to match the denomination to the order of presidency was abandoned. Theodore Roosevelt appears on the 30¢ stamp, William Howard Taft on the 50¢ stamp, Woodrow Wilson on the $1, Warren G. Harding on the $2, and finally Calvin Coolidge on the $5. In addition to the 29 presidents who appear on these stamps, Benjamin Franklin, the first **Postmaster General**, is depicted on the ½¢ stamp; the first First Lady, Martha Washington, is on the 1½¢ stamp; and the 4½¢ stamp shows the official residence of the Presidents, the White House. Thus the Presidential Series contains a total of 32 stamps issued in sheet format (*Scott* 803-834).

While other designers receive credit for the other stamps in the series, Miss Rawlinson's design is clearly the basis for them all. Though all the stamps in the series are similar, they are not identical. Values from ½¢ to 9¢ have no border, as in Rawlinson's design (fig. 2). The 10¢ through 19¢ values have a single line border (fig. 3), and the 20¢ through 50¢ values have a double line border (fig. 4). The dollar values were bicolored, with designs significantly different from the cent values (fig. 5).

Figure 2

This 5¢ James Monroe (810), like all the Prexie stamps through the 9¢ stamp, has no frame line around the design.

Figure 3

This 16¢ Abraham Lincoln (821), like all the Prexie stamps from 10¢ through the 19¢, has a single line frame around the design.

Figure 4

This 25¢ William McKinley (829), like all the Prexie stamps from 20¢ through the 50¢, has a double line frame around the design.

Figure 5

This $5 Calvin Coolidge (834), like all the Prexie dollar stamps, is bi-colored.

All sheets of stamps from ½¢ to 50¢ cent were printed on the rotary press (ch. 36) using 400 subject plates, and were perforated 11 x 10½. Both ordinary plates and **electric-eye plates** were used. The dollar values were printed on the flat plate press (ch. 35) using 100 subject plates, and perforated 11. Color varieties abound in the Presidential Series. The $1 Wilson offers two interest-

Figure 6

A used joint line pair of the 1½¢ Martha Washington (849).

ing varieties for specialists. In 1951 it was accidentally printed on watermarked paper (832b), and then in 1954 it was issued in an experimental dry printing format (832c). According to the *Precancel Stamp Society Catalog of US Bureau Precancels*, there are 2,835 different Bureau **Precancels** of Presidential Series stamps! In addition, two stamps in the series, the ½¢, and the 1½¢, were overprinted for use in Canal Zone.

The first Prexie stamp, the 1¢ Washington sheet stamp (804) was issued on April 25, 1938. The rest of the sheet stamps were issued by the end of 1938, and with a few exceptions, were issued in order of their denomination. All of the Prexie stamps were issued in Washington, D.C., except the ½¢ Franklin which made its appearance in Philadelphia.

The Presidential Series contains nine coil stamps with vertical perforations (839-847), and four coils with horizontal perforations (848-851, fig. 6). The coil stamps were printed on the rotary press from plates of 170 subjects for the vertically perforated stamps, and from plates of 150 subjects for the horizontally perforated stamps. They were issued in January 1939.

The 1¢, 2¢, and 3¢ stamps were issued as booklet panes (804b, 806b, and 807a, fig. 7). The panes were assembled in various combinations into booklets with a variety of different covers. *Scott* lists 18 different booklets for Prexie stamps (BK86-BK103). The first Presidential booklets were issued in January 1939.

Figure 7

The 3¢ Thomas Jefferson was issued in booklet pane format (807a) as shown here. It was also issued in sheet and coil format. Paying the 3¢ first class rate, the 3¢ Jefferson is was the most commonly used and familiar Prexie design.

Presidential Solo Usages

½¢ Franklin - [While this stamp could not be used "solo", it was used with others to pay three different common 3rd class rates at the time: 1.5¢, 4.5¢, and 7.5¢.]

1¢ Washington - Domestic Postcard (until January 1952), Certificate of Mailing - no insurance (until January 1954).

1½¢ Martha Washington - Domestic Third Class for two ounces (until January 1949), International Printed Matter for two ounces (until October 1953).

2¢ Adams - Domestic First Class Local Delivery, per ounce (until January 1949), Domestic Post Card after January 1952.

3¢ Jefferson - Domestic First Class, per ounce (until July 1958), International Post Card (until October 1953).

4¢ Madison - International Post Card (after November 1953), Domestic Air Mail Post Card (January 1949 through July 1958).

4½¢ White House - Domestic Third Class (1½¢) plus Minimum Insurance (3¢), November 1944 through December 1948.

5¢ Monroe - International Surface (per ounce) Until October 1953, Domestic Air Mail (per ounce) October 1946 through December 1948.

6¢ Adams - Domestic Air Mail (per ounce) until March 1944, and January 1949 through July 1958.

7¢ Jackson - Domestic Third Class (2¢) plus Minimum Insurance (5¢) after January 1949.

8¢ Van Buren - International Surface (two ounces: 5¢ first ounce plus 3¢ second ounce) until October 1953, International Surface (per ounce). After November 1953, Domestic Air Mail (per ounce) March 1944 through September 1946.

9¢ Harrison - Domestic First Class (three ounces) until July 1958.

10¢ Tyler - International Uniform Air Mail to the Western Hemisphere (per half ounce) after October 1946.

11¢ Polk - International Surface (three ounces: 5¢ first ounce plus 3¢ per ounce for the next two ounces) until October 1953.

12¢ Taylor - International Air Mail to Central America (per half ounce) until March 1945, Military Air Mail (2 ounces) December, 1941 through September 1946.

13¢ Fillmore - Domestic Surface (3¢ per ounce) plus Special Delivery (10¢) through October 1944.

14¢ Pierce - International Surface (four ounces: 5¢ first ounce plus 3¢ per ounce for the next three ounces) until October 1953.

15¢ Buchanan - International Uniform Air Mail to Europe (per half ounce) after October 1946.

16¢ Lincoln - Domestic Surface (3¢ per ounce) plus Special Delivery (13¢) November 1944 through December 1948.

17¢ Johnson - Domestic Local Delivery (2¢ per ounce) plus Minimum Registration (15¢) until March 1944.

18¢ Grant - Domestic Surface (3¢ per ounce) plus Minimum Registration (15¢) until March 1944.

19¢ Hayes - Domestic Air Mail Post Card (4¢) plus Special Delivery (15¢) January 1949 through December 1951.

20¢ Garfield - Air Mail to or from Hawaii (per half ounce) until January 1945. International Surface (5¢) plus International Registration (15¢) February 1945 through December 1948.

21¢ Arthur - Domestic Surface plus Registration (various combinations) until March 1944.

22¢ Cleveland - First Class Local Delivery (2¢ per ounce for two ounces) plus Minimum Registration (15¢) plus Return Receipt (3¢) until March 1944.

24¢ Harrison - Domestic Surface plus Registration (various combinations) until March 1949.

25¢ McKinley - International Air Mail to Africa, Asia, Australia & Oceania (per half ounce) after October 1946.

30¢ Roosevelt - International Air Mail to Europe (per half ounce) April 1939 through October 1946, with various interruptions during World War II.

50¢ Taft - Air Mail to or from the Philippines (per half ounce) until December 1941.

$1 Wilson - Air Mail to/from Hawaii (20¢ per half ounce for 2.5 ounces) until January 1945.

$2 Harding - International Air Mail Rate to Africa, Asia, Australia & Oceania (25¢ per half ounce for 4 ounces) after October 1946.

$5 Coolidge - Air Mail to or from the Philippines (50¢ per half ounce for 5 ounces) until December 1941.

Notes on Collecting

The denominations of these stamps were clearly dictated not by postal need, but by the desire to present our nation's presidents on denominations that matched the order of their terms in office. Some of these stamps did not pay any obvious rate and therefore did not meet any obvious postal need at the time of issue. One interesting and popular approach to collecting the Prexies is to attempt to find each stamp, used singly on a piece of mail, paying some recognizable rate or fee. This is called a *solo usage*.

Other strategies for collecting Prexie stamps include: collecting them by color variety, Bureau or local precancel, by plate number, and by *EFO* type. Philatelically inspired covers may be collected as first day cover, first flight covers, and *Highway Post Office* first trips. Postal history may be collected by denomination, by rate such as air mail, special delivery, or registry, or by era such as World War II or first year usage.

Almanac

1937 – A national competition is announced by the U.S. Treasury Department on July 14 to design a new "Presidential Series" of regular postage stamps. Over 1,200 entries are submitted.

1937 – The design competition ends on September 15 with 25-year-old artist, Elaine Rawlinson of New York City, declared the winner. She receives a $500 prize for her simple elegant design, which included the President's right bust and his years in office. Thus, the Prexies became the first series of stamps to be designed by a woman.

1938 – The first Prexie sheet stamp, the 1¢ George Washington is issued on April 25. The next 31 sheet stamps are issued throughout 1938, generally in order of denomination.

1938 – On December 1 the Post Office Department announces dates throughout 1939 for the issuance of the Prexie coils, both horizontal and vertical, and booklet stamps.

1939 – Two Prexies, the ½¢ and 1½¢, are issued on September 1 with overprints for emergency use in the Canal Zone to provide fractional postage for new third class rates.

1954 – The first of the Liberty Series stamps are issued April 9, which would gradually replace the Presidential Series over the next six years.

1956 – The last of the 3¢ Jefferson stamps, the workhorse of the Presidential Series, is sent out to postmasters on May 16. In total, over 130 billion 3¢ sheet stamps, coils, and booklet panes were printed.

1960 – The last of the Prexie issues (the 15¢ sheet stamp and the 6¢ coil) are delivered to post offices around the country on June 30.

What Others Have Said

The new Presidentials...on again, off again.

"Much has appeared in the philatelic press in regards to the so-called Presidential series with portraits of Washington to Coolidge inclusive. Of course Mr. Hoover would be omitted because our present laws do not permit the portrait of a living person on our stamps. The nearest approach we have had in honoring a living dignitary is by simply mentioning his name as in the case of Col. Lindbergh and Admiral Byrd. Anyway the news has told us that we would have the new set and we would not. As a matter of interest, one of the earliest philatelic activities of President Roosevelt was to request such a series...he made suggestions for their design...Lately the question has arisen as to whether some of the Presidents are worthy of such an honor and for the time being at least the issue has been sidetracked, no doubt at the suggestion of the President."

—*Philip H. Ward Jr.,* "Editorial – Proposed Presidential Series," Mekeel's Weekly, 1935. *Ward was one of the most prominent stamp dealers of his time and an officer of the APS.*

The 5th Bureau series must be taken seriously...finally!

"In a Post Office release dated March 7th, Postmaster General Farley announced that the portrait of every deceased President...would appear on a new regular series of 31 stamps. The 5th Bureau series evidently must now be taken seriously, although it has taken four years for the Department to get worked up sufficiently to take this step.... To get everybody in as long as he is dead, six more denominations had to be provided...merely to provide a place for our past executives. [There will no demand for] the 16¢ and 19¢ denominations...The writer cannot see any excuse for a Presidential series as a regular issue. There is a valid excuse from an educational point of view for such a set of stamps, but it would logically be commemorative and in low denominations."

—*Hugh M. Southgate,* "The Presidential Series," The Bureau Specialist, 1938. *Southgate was the President of the BIA at the time.*

Presidentials serve as proud emblems of the United States

"The very last regular issued Prexy – the Macon, Georgia, Bureau precancel on the 1½-cent Martha Washington coil—is...scarce. If regulations were followed, at least 250,000 were printed. The order was shipped from the Bureau to Macon in November 1960, at a time when there was no plausible usage for the stamps, because the minimum per-piece rate for third class bulk mail had risen to two-cents on January 1, 1959, and the compatible nonprofit bulk rate was 1¼ cents. Probably fewer than 50 exist; it has a...value of $150 as a single stamp or $350 as a pair. Although the final stamp was issued in 1960, several denominations of Prexies remained in use well into the later Liberty series era. Even after they essentially had disappeared from mail, postal officials regarded them as highly proud emblems of the United States [as they brought them to the 1979 Universal Postal Union Congress in Rio de Janeiro in leather bound presentation booklets.]"

—*Ken Lawrence, "The Culture of Presidential Series Collectors,"* American Philatelist, *1995.*

Why We Collect Them

"It seems likely that one of the factors encouraging so many of today's...[collectors] to become interested in the Prexies is that they were among the first stamps to be acquired...as children in the 'forties and 'fifties. The Prexies offer a dose of nostalgia, remindful to many of days of youthful enthusiasm, and it is a joy to discover that these old friends can once again become the focus of collecting...."

—*Richard W. Helbock,* Prexie Postal History, *1988.*

Examples of Postal Usage

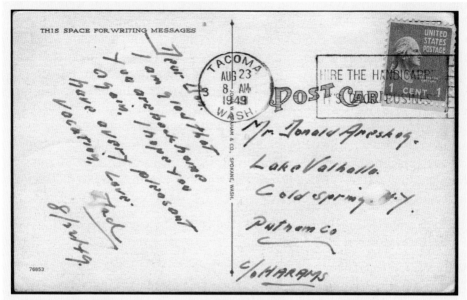

The 1¢ Washington (804) on a 1949 post card. This stamp paid the post card rate until it was raised to 2¢ on January 1, 1952.

Figure 9

A 1952 airmail cover bearing a 6¢ John Quincy Adams (811). This Prexie stamp paid the domestic airmail rate from January 1, 1949 until July 31, 1958.

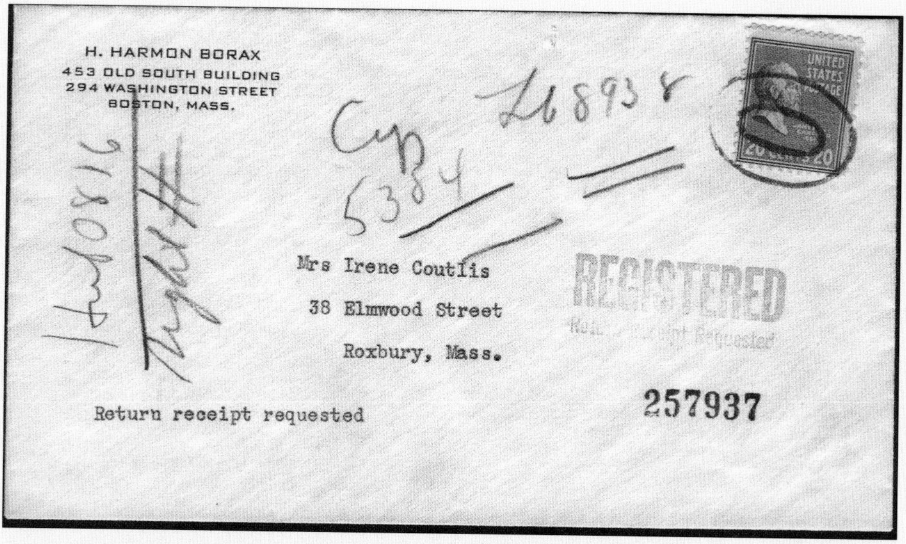

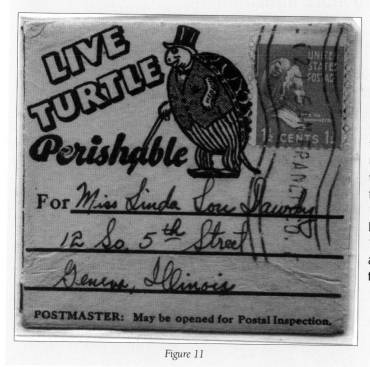

Figure 10

Registered cover, bearing a 20¢ James A. Garfield (825), paying the 3¢ first class postage, 15¢ registry fee and 3¢ for return receipt service. Mailed on January 9, 1942 in Boston, Massachusetts it is properly postmarked on the back, with only a mute cancellation on the stamp.

A 1½¢ Martha Washington (805), used to pay the third class rate for up to two ounces, which was in effect from April 15, 1925 until December 31, 1948. This package contained a live turtle.

Figure 11

Figure 12

A 5¢ Monroe (810) on censored international surface mail to a member of the French Navy in 1945.

Where to Find More Information

- *The Prexies* by Roland E. Rustad is the definitive resource for the Presidential Series.

- *Prexie Postal History* by Richard W. Helbock provides numerous examples and explanations of how these stamps were used to carry the mail.

- "Presidential Issue Usages," by Leonard Piszkiewicz, et al., provides essential usage information.

- *Encyclopedia of Plate Varieties on U.S. Bureau-Printed Stamps* by Loran C. French provides detailed information on many plate varieties.

Chapter 12
Liberty Series

The Liberty Series, the definitive (ordinary) stamps in general use from 1954 through 1973, takes its name from the 3¢, 8¢, and 11¢ values picturing the Statue of Liberty (fig. 1). Though in common use for more than two decades, some stamps remained on sale through the 1980s. Many stamps with the same face design were produced by different production methods. Collecting the "Liberties" for their rich historical stories and their many different varieties provides the U.S. stamp collector with many challenges and opportunities.

The 1938 Presidential Series was in service for 15 years when word came toward the end of 1953 that a new series of stamps would be forthcoming. The first to be issued, on April 9, 1954, was the 8¢ red, white, and blue Statue of Liberty stamp (*Scott* 1041). The premiere of the first stamp of the new "ordinary series" was actually broadcast on national television with President Dwight David Eisenhower presiding! In the philatelic world, the excitement was enhanced as it was going to be a two-color definitive stamp, a rare occurrence at the time. The series differed radically from the Presidentials, featuring "warm portraits" of its subjects, as compared to "hard profile busts" of the earlier series. Famous portrait artists and photographers' works were used as the basis for the designs, such as the work of Rembrandt Peale for the 5¢ James Monroe and the 15¢ John Marshall.

Figure 1

The Liberty Series derives its name from the three stamps depicting the Statue of Liberty. The 3¢ stamp shown here paid for one ounce of First Class mail from the time of its issue until 1958.

Much was made of the fact that the Liberty series would contain only 18 different denominations, whereas the Prexies had 32 different values. The denominations for the Liberties were selected to ensure no more than two stamps were necessary to pay up to 60¢ in postage, nor more than three for up to $1.60.

A study had determined that some of the Presidential denominations actually saw very little service in carrying the mail and that those denominations were not needed in this new series.

Figure 2

A joint line pair of the 1¼¢ Palace of the Governors coil (1054A) with small holes.

Figure 3

The $5 Hamilton (1053), issued on March 19, 1956 was printed on the flat plate press at the Bureau of Engraving and Printing in black ink and is often considered one of the most beautiful twentieth century portrait stamps. The vignette was engraved by Charles A. Brooks.

The Liberties started out as a set with 17 different subjects and 18 denominations, printed in three formats of sheet panes, booklet panes, and coils. This would have resulted in a complete set that would have totaled no more than 30 different stamps, a smaller set than the Presidentials, which had 49 different stamps. But over time, the Liberty Series developed into a series that contained more than 60 different varieties, even though only eight denominations were added to the original plan (1¼¢ (fig. 2), 2½¢, 4½¢, 8¢ Pershing, 11¢, 12¢, 15¢, and 25¢). This occurred because as each stamp was reprinted, unlimited printing being one of the hallmarks of an ordinary series, technological changes were occurring at the Bureau of Engraving and Printing (BEP). A variety of papers, perforations and *phosphor tagging* was utilized, each creating a "new stamp" to be obtained for one's collection.

All stamps were produced by the BEP, and most were printed by the *rotary press*. The 8¢ Statue of Liberty was printed on both the *flat plate* (1041) and the rotary presses (1041B), and both versions were released on April 9, 1954. Four years later, Postmaster General Arthur Summerfield announced a third version of the stamp (1042) would be released on March 22, 1958, printed on the new *Giori* Press. The Giori press was exciting because it could print the two color stamp in a single press run, whereas previously a two color stamp required two separate passes through the press, one for each color. These two trips through the press created two plate numbers for each stamp, while the Giori printings, with only one pass through the press, utilized a single plate number. One of the last stamps of the series to be issued, on June 15, 1961, the 11¢ Liberty (1044A), was also printed on the Giori Press. The $5 Hamilton (fig. 3) was printed only on the flat plate press.

It was not until the 1963 *Scott* that the following statement appeared:

In 1953 the Bureau of Engraving and Printing began experiments in printing on "dry" paper [moisture content 5–10 per cent]. In previous "wet" printings, the paper had a moisture content of 15–35 per cent. The new process required a thicker, stiffer paper, special types of inks, and greater pressure to force the paper into the recessed plates. The "dry" printing show whiter paper, a higher sheen on the surface, feel thicker and stiffer, and the designs stand out more clearly than on the "wet" printings.

This acknowledgement by *Scott* came almost ten years after these different printings were first reported in the philatelic press. The new **dry** printing varieties were experimental in 1953, but by the end of the decade all U.S. stamps were being printed by the dry printing method. None of the Liberty series dry printed stamps were ever intended to be new stamps, different from the earlier **wet** printed stamps. They were simply created as advances in printing technology occurred. Certainly the general stamp buying public, and postal window clerks themselves, had no idea there were two different varieties of the same stamp. Only as word started appearing in the philatelic press did collectors become aware that to be "complete" they needed both printings. Even *Scott* editors took a long time to recognize their existence, but today all 14 stamps, printed both wet and dry, have both varieties listed.

Most of the wet printed stamps have ink impressions that are much darker and with less clear designs than their dry printed counterparts. On the dry printed stamps, the ink impressions are crisper, and the designs much sharper and clearer. Regarding the paper itself, the designs of the wet printed stamps can be seen through the backs of the stamps, whereas the dry printings are nearly opaque.

The phosphor tagging of stamps, applied to facilitate automatic mail handling, was a process pioneered in 1963 and adopted for regular use by 1968. The advent of tagged versions of a stamp unintentionally produced new varieties that are listed separately in *Scott* even though they appear to be identical to the naked eye. The Liberties have many tagged varieties. The first listings of tagged varieties appeared in the 1966 *Scott*. The first Liberty series stamp to be tagged was the 4¢ Lincoln stamp (1036b), issued November 2, 1963. There are three types of tagging on the Liberty issues, referred to as **Tagging - Type I, Type II**, and **Type III**.

Two perforation varieties are found on the Liberty series coil stamps. The coils were initially issued with normal size (**large holes**) perforation holes and then appeared with **small holes**, even though they were of the same perforation gauge.

The bicolor Liberties and the $5 Hamilton were dry printed on pregummed paper using **sheet-fed** presses. They were perforated on **L perforators** and had

Figure 4

The Liberties were produced with a number of different electric-eye markings. The dry printed 1¢ Washington plate block on the left exhibits electric-eye markings, while the wet printed plate block on the right exhibits none.

no *electric eye markings*. All other Liberty sheet stamps were printed on *web-fed* presses and perforated on electric-eye equipment, utilizing three different formats of electric eye markings (fig. 4).

Some Liberty series stamps are found as printing *errors* or *freaks*. Five of the coil stamps (1¢, 2¢, 3¢, 4¢, and 25¢) have been found *imperforate* in long strips or full coils. There are also imperforate error examples of several sheet stamps.

The final issue in the Liberty Series was issued on February 25, 1965 in Boston, the 25¢ coil featuring Paul Revere (1059A). While most of the Liberty stamps went off sale by the mid-1970s, this vending machine favorite remained on sale officially until April 30, 1987, a remarkable 22-year run, well after most of the Liberties went off sale in the late 1970s. It then reappeared when the First Class postage rate increased to 25¢ in 1988!

Second only to the Washington-Franklin Issue of 1908–1922, the Liberties provide collectors with the most opportunities to find varieties of face-same stamps.

Notes on Collecting

There are a variety of ways to collect the Liberties. A basic collection of mint or used examples is readily available. Only the purchase of the $5 Hamilton (1053) in mint condition will incur more than a modest expenditure.

The original announcement about the 18 stamps meeting all rates in frankings of not more than three stamps, presents a challenge to the postal history collector to assemble a collection of covers showing the various rates in all possible combinations.

Historically, the BEP dampened its paper to facilitate the transfer of the ink. This "wet printing" ended and was replaced by "dry printing" in the late 1950s, while the Liberties were still in production. The Liberties are the only definitive series that can be collected both as wet and dry printings.

Due to the discovery of new varieties of the Liberty Series, collectors have a formidable task of assembling a mint, used, and on-cover collection of each of the more than 60 varieties. Of the many varieties created by the reprinting of various Liberty series stamps over two decades, one of the most notable is the "**Look Coil**," in which coil rolls of 3,000 3¢ Liberty coils were produced expressly for use by Look magazine on their promotional mailings. Most were used on these mailings from a production center in Des Moines, Iowa. Even though millions of these covers were mailed, only a few have survived. Adequate numbers of a reprint of the coil, however, fell into philatelic hands so that a single mint copy is available for a few dollars. The thrill of the hunt for used copies on Look covers extends to this day.

Figure 5

The souvenir sheet issued for the Fifth International Philatelic Exhibition held in New York in 1956 depicted two Liberty stamps, both valid for postage.

Although not officially part of the Liberty series, the **souvenir sheet** issued in honor of the Fifth International Philatelic Exhibition (FIPEX, 1075), features enlarged imperforate reproductions of the 3¢ and 8¢ Statue of Liberty stamps (fig. 5). Some collectors include the 2¢ **Postal Card** (UX44) as part of the Liberty Series as well. This postal card was the first "commemorative" postal card to be issued.

Almanac

1954 – The first stamp in the series, the 8¢ Statue of Liberty (1041 and 1041B) is issued on April 9.

1954 – The 2¢ Jefferson coil (1055) is issued on October 22.

1961 – The final issue, the 11¢ (1044A), also showing the Statue of Liberty, is issued in Washington, D.C. on June 15.

1984 – On January 31 the 2¢ Jefferson coil is formally removed from sale after thirty years.

What Others Have Said

In God We Trust

"At the request of thousands of persons who have urged the Post Office Department to issue a regular stamp with a religious statement, the new 8-cent Statue of Liberty stamp will carry the inscription of 'In God We Trust' arched over the symbolic torch bearer....Under this symbol of freedom...is the word 'Liberty.' The red, white and blue stamp will be the first in a series of ordinary stamps that will eventually replace the series established in 1938....'The symbolism of God and Country in this .75 by .87 inch stamp,' Postmaster General Arthur E. Summerfield said, 'marks the first time that a religious tone has been incorporated into a regular or ordinary stamp, as distinguished from a commemorative stamp which is discontinued after the initial printing order.'"

—*USPOD News Release #2092, 1954.*

Eighteen Stamps for the Series

"The news long awaited by stamp collectors of the nation has at last been broken by the Post Office Department. Revealed are the designs which will be used on the twelve stamps still to be issued in the Liberty Series for regular postage...."

—*"Additional Liberties Revealed – Series of Eighteen to have 6 Presidents, 6 Historical Shrines, 6 Famous Americans," Linn's Stamp News, 1955.*

Telling the Difference

"Now, what do we mean by 'dry' and 'wet?' Essentially...the process of recess-printing from intaglio plates has required that the paper used in printing be dampened before receiving or taking up an impression from the inked plate; that is, it was so up to the successful introduction of dry-printing...The difference in paper criterion is perhaps the one best criterion [for telling them apart]....The general appearance or tone is softer in the wet printed, and in the dry-printed the lines are sharper and stand out more....You may be able to feel the difference by running your fingers over the design..."

—*George W. Brett, "The Recognition and Differentiation of Dry and Wet Intaglio Engraved Stamps Produced at the Bureau of Engraving and Printing," Stamps Magazine, 1955.*

Typical New Issue Announcement

"The 12-cent Benjamin Harrison regular postage stamp, to be issued June 6, 1959, at Oxford, Ohio, will feature the likeness of the twenty-third President of the United States.....reproduced from a photograph taken by Charles Parker...Victor S. McCloskey, Jr. of the Bureau of Engraving and Printing designed the central subject and lettering, and Charles R. Chickering the frame….When the 12-cent Harrison stamp appears, the current regular issue will be brought more closely to the intended balance. Originally there were six Presidents, six outstanding Americans, and six shrines…As now issued and announced there will be seven Presidents, eight noted Americans, and eight shrines…"

—*USPOD News Release #65, 1959.*

Be familiar with the gum and paper varieties

"Most of the Liberties were manufactured in the days when gum was applied after printing, but a couple of designs remained in use long after the series as a whole had been phased out, and in the late 1970s appeared with dull gum finish. These include the 2-cent Jefferson coil and the 25-cent Revere coil. Because the Bureau was experimenting with several different dull gum formats, collectible dull gum varieties exist on the 2-cent coil. Some Liberty series stamps have been reported on thin, almost transparent paper, but the most celebrated paper type in the series is the 2-cent Jefferson sheet stamp dry-printed on Silkote paper [see glossary]. Only 50,000 stamps were printed on this special stock, from just two plates, 25061 and 25062 (which are common plates on ordinary stamp paper), so it is a key Liberty Series stamp."

—*Ken Lawrence, "Collecting the Liberty Series,"* The United States Specialist, *1992.*

Examples of Postal Usage

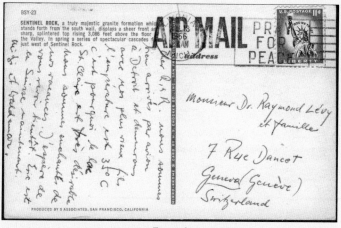

Figure 6

An 11¢ Liberty, issued on June 15, 1961, paid the 11¢ International Air mail Post Card rate on this July 18, 1966 post card to Switzerland.

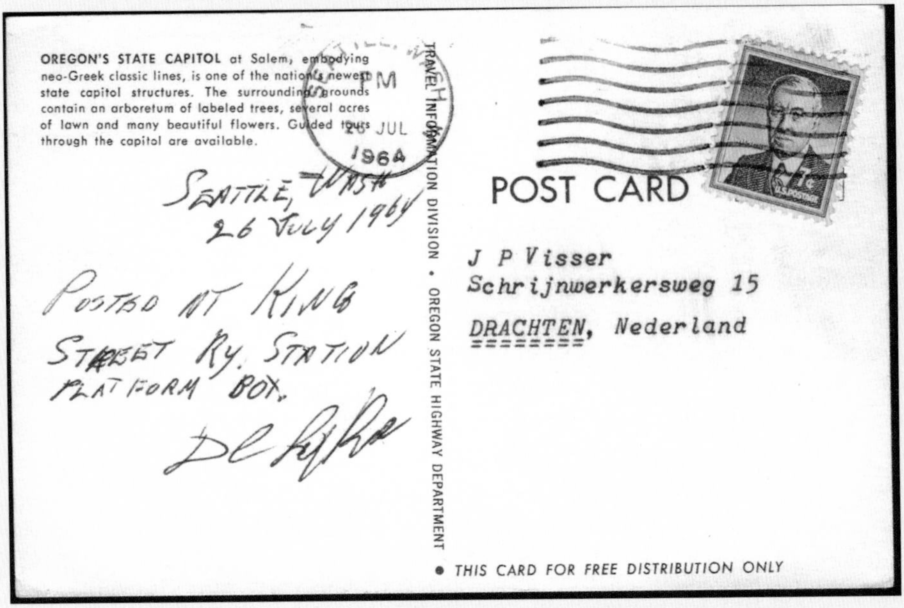

Figure 7

A 7¢ Wilson issued on January 10, 1956 paid the 7¢ surface (ship) rate on this July 26, 1964 post card to the Netherlands.

Figure 8

This 1963 certified mailing using a 30¢ Robert E. Lee stamp to pay the 20¢ certified mail fee and the 10¢ return receipt service. The First Class postage was paid by a 5¢ Washington that is not a Liberty Series stamp.

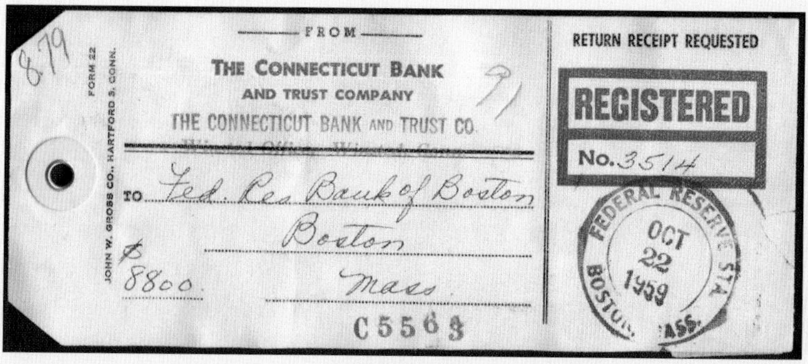

Figure 9a

A Registry tag used in 1959 on a mailing to the Federal Reserve Bank of Boston with an indicated value of $8,000.

Figure 9b

The reverse of the Registry tag shown in Figure 9a, with $8.79 in postage paid with Liberty Series stamps.

Where to Find More Information

- The United States Stamp Society maintains a 1954 Liberty Series Study Committee, a group comprised of enthusiastic collectors of the Series as well as those who have conducted research and published informative papers about different aspects of the series. It may be accessed through a link on the USSS site: www.usstamps.org, or directly at http://members.aol.com/raustin13/study grp/liberty.htm. Visitors to the site can post their questions, read about the Liberty series, and see many great photos.

- *Encyclopedia of Plate Varieties on U.S. Bureau-Printed Stamps* by Loran C. French provides detailed information on many plate varieties.

- A major new book on the Liberty Series by Tony Wawrukiewicz, David Eeles, and Ken Lawrence, to be published by the APS, was in preparation in 2005.

Chapter 13
Prominent Americans Issue

In April 1965 Postmaster General John A. Gronouski announced plans for a new series of definitive postage stamps, the Prominent Americans. The series would recognize people who played an important role on the American scene. In compiling the list of honorees, the Postmaster General consulted a number of advisers, including his *Citizens Stamp Advisory Committee*, American historians Catherine Drinker Bowen and Bruce Catton, and others. Eighteen individuals were initially chosen, with seven others added before the series ended (fig. 1). The Prominent Americans have *Scott* numbers from 1278 to 1305C, 1393 to 1395, and 1397 to 1402. The series includes a 1¢ Thomas Jefferson, 1¼¢ Albert Gallatin, 2¢ Frank Lloyd Wright, 3¢ Francis Parkman, 4¢ Abraham Lincoln, 5¢ George Washington, 6¢ Franklin D. Roosevelt, 6¢ and 8¢ Dwight D. Eisenhower, 7¢ Benjamin Franklin, 8¢ Albert Einstein, 10¢ Andrew Jackson, 12¢ Henry Ford, 13¢ John F. Kennedy, 14¢ Fiorello LaGuardia, 15¢ Oliver Wendell Holmes, 16¢ Ernie Pyle, 18¢ Elizabeth Blackwell, 20¢ George C. Marshall, 21¢ Amadeo P. Giannini, 25¢ Frederick Douglass, 30¢ John Dewey, 40¢ Thomas Paine, 50¢ Lucy Stone, $1.00 Eugene O'Neill, and $5.00 John Bassett Moore.

The series was introduced on November 10, 1965 with the issuance of the 4¢ Lincoln stamp. It was the seventh regular stamp series issued since the Bureau of Engraving and Printing (BEP) took over the production of postage stamps in 1894. Over the next nine years a total of 25 stamp designs would be issued. In addition, the 6¢ Eisenhower would be reissued as an 8¢ stamp and the 5¢ Washington would be

Figure 1

The 27 stamp designs of the Prominent Americans Series include one stamp that was redrawn, and one stamp issued as a new denomination.

redrawn. The stamps of the Prominent Americans Issue were in general use until the introduction of the Americana Issue (ch.14) in the late 1970s. Some Prominent Americans continued to be produced until the mid-1980s, gradually being replaced as the Great Americans Issue (ch.15) was introduced. Two stamps were replaced while the series was current. Dwight D. Eisenhower replaced both Franklin D. Roosevelt on the 6¢ value and Albert Einstein on the 8¢ value, both at a time when the First Class postage rate was increased to those denominations.

All of the designs were issued as sheet stamps with the exception of the deep claret 8¢ Eisenhower stamp. There are two 8¢ Eisenhower stamps, a tri-color stamp, issued only in sheet format (1394) and the deep claret (mirroring the 6¢ Eisenhower design) issued only as booklet (1395) and coil (1402) stamps. A total of six denominations were produced as booklet panes for single and *combination booklets*, and nine denominations were released in coil rolls. All of the stamps were intaglio printed. The stamps were in production during the period when the Post Office Department (POD) was reorganized into the United States Postal Service (USPS). It was a time of considerable technological changes in stamp production and mail handling that is reflected in numerous gum, perforation, *luminescence*, and Bureau *precancel* varieties produced for the sheet, coil, and booklet formats of the series.

Designs
The Prominent Americans Issue lacks uniformity of design. Unlike other definitive stamp series that exhibit some common design element, each stamp in the Prominent Americans is uniquely designed. Previous issues had one or two individuals create the series design. However the Prominent Americans Issue .utilized 13 different individuals to produce the diverse designs. The unifying factor of the series was the recognition of the individuals portrayed. In the words of the USPS, "The men and women honored by the Prominent Americans Series of United States postage stamps are as diverse as their contributions to the growth and development of America."

The concept was noble, but stamp collectors had been spoiled by the simplicity and uniformity of their definitive stamps, so the initial criticism, after the release of the first three stamps (4¢ Lincoln, 6¢ Roosevelt, and 5¢ Washington), was harsh. Some mocked the effort, calling the stamps the "Ugly Americans."

The Washington stamp, based on a portrait by Rembrandt Peale, was issued in both a sheet (1283) and coil (1304) format in 1966. The *engraving* of the facial features seemed to suggest an unflattering "pocked marked" and "unshaven" appearance. Because of the criticism of the original design, a redrawn "clean shaven" sheet stamp was released November 17, 1967 (fig. 2).

Figure 2

The original 5¢ Washington stamp (1283 on left) and the redrawn 5¢ Washington stamp (1283B on right).

When the **First Class** letter rate changed from 5¢ to 6¢ in January 1968 there was little need for 5¢ stamps. Even when the First Class letter rate eventually rose to 15¢ in May 1978, there was still a good supply of original design 5¢ coil stamps (1304) on hand. Nevertheless, a redrawn 5¢ coil stamp (1304C) appeared unannounced in the early months of 1981. One reason for the issuance of the new coils was the anticipation of a 5¢ increase from the then current 15¢ First Class rate. The Disabled American Veterans (DAV) for their charitable response envelopes used a significant quantity of the new coil. It is speculated that the redrawn coils were created at the request of the charitable organization. As it turned out, the rate was increased only by 3¢ in March 1981 and the DAV mailings used a strip of three of the new coil and a single 3¢ Parkman coil stamp. The plates for the redrawn 5¢ coil went to press only one time, on December 2, 1980. In November 1981 the First Class rate was increased to 20¢. Surprisingly, when additional quantities of 5¢ coils were needed, new plates were made with the original "dirty face" design and they appeared in strips of four on the next DAV mailing.

Sheet Stamps

All but one of the Prominent Americans sheet stamps was printed on the BEP's **Huck-Cottrell** Presses. The exception was the black, red, and blue-gray 8¢ Eisenhower stamp (1394), which was printed on the BEP's 3-color Intaglio **Giori press** (ch. 37).

Marginal markings play an important role in the production process. In addition to the plate numbers that appeared in the four corners of the sheets (one number per pane of 100 stamps), two types of *electric-eye* marks appear on the sheet. The thick vertical lines between the right and left panes termed dashes and the horizontal lines opposite each row of stamps called frame slugs were used in the sheeting and perforation process. Two other marginal markings, "USE ZIP CODES" and "MAIL EARLY IN THE DAY" appeared on sheet panes beginning with BEP plate number 29600. The lower right pane of 100 of the 21¢ Giannini stamp, shown in Figure 3, illustrates these markings. These markings appear on all panes for some Prominent Americans denominations. Some denominations are known both with and without the markings, and some have no "ZIP" or "MAIL EARLY" markings at all.

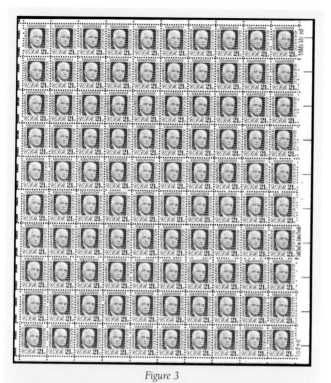

Adhesive gum was applied to the colorless wove paper stamp **web** during the print run on the Cottrell press. The gum was a resin-dextrin adhesive with a "shiny" appearance and it was used in the production of all the sheet stamp denominations and most of the coil and booklet stamps. During the perforating process, the shiny-gummed paper was subjected to **gum breakers** to reduce the effects of paper curling.

The BEP had been experimenting with a matte-textured resin-dextrin adhesive in a polyvinyl acetate (PVA) solvent emulsion. This "dull" adhesive gum was humidity resistant and eliminated paper curling as well as the need for separator tissue used in stamp booklets. Because of these characteristics, the web rolls could be pre-gummed and on-press gumming could be eliminated. Paper preprinted with "dull" gum was introduced by the BEP in late 1970 and eventually was used for the production of several Prominent Americans stamps. On sheet stamps, the dull gum is known on the 5¢ Washington (original and redrawn versions), 15¢ Holmes, 20¢ Marshall, 25¢ Douglass, 40¢ Paine, 6¢ Eisenhower, and the 7¢ Franklin. On booklet panes dull gum is found on the 1¢ Jefferson, 6¢ and 8¢ Eisenhower, 2¢ Wright, and 15¢ Holmes. Dull gum is found on all the coil stamps except the 1¢ Jefferson, 4¢ Lincoln, and the 6¢ Roosevelt. The "matte" surface of the gum gave an almost "not gummed" appearance to the stamps so a light yellow or cream coloring was added to some of the gum formulation creating several "dull" gum varieties. The paper used to produce the multicolored 8¢ Eisenhower sheet stamp was pre-gummed with shiny gum, but did not require gum breakers.

Figure 3

Lower right pane of 100 of the 21¢ Giannini stamp, showing marginal markings, including ones used in the "electric eye" perforating process.

The application of ***phosphorescent tagging*** to postage stamps was still in its formative stage when the first of the Prominent Americans went to press. Begun in 1963, it would coat stamps so that the ultraviolet sensor unit on the Mark II Facer-canceller machine could locate and cancel the stamp (ch. 54). After January 1, 1967 most regular stamps were tagged. Although almost half of the Prominent Americans denominations were initially produced without tagging, eventually all of the sheet stamps received tagging except the 1¼¢ Gallatin stamp which was used to pay the Third Class non-sorted mail rate. Three different types of ***overall tagging*** exist on the Prominent Americans sheet stamps: ***Tagging Type II***, ***Tagging Type IIA***, and ***Tagging Type III***.

Generally, the color shades of the Prominent Americans stamps were fairly uniform. Two stamps, however, are recognized with listed color varieties. The 25¢ Frederick Douglass stamp was initially issued "rose lake" (1290). It also exists as "magenta" (1290b). The magenta stamp was produced inadvertently when, according to the BEP, the ink for the Douglass stamps may have been added to an inadequately cleaned ink fountain that had been used to produce the 15¢ Holmes magenta colored stamp.

Around 1981 the BEP began to use lead-free inks, which were generally identical in color shade to the previous inks. However it was difficult to find a lead-free match for the original "deep olive" shade used on the 20¢ Marshall stamp (1289). Several shades exist, including a "black olive" on shiny gum (1289b).

There are several other denominations that exhibit shade varieties that remain unlisted. There are two strikingly different color shades on the 7¢ Franklin, which correspond to the shiny and dull gum varieties. The $1 Eugene O'Neill stamp is listed as "dull purple," though collectors have reported as many as eight other shade varieties. The "blackish lilac" shade is clearly different than the listed "dull purple," and was acknowledged by the BEP as a color error in *Linn's Stamp News*, September 18, 1995.

Stamps printed on the Huck-Cottrell press went to the ***web-fed electric-eye*** perforator, which produced 11 x 10½ perforations on vertical stamps and 10½ x 11 on horizontal stamps. The perforations, with imperfect corners and holes, extend though the narrow margin but not though the wide margin. This electric-eye perforating machine normally applied gum breaker ridges, added perforations in both directions and finally, cut the roll into sheets in a single process.

The 8¢ multicolored Eisenhower stamps, printed on the Giori press were perforated on the ***L perforator*** with 10.94 perforations that extended completely through the margins of the pane.

Booklet Stamps

Prominent Americans booklets were made from six different stamp denominations, all with overall tagging. A total of 12 different booklets were produced from 1967 through 1978 that contained various combinations of Prominent Americans stamps. Three booklets contained stamp panes of a single denomination, the two 8¢ claret Eisenhower (BK121 and BK123) and the 15¢ magenta Holmes (BK117A). Seven others contained combinations of two different Prominent Americans stamp panes (BK116, BK117, BK117B, BK118, BK119, BK120, and BK122) and additionally, the 2¢ Wright was combined with the 13¢ Liberty Bell stamp of the Americana Issue in one booklet (BK127), and with the 11¢ carmine Jet air mail stamp in another (BKC22). Booklet stamps have always been made for public convenience usually for use on letters and post cards. A key to understanding Prominent Americans booklets is the First Class postage rates. From 1967, when the series' first booklet was issued until mid 1978, when the last Prominent Americans booklet was issued, there were five changes to the First Class letter and six to the post card rate. In almost every case, the variety of panes and pane combinations was introduced to provide convenient booklets to accommodate these rate changes and to make booklets that could be sold in vending machines without the need to give pennies in change.

In order to price many of the booklets in whole dollar amounts, the POD continued the practice begun with the 5¢ Washington booklet of 1962 of substituting service messages or "slogan" labels for stamps on some of the booklet panes. Figure 4 illustrates the four slogans (identified by *Scott* as numbers 4, 5, 6, and 7) used on Prominent Americans booklet panes.

Booklet stamps were printed on the Huck-Cottrell press from 320, 360, and 400 subject rotary plates. Each roll produced approximately

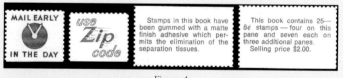

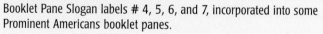

Figure 4

Booklet Pane Slogan labels # 4, 5, 6, and 7, incorporated into some Prominent Americans booklet panes.

6,000 sheets of plate impressions. Booklet construction changed over the life of the series as technological improvements were introduced (ch. 47 and 48). Initially the printed rolls were perforated on the Harris-Seybold electric-eye perforator, and then hand collated into booklets. While most of these booklets were available over the counter at local post offices, four booklets were produced solely for dispensing in automatic vending machines (BK117, BK122, BK129, and BKC22).

Printing on dull-gum paper was initiated for regular postage stamp booklet production with the experimental $2 booklet (BK119) containing 1¢ Jefferson and 6¢ Eisenhower stamps without **interleaving**, issued March 1, 1971. In 1974 mechanical collation replaced hand collation, which was made possible because the dry dull-gum eliminated the need for interleaving. The 90¢ combination 13¢ Liberty Bell and 2¢ Frank Lloyd Wright booklet (BK127) was collated by this process.

In 1976 the BEP purchased **Goebel booklet-forming machines** that performed many steps in the booklet making process. This machine, capable of producing 15,000 booklets per hour, was used to make the $3.60 booklets (BK117A) containing three panes of eight 15¢ Holmes stamp. This was the last booklet to use a Prominent Americans stamp.

Coil Stamps

The coil stamps were printed on Cottrell presses from pairs of 432 subject plates, 18 subjects across by 24 in the rotary direction. The two curved plates produced **joint lines** on coil stamps at the seam between the two plates. The joint lines appear at 24 stamp intervals. Like the sheet stamps, coils received an overall phosphor tagging, except for those issued with Bureau precancels.

The web for coil stamps was fed through a Huck coiling machine that produced gauge 10 perforations on **endwise** and **sidewise** coil stamps. The web was then slit into individual strips that were counted, cut, rolled into coils, and bound with a strip of masking tape. All rolls, regardless of size, were then hand wrapped in cellophane.

The coil stamps have many collectable varieties. Two denominations were issued as vertical coils and nine were issued as sidewise coils. Some coil stamps were produced with both shiny and dull gum and some were precanceled, on the Cottrell press. While large rolls were prepared for commercial mailings, the smaller 100 stamp rolls were issued for public convenience. Like booklet stamps, the issuance of coil stamps reflected the need for new denominations as postal rates changed.

15¢ Holmes Die Types

One interesting feature of the series is the Oliver Wendell Holmes 15¢ stamp that was actually produced from three different designs (Die types, fig. 5). The Type I die produced sheet stamps (1299) were issued March 8, 1968. A decade later, on May 29, 1978, the First Class letter rate was increased to 15¢. Even though the new 15¢ Fort McHenry Flag stamp was in production, it was decided to continue to produce Holmes sheet stamps and to issue new Holmes stamps in coil and booklet format in order to more fully and economically utilize BEP presses. The coil version (1305E), using the same Type I die used on the sheet stamp, and a booklet (1288B) made from a new die (Type III), were issued on June 14, 1978. The Type III die used for the booklets stamps was smaller than Type I in order to accommodate size requirements for stamps produced in

Figure 5

The 15¢ Holmes die types (from left to right): types, I and II (used on sheet and coil stamps) and type III (used on booklet stamps).

booklet form on the new Goebel booklet forming machines. Type III is characterized by a significant reduction the length of Holmes' tie.

It was long recognized that the original Holmes die was cut in a fashion that, when transferred to the printing plates, produced inking problems. Missing ink or "white spots" from wiping pressure, and ink spreading or "mashing out" due to printing pressure often can be seen with the naked eye. With the increasing need for 15¢ stamps, BEP decided to correct the problem by creating a new die. This new Type II die appeared similar to the original design, but it had modifications of the lettering, numerals, and chest areas. The most distinguishing characteristics of Type I are that the cent sign is left of center of the "E" in postage, all engraved lines in the tie touch the right outline of the tie, and the tie touches the robe. In Type II, the cent sign is centered under the "E", the third engraved line from the bottom in the tie is short, and the other tie hatch lines are incomplete. The tie does not touch the robe. Type II sheet (1288d) and coil (1305Ei) stamps were issued without notice.

Bureau Precancel

Many Prominent Americans sheet and coil stamps exist as Bureau or *local precancels* (ch. 29). As Bureau precancels they exist both with the traditional "City and State between horizontal lines" precancels, applied by the Cottrell press, and, beginning in September 1978, with two parallel lines only. These later precancels, which replaced the traditional city and states Bureaus are known as **National Bureau precancels**. They could be used on precanceled mail at any post office.

Figure 6

Bureau Precancels on the 3¢ Parkman coil: a "city and state" type, a "National Bureau" with lines only, and a Service Inscribed precancel.

The BEP also experimented with *service inscribed* precancels which identified the specific use for which the stamps were intended, for exam-

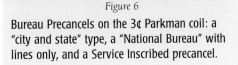

ple, "Bulk Rate", "PRESORTED FIRST-CLASS", and "Non-profit Org." The 3¢ Francis Parkman stamp is illustrative. The sheet stamp was issued with the city/state precancel while the coil version was issued with city/state, "national" and "service inscribed" precancels (fig. 6).

Notes on Collecting

The seven postal rate changes that took place during the 15-year life of the series, make it one of the most challenging from the perspective of postal history. Some collectors attempt to document these rate changes with appropriate covers. They may try to collect letters postmarked on the last day of the old rate, and the first day of the new rate utilizing various stamps in the series. Also during the life of the Prominent Americans new mail services and classes were introduced, including new types of bulk rate, and pre-sort, as well as **Priority Mail** and **Express Mail**. Finding examples of Prominent Americans stamps used for each of the mail classes, services, and fees in existence at that time provide an on-going challenge.

As with other stamp series, one can collect unused and used Prominent Americans in all three production formats. Coil stamps can be collected as singles, pairs, or as joint-line pairs. Booklet stamps can be collected as panes, with **exploded booklet** covers or as intact complete booklets. Numerous Prominent Americans exist as **Errors**, **Freaks** and **Oddities** (ch. 52). Some errors exist with tagging missing. Imperforate errors exist. Freaks include miscuts, **foldovers**, and smeared ink. An interesting Bureau precancel collection can be formed with both "city and state" and "national" precancels.

Almanac

1965 – On April 25 the POD announces plans to issue a new series known as the Prominent Americans Series.

1965 – The first Prominent Americans sheet stamp, the 4¢ Lincoln, is issued on November 10.

1966 – The first Prominent Americans coil stamp, the 4¢ Lincoln, is issued on May 28.

1967 – Most stamps issued beginning January 1 are produced as **tagged** stamps.

1968 – First Prominent Americans booklet (BK117) becomes available January 9, a $1 Combination Booklet for vending machines, with three panes of 6¢ Roosevelt stamps (1284c), and one pane of 2¢ Wright stamps (1280a).

1971 – Two dollar booklets containing 1¢ Jefferson and 6¢ Eisenhower stamps printed on dry dull-gum paper are issued without interleaving paper on March 1.

1978 – "National" Bureau precancels with lines only, valid on precanceled mail at any U.S. post office, begin production at the BEP on October 4.

What Others Have Said

The USPOD thought this was a beautiful stamp...

"Don't you agree with me that the stamp [4¢ Lincoln] captures some of the homespun quality of Abe Lincoln? I hope that this stamp will help to rekindle in Americans the memory of the man who preserved these United States."

—*Asst. Postmaster General Richard J. Murphy, dedication of the Lincoln stamp, New York, New York, November 19, 1965.*

...And then there was the stamp collecting public

"If the results achieved so far both in design and color selection are sustained throughout, this series may well be renamed 'The Ugly Americans.' With all the artistic talent available are these truly representative of our best effort? Will these labels, to be attached by the billions to mail matter sent worldwide, create or sustain an image of this nation and of its past 'greats' that is so anxiously sought? The head of the 4¢ looks like a teen-ager fixed up with fake whiskers and a beard to create a 'Lincoln' for the Junior High Assembly. And everybody knows that Lincoln was born in a log cabin. So why clutter up the stamp with all that messy backdrop. If any American has earned a place of dignity in our symbols, it is our 16th President; but he doesn't get it here."

—*Robert C. Masters, "The Editor's Corner," The United States Specialist, 1966.*

U.S. 6-cent Eisenhower counterfeits are reported

"[There have been reports of]...counterfeits of the U.S. 6-cent Eisenhower (Scott 1393), which was originally issued Aug. 6, 1970....the counterfeit stamps are rather crude in many respects and do not even come close to resembling the originals except as to design. Alert philatelists will easily spot the differences once they know of their existence....the color of the genuine stamps is a dark blue gray, whereas the counterfeits [are] more blue than gray. Being printed by photographic process the lines do not show as distinctly as the engraved stamp...[some] were almost completely lost in the lithographed counterfeit."

—*James A. DeVoss, "U.S. 6-cent Eisenhower Counterfeit," American Philatelist, 1971.*

The 5¢ Washington creates a modern day postal history rarity

"The stamp design (1283) was criticized widely by the public because it made Washington's face appear dirty or unshaved and thus undignified....To salvage the design, artist Steven Dohanos...removed enough of the etched pattern to lighten Washington's facial features....[With regard to the 5¢ shaved coil] In my opinion, all non-philatelic usages of this stamp, whether by DAV or other mailers, are scarce and desirable. Once the Prominent Americans Series achieves exhibition status, these surely will be key items to display. If someone can find an example postmarked earlier than February 10, 1981, he or she will have an outstanding treasure of modern philately."

—*Ken Lawrence, "Who Shaved George Washington's Face?" American Philatelist, 1993.*

Examples of Postal Usage

Figure 7

A 7¢ Franklin stamp, postmarked "OCT 13 1975," pays the post card rate during the 3½ month period (September 14 to December 31, 1975), when the card rate was 7¢.

Figure 8

Letter to Vienna, Austria, postmarked "Sep 4 1973" franked with four Prominent Americans totaling $1.58 that paid the 95¢ registry fee and three times the 21¢ per ½ oz. international air mail rate.

Where to Find More Information

- The USPS produced *Prominent American Series: Issues of 1965–1975* which tells the story of each stamp.

- Bob Winter's *Prominent Americans Series Bureau Precancel 1965–1973*.

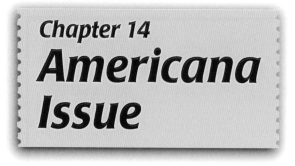

Chapter 14

Americana Issue

In 1971, the newly created United States Postal Service (ch. 33) took the extraordinary step of hiring a private firm – Kramer, Miller, Lomden, and Glassman of Philadelphia, Pennsylvania – to design a concept for a new series of definitive postage stamps, which would feature the culture and history of the United States. On October 31, 1975, the eve of America's bicentennial year, a new stamp was issued in **booklet** form depicting the Liberty Bell (Scott 1595, fig. 1). It heralded the beginning of a new series of definitive postage stamps called the Americana Issue, intended to replace the Prominent Americans Series (ch. 13). By the time the last Americana stamp was issued in 1981, twenty-five different designs had appeared on stamps in sheet, coil, and booklet format. They depicted American culture and history, many of them with a distinct bicentennial flavor. Sometimes the same design appeared in more than one format, and indeed, the 15¢ Ft. McHenry Flag appeared as a sheet stamp (1597), a booklet stamp (1598), and a coil stamp (1618C). The Americana Issue has Scott numbers ranging from 1581 to 1619, and 1811 to 1816.

Figure 1

The Americana Issue was launched in 1975 with two booklets (BK127 and BK128) containing 13¢ Liberty Bell stamps. Shown here is a pane of seven stamps plus a label (1595b) from the $2.99 booklet (BK128).

As with previous U.S. definitive series, the Americana Issue stamps are tied together by a common design element. Each Americana stamp features an inscription that wraps around two adjoining sides. When stamps are properly arranged in blocks of four, the stunning visual effect is that of a frame enclosing four related vignettes (fig. 2, 3, 4, 5, and 6). The casual user of these stamps probably did not appreciate this subtlety, which may be one of the reasons that the series was not popular with the public and became the shortest-lived definitive series of the twentieth century. There are also five Americana stamps with fractional cent denominations, which appear only as coils (1613-1615C and 1813, fig. 7) and cannot be arranged to create the wrap-around framed effect. Many of the stamps were printed on colored paper, a first for a definitive series.

Figure 2

The 1¢ (1581 and 1811), 2¢ (1582), 3¢ (1584), and 4¢ (1585) stamps have a "Roots of Democracy" theme: "The Ability to Write," "Freedom to Speak Out," "To Cast A Free Ballot," and "A Public That Reads."

Figure 3

The 9¢ (1590, 1590A, 1591, and 1616), 10¢ (1592 and 1617), 11¢ (1593), and 12¢ (1594 and 1816) stamps have a "Rights and Freedom" theme: "Right of the People Peaceably to Assemble," "People's Right to Petition for Redress," "Liberty Depends on Freedom of the Press," and "Freedom of Conscience · An American Right."

Figure 4

The 13¢ Eagle and Shield (1596), 13¢ Liberty Bell (1595 and 1618), 15¢ (1598 and 1618C), and 16¢ (1599 and 1619) stamps have a "Symbols of America" theme: "One Nation Indivisible · E Pluribus Unum," "Proclaim Liberty Throughout All the Land," "Land of the Free · Home of the Brave," and "I Lift My Lamp Besides the Golden Door."

Figure 5

The 24¢ (1603), 28¢ (1604), 29¢ (1605), and 30¢ (1606) stamps have a "Historic Places and Signaling Devices" theme: "Midnight Ride · One If By Land, Two If By Sea," "Remote Outpost · New Nation Building Westward," "Lonely Beacon · Protecting Those Upon the Sea," and "American Schools · Laying Future Foundations."

Figure 6

The 50¢ (1608), $1 (1610), $2 (1611) and $5 (1612) stamps have an "America's Light" theme: "America's Light Sustained By Love of Liberty," "America's Light Fueled By Truth and Reason," "America's Light Will Shine All Over the Land," and "America's Light Leads Her Generations Onward."

Figure 7

Five Americana designs appear only on coils with fractional denominations. The 3.1¢ (1613), 7.7¢ (1614), 7.9¢ (1615), 8.4¢ (1615C), and 3.5¢ (1811) have a "Music" theme: "Listen With Love to the Music of the Land", "Marching in Step to the Music of the Union," "Beat the Drum for Liberty and the Spirit of '76," "Peace Unites a Nation Like Harmony in Music," and "The Music of America is Freedom's Symphony."

The Bureau of Engraving and Printing (BEP) printed all the Americana Issue stamps. The **Cottrell Press** printed all of the single color stamps in this series except for the two Dome of Capitol 9¢ booklet stamps (1590 and 1590a), and the 16¢ Statue of Liberty coil stamps (1619), which were printed on the **B press**. The Dome of Capitol booklet stamps appear *se-tenant* on *panes* with stamps that are not a part of the Americana Issue.

The multi-colored 13¢ Eagle and Shield (1596) was printed on the **Andreotti press**. Multi-colored Ft. McHenry Flag sheet stamps (1597) were printed on the **A press**, while the Ft. McHenry Flag booklet stamps (1598) were printed on the B press. The 50¢ through $5 values were printed in two steps on sheet-fed presses, first on a Miller offset press and then on a Giori I-8 currency press. It is a two-step process such as this that creates the potential for printing an inverted stamp. That is how the most spectacular and well-known Americana error variety was created – the rare $1 Candlestick with brown color inverted (1610c, fig. 8).

Figure 8

The "Candlestick" invert.

There are varieties of Americana Issue stamps, the most common of which involves gum. Many Americana stamps have either shiny or dull gum. They are listed in *Scott*, but are not identified by separate numbers. There is a significant paper variety on the 2¢ stamp. Because of a rate change in the fall of 1981, the BEP was required to produce significant quantities of 2¢ stamps that customers could use in conjunction with their existing 18¢ stamps to pay the new 20¢ first class rate. Since the BEP did not have a sufficient stock of the properly tinted paper, it used an ordinary white paper described by *Scott* as "cream paper," resulting in a new variety (1582a). Some 1¢ stamps were also printed on this paper (1581c), apparently by mistake. **Tagging** was routinely applied to all Americana Issue stamps, but errors were created for many denominations when tagging was not successfully applied. **Color omitted** errors exist on the 50¢, $1, and 13¢ Eagle and Shield, as well as the 15¢ Fort McHenry sheet and coil stamps. There are a number of **imperforate** errors, and abundant freaks, especially misplaced perforation **freaks**. The 13¢ Eagle and Shield is perforated in two varieties. On the stamp as originally issued (1596) the 11.2 **bullseye perforations** meet perfectly in the corners. However, the Andreotti press on-line perforator was out of service during one printing of this stamp, so the BEP's **L perforator** was used instead. The resulting perforations are 11, do not met perfectly at the corners, and go all the way to the edge of the selvage (1596d).

Figure 9

The 13¢ Liberty Bell precanceled with the post office name (Chicago IL), with bars only, and as "Service Inscribed."

During the Americana years, booklet production at the BEP was undergoing rapid change (ch. 48). The two booklets that launched the Americana Issue in 1975 contained 13¢ Liberty Bell stamps. The first, for use in **vending machines**, which contains six 13¢ and six 2¢ stamps

(BK 127), sold for 90¢. A second (BK128), containing 23 13¢ stamps, was priced at $2.99 for over the counter sales. Another vending machine booklet containing 13¢ Liberty Bell stamps (BK 129) was issued in 1976. A fourth booklet (BK130), also for vending machine use, contains 15¢ Ft. McHenry flag stamps. The final vending booklets, the first folded booklets produced by the BEP on its new **Goebel booklet forming machine**, contained a single **se-tenant** pane with one 9¢ Freedom to Assemble stamp along with seven 13¢ stamps not part of the Americana Issue. Panes in these Goebel booklets exist in two perforation varieties, 11 x 10½ (BK131) and 10 (BK132).

Bureau Precancels (ch. 29) changed significantly during the era of the Americana Issue. The last of the traditional Bureau Precancels, overprinted with post office names, appear on Americana Issues. The Americana stamps were likewise the first to appear with the plain lines of **National Bureau Precancels** and **service indicators** (fig. 9).

Notes on Collecting

All of the basic Americana series stamps can be purchased at a modest price. Many varieties are also available at a modest cost and a collector can put together an impressive collection on a modest budget. The only exception is the $1 Candlestick invert that requires many thousands of dollars to obtain.

While the Americana Issue was short-lived, it was in service during a time of frequently changing rates. Thus it is a challenge to collect Americana Issue postal history properly paying the various rates.

Almanac

1975 – First of the Americana Issue stamps is issued on October 31 to pay for the upcoming domestic rate increases.

1975 – First definitive stamp printed on colored paper is released on November 13, the 11¢ Freedom of the Press (1593).

1975 – Domestic First Class letter rate increases from 10¢ to 13¢ on December 31.

1978 – Domestic First Class letter rate increases from 13¢ to 15¢ on May 29.

1981 – Domestic First Class letter rate increases from 15¢ to 18¢ on March 22.

1981 – Domestic First Class letter rate increases from 18¢ to 20¢ on November 1.

1983 – The last variety of an Americana definitive is introduced, a service inscribed precancel of the 12¢ stamp.

1985 – Domestic First Class letter rate increases from 20¢ to 22¢ on February 17.

1987 – The last Americana Issue, the $5 Railroad Lantern (1612), is withdrawn from sale on October 31.

What Others Have Said

The Americanas are heralded as an exciting new concept...

"The flood of new regular issues... that threatens to engulf collectors late this year can also be beneficial....We stand at the threshold of a new series – the Americana series – which design-wise at least, promises an exciting new concept – objects and places associated with American culture rather than mere portraiture alone. Moreover, many of these stamps will be quality intaglio productions."

—*Barbara Mueller, "Realistic Goals for the New Americana Series,"* The United States Specialist, *1975.*

...and although short lived, had an enriching effect on our hobby

"The Americana Series of definitive postage stamps ... represented a radical departure from all that had proceeded it, both in conception and in execution. Ultimately the 1975 to 1983 Americana Series failed, a victim of the economic inflation that wracked the late '70s and the Postal Service's overambitious goals -- trying to do too many things with this series all at once. On another level, the Americana Series enriched our hobby with a variety of collectibles, from decimal-denominated precancels ... to legendary errors like the $1 Candlestick stamp with intaglio brown inverted. Such items probably added more to the lore of the U.S. stamp collecting than other, more successful series."

—*Ken Lawrence, "Americana Series 1975-83,"* American Philatelist, *1995.*

The $1 Rush Lamp Americana had volumes written about it

"There seem to be two major color varieties of the candleholder and lettering. One is a dark brown which sometimes appears to be almost black. The other is a lighter reddish brown. Between these two extremes there are at least a dozen other shades which can be classified as either a shade of dark brown or a shade of reddish brown, thus giving credence to the theory that there was a change in ink formulation....It would not be unreasonable to assume that the different shades of each color were at least partly due to the kind of paper used and the amount of ink laid down on the paper....Numerous...collectors have noted the many color variations on the $1 Americana's."

—*Howard A. Moser, "Notes on Aspects of the $1 Rush Lamp Americana Stamp Normal and Invert,"* The United States Specialist, *1995.*

The Americana Series is not dead yet!

"New rates have created a need for 6¢ and 12¢ U.S. postage stamps, and recent announcements indicate some surprises to meet those needs. First, a new 12¢ issue in sheet and coil formats will be issued April 8 in Dallas, Tex. Despite reports that the Americana Series was finished, the new 12¢ design is an Americana definitive issue which is likely to represent the final release for that regular series. The 12¢ stamp meets the new postcard rate...the need for 12¢ stamps...prompted the decision to issue the 12¢ Americana, which has been designed and available for some time. [The] design has been on file all the time, and is now being pushed out to help with the rate-change crunch."

—*"Americana definitive to debut in Dallas,"* Linn's Stamp News, *1981.*

Examples of Postal Usage

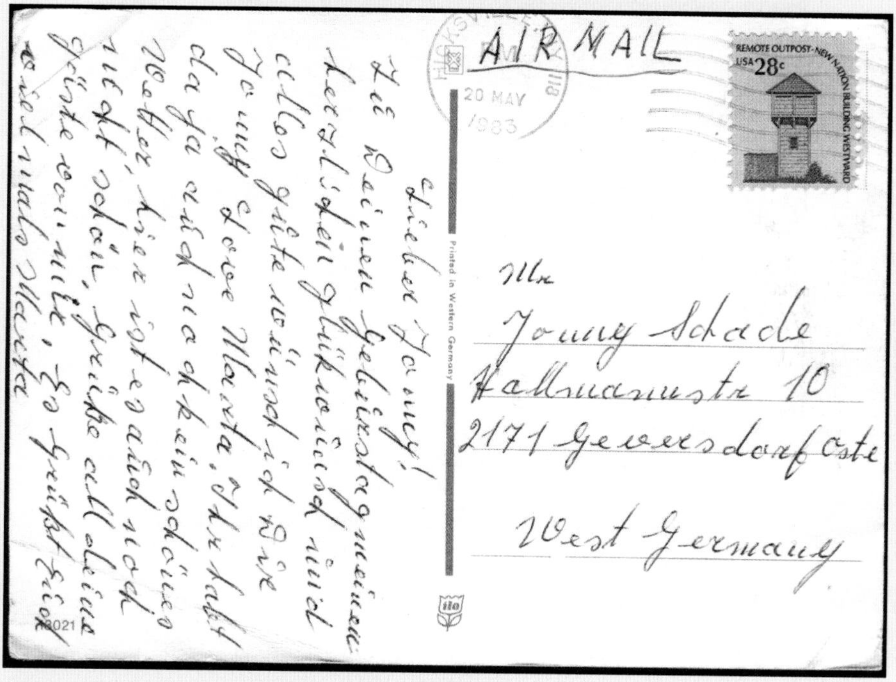

Figure 10

A 28¢ Remote Outpost stamp postmarked "20 May 1983" on an airmail postcard to Germany.

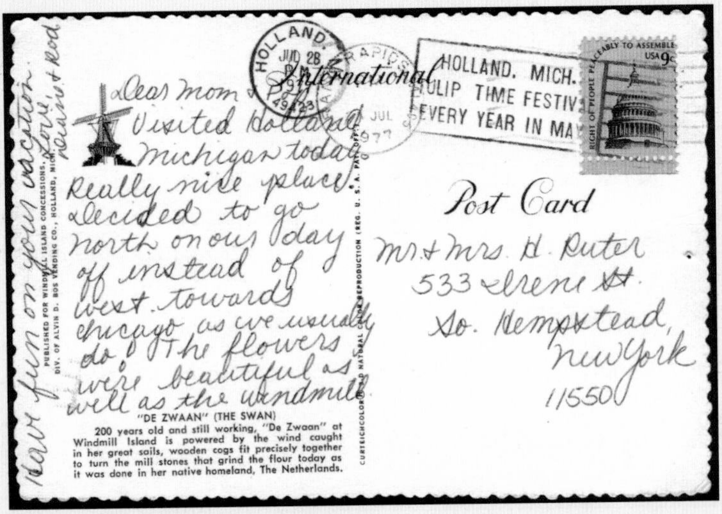

Figure 11

A 9¢ Right to Peaceably Assemble stamp paying domestic postcard rate post-marked twice on July 28, 1977.

Figure 12

A 13¢ Liberty Bell coil stamp on a commercial First Class cover.

Where to Find More Information

- "Americana Series 1975-83" by Ken Lawrence is the most detailed description of the Americana series published to date.

- The "Americana" Series reference manual depicted in the "at-a-glance system" by Art (Aaron) Maniker is a highly useful and comprehensive resource on the series.

- The Americana Series: Issues of 1975-1981 by the U.S. Postal Service.

Chapter 15
Great Americans Issue

The Great Americans definitive series (fig. 1), a set of stamps with sixty-three designs, issued between 1980 and 1999, comprises the largest set of face different ordinary stamps issued through the beginning of the twenty-first century. Sixty-two of the stamps honor individuals. One honors a couple, Lila and DeWitt Wallace (Scott 2936). The general public, and even many collectors, had no knowledge of most of the individuals portrayed. The subjects were chosen from among the many suggestions submitted to the *Citizens' Stamp Advisory Committee*, but appear to have been selected to satisfy various political agendas. There are Native Americans, various minorities, and women from all walks of life (fig. 2). There was no apparent unifying theme in the selection of subjects.

Figure 1

Walter Lippmann, a writer perhaps best known for his nationally syndicated newspaper column, appeared on the Great Americans stamp (1849) issued in Minneapolis, Minnesota on April 19, 1985.

The Great Americans are characterized by their standard definitive size, simple design lines, and monochromatic colors. They offer more complicated varieties than typically found in previous definitive series. *Scott* lists the Great Americans in three different groups: 1844 to 1869, (a series of 25 stamps was anticipated when *Scott* set aside numbers 1844 to 1869 for the new series) 2168 to 2197, and 2933 to 2943.

Stamps in the first group were initially issued between 1980 and 1985. Stamps in the second group were initially issued between 1986 and 1994, with some varieties coming in later years. In some cases when stamps went back to press in later years new varieties were created. The stamps in the third group were issued between 1995 and 1999. Other than the years when these stamps were initially issued, there is no apparent significance to these three groups, and certainly no distinguishing characteris-

Figure 2

A characteristic of the Great Americans Issue is the diversity of Americans honored.

tics. When the original block of sequential numbers set aside by the *Scott* editors was used, the editors assigned a new block of numbers, and then another.

The Bureau of Engraving and Printing (BEP) printed Great Americans on several different printing presses. Private contract printers also produced them. Great Americans are grouped here on the basis of BEP or private production, and, in the case of BEP production, on the basis of the printing press used.

Scott Listings of Great Americans

Some specialists question the adequacy and accuracy of *Scott* listings for this series. Throughout this chapter only *Scott* whole number references are used. This approach will provide readers with basic information, while acknowledging the *Scott* numbering of varieties in this series is problematic. Some have published articles challenging the accuracy of the perforation gauge measurement reported by *Scott* for some stamps.

What are "*Scott* whole numbers"?
When a series of stamps is announced, *Scott* typically reserves a group of catalogue numbers for the stamps in that set, and assigns numbers as stamps are issued. Capital letter suffixes are sometimes used, e.g., 1031A, in order to create additional catalogue "whole numbers" for the series or set when the quantity of reserved numbers is not sufficient. Lower case suffix letters, e.g., 2192a, indicate a variety of a stamp, perhaps due to ink color, paper, tagging, etc. Therefore, using only *Scott* "whole numbers" refers to the basic stamp, ignoring its varieties.

BEP Cottrell Press Stamps

The Great Americans Series premiered on December 27, 1980, with the issuance of the 19¢ Sequoyah stamp (1859). This value fulfilled the need for a stamp to pay the international post card rate effective January 1, 1981. It was printed at the BEP on the *Cottrell* presses, the standard press of the day. The last Great Americans to be printed on a Cottrell was the 3¢ Henry Clay (1846), issued July 13, 1983.

A total of twelve Great Americans was printed on the Cottrell presses: the 2¢ Stravinsky (1845), 3¢ Clay (1846), 4¢ Schurz (1847), 5¢ Buck (1848), 13¢ Crazy Horse (1855), 17¢ Carson (1857), 18¢ Mason (1858), 19¢ Sequoyah (1859), 20¢ Bunche (1860), 20¢ Gallaudet (1861, fig. 3), 35¢ Drew (1865), and 37¢ Milikan (1866). They are all perforated 11x10.5 and display *overall tagging*.

An early morning fire on March 5, 1982 at the BEP annex caused substantial damage to four of the five Cottrell presses. The 13¢ Crazy Horse stamps were on Cottrell press #804 at the time. As a result of the fire, two of the four presses were scrapped, necessitating the switch of the Great Americans to the A press.

BEP A and I-8 Press Stamps

The first stamp of the Great Americans Series printed on the A Press was the 1¢ Dix (1844, fig. 4). Although plates for the Dix stamp were made for use on the Cottrell press, they were never used. Instead, the first stamps were printed on the BEP's A press and are **block tagged**.

Printing was done at a single **intaglio** station that produced a **web** with **floating plate number** positions. **Marginal markings,** to guide sheet cutting machines, were also printed on the web. The panes of stamps contained no top or bottom **selvage**; only straight edge cuts at the top and bottom.

Figure 3

A plate block of the 20¢ Gallaudet (1861), printed on the Cottrell press with a representative plate number. The horizontal lines in the selvage are electric eye markings. The small spot of color that appears above the center of the upper electric eye bar is a corrosion stain. The green ink used to print the Gallaudet stamps is very corrosive. It created a depression in the plate, which printed the spot.

When the Dix stamp first went to press, the A press was equipped with an **in-line harrow perforator**, gauge 11. (Some specialists contend this is gauge 11.2 but it is listed in *Scott* as perf 11.) This perforator produced bullseye perforations that met perfectly at the corners of the stamps. They do not cross into the edge of the selvage.

In December 1983, the harrow perforator broke down and the remainder of the press run of Dix stamps was perforated on the BEP's off-line **L-Perforators**, gauge 10.9 as listed in *Scott* (some specialists contend it should be listed as 10.8). Perforations were applied first in one direction and then in the other, so the perforations do not meet perfectly at the corners.

Additional 1¢ Dix varieties were created when the BEP created a new **sleeve**. Since the intention was to use the **off-line perforators, electric eye** marginal markings were added.

Figure 4

A block from the top of a post office pane of 1¢ Dix (1844). Note printing sleeve number 1 at the top of the selvage where the floating plate number format left it when the roll was cut into panes of 100. There is no top or bottom selvage with this format. The illustration also shows the bulls eye perforations characteristic of the first press runs of the Dix stamp.

Ten additional Great Americans were printed from the A press with floating marginal markings, **block tagging**, and L-perforated gauge 10.8, 10.9, or 11 depending on the stamp. These stamps are the 6¢ Lipmann (1849), 7¢ Baldwin (1850), 9¢ Thayer (1852), 10¢ Russell (1853), 14¢ Lewis (1856), 20¢ Truman (1862), 22¢ Audubon (1863), 30¢ Laubach (1864), 39¢ Clark (1867), and 40¢ Gilbreth (1868). Some of them exist with both large and small block tagging.

In 1985 the A Press lacked sufficient capacity to produce all of the stamps needed. Therefore the BEP's I-8 sheet-fed currency presses were placed into service to produce the 8¢ Knox (1851), 11¢ Partridge (1854), and 50¢ Nimitz (1869). The paper stock used on these sheet fed presses was pre-gummed and shinier than gum used on other stamps in the series. Since the I-8 presses had no capacity for phosphor tagging, these stamps were overall tagged on other presses.

In 1986, the BEP changed the layout of definitives to appeal to collectors who longed for the traditional plate blocks of four. The A press printing sleeves were reconfigured to enable a return to plate blocks of four with corner numbers. Twenty new designs debuted with this layout: 1¢ Mitchell (2168), 2¢ Lyon (2169), 3¢ White (2170), 4¢ Flanagan (2171), 5¢ Black (2172), 10¢ Red Cloud (2175), 14¢ Howe (2176), 15¢ Cody (2177), 17¢ Lockwood (2178), 21¢ Carlson (2180), 23¢ Cassatt (2181), 25¢ London (2182), 28¢ Sitting Bull (2183), 45¢ Cushing (2188), 56¢ Harvard (2190), 65¢ Arnold (2191), $1 Revel (2193), $1 Hopkins (2194), $2 Bryan (2195), and $5 Harte (2196).

In 1986, when the $1 Bernard Revel stamp debuted, a great scandal occurred. Unbeknownst to anyone, BEP engraver Kenneth Kipperman added an unauthorized mark to the *die*, a Star of David at the juncture of Revel's beard and moustache. The star's discovery touched off an internal investigation into the BEP's stamp dies of the previous 10 years.

In 1987, the $5 Bret Harte stamp became the first definitive stamp issued in miniature sheet format. The stamps were issued in panes of 20 stamps that were intended to reduce waste at Philatelic Centers and Philatelic Sales Divisions. Previously, when collectors purchased a plate block of four, the USPS was left with 96 stamps from each high valued stamp pane to sell or, more commonly, destroy. With the new miniature sheet format, four plate blocks could be sold with only four stamps left for disposal.

A front-page story in *Linn's Stamp News* on July 16, 1990 announced the discovery of a major plate variety on the $1 Johns Hopkins stamp. The variety manifests itself as a large spot on the subject's shirt just below his bow tie. It was described in the article as "the easiest plate variety to identify on a modern U.S. stamp." After the flaw was discovered, the BEP re-entered the design on the printing sleeve, limiting the availability of this now rare variety.

Another five values, previously issued with floating plate numbers were now printed with traditional plate number blocks of four: 20¢ Truman (1862), 22¢ Audubon (1863), 30¢ Laubach (1864), 39¢ Clark (1867), and 40¢ Gilbreth (1868). These 25 values were perforated on the **Bobst-Champlain** perforators that produced characteristic bullseye perforations.

During the latter part of the A press' use, the BEP experimented with phosphor-coated paper. The 15¢ Cody (2177) was the only Great Americans stamp printed on this paper.

The practice of overall tagging resumed in 1990. Eight values that had previously been released with block tagging were reissued with overall tagging. They were the 10¢ Red Cloud (2175), 15¢ Cody (2177), 20¢ Truman (1862), 23¢ Cassatt (2181), 30¢ Laubach (1864), 45¢ Cushing (2188), 50¢ Nimitz (1869), and $1 Hopkins (2194). Two new designs were added, the 5¢ Marin (2173) and 40¢ Chennault (2187).

Stamps were tagged with phosphor to trigger the post offices' optical facer-cancellers. With the lack of human handling, patrons could abuse the system by using lower value tagged stamps to fool the optical readers. In August 1997, the *San Francisco Chronicle* broke a front-page story exposing this perceived flaw in the USPS' revenue protection program. They mailed a sampling of letters that were franked with Great Americans, including 72 under-franked envelopes bearing 10¢, 20¢, and 23¢ values, at a time when the first class rate was 32¢. All of the stamps were phosphor tagged and successfully processed through the facer-canceller machines. Seventy made it to their final destinations and only one was assessed postage due, showing the vulnerability of the system. Lost revenue prompted the Postal Service to produce untagged low value stamps. The 4¢ Father Flanagan was the first to appear intentionally without tagging (2171). These values are listed as untagged by *Scott*.

BEP C and D Press Stamps
The BEP had problems with the A press, especially with the unreliable ink dryers. Production was completely switched to the **C and D presses** in 1991. These presses, made by Goebel, have 3-color intaglio stations, each typically printing a different single color. In addition, the D press has six offset printing stations. C and D press printing sleeves were interchangeable. Four previously issued stamps were printed from these presses with overall tagging: Cody (2177), Cassatt (2181), Red Cloud (2175), and Nimitz (1869). Seven values were later printed on **coated paper** from the C and D presses including Cassatt (2181), Red Cloud (2175), Chennault (2187), Humphrey (2189), Wilkie (2192), Hopkins (2194), and $5 Harte (2196).

BEP F Press Stamps

In late 1992 the *F press*, a 4-color offset, 3-color intaglio combination press, began producing Great Americans stamps on a paper with *taggant* applied over uncoated paper. When viewed under short wave ultra-violet light, the taggant appears mottled due to the unevenness of the surface of the paper. Seven previously issued stamps appear in this format: Hopkins (2194), Cassatt (2181), Nimitz (1869), Humphrey (2189), Wilkie (2192), Red Cloud (2175), and Truman (1862). One new stamp appeared in this format, the 46¢ Ruth Benedict (2938). In 1995, the BEP added a second ink supplier, which created new shades on some stamps.

Great Americans Produced by Private Contractors

After 1991 contract suppliers produced several Great Americans, the first being the 35¢ Chavez (2186), issued April 3, 1991. Private contractors could produce stamps at lower costs than the BEP. In the Executive Summary of a June 1991 report of the U.S. General Accounting Office entitled *Postage Stamp Production: Private Sector Can Be a Lower Cost Option Source*, costs of BEP produced Red Cloud stamps were compared to those of the new 35¢ Chavez stamp. Both stamps were intaglio printed and the *Canadian Bank Note Company* produced the Chavez stamps.

The costs for the Chavez stamp were $1.70 per 1000 compared to $1.90 per 1000 for the BEP printed Red Cloud stamps. The move toward the use of contract printers was irreversible. In addition to the Chavez stamp the following Great Americans were contract printed: 20¢ Apgar (2179), 29¢ Warren (2184), 29¢ Jefferson (2185), 32¢ Hershey (2933), 32¢ Farley (2934), 32¢ Luce (2935), 32¢ Wallace (2936), 55¢ Hamilton (2940), 55¢ Morrill (2941), 77¢ Breckenridge (2942), and 78¢ Paul (2943). Private contractors printed ten of the last eleven Great Americans to be issued.

Notes on Collecting

The collector of Great Americans stamps is challenged by the many different varieties that were created by constantly changing production processes. Tagging is a key to understanding the various printings. Therefore a collector of Great Americans will want a short wave ultra-violet light, and some knowledge of phosphor tagging terminology (ch. 54). A basic understanding of the presses involved will also help (ch. 37).

Since there are stamps with 63 different designs, a collector might pick a specific one, and study its many different varieties of tagging, perforations, gum, paper, and ink color. If, for example, one collects the varieties of the $1 Hopkins, the following articles would aid research: "New varieties of $1 definitives cropping up" by Fred Baumann, *Stamp Collector*, November 23, 1998; "$1 Johns Hopkins stamp has low-glow gum" by Michael Schreiber, *Linn's Stamp News*, February 9, 1998; "Five different $1 Hopkins" by Charles Snee, *Linn's Stamp News*, July 1, 2002.

EFOs abound in this series. Figure 5 shows the Robert Millikan stamp (1866). One image shows the correct design with the subject's name running up the left side of the stamp. The other, with the name running up the right side, is a result of a 5mm shift of the vertical perforations.

Figure 5

A 37¢ Robert Millikan (1866) EFO. The stamp on left is correctly perforated, with the subject's name running up the left side of the design. The stamp on the right, with the name running up the right side of the design, is a result of a 5mm shift of the vertical perforations.

Almanac

1980 – Without fanfare, the first Great Americans stamp, the 19¢ Sequoyah (1859) is issued December 27.

1986 – The 25¢ Jack London stamp (2182) is issued January 11, the first in the second of the three *Scott* groups of Great Americans (2168 to 2197).

1987 – On August 25 the $5 Bret Harte (2196) becomes the first definitive issued in miniature sheet format.

1990 – On February 18 the 5¢ Luis Muñoz Marin (2173) debuts as the first stamp with biographical information in the selvage.

1995 – On July 11 the 55¢ Alice Hamilton (2940) is the first stamp to be issued in the third and final group of *Scott* numbers (2933 to 2943).

1999 – On July 17 the 55¢ Justin S. Morrill (2941) becomes the 63rd and final stamp in the 15-year life of the Great Americans Series.

What Others Have Said

The first in a new series
"The U.S. Postal Service has released design details for the Sequoyah regular postage stamp, which will be issued December 27, 1980 at Tahlequah, Oklahoma. The 19-cent denomination of the Sequoyah stamp meets the new international rate for postcards which becomes effective January 1, 1981....The

Sequoyah stamp will be the first issue in a new series of stamps that will gradually replace the current Americana Series. The new Series will be called the Great Americans Series."

—"U.S.P.S. to issue Sequoyah stamp Dec. 27, 1980 – News, Views and Comments," *Stamps Magazine, 1980. This was a sea-change news release, since announcement of a new regular series was buried in the text announcing the release of a single stamp.*

Bernard Revel and John Hopkins – side-by-side at the same time.

"The $1.00 Johns Hopkins regular stamp goes on sale June 7 in Baltimore, Maryland. The stamp honors the successful Maryland merchant, banker and investor, who bequeathed $7 million to found Johns Hopkins University....The stamp is being produced in the same format as the $5.00 Bret Harte, 20-stamp miniature sheet (four rows of five stamps each). A single-digit number appears in each of the four corners on the selvage...Post Offices with authorized philatelic centers will receive an automatic distribution....The Bureau will fill currently unfilled requisitions for the $1.00 Bernard Revel stamp with the Johns Hopkins stamp...All other post offices requiring fewer than 20,000 stamps should requisition them immediately from their stamp distribution offices..."

—USPS Postal Bulletin #21724, 1989. *This bulletin announcement illustrates some of the various procedures by which local postmasters obtained their stock of the new stamp.*

Some Great American are more difficult to study than others

"The $5 Bret Harte has been distributed in stacks of 100 panes protected by a piece of cardboard...the whole sleeve has produced 16 panes of 20 stamps, instead of 8 panes of 100. Panes are arranged two by two on the sleeve horizontally, and the inscription © USPS 1986 is alternating in lower and then upper positions. Each pane has a plate number in each corner. The only obvious difference between the 16 panes lies in the position of the copyright inscription (upper or lower)...let us note that research on the $5 Harte will be extremely difficult; with its high face value the stamp is not distributed widely, and panes in each stack of 100 appear to be identical."

—*Michel Rybalka, "Remarks on Some Recent Issues,"* The United States Specialist, 1988.

Some Great Americans subjects become controversial subjects

"The Great American Series...is alive and well....The Great Americans are avidly collected by those interested in production varieties, Americana and other topicals. The Postal Service has used the series to give overdue recognition on stamps to women, black Americans and Indians. Indeed, the first...stamp honored an Indian, but white males still dominate the Great Americans. Some Great Americans stamps became controversial simply because the people they depicted were controversial, and from both sides of the political spectrum, namely the 10¢ Richard Russell of 1984 and the 29¢ Earl Warren of 1991. To their detractors, Russell was an opponent of civil rights and Warren an activist liberal. Both stamps were replaced by other Great Americans, the 10¢ Red Cloud of 1987 and the 29¢ Thomas Jefferson of 1993."

—*Michael Schreiber,* "*Great Americans to continue with Hershey,*" Linn's Stamp News, *1994.*

Why so many designs?
"The reason for all these stamps is not demand for sheet definitives (now at an all-time low, it seems), but rather the need to accommodate the demand for a downsized, cut-rate commemorative."

—*Fred Bauman*, Stamp Collector, *1997.*

Examples of Postal Usage

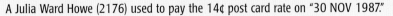

Figure 6
A Julia Ward Howe (2176) used to pay the 14¢ post card rate on "30 NOV 1987."

Figure 7

A combination of values is used to pay the ½ to 1-ounce international air mail rate of 95¢ in effect in 1992.

Figure 8

A pair of $1 Revel stamps used in 1988 paying 85¢ certified mail fee, 25¢ First Class letter rate, and 90¢ return receipt requested.

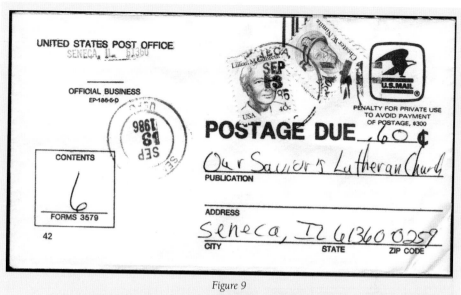

Figure 9

Great Americans used at Seneca, Illinois to collect postage due in 1986.

Where to Find More Information

- "The Great Americans Series" by Ken Lawrence is the most informative article about the series, but lacks details on those stamps issued from 1993 through 1999.

- Stephen G. Esrati published highly detailed listings and narratives about the Great Americans in a series of newsletters entitled *The Great Americans* from 1992 through 1999.

- The relevant volumes of *Linn's U.S. Stamp Yearbook*, edited by Fred Boughner or George Amick.

Chapter 16
Transportation Coils

On May 18, 1981, without fanfare, a stamp was issued which broke an 80-year-old custom – a coil stamp was issued with its own unique design (*Scott* 1907). It pictured a surrey from the 1890s, a unique, new design for a U.S. postage stamp. Until then, stamps in convenient coil rolls were always of the same design as definitive stamps that were in circulation at the time (ch. 49). Although the stamp was printed in brown ink, the first brief announcement from the United States Postal Service (USPS) indicated it would be printed in black ink with few other details provided.

Figure 1

This strip contains a gap between the precancel lines, which happens to occur at the same place as the joint line. However, the precancel gap and the joint line do not typically coincide.

There were to be 50 more coil stamps issued through the next 15 years, each depicting a different conveyance of transportation, ranging from a 1770s carreta (2255), a Southwestern term for a two-wheeled cart, to a 1933 Stutz Bearcat (2131). Conveyances depicted are as entertaining as a 1900s circus wagon (2452), as somber as an 1860s ambulance (2128 and 2231, fig. 1), and as utilitarian as a 1920s tractor (2127, fig. 2). Stamp collectors who are interested in the movement of the mails may take special interest in the stamps depicting a 1880s mail wagon (1903), a 1910s **Star Route** truck (2125), and a 1920s railroad mail car (2265).

The Bureau of Engraving and Printing (BEP) printed most Transportation Coils, though a few of the last issues in the 1990s were printed by private contractors. The line **engraved intaglio** printing method was used to produce most of them, though a few of the last ones were

Figure 2

These stamps, from the second group of Transportation coils, issued between 1985 and 1987, have the Service Indicator printed in a different color ink than the color of the basic design. They are all classified as precancel stamps.

gravure printed. The Transportation Coils offer a large number of varieties to collect, such as *precanceling*, *tagging*, paper, and gum. One of the more fascinating features of the Transportation Coils is the tiny plate numbers printed at the bottom of stamps at given intervals. Stamps with these numbers are known as *Plate Number Coils* (PNCs) and appear at intervals of 24, 48, or 52 stamps, depending upon the press employed (ch. 50).

Transportation Coils exist in an unprecedented array of denominations, i.e. 5¢, 5.2¢, 5.3¢, 5.5¢, 5.9¢, etc. Never before had stamps been issued in so many fractional cent values. This was done to provide stamps with face values exactly matching the

Figure 3

The precanceled version of the 4¢ Stagecoach coil (1898b), with the inscription, "Nonprofit Org." indicating it was for use by nonprofit organizations. Nonprofit organizations paid lower Third Class rates than did commercial businesses. Note the clipped perforations, indicating that this stamp was applied by an affixing machine to a piece of bulk mail.

rates (often fractional cents) for various categories of *Third Class* mail, also known as bulk rate mail and quantity-discount mail, but perhaps most commonly known as "junk mail". As these rates changed, new stamps with new values were often issued.

Many Transportation Coils were issued as precancels, intended for use on bulk mailings that would bypass canceling equipment. Sometimes the precancel consisted of an overprinted pair of black horizontal lines, with or without the words of a *Service Inscription* between them (fig. 3). Sometimes the precancel consisted of the words of a Service Inscription that were an integral part of the stamp design. Other times the precancel consisted of both overprinted back lines and a service inscription that were an integral part of the design (fig. 4)! Until 1988, precanceled stamps with horizontal black line overprints were not available to collectors directly from the Postal Service, as bulk mailers required permits to purchase and use them. To satisfy collector demand, unprecanceled versions of these stamps were issued and sold to them via the Philatelic Sales Agency.

Figure 4

A sleigh from the 1880s is depicted on the 5.2¢ stamp. The stamp on the left (1900) is without overprinted precancel lines. The one on the right (1900a) has overprinted precancel lines. Note the Service Inscription, "Auth Nonprofit Org" appears on each stamp.

Figure 5

The 20¢ Fire Pumper (1908) was issued on December 10, 1981. It paid the 1 oz. First Class rate, which had been raised to 20¢ on November 1. Note the comparatively small size of the numeral of value, followed by a "c." This is chacteristic of the first Transportation coils, issued in the years 1981-84.

Figure 6

The 3¢ Conestoga Wagon (2252), issued on February 29, 1988, was often used in conjunction with a 22¢ stamp to meet the First Class rate of 25¢, which went into effect on April 3. Note the numerical value is not followed by a "c" or "¢."

Some large mailers, such as Reader's Digest and the Disabled American Veterans, used large quantities of low value stamps on return envelopes. It was their belief that such use encouraged a greater response from the public.

The Transportation Coils are listed in *Scott* as four distinct groups, based primarily on the years during which they were issued. The four groups tend to have some distinguishing characteristics, which are described in the details as follows.

The First Group of Transportation Coils (1897–1908)

The first coils in the series met the rates for first class postage needs. In addition, between March 22, 1981 and January 9, 1983 there were six changes in postage rates for bulk mail, both regular (commercial) bulk and non-profit bulk. Five of the six rate changes were marked by the issuance of new stamps.

This first group of Transportation Coils is distinguished by a comparatively small value, followed by a "c." An example is the 20¢ Fire Pumper (1908, fig. 5). Stamps from the later groups express values in larger sized numbers, and lack either a "c" or a "¢" (fig. 6). The earliest stamps were printed on the *Cottrell press*, a *rotary press* on which two plates were joined together to make a sleeve. The gaps between the two plates left depressions in which ink could accumulate, thus creating *joint lines* (fig. 7). Later stamps were printed on the *B press*, which used a single sleeve. Thus there were no joint lines on B press stamps.

Some stamps in this group were printed on both presses.

Five of the 14 stamps in the first group are **Service Inscribed**, that is, have incorporated into their designs words ("Auth Nonprofit Org" or "Bulk Rate") that specify the service for which they were intended (1900 [fig. 4], 1901, 1903, 1904, and 1905). These same five stamps also exist overprinted with two horizontal parallel lines as a pre-cancel. Three other stamps in the first group (1898Ab [fig. 3],

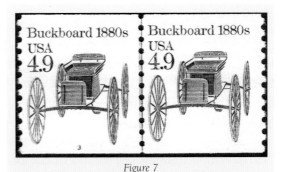

Figure 7

The joint line between these two 4.9-cent Buckboard (2124) stamps is a telltale sign of the Cottrell Press. Some collectors collected pairs, like this one, before the standard collectible size evolved to a strip of five with the number in the middle.

1902a, and 1906a) exist with a precancel overprint that consists of both parallel lines and words indicating the intended use ("Nonprofit Org", "Blk. Rt. CAR-RT", or "PRESORTED FIRST CLASS"). All stamps with precancel overprints were made available to collectors without the overprints.

The double line precanceling produced on the Cottrell press was applied by a series of mats that were of somewhat different size than the plates used to print the stamps. As a result, coils strips exist with gaps (breaks) in the otherwise continuous horizontal precancel lines (fig. 1). These gaps represent the spot where precanceling mats came together. Enthusiasts collect these gaps by their location on a strip of stamps in relationship to the location of the joint line produced where the plates used to print the stamps came together. Because of a change in methodology, precancel gaps are not found on stamps from the B press.

The designs for the 1¢, 2¢, and 4¢ were redesigned in order to facilitate printing on the B press. The 1¢ (2225) and 2¢ (2226, fig. 8), values are readily distinguished by their larger numerical value, and the absence of the "c." The new design for the redesigned 4¢ value (2228) is somewhat smaller than the original design and not easily distinguished from the original because the small "4c" was retained.

Figure 8

The first of the two Locomotive stamps (1897A), issued in 1982, has a smaller numeral and a "c." The re-engraved version (2226), issued in 1987, has a larger numerical digit and no "c."

In this first group, stamps issued with overprinted precancels were not **tagged**. It was not necessary to tag these stamps as they were not intended to be canceled in mail processing equipment. All other stamps in the group, including those issued without overprinted precancel lines intended for collectors, were tagged. Stamps printed on the Cottrell press were **overall tagged** while those printed on the B press were block tagged.

The Second Group of Transportation Coils (2123–2136)

The bulk rate changes of February 17, 1985 resulted in a second group of Transportation Coils, as did additional rate changes in 1986. Stamps in this group are distinguished from those of the first group by larger numerals, and the absence of the "c" symbol (fig. 6).

The second group of stamps was designed to be printed on the B press. Since that press was printing the huge quantity of first class stamps required by the change in first class rates which had also been implemented on February 17, 1985, the 3.4¢, 4.9¢, 8.3¢, 12¢, and 14¢ values were printed on the Cottrell press. Later printings of the 8.3¢ (2231), 12¢ (2132b), and 14¢ (2134b) stamps were made on the "B" press. These B press stamps have slightly narrower designs than those printed on the Cottrell press. There is a joint line to the right of the plate number on Cottrell printings, and none on the B press stamps.

When the second group of Transportation Coils was introduced in 1985, seven values were precanceled with two overprinted horizontal lines and a service inscription between the lines. In this respect they are similar to precancels of the first group. These stamps, printed and precanceled on the Cottrell press, exist with gaps in the precancel lines, just like the Cottrell printed stamps in the first group. However, by 1987, service inscriptions were printed in a different color than those used in the rest of the design, and the overprinted horizontal lines were eliminated. The 5.5¢, 7.1¢, 8.5¢, and 10.1¢ stamps (2125a, 2127a and b, 2129a, and 2130a; fig. 2) appear in this format. Fractional cent values without service inscriptions were provided for collectors who were still not permitted to use service inscribed stamps. As in the

Figure 9

The 10¢ Canal Boat (2257), reprinted several times, exists with several varieties of tagging and gum.

first group, unprecanceled stamps printed on the Cottrell press were overall tagged while those printed on the B press were block tagged.

Two stamps in this group saw double duty, each precanceled with two different service inscriptions that served different purposes. The 10.1¢ Oil Wagon (2130a) has "Bulk Rate" or "Bulk Rate Carrier Route Sort" service inscriptions, while the 7.1¢ Tractor (2127) exists with "Nonprofit Org." (2127a) and "Nonprofit 5-Digit ZIP+4" (2127b) service inscriptions.

Figure 10

The Canoe (2453) and Tractor Trailer (2457), issued late in the Transportation Series, represent the institutionalization of false franking. The mailer paid the difference between the actual rate and the face value of the stamp. Transportation Coil stamps are most typical collected in strips of five, with the PNC in the middle.

The Third Group of Transportation Coils (2252–2266)

The bulk rate changes of April 3, 1988 made most of the fractional denominations of the second group obsolete. The general appearance of the third group is similar to the second group but for the service inscriptions which were made an integral part of the design. Also, the horizontal lines designating precancels were eliminated. Stamps of the third group were all printed from a single plate on either the B or the **C press**, which eliminated the joint lines!

The group is characterized by a wide variety of paper and gum, particularly on stamps reprinted several times as the USPS experimented with new paper suppliers. The 10¢ Canal Boat (2257, fig. 9), for example, was printed at least seven times between 1987 and 2000. It features block tagging, overall tagging, **mottled tagging**, **solid tagging**, and **prephospered paper.** In addition there are three gum varieties: dull gum, shiny gum, and low gloss dull gum.

Figure 11

The 4¢ Steam Carriage (2451) had its value expressed "04" rather than simply "4". This unconventional method of expressing monetary value was soon abandoned.

Stamps printed for collectors without a service inscription were no longer provided. The sole exception is the 17.5¢ racing car (2262).

Fourth Group of Transportation Coils (2451–2468)

The *Postal Bulletin* of May 2, 1991 announced that the 5¢ Canoe stamp (2453) would be used for all rate categories of bulk non-profit third-class mail while the 10¢ Tractor Trailer (2458) to be issued the same day would be used for all first-class presort and bulk regular third-class mail (fig. 10). After a decade of attempts, the USPS no longer sought to exactly match rates with the face value of stamps—there would be no more fractional values. Instead, mailers would affix these 5¢ or 10¢ stamps, and then pay, at the time of mailing, any difference between the face value of the stamp used and the actual postage rate.

The 4¢ Steam Carriage (2451, fig. 11) has its value preceded by a zero, being expressed as "04" rather than simply "4". Some of the 5¢ stamps (2452, 2452B, 2453, and 2454) also have their values expressed in this manner.

Reflecting changing times, some stamps, Circus Wagon (2452B and 2452D) and Canoe (2454) were printed by private firms instead of the BEP. In 1995 the year date was added to the lower left corner of stamps. This innovation appeared on the 5¢ Circus Wagon (2452D) printed by Stamp Venturers, the 20¢ Cog Railway (2463), and the 32¢ Ferryboat (2466).

Notes on Collecting

The Transportation Coils may be collected as singles, pairs, or as plate number strips of three or five. Some collect strips of seven in order to show precancel gaps to the right of the plate number. Others chose to pursue first day covers or postal history. It is something of a challenge to assemble a complete set of the fractional values of the transportation coils on cover paying the proper rate. The 3.4¢ school bus (2123) of the second group is particularly difficult to locate. It is an even greater challenge to acquire plate number coils paying the proper rate.

A number of Transportation Coils exist as errors. There are imperforate errors and errors that lack intended tagging. A significant and affordable color error exists on the 32¢ Ferryboat (2466b), which can be found printed with bright blue ink instead of the intended shade of blue. Some specialists refer to this color error as "Bronx Blue."

Splices appear on at least some rolls of 10,000 stamps. First reported in 1989, they are known on the 1¢ re-engraved Omnibus (2225), the 3¢ Conestoga Wagon (2252), the 10¢ Canal Boat (2257), the 10.1¢ Oil Wagon (2130), the 13.2¢ Coal Car (2259), the 16.7¢ Popcorn Wagon (2261), and the 5¢ Circus

Wagon (2452) printed by American Bank Note and Stamp Venturers, as well as the 5¢ Canoe printed by Stamp Venturers (2454).

The challenge of collecting postal usage of the Transportation Coils is to find each value properly used on a cover during the period that the rate was in effect. Bulk rate mail stamps are especially challenging, as there was often a delay between the implementation of a new postal rate and the appearance of a stamp to pay that rate. For that interim period, the post office allowed mass mailers to use lower values and to pay the difference in cash. The stamps on the cover would underpay the rate, resulting in a *"false franking"*.

Almanac

1981 – The first Transportation Coil, the 18¢ Surrey (1907), is issued without fanfare on May 18.

1991 – The canoe stamp and the tractor trailer stamp are issued May 25, ending the necessity for many new fractional Transportation Coils when rates change.

1995 – A 5¢ circus wagon stamp (2452D) is issued March 20 with the date 1995 in the lower left corner, setting the precedent for the year date to appear on all future issues.

1995 – The last Transportation Coil, the 20¢ Cog Railway (2463) is issued June 9.

What Others Have Said

Transportation coils are handsome, interesting, and valid for first class postage.
"Taken as a group, these elegant line engraved stamps are the handsomest U.S. definitive set since the Presidentials. As collectible objects, they might ultimately prove the most interesting regular stamps since the Washington-Franklins. The most elusive of the transportation coils are the decimal denominated stamps...typically used in precancel form. However, they are available to collectors unprecanceled, and thanks to a decree last summer by then Postmaster General William Bolger, they are perfectly valid for first class postage."

—*Michael Laurence*, Linn's Stamp News, 1985.

The endless hunt for Transportation Coil varieties
"The Cottrell presses recently have been retired and the B press has taken their place. Since it uses a 'sleeve' with no 'seam', no 'joint line mark' is printed. The small plate number continues to be printed in the normal location at the bottom of the stamp, at intervals of 52 stamps instead of the Cottrell press 24. Collecting

the Transportation series...has become one of the greatest challenges of modern U.S. philately because of the many errors and varieties that have come to light. One [type] of these relates to the 'small number' itself."

—*Frank Shively, Jr., "Transportation Coils – 'Small Number' varieties," The United States Specialist, 1986. Shively goes on to describe the many errors and varieties found to date.*

No more collector versions of the Transportation Coils
"The 33rd face-different stamp in the ongoing United States Transportation coil series, a 16.7¢ Popcorn Wagon, will be released as a service-inscribed stamp only. No tagged and non-inscribed collector version will be released....this means that all future fractional coil stamps will be available only as service inscribed stamps. There will be no more collector versions that are tagged and non-inscribed."

—*Wayne Youngblood, "Service-inscribed-only coil calls for USPS clarification," Linn's Stamp News, 1988.*

U.S. Stamp collectors rebel and the USPS listens
"A furor erupted among collectors when the U.S. Postal Service announced that the tagged collector edition of the 11-cent caboose wasn't valid as postage because of the bulk-rate legend in the stamp's inscription. By extension, this decision demonetized the collector editions of nine earlier decimal denominated coils, too. The outcry against this policy and an editorial crusade in the weekly philatelic press caused the ruling to be withdrawn. Nevertheless, to avoid ambiguity, the next three years' new stamp issues put service inscriptions only on the precancels, and omitted them from the tagged stamps, beginning with the 7.4 cent baby buggy."

—*Ken Lawrence, "A Tribute to the Transportation Coils," American Philatelist, 1991.*

Collecting the Transportation series by method of transportation portrayed
"I...served as chairman of the Transportation Series subcommittee for the Citizens' Stamp Advisory Committee. The subcommittee had the responsibility to present to the full committee periodically another group of vehicles to be considered as subject matter for the series. Our subcommittee worked very hard trying to have a variety of subjects in several ways. One way was whether the vehicle would be carrying a single person, a group of people or cargo. Another way was the means of power or whether it would run by human power, an animal, a motor or any other way. Originally, the vehicles had wheels but that was broadened to include runners, rudders, pulleys and wings."

—*Mary Ann Owens, "U.S. Transportation Series Coils from a Thematic Point of View," The United States Specialist, 1992.*

Examples of Postal Usage

Consumer Products Offer
P.O. Box 795
Melville, N.Y. 11747

14

Ambulance 1860s
8.3 USA

CAR-RT SORT ** CR06
AUDREY MOORE
92 W 14TH
CHGO HEIGHTS, IL 60411

REQUEST FOR INFORMATION . . .

Figure 12

The commercial mailer of this piece paid a rate of 8.3¢ using the 1985 Ambulance coil (2128). The 8.3¢ rate for Carrier Route Presort was in effect from February 17, 1985 until April 2, 1988. To qualify for this discounted rate each piece had to be part of a group of ten or more pieces sorted to the same carrier route, rural route, highway contract route, post office box section or general delivery unit. The service indicator, "Blk. Rt. CAR-RT SORT" indicates the level of sorting required. Because this stamp is a precancel, it did not receive an additional cancellation or postmark.

PO Box 193
Yarmouth Port, Massachusetts 02675

Tow Truck 1920s
8.5 USA

PLANNING

POSTMASTER: *Please Expedite.*
Official Survey Documents Enclosed

Figure 13

A nonprofit organization used a 1987 8.5¢ Tow Truck (2129) on this cover. This rate was in effect from April 20, 1986 until April 2, 1988. Note the stamp was "clipped" by the affixing machine that attached it.

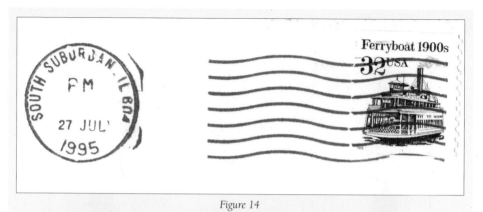

Figure 14

Not all Transportation Coils were issued for use on bulk mailings. This 32¢ Ferryboat (2466), photographically cropped, was issued June 2, 1995 to meet the First Class rate.

Where to Find More Information

- *Linn's Plate Number Coil Handbook*, by Ken Lawrence, is considered the "bible" for transportation coil collectors, containing all of the essential details on each of Transportation Coil covered.

- The Plate Number Coil Collectors Club (PNC3) has a web site (www.pnc3.org) that includes detailed catalog information.

- *Coil Line* is the monthly publication of the Plate Number Coil Collectors Club, (PNC3). Published monthly since May 1988, a run of this set of journals is invaluable to the Transportation Coil specialist.

- *The Transportation Coils and other Plate Number Coil Issues* by Joseph Agris has many useful illustrations and some beautiful color plates.

- *The 1995 Plate Number Coil Catalog*, edited by Richard J. Nazar contains dated pricing and quantity information, but is still a useful resource.

- The relevant volumes of Linn's *U.S. Stamp Yearbook*, edited by Fred Boughner or George Amick.

Chapter 17
Late Twentieth Century Definitives

Throughout most of the twentieth century definitive stamps were issued in sets with clearly defined themes and common design elements. Examples include the Prexies, Great Americans Series, and Transportation Coil Series. Categorizing these stamps is easy! But during the late twentieth century many definitives were issued without a common theme, design, or name.

Most, but not all of these late twentieth century definitives can be broadly categorized as follows: American Culture, Scenes and Transportation (fig. 1), Expedited Mail (fig. 2), Flags (fig. 3), Flora, Fauna and Wildlife (fig. 4), miniscapes (fig. 5), and rate change issues (fig. 6). These definitives were issued in a variety of formats including sheets, coils, and booklets (including ATM sheetlets), with **self-adhesive** or **water-activated** gum. They were printed by an increasing number of private contractors as well as the Bureau of Engraving and Printing (BEP). Since a variety of perforation sizes was used, collectors for the first time since the 1930s, needed to dust off their perforation gauges to properly identify some stamps available at a post office!

In 1995 the United States Postal Service (USPS) announced that future definitive issues for nonprofit bulk mail would be comprised of "American Scenes." Stamps for bulk mail (also known as **Standard Mail**) would feature "American Transportation" and stamps for First Class presorted mail would illustrate "American Culture." All these stamps were to be issued in non-denominated form, their assigned values not printed on their face.

American Culture (First Class-Presorted)
Figure 1a illustrates the non-denominated 25¢ Diner self-adhesive coil (*Scott* 3208A) issued September 30, 1998 as part of the American Culture series. A variety with water-activated gum (3208) had previously been issued on June 5. The stamps were intended to cover any of the various rates charged for presorted first-class letter mail. The USPS considered these stamps **precancels** based on the presence of the "Presorted First-Class" service inscription. The Diner stamp

replaced the two 25¢ Juke Box stamps (2911 and 2912) issued March 17, 1995, the same day two 15¢ Automobile Tail Fin postcard presorted rate coils (2908 and 2909) were issued. The Automobile Tail Fin stamps carry the service inscription "First-Class Card," as shown in fig. 1b.

American Scenes (Non-Profit Bulk)
The first stamp issued with the American Scenes designation (2902) was a non-denominated 5¢ Butte nonprofit rate coil on March 10, 1995. Figure 1c illustrates the American Scenes 5¢ Wetlands self-adhesive coil (3207A) issued December 14, 1998 for use by nonprofit organizations on presorted bulk mail. A variety with water-activated gum (3207) had previously been issued on June 5.

American Transportation (Standard Mail)
The first stamp issued with the American Transportation designation (not to be confused with the Transportation Coil Series, ch.16) was a non-denominated 10¢ Automobile bulk rate coil (2905) on March 10, 1995. Figure 1d illustrates the 10¢ Green Bicycle self-adhesive presorted standard mail coil issued on August 14, 1998. A variety with water-activated gum (3229) was issued the

Figure 1a   *Figure 1b*   *Figure 1c*   *Figure 1d*

Stamps which illustrate American Culture, Scenes, and Transportation.

same day. The "PRESORTED STD" service inscription indicates that it is for a class of mail called "Standard Mail" created July 1, 1996 by the merging of Third- and Fourth-Class mail. The difference between the assigned 10¢ value and the actual charge for postage, which was based on weight and degree of presorting, is paid at time of mailing.

Priority Mail, a subclass of First Class mail, began service in 1985. It provides a postage savings for items weighing 13 ounces or more. The first stamp specifically intended for use on priority mail was the 1989 $2.40 Moon Landing stamp (2419). In 1991, it was replaced by a $2.90 Bald Eagle design (2540, fig. 7), which sported an Olympic emblem. Figure 2a illustrates the Space Shuttle Landing (3261) Priority Mail self-adhesive issued November 9, 1998. This $3.20 stamp covered the Priority Mail flat rate effective January 10, 1999 for items weighing up to two pounds. The stamp includes in its design ***Scrambled Indicia*** which are hidden images that can only be viewed with a special lens. Using the special decoder lens, the names of the six NASA space shuttles are visible, with space shuttle "Endeavour" misspelled "Endeavor." In addition, a microprinted "USPS" can be found on the right wing of the landing shuttle.

Express Mail is an expedited delivery service provided by the Postal Service to the general public since 1977. In 1983, the USPS issued the first **Express Mail** stamp (1909). It depicts a Bald Eagle with the moon as a backdrop. At $9.35 it was the highest face value postage stamp issued until that time. It was valid for all mail services and issued in booklet panes of three. On August 9, the USPS announced that postal clerks could break the $28.05 booklet panes and sell singles for just 30 days. In an October 27 postal bulletin, the USPS changed policy, allowing the $9.35 stamps to be purchased as singles on an ongoing basis. On April 29, 1985, a second booklet pane of three replaced the $9.35 stamp with a $10.75 Bald Eagle stamp (2212), depicted in figure 2b. Figure 2c illustrates the Space Shuttle Piggyback (3262) Express Mail self-adhesive, issued November 19, 1998, depicting the space shuttle Endeavour being carried piggyback on a modified Boeing 747. The $11.75 stamp covered the Express Mail basic rate, effective January 10, 1999. It also contained the names of the six space shuttles as "Scrambled Indicia," with "Endeavour" again misspelled, as well as a microprinted "USPS" that can be found on the right side of the Boeing 747.

Figure 2a

Figure 2b

Figure 2c

The Bald Eagle and Space Program are common themes on Expedited Mail stamps.

American Flags

Since the 1963 5¢ Flag Over the White House (1208, fig. 3a) sheet was issued, the American flag has appeared regularly on U.S. stamps. "Flag" definitives, issued in sheets, coils, and booklets, have been printed and sold in far greater quantities than any other postage issues. The 1985 22¢ Flag Over the Capitol booklet stamp (2116) has the distinction of being the first definitive stamp to be issued in a size previously used only for commemoratives. The Flag Over the Capitol (2115) was also issued as a regular sized definitive, shown in figure 3j.

Many of the "Flag Over the..." designs used since 1963 are illustrated in figure 3, showing the progression of postage rates from the 5¢ Flag Over the White House (fig. 3a) issued January 9, 1963 to the non-denominated 34¢ Flag Over Farm (fig. 3s), issued December 15, 2000. The "Flag Over the..." stamps have

Figure 3a

Figure 3b

Figure 3c

Figure 3d

Figure 3e

Figure 3f

Figure 3g

Figure 3h

Figure 3i

Figure 3j

Figure 3k

Figure 3l

Figure 3m

Figure 3n

Figure 3o

Figure 3p

Figure 3q

Figure 3r

Figure 3s

American Flag stamps illustrate the many increases in the First Class Rate from 1963 through the end of the century.

included the following design elements:

White House (1208, 1338A, and 1338G), shown in figures 3a through 3c; 13¢ Independence Hall (1622), shown in figure 3d; U.S. Capitol (1623 and 2115), shown in figures 3e and 3j; 18¢ Purple Mountains (1893), 18¢ Grain (1890), 18¢ Sea (1891), and 20¢ Supreme Court (1894), shown in figures 3f through 3i, respectively; and, 22¢ Fireworks (2276), 25¢ Yosemite National Park (2280), 29¢ Mount Rushmore (2523), 29¢ Olympic Rings (2528), 32¢ Porch (2914), 32¢ Field (2919), 33¢ City (3278), 33¢ Chalkboard (3283) and (34¢) Farm (3449) shown in figures 3k through 3s, respectively.

Flora, Fauna, and Wildlife

The 18¢ dark brown American Wildlife (fig. 4a) booklet (1880–1889), picturing ten different animals, was issued May 14, 1981. On January 8, 1982, the Rocky Mountain Bighorn design from that booklet was issued in a booklet consisting of only that design, but with a value of 20¢ (1949, fig. 4b). Initially printed on the **Cottrell press**, the Bighorn was subsequently printed on the multicolor B press in 1983 (1949c). The latter stamp is between ¼ mm and ½ mm narrower than the stamp printed on the Cottrell press.

Flora & Fauna, depicting the animal and plant life characteristic of the United States, was originally announced as a Wildlife series. Intended to replace the Great Americans series (ch. 15), a $2 multicolor Bobcat (fig. 8, 2482) stamp was issued on June 1, 1990. In 1991, when lower value definitives began to be issued, the USPS depicted all values less than 10¢ with a leading zero and no cents sign, as illustrated in figure 4c by the 01 (cent) American Kestrel stamp (2476). In 1995, that decision was

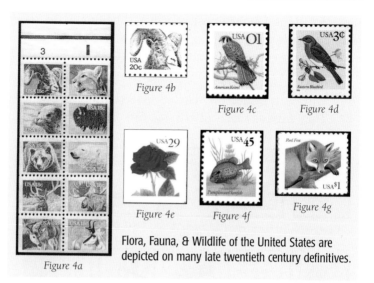

Figure 4b

Figure 4c

Figure 4d

Figure 4e

Figure 4f

Figure 4g

Flora, Fauna, & Wildlife of the United States are depicted on many late twentieth century definitives.

Figure 4a

reversed and values less than 10¢ once again included a cents sign, as illustrated by the redesigned 3¢ Eastern Bluebird (fig. 4d, 3033). Through the years, flora, as exemplified by the 29¢ Red Rose (fig. 4e, 2490), and fauna, as exemplified by the 45¢ Pumpkinseed Sunfish (fig. 4f, 2481) and $1 Fox (fig. 4g, 3036) have been issued as part of the Flora & Fauna series.

Figure 5a   Figure 5b   Figure 5c

Mini-scapes illustrate landscape scenes and familiar objects.

Mini-scapes

The mini-scape issues served as an alternate to both the Great Americans (ch. 15) and Flag definitive issues. They portray everyday American landscape scenes and familiar everyday objects. The first issued was the 15¢ Beach Umbrella (fig. 5a, 2443), as a booklet pane of 10 on February 3, 1990. This was the first USPS postcard rate stamp to be issued in solely booklet form, primarily for vacationers and tourists. In 1991, two more mini-scapes were issued, the 19¢ Hot-Air Balloon (fig. 5b, 2530) in both sheet and booklet form on May 17, and the 19¢ Fishing Boat coil (fig. 5c, 2529) on August 8.

Non-Denominated Stamps

Non-denominated stamps were printed in anticipation of increases of unknown amounts in postal rates, when it was believed there would be insufficient time to produce denominated stamps for the new rates after they were announced. Letters of the alphabet were used as part of the design on these stamps, which represented the assigned postage value. The first in the series were the "A" stamps, which were issued in 1978 with an assigned postage value of 15¢. They appeared in sheet, booklet, and coil form (1735, 1736, and 1743 respectively). The orange "A" stamp is shown in figure 6a.

"B" stamps were issued on March 15, 1981 with an assigned postage value of 18¢. They exist as sheets (1818, fig. 6b), booklets, and coils. Just seven months later the rates changed again and "C" stamps were issued on October 11 with an assigned postage value of 20¢. With the "C" stamp, the phrase "Domestic Mail" was added to the design since, under Universal Postal Union (UPU) regulations, stamps without denominations were not valid

Figure 6a   Figure 6b   Figure 6c   Figure 6d   Figure 6e

Figure 6f   Figure 6g   Figure 6h   Figure 6i   Figure 6j

Rate Change stamps shown alphabetically, as issued.

for international mail. The brown "C" booklet stamp (1948), significantly smaller than the "A" and "B" stamps, is shown in figure 6c.

The "D" stamps (fig. 6d, 2113) were issued in 1985 with an assigned postage value of 22¢. They have the same format as the "C" stamps. Printed in 1981 immediately after the rate had changed to 20¢, the "D" stamps had been stored for four years in the Philatelic Sales Division's cave beneath Kansas City, Missouri.

In 1988, the "E" stamps were issued with an assigned postage value of 25¢ and became the first rate change issue with a theme – "E" for Earth, showing an image of the earth in full color. The multicolored "E" booklet stamp (2282a) is shown in figure 6e.

"F" stamps were issued in 1991 with an assigned postage value of 29¢. On the "F" stamp, for Flower or Flag, "Domestic Mail" was replaced with "For U.S. Addresses Only", as clarification that the stamp was only valid to addresses within the U.S. and not for letters mailed in the U.S. to foreign destinations. The perf. 10 "F" coil (2518), is shown in figure 6f.

"G" stamps (Old Glory) were issued in 1994 with assigned postage values of 5¢, 20¢, 25¢, and 32¢. Figure 6h depicts the 32¢ Old Glory (2887) self-adhesive stamp.

"H" stamps (Uncle Sam's Hat) were issued in 1998 with an assigned postage value of 33¢. An "H" self-adhesive sheet stamp (3260) is shown in figure 6f. The design was also issued in booklet (3267, 3268, and 3269) and coil (3264 and 3265) forms.

In 2000, the First Class postage rate increased from 33¢ to 34¢. The Flag Over Farm (fig. 3s) and Statue of Liberty non-denominated stamps were issued in lieu of an "I" stamp, a departure from the alphabetical pattern used for previous rate change stamps.

"Make-up Rate" stamps were intended for use on First Class mail, with the stamp equal in postage value to the amount of the increase over the most recent rate. For example, the 1¢ Weathervane (fig. 6j 3257) stamp issued in 1998 pays the 1¢ difference between the 32¢ First Class rate in 1997 and the new 33¢ First Class rate in 1998, allowing postal customers to use up their 32¢ stamps. The 4¢ "F" bistre and carmine make-up rate stamp (2521, fig. 6g), was issued on January 22, 1991. The wordy design and punctuation were controversial and derided.

Notes on Collecting

Many of the late twentieth century definitives have been issued in various forms: self-adhesive coils and booklets, and water-activated sheets, coils, and booklets (including ATM sheetlets). In addition, multiple printers were often engaged in printing the "same" issue, increasing the number of varieties. This gives collectors a wonderful challenge, seemingly endless at times, to acquire one copy of every possible variety of each issue.

As an example, the "Flag Over the Porch" stamp issued with a large blue "1995" in the lower left corner of the stamp was produced as a water-activated sheet and coil and a self-adhesive coil and booklet. Within a booklet, the shape of the perforations may differ based on position or orientation of the stamp on the pane – each could be considered a different variety, particularly when they are collected on-cover. A total of six formats with year, color, and size variations were issued for the "Flag Over the Porch": large blue 1995, small blue 1995, red 1995, blue 1996, red 1996, and red 1997. Finding used on- or off-cover or unused examples of each "Flag Over the Porch" variety presents a major challenge.

During the late twentieth century, the USPS used several private contractors (ch. 38), in addition to the BEP to produce stamps. In many cases, definitives were printed, or reprinted, by different contractors. *Scott* identifies the specific contractor responsible for each stamp, making it possible for the collector to collect the stamps of any particular contractor.

Assembling an on-cover collection can also be a challenge, particularly if attempting to obtain all the varieties. Many of the Express Mail and Priority Mail stamps are difficult to find in good condition on-cover. This was caused by the USPS' design of their cardboard carriers for these classes of mail, where the stamp was typically placed directly over an invisible "string" that allowed the recipient to easily tear open the package, but which destroyed the stamp in the process!

Almanac

1977 – Express Mail is first offered to the general public on October 9.

1978 – The "A" rate (15¢) non-denominated definitive is issued May 22.

1981 – The "B" rate (18¢) non-denominated definitive is issued March 15.

1981 – The 18¢ American Wildlife booklet is issued May 14.

1981 – On October 11 rates change and the "C" rate (20¢) non-denominated definitive is issued.

1983 – The first Express Mail stamp (1909), a $9.35 stamp in a booklet (BK140B) of three is issued August 12.

1985 – The "D" rate (22¢) non-denominated definitive is issued February 1.

1985 – Priority Mail is introduced February 17 with a $2.40 1-lb rate nationwide.

1988 – The "E" rate (25¢) non-denominated definitive is issued March 22.

1990 – The first mini-scape stamp, the 15¢ Beach Umbrella (2443), is issued February 3.

1991 – The "F" rate (29¢) non-denominated definitive is issued January 22.

1994 – The "G" (32¢) rate non-denominated definitive and 3¢ Make-up rate definitive are issued December 13 for the rate increase on January 1, 1995.

1996 – Classification reform goes into effect July 1 with all prior Second Class mail renamed Periodicals, Third Class mail renamed Standard Mail (A), and Fourth Class Mail renamed Standard Mail (B).

1998 – The "H" (33¢) rate non-denominated definitive and 1¢ Make-up rate definitive are issued November 9.

2000 – The alphabetic pattern ends at "H" on December 15 as the Flag Over Farm and Statue of Liberty stamps are issued, instead of "I" non-denominated definitives, to pay the 34¢ First Class rate in the new millennium.

What Others Have Said

Wildlife Booklet positions

"In case you were wondering, there are 48 booklet pane positions per plate and thus a calculated 768 different Wildlife booklet pane positions that have passed across USPS counters. My best advice is don't try to find and plate too many of the non-JL position panes as you will probably go broke trying and then you won't be able to afford the doctor's fees to correct your resulting eyesight problems!"

—*Bruce H. Mosher, "Discovering U.S. Rotary Printed Booklet Pane Varieties,"* The United States Specialist, *1982.*

U.S. Flag Stamps

"The Stars and Stripes and Yosemite National Park combine to pay tribute to America's heritage of individual freedom and natural beauty. Certainly, nothing represents our country better than the U.S. Flag. The Stars and Stripes has been featured on approximately 33 stamps and has been a recognizable design element in at least another 43 stamps, making it easily America's most popular stamp subject since its first appearance on a U.S. postage stamp in 1869."

—*USPS Mint Set of Definitive Stamps 1987–88, about the Flag over Yosemite issue.*

Non-denominated Stamps

"The Postal Service had requested an increase in the prime rate to 16¢ for business mail, and confidently stockpiled huge quantities of 16¢ Statue of Liberty sheet and coil stamps...to meet that rate....But the PRC approved a uniform increase for all mailers to 15¢, so those stocks were virtually useless. Contingency A-rate stamps and stamped envelopes that had been printed in 1975 and 1976 were issued to meet the need until supplies of denominated 15¢ stamps and envelopes could be produced....The New Yorker magazine ridiculed the A-rate stamp: 'It is an alarming pumpkin-orange in color, and it has the texture of the sort of gummed address label that Uncle Ned orders by the thousands from the Shopping Mart in the back of Time Magazine'....No doubt many postal customers agreed, but collectors seemed to enjoy having something new and different."

—*Ken Lawrence, "Alphabet soup: U.S. non-denominated Stamps and Postal Stationery,"* Scott's Stamp Monthly, *1995.*

Priority Mail looks very important but it's often very slow

"Priority Mail, the fastest growing two-day mail service offered by the U.S. Postal

Service, is not always a bargain. That's the conclusion of The Star-Ledger of Newark, N.J. which recently tested Priority Mail services from eight New Jersey towns. It found that half of the time Priority Mail envelopes were delivered on the same day as letters mailed at regular first-class rates. The newspaper deposited first-class letters and Priority Mail envelopes to seven cities at the same time in response to a reader's complaint about the poor mail service. It found that regular mail beat priority mail to both New York, and St. Petersburg, and tied regular mail in Pacific Palisades, California. 'Given these results, why would anyone use Priority Mail?' The Star-Ledger asked. It quoted postal spokes-woman Sandra Harding as offering one explanation. 'A lot of people like the importance given to the packaging. The free packaging makes it wonderful,' she told the newspaper. 'It will look important and get special handling'."

—*Bill McAllister, "It looks important but it's slow," Linn's Stamp News, 1997.*

Examples of Postal Usage

Figure 7

A corner, cut from an envelope, sent by Priority Mail from SUMMAS WA postmarked June 2, 1992. The American Bald Eagle shown on the $2.90 stamp (2540) and label has been the symbol of Priority Mail since its inception. Some collectors will cut down large envelopes, such as the piece illustrated, in order to more easily show them in their collections.

Figure 8

A 1993 Certified Letter from "MATAMORAS PA." It is franked with a 29¢ "Flag Over Pledge of Allegiance" paying the first class rate, and a $2.00 Bobcat (2482), paying the $1 certified mail fee and $1 return receipt fee.

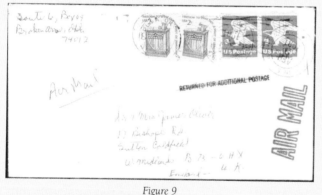

Figure 9

Two B rate (18¢) definitives (1818) used on an air mail letter postmarked "TULSA OK / APR 8 1981." The international air mail rate to England was 40¢ in 1981. The envelope was struck with the auxiliary marking "RETURNED FOR ADDITIONAL POSTAGE", which was subsequently crossed out after the addition of two 2¢ "Freedom to Speak" definitives (1582). The non-denominated B rate definitives were not valid for international postage in 1981, but it appears they were accepted nonetheless.

Where to Find More Information

- The relevant volumes of *Linn's U.S. Stamp Yearbook*, edited by Fred Boughner or George Amick.

Chapter 18
Nineteenth Century Commemoratives

Ordinary postage stamps had already been around for nearly 50 years when an enterprising Postmaster General (PMG), John Wanamaker, had the idea to issue a series of stamps, which commemorated an historical event. They were to become the first U.S. *commemoratives*, which were issued in 1893. A set of 16 stamps, they honored both the 400th Anniversary of Columbus' voyage and the great 1893 Chicago Columbian Exposition. The second and last set of commemoratives of the nineteenth century, a series of nine stamps to honor another major international exposition being held in Omaha, was issued in 1898. These two sets of commemoratives prepared the way for the rapid growth of commemorative issues in the twentieth century.

One of the long-standing debates among U.S. collectors is, "What is the first U.S. commemorative issue?" The 1876 U.S. Centennial Exposition, held in Philadelphia, had two special stamped envelopes issued in its honor, and they certainly are a "commemorative issue." Some collectors suggest that the black Lincoln (memorial) stamp issued in 1866 (*Scott* 77), the year after Lincoln was assassinated, should be considered as the first commemorative. Yet, certainly as far as catalogue listings go, most generally agree that the 1893 Columbians were the first commemoratives.

Stamp collectors should pay homage to PMG Wanamaker, who served from March 7, 1889 to March 6, 1893. He announced his intention to produce "a special series of stamps with illustrations to commemorate the discovery of America by Columbus" in his annual report to Congress for the fiscal year ending June 30, 1892. The idea paved the way for a monumental change in the stamp program: stamps to commemorate, memorialize, and honor people, places, and events. Until that time, stamps contained portraits of Benjamin Franklin, George Washington and others (deceased) thought to be great American leaders, or various objects in the case of the 1869 Pictorials.

Mr. Wanamaker signed the contract with the American Bank Note Company (American) to produce the series of stamps on September 27, 1892. He announced that these "new stamps will be of the same height as the present series, but twice as long, the increased size thought necessary in order to properly display the illustrations." The "present series" referred to the **Small Bank Notes** (219–229, ch. 6) also printed by American.

After the initial series of 15 stamps had been announced, a 16th was required when PMG Wanamaker issued an official order that, effective January 1, 1893, the new fee for sending a **registered** First Class letter would be 8¢, a reduction from the existing 10¢ fee. All of the Columbians debuted on January 2, 1893, except the 8¢ value, which was issued in March. The official release date was Sunday, January 1, when most post offices were closed.

All of the printing plates for the 1¢ value, and some of the plates for the 2¢ value, contained 200 subjects, while the remainder of the plates for the 2¢ value, and all of the plates for the other values contained 100 subjects. The sheets of 200 were divided into panes of 100, which is the size in which all of the values were issued to postmasters, making the post office panes quite large. The stamps are all perforated 12 and printed on unwatermarked paper.

Reporting in the December 1892 issue of *The Metropolitan Philatelist*, J.W. Scott noted that the work of printing the stamps had begun in late September. "Requisitions for them from post offices throughout the country will be filled by next week, so that the stamps may be on sale by January 1, 1893." A special stamp requisition form was printed and distributed which listed all of the Columbian stamps and stamped envelopes that could be ordered.

Figure 1

The 1¢ Columbian depicts a clean shaven "Columbus In Sight Of Land."

The illustrations for the stamps were all selected from famous paintings. They form a veritable gallery of fine art, featuring works found in great museums and key government buildings. It may be unfortunate that the beautiful engravings on each stamp were not arranged in chronological order to tell the story of Columbus and his voyages. But Mr. Wanamaker felt there was a very good reason for the stamps being out of chronological order: he wanted the stamps with the most important parts of the story to be on the denominations most frequently used, hence the selection of the low values for the best known portions of the story. It is interesting to

Figure 2

The 2¢ Columbian, of which almost one and a half billion were printed, depicts the "Landing Of Columbus."

note that on the 1¢ stamp, which shows Columbus Sighting Land (fig. 1), Columbus is depicted as clean-shaven. But on the 2¢ (fig. 2), which pictures Columbus Landing in the "New World" just a few hours later, he has grown a full beard! Such observations started the tradition of finding odd or allegedly impossible situations depicted on United States stamps.

The $15.00 face value of the dollar-values of the Columbian set was out of reach of most Americans. There was no proper domestic use for the dollar-value stamps according to the postal rates in effect on January 1, 1893. For example, a Fourth Class package weighing the maximum permissible weight of four pounds would cost only 64¢ to mail. Since the dollar value stamps were not to be found on normal mail, there was much scheming by collectors and dealers to find ways to obtain the coveted dollar denominations in used condition. In March 1894, the *New York Sun* published a scandalous story entitled "Columbian Stamp Frauds" with the subhead, "A Conspiracy between Stamp Sellers and a Fourth-Class Postmaster." The story dealt with a particular Post Office Department (POD) provision of the era, namely, that Fourth Class postmasters, those at the very smallest post offices, earned part of their salary based on how many stamps they sold and cancelled at their post offices. The article noted that Charles H. Mekeel, of St. Louis, one of the leading stamp dealers of his day, had a warrant issued for his arrest. Because the dollar-value Columbians were already worth more than face value in used condition, Mekeel worked out an arrangement with Fourth Class Postmaster Baker, of Shrewsbury, Illinois. One of Mekeel's employees, a certain W.L. Scott (who was not related to the famed J.W. Scott of the *Scott Catalogue*) would bring letters and packages to Baker bearing dollar values far in excess of the required postage. Baker would arrange to cancel them neatly and lightly, and they would be delivered through the mails to Mekeel. Baker would give Scott a kickback, a percentage of the profit he was making by selling the stamps. Mekeel would carefully soak the stamps and have copies of the much desired and in-demand used Columbians to sell to collectors. The court case was dismissed in November when the judge found it was not really illegal for the postmaster to share his profits with anyone to whom he so chose to give his money!

There were many complaints about the size of the new 1893 stamps. Until January 1, 1893, all stamps were about half the size of these new "commemoratives." The public, particularly the business community, condemned the fact that people had to lick stamps that were twice the size of any regular postage stamps that had ever been issued before. The size of these stamps was labeled "special delivery size," a name taken from the blue special delivery stamps of 1885 and 1888 (E1 and E2). Licking such a large size stamp for an occasional special delivery mailing was apparently acceptable, but not for everyday letters. This brings up another important piece of "Columbians" history. A new orange special delivery stamp (E3) had to be issued to replace the original blue versions, because the 1¢ deep blue Columbian stamp was sometimes mistaken for the 10¢ special delivery stamp and vice versa. The orange special delivery is often referred to as the "17th Columbian" issue.

Complaints about the set quickly crescendoed, and activity around the Columbians became so frenzied that legislation was actually written and introduced on the floor of the U.S. Congress to halt their sale. In a concisely worded resolution, Colorado Senator Edward O. Wolcott (1889–1901), presented the following to the United States Senate: "That the Postmaster General of the United States be instructed to discontinue the sale of the so-called Columbian stamps except to such persons as may specifically call for them, and be instructed to keep on sale the ordinary postage stamps in use before the printing of the so-called Columbian stamps." Fortunately for collectors, the legislation never passed.

The Columbians reappeared on their 100th anniversary in 1992 on a set of five souvenir sheets (2624–2629). The colors and dates on the stamps were changed so there would not be any confusion between the singles from the perforated souvenir sheets and the original stamps.

The Columbians came to be issued because PMG Wanamaker was a marketing expert (founder of the chain of Wanamaker's Department Stores before he became PMG). The other commemoratives issued in the nineteenth century came about because his successor five years later, PMG James A. Gary, responded favorably to a request from Edward Rosewater, the publisher of the *Omaha Daily Bee*, who was serving as Chairman of the Publicity Committee for the 1898 Trans-Mississippi Exposition being held in Omaha to promote development of the Midwest and West. Coming just five years after the Columbians, these proposed nine new commemoratives unleashed a furor of protest. But PMG Gary stood firm by his decision and the nine stamps appeared.

Figure 3

The 10¢ Trans-Mississippi Exposition Issue depicts "Hardships of Emigration." Like the other stamps in the series it was designed by R. Ostrander Smith.

The designs of the Trans-Mississippi stamps have no explicit connection to the Exposition (fig. 3). In fact they do not even have a date on them. Compare this to the Columbians, which at least contain the dates 1492–1892, indicating that the stamps celebrate the 400th anniversary of "something." And while the Columbians all include a caption identifying a Columbus related illustration on each stamp the Trans-Mississippi stamps have only the caption of the painting or photograph used on each stamp, all without obvious relationship to each another.

All of the values of the Trans-Mississippi stamps were printed from plates of 100 subjects, with each plate containing **guidelines**, **arrows**, **plate numbers**, and BEP **imprints**. Sheets were cut in half and issued to post offices in panes of 50. Each pane of 50 thus had ten stamps with straight edges on either the left or the right side. Unlike the Columbians, there are no Trans-Mississippi stamps with straight edges on the top or bottom of the stamp. All of the paper used for the Trans-Mississippi stamps have the double-line USPS watermark.

The Trans-Mississippi stamps were all supposed to be printed in two colors, the borders in various colors, and the vignettes in black. But the BEP reported to the PMG that they, "found it impossible to furnish satisfactorily or in the time desired supplies of the several denominations in two colors." So the stamps were produced in a variety of single colors, and for the most part judged to be of poor quality and design. One of the deans of American Philately, John N. Luff, wrote at the time, "The stamps are poorly conceived and executed, overloaded with ornaments, heavy in color and blurred in printing." Yet, over the course of the next 100 years, many collectors have come to agree that the $1 value, which is titled "Western Cattle in Storm," and which is from an engraving entitled "The Vanguard" by C.O. Murray and a painting by J.A. MacWhirter, is one of the most, if not the most, beautiful stamp issues ever released. It took 100 years, but the Post Office eventually released the Trans-Mississippi stamps in two colors as originally intended. On their 100th birthday in 1998, the set of nine two-color Trans-Mississippi stamps appeared on two souvenir sheets (3209 and 3210).

The $1 and $2 values never had the sales to collectors that were anticipated. Ironically, the stamps, which were on sale from June 17 through December 31, 1898, were available to the public at the same time that the 1893 dollar-value Columbians were still available from the Washington, D.C. post office. Collectors were able to obtain the Columbians at face value until the turn of the century. Although officially withdrawn from sale on December 31, 1900, some Columbian stock remained on sale until the early 1900s, when the remainder was destroyed.

Notes on Collecting

Our oldest commemoratives, the Columbians, offer something for every collector, especially the 2¢ Columbian. They are readily obtainable on cover at very reasonable prices. However one dated "January 1, 1893" or "January 2, 1893", a first or second day cover, would sell for many thousands of dollars.

The 2¢ Columbian also offers collectors the challenge of finding what is called the "broken hat variety," a break-like mark in the hat worn by the person standing third to the left of Columbus (fig. 11, ch. 46). This variety was caused by an abnormal relief on a transfer roll.

Some collectors have formed specialized collections of the 2¢ Columbian, of which almost 1.5 billion were sold. This compares to 449 million of the 1¢, and 35 million or less for each of the rest of the set. The dollar values were issued in quantities of 55,000 to as few as 26,000.

Some of the higher face-value stamps of both the Columbians and Trans-Mississippi are financially out of reach for many collectors. For collectors on a limited budget, purchasing "space fillers," copies of the stamps that are in some way damaged, may be an alternative. A space-filler, depending on the extent of the damage, might sell for as little as 10% of catalogue value. Collectors should be cautious when purchasing any high value stamp. Hidden damage to the paper, gum or ink renders a stamp worth but a fraction of its catalogue value. Consider submitting expensive stamps for *expertizing* as a condition of purchase.

Nineteenth century commemoratives are collected in a number of formats. There are listings in *Scott* for plate number strips of three, four, and six stamps as well as plate blocks of six or eight stamps. *Scott* should be consulted for the complete details of these collectable formats. These formats of plate number strips are collected only on certain stamp issues.

Almanac

1892 – On December 5 the PMG announces that on January 1, 1893, the POD will place on sale at post offices a new series of postage stamps known as the Columbian Series.

1893 – January 1, a Sunday, is the official first day of sale of the Columbian stamps, for those post offices open for business.

1893 – The 16th Columbian stamp, the 8¢ value, goes on sale March 2.

1897 – PMG James A. Gary announces on December 23 a series of stamps to honor the 1898 Trans-Mississippi Exposition running from June 1 to November 1, 1898 in Omaha.

1898 – June 17 is the actual first day of issue for the Trans-Mississippi commemoratives, which were originally scheduled for release on June 1, but delayed due to production changes.

1992 – On May 24 the USPS issues the Columbian Souvenir Sheets, miniature sheets reproducing the 16 original commemoratives. The stamps are almost identical to the originals, except for the date "1992" instead of "1892" at the upper right corner.

1998 – On June 18, the 100th birthday of the Trans-Mississippi commemoratives, the USPS issues all nine stamps in two souvenir sheets. The designs are identical to the 1898 stamps, but are printed in the originally intended two colors, distinguishing them from the original single color stamps.

What Others Have Said

Raised the standards

"On the whole, stamp collectors were by no means averse to receiving the beautifully engraved Columbians series into their albums. They have added considerably to the general interest of a collection of the world's postage stamps, and to those who require an apology to their uninitiated friends for collecting postal emissions, this handsome and instructive series has proved of real utility….the Columbian issue had the effect of raising the pictorial standard of most of the subsequent issues of this nature."

—*Fred J. Melville*, United States Postage Stamps, 1870–1893, 1894. *A notable nineteenth century collector commenting on the debate of whether or not the Columbians were too much and overdone.*

Stamp collectors pay the freight

"The issue was designed primarily to advertise the 'World's Fair' or Columbian 'exposition' [sic]…. A secondary purpose, it seems to this writer, was to make the stamp collectors of the country 'pay the freight' as it were. It was frankly stated at the time the stamps were projected, that an enormous profit would come to the government from the sale of sets of the stamps. That such was the case is easy to believe, as it required fifteen good dollars to buy from the post office the five 'dollar values.'"

—*Frank E. Goodwin*, Goodwin's Specialized United States, 1919. *A notable collector and philatelic author, suggesting that, indeed, the Columbians were designed to take advantage of stamp collectors.*

Stamp collectors are the greatest

"The beauty and unique character of the new Columbian stamps will cause their sale in large quantities, simply for use in collections; and not only will they be purchased in single or partial sets by collectors, but in view of the limited time in which they will be issued, they will be accumulated in great quantities by dealers and others to meet future demands...The introduction of the new stamps, though not designed primarily for that object, will be proven to be a revenue measure of the highest importance to the public service. The net profit to be derived from their issue, that is the extra amount beyond the ordinary revenue that would have resulted from the sale and use of ordinary stamps, may be fairly placed at $2,500,000."

—PMG John Wanamaker, "The Report of the Postmaster General - 1892" predicting his windfall profits to come in the next fiscal year, based on his proposal for the Columbians.

The very peak of desire

"This stamp, the top value of the whole Columbian series [fig. 4], certainly can be said to represent the very peak of desire for a great many collectors. It probably is normal for most collectors to acquire this stamp as the last in their set of Columbians....it is only natural that a considerable degree of pride goes with the completion of the set."

Figure 4

The $5 Columbian Exposition Issue.

—Lester Brookman, The Nineteenth Century Stamps of the United States, 1947. This very passionate statement is one of the most commonly held feelings among many United States stamp collectors.

I had the power

"I found that I had the power to authorize this issue and did it because I want to help the people of the West. The...Exposition means a great deal to the people of that section of the country, and its character is decidedly an International one, no less than 15 countries having promised their support....I do not consider philatelists greater patriots on account of the interest they take in the stamps of their country. No one is compelled to buy the high values unless he wishes to do so."

—PMG James A. Gary responding to stamp collectors' protests that so soon after the Columbians were issued in 1893, collectors were being slapped with more high value commemoratives.

Figure 5

The popular $1 Western Cattle in Storm is based on a painting by John H. MacWhirter depicting cattle in the Scottish highlands during a snowstorm.

For many, the $1 Cattle in Storm (fig. 5) is the most beautiful U.S. stamp ever issued

"It is readily understood why the Department would want a design representing Western Cattle. It had been and was one of the most necessary and progressive industries on the Western Plains....It is interesting to note that this stamp is considered one of the finest produced by the Bureau of Engraving and Printing, as well as one of the most popular and most eagerly sought after designs. Many polls among serious students of our engraved stamps have placed this design and its execution either first or near the top of all of our stamps for its single beauty and appeal. It was chosen from among all the stamps produced by the Bureau of Engraving and Printing to be exhibited at Exposition Filatelica International Efimex 68 Mexico...."

—*Robert C. Lorenzen and Walter A. McIntire, "The Trans-Mississippi Series – The One-Dollar Trans-Mississippi Issue," The United States Specialist, 1972.*

Examples of Postal Usage

Figure 6

A 1¢ Columbian used on a piece of Third Class mail in 1894 from Crawfordsville, Ind.

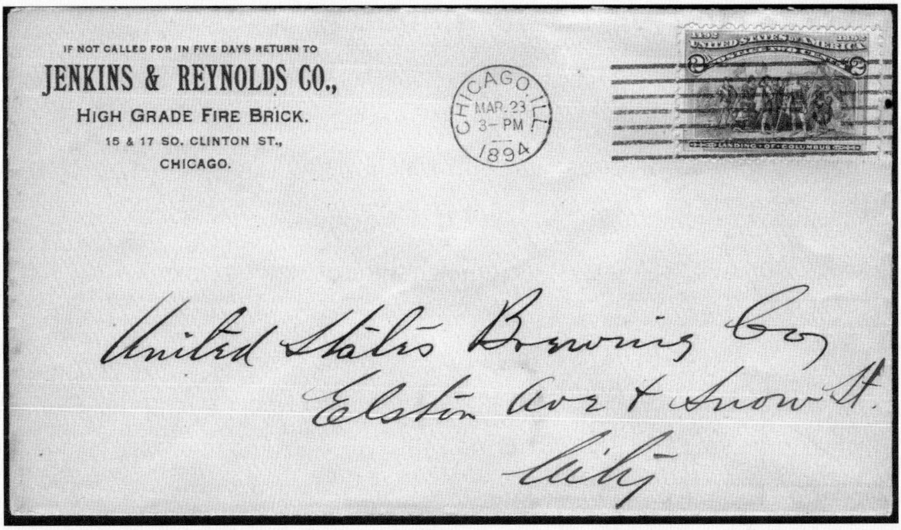

Figure 7

A 2¢ Columbian used on a piece of First Class mail from Chicago in 1894.

Figure 8

A 2¢ Trans-Mississippi with a Barry machine cancel from Brooklyn, N.Y. in 1898.

Where to Find More Information

- *The Nineteenth Century Postage Stamps of the United States* - Volume II, by Lester Brookman.

- John N. Luff's *The Postage Stamps of the United States*.

- "Wanamaker's Columbians," by Louis J. Heizmann.

- Thomas Corette's "The 2-Cent Columbian 'Broken Hat': Accidental or Deliberate?"

- Randy L. Neil's *The Trans-Mississippi Issue of 1898*.

- George B. Sloane's "The Trans-Mississippi Issue of 1898 (The So-Called Omaha Issue)," in Volume 9 of *The Stamp Specialist*.

- *Linn's U.S. Stamp Facts – 19th Century*.

Chapter 19
Twentieth Century Commemoratives 1901-1933

"Come to the Fair!"

That invitation might well be regarded as the theme of the majority of the commemorative stamps issued during the first two decades of the twentieth century - a time in our nation's history when a fair or exposition was truly an exciting event, and great entertainment! U.S. commemorative postage stamps helped spread the invitation, "Come to the Fair!"

The first commemoratives of the twentieth century (*Scott* 294-299, fig. 1) were also the first bi-colored postage stamps printed by the Bureau of Engraving and Printing (BEP). Issued to publicize the 1901 Pan-American Exposition held in Buffalo, New York (at which President William McKinley was assassinated), they depict state of the art transportation, including an electric auto-

Figure 1

The first commemoratives of the twentieth century – the six Pan-American Exposition stamps (294-99).

Figure 2

The 10¢ Louisiana Purchase Exposition stamp (327).

mobile used by the B&O Railroad in Washington, D.C. to deliver train passengers to their final street address destination.

The Louisiana Purchase Exposition Issue publicized the 1904 World's Fair held in St. Louis. Five single color stamps were issued in values of 1¢, 2¢, 3¢, 5¢ and 10¢ (323-327). These stamps feature men who were intimately involved in the Louisiana Purchase in 1803: Robert Livingston, Thomas Jefferson and James Monroe. The 10¢ value (fig. 2) depicts a map of the Louisiana Purchase, the first map to appear on a U.S. stamp. The subject of the 5¢ stamp may be puzzling at first, as it depicts William McKinley, who had nothing to do with the Louisiana Purchase. He earned his place on the stamp because he was the President who signed the legislation giving Federal sanction to the Exposition. This stamp essentially became a memorial to the then recently martyred president.

The Jamestown Exposition of 1907 was held in Hampton Roads, Virginia. It honored the tercentenary of the founding of Jamestown, and was celebrated with three stamps with values of 1¢, 2¢, and 5¢ (328-330).

The Alaska-Yukon-Pacific Exposition was held in Seattle, Washington during 1909. Secretary of State William H. Seward, who negotiated the purchase of Alaska from Russia in 1867, is depicted on the Alaska-Yukon-Pacific stamps (370 and 371). The design of the Alaska-Yukon-Pacific stamp was also produced and sold as an imperforate stamp, as well. A number of stamps of this time period were made available as imperforates, as they were intended for perforation and manufacture into coils by private companies. Those privately perforated coils were then sold for use in private vending and affixing machines.

Figure 3

An imperforate pair of the Hudson-Fulton Celebration Issue (373).

The Hudson-Fulton Celebration was held in New York September 25 - October 11, 1909. Though not a fair or exposition in the traditional sense, this massive celebration, which stretched the length of the

Hudson River from Staten Island to Troy (a distance of over 150 miles), had all the flavor of a fair. It was a combined commemoration of the tercentenary of Henry Hudson's discovery of the Hudson River, and the centenary of Robert Fulton's steamship, "The Clermont," which plied the waters of the Hudson. Hudson's ship, "The Half Moon" and Fulton's steamboat, "The Clermont" (or at least the reproductions of them built for the celebration) are anachronistically depicted side by side on stamps (372 and 373) that were issued both in perf. 12 and imperforate form (fig. 3). For the first time in U.S. history more than one set of commemoratives, celebrating more than one topic in a single year, was issued in 1909.

San Francisco was home to the Panama-Pacific Exposition in 1915. Four values honoring this exposition were issued in 1913. However, the 10¢ stamp of the series exists both as "orange yellow" and "orange", creating a total of five major *Scott* numbers for these stamps (397-400A). The stamps issued in 1913 in advance of the Exposition were perforated 12, the standard practice of the day. However, by the time additional stamps were printed, beginning in late 1914, the BEP had switched to use of perf. 10. Many collectors at the time were not even aware of this change in perforation, but the additional Panama-Pacific stamps, issued in 1914-1915 as perf. 10 have different *Scott* numbers (401-404).

Other commemoratives issued during this time period were issued for the centennial of Lincoln's birth (367, 368, and 369) and to commemorate the victory of the Allies in World War I (537).

Fairs and expositions receded from their prominent place in American culture as the third decade of the twentieth century began. Never again would fairs and expositions so thoroughly dominate the American imagination – or our stamp program.

Figure 4

A block of the Ericsson Memorial Issue (628), with the initials of the siderographer who made the printing plate, Clyde V. De Binder.

New patterns emerged for commemorative stamps during the late 1920s and early 1930s. More commemorative stamps were issued, but the trend was toward issuing fewer stamps for each event commemorated. Some of those events might today be considered obscure, or perhaps even inappropriate for commemoration, but stamps were issued in response to political pressures. For example, many today probably do not know who the Huguenots or the Walloons were, but they were honored together with a set of three stamps (614-616). The Huguenot-Walloon stamps set something of a precedent for honoring immigrant groups. Two 1925 bi-colored stamps (620-621) honored the Norwegians. Because Michael Eidsness (Superintendent of the Stamps Division in 1925) was a Norwegian, this probably helped the efforts to issue these stamps. The 1926 Ericsson Memorial Issue (628) was considered a tribute to the Swedes (fig. 4). The 1930 von Steuben Issue (689) could be considered a tribute to the Germans (fig. 5). The next year, in 1931, the Polish community was recognized with the Pulaski issue (690, fig. 5). Von Steuben and Pulaski were generals who aided Washington in the Revolutionary War.

The 150th anniversary of the American Revolution was celebrated during the 1920s. All agreed it was an event worthy of postal commemoration. Indeed some the stamps issued commemorated Revolutionary events about which every schoolboy or girl of the day knew, such as the battles of Lexington and Concord (617-619) and Yorktown (703). However, along with these well-known engagements, political pressure brought about the philatelic recognition of such relatively minor events as the Battle of White Plains (629) and the Battle of Bennington (643). From the perspective of modern day sensibilities perhaps the most puzzling revolutionary commemorative is the one issued for Major John Sullivan (657), who, if he were in the military today, would perhaps receive disciplinary action for his brutality toward Native Americans.

Figure 5

Two of the so called "2¢ Reds," the von Steuben Issue (689) and the Pulaski Issue (690).

Three highly unusual commemoratives were issued in 1928. Postmaster General Harry New, who almost reflexively resisted issuing commemoratives because he considered them too expensive, agreed to overprint the ordinary 2¢ and 5¢ stamps then in use, to honor the Sesquicentennial of the discovery of Hawaii by Captain James Cook (647 and 648). The commemorative overprint reads, "Hawaii 1778-1928". Postmaster General New opened up a "can of worms" with this decision that he probably lived to regret. Bowing to the demands of what he called "stamp cranks," he agreed to one more overprint. The 2¢ ordinary stamp was overprinted "Molly Pitcher" (646) honoring the mythic heroine of the Revolutionary War Battle of Monmouth in New Jersey. There has never again been a commemorative overprint.

The 200th anniversary of George Washington's birth occurred in 1932. On January 1 of that year a set of 12 stamps was issued in his honor (704-715). They depict Washington from his youth to his retirement, as portrayed by various artists. Perhaps the most famous portrait of Washington used in the series is the one by Gilbert Stuart, which appears on the 2¢ stamp. They were issued in huge quantities, as the Post Office Department (POD) wanted them to be sold at post offices for a few months in place of the regular Fourth Bureau issues current at the time.

Pan-American Inverts

Three of the Pan-American Exposition stamps exist as inverts: the 1¢, 2¢, and 4¢. The 1¢ and 2¢ were produced by accident and discovered by the public. The 4¢ invert was created intentionally at the BEP after it was erroneously reported that the public had discovered inverts of this denomination. Because these stamps were printed in two colors they required two separate trips through the flat plate press. First the black vignette was printed. Then the colored frame was printed from a second plate. The inverts occurred when sheets on which the vignette were already printed were rotated 180° from the proper orientation prior to the printing of the frame. These three classic inverts were reproduced 100 years later on a 2001 Souvenir Sheet (3505).

The first stamp honoring an Olympic Game (716) was issued for the 3rd Winter Olympics held in 1932 in Lake Placid, New York. This stamp was criticized because of what today would be called a major design error. The designer, A.R. Meissner, obviously knew little about skiing, for the ski jumper on his stamp is shown using poles, and is depicted in an unnatural crouching position! That spring two more stamps were issued to commemorate the 10th (Summer) Olympic Games held in Los Angeles. Thus began a tradition of issuing Olympic stamps that would greatly expand later in the century.

Other commemoratives of these years covered a number of other subjects, such as the Canalization of the Ohio River (681), Arbor Day (717), and the Georgia bicentennial (726). But one thing is certain; there would never again be as much restraint in the issuing of new commemoratives as there was during the first third of the twentieth century.

Most of the commemoratives issued from 1901 to 1933 were printed on the flat plate press. However, as this period came to a close, the rotary press, clearly in the ascendancy, was used with increasing frequency for the printing of commemoratives stamps.

Early in the century all commemoratives were perforated 12. However, the BEP changed its preferred perforation gauge to 10 while the Panama-Pacific stamps were still being produced. By the time of the next commemorative about four years later (Victory Issue, 537) the perforation gauge had again changed, this time to 11, and there it remained for the remaining flat plate printed commemoratives under consideration in this chapter. The commemoratives printed on the rotary press were perforated 11 x 10½, the preferred perforation for rotary press printed stamps in those years.

Most of the stamps of this era were designed by the great BEP designer Clair Aubrey Huston. The Pan-Americans were designed by Raymond Ostrander Smith, and the Hudson-Fulton stamp by M.W. Baldwin, but Huston designed all the remaining commemoratives until the 2¢ Aeronautics Conference Issue of 1928. Huston shares the design credit for that stamp (649) with A.R. Meissner, a rising star at the BEP who would help fill Huston's shoes upon Huston's retirement in 1933.

Notes on Collecting

All of the commemorative stamps issued for fairs and expositions during these years exist on covers with special cancellations from the event being commemorated. Most are illustrated in *Scott*. Such covers command a premium in the market over regular covers. Post cards from these fairs, especially with appropriate stamps and cancellations are popular collectables (see Examples of Postal Usage).

All of the imperforate stamps of these years (both ordinary and commemorative) were primarily intended to receive private perforations and manufacture into coils by private companies. In reality the Alaska-Yukon-Pacific stamps and the Hudson-Fulton stamps were not well-suited for this purpose because of their larger size. Most of these stamps that exist with private perforations were produced as a favor to collectors and few of them were actually used in vending or affixing machines. Finding them used on cover is a collecting challenge!

The paper used to print these commemoratives was the same paper used for ordinary stamps during this time. The Pan-American through Hudson-Fulton stamps were printed on double line watermarked paper. Reflecting a change in BEP policy, the Panama-Pacific stamps were printed on single-line watermarked paper. Subsequent commemoratives were all printed on unwatermarked paper.

The stamp issued to honor the Battle of White Plains in 1926 was also issued in the form of a souvenir sheet for the International Philatelic Exhibition held in

New York October 16-23, 1926. This was the first U.S. souvenir sheet. Individual stamps from the pane of 100 (629) and from the souvenir sheet (630) are both perforated 11, and are distinguishable only when there is selvage attached or when 629 is identifiable by being found in a multiple of 26 or more, or in horizontal or vertical strips of six stamps or more.

There are collectible printing varieties of some of these commemoratives. For example, the 5¢ Huguenot-Walloon depicted in figure 6 shows a well-known relief break. A relief break occurs when a transfer roll deteriorates during the process of making a printing plate, whereby some of the steel breaks off the roll. The result shows up on the printed stamps. In this case the transfer roll deteriorated gradually while the plate was being made and the result shows up progressively on several stamps from the upper right pane of plate 15754.

Figure 6

Detail from the 5¢ Huguenot-Walloon Issue (616). The "broken circle" beneath the "5" was caused when a fragment of steel on the transfer roll gradually broke away as the printing plate was being made.

Most of the commemoratives issued from the late 1920s through the early 1930s were printed in red. They are sometimes referred to collectively as "2¢ Reds."

One fascinating collecting challenge is to assemble a collection of 1932 covers featuring different rates and usages of the Washington Bicentennial series, which was sold to the public in lieu of the regular bureau issue definitives of the time.

Almost any collector on a modest budget can obtain a complete collection of these thirty years of commemoratives in used condition. Many of them are very reasonably priced. Only the White Plains Souvenir Sheet provides a financial challenge for many collectors. Ironically, it is actually catalogued less in mint condition, than in used, as used copies were easily spoiled or destroyed.

Almanac

1901 – The Pan-American Exposition Series goes on sale May 1.

1901 – The first Pan-American inverts are discovered May 4.

1909 – The first definitive-sized commemorative is issued February 12 to honor Abraham Lincoln's 100th birthday.

1913 – The perf. 12 Panama-Pacific Exposition Issue goes on sale January 1.

1914 – The earliest documented use (EDU) of any perf. 10 Panama-Pacific Exposition Issue, the 1¢ green, is December 21.

1924 – The Huguenot-Walloon Issue goes on sale May 1 in eleven cities.

1926 – The White Plains souvenir sheet (630) is issued October 18 at the second International Philatelic Exhibition in New York City.

1927 – Two Revolutionary War related issues are released on the same day, August 3, commemorating the battle of Bennington (Vermont Sesquicentennial) and the Burgoyne Campaign.

1929 – In another record setting year, five different events are commemorated. This includes the Ohio River Canalization, honored by an October 19 stamp, the last issued before the Great Depression.

1932 – The Washington Bicentennial Issue is released on January 1, a day when most post offices are closed.

1933 – A philatelic era ends on February 12 as C.A. Huston's last stamp is issued, the Georgia Bicentennial, and he retires from the BEP.

1933 – Franklin D. Roosevelt, member #11590 of the American Philatelic Society, becomes President of the United States on March 4, ushering in a unique philatelic period.

What Others Have Said

The Pan-American Inverts
"The new issue was in use only a few days when the 2¢ was reported with the center inverted. Consternation was in order at the Post Office – the Bureau was incredulous.... A stigma has always been attached to the four cent orange brown and black with center inverted [sic]. This stamp was never issued legitimately, but was "created.""

—*George B. Sloane, prominent philatelist.*

The Lincoln Centennial Stamp
"Resolved by the Senate and the House of Representatives... That the Postmaster General is hereby authorized to design and issue a special postage stamp, of the denomination of two cents, in commemoration of the one-hundredth anniversary of the birth of Abraham Lincoln."

—*Joint Resolution of Congress passed January 22, 1909.*

Too many stamps?

"The [Post Office] Department is not in favor of legislation of this kind. In fact, it discourages such legislation. Naturally the postal service can have too many varieties of postage stamps. In order to prevent this condition from arising it is believed that the best interests of the Government and all concerned would be better served if the preparation and issuance of special stamps were left to the discretion of the Department where it is now placed by existing law rather than following any other procedure."

—*Letter from Postmaster General Harry New, January 14, 1925, responding to legislation mandating the issuance of stamps for the Lexington-Concord Sesquicentennial, and expressing his feelings about commemorative stamps and the role he felt should be played regarding them by Congress and the Post Office Department.*

Clout Wins the Day

"The desirability of having a special postage stamp for the Battle of the Monongahela [Braddock's Field] has already been brought to my attention by Representative Kelly… Very careful consideration will be given the matter with a view to issuing a stamp for the anniversary of this important historical event…"

—*Letter from Postmaster General Brown on April 10, 1930 to Labor Secretary Davis, regarding the request of Rep. Clyde Kelly, chairman of the Committee on Post Offices and Post Roads, that a stamp (688) be issued to commemorate an obscure battle near Kelly's hometown.*

The Washington Bicentennial Series

"Although the celebration was officially scheduled to open on George Washington's 200th birthday, on February 22, 1932, and close with Thanksgiving Day, November 24, 1932, first day covers were canceled on January 1, 1932… The Postmaster General approved the designs of portraits selected by the Directors of George Washington Bicentennial Commission, and it was decided to restrict the issue to 12 stamps, of the same size of the regular stamps, so there would be no additional cost in effecting their distribution."

—*Paul Gouled, "The Parenthood of the Bicentennial Series," Stamps Magazine, 1932.*

Examples of Postal Usage

Figure 7

A cover bearing a 2¢ Pan-American (295) addressed to Canada, canceled at Buffalo, New York, by a Barry canceling machine, using a slogan that publicizes the Pan-American Exposition. Though canceled in Buffalo, it is not an exposition cancel.

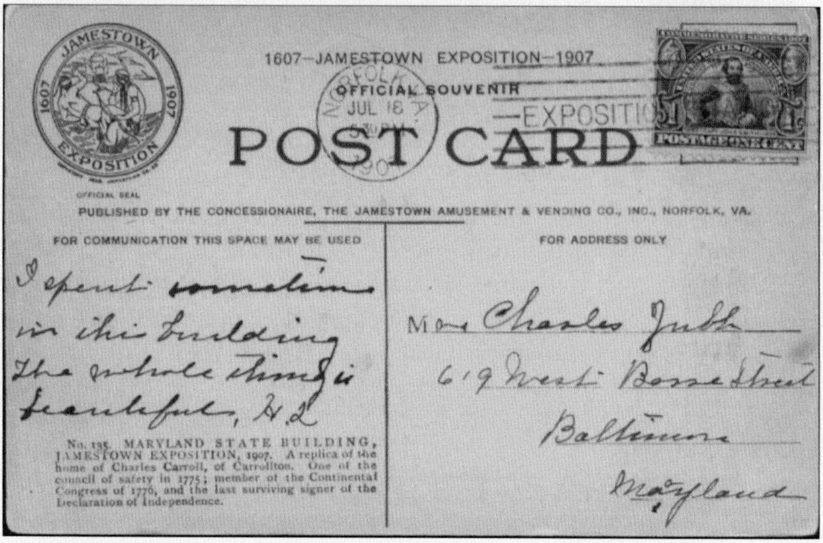

Figure 8

A 1¢ Jamestown Exposition Issue (328) used on an official post card, and canceled at the Exposition Station.

Figure 9

A third-class cover bearing a 1¢ Panama-Pacific Exposition Issue, perforated 12 (397). Panama-Pacific stamps were also issued perforated 10. Note the absence of a date in the dial. This was a common practice in canceling 3rd class mail.

Figure 10

The 5¢ Ericsson Memorial (628) paying the Universal Postal Union (UPU) rate for foreign surface mail. The Ericsson Memorial depicted on the stamp is located in Washington, D.C.

Figure 11

Molly Pitcher (646) on a First Class cover. Molly Pitcher is one of only two subjects commemorated by the overprinting of ordinary stamps.

Where to Find More Information

- The classic text on these stamps is Max G. Johl's *The United States Commemorative Stamps of the Twentieth Century*.

- For a more recent treatment see Gary Griffith's two volumes: *United States Stamps 1922-26* and *United States Stamps 1927-32*.

- For a guide to cachets on First Day Covers of these stamps see the multi-volume *Planty Photo Encyclopedia of Cacheted First Day Covers* by Michael A. Mellone.

- *Encyclopedia of Plate Varieties on U.S. Bureau-Printed Stamps* by Loran C. French provides detailed information on many plate varieties.

- The commemoratives of 1909 are covered in a valuable website, www.us1909.com/.

Chapter 20
Twentieth Century Commemoratives 1933-1971

The inauguration of Franklin D. Roosevelt on March 4, 1933 ushered in a new era in U.S. stamp collecting, while the end of the old U.S. Post Office Department (POD) on June 30, 1971 brought an era to a close. Between those two milestone events was issued an ever widening array of *commemorative* postage stamps. The first stamp issued by the Roosevelt administration was the 3¢ "Peace of 1783 Issue" (*Scott* 727) on April 19, 1933 (fig. 1) commemorating the proclamation of peace which had ended the Revolutionary War 150 years earlier. Sometimes called the "Newburgh Issue," it depicts the Hasbrouck House overlooking the Hudson River in Newburgh, N.Y. where George Washington issued his Proclamation of Peace. The last commemorative stamp issued by the old POD was the 8¢ Antarctic Treaty Issue (fig. 2), released on June 23, 1971. The number of stamps issued during the 38 years between these two stamps nearly matches the total number of stamps issued from the time of the first regular stamps in 1847, until Roosevelt became president.

Figure 1

The "Peace of 1783" issue was the first stamp issued by FDR's postal administration. Like so many of the commemorative stamps issued in the 1930s it is printed with violet ink.

The Roosevelt Years

Franklin D. Roosevelt, the 32nd President of the United States, was an ardent stamp collector. His well-known philatelic activities encouraged many depression era Americans to become interested in this "new" hobby. The public's desire for philatelic information resulted in large-city newspapers beginning or expanding their philatelic reporting. Membership in philatelic organizations increased significantly, as did the circulation of many stamp publications. Collector enthusiasm for stamps and supplies resulted in prestigious department stores opening stamp departments, and customers flocking to the many private stamp stores that could be found in almost every American city. Post Office Department revenue increased as collectors

The 8¢ Antarctic Treaty issue (1431), the last commemorative issued under the United States Post Office Department, was printed on the Giori Press.

The stamp honoring the birth of the United Nations (928) was issued only days after Roosevelt's death. In 1970 another stamp (1419) was issued for the organization's twenty-fifth anniversary.

bought and "retained" stamps, while both the POD and the White House were inundated with letters covering a variety of philatelic topics. What had once been considered a child's pastime was now the proud hobby of many adults. Stamp collecting had come of age, reaching a pinnacle during this era.

FDR had an eclectic collection of tremendous size and broad scope. His U.S. collection contained a huge variety of material, including covers addressed to him by ordinary citizens! FDR was also an avid collector of foreign stamps. FDR's stamp collection contained some important philatelic gems. It was also filled with many "seconds," stamps that were poorly centered, thinned, creased, badly perforated, or heavily cancelled. None of these "faults" bothered FDR who regarded every stamp as a source of information about a nation and its people. In short, Roosevelt collected what he liked, a good principal for any collector! His collection provided FDR with both joy and relaxation in challenging times with an uncertain future.

James A. Farley, FDR's first Postmaster General (PMG) announced within a week of the president's inauguration that the administration's first new stamp, with a design personally approved by Roosevelt, would be the Newburg, or "Peace Stamp" mentioned above. The president remained intimately involved with the issuance of new stamps throughout his administration, suggesting issues and designs, modifying designs, and personally approving more than 200 stamps. In his last official directive as President, FDR approved the 5¢ United Nations Conference commemorative (928, fig. 3). The quotation marks around the wording "Toward United Nations, April 25, 1945" and FDR's name were added to the stamp's design after his death. Even with these last minute changes, the stamp was issued on schedule at the first meeting of the U.N. Conference in San Francisco, only thirteen days after FDR's death.

The early Roosevelt years saw a scandal in the POD as a result of the actions of PMG Farley. Beginning with the Newburgh Peace Issue (727), Farley went to the Bureau of Engraving and Printing (BEP) and had removed from the presses a few sheets of each issue that had been properly printed, but not perforated, gummed, or divided into post office size **panes**. He paid face value for them. These sheets, unavailable to the public in this format, were given as gifts to FDR and some high-ranking government officials, as well as to members of the Farley family. This practice continued with each new issue through the Trans-Mississippi Philatelic Exposition Issue Souvenir Sheet, issued October 10, 1934.

Farley agreed to send an imperforate sheet of the "Mothers of America" stamp (737), issued on May 2, 1934, to the friend of a friend, after receiving the $6 face value payment. A short time later, this individual tried to secure a loan, using the imperforate sheet as collateral by explaining the stamps were rare and therefore worth several thousand dollars. The loan was declined.

Figure 4

This is known as a "vertical gutter pair." It was cut from a large "Farley" press sheet that originally contained 20 of the 1¢ National Parks Souvenir Sheets, each souvenir sheet consisting of six stamps. The piece illustrated was cut in such a manner that it includes one stamp from each of two different souvenir sheets, with a "gutter" running vertically between them.

A storm of protest grew against what was seen as highly unethical behavior on the part of Farley. Stamp collectors objected to specially created stamps for government officials that were unavailable to collectors. These objections become so strong that on January 9, 1935, FDR instructed Farley to discontinue the practice of releasing stamps in special conditions. But the controversy continued to grow unabated, resulting in the POD announcing on February 5, 1935 that all of the imperforate sheets would be issued in sufficient quantity to satisfy public demand. The publicity surrounding these stamps had created huge demand, resulting in both collectors and dealers buying unprecedented quantities of stamps (fig. 4). What had started as an embarrassing scandal for the young Roosevelt administration had become a very profitable enterprise for the United States Post Office Department!

Stamps with Agendas

Figure 5

The National Recover Act (NRA) issue of 1933 depicts a farmer, businessman, laborer and female worker. The design for this stamp was taken from a poster on which President Roosevelt was the second of the four people. By the time the design of the stamp was approved the president had gone incognito as a "businessman."

The use of commemorative stamps to promote political and civic agendas began in earnest during the middle of the twentieth century. Perhaps one of the more obvious examples is the National Recovery Act (NRA) stamp (732). Issued on August 15, 1933 (fig. 5), its sole purpose was to call attention to the NRA and to encourage U.S. citizens to support it. FDR is clearly identifiable in the watercolor that is the basis for this design, which was altered to disguise FDR as a businessman by giving him a hat and mustache.

Another example of stamps serving political purpose is the Overrun Countries series (909–921, fig. 6), issued in 1943 and 1944 - probably the darkest period of WW II. These 5¢ commemoratives, featuring the flags of countries occupied by the Axis Powers, paid the international surface rate, and were clearly intended to inspire hope in the countries to which they carried mail. This theme of hope was further emphasized by the common frames of these stamps, which depict a Phoenix rising from the ashes, and a woman who has been liberated from her shackles. Because the BEP lacked the multicolor capabilities necessary to produce these stamps, The **American Bank Note Company** (ABNC) was called upon to print them.

Figure 6

The 13 "Overrun Countries" stamps were printed by the American Bank Note Co., an anomaly in a time when the BEP printed all other U.S. postage stamps. The stamp honoring Denmark (920) is depicted here.

Another commemorative series with an "agenda," the "Champion of Liberty" stamps, was issued by the Eisenhower postal administration from 1957 to 1961. Appearing at the height of the "Cold War" they may rightly be regarded a propaganda weapon in that war, and as a minor but real instrument of U.S. foreign policy. Nineteen commemoratives honored ten "Champions of Liberty" from around the globe, including President Ramon Magsaysay of the Philippines (fig. 7); Simon Bolivar, a South American freedom fighter; Lajos Kossuth, a Hungarian freedom fighter; José de San Martin, a South American soldier and statesman; Ernst Reuter, the Mayor of post-war Berlin; Thomas Masaryk, the founder and President of Czechoslovakia; Ignacy Paderewski, a Polish statesman and musician; Gustaf Mannerheim, President of Finland; and Giuseppe Garibaldi, an Italian freedom fighter. Perhaps the most well known "Champion of Liberty", Mahatma Gandhi of India, was represented on the last two stamps in the series (1174 and 1175). While the Gandhi stamps were issued six days into the new Kennedy administration, they were actually a product of the Eisenhower postal administration. Most of the "Champion of Liberty" stamps were issued not only as 4¢ stamps, which paid the domestic rate, but also as 8¢ stamps, the rate for international surface mail at the time. The sole exception was the Magsaysay stamp (1095) which was issued only as an 8¢ commemorative, and which was the largest postage stamp ever issued until that time. Issuing "Champion of Liberty" stamps in a value of 8¢ was an attempt to insure that they would carry the message of freedom around the world during the cold war.

Figure 7

Ramon Masaysay, a "Champion of Liberty" is honored on this 1957 commemorative. With a denomination of 8¢ it was intended for use on international mail. This was the largest commemorative stamp issued to that time.

Many other commemoratives stamps in these years promoted a political or civic agenda. They include: "Win the War" (905) in 1942, NATO (1008) in 1952, "Atoms for Peace" (1070) in 1955, "Soil Conservation" (1133) in 1959, "Alliance for Progress" (1234) in 1963, "Stop Traffic Accidents" (1272) in 1965, and "Plant for a More Beautiful America" (1318) in 1966. Then, near the end of this era, it was the Viet Nam protests of the 1960s and the civil unrest that accompanied uneasy race relations of these years that helped inspire the "Law and Order" commemorative (1343) issued in 1968, late in the Johnson administration.

Historical milestones

The 1940s witnessed a dramatic increase in the number of commemoratives issued. In 1941 the POD issued only one commemorative stamp, the Vermont Statehood 150th anniversary (903). However by 1948 and the beginning of post war prosperity, the number of new commemoratives exploded to an

Figure 8

This 1948 commemorative (968), celebrating someone's definition of the centennial of the Poultry Industry, was roundly criticized and ridiculed. It was designed by veteran BEP designer Charles R. Chickering.

Figure 9

Issuing commemoratives for significant statehood anniversaries became an established practice during the middle years of the twentieth century. This stamp, issued in 1963, honored the 100th anniversary of West Virginia statehood.

unprecedented 28. A storm of protest by collectors descended on many of these issues, but the most vigorous protest was reserved for the so-called "Chicken stamp." The Poultry Industry Centennial stamp (fig. 8) was not only accused of being ugly, but also of inappropriately promoting commercial interests. Other commemoratives were less controversial, including those issued to honor states celebrating major anniversaries of statehood (fig. 9).

The Famous Americans Issues of 1940 (859-893) commemorated 35 individuals in seven categories: authors, poets, educators, scientists, composers, artists, and inventors. It was the longest commemorative set issued up until that time. Five stamps with unique frame designs were issued in each category, with values of 1, 2, 3, 5, and 10 cents. While not generally considered a part of the Famous Americans, stamps were later issued (between 1947 and 1950) commemorating Thomas Edison (945), George Washington Carver (953), William Allen White (960), Harlan Stone (965), Joel Chandler Harris (980) and Edgar Allen Poe (986) and Samuel Gompers (988). They used the same, or very similar, frames as the Famous Americans, and many are closely related by subject.

Innovations

In 1957, PMG Arthur Summerfield created the Citizens' Stamp Advisory Committee. It was given the responsibility of recommending stamp subjects, and ensuring the artistic merit of designs. This resulted in a number of philatelic innovations. In one example, the 4¢ 48-Star Flag commemorative (1094) was the first stamp to prominently feature the American flag. It was printed on the new **Giori press** which simultaneously applied different colored inks in the printing process. This was the BEP's first truly full color stamp. While the commemorative was successful, it was very controversial at the time. The idea of postmarking this stamp was considered by some patriotic citizens as a "desecration" of the flag. As a result, when the stamp was released on July 4, 1957, First Day Covers were not cancelled publicly.

In another philatelic first, the St. Lawrence Seaway Issue (1131) of 1959 was issued simultaneously with a stamp of the same design issued by Canada. This was only the first of a number of such **joint-issues** that would be issued in the ensuing years.

The first Christmas stamp (1205) was issued in 1962. The 1964 Christmas stamp (1254-1257) was the first **se-tenant** issue in U.S. history. Each of the four stamps in the block illustrates a different plant traditionally associated with Christmas.

The five Civil War Centennial commemoratives (1178-1182) were issued from 1961 to 1965, honoring each of five battles (Ft. Sumter, Shiloh, Gettysburg, The Wilderness, and Appomattox), on their respective 100th anniversaries.

The first commemorative printed using the **photogravure** method was the Thomas Eakins commemorative (1335). It was printed by Photogravure & Color Company, not the BEP. This was the first stamp since 1894 not to be printed by the BEP (except for the Overrun Countries, 909-921). The Eakins stamp might be called the "beginning of the end" for stamp production at the BEP, as the Post Office increasingly sought outside contractors to print stamps.

Commemoratives issued early in the period of 1933-1971 were all single color products of either the **flat plate** or the **Stickney Rotary Press**. The Giori Press brought full color capabilities to the BEP in the 1950s. By 1971 virtually all commemoratives were in full color.

Notes on Collecting

In general, the commemoratives from this era are probably the easiest in the entire catalogue to acquire. All are readily available from a wide variety of philatelic sources. Virtually all can be purchased in unused condition and they are generally the most inexpensive stamps that can be bought by collectors. Because there are large quantities of high quality stamps available, the collector does not need to be worried about faulty stamps that have been repaired, re-gummed, or re-perforated. Thus, no expertizing certificate needs to be considered before purchasing any of these commemoratives.

When collecting any of the se-tenant commemoratives, consult *Scott* to determine the order of the arrangement of the stamps in a block of four: each se-tenant issue is listed and illustrated in the catalogue in a specific order to be a proper se-tenant block. Those who collect particular issues often seek those stamps on covers to foreign destinations or utilizing special services such as air mail or *special delivery*.

Almanac

1933 – James A. Farley is sworn in as Postmaster General of the United States on March 4, the same day that the stamp collecting Governor of New York State, Franklin D. Roosevelt is sworn in as President, creating a President-PMG team that favored stamp collecting.

1933 – The 1¢ and 3¢ "Chicago Souvenir Sheets" are issued August 25, the first of six souvenir sheets to be issued in a four-year period, before a decision to restrict their issuance is finally made in 1937.

1942 – The first stamp to use foreign language characters as part of its theme, the Chinese Resistance Commemorative (906), is issued July 7.

1962 – One of the most well known examples of a stamp error appears on October 23 with the Dag Hammarskjöld commemorative (1203). When originally released a small number was discovered with the yellow background inverted and shifted to the right.

1962 – On November 16 Postmaster General J. Edward Day orders 40 million more errors of the Dag Hammarskjöld commemorative printed (1204), eliminating any potential philatelic premium.

1963 – The 5¢ City Mail Delivery stamp (1238) is issued October 26, the first commemorative to be *tagged*. Invisible luminescent ink activated ultraviolet sensors during processing, permitting automated stamp canceling. The stamp features a reproduction of Norman Rockwell's 1863 Letter Carrier.

1967 – The Accomplishments in Space issue (1331 and 1332), released September 29, is the first to have a continuous design that fills two stamps. It portrays Edward White II as the first American to walk in space.

1968 – Legislation to permit the reproduction of postage stamps in color in publications is signed into law by President Lyndon Johnson on June 20.

1971 – On July 1, officially dubbed "Postal Service Day", the United States Post Office Department fades into history after 200 years of service, and becomes the U. S. Postal Service.

What Others Have Said

Farley's "Follies"

"March 15 – the first day sale of the imperforate sheets of stamps – was typically a dealer's day with a total of first day sale of this Farley issue considerably in excess of $500,000. Single orders for five or ten thousand dollars were not uncommon....The authorities seemed to have forgotten that collectors asked primarily that the original presentation sheets be withdrawn and that the wholesale distribution be made only in the event that the original imperf sheets could not be recalled. It might appear that the revenue-acquiring aspect was of greater interest to the (Post Office) Department (than whether the original sheets could be recalled)."

—*Albert Kunze, "From the Nation's Capital,"* Stamps Magazine, 1935. *From an article reviewing the first day sale of the Farley reprints.*

A change in the *Scott* Catalogue (and stamp journalism!)

"The most noticeable improvement in this new edition is inclusion of illustrations of the postage issues. The illustrations are now permitted by the government provided they differ in size from the original stamps. If small-sized ones are to be used they must be less than three-fourths the size of the originals while if large sized ones are used they must be at least one and a half times the size of the originals. We have used the over-size illustrations for this Catalogue."

—*Hugh M. Clark, editor, From the Introduction to* Scott Catalogue of United States Stamps Specialized – 1939. *Prior to this time, it had been illegal to print a complete picture of a U.S. postage stamp, even in stamp catalogs or albums. Even advertisements that might show a letter on a table had to be retouched so that the stamp, no matter how small, could not be readily identified. Now illustrations, if larger or smaller than the actual stamp, could fill stamp albums and catalogs, aiding identification and greatly promoting the hobby of stamp collecting.*

The Philatelic Truck

"The Post Office Department's new philatelic truck will start its nationwide tour from the White House Tuesday morning. President Roosevelt, the nation's number one stamp collector, will be the recipient of a sheet of postage stamps which will be presented to him from the truck by the Postmaster General in ceremonies incident to the departure of the first traveling exhibit ever authorized by the Post Office Department. The truck is scheduled to appear in cities and towns in every state in the Union."

—*Post Office Department Information Service announcement dated May 6, 1939.*

It's time to honor "Heroes of Peace"

"America, a nation rich in great personalities, gave philatelic recognition to many of her military characters, explorers and statesmen. It is strange that, with few exceptions, a peace loving nation such as ours never, during the almost one hundred years postage stamps were issued by our government; saw fit to pay homage philatelic to her "Heroes of Peace." Consequently, it was quite natural...that hundreds of requests and suggestions for the issuance of stamps honoring famous men and women reached the Post Office Department from various organizations and individuals....The Famous American series was the culmination of these suggestions and requests rather than the conception of any one particular individual or organization."

—*George H. Hahn*, United States Famous Americans Series of 1940.

Whew! What a year 1948 was for commemorative stamps!

"This past year has been an eventful one for stamp collecting in the United States. We've seen 28 commemoratives issued in rapid succession—23 of them during the past six months – and we are all a little breathless....It's all over now, and we're looking into 1949 with certain trepidation...There is no doubt that the commemoratives issued in 1948 provided stamp collecting with a wealth of good advertising. There is ample evidence that every new stamp recruited new collectors."

—*William W. Wylie*, Western Stamp Collector, *1949. Wylie was a major spokesman of the hobby at the time, editorially bemoaning the 28 commemorative issues of 1948. Ironically only five commemoratives were issued in 1949.*

The birth of Christmas Stamps

"As Postmaster General, I find the philatelic part of my position a pleasure – not a chore....In my view, postage stamps are not suitable as signboards for commercial enterprises.... I am interested...in creating good precedents for the future...two subjects stand out far and above all the rest in public enthusiasm. The public obviously likes us to have a stamp with American flag – and the public would like to have a special Christmas stamp. We receive nearly 1,000 letters a year on (issuing a Christmas stamp). So, following the recommendation of the Citizens' Stamp Advisory Committee, less than two weeks ago...this coming Christmas season, there will be a special stamp especially appropriate for use on Christmas cards...."

—*Postmaster General J. Edward Day, May 26, 1962 at the Banquet of COMPEX at the La Salle Hotel in Chicago. This is the earliest known official announcement of the USPOD's decision to issue a Christmas stamp.*

Se-tenant stamps are introduced and popularized in the late 1960s.

"Postmaster General Lawrence F. O'Brien's announcement that a 10-stamp set featuring early American Flags is to be issued later this year will certainly attract public attention to our hobby....one pane will include five copies of each flag in the 10-stamp series. The historic import of this flag series may prompt many of our teachers to encourage their students to obtain panes containing the 10 different flags. When reproduced in full color, each will become a visual aid in the study of early American history....Remember last year's space stamp "twins"...the appeal of the "twin" design, when viewed by the casual postal patron, most certainly prompted thousands to explore the field of philately."

—*James M. Chemi, "Timely Observations," The American Philatelist, 1968. Chemi, editor, used his monthly column to editorialize on issues. He devoted this column in praise of the newly emerging se-tenant designed stamps coming from the USPOD.*

The Initial step to photogravure in U.S. Stamp Production

"On June 10, 1967, Postmaster General O'Brien announced plans for issuance this fall of the first United States postage stamp to be produced by the photogravure method of printing. The stamp selected for the gravure experiment is...Thomas Eakins' 'The Biglen Brothers Racing'....The painting contains many dark values, so, in searching for a way to brighten these values, the Citizen's Stamp Advisory Committee suggested that the design of the stamp be surrounded by a metallic gold frame which will be the *selvage* of the stamp....Resultant complex production problems [determined that] The Eakins stamp will not be printed by the Bureau of Engraving and Printing but will be commercially produced under contract to the Photogravure and Color Company, Moonachie, New Jersey. However the Bureau of Engraving and Printing will assert quality control."

—*The United States Specialist, 1967. An historic announcement which came full circle when the BEP stopped producing any U.S. postage stamps in 2005.*

Examples of Postal Usage

Figure 10

The 3¢ Navy (792) on this 1937 hotel cover was used about seven months after it was issued. Sets of stamps honoring the Army and Navy were issued in 1936 and 1937.

Figure 11

Commemoratives honoring Abraham Lincoln are used on this 1942 cover from Iowa City, Iowa to pay 6¢ air mail postage, and 10¢ for Special Delivery.

Figure 12

This 1959 cover to Switzerland used an 8¢ Champion of Liberty Stamp (1137). The Los Angeles sender used the stamp, with its message of freedom, as the POD hoped he would - on mail to a foreign country.

Figure 13

Use of a roller cancel to cancel this 1968 "Law and Order" stamp (1343) is unusual since roller cancels were generally reserved for larger pieces of mail that could not go through traditional letter canceling machines.

Where to Find More Information

- *United States Postage Stamps 1945-1952* by Sol Glass has introductory information, design, first day sale ceremonies, statistical data, plate record data and hundreds of photographs that include approved and rejected designs of the commemorative and air mail stamps issued from 1945 to 1952.

- *Farley's Follies* by Ralph Sloat provides a detailed reconstruction of the events leading up to the controversial imperforate Farley issues. It covers the period from Farley's nomination to his resignation and beyond, with transcripts of Congressional debates, personal correspondence, news items and photographs.

- *Franklin D. Roosevelt and the Stamps of the United States 1933-45* by Brian C. Baur present interesting information on the inside stories behind the stamps issued during the FDR administration.

- *Franklin D. Roosevelt: The Stamp Collecting President* by Brian C. Baur discusses how stamps impacted the life of FDR with attention to what was in his collection.

- *Handbook on U.S. Luminescent Stamps* by Alfred Boerger and John Stark provides useful information on understanding and detecting the early stamps with luminescent papers or inks.

- *Sloane's Column* compiled by George Turner is a complete collection of 1,350 columns on an interesting and wide variety of philatelic topics written between 1932 and 1958, by one of the most highly regarded American philatelic writers.

- *Stamping Our History - The Story of the United States Portrayed on Its Postage Stamps* by Charles Davidson and Lincoln Diamant covers nearly 150 years, illustrating and discussing stamps that portray the great epochs of the United States. It is well illustrated with large full color photographs, some enlarged over 2,000%.

- *Stamp Romances: The Lore and Legend Associated with the 1934 National Parks Series of Stamps* by Albert F. Kunze provides colorful stories inspired by the park portrayed on each of the ten stamps.

- *Encyclopedia of Plate Varieties on U.S. Bureau-Printed Stamps* by Loran C. French provides detailed information on many plate varieties.

Chapter 21
Twentieth Century Commemoratives 1971-2000

This chapter covers commemoratives, starting with the first one issued by the new United States Postal Service (ch. 32), the 8¢ American Revolution Bicentennial Commission Emblem, on July 4, 1971 (*Scott* 1432), and concluding with the last one of the twentieth century, the 33¢ Legends of Hollywood commemorative portraying actor Edward G. Robinson (fig. 1), issued on October 24, 2000 (3446).

The **se-tenant** issues dominated the commemorative landscape in the final third of the twentieth century. Some 140 se-tenants were issued, often as blocks of four, but also as blocks of eight, nine and ten, as pairs, and strips of three, four, five, six, ten, and panes of fifty. Topics include historical, technological, cultural, floral, fauna, artistic, holiday, or fantasy themes.

Commemorative stamps in these years include some that blurred the traditional and once distinct line between commemorative and the ordinary (definitive) stamps. The first Love stamp (1475) was issued in 1973. Starting in 1984, Love

Figure 1

The first commemorative issued by the USPS in 1971 (also the first Bicentennial stamp), and the last commemorative of the twentieth century (Edward G. Robinson). Notice the hard to read printing on the Robinson stamp, and the dramatic increase in postage from 1971 to 2000, from 8¢ to 33¢. The bicentennial stamp was issued in then traditional panes of 50. The Robinson stamp was issued in a new format size of 20.

Figure 2

The first semi-postal, issued in 1998 for Breast Cancer Awareness (B1). Notice the small bits of backing paper protruding from beneath the die-cut simulated perforations on this self-adhesive stamp.

stamps were issued regularly, and provided the finishing touch to Valentine's Day cards, wedding invitations and love letters. They featured a wide range of designs including flowers, animals, cherubs, love letters, and abstract art. A Christmas stamp was first issued 1962, and has been issued annually since then. The concept of a holiday stamp began to evolve in 1972 with issuing both a traditional and contemporary stamp each year. The holiday program was then expanded to include stamps in observance of Hanukkah, Kwanzaa, and Eid. All of these Love and holiday stamps, called "special issues" by the USPS, proved very popular with the general public.

The Breast Cancer Awareness issue of 1998 (B1) has all the appearance of a traditional commemorative stamp, but is actually the first *semi-postal* ever issued in this country (fig. 2). Congress passed a controversial bill in July, 1997 directing the USPS to issue a stamp to benefit breast-cancer research. A semi-postal has two values associated with it. The first is its postal value, and the second is the amount given in support of a designated cause or charity. When the Breast Cancer Awareness stamp was released on July 29, 1998 it had a face value of 40¢. Its postal value was 32¢. The remaining 8¢ was the surtax for cancer research. Because of changing postal rates, the cost of the stamp, its postal value, and the amount of the surtax, changed several times through the years. When sales were suspended on January 1, 2004 (the federal law authorizing this fund raising activity had expired), it had been responsible for raising more than $35 million for research from the sale of over 485 million stamps. New legislation, encouraged by the popularity of this semi-postal, extended the sale of the Breast Cancer Awareness issue, and allowed for other charities to be supported in this way.

One way of categorizing the commemorative stamps of the last third of the twentieth century is according to quantities "retained," as defined by USPS survey. According to the USPS the number one favorite was the 29¢ Elvis commemorative (fig. 3), first issued in panes of forty on January 8, 1993 (2721). The USPS distributed 517 million stamps in two printings. Other Elvis stamps were issued in panes of thirty-five that also honored other entertainers, with

14.3 million stamps printed (2724), and as a booklet stamp with 102 million stamps printed (2731). It was estimated by the USPS that 124 million stamps were "retained" by both collectors and Elvis fans. The other top five most popular commemorative stamps, in terms of retention, were: the 1992 Wildflowers (2647-2696) with 76.2 million printed, the 1993 Legends of American Music Series, Rock and Roll/Rhythm & Blues (2724-2737) with 75.8 million printed, the 1995 Civil War (2975) with 46.6 million, and the 1994 Legends of the West (2869) with 46.5 million. The remainder of the top 10, in descending order, are: 1995 Marilyn Monroe (2967), 1997 Bugs Bunny (3137),

Figure 3

The 1993 Elvis stamp is considered by the USPS to be the most popular stamp of all time. The one picture here (2721) came from a pane of 40 stamps. Another 1993 Elvis stamp, of almost identical design, is one of seven honoring American musicians. It appeared on a pane of 35, and in booklet form.

1992 Summer Olympic Games (2637-2641), 1997 The World of Dinosaurs (3136), and the 1996 Centennial Olympic Games (3068). The USPS measured retention by evaluating responses from quarterly surveys mailed to 60,000 households that correspond to U.S. Census statistics. These statistics however, are disputed by some who point out that storing a few panes of stamps in a closet for a few years and then using them for postage, does not qualify as "retention," let alone "collecting."

The American Revolution bicentennial celebration was the occasion for the USPS to release an unprecedented 113 commemorative stamps. The number of stamps issued seems even more staggering when one realizes that no commemorative stamps were issued for the centennial of the American Revolution, and only sixteen were issued during America's sesquicentennial era of 1925 to 1933.

Bicentennial commemoratives were released over a six-year period, beginning with the American Revolution Bicentennial Commission Emblem stamp issued July 4, 1971 (1432). Other Bicentennial issues included the 1972 Colonial American Craftsmen, issued as a block of four (1456-1459). In 1973 the Communications in Colonial Times was issued as four stamps (1476-1479). There was also a Boston Tea Party block of four stamps which, as a unit, illustrates a complete scene (1480-1483). In 1975, with the 200th anniversary celebration only one year away, there were five commemorative sets released. The first was the First Continental Congress as a block of four (1543-1546); then the Contributors to the Cause, also as a block of four, and the first to have explanatory printing on the reverse (1559-1562); the Lexington Concord Battle (1563); the Bunker Hill Battle 200th Anniversary (1564); and finally the Military Uniforms, issued as a block of four (1565-1568).

The bicentennial commemoratives issued in 1976 eclipsed the total number released since 1971. The first bicentennial commemorative of 1976, issued January 1, was the Spirit of '76, issued as a strip of three (1629-1631). It features a painting by Archibald Willard painted for the Centennial celebration in 1876. Originally titled *Yankee Doodle*, its name was later changed to *The Spirit of '76*. On February 23, a pane of the 50 stamps was issued portraying the state flags arranged in the order in which states joined the union. This was the first time that a pane with 50 different stamps had been issued (1633-1682). On May 29 there were four **souvenir sheets**, each with five stamps set inside a design that covered almost the entire pane. One, with 13¢ commemoratives, featured the Surrender of Cornwallis at Yorktown (1686). Another, with 18¢ commemoratives, featured the signing of the Declaration of Independence (1687). The third, with 24¢ commemoratives, depicted Washington Crossing the Delaware (1688), while the fourth souvenir sheet, with 31¢ commemoratives, depicts Washington Reviewing the Army at Valley Forge (1689). These four souvenir sheets were issued at Interphil, the International Stamp Show held in Philadelphia in 1976. On June 1, a joint issue with Canada illustrating Benjamin Franklin and a map of North America (1690) was issued. Standing at

Figure 4

Issued on July 4, 1976, this strip of four depicting the signing of the Declaration of Independence (1691-94), is among the many stamps issued for the American Bicentennial.

the heart of the Bicentennial stamps, and issued on July 4, 1976, was the issuance of an unprecedented strip of four commemoratives featuring a single design, the signing of the Declaration of Independence (1691-1694, fig. 4).

Even after the bicentennial was celebrated on July 4, 1976, American Bicentennial Issues continued with ten additional ones appearing before the end of the year. The ten included: Washington's Victory over Lord Cornwallis at

Princeton (1704); the 200th anniversary of Marquis de Lafayette arriving on the coast of South Carolina (1716); Skilled Hands for Independence, issued as a block of four featuring a Seamstress, Blacksmith, Wheelwright, and Leatherworker (1717-1720); General Herkimer at the Battle of Oriskany (1722); Members of the Continental Congress in Conference Drafting the Articles of Confederation (1726); Surrender of General Burgoyne at Saratoga (1728); and, finally, one of the Christmas Issues featuring Washington in prayer at Valley Forge (1729).

Sports in general and Olympic games in particular, were regularly commemorated during this period. The first Olympic stamps (three of them) appeared in 1932. There was one stamp in 1960. But 79 Olympic stamps appeared between 1971 and 2000. According to USPS surveys, the 1992 Summer Olympics (2637-2641) and the 1996 Centennial Olympic Games (3068) were among the all-time top ten most retained commemoratives stamps.

During these years commemoratives appeared in previously unseen formats. For example, on the occasion of AMERIPEX '86, the International Stamp Show held in Chicago, four Miniature Sheets measuring 120 by 207 mm were issued with nine commemorative stamps each. The Ameripex '86 Issue (2216-2219) has a Presidential theme, illustrating 35 Presidents and the White House.

Four additional panes of 50 different subjects were issued. In 1982, the State Birds and Flowers were issued with two different perforations, the first (1953-2002) with 10½ x 11¼ perforations; and a second (1953A-2002A) with 11¼ x 11 perforations. In 1987 the North American Wildlife pane (2286-2335) was issued with 50 different stamps portraying birds, animals and insects from all areas of the U.S. Finally, in 1992, Wildflowers (2647-2696) was released, which holds the honor of being the second most popular commemorative stamp retained by admirers.

In 1978 a new series of commemoratives was launched honoring Black Americans. The first honored Harriet Tubman (1744). Stamps in this series continued to be issued annually through the end of the century and beyond. Honorees included Martin Luther King, Jr. (1771), Scott Joplin (2044) and A. Phillip Randolph (2402).

As the new millennium approached, the release of "Celebrate the Century" panes created great interest and excitement among collectors and the general public. Ten panes each documented one of the decades of the twentieth century with 15 stamps (3182-3191). Eight topics were covered in each decade: art, sports, historical events, technology, entertainment, science, political figures, and lifestyles, which facilitated comparison between the decades. The back of each stamp was printed with additional information regarding its subject.

By the 1990s it became commonplace for commemoratives to be issued in panes of twenty, often with a decorative banner that was not valid for postage. Topics included Legends of the West (2869 and 2870), Civil War (2975), Comic Strips (3000), Classic Aircraft (3142), and American Art (3236). The 1999 Sonoran Desert issue (3293) and the 2000 Pacific Coast Rain Forest (3378) were issued in a format in which the individual stamps constituted small portions of a design that covered nearly the entire pane, similar to the bicentennial souvenir sheets.

Collectors who could not afford the classic nineteenth century commemoratives were treated to panes that featured reproductions of the 1893 Columbian Exposition (2624-2629) and 1898 Trans-Mississippi Stamps (3209 and 3210).

Another popular series commemorated WW II with five panes (2559, 2697, 2765, 2838, and 2981) issued between 1991 and 1995. Each has ten stamps attached to a central panel illustrating a map of the world showing the expansion and contraction of Axis control (fig. 5).

Figure 5

The second in a series of panes commemorating the 50th anniversary of World War II. This one, from 1992, has ten stamps that depict military engagements abroad, and life on the "home front."

Another popular series, Legends of Hollywood, highlights a different silver screen celebrity on each pane. Those so honored were: Marilyn Monroe, James Dean, Humphrey Bogart, Alfred Hitchcock, James Cagney, and Edward G. Robinson.

Of course not all of the commemoratives of these years broke new ground in terms of subject. States continued to be honored on significant anniversaries of statehood, and stamps continued to honor such national leaders as Robert F. Kennedy (1770), Everett Dirksen (1874), Franklin D. Roosevelt (1950), Dwight Eisenhower (2513), and Richard Nixon (2955).

The classic 1869 U.S. Abraham Lincoln stamp is reborn in these four larger versions commemorating World Stamp Expo'89, held in Washington, D.C. during the 20th Universal Postal Congress of the UPU. These stamps show the issued colors and three of the trial proof color combinations.

©USPS 1988

Figure 6

This souvenir sheet (2433) was issued to honor World Stamp Expo '89, held in Washington, D.C. November 17 through December 3, 1989. The souvenir sheet was issued on opening day.

Souvenir Sheets

Souvenir Sheets had been traditionally associated with major philatelic events. And indeed such souvenir sheets were issued from 1971-2000, including: American Bicentennial (1686-1689) (Interphil), Canadian International Philatelic Exhibition '78 (1757), and World Stamp Expo '89 (2433, fig. 6). The Interphil Sheets were the first to not include or reflect the fact that they were issued to honor a major stamp show.

By the 1990s the concept of "Souvenir Sheet" expanded to include: 1994 World Cup Soccer Championships (2834), Norman Rockwell (2840), Bureau of Engraving and Printing (2875), Cycling (3119), and Space (3409-3413).

Booklet Commemoratives

Prior to 1986, only one (air mail) commemorative appeared in booklet form (the 1927 Lindbergh Air Mail, C10a). On January 23, 1986, Stamp Collecting (2198-2201) appeared in the popular and convenient booklet format. The booklet had two panes of four different vertical stamps, and was issued as a *joint-issue* with Sweden to celebrate the 250th anniversary of the Swedish Post Office and the 100th anniversary of the Swedish Philatelic Society. While Stamp Collecting appeared only in booklet form, some subsequent issues appeared in both regular pane format and in booklet form. A unique booklet format was used to honor several Warner Bros. cartoon themes, including Bugs Bunny (3137), Sylvester & Tweety (3204 and 3205), and Daffy Duck (3306).

Notes on Collecting

During the final 29 years of the twentieth century, the USPS issued more than 2,000 new stamps, averaging over 69 annually. By comparison, in the entire previous 124 year history of the United States Post Office Department, less than 1,500 issues had been produced, averaging 11½ each year.

Improved printing techniques have resulting in most stamps being produced with very fine, or better, centering. The majority of commemoratives between 1977 and 1981 are modestly priced even in unused condition, while later stamps, between 1987 and 2000, with a higher face value, are priced proportionally higher. The various panes, souvenir sheets and high denomination special issues cost only slightly more. Because they appear in many different sizes and shapes, perhaps the greatest challenge is obtaining the proper mount to protect and display them.

There are two commemoratives in this era priced well above all others. The first is a variety of the John Paul Jones commemorative issued in 1979, printed by J.W. Fergusson & Sons. After printing, the sheets were taken to the **American Bank Note Company** (ABNC) to be perforated 12 x 12. However, after only one day's use, the horizontal pins broke and were replaced with perforation 11 pins, creating the 11 x 12 perf. (1789). Later the perforation 12 vertical pins were replaced by perforation 11 pins, resulting in the 11 x 11 variety (1789A). By the beginning of the twenty-first century only four panes (200 stamps) have been reported of the 12 x 12 perf. (1789B), making it one of the rarest U.S. commemoratives. The other higher priced commemorative is the "recalled" Legends of the West pane (2870), of which 150,000 were made available through a special drawing conducted by the USPS, as described in chapter 33.

During the 1990s uncut **press sheets** of selected issues were sold to collectors. This was the first time since the Farley Special Printings of the 1930s that collectors could purchase full uncut sheets.

The 1970s was a period of substantial stamp price increases due to speculation. By the late 1970s, double-digit inflation and poor performance of traditional financial investments had many investing in tangible assets. Large investment capital quickly entered and overwhelmed the stamp market. To illustrate the dynamic growth of capital entering the stamp market, the 1979 Salomon Brothers survey recorded stamps values rising 60.9% during those preceding 12 months, compared with only 5.3% for stocks and 3.3% for bonds. Stamps had also greatly exceeded the 10.5% rate of inflation. For a few years substantial profits from stamps seemed guaranteed - after all, U.S. postage stamps had never before decreased in value. However, by the early 1980s that is exactly what happened. Significant corrections to stamp valuations were made as the economy changed and investors abandoned the stamp market. "In 1981, the market was thinned of most speculative buyers and, once again, the market is now based on collectors, who buy to meet specific requirements," wrote Stephen Datz in the spring of 1982, describing how the stamp market was rapidly leveling off as the investors left after creating an unprecedented collapse in the stamp market.

Almanac

1974 – The first diamond-shaped stamps are issued June 13 as a block of four - the Mineral Heritage Issue (1538-1541).

1974 – The first self-adhesive stamp, the 10¢ Christmas Dove (1552), is issued November 15 as an experiment. It would be nearly 30 more years before self-adhesive stamps became commonplace.

1975 – Two Christmas stamps (1579 and 1580), issued October 14, are the first *non-denominated* stamps. A postal rate increase was due to be implemented during the production of the holiday issues, but postal officials had not yet established the new *First Class* rate. Thus, the commemoratives simply read "US Postage" recognizing they would be valid for the First Class rate in effect when issued.

1981 – The one ounce First Class postage rate is increased to 18¢ on March 22. This is the shortest duration of any First Class rate, lasting little more than seven months. Because of this, the James Hoban commemorative (1935 and 1936) is issued twice, one at 18¢ face and the other at 20¢ face.

1984 – The Health Research (2087) commemorative, issued May 17, is the first stamp to use truly metallic ink, which can be seen in the *gravure* colors that include a silver hue found only on the border.

1985 – The Jerome Kern commemorative (2110), issued January 23, is the first stamp issued with a face value of less than one dollar that did not include either the word "cent(s)" or the "¢" symbol.

1992 – On July 24 the USPS issues its first stamps (29¢ American Wildflower commemoratives) with *micro-printing* - extremely small letters or numbers somewhere in the design.

1993 – On January 8 the first stamp is issued with artwork selected by "vote" of the public. The choice is between a youthful Elvis watercolor by Mark Stutzman or a more mature Elvis painted by John Berkey. Nearly 1.2 million ballots are returned to the USPS in 1992, with more than 75% of voters choosing the young Elvis (2721).

1997 – The first two triangular stamps, Sailing Ship and Stagecoach (3130 and 3131), are issued March 13 as the Pacific '97 commemoratives.

1997 – The Department of the Air Force commemorative (3167), issued September 18, is the first stamp with a hidden three-dimensional image, a *Scrambled Indicia*. When the USPS *stamp decoder* lens is placed over the stamp, the repeated phrase "USAF" can be observed. By the end of 2000, there are 25 stamps with hidden images or phrases. Primarily used as a security feature to thwart counterfeiting, it is also used to appeal to both collectors and young adults who might become collectors.

1999 – To commemorate Valentines Day, two Love stamps (3274 and 3275) are issued January 28 with irregular margins, emphasizing the shape of the heart. To highlight this unique shape, the stamps are printed using a self-adhesive feature that permits a clean straight edge not possible on typical perforated stamps (fig. 7).

2000 – A circular stamp is issued honoring Space Achievement and Exploration (3412) on July 7. With a face value of $11.75, it is the first stamp to contain a hologram.

2000 – The first pentagon-shaped stamps are issued July 11 on the Exploring the Solar System (3410) Souvenir Sheet.

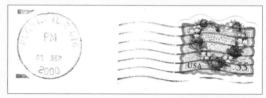

Figure 7

This 55¢ LOVE stamp (3275) and its cancellation are photographically cropped from an envelope that contained a wedding invitation. Some love stamps, like this one issued in 1999, paid the First Class postage for 2 ounces, a typical weight for a mailing containing a wedding invitation, response card, and envelope. The 1999 LOVE stamps were the first to have an irregular margin.

What Others Have Said

Issuing only Commemorative Stamps

"I would like nothing better than to see all stamps in a commemorative format. If you give a stamp designer a bigger canvas, and a stamp printer a larger piece of paper, you increase the probability of excellence. But that's an impossible dream because of other factors working against such an idea. To convert all of those sheet definitives to commemoratives would double both the printing time required and its costs."

—*Don McDowell, USPS Stamps Division Manager commenting on the popularity, and production issues, of commemorative stamps in 1983.*

BEP groups four commemoratives in the same press sheet

"For the first time in its history, the U.S. Postal Service has used a special 'quadrant' printing method to simultaneously produce four different commemorative stamps with one gravure press operation. The stamps honor the Federal Deposit Insurance Corporation (FDIC), the Credit Union Act of 1934, Soil and Water Conservation and the National Archives. For first-time stamp designer Michael David Brown...the design of the quadrant stamps proved to be an artistic challenge - to create four designs that could be printed in the same sheet from the same six inks....Brown met the challenge with four designs which, in his words, 'graphically and conceptually' symbolize the vital roles of the Federal entities depicted.... 'I tried to capture what I pictured as the most important or outstanding feature for each agency represented,' he said."

—*Carl Burcham, "Quadrant Printing," The United States Specialist, 1984.*

World Stamp Expo '89 featured 11 different First Day ceremonies

"To celebrate the opening of World Stamp Expo '89, a miniature souvenir sheet will be issued on the first day of the event. The imperforate sheet features reproductions of the classic 90-cent Lincoln stamp of 1869 and three ***color trial proofs*** of the same design in a block of fours. This is the first of eleven stamps and postal stationery items to be released by the postal service throughout the exposition."

—*"World Stamp Expo '89 Will be an Historic Event," American Philatelist, 1989.*

Celebrate the Century

"Unveiling 30 stamps in 30 days is an unprecedented undertaking for the Postal Service. This will set the stage for the voting periods to follow where the public will have the opportunity to select which stamps will honor the latter decades of the passing century."

—*PMG Marvin Runyon, commenting on December 11, 1997, on the Celebrate the Century Program in which the stamps used for each decade, beginning with the 1950s, were voted on by the public.*

First Image Cut Stamp

"....with the Victorian-Love stamps, we have the first stamps in US postal history cut to shape of the image....they mark a radical change in US stamps."

—*Azeezaly S. Jaffer, Executive Director, Stamp Services, USPS, USA Philatelic: The Official Source for Stamp Enthusiasts, 1999.*

Design Feature of the 32¢ Alfred Hitchcock Commemorative

"It's sort of an inside joke. Most of the general public doesn't know what the Royal Mail's stamp designs look like, so whether or not anyone would pick up on it we didn't know. But we thought it would be fun to do."

—Terrence McCaffrey, head of stamp design for USPS, commenting on the use of the outline caricature of the British-born Hitchcock in the upper left corner of the stamp (3226). It was intended to be a subtle spoof of Great Britain's practice of putting a small silhouette of the queen on its commemorative stamps.

Examples of Postal Usage

Figure 8

An Apollo-Soyuz (1570) used to pay the 10¢ First Class postage rate in 1975. The stamp is the American version of a joint American-Soviet issue honoring the Apollo-Soyuz project.

Lexington & Concord (1563), one of the Bicentennial stamps, used on a cover addressed to a prominent philatelic journalist, James Chemi, who at that time was the editor of the American Philatelist. Some collectors seek covers addressed to prominent individuals.

Figure 9

Figure 10

Finding a post card rate commemorative properly used on a post card, such as the 1984 Summer Olympics 13¢ here (2048), may be a bit of a challenge, but it can be done.

Where to Find More Information

- *The Postal Service Guide to U. S. Stamps* published annually by the USPS contains full color illustrations of all stamps and retail pricing information.

- The relevant volumes of *Linn's U.S. Stamp Yearbook*, edited by Fred Boughner or George Amick.

Chapter 22
Twenty-first Century Stamps

The first stamp of the new millennium (*Scott* 3466, fig. 1), issued on January 7, 2001, featuring a traditional subject, the Statue of Liberty, was printed by the Bureau of Printing and Engraving (BEP). But reflecting changes that had been accelerating in previous decades, that stamp was ***self-adhesive***, and would be among the last stamps to be printed by the BEP. Like so many of the definitive stamps issued at the beginning of the new century, this stamp was issued in two additional varieties (3476 and 3477); all three were coils. A very similar stamp was issued in booklet format (3485a, b, c, and d).

Figure 1

The first stamp of the twenty-first century featured the Statue of Liberty, a subject first used on a stamp in 1922.

Definitive Issues

As the twenty-first century began, and as the total number of different postage stamps issued since 1847 approached 4,000, the stamp program of the U.S. Postal Service (USPS), like the wider American society, was profoundly affected by the events of September 11, 2001. Only 43 days after the terrorist attacks, the United We Stand definitives (3549, 3549B, 3550, and 3550A) were issued on October 24, 2001. Reflecting a renewed patriotic use of the flag, the flag appeared on the three varieties issued that day, a booklet of 20 (3549, fig. 2), a coil of 100 (3550), and a coil of 10,000 (3550A).

A new low-denomination definitive stamp series, the American Design, began in 2002. This series, which was anticipated to extend over a number of years, featured various furniture and other objects considered to be Americana. The 5¢ Toleware Coffeepot (3612) issued in 2002 was the first release of the American Design series. The 10¢ American Clock (3751) and 1¢ Tiffany Lamp (3757) joined this series in 2003. The 4¢ Chippendale Chair (3750) and the 2¢ Navajo Jewelry (3749) stamps became part of the series in 2004.

High-denomination definitive stamps, for Priority and Express Mail service, which previously used a space or eagle theme, were replaced in 2001 with the

Figure 2

Washington Views Issue, featuring familiar views of the nation's capital. The $3.50 U.S. Capitol Dome (3472) and the $12.25 Washington Monument (3473) were the first to be issued, both appearing on January 29, 2001. In 2002, rate increases provided an opportunity to portray new scenes. The Jefferson Memorial (3647) was featured on the $3.85 stamp for Priority Mail, which has a facsimile of Thomas Jefferson's signature as Scrambled Indicia. The U.S. Capitol was used again, with a different view of the dome, at dusk, for the $13.65 Express Mail stamp (3648, fig. 3).

Commemorative stamps

Commemoratives stamps in the early years of the twenty-first century utilized traditional, innovative, as well as controversial subjects. Among the traditional themes was the 34¢ Greetings From America (3561–3610) pane of 50, with each stamp on the pane honoring a specific state. Issued on April 4, 2002, the stamp honoring New York State was originally designed to include an image of the World Trade Center, which was hurriedly altered. Less than three months after the Greetings from America stamps were issued First Class postage rose to 37¢, resulting in USPS officials reissuing them (3696–3745) on October 25, 2002 with the higher value of 37¢. The back of each commemorative has a wealth of information pertaining to each state that included: the state bird, flower, tree, capital, and date of statehood.

Prestige booklets debuted just as the twentieth century was drawing to a close. The first one, U.S Navy Submarines (3372–3377), was issued in 2000. The Old Glory prestige booklet appeared (3776–3780) in 2003. These booklets, printed on stiffer paper stock, contained stamps as well as text and illustrations.

The release of the Lewis and Clark Bicentennial commemoratives on May 14, 2004, was the first time in history that three

Figure 3

The Express Mail stamp issued on July 30, 2002 was printed by Banknote Corporation of America.

stamps were released on the same day in 11 states. The sites selected were located along the route of the Lewis and Clark Expedition. Two of the three stamps, featuring portraits of the explorers, were sold in a prestige booklet of 20 stamps (3855 and 3856, BK297) at $8.95, $1.55 above face value, creating considerable controversy. While both booklet stamps were subject to this premium, a pane of 20 featuring both explorers (3854, fig. 4) surveying the countryside was sold at face value.

Figure 4

The Lewis and Clark Expedition was honored on this 2004 commemorative, a portion of which was printed by the traditional intaglio method.

These commemoratives, very popular both with stamp collectors and the general public, have been described as the most beautiful stamps issued by the USPS in many years. Their frames have been compared to those used on the *Series of 1922*.

Political influence, long a factor in the selection of subjects for stamps, continued to exert itself into the twenty-first century, even succeeding in overruling the *Citizens' Stamp Advisory Committee* (CSAC), which has established formal rules covering the subject matter of U.S. stamps. Rule #12 of the CSAC states, "No stamp shall be considered for issuance if one treating the same subject has been issued in the past 50 years." While the Special Olympics (3771) is an important subject, it appeared for the fourth time (in 25 years) on February 13, 2003. This stamp, originally requested by Timothy Shriver, president of the Special Olympics, was initially denied. Shriver appealed to John Walsh, a member of the Postal Service Board of Governors who went to Terrence McCaffrey, manager of stamp development, without satisfaction. Walsh approached Postmaster General John Potter who ordered the rule be waived.

The "Nature of America" souvenir sheet series illustrates and interprets a variety of natural ecosystems found in the United States and its territories. The plant and animal species, and their interactions, portrayed on each sheet were recommended by scientists. The same design team was used for all the Nature of America panes to give the series consistency. The back of each pane includes descriptive information on the plant and animal life portrayed on the front. Each of the ten self-adhesive stamps illustrates a subject integral to the overall mural. The series began in 1999 with the Sonoran Desert (3293), and the Pacific Coast Rain Forest (3378) in 2000. The 2001 pane depicts life on the

Great Plains Prairie (3506) while the Longleaf Pine Forest (3611) was featured in 2002. The Artic Tundra (3802) was issued in 2003 and the sixth issue, the Pacific Coral Reef (3831), was issued January 2, 2004. The seventh issue, the Northeast Deciduous Forest (3899) was issued in 2005.

Frida Kahlo was the first Hispanic woman to be the subject of a commemorative stamp (3509). Issued June 21, 2001, the stamp features a self-portrait painted in 1933. A painter and feminist icon, the stamp was controversial because of Kahlo's leftist political beliefs.

Semi-postal stamps

The first *semi-postal* stamp of the new millennium, and only the second semi-postal stamp ever, Heroes of 2001 (B2, fig. 5) was a response to the events of September 11. It was issued on June 7, 2002 at a first day ceremony held at Battery Park in New York City. The Senate passed legislation for this 45¢ semi-postal in October 2001. Initially 11¢ of the sale price went to a relief fund created by the Federal Emergency Management Agency. The charitable amount became 8¢ when First Class rates rose on June 30, 2002. The fund assisted the rescue personnel, or family members of those killed or permanently disabled in the line of duty in connection with the terrorist attacks of September 11, 2001. The stamp depicts details of Thomas Franklin's photograph of three firemen raising the U.S. flag

Figure 5

A portion of the proceeds from the sale of the "Heroes" semipostals was used to aid rescue workers and their families.

at "ground zero", the World Trade Center site, in New York City. Authorized for sale through December 31, 2004, more than 128 million "Heroes of 2001" stamps were sold which raised more than $10 million.

On October 8, 2003, the 45¢ Stop Family Violence (B3) was issued to prevent domestic violence and to protect its survivors. Funds raised from this semi-postal were administered by the U.S. Department of Health and Human Services. The image on this semi-postal, drawn by 6-year old Monique Blias of California, depicts a distraught woman. Her drawing won the international 2003 Asiago Award for Young Artists.

Customized Postage

The President's Commission on the USPS in a report issued July 23, 2003 recommended, among other things, that the USPS issue personalized stamps for sale at premium prices. A test marketing of what the USPS called **customized postage** (ch. 61) was conducted from July 22 to September 30, 2004. A private company, Stamps.com, sold postage with the brand name PhotoStamps™. Individuals were allowed to create postage with their own designs, images, or photographs. The image covered about two-thirds of the stamp with the remaining portion containing indicia information, bar code, a readable and unique serial number as well as the postage value. The USPS permitted seven denominations to be issued. The rates, and the total number of panes sold were: 2,852 for 23¢ for postal cards, 136,981 for 37¢ first-class letters, 1,491 for 49¢ large envelopes, 2,520 for 60¢ 2-ounce letters, 1,426 for 83¢ 3-ounce letters, 1,481 for $1.06 4-ounce letters and only 369 for $3.85 flat rate Priority Mail. The $3.85 value with only 7,380 stamps might be considered a modern rarity. A premium was charged for each stamp. For example, a 37¢ stamp sold for 85¢. A total of 147,120 panes (2,942,400 stamps) were sold during the 52-day test period, generating over $1 million in revenue for the USPS.

The most popular images submitted by customers were baby pictures, followed by family members, then pets. Near the end of the test period Stamps.com loosened its restriction to include images of adults. Each image submission was reviewed for its suitability; however, controversial images still appeared. After further consideration by the USPS customized postage was again permitted, beginning May 30, 2005. Almost immediately the number of private venders issuing customized postage began to grow.

Notes on Collecting

As one or more private contractors print a particular stamp, there has been a corresponding increase in varieties. For example, a stamp with the same design may appear as: **water-activated** or self-adhesive; as sheet, coil, or booklet stamps; with color variations; serpentine die cut variations; cropped design; and differences in the backing paper. For example, the 37¢ Flag coil stamp has varieties printed by the BEP (3622, 3632), Sennett Security Products (3631), Banknote Corporation of America (3633), and Guilford Gravure (3633A), each with distinguishing characteristics. One of the best parts of collecting twenty-first century stamps is that they are delivered to your home or office six days a week. Check your mail for some great twenty-first century collectibles!

Almanac

2001 – The USPS issues 42 definitive stamps, the highest number ever for a single year.

2002 – The USPS issues 242 varieties of stamps and postal stationary - a new record.

2002 – The cent symbol last used in 1985, returns as a "c" next to the numeric value on the 5¢ Toleware Coffeepot (3612). It is reintroduced to avoid confusing low-value stamps with those having dollar-values.

2003 – The Bureau of Engraving and Printing, once the sole producer of postage stamps, prints only the 37¢ Flag coil self-adhesive (3632).

2004 – The USPS tests the production, sale, and usage of computer-generated personalized postage featuring personalized images.

2005 – All postage stamps are issued in a self-adhesive format only, retiring the traditional water-activated adhesive.

2005 – The BEP produces its last postage stamp (3632) June 10. All subsequent postage stamps and postal stationary are produced by private firms.

What Others Have Said

Release of the United We Stand definitive in just 43 days

"It is fitting that the U.S. Postal Service - which has served the people of this nation since the dawn of our republic - is planning to issue the United We Stand stamp. For our primary job has always been to bind the nation together. Today, more than ever, the people of America are united in their purpose, their pride and their determination. This postage stamp is graphic representation of that unity."

—*Robert Rider, chairman of the USPS Board of Governors at the unveiling ceremony for the United We Stand (3549, 3549B, 3550, and 3550A) definitive on October 2, 2001. The stamp was issued on October 24, only 43 days after September 11. Nearly 4.8 billion stamps were produced.*

Heroes of 2001 semi-postal violates a USPS guideline

"A number of Linn's readers were quick to point out that the Heroes design shows three living individuals – an apparent contradiction of the USPS Guideline that 'no living person shall be honored by portrayal on U.S. Postage.' For the USPS, however, shades of meaning allow it to get around this rule. 'The key word in this guideline is 'honored" the Postal Service said March 12…In the case of the Heroes of 2001 design it simply was the best and most powerful image to use."

—*Charles Snee, "New Heroes Stamp to be issued June 7 in New York, nation's second semipostal remembers Sept 11,"* Linn's Stamp News, *2002.*

Twenty-first Century Private Stamp Printers add many surprises to new issues

"When a stamp printer produces an issue in a style or format that is new to the company, we can look forward to some unusual and sometimes puzzling features on the stamps….The 21¢ Bison Coil [3467–3468] assigned by USPS to Avery-Dennison is Avery's first venture into the small roll PSA [pressure sensitive adhesive] coil world and it is not disappointing the PNC variety specialists….At a very early stage, a collector found and reported a large nine-digit number printed at 35 stamp intervals on the backs of two or three adjacent stamps. The number is printed by black dot matrix…[and] serves as an internal accounting device….Avery is using it as a wastage control and to track the quantity of stamps process and shipped."

—*Alan Thomson, "Hunting the Bison: Hunting for Answers,"* The United States Specialist, *2001.*

Design Feature of the 37¢ Houdini Commemorative

"We wanted the kids to be able to see it. So we decided to go back to the Scrambled Indica. Dick [Richard Sheaff] added the chains to the design so that when you look at the stamp with the decoder, there's the subject wrapped in chains. It's a nice little play on Houdini and who he was."

—*Terrence McCaffrey, manager of stamp development, commenting on the use of Scrambled Indica to produce the disappearing chains that wrap Houdini (3651).*

The Greatest Honor of All

"I think a commemorative postage stamp is probably the greatest honor of all. As wonderful as the Grammy's and the Oscar's are, I think this tops them all."

—*Ginny Mancini, commenting on the stamp (3839) honoring her husband, composer/arranger Henry Mancini, on April 9, 2004, four days before its issuance.*

Examples of Postal Usage

Figure 6

A 23¢ Washington stamp (3617) printed by Avery Dennison, and bearing plate number V46, pays the post card rate.

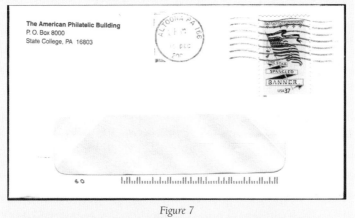

Figure 7

The 1893 Silk Bookmark stamp (3778) from the Old Glory Prestige Booklet (BK293), printed by Ashton-Potter, used on a mailing from the American Philatelic Building.

Where to Find More Information

• The relevant volumes of *Linn's U.S. Stamp Yearbook*, edited by George Amick.

Chapter 23
Air Mail Stamps

The history of aviation and *air mail* stamps are intertwined. The designs of air mail stamps depict the progress of aviation from early balloon ascensions to space flights. Air mail stamps illustrate the expansion of air mail service from the first regularly scheduled domestic air mail service in 1918, to its expansion around the world.

On May 15, 1918 President Woodrow Wilson and other dignitaries gathered in a Washington, D.C. park to watch an army pilot take off with the first regularly scheduled air mail. The plane took off late and instead of heading north toward Philadelphia and then on to New York, flew south and landed in a field! Fortunately for the publicity conscious Post Office, the southbound mail from New York did arrive uneventfully in Washington.

Figure 1

The first air mail stamp (C3), was the first of three issued in 1918, in conjunction with the first regularly scheduled air mail service, a route between Washington and New York.

Only two days previously, on May 13, the first air mail stamp was issued (*Scott* C3, fig. 1). This 24¢ stamp was intended the pay for air mail service on the new route between New York and Washington, and included 10¢ for **Special Delivery** service. The stamp depicted a Curtiss "Jenny," which actually carried mail on the new route. There had been close to one hundred pioneer air mail flights in the United States between 1910 and 1916; however this stamp boldly proclaimed the long awaited regularly scheduled service.

Instant fame came to our first air mail stamp when a pane of 100 was sold with the airplane upside down! Postal officials who tried desperately to get it back from its purchaser, William T. Robey, greeted it with chagrin. Robey, who bought it at a Washington, D.C. post office for its face value of $24, quickly sold it to legendary stamp dealer Eugene Klein for $15,000. Klein resold it to "Colonel" H. R. Green for $20,000. Green subsequently broke up the pane.

Twenty-four cents was a lot of money to mail a letter at a time when regular *First Class* mail was only 3¢, thus the air mail service was not heavily used. To promote greater use, the cost of the New York-Washington air mail was reduced to 16¢ on July 15 and then again on December 15 to 6¢ (but without special delivery service included). Stamps were issued for these reduced rates (C2 and C1).

Over the next few years air mail service expanded across the country. From its inception, the goal was to have trans-continental air mail service. On July 1, 1924, this goal was accomplished, with the establishment of regularly scheduled day and night service between New York and San Francisco. The Post Office issued a set of three air mail stamps for use on this transcontinental service (C4-6, fig. 2). The country was divided into three zones, New York-Chicago, Chicago-Cheyenne, Cheyenne-San Francisco. The rate was 8¢ per zone, hence the denominations of 8¢, 16¢, and 24¢ so that there was a stamp to pay each possible combination.

Figure 2

The first of three air mail stamps issued in 1923 (C4-6) for use of the New York – San Francisco transcontinental route.

The next milestone in flying the mail occurred when the Post Office Department signed contracts with private air companies to carry the mail. The first **contract air mail** routes (CAMs), began operating in February 1926. A set of three stamps, intended for use on these routes was issued (C7-9, fig. 3), each

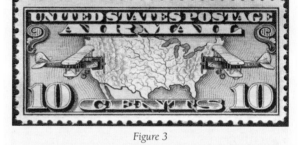

Figure 3

The first of three air mail "map" stamps (C7-9) issued in 1926 and 1927 for use on contract air mail routes (CAMs).

with a design that showed the map of the U.S. The 10¢ paid the rate for a one-ounce letter on a "contract" route of 1000 miles or less, while the 15¢ value paid for routes of 1000 to 1500 miles. The 20¢ value was for use on contract routes over 1500 miles, although no contract routes of this length were actually established during this rate period.

The country was mesmerized in May of 1927 when Charles Lindbergh flew non-stop from Roosevelt Field on Long Island to Paris. One of the most popular air mail stamps ever issued was placed on sale less than a month later (C10), showing his plane, the "Spirit of St. Louis." On May 26, 1928, this 10¢ stamp was issued in booklet format (C10a, fig. 4), the first ever air mail **booklet**.

Lindbergh's 1927 solo flight across the Atlantic was honored with a single stamp, and this booklet pane (C10a) of the same design.

Figure 4

Figure 5

The "Beacon" stamp (C11) was issued to meet the reduced air mail rate, effective August 1, 1928. Lights like the one shown on this stamp were erected across the country to make night flying possible.

The air mail rate was reduced from 10¢ per ½ ounce to 5¢ for the first ounce on August 1, 1928. Stamps issued to meet this rate were the beautiful "Beacon on Rocky Mountains" (C11, fig. 5), and the Winged Globe in both *flat plate* and *rotary press* formats (C12 and C16).

Two flights of the German Graf Zeppelin airship were commemorated by U.S. air mail stamps. A set of three (C13-15) was issued for use on the Europe-Pan America roundtrip flight in 1930 (fig. 6). The denominations, 65¢, $1.30, and $2.60 paid various rates for post cards and letters on different segments of the trip. The 65¢ stamp paid the rate for post cards sent by steamer to Germany and then by Zeppelin from Friedrichshafen to Seville, Spain, or

Figure 6

Issued during the depression year of 1930, this 65¢ stamp was one of three high denomination Graf Zeppelin stamps (C13-15) that carried mail on a special flight of the German airship.

via the zeppelin from Lakehurst, New Jersey, to Seville or Friedrichshafen. The other two values were primarily for use on letters, but the $1.30 value could also be used for post cards on certain segments of the flight.

In 1933 a 50¢ stamp (C18), fondly called the "baby zep," was issued for use on the Century of Progress flight. This flight was a "good will" flight by the Graf Zeppelin from Friedrichshafen, via Spain, South America, and the southern U. S., to the World's Fair being held in Chicago. Dispatch points in the U.S. were Miami, Akron, and Chicago.

On November 22, 1935, with a war threat with Japan growing, air mail service across the Pacific was inaugurated by the Post Office Department – Pan Am being selected as the inaugural carrier. A 25¢ trans-Pacific air mail stamp (C20, fig. 7) was issued, paying the rate for each of the three trans-Pacific zones: San Francisco to Hawaii, Hawaii to Guam, and Guam to the Philippine Islands. Thus, a ½-ounce letter from San Francisco to the Philippines was charged 75 cents. On February 15, 1937 a stamp (C21) was issued in a denomination of 20¢ for the reduced rate between San Francisco and Hawaii and also between Hawaii and Guam. At the same time the rate from the U.S. mainland

Figure 7

The first of three stamps (C20) issued in 1935 and 1937 for trans-Pacific air mail.

to the Philippine Islands was reduced to 50¢ and service was extended to Hong Kong. The rate from Hawaii to Hong Kong was also set at 50¢. A Trans-Pacific stamp (C22) was issued to pay these 50¢ rates. A combination rate of 70¢ was required for a letter flown from San Francisco to Hong Kong.

Air mail across the Atlantic did not begin until May 20, 1939, when Pan Am flew from New York to Marseilles, France via Horta (in the Azores) and Lisbon, Portugal. This service lasted a very short time due to the advent of World War II. A 30¢ air mail stamp (C24) was issued for this trans-Atlantic service.

A series of seven stamps, in different denominations but with the same design, was issued during the World War II years (C25-31). Known as the Transports, they depict a Twin-Motored Transport Plane and paid a wide variety of air mail rates. The airplane depicted on these stamps is an artist's rendition, rather than an actual plane.

In the years following World War II many air mail *commemoratives* were issued. For example, a set of three (C42-C44) issued in 1949 honors the 75th anniversary of the Universal Postal Union (fig. 8). The 50th anniversary of air mail service was honored in 1968 with a stamp (C74) depicting the same Curtiss Jenny used on the first air mail stamp.

Figure 8

Following World War II commemorative air mail stamps became popular. This one (C42), depicts the Post Office Building in Washington, D.C. and is one of three stamps issued to honor the 75th anniversary of the Universal Postal Union.

Many commemoratives have been issued honoring famous aviators. Amelia Earhart, who lost her life in the Pacific in 1937, is honored on a 1963 stamp (C68). Robert Goddard, an early experimenter with rocketry, was honored in 1964 (C69). The Wright Brothers (C91-92), Octave Chanute (C93-94), Wiley Post (C95-96), Blanche Stuart Scott (C99), Glenn Curtiss (C100), Alfred V. Verville (C113), Lawrence Sperry and his father, Elmer Sperry (C114), Samuel Langley (C118), Igor Sikorsky (C119), Harriet Quimby (C128) and William T. Piper (C129) were also honored.

In July 1969, America first put a man on the Moon. Planning ahead, the Post Office Department sent the *die* for a colorful new air mail stamp (C76) commemorating this epoch flight aboard Apollo 11, the space ship that carried the astronauts into moon orbit. The lunar module "Eagle" carried the die to the Moon's surface. Later, back on Earth, the printing plates for the new stamp were prepared using this die (fig. 9).

Figure 9

The First Man on the Moon issue (C76) was produced in 1969 from a die carried to the moon on Apollo 11.

The category of domestic air mail service was, for all intents and purposes, eliminated on October 11, 1975. Thereafter all domestic First Class mail would be forwarded by the quickest means possible. Thus a separate air mail service was unnecessary. After 1975 air mail stamps were only issued for international service. The USPS Board of Governors officially abolished domestic air mail service 18 months later, on May 1, 1977.

Figure 10

Issued in 1999, the Niagara Falls stamp (C133) was the first air mail stamp to use a silhouette of a jet plane instead of the words air mail.

On May 12, 1999 a new kind of air mail stamp was first issued (fig. 10). The design no longer included the words "airmail" or "air mail," but did include a small silhouette of a jet plane next to the value. Although considered air mail stamps, and listed in *Scott* as such, they may be used for any postal service.

Two stamps were issued in the 1930s to pay the combined air mail postage and special delivery fee. The first was issued on August 30, 1934 (CE1), and the second on February 10, 1936 (CE2). Both are 16¢ stamps (6¢ air mail plus 10¢ special delivery). The second was issued in red and blue to replace the earlier dark blue stamp, making it easier for postal clerks to recognize the stamp and provide the appropriate service.

A $1 stamp was issued on April 4, 1968, to pay for airlift charges on parcels sent to, and received from, servicemen overseas and in Alaska, Hawaii, and Puerto Rico. Although inscribed "Airlift," it was valid for all regular postage, and so it is listed by *Scott* as a regular stamp (1341) although some collectors consider it an air mail stamp.

Notes on Collecting

The first air mail stamp listed by *Scott*, C1, the 6¢ orange "Jenny," was not the first air mail stamp issued. The 24¢ stamp (C3) was the first issued, on May 13, 1918. *Scott* lists the set (C1-3) in order of denomination rather than chronologically.

The 24¢ "Jenny" was printed by two different passes through the printing press. **Misregistrations** created numerous stamps where the blue "Jenny" is higher, lower, or further left or right than normal, creating collectible varieties sometimes called the "fast plane" or "grounded plane." A similar phenomenon occurs on the Beacon on Rocky Mountains (C11).

A popular air mail collecting specialty is first flight covers. The establishment of new air mail routes was generally announced sufficiently in advance to allow collectors to prepare covers to be flown on the first flight. Rubber stamped cachets are common.

The Graf Zeppelin Issue (C13-15) is the key to a complete set of air mail stamps. Issued with a high face value during the Great Depression, only 61,296 complete sets were sold. They are readily available today, but are the most expensive air mail stamps to obtain.

The air mail rate was reduced from 10¢ per ½ ounce to 5¢ for the first ounce on August 1, 1928. Therefore the Lindbergh booklet pane stamp had an intended period of usage of only a little more than two months. Finding the stamp properly used on cover during this time is difficult. Even more difficult is finding a cover properly using the 44¢ "New Sweden" air mail stamp (C117), issued on

March 29, 1988. The foreign air mail rate increased to 45¢ on April 3. Hence, the intended period of use was just five days!

The 80¢ Hawaii air mail stamp issued in 1952 paid the domestic air parcel rate for a 1 pound package to zone eight (more than 1,800 miles). Though the stamp had a long life with many applications, collectors especially seek it used on shipments from Hawaiian flower growers.

Putting together a collection of domestic air mail covers, illustrating the different air mail stamps and domestic rates of the 1960s and 70s would not be expensive, but the covers may not be easy to find!

Almanac

1877 – The "Buffalo Balloon" air mail semi-official stamp (CL1) is used June 18 on mail carried aloft by Samuel Archer King in a flight from Nashville to Gallatin, Tennessee.

1911 – The 25¢ semi-official "Rodgers Aerial Post" stamp (CL2) is used in October on mail flown on some western segments of the coast-to-coast flight of the *Vin Fiz Flyer*.

1918 – First official air mail stamp is issued May 13, the 24¢ "Jenny" (C3).

1918 – On May 14 William T. Robey purchases the **inverted Jenny**, known only in one pane of 100 stamps.

1918 – First regularly scheduled air mail service between New York and Washington, via Philadelphia, begins May 15.

1918 – On July 11 the 16¢ "Jenny" stamp (C2) is issued for the reduced air mail rate, effective July 15 on the New York-Philadelphia-Washington route, which includes Special Delivery.

1918 – On December 10 the 6¢ "Jenny," (C1) is issued for a pending reduction in the air mail rate.

1918 – The first New York-Philadelphia-Washington flight at the 6¢ rate occurs on December 16.

Semi-official Air Mail Stamps

Two privately issued air mail stamps are forerunners of regular U.S. air mail stamps. Though not issued by the Post Office Department, they are considered semi-official. The first (CL1) was issued for mail carried on the "Buffalo Balloon" on June 18, 1877 from Nashville to Gallatin, Tennessee. The second (CL2) was issued for mail carried on an airplane named the "Vin Fiz Flyer" as it crossed the country in 1911. Aviator Calbraith Perry Rodgers attempted to fly coast-to-coast in 30 days in order to win a prize of $50,000 offered by newspaper publisher William Randolph Hearst. Rodgers completed the flight – but it took more than 30 days.

1919 – Specific air mail rates eliminated July 18. Until July 1, 1924 mail is carried by airplane on a space available basis, but the service is not guaranteed.

1926 – Mail begins flying on planes of private "contract" carriers February 15. A complex system of rates is used.

1927 – A simplified and uniform rate of 10¢ per half ounce becomes effective February 1 for air mail.

1928 – Air mail rate is reduced on August 1 to 5¢ for the first ounce and 10¢ for each additional ounce. The 5¢ Beacon Air Mail stamp (C11) is issued on July 25 for this rate.

1934 – Post Office Department cancels all existing air mail contracts on February 19 due to an outcry over bidding irregularities. United States Army carries air mail. Due to their inexperience, numerous Army aviators are killed in accidents. The Post Office eventually issues new closely controlled contracts to private carriers.

1969 – The 10¢ "Moon Landing" stamp (C76) is issued September 9 using plates made from master die that was carried to the Moon.

1975 – Domestic air mail service category is eliminated October 11, all domestic mail being transported by the fastest available method at the surface rate.

1977 – Domestic air mail rate is officially abolished May 1.

1999 – First air mail stamp with a small silhouette of a jet plane replacing the word "airmail" is issued May 12, the 48¢ "Niagara Falls" stamp (C133), paying the rate for an air mail letter to Canada or Mexico.

What Others Have Said

The Post Office carries mail by Air for the first time

"The first aerial dispatch of United States mail occurred in September last, when 43,000 pieces were carried from Aeroplane Postal Station No. 1 on Nassau Boulevard to Mineola, Long Island. The progress being made in the science of aviation encourages the hope that ultimately the regular conveyance of mail by this means may be practicable. Such a service, if found feasible, might be established in many districts where the natural conditions preclude other means of rapid transportation."

—*PMG Frank H. Hitchcock, 1911.*

U.S. Air Mail Service is the only practical aeroplane service in the world

"The Air Mail Service of the United States is the only practical commercial aeroplane service in the world. No service in foreign countries compares with it in magnitude, in continuous dependability and its benefits to commerce. Its record of performance during the fiscal year 1919 was 96.54 per cent, and this record was obtained with more than 30% of the trips made in rain, fog, mist or other conditions of poor visibility."

—*PMG Albert Burleson, 1919.*

Public demand leads to issuing the Lindbergh air-mail stamp in booklets
"Owing to the enormous demand for air-mail stamps in book form, the department has decided to issue the Lindbergh air-mail stamps in books containing six stamps, arranged in two sheets of three stamps each and interleaved with paraffin paper. The price of the new books will be 61 cents each and they will be first placed on sale at Washington, D. C., on May 26, 1928. Furthermore, on account of the Midwestern Philatelic Exhibition at Cleveland, Ohio, it has been decided to include the sale of these books at Cleveland on May 26, which is the last day of the exhibition."

—*R. S. Regar, Third Assistant Postmaster General, May 14, 1928.*

How quickly the 24¢ Jennys were printed – proving that haste makes inverts
"The production and distribution of this stamp probably set a record for speed. There was a span of just 5 days from the time the experimental air service was authorized by Act of Congress (Friday, May 10, 1918) until the first flights were started. President Woodrow Wilson signed the bill on Saturday, May 11th. On Sunday, May 12th, the stamps are reported to have been on the presses of the Bureau of Engraving and Printing. The first lot was delivered to the Washington postmaster Monday, May 13. The following day the offices in the three cities put supplies of the stamps on sale at 9 am. And near the noon hour on Wednesday, May 15th, the planes carrying the mail departed on their initial trips."

—*Henry Huff, "C3 – The 24c Air Mail Stamp of 1918,"* The Bureau Specialist, *1948.*

The 20¢ "Map" Stamp of 1927
"There was never a contract route that exceeded 1,500 miles in length during the period prior to February 1, 1927. So, no need existed for a 20-cent air mail stamp until then. On that date...the air mail rate became 10 cents a half-ounce, regardless of distance and whether carried on Government operated or contract routes. Since many letters weighed more than a half-ounce The Post Office Department issued the 20-cent Map air mail stamp on January 25, 1927, seven days prior to the new rate....Is it easy to find on commercial air mail covers? No! But it is worth searching for especially on covers used during the early months of 1927. Just remember the date, February 1, 1927, when the rate changed and start searching."

—*Philip Silver, "Random Thoughts on U.S. Air Mails,"* The Aero Philatelist, *1977.*

Examples of Postal Usage

Figure 11

A 1925 cover carried from San Francisco to Chicago on the transcontinental route. The 16¢ stamp (C5) pays the postage for a letter carried through two of the route's three zones.

Figure 12

The Transports (C25-31) were in common usage during World War II. The "examined" cover shown here was sent from Kentucky to London, England in 1943. The postage is paid by a 30¢ Transport (C30).

Figure 13

The Alaska Statehood air mail commemorative (C53) used on a 1959 cover to pay the domestic air mail rate of 7¢.

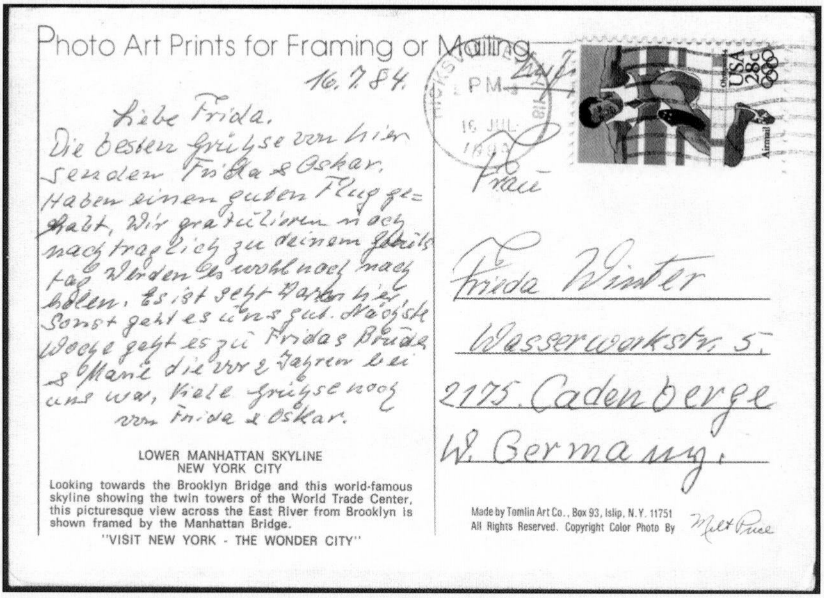

Figure 14

A 1984 Summer Olympics air mail (C102) used to pay the international air mail rate of 28¢ on a post card from Hicksville, NY to West Germany.

Chapter 23 | Air Mail Stamps

Where to Find More Information

- *The American Air Mail Catalogue* has been published in several editions through the years by the American Air Mail Society. It contains valuable information not only about air mail stamps, but also related topics such as pioneer flights, government flights, contract air mail routes (CAMs), and foreign air mail routes (FAMs).

- *The Transports* by G. H. Davis is a thorough study of the 1941-1944 Transport Air Mail stamp issue.

- *Via Airmail, An Aerophilatelic Survey of Events, Routes, and Rates.* Simine Short, Editor.

- *Airmail Antics* by Fred Boughner tells the story of air mail service from its inception in 1918 through 1934.

- *The Inverted Jenny: Money, Mystery, Mania* by George Amick is a thorough account of the inverted Jenny.

- *Flight of the Vin Fiz* by E. P. Stein.

- *The Aero Philatelist Annals* was published from 1953 until 1971 by an outstanding organization of air mail collectors. In it are some of the best articles on our early air mail stamps found anywhere.

- The *Airpost Journal* published monthly since 1931, by the *American Air Mail Society*.

- *Encyclopedia of Plate Varieties on U.S. Bureau-Printed Stamps* by Loran C. French provides detailed information on many plate varieties.

Chapter 24
Special Usage Stamps

Special Usage stamps, sometimes called Service Indicator stamps, are stamps intended for one specific function, which is generally specified on the face of the stamp. Although there are exceptions, Special Usage stamps are generally valid only for the specified function. These stamps are listed in the so-called "back-of-the-book," a reference to the physical location of their listings in *Scott*. Each category of Special Usage stamps has a distinctive letter-prefix as part of its catalogue number. A description of the various services named in connection with these stamps is provided in chapter 59.

Special Usage stamps can be divided into two major types: those sold directly to the general public for their use, and those intended only for use by post office or other governmental personnel, and thus not generally sold directly to the public. The gauges of perforations used for many Special Usage Stamps, the printing contractors, the types of presses used, and the varieties of paper used all parallel the developments of other postage stamps.

Stamps Sold to the Public

Special Usage stamps sold directly to the public include: Air Mail, Air Mail Special Delivery, Special Delivery, Special Handling, Registration, Certified Mail, Parcel Post, and Savings Stamps. While one or more stamps have been issued for each of these usages it was generally permissible, with some exceptions, to pay for services represented by these Special Usage stamps with regular stamps. Air Mail and Air Mail Special Delivery stamps are treated separately (ch. 23) and are not included here.

Special Delivery was a postal service provided from 1885 until 1997. Mail receiving this service would be delivered by special messenger to the addressee immediately upon arrival at the destination post office. There were, however, limitations on the hours during which Special Delivery service was provided, and on the distance that a messenger would travel. Mail given this service did not have to wait for the next regular delivery, a huge benefit to business and commerce during the late nineteenth and early twentieth centuries, and continued to be commercially important into the 1960s. Special Delivery provided no special treatment for mail prior to its arrival at the destination post office.

Initially this service was only available at selected, larger post offices. Later the service became available at all post offices.

Scott lists 23 Special Delivery stamps with an "E" prefix (fig. 1). The first 19 Special Delivery stamps illustrate an interesting progression in the methods of delivery used by Special Delivery messengers: a messenger on foot, a messenger on bicycle, a messenger on motorcycle, and finally a truck. This progression is interrupted by one stamp, E7, issued in 1908, depicting the Helmet of Mercury. This once unpopular stamp has been dubbed the "Merry Widow" by collectors, because of its perceived similarity to a hat inspired by the Merry Widow operetta. In the 1950s Special Delivery stamps were issued showing a letter being transferred from one hand to another (E20 and E21). The last two Special Delivery stamps (E22 and E23), issued in 1969 and 1971 respectively, feature a two-color design showing reversed arrows.

Figure 1

The first and the last Special Delivery Stamps, issued in 1885 and 1971 respectively.

Payment of the Special Delivery fee entitled a piece of mail to one attempt at special delivery. If that attempt was unsuccessful the piece of mail reverted to regular mail and was subsequently delivered in the ordinary manner. Through the mid-1940s once an attempt at delivery was made, the mail was generally marked with some variation of a "Fee Claimed" handstamp, indicating both that no further attempt at special delivery should be made, and that the post office so stamping the item was receiving the appropriate fee, from which the messenger was paid.

BEP designer Raymond Ostrander Smith had himself photographed on a bicycle. That photo was used as the model for the Special Delivery stamps (E6, and E8-11) which he designed showing a Special Delivery messenger on a bicycle. Two stamps have been issued to pay the combined Air Mail - Special Delivery fee (CE1-2) and are discussed in ch. 23.

Figure 2

The first Special Handling stamp, issued in 1925.

Figure 3

Only one Registration Stamp was ever issued.

Figure 4

Only one Certified Mail stamp was ever issued.

Special Handling is a service introduced in 1925 in which payment of the Special Handling fee entitles packages to the same expeditious treatment given *First Class* mail. In 1925 all day old chicks and baby alligators sent through the mail were required to be sent Special Handling. The Special Handling fee in 1925 was 25¢, and a deep green colored stamp of this denomination was issued that year (fig. 2). Later it was issued in light green. In April 1928 the rate structure was modified requiring 10¢, 15¢, and 20¢ stamps. They were issued in the same design as the 25¢ stamp, but were only printed in light green. All Special Handling stamps were printed on the flat plate press. Until 1955 Special Handling stamps were printed using the *wet* process. In 1955 the three lower value Special Handling stamps were reprinted from the original printing plates, using the *dry* process. *Scott* uses the prefix "QE" for the four Special Handling stamps.

Registration is a service providing special security for mailed matter. The only Registration stamp (F1, fig. 3) was issued in 1911.

Certified Mail is a service first offered in 1955. The purpose is to provide proof of mailing and delivery of First Class mail. There is only one Certified Mail stamp (FA1, fig. 4), issued in 1955.

Parcel Post, also known as *Fourth Class mail*, and more recently as Standard Mail (B), is a service the Post Office began providing for domestic packages on January 1, 1913. Twelve Parcel Post stamps were issued for this service (prefix "Q"), beginning in late November 1912. This series, designed by the BEP's Clair Aubrey Huston, is a favorite of many collectors. The various vignettes are something of a time capsule of 1913 America, with many of them relating to the movement of the mail (fig. 5). For the six months beginning January 1, 1913, only Parcel Post Stamps could be used for Parcel Post service, and they could not be used for any other service. This restriction was lifted on July 1, 1913 when Parcel Post stamps and regular stamps could be used interchangeably. The 20¢ Parcel Post stamp (Q8) depicts "Aeroplane Carrying Mail" and is the first stamp to depict an airplane.

Figure 5

One of 12 Parcel Post stamps issued in 1913, this one depicting a rural mail carrier on his route.

Savings Stamps is a generic name given to a category of stamps purchased by the public that served the dual purpose of creating personal savings and making a loan to the government. The Post Office operated a Postal Savings System from 1910 until 1966. In connection with that system the Post Office Department issued Postal Savings Stamps, (prefix "PS") from 1911 to 1941, and Savings Stamps (prefix "S") from 1954 to 1961. War Savings Stamps (prefix "WS"), and a Treasury Savings Stamp (prefix "TS"), issued by the Treasury Department, helped finance both the First and Second World Wars.

Stamps Not Sold to the Public

Special Usage stamps that were generally not sold directly to the public include: Postage Due, Parcel Post Due, Official stamps, Newspaper and Periodical stamps, and Postal Note stamps.

Postage Due stamps were an accounting device, which facilitated the collection of money owed to the Post Office from the recipients of mail. "Postage Due" was assessed on mail that was entirely unpaid or insufficiently prepaid, and, beginning in 1928, on business reply mail. Formulas for assessing the amount of postage due have varied over the years. The first Postage Due stamps were used in 1879, although post due charges were assessed and collected prior to the introduction of the stamps. The last Postage Due stamp was released in 1985. The dominant design feature of all postage due stamps is their value. Since these stamps were considered purely utilitarian, none of them feature any portraits or other special commemorative elements.

Figure 6

The first and last Postage Due stamps, issued in 1879 and 1985.

The first Postage Due stamps were printed by the ***American Bank Note Co.*** (ABNC), with the BEP assuming responsibility for production in 1894. *Scott* lists 103 Postage Due stamps, using the prefix "J" (fig. 6).

Figure 7

One of five Parcel Post Postage Due stamps, issued in 1913. Note the strictly utilitarian design.

This Official stamp issued for use by the Navy in 1873 was printed in a color Scott calls "ultramarine." Official stamps of the same design were issued for use by other governmental departments, but each department was printed in a different color. For example, Agriculture was yellow and Interior was vermillion.

Figure 8

Figure 9

One hundred dollar Newspaper and Revenue stamp issued in 1896.

Parcel Post Due stamps are analogous to regular Postage Due stamps, but facilitated the collection of money due to the Post Office from recipients of Parcel Post. The five Parcel Post Due stamps (*Scott* prefix "JQ") were required for the collection of Parcel Post Due for the first six months of 1913 (fig 7). Beginning July 1, 1913 they could also be used as regular Postage Due stamps, and even as regular postage stamps! Like regular Postage Due stamps they were considered utilitarian and prominently feature a large numeral indicative of value.

Official Stamps are issued for the exclusive use of governmental personnel, and are not valid for payment of postage by the public. Their purpose is to monitor postal use by government departments. The *Scott* prefix for Official stamps is "O". Official Stamps, first issued in 1873, were a response to perceived abuse and lack of control in the formerly used franking (signature) system. The **Continental Bank Note Co.** (CBNC) printed the stamps issued in 1873 for the Agriculture, Executive, Interior, Justice, Navy, Post Office, State, Treasury, and War Departments. The same designs were used for all of the departments, except Post Office (fig. 8). A distinctive color was used for the stamps of each department. In 1879 the American Bank Note Co. took over stamp production, and printed some Official stamps of the 1873 series on soft porous paper. The use of these Official stamps ended in 1884. Official stamps were once again issued for use by government departments in 1983. Unlike the earlier stamps they are not departmental specific, and all bear the Great Seal of the United States

In 1910 and 1911 Official stamps were issued for use by the Postal Savings System. Six stamps with the same utilitarian design were issued. The use of these stamps was discontinued in 1914.

Newspaper and Periodical Stamps were first issued in September 1865 to evidence payment of postage on bulk shipments of newspapers and periodicals. These large stamps were affixed directly to bundles of newspapers or periodicals. In 1875, the system changed and new smaller sized stamps were printed by the American Bank Note Co., and later by the BEP. These stamps, instead of being affixed directly to bundles, were placed in receipt books as evidence of payment, and were kept by the Post Office. The *Scott* prefix for these stamps is "PR". Two $100 stamps were issued (fig. 9). Except for revenue stamps, they are the highest denomination stamps ever issued. The use of Newspaper and Periodical stamps was discontinued in 1898.

Postal Note stamps (prefix "PN") were issued in 1945. They were used as a supplement to the Money Order Service as a means of sending amount under $1. Issued in 18 denominations, any amount from 1¢ to 99¢ could be constituted using no more than two stamps. The stamps were affixed to the portion of a U.S. Postal Note canceled by the clerk and retained by the Post Office. Use of Postal Note stamps was discontinued in 1951. These black, utilitarian stamps, printed on a rotary press, feature the words, "Postal Note" and its denomination (fig. 10).

Figure 10

One of 18 Postal Note stamps issued in 1945.

Notes on Collecting

All Special Delivery stamps are available in used condition at a modest cost. Early mint stamps are expensive. Special Handling, Parcel Post Due, Registration, Postal Note, and Certified stamps are available in used condition at modest prices. Some mint stamps are more costly. A complete collection of used Parcel Post stamps can be assembled for a modest cost. Mint examples of the higher values are somewhat expensive. There is a wide range of values for Official Stamps, Newspaper and Periodical Stamps, and Postage Due stamps. Many of them can be obtained for several dollars or less, while others require thousands of dollars.

Plate blocks of Parcel Post stamps exist both *without* a marginal **imprint** in earlier printings, and *with* a marginal imprint stating the denomination in words in later printings.

Numbers are assigned to Registered and Certified mailings at the time of mailing and appear on both the mailed item and its receipt. City specific Registry labels containing pre-printed numbers were used on registered mail to foreign destinations in designated foreign exchange cities during 1883–1911, and are eagerly sought by some collectors. These numbers are an important part of postal record keeping and control. Numbers were once assigned, in sequence, to Special Delivery mail as it arrived at the destination post office. The numbers were either stamped on the mail using a sequential numbering device or were written by hand.

Parcel Post rates are based both on weight and distance traveled. With a few minor exceptions, most notably the 1926-1927 air mail rates, the factor of distance has not applied to any other category of domestic mail since 1863.

Higher denomination Postage Due stamps are most commonly found on "Postage Due Bills". They were used in connection with the **Business Reply Mail** service, in order to collect the postage due on a large stack of business reply envelopes.

In 1879 the American Bank Note Co. took over stamp production from Continental Bank Note Co., and printed some Official Stamps of the 1873 series on soft porous paper. The paper used by American Bank Note does not glow under short wave UV light. After more than a century it is often difficult to distinguish stamps produced earlier by the Continental Bank Note Co., which *do* glow under short wave UV light, from those produced later by the American Bank Note Co., except by using UV light, which enables positive identification.

In 1899 the government sold 26,989 sets of discontinued Newspaper and Periodical stamps to the public for $5 per set. This is the source of the majority of stamps in the market today.

Almanac

1855 – The nationwide registration of mail begins July 1.

1865 – Newspaper and Periodical stamps are introduced in September.

1873 – The first Official stamps are issued on July 1.

1879 – Postage Due stamps are introduced on July 1.

1884 – Departmental official stamps are declared obsolete on July 5.

1885 – Special Delivery is instituted on October 1, using distinctive stamps.

1894 – The BEP assumes responsibility for printing postage stamps on July 1.

1898 – Use of Newspaper and Periodical stamps is discontinued.

1911 – Postal Savings System begins operation.

1911 – The only Registration stamp ever issued is released on December 1.

1913 – Parcel Post service is introduced on January 1.

1925 – Special Handling service and stamps are introduced.

1945 – Postal Note stamps are introduced on February 1.

1951 – Postal Note stamps are discontinued on March 31.

1955 – Certified Mail service is initiated on June 6 and the only stamp ever issued for this service is issued.

1966 – Postal Savings System is abolished on March 28.

1983 – Modern Official stamps, with penalty inscription, are introduced January 12.

1997 – Special Delivery service is terminated on June 7.

What Others Have Said

Establishment of Special Delivery service proposed

"Letters are now delivered by carriers at stated hours during the day from about 7 A.M. to 6 P.M., the frequency of trips varying in different cities…. Letters received, therefore, after the carriers go out on their trip, whatever their importance, must lie in the office until the next trip. After the close of the deliveries for the day, carriers' letters must lie over until the next morning delivery, which delay in many instances, fails to meet the wants of the writer or the object of the communication. Out of this want for a more speedy delivery have grown… private enterprises… and are diverting from the legitimate revenues of the Department thousands of dollars a year. The patronage bestowed on these enterprises evidences a public demand for a more speedy delivery for a certain class of correspondence."

—*Frank Hatton, First Assistant Postmaster General, 1883.*

How the early Special Delivery stamps were printed

"The Special Delivery stamps of 1895 (*Scott* E-5) and 1902 (*Scott* E-6) were printed from plates of 100 subjects, having vertical and horizontal guide lines. The sheets were cut vertically through the center on the guideline into panes of 50 stamps each. Therefore, we have guide lines unperforated on the vertical edges and guide lines on the perforated tops or bottoms of the stamps. In 1908, a new style Special Delivery stamp was issued showing a Helmet of Mercury. This stamp, which had a very short life, was printed from plates of 280 subjects, divided by vertical and horizontal guide lines into panes of 70 subjects each.

The sheets were cut along the guide lines which are found on unperforated edges. All Special Delivery stamps from 1911 through the 20 cent black of 1925 were printed from plates of 200 subjects and provided with vertical and horizontal guide lines. The sheets were cut...into panes of 50 stamps each. The...guidelines are found on unperforated edges of the stamps."

—*J. H. Davis Reynolds and John L. Steele, Jr., "Guide Line and Other Plate Markings,"* The United States Specialist, 1970.

The 10¢ Registry Fee Nov. 1, 1909 to March 31, 1923

"Just why the old 10¢ fee was reinstated [from 8¢] is unknown; perhaps it was because of a desire to deal with a round figure. Simultaneous with the increase in fee was an increase in the indemnity limit from $25 to $50....one stamp, the first and only of its kind, was issued to pay the registry fee exclusively. Known now to collectors as Scott No. F1, it first appeared on Dec. 1, 1911. Since postal employees and the public alike blithely ignored its existence and used ordinary stamps in place of it, the little blue eagle stamp was abolished by an order of the Postmaster General dated May 28, 1913. However, continuation of their use was permitted until supplies were exhausted. This stamp is quite common on cover; it is often found used as late as 1920 by philatelists seeking to create an unusual cover."

—*Barbara Mueller, "U.S. Registry Fees, 1855-1955 – Their Philatelic and Postal Significance,"* Twenty-First American Philatelic Congress Book, 1955.

The people complain, and the Post office listened – they lifted the restriction!

"The Postmaster General declares that the success of the Parcel Post is the greatest and most immediate that was ever scored by any new venture in this country and that the Bureau of Engraving and Printing has had to increase its daily output of Parcel Post stamps from five million a day to ten million stamps a day to meet the unusual demand. The use of special stamps for this service has been the subject of a good deal of criticism. It is presented that the special stamps were used to facilitate the accounting that was necessary in connection with this new and special service. Many newspapers attack this distinctive stamp regulation, as an example... 'A postage stamp is simply the formal receipt which the Government gives for money paid in advance. A ten-cent postage stamp signifies only that the Government has received ten cents for the benefit of the Post Office Department. Its meaning is exactly the same, no matter what class of mail matter it be affixed. Why, then, should the people be put to the unnecessary trouble of securing a distinctively colored stamp when they desire to use the parcel post?'"

—*Charles H. Mekeel, "Parcels Post,"* The Philatelic Journal of America, 1913.

Millions of certified mail forms distributed nationwide

"Certified Mail, a new service of the Post Office Department designed to give mail patrons most of the advantages of registered mail but at a lower cost and less trouble, will go into effect around June 1st 1955, or shortly thereafter, Postmaster General Arthur H. Summerfield has announced. (The exact date will be announced as soon as arrangements for distribution of millions of forms are completed.)....A special 15-cent "Certified Mail" stamp will be issued, but ordinary stamps may be used."

—*"Certified Mail to Start About June 1st,"* Stamps Magazine, *1955.*

Examples of Postal Usage

Figure 11

A 1905 Special Delivery cover. The sequential number, #65169 was applied when the cover arrived at the destination post office and was part of the Post Office's record keeping system. This cover was delivered as part of a regular mail delivery because the establishment was "closed" when the Special Delivery messenger attempted to deliver it. Payment of the Special Delivery fee only paid for one special delivery attempt. The auxiliary marking, "Fee claimed at Chicago, Ill." indicates that an attempt was made at delivery.

Figure 12

A Special Delivery stamp (E20) used on a 1957 cover. The Special Delivery fee was increased to 20¢ in 1952. The charge for Special Delivery was in addition to the regular first class postage.

Figure 13

Registered cover using the Registration stamp (F1) and a 2¢ Washington-Franklin stamp. The registration fee was charged in addition to the first class postage.

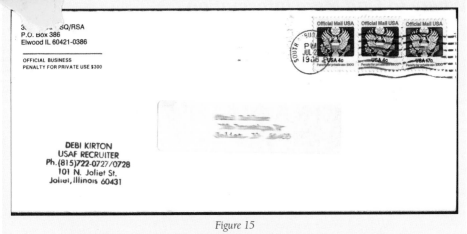

Figure 14

The 2¢ Parcel Post stamp (Q2) depicting a city carrier, used to pay the First Class rate on September 9, 1913, shortly after such usage became permissible. Properly used Parcel Post stamps are more commonly found from the period after July 1, 1913, when they could be used for other classes of mail beside Parcel Post.

Figure 15

Official stamps (0128 and 0130) used on 1988 Air Force recruiting brochure.

Figure 16

Two Postage Due stamps (J81) used in 1942 to collect 4¢ due on a piece of Business Reply Mail. The sender properly paid no postage on this piece of mail. The recipient paid the first class postage rate of 3¢, plus a 1¢ fee, as evidenced by the postage due stamps attached.

Where to Find More Information

- The United States Stamp Society published two relevant research papers: *Printing History of Postage Dues, Series of 1894 and 1930 Flat Plates*, and *Printing History of Special Delivery, Parcel Post, Parcel Post Due, Special Handling, Registration, Official Mail and Postal Savings Flat Plates* both by Wallace Cleland.

- The story of the Registration Stamp is told in Robert L. Markovits' *United States: The 10¢ Registry Stamp of 1911*.

- Henry Gobie's two books, *The Speedy: A History of United States Special Delivery Service* and *U.S. Parcel Post: A Postal History* are useful studies of Special Delivery and Parcel Post, respectively.

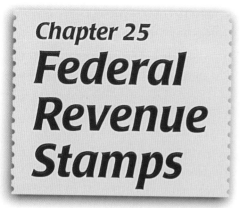

Chapter 25
Federal Revenue Stamps

Revenue Stamps tell the story of our country! They are a reflection of the wars we have fought, our political debates about how to finance government, and even our clashes over cultural values. Benjamin Franklin observed in 1789 that, "In this world nothing is certain except death and taxes." Revenue stamps have helped facilitate the collection of some of those taxes.

Revenue stamps were a contributing factor to the start of the Revolutionary War. The British imposed taxes on their North American colonies by the Stamp Act of 1765, to defray the cost of maintaining standing armies on the American continent. These taxes aroused strong opposition in the colonies and all stamp distributors were forced to resign their offices by January 1766. The Act was repealed that March. In 1773 a tax was levied on imported tea, and the famous tea party was held in Boston. The tax levied on tea, however, did not involve stamps.

In the early years of the republic, long before the days of the income tax, the primary options the Federal government had for revenue were tariffs, excise taxes (taxes on products), and documentary taxes (taxes on documents). What and who should be taxed (cultural and political questions) and at what rates (a financial question) were burning questions for the new nation.

Early Embossed Stamps
A tax was imposed on distilled spirits, both imported and domestic. As early as 1791, *embossed* revenues known as "Supervisors' Seals" were used on certificates for these taxes. The tax was unpopular and led to the so-called Whiskey Rebellion of 1794 in western Pennsylvania. In 1794 tax stamps were introduced in association with federal licenses to sell liquor. The embossed stamps are known with a value of $5.

On July 1, 1798 excise taxes were imposed on vellum, parchment, and paper. Embossed stamps of various denominations were issued with the

Figure 1

An example of the ten-cent Pennsylvania First Federal Issue embossing, (RM176), graphically cropped from a promissory note. In spite of their age, documents with the more common embossed revenues are not expensive.

names of each of the sixteen states, but were used to collect federal taxes, not state taxes. This series is known as the First Federal Issue (fig. 1).

The Second Federal Issue, replacing the first on March 1, 1801, also consisted of embossed stamps, but did not include state names. The stamps have two parts: one applied in the General Stamp Office and the other in the Office of the Commissioner of Revenue. They were used until June 30, 1802 when these taxes were abolished.

A Third Federal Issue was used from January 1, 1814 until December 31, 1817. Unique embossed designs were used for each denomination, five cents through five dollars. Federal licenses to work a still had their own embossed and printed designs during this period.

Documentary and Proprietary Stamps

The Civil War created a large array of revenue stamps. The history of adhesive revenue stamps for payment of federal taxes essentially began with the Revenue Act of 1862. The North started to tax many items to help finance the Civil War. Documentary taxes were levied on various documents. Excise taxes were levied on various manufactured items, and many *Proprietary Revenue Stamps* were issued to collect these taxes.

Figure 2

A fully perforated "First Issue" revenue stamp (R9c) originally designed for use on express receipts, but after December 25, 1862, usable to pay any documentary tax. The two-cent blue express stamp is also known imperforate and part-perforate.

The classics of the U.S. revenue field, which grew out of the Revenue Act of 1862, are the adhesive stamps known as the First, Second, and Third Issues. The First Issue adhesive stamps (*Scott* R1 through R102) were printed between 1862 and 1871 by **Butler & Carpenter** of Philadelphia. They primarily paid documentary taxes, although several proprietary and playing card stamps are included in this group. Except for the $200 value they were all printed in a single color, and most were designated for a particular purpose, such as "Power of Atty." and "Life Insurance". Initially these stamps could only be used for the purpose specified on the stamp; however this requirement was lifted after December 25, 1862, when the documentary stamps could be used interchangeably. The requirement was lifted, partially due to the difficulty of maintaining appropriate stocks of the various stamps. All of the various First Issue revenues are known *perforated*; some of them are also found imperforate or part perforate (fig. 2).

In response to attempts by some to remove cancels and fraudulently re-use stamps, new designs were issued in 1871 with blue frames, or multi-colored frames in the case of the $200 and $500 "Persian Rugs," and a **vignette** printed in a somewhat fugitive black ink. These are known as the Second Issue (R103–133). The resulting uniformity of appearance confused taxpayers, so still another set of new stamps appeared quickly with frames in different colors. These are the Third Issue (R134–150, fig. 3).

The 70¢ value from the beautifully engraved "Third Issue." The Third Issue replaced the confusing Second Issue only a few months after its issue.

Figure 3

All of the documentary taxes, with the exception of the tax on bank checks, were repealed in 1872. Only 2¢ stamps (R151 and 152) continued in use through June 30, 1883, when the remaining taxes ended.

Figure 4

When the Spanish-American War began at the end of the nineteenth century, documentary taxes were re-instituted. Stamps were issued for use from 1898 until 1902 (R153–194) and include the popular "Battleship" stamps (R161–172) that helped an aroused public to "Remember the Maine!"

Documentary taxes were issued again, for government expansion purposes, from 1914 to 1916, resulting in the stamps known as R195–227. With the advent of World War I came the War Revenue Act of 1917, resulting in the "workhorse" Series of 1917 (R228–286). Issued in several different perforation gauges, the Series of 1917 was used until 1940 (fig. 4), when it was replaced by the "dated reds" (R288–732). These "dated reds" (fig. 5), with face values ranging from 1¢ to $10,000, were issued annually with an overprint ("Series 1940", "Series 1941", etc.) until 1958. However the lower values (1¢ through $20) in the Series of 1954 were not **overprinted** with a year date. Neither was a second set of the high vales ($30 through $10,000) from the Series of 1958.

The Series of 1917 exists with several different perforation gauges, reflecting the efforts of the BEP to find perforations that were "just right." This one (R228) is perf. 11.

Figure 5

The so-called "Dated Reds" Documentary stamps were issued every year from 1940 through 1958. All the stamps have the same design, but were overprinted with the year of issue. This one is from 1944 and has a perforated cancel. These stamps have face values up to $10,000!

Figure 6

Spanish American War "battleship" revenues (RB20–31) were used to pay taxes on proprietary articles. The 3³/4¢ stamp (RB29) is shown here. Two different perforation types exist for these stamps: rouletting and hyphen-hole perforation. This example is rouletted, and has atypically large margins.

Figure 7

A private die proprietary stamp (RO57c), used by the Cannon Match Company of Stillwater, Minnesota. In general, four distinct types of paper were used in printing private die stamps, and the letter "c" in the catalog listing classifies this one as having been printed on pink paper.

These stamps, with no overprint, remained in use through the end of 1967. There was a final documentary issue commemorating the centenary of the Internal Revenue Service in 1962, which was reissued the following year with the centenary date removed (R733–734). Documentary revenues were no longer used after 1967. The gradual disappearance of these, and most other Federal revenue stamps, is paralleled by the ascendancy of the income tax to finance our government, a tax that does not require the use of stamps.

When the black and blue Second Issue documentary stamps appeared in 1871 a similar issue of green and black stamps was printed for proprietary items (RB1–10). In 1875 a solid-color series of Proprietary stamps was issued (RB11–19). These stamps can be found on silk and watermarked papers, some of the latter in *rouletted* as well as perforated versions. The "Battleship Maine" design that was used for documentary stamps during the Spanish American War was also used on proprietary stamps (fig. 6).

A simple black design was used on proprietary stamps resulting from the Act of 1914 (RB32–64). The final series of proprietary stamps, printed in dark blue, was issued from 1919 to 1921 (RB65–73).

The Tax Act of 1862 provided that a company taxed under the proprietary schedules could propose a stamp design for its own use! If approved, the company paid to have a die made and stamps produced. In return, the company could have advertising on its stamps, and buy them at a discount from the cost of the generic proprietary stamps. Called *Private Die Proprietaries*, they are also known as Match and Medicine stamps. There are

186 stamps for matches (RO, fig. 7), one for canned fruit (RP), 315 for patent medicines (RS), 33 for perfumes (RT), and 16 for playing cards (RU).

Tobacco and Alcohol Stamps

The first tobacco *taxpaids* appeared in 1868 and indicate payment of taxes on manufactured (cured, cut, and packaged) tobacco. They are denominated in ounce and pounds. For example, there are stamps to pay the tax of sixteen cents per pound for tobacco with stems, and thirty-two cents per pound for tobacco without stems. Various series of "taxpaids" were produced until the use of such manufactured tobacco stamps was discontinued in 1959.

Chewing tobacco was often packaged in tinfoil, or lead coated tinfoil. Payment of the tax was indicated by a stamp printed directly on the package. Paper wrappers with revenue imprints were used briefly from 1868 to 1869 and from 1878 to 1881.

Figure 8

A cigarette tax stamp, Series 109, the "109" denoting the year 1939.

The tax on snuff has been paid with an interesting array of stamps. From 1868 until sometime in 1870 thirty-two cents per ounce manufactured tobacco stamps were used to pay the tax on snuff. After 1870, stamps were printed specifically for use on snuff packages. Overprinted tobacco stamps from 1869 to 1871 were used in 1872, and then another series of snuff stamps was introduced. Snuff stamps were discontinued in 1959.

Taxpaid stamps were issued for cigars beginning in 1865. Until 1868 the tax was based on the value per thousand cigars, when the tax became $5 per thousand regardless of value. Beginning in 1917 tax rates were divided into five classes based on retail price. In 1932 a numbering system was introduced for cigar, snuff, manufactured tobacco, and cigarette stamps. Stamps issued in 1932 were designated as series 102. Stamps from 1933 were series 103, and so on (fig. 8). Small cigars were grouped with cigarettes until 1897, when they were put into a separate tax class.

There were taxpaid stamps for domestic cigarettes during the same period as cigars. Imported cigars and cigarettes had different tax rates and stamps (fig. 9). Stamps were issued from the late 1800s for "Imported Opium" and "Smoking Opium" made domestically from imported opium (fig. 10).

Four stamps were issued for use on packages of cigarette tubes (RH1–4). The first two of these were overprinted 1917 documentary issues.

Figure 9

A custom cigar stamp of the Series of 1875, used to pay the tax on a box of 25 imported cigars. The series of holes punched around the central portrait of William Henry Harrison was used to discourage washing and subsequent re-use.

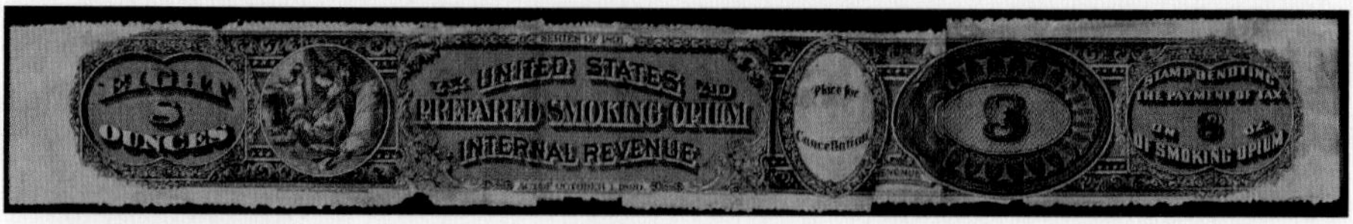

Figure 10

To help combat a nineteenth century drug problem a tax was levied in 1864 on prepared opium for smoking. Stamps were first issued in 1879. This is an eight ounce stamp from the series issued in 1890, when the tax was $10 per pound.

Tobacco sales tax stamps were used to pay the tax on tobacco sold over individual quotas. Overprinted stamps of the 1917 documentary issue (RJ1–11) were used in 1934 and 1935, until this tax was eliminated.

Tobacco has been heavily taxed, but so too has alcohol! Beer received its first stamps in 1866 (fig. 11). Cordials and wines had to wait until 1914 (RE1–204). Fermented fruit juice joined the list with taxpaid stamps in 1933 (REF1–10).

Figure 11

A 25¢ Beer Stamp (REA3) from 1866. Some Beer Stamps are taxpaids.

Strip stamps placed over the tops of liquor bottles until 1985 were once familiar to consumers (fig. 12). These strips were not used to collect the liquor taxes, but were more for federal control purposes. There are also stamps for industrial-proof alcohol and imported wines. Other stamps were required for moving and warehousing alcohol.

Figure 12

A Bottle Stamp, for use on a one quart container. The red stamps came into use in 1934.

Distilled Spirits and Excise Tax stamps (RX), paying taxes on batches of distilled spirits, were used from 1950 to 1959. Rectification Tax stamps (RZ) were issued in 1946 to cover a tax on distilled spirits when they were distilled again.

Taxes are still levied on tobacco and alcohol; however, stamps are no longer used to collect these taxes.

Still More Tax Stamps!

"Special Tax stamps" arose out of the Civil War Revenue Act of 1862. Taxes were imposed on various occupations for which "licenses" were issued from 1862 to 1866. In 1867 the title of these fill-in-the-blank forms was changed to "receipt" to avoid an apparent conflict between federal and state law. In 1873 these "receipts" gave way to the "Special Tax Stamp."

Very large Special Tax stamps began to be printed by the Bureau of Engraving and Printing (BEP) in 1873. Many unused copies are available today as punched (cancelled) remainders because Hiram Deats and E.B. Sterling rescued a large quantity of them in 1890 from destruction by the government.

Special Tax stamps have been issued through the years for dispensing of opium, dealing in oleomargarine, and ownership of a yacht, or certain equipment such as coin operated amusement devices (fig. 13). Some Special Tax stamps persisted into the twenty-first century.

Future Delivery tax stamps (RC) were used on futures contracts on the commodities exchanges. Series 1917 documentary issues were overprinted for this purpose and were used from 1918 until 1938.

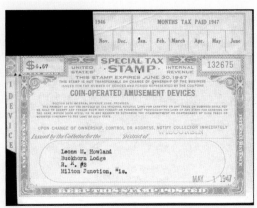

Figure 13

A special tax stamp licensing coin operated amusement devices to a bar in Wisconsin in 1946–1947.

Stock Transfer stamps (RD), for use with transactions on the national stock exchanges, were also initially 1917 documentary stamps that were overprinted. They were used until 1940, when a "dated green" series of Stock Transfer stamps was issued. The last "dated greens" were issued in 1952.

Some stamps in the First Issue were issued for use on playing cards, though some producers preferred to use the proprietary issues. There was no tax on playing cards after June 30, 1883, until the Wilson bill of 1894 that instituted a tax of two cents per pack. Two stamps (RF1 and 2) were issued that year for packs on hand and new shipments, respectively. The tax rate was changed several times and different designs and overprints were used until 1965 (RF 3–29, fig. 14).

A tax of 50% on the net profit on transfer of silver bullion was in effect from 1934 until 1963. The early Silver Tax issues used in connection with payment of this tax were overprinted 1917 documentary stamps (RG1–57). "Dated silvers" (RG58–132) were issued beginning in 1941.

Figure 14

A used playing card stamp from the 1931 issue (RF25). This was the last playing card stamp denominated in a monetary value.

Potato tax stamps were issued in connection with the Potato Act of 1935. One type (RI 14–18) was issued for potatoes that were tax exempt. Another type (RI 1–13), never actually used, was designed to pay the tax of three-quarters of a cent per pound on amounts that exceeded a grower's allotment. In 1936 distribution of the tax was declared to be unconstitutional and was eliminated.

Narcotic tax stamps (RJA1–106) were used on containers of opium, coca leaves, and their derivatives from 1919 until 1971. The first stamps were overprinted stamps from the 1914 and 1917 documentary series, and the 1919 proprietary series. These stamps are known as RJA1–41. From 1920 until the expiration of the tax in 1971 stamps were generally strips designed to run over the stoppers and caps of medicine bottles (RJA42–106).

Motor Vehicle Use revenue stamps (RV1–53) were used during the Second World War. They were pasted to the inside of windshields so all stamps, except the first, had gum on the face of the stamp. Boating tax stamps (RVB1 and 2) were issued in 1960.

Figure 15

Stamp for a half barrel of mixed flour.

Some products were occasionally subject to Federal taxation more for regulatory than financial purposes. Among these products were: adulterated butter, processed butter (rancid butter reprocessed for human consumption), a blend of wheat flour ground together with flour from another grain or material called "mixed flour" (fig. 15), oleomargarine (a tax being imposed at the urging of butter producers), and filled cheese (an inferior cheese made from skim milk with a lard or oleomargarine filling).

Perhaps some of the most unusual revenues are taxpaid stamps associated with cotton. The Tax Act of 1862 included a tax of a half-cent per pound on raw cotton, and the rate increased several times before the tax was repealed in 1868. Payment of the tax was normally indicated by long, harpoon-like metal shafts that could be driven into the bale, or by parchment or canvas tags held by wire with a metal point driven into the bale.

The Agricultural Adjustment Act of 1934 imposed a tax on quantities of cotton produced over allotted quotas. Metal tags were attached to bales on which no tax was due. These tags were used until distribution of the tax was declared unconstitutional and the law was repealed.

Other federal tax stamps have come and gone through the years. At the beginning of the twenty-first century there was only one federal tax stamp in use: the Firearms Transfer Tax stamps (RY), introduced in 1934.

Revenue Stamped Paper

Not all printed tax stamps are adhesive stamps. During the Civil War era some tax stamps were printed directly on documents, most commonly checks, and are known as **Revenue Stamped Paper**. This method of tax collection was used again during the Spanish-American War. These stamps exist in various denominations, designs, and colors. They are located in the RN section of *Scott* (fig. 16).

A Fee, not a Tax

Not every tax requires a revenue stamp, and not every revenue stamp pays a tax. While the distinction between stamps that pay taxes and those that pay fees is

Figure 16

An attractive bank draft from the Civil War tax era bearing an imprinted revenue to pay the two-cent check tax (RNJ-9). This imprint design, containing the instructive clause "Good for check or sight draft only" in small letters at the bottom, is quite rare.

not always clear, Consular Service Fee stamps (RK1–40), clearly accounted for fees (not taxes) paid to issue consular documents from 1906 into late 1955. Custom Fee stamps (RL1–8) had a similar use at the New York Custom House

Figure 17

Fees raised by "duck stamps" help to conserve wetlands, the habitat of ducks. This used copy of the 1963 Hunting Permit stamp (RW30), was cancelled, as required, when the hunter wrote his name across it.

from 1887 until 1918. They indicate collection of miscellaneous fees, but not customs duties.

Other stamps that paid fees include the ten different Camp stamps used by the National Forest Service from 1985 through 1988 (RVC). Two denominations of Trailer Permit stamps (RVT1–2) were used from 1939 into the early 1950s to pay the fee for a house trailer attached to a motor vehicle entering a national park or monument.

Hunting Permit stamps (RW), often referred to as "duck stamps" were first issued in 1934, with a face value of one dollar. They have survived into the twenty-first century, though the cost has risen over the years (fig. 17). A contest is conducted annually to choose a design for that year.

Notes on Collecting

All *Scott* listed revenues have an "R" in their catalogue number prefix. Items of embossed revenue paper are listed with a prefix of RM. Many adhesive revenue stamps use only an R in their prefix. Others use an R with one or more other letters, for example, RC for Future Delivery stamps, and RD for Stock Transfer stamps. Not all revenue stamps have been listed by *Scott*; however, *Scott's* trend has been to increase its coverage of them.

Many revenues have interesting cancels. Railroads, insurance companies, mining companies, steamships, and the like, applied their cancels to First Issue stamps.

Obsolete Revenues

Between 1954 and 1978, the Internal Revenue Service donated over 7 million obsolete twentieth-century revenue stamps to the Smithsonian Institution. In late 2004, following a lengthy debate, the National Postal Museum decided to sell at public auction those not retained for the national collection.

The Spanish American War "battleship" issue can be found with many printed and **hand-stamped** cancels of, for example, railroads and patent medicine companies. Some collectors collect Wine stamps with different winery cancels, playing card stamps from different manufacturers, or different automobile makes and models on the back of the Motor Vehicle Use stamps.

Some include, in their collections of taxpaid stamps, the Treasury Department prescription blanks for medicinal alcohol that were used during Prohibition. These were printed by the Bureau of Engraving and Printing and were used to obtain legal, taxed alcohol for medicinal purposes.

Perhaps the easiest proprietary stamps to find on an item are playing card revenues on unopened packs.

Collectors may be interested in **collateral** items that are not revenue stamps, but are part of the history of government taxation. Such items include lock seals that were inserted into distillery warehouse padlocks to cover the keyholes, and hydrometer labels used to determine the percent of alcohol in a liquid.

It is sometimes difficult to find revenue stamps in good used condition. Many collectors have seen an old cigar box with the remnant of a stamp divided between the lid and the side of the box. Other stamps have been varnished over, tacked up on the wall of a tavern or otherwise "roughed-up" in the course of fulfilling their function. Collecting these stamps while still attached to the original object, a pack of cigarettes for example, is another challenge. Whenever a stamp is found still attached to the original object, it is generally advisable to not remove it from the object.

There is a growing interest in collecting revenues on documents or other items. Certainly, embossed or imprinted revenues should not be cut off their documents, and it is generally better to leave adhesive items on documents as well. Collecting proprietary revenues on bottles and packages presents a logistical problem, but is worth the effort.

The **National Bank Note Company** began its printing contract on September 1, 1875, and its successor, the **American Bank Note Company**, succeeded to the contract in 1879. The Bureau of Engraving and Printing assumed the work in October 1880.

Almanac

1791 – Embossed supervisor's seals, the first federal revenue stamps, are introduced for imported distilled spirits on July 1.

1798 – First Federal Issue is used for the first time on July 1.

1801 – Second Federal Issue is introduced on March 1.

1814 – Third Federal Issue is introduced on January 1.

1862 – Revenue Law of July 1, 1862 becomes effective on October 1, requiring use of revenue stamps.

1862 – Requirement to match usage to purpose specified on stamp is lifted December 25, except for proprietary stamps, which still could not be used for documentary purposes.

1865 – First cigar revenue stamps are issued, while the last ones were issued in 1959.

1868 – Tobacco stamps are issued and continue in use until 1959.

1868 – Distilled spirits stamps are issued and continue in use until 1985.

1870 – Snuff stamps are placed in a separate category from tobacco issues, and are issued until 1959.

1873 – Large Special Tax stamps are printed by the BEP.

1883 – Documentary and proprietary taxes introduced in the Revenue Law of 1862 and subsequent amendments are repealed on July 1.

1886 – Federal excise taxes on oleomargarine begin. Tax on domestic oleomargarine ends in 1950 and on imported oleomargarine in 1977.

1894 – Playing card tax imposed by the Wilson Bill begins August 1, lasting until June 22, 1965.

1898 – Spanish American War tax period begins July 1, ending for many items on July 1, 1901, and the remainder of items on July 1, 1902.

1914 – Documentary and proprietary stamp taxes reestablished on December 1 by the Emergency Revenue Law of October 22, 1914; repealed in 1916.

1917 – An Act to provide revenue to defray war expenses and for other purposes establishes new proprietary taxes November 1; repealed November 23, 1921.

1917 – An Act to provide revenue to defray war expenses, and for other purposes, imposes various documentary taxes effective December 1; repealed on December 31, 1967.

1934 – Hunting Permit stamps, "duck stamps", are first issued on July 1.

1942 – Motor Vehicle Use revenue stamps are introduced on February 1.

What Others Have Said

A hydrometer is used to determine the specific gravity and purity of liquids
"Hydrometer labels are very pretty indeed and make a very nice showing in collected form. They are printed in black on white bond paper, the paper being sometimes thick and sometimes thin. Not all series appear on both papers. The

labels are oblong measuring 77 by 28 mm. There is a wavy line that runs entirely around the label. The frame measures 1¼ mm. In an oval at the left, is a portrait of Washington (except in the case of two printings, which bear the pictures of the then current Commissioner). In the main body at the top are the initials U.S. in large fancy letters with words INTERNAL REVENUE in white words on a black band across the center of the initials. Below, is STANDARD HYDROMETER in open letters and underneath it the signature of the Commissioner....[they] were issued by the Bureau and sent free to the manufacture of the hydrometer tube. They were placed in the tube and sealed when manufactured."

—*Paul R. Fernald, "Hydrometer Labels,"* The Bureau Specialist, *1947.*

Why are the 33⅓¢ beer stamps so scarce?

"The 33⅓ cents beer stamps have always been used less than any other denomination of these (beer) stamps. It was discovered, several years back, in the mining towns of California and Nevada, that a pack-mule could more conveniently carry a burden of two kegs of beer, each measuring a third barrel or weighing ten gallons, on either side, and as kegs of this size are used only in these districts, hence the scarcity of that denomination."

—*Robert S. Hatcher,* American Philatelist, *1888.*

Scott listed tobacco stamps

"There are two series of revenue stamps listed by Scott that are related to tobacco products. The stamps would belong in a topical collection related to either tobacco or smoking. One can find the Cigarette Tubes tax stamps midway through the listings for revenue stamps in Scott. They are the RH and RJ numbers. The first of these two categories has a grand total of four stamps. The stamps represented the payment of tax on cigarette tubes. Scott defines them as 'hollow tubes of paper. Each with a thin cardboard mouthpiece attached. They were sold in packages so that buyers could add tobacco to make cigarettes'....They are certainly not an expensive group to go after. But they can be challenging."

—*Richard Friedberg, "Cigarette Tubes and Tobacco Sale tax stamps,"* Linn's Stamp News, *1989.*

The challenge of revenue stamps

"It is by various and numerous channels that monies flow into Uncle Sam's coffers. Have you ever paused to consider how many of these methods employ stamps or have been checked by the use of stamps? These stamps, evidences of taxation, which the government uses, are the basis for the philatelist's revenue collection. One finds it quite an absorbing game to obtain just one stamp to illustrate each method used to collect revenue. The intensity of the game increases as one broadens out to find one stamp from every issue. Even so limited a general collection as just mentioned becomes a truly man-sized job."

—*George T. Turner, "What Comprises a Revenue Collection?"* American Philatelist, *1941*.

Examples of Revenue Usage

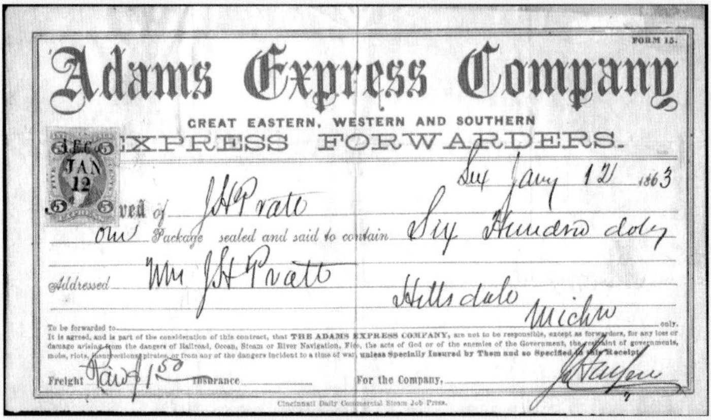
FORM 15.

Adams Express Company

GREAT EASTERN, WESTERN AND SOUTHERN

EXPRESS FORWARDERS.

Freight

Insurance

For the Company,

Cincinnati Daily Commercial Steam Job Press.

Figure 18

An Early Matching Usage of an imperforate 5¢ First Issue express revenue used on an Adams Express receipt early in 1863. This is an EMU (Early Matching Usage) – a term usually applied to a First Issue stamp used in the last few days of 1862 or early 1863 when the stamp is used on the type of document for which it was intended. RMU is the acronym for "Required Matching Usage", and applies to stamps used from October 1 through December 25, 1862 when the matching of the stamp and the document was required. Note the printed express cancel on the stamp.

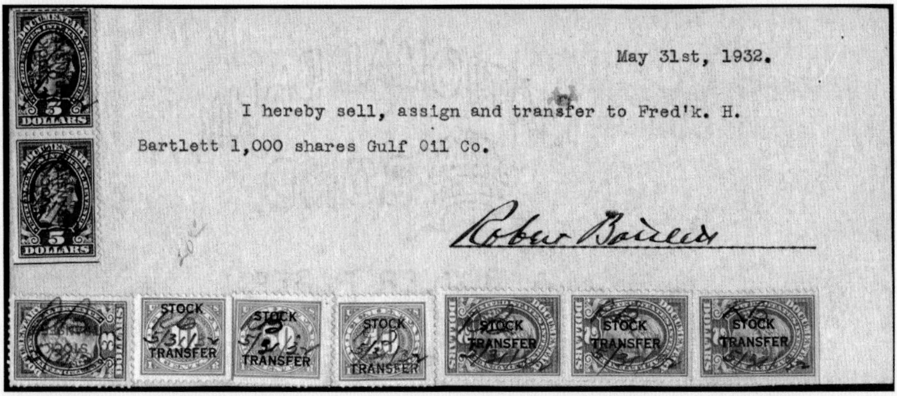
May 31st, 1932.

I hereby sell, assign and transfer to Fred'k. H. Bartlett 1,000 shares Gulf Oil Co.

Figure 19

An order to sell 1,000 shares of Gulf Oil in 1932. The stock transfer stamps pay a tax of $20.

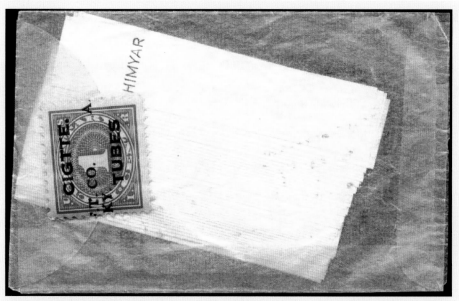

Figure 20

A cigarette tubes tax stamp (RH1) on a packet of tubes. The stamp is an overprinted documentary stamp from the Series of 1917.

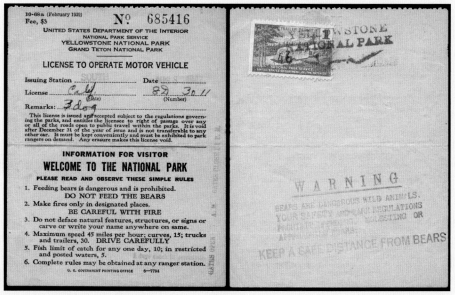

Figure 21

"License to Operate Motor Vehicle" issued in Yellowstone National Park in 1943, with a Trailer Permit stamp (RVT2).

Where to Find More Information

- Richard Friedberg's *Introduction to United States Revenue Stamps* is a basic text, full of information needed to understand revenue collecting.

- *An Introduction to Revenue Stamps* by Bill J. Castenholz is another good, well illustrated, introductory book.

- *The Revenue Stamps of the United States*, by Elliot Perry writing as Christopher West, goes into some detail concerning nineteenth century issues and illustrates most of the general issue proprietary and documentary stamps.

- *An Historical Reference List of the Revenue Stamps of the United States, Including the Private Die Proprietary Stamps (The Boston Revenue Book)*, written by George L. Toppan, Hiram E. Deats and Alexander Holland is an indispensable reference for the Civil War era documentary and proprietary revenues. Modern reprints are readily available.

- *Springer's Handbook of North American Cinderella Stamps Including Taxpaid Revenues* by Sherwood Springer is a must for collectors of taxpaid revenue stamps.

- *A Catalog of United States Revenue-Stamped Documents of the Civil War Era by Type and Tax Rate*, by Michael Mahler is a gorgeous book filled with illustrations and information on the Civil War documentary taxes.

- *Civil War Era Occupational Licenses, 1863-1873* by John Alan Hicks explores the various forms used in the collection of taxes on occupations.

- *The Springfield List of United States Internal Revenue Stamps, Hydrometers, Lock Seals and Etc.*, by J. Delano Bartlett and Walter W. Norton.

- Two specialized catalogs of taxpaids are *United States Internal Revenue Tax-Paid Stamps Printed on Tin-Foil and Paper Tobacco Wrappers* by John Alan Hicks, and *History of Oleomargarine Tax Stamps and Licenses in the United States*, by Carter Litchfield.

- Most of the nineteenth century general issues are illustrated in color at: www.theswedishtiger.com/usstamps.

- The American Revenue Association maintains a helpful website at: www.revenuer.org.

- There is a general reference to *Scott* Listed revenues at: www.rdhinstl.com/revs.htm.

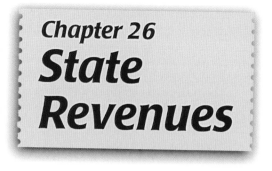

Chapter 26
State Revenues

Most people are familiar with those intimidating tags sometimes attached to a pillow or mattress. They have an official looking stamp affixed, warning that they are not to be removed under penalty of law. What most of those people may not realize is they have encountered a state revenue stamp!

Revenue stamps have been issued by federal (ch. 25), state, and local governments to document the payment of various taxes and fees, as well as for purposes of control and accounting. State Revenue stamps include not only stamps issued by states, but by local jurisdictions as well, including Indian Reservations.

The history of state revenues dates back to the Colonial Period when revenue stamps were issued by the Colony of Massachusetts in 1755. Most were embossed, in the style of notary seals. New York Colony also used embossed stamps from 1757 to 1760, while Delaware, Maryland, and Virginia used embossed stamps to collect state taxes intermittently between 1793 and 1856.

Figure 1

California issued the first adhesive revenue stamps in the United States in 1857. This one was designated for use with a Second of Exchange bill, paying a tax of 60¢ for an amount above $200, but less than $300.

There are imprinted revenues from what is now California from the 1820s and 1830s, while it was a part of Mexico. They are known as *papel sellado*. In 1857 California obtained the distinction of being the first state in the Union to issue adhesive revenue stamps (fig. 1). The stamps were used to pay California state taxes on various transactions and predate Federal adhesive revenues by about five years.

Nevada issued stamps to pay documentary taxes in 1865. Louisiana issued stamps for a tax on lottery tickets in 1866. Alabama produced two denominations of stamps to pay the tax imposed in 1867 on documents bearing the seal of a public officer.

States and localities have taxed a broad array of products and services, and produced many stamps to facilitate payment. Stamps have been used to pay taxes on, among other things, financial transactions (fig. 2), oysters, dog food, fertiliz-

Figure 2

A $2 New York State stamp used to pay a stock transfer tax.

er and dry cleaning. Other stamps denote a fee paid for licensing, or a service such as an inspection of the quality of a product.

The twentieth century witnessed a rapid growth both in the number and types of state revenue stamps. There is a great variety of state revenue stamps which includes: Florida Peat and Humus stamps, an early Wyoming sportsman's license, **perfins** in cigarette decals, Maryland perfins, Bellingham, Washington Condition Sales stamps, a plate variety in the North Carolina Cleaning & Pressing stamps, and Oklahoma documentaries.

State Revenue stamps are generally not *Scott* listed. *Scott* does list state duck hunting permit stamps, but state stamps for hunting other types of game are not listed.

Notes on Collecting

There are no published albums for these stamps, so one cannot collect them by filling in blank spaces. Additionally, there are too many different stamps for anyone to collect all of them, and new items are frequently discovered. State revenues are for collectors with perseverance, who are not afraid of the unknown. But it is well worth the effort, as many of these stamps are beautiful, and it is possible to inexpensively own rarities.

Almanac

1857 – California issues the first adhesive revenue stamps in the United States.

1865 – Nevada issues adhesive revenues.

1866 – Louisiana issues lottery ticket stamps.

1867 – Alabama issues stamps for a tax on seals of public officers.

1938 – The first state duck stamp is issued in Ohio.

What Others Have Said

State Revenues provide an almost endless array of varieties

"There is the fascination of state revenues themselves; the endless varieties of issues: Upland Game Bird stamps, Frog licenses, Honey tax, Canned Dog Food, Oysters, Perfume, Apple and on and on. You name it and there is probably a state that once taxed it and produced a stamp for it."

—*Gerald Abrams, welcoming the State Revenue Society as an American Revenue Association chapter, December 1975.*

The District of Columbia issued Beverage Tax paid stamps

"As a group they differ from any other issues with which I am acquainted, in as much as there are four sets of stamps for different kinds of beverages. The stamps for the same amount of liquid are identical in design for all four kinds but each set has its own color and price. The stamps of a set are identical except for the large numeral in the center denoting the amount of liquor in the container. There are stamps for eight different capacities of containers between 1 gallon and 1/80th of a gallon....the Alcohol stamps are yellow; Spirits – red; Champagne – purple and Wines – Green. The stamp is the regular double size; horizontal; 200 subjects to the sheet or 50 subjects to the pane. They are a flat plate product, perforated 11 and printed on unwatermarked paper....The first use of these stamps was in May 1934."

—*Hugh M. Southgate, "District of Columbia Beverage Tax Paids,"* The Bureau Specialist, *1937.*

Fruit Tax Stamps used to develop funds to promote the sale of Washington fruit

"The Washington State Fruit Commission...used tax stamps on bills of lading and transportation certificates from 1947 through 1952. The funds derived from the sale of these stamps were used to promote the sale of Washington grown apricots, cherries, peaches, prunes and Bartlett pears. The procedure was similar to the one used by the Washington State Apple Commission....The fruit stamps were printed with a border and top panel in yellow-green for the two 1947 issues, and in deep blue for the 1948 issue. The panel on the two-value 1949 set is in orange and on the 1951 set is red....Originally, shippers of soft fruit affixed the stamps on the railroad bills of lading or on the Commission's copy of the Certificate of Transportation used by truckers."

—*Fred E. Carver, "State Fruit Tax Stamps for Promoting Sales,"* American Philatelist, *1961.*

New York produced revenue stamps to try and restrict the processing of fish
"He noticed a hitherto unchronicled tax stamp on a tin of Processed Fish Pate. A 25 x 33mm. 5¢ stamp printed in black on blue paper, perf. 12 and reading: STATE OF NEW YORK / CONSERVATION DEPARTMENT / ALBANY, N.Y. /PROCESSED/ TROUT AND GAME STAMP / PAID 5 CENTS. The stamps were a rather short-lived issue and of no denomination other than 5¢. They were printed in gummed sheets of 100 overprinted with a different consecutive serial number in red figures 4mm high. The stamps were in use in New York only from April 13, 1941 to March 2, 1944. These stamps were apparently an excise tax with the added intention of restricting the wholesale processing and sale of certain species of trout and game birds....The Conservation Department ran into difficulties of enforcement, both legal and technical."

—*George D. Cabot, "The Story of the Discovery of the Trout and Game Stamp,"* Fourteenth Philatelic Congress Book, *1948.*

Examples of Revenue Usage

Figure 3
Federal Hunting Permit Stamp or "Duck Stamp" (RW19), used on the same document with a 1952 Virginia Bear and Deer Hunting Stamp.

Figure 4

This mattress tag has a Pennsylvania revenue, an Indiana inspection stamp and a Detroit Department of Health municipal revenue on it.

Figure 5

Detail of a stock certificate showing a 10¢ Florida Documentary Tax Stamp.

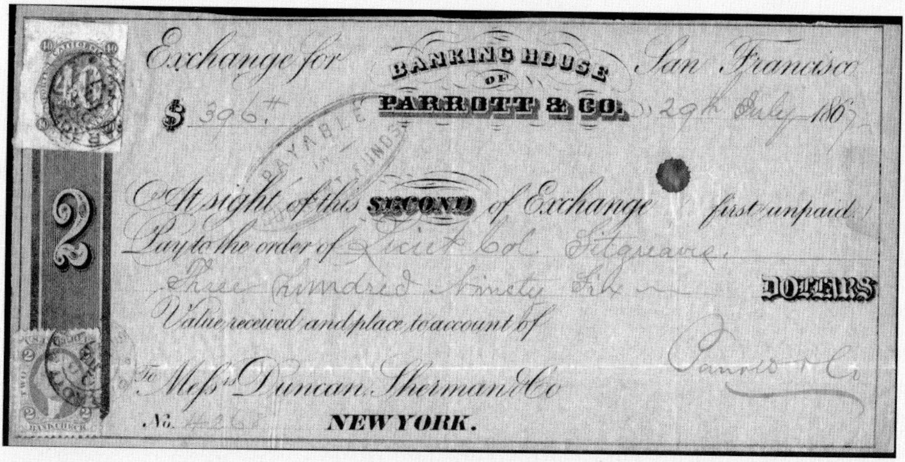

Figure 6

"Bill of Exchange" which has a federal revenue stamp and a stamp from the second California state series attached.

Where to Find More Information

- The State Revenue Society has a website at: www.hillcity-mall.com/SRS/. One of the valuable features of this site is an online catalog of city and county revenue stamps.

- Elbert S. Hubbard's *State Revenue Catalog*.

Chapter 27
U.S. Possessions, Usages Abroad, and Occupied Areas

American postal service has followed the flag around the globe to a number of U.S. possessions. It has also been present "off-shore" both for civilian populations and for the American military.

Possessions

The term "U.S. Possessions" may be somewhat misleading since not all of these far-flung places are, or ever were, United States "possessions" in the strict sense. In Scott, they include the Canal Zone, Cuba, Danish West Indies, Guam, Hawaii, Philippines, Puerto Rico, and Ryukyu Islands. The postal history of each possession is tied to a very specific period of time. Many of these areas have extensive postal histories before or after the period of time presented here.

Spanish-American War yields four possessions

The Spanish-American War of 1898–1899 left quite a legacy for stamp collectors. Stamps were issued for use in the former Spanish possessions that America acquired as a result of winning the war: Cuba, Guam, Philippines, and Puerto Rico. In addition, there are many revenue stamps issued to finance the war (ch. 25).

Cuba U.S. administration of Cuba lasted almost three and a half years, ending when U.S. military rule was replaced by full Cuban autonomy in 1902. In 1899 several stamps of the Series of 1894 (ch. 7) were overprinted for use in Cuba. They were quickly replaced by five pictorial stamps printed by the Bureau of Engraving and Printing (BEP), which are simply inscribed "Cuba."

Guam Unlike Cuba, which the United States held in trust only briefly, Guam was ceded to the U.S. after the Spanish-American War. It remains a U.S. possession and its residents are U.S. citizens. In 1899, selected Series of 1894 stamps were overprinted "GUAM" for use on that island. Guam was supplied with non-overprinted U.S. stamps beginning in 1901, and continues to use U.S. stamps today. For one year, from April 8, 1930 until April 8, 1931, locally printed stamps and overprinted U.S. Philippine stamps (GUAM GUARD MAIL) were used for local service.

Philippines Series of 1894 stamps were overprinted for use in the Philippines in 1899 (fig. 1). When the Series of 1902 (ch. 8), was released, each denomination was overprinted for use in the Philippines. Beginning in 1906, the BEP printed several series of stamps inscribed "Philippine Islands – United States of America." One of the more interesting of these is Scott 357, issued on May 3, 1932. It was intended to depict Pagsanjan Falls in the Philippines, and the stamp carries a banner with that identification; however, the **vignette** actually depicts Vernal Falls in Yosemite National Park! In 1935, the Philippines became a "Commonwealth" of the United States. This status ended after World War II when, in 1946, the Philippines became an independent nation. During the "Commonwealth"

Figure 1

Block of four 3¢ Jackson stamps from the First Bureau Issue, overprinted for use in the Philippines. Similar overprints were made for use in Puerto Rico, Guam, and Cuba.

period some earlier stamps were issued with a "Commonwealth" overprint. Also a variety of new pictorial issues was prepared by the BEP, including six stamps issued to commemorate the 33rd International Eucharistic Congress, held in Manila in 1937. The Philippines endured Japanese occupation. The Japanese both overprinted earlier Philippine issues and printed their own stamps. The Japanese added insult to injury by overprinting one BEP printed stamp in 1942 to read, "Congratulations / Fall of / Bataan and / Corregidor / 1942." After liberation, the same issue was overprinted VICTORY.

Puerto Rico Residents of Puerto Rico are U.S. citizens, and Puerto Rico remains a U.S. commonwealth. Series of 1894 stamps were over-printed "Porto Rico" and then "Puerto Rico." Puerto Rico today uses U.S. stamps.

Other U.S. Possessions
Hawaii Our 50th state began its philatelic life as an independent kingdom. Hawaii's first stamps, the so-called "Hawaiian Missionaries," were issued in 1851-1852 and are exceedingly rare and valuable. Fortunately for those collectors who will never own any of them, these four stamps, and a unique cover bearing two of them, are reproduced on a mini-sheet issued by the U.S. Postal Service in 2002 (fig. 2). Until 1859, domestic mail was free in Hawaii, so the stamps issued up to that time were needed only for international mail, primarily to the United States.

The "Grinnell" Missionaries

In 1919 a group of allegedly authentic Hawaiian Missionaries surfaced in California. Known as the "Grinnell" Missionaries after their 1919 owner, they have been surrounded by mystery and controversy. Famed collector Alfred Caspary purchased them but concluded they were fakes and returned them. A California judge agreed in 1922 that they were fakes. The defenders of their authenticity continued to press their case through the years, but were dealt a blow in 2004 when the Royal Philatelic Society in London also concluded that they are fakes.

In 1893 American plantation owners led a coup against Queen Lilinokalani. A provisional government was formed and some royal stamps were overprinted "Provisional Govt. 1893." In 1894 a republic was declared and American plantation owner Sanford B. Dole (of pineapple fame) became president. The Republic of Hawaii issued nine stamps, including one honoring Dole (79, fig. 3). After annexation by the U.S. in 1898, the island's inhabitants used U.S. stamps. In addition to postage stamps, postal stationery was issued by the kingdom, the provisional government, and the republic.

Canal Zone As a result of the rich and colorful history of the Canal Zone, collectors have been given 75 years of great stamps. The first stamps issued for use in the Canal Zone, in 1904, began life as Columbian stamps. They were subsequently overprinted "Panama" by the new break-away republic, and then overprinted a second time – "Canal Zone." These were quickly followed, still in 1904, by five stamps from the Series of 1902 overprinted "Canal Zone / Panama." Over the course of the next twenty years some sixty Republic of Panama stamps were used with

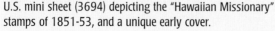

Figure 2

U.S. mini sheet (3694) depicting the "Hawaiian Missionary" stamps of 1851-53, and a unique early cover.

Figure 3

25¢ Republic of Hawaii stamp honoring President Sanford Dole (79).

some variation of a "Canal Zone" overprint (fig. 4). Beginning in 1924, stamps of the Series of 1922 (ch. 10) were overprinted for use in the Zone. The U.S. Sesquicentennial stamp of 1926 was overprinted for the same purpose. Beginning in 1928, the BEP printed stamps specifically for the Canal Zone. These stamps are a virtual pictorial history of the Panama Canal. Some of the stamps honor men such as William Gorgas, George Geothels, and of course Teddy Roosevelt. Others depict the construction and operation of the canal (fig. 5). One stamp, the 1962 Thatcher Ferry Bridge stamp (157), exists as a printing error with the bridge omitted! Though this stamp is of the same vintage as the infamous and massively reprinted U.S. Dag Hammarskjöld invert (1204), the Thatcher Ferry Bridge error was not intentionally reprinted by postal authorities. The Canal Zone Postal Service ceased operations on September 30, 1979.

Figure 4

An early Republic of Panama stamp overprinted for use in the Canal Zone.

U.S. Virgin Islands The Danish West Indies (DWI) was purchased from Denmark in 1917, and became known as the U.S. Virgin Islands. Safeguarding the Panama Canal was one justification for the purchase. Denmark had issued stamps for use in its colony, and U.S. Postal officials honored those stamps for the first six months following the transition to U.S. sovereignty (March 31, 1917 to September 30, 1917). U.S. stamps were also available for use during this period. *Mixed frankings* of U.S. and DWI stamps were permitted, and such frankings are highly sought after today! Three playing card revenue stamps are the only U.S. stamps issued specifically for this territory.

Figure 5

A 1939 5¢ Canal Zone stamp showing "Gailliard Cut – After." The "before" version is found on the 3¢ stamp in the same series.

American Samoa The U.S. extended its influence to the port of Pago Pago in East Samoa before 1898. The old kingdom of Samoa was divided with the U.S. taking possession of the eastern portion. Only U.S. postage has been used there since 1898.

Finally, some collectors might include, in the category of U.S. possessions, those stamps of more recent vintage issued by the Marshall Islands, Micronesia, and Palau which were once part of the post World War II U.S. Pacific Trust Territory. These stamps are not *Scott Specialized* listed.

Usages Abroad

U.S. postage has occasionally been used outside the U.S., in areas which are not possessions. The three authorized ways this can occur are when postal services are extended to U.S. civilian or military personnel while on duty in foreign countries, by special agreement by a host country to permit the operation of a U.S. post office on its territory, and on U.S. flag and naval ships.

Figure 6

A 10¢ on 5¢ blue Washington-Franklin (K5) overprinted for use by the U.S. Postal Agency, Shanghai, China.

Usages abroad can be found as early as the first stamps issued in 1847. Some were used in Canada to pay all or part of postage from that country to the U.S. By international agreement, the stamps of one country can be used on mail from that country's embassies and consulates back to the home country when they are carried to the home country by diplomatic pouch and then placed in the mails. For example, there are covers bearing 1873 Department of State Official stamps with Washington, D.C. postmarks which actually originated abroad.

During the nineteenth century it was common for major powers to establish postal agencies in foreign nations. The U.S. Postal Agency most familiar to collectors operated in Shanghai, China from 1867 until December 1922. It was used by businesses, merchants, and residents of China sending letters to relatives in the U.S. In 1919, Washington-Franklin stamps were overprinted SHANGHAI/CHINA by the BEP for use at the Postal Agency in Shanghai (K1-16, fig. 6). In 1922 two Washington-Franklin stamps were locally overprinted (K17 and K18). U.S. Postal Agencies also operated with the occupation of Vera Cruz, Mexico, in 1916 and the ***American Expeditionary Force*** (AEF) in Siberia at the end of World War I. No stamps were surcharged in connection with those operations, although postmarks do exist. Baranquilla, Colombia was the location of the last regular U.S. Postal Agency, which operated from at least 1931 until 1945.

There have been other authorized usages abroad. For example, the 1978 U.S. souvenir sheet (1757) honoring the Canadian National Show, CAPEX, was canceled at the exhibition station. Maritime mail, both civilian and naval, represents usage abroad. Some ships had operating U.S. post offices from 1891 into the 1930s. Most U.S. civilian ships and larger naval vessels are equipped to receive mail bearing U.S. stamps. Such mail may bear the marking **Paquetbot** or Posted at Sea or Sea Post.

Occupied Areas

The United States administered the Ryukyu Islands from 1945 until they reverted to Japanese sovereignty in 1972. Over two hundred stamps were issued during these years. They are listed in Scott.

During and after Word War II stamps known as AMG (**Allied Military Government**) were issued for use in liberated Europe. While the *Scott Specialized Catalogue of United States Stamps & Covers* does not list these stamps, they are listed in other catalogs under the countries where they were used: Italy, France, Germany, and Austria. However, since most of the 132 AMG stamps were printed at the BEP in Washington (and all were printed by order

Figure 7

This AMG stamp was printed by the Bureau of Engraving and Printing in Washington, D.C. for use in Berlin and in the British and American Zones of Germany after World War II. Similar but distinct versions of the stamp were printed in Europe.

of the U.S. War Department and under U.S. supervision) there is a good rationale for including them in U.S. collections (fig. 7).

Notes on Collecting

Overprinted U.S. Special Delivery stamps, Postage Dues, and stamped envelopes were issued for use in Cuba, and the Philippines. Guam was given overprinted Special Delivery stamps, and Puerto Rico received overprinted Postage Dues.

Caution should be exercised in using Scott catalogue numbers to identify the stamps of U.S. Possessions. The same catalogue number can be used for each possession (as well as the United States proper), so one should always be clear which possession is being referenced. For example, Special Delivery Stamps were issued for Cuba, Guam, and Philippines. Therefore each of those possessions has a stamp with the *Scott* number E1.

Values for U.S. Possession stamps range from the astronomically priced Hawaiian Missionaries to some surprisingly affordable stamps, including all of Hawaii's "republic" stamps. The beautifully engraved stamps produced by the BEP beginning in the 1920s for use in the Philippines and the Canal Zone are very modestly priced. Even some of the Series of 1894 overprints can be purchased for less than one dollar in used condition. Some Canal Zone overprints on Columbia and Republic of Panama stamps have been extensively counterfeited, and caution is advised when purchasing these stamps. Fake overprints also exist on "Shanghai" stamps.

The 1979 U.S. postal card depicting Honolulu's Iolani Place (UX81) bears a striking similarity to the postal card issued by the Republic of Hawaii (UX8).

Almanac

1851 – First Hawaiian stamps, the so called "Missionaries", are announced for sale on October 1.

1894 – Republic of Hawaii is established on July 4 and stamps are subsequently issued.

1898 – U.S. establishes postal facilities in the Philippines on May 1.

1898 – On December 10 Spain renounces all claims to Cuba, cedes Guam and Puerto Rico to the U.S. and transfers sovereignty of the Philippines to the U.S.

1899 – U.S. Military Authority established in Cuba on January 1, and U.S. stamps are issued.

1899 – Philippines Postal service is separated from the San Francisco post office on May 1.

1899 – Series of 1894 stamps overprinted "Guam" are put into use on July 7.

1900 – Hawaii becomes a territory using U.S. stamps on June 14.

1901 – Regular U.S. stamps are first used in Guam on March 29.

1902 – Cuba assumes self-rule as a Republic on May 20.

1904 – On June 24 the Canal Zone Postal Service is established, which issues its first stamps.

1917 – Danish West Indies purchased by U.S. and renamed U.S. Virgin Islands on March 31. Danish stamps remain valid for postage until September 30, 1917.

1919 – Overprinted stamps are placed on sale at the U.S. Postal Agency in Shanghai, China on July 1.

1935 – Stamps first appear on November 15 identifying and celebrating the Philippines as a "Commonwealth" of the United States.

1943 – The first AMG stamps appear on September 17 for use in Italy.

1946 – The Philippines becomes an independent republic on July 4.

1948 – First Ryukyu Islands stamps are issued July 1.

1979 – The Canal Zone Postal Service ceases operation (succeeded by Panama Postal Service) on September 30.

What Others Have Said

Canal Zone – The New York and Canal Zone Railway Post Office
"Mail service has been established on steamers of the Panama Railroad and Steamship Company between New York, NY and Colon, Panama, the railway post office being maintained there being known as the "New York and Canal Zone R.P.O.". Clerks are assigned to this line and handle in transit all mails to and from New York, NY and post offices in the Canal Zone. This improvement is regarded as one of importance in caring for mails to and from…the Canal Zone…"

—*"Railway Mail Service,"* Post Office Department, Annual Reports for the fiscal year ended June 30, 1908.

Cuba – Order of July 21, 1898 of President William McKinley
"In view of the occupation of…Cuba by the forces of the U.S., it is ordered that postal communication between the U.S. and that port, which has been suspended since the opening of hostilities with Spain, be resumed, subject to such military regulations as may be deemed necessary….the revenues derived from such service are to be applied to the expenses of conducting it, and U.S. postage stamps are therefore to be used."

—*George S. Hill, "History of the American Postal Service in Cuba,"* The Collectors Club Philatelist, *1937.*

Danish West Indies/Virgin Islands – The USPOD wastes no time!
"After the U.S. bought the Virgin Islands from Denmark on March 31, 1917, the local post offices continued to use the Danish canceling devices until new ones were made. Apparently the Post Office Department wasted no time in sending booklets to the new territory, for booklet stamps are found canceled in April and May with the old cancellers."

—*Richard Larkin, "Booklet stamps on cover,"* The United States Specialist, *1985.*

Guam – United States Stamps Overprinted for Use in Guam
"The total face value of the stamps overprinted was $950.00. Under normal conditions, these would have been sufficient to supply all ordinary and legitimate postal needs at Guam for 2 years….When the box of stamps was taken

from the safe and opened, it was found that they were not in the best of condition. A large number of the sheets were stuck together. When packed and sealed in the box at the Bureau [of Engraving and Printing] no one thought of the climatic conditions in the South Pacific, and the necessary precautions were not taken to keep the sheets of stamps from sticking together. Shortly thereafter, [when the] orders for [the replacement] stamps were received… [they] were found to be for ten times…. [the original order, and hence, more than $9500 of stamps were sent to Guam]."

—*Arthur J. Trumbull, "United States Stamps Overprinted for use in Cuba, Guam Puerto Rico and the Philippines," U.S. Possessions Stamp Exhibition, 1949.*

Hawaii – A relatively unknown transition period
"The Republic of Hawaii was annexed by the United States on August 12, 1898,–hence as part of the United States why should not a 2c U.S. stamp be used on a letter from Hawaii almost three months later? But then,–why was there a Hawaiian issue of 1898? Investigation shows that the Hawaiian Islands did not actually become part of the United States until 'Territory Day', June 14, 1900. On that day, the two postal systems became one, as per order of the Postmaster General dated April 30, 1900, and the cancellation 'Honolulu, H.I.' became 'Honolulu, T.H.' Between the date of annexation and Territory Day, Hawaii remained an independent postal system and a member of the Universal Postal Union with the customary 5c letter rate of the United States, as to any other foreign nation."

—*George P. Howard, "Cover Collecting," The United States Specialist, 1955.*

Philippines – Who were these great men on Philippines stamps?
"All Philippine postage stamps issued between 1899 and July 4, 1946, bear the [inscription] "UNITED STATES OF AMERICA". Some of these stamps bear the portraits of American national heroes. The issues of 1899 to 1903-04 are stamps of the United States overprinted PHILIPPINES. On stamps of the issues of 1906 to 1926 appear portraits of McKinley, Lawton, Lincoln, Sampson, Washington, Franklin and Dewey. How many American collectors know what made each of them a distinguished American citizen? The names of some of them are familiar to us. But how many know anything about Lawton, or why his portrait was chosen for a Philippine stamp?"

—*Arnold W. Warren, "The Forgotten Philippines," American Philatelist, 1948.*

Ryukyu Islands – Only 22 days to print and distribute stamps
"…on August 23rd 1958, Lt. Gen. Donald P. Booth, United States High Commissioner, announced that the United States dollar would replace the B-yen as the official currency of the Ryukyu Islands….the conversion was set as

September 15. Thus the Postal Services Agency had only 22 days to design, print and distribute a wide variety of dollar denomination stamps....to the 81 post offices scattered about the three island groups...."

—*George MacLellan, "New Data on the...1958 Ryukyu Provisionals," S.P.A. Journal, 1970.*

Examples of Postal Usage

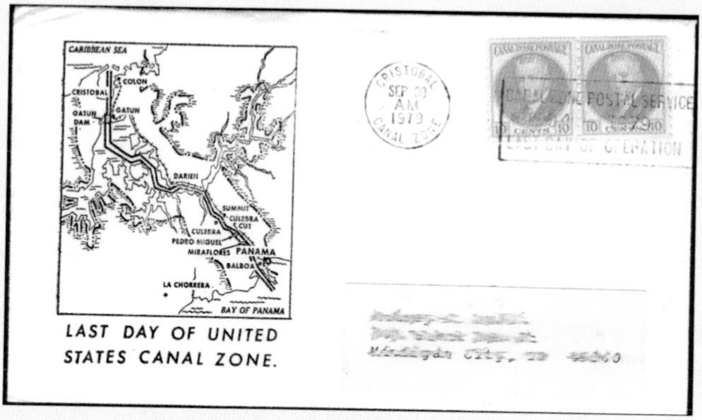

Figure 8

A philatelicaly inspired Canal Zone cover, bearing a pair of the Major General Harry Foote Hodges 10¢ coil stamps (161). It is cancelled at Cristobal, C.Z. on the last day of operation of the Canal Zone Postal Service, Sept. 30, 1979.

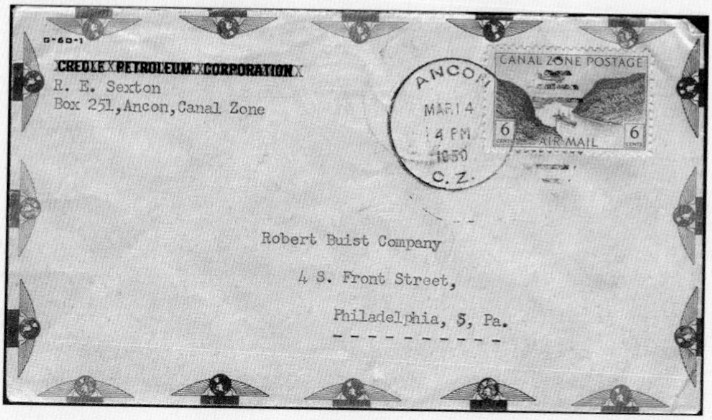

Figure 9

An air mail cover, commercial usage, franked with a BEP printed stamp, from Ancon, Canal Zone to Philadelphia. The stamp (C8) is one of a series depicting a plane flying over Gaillard Cut. Domestic rates applied to and from the Canal Zone. The air mail rate for a single weight letter in 1950 was 6¢.

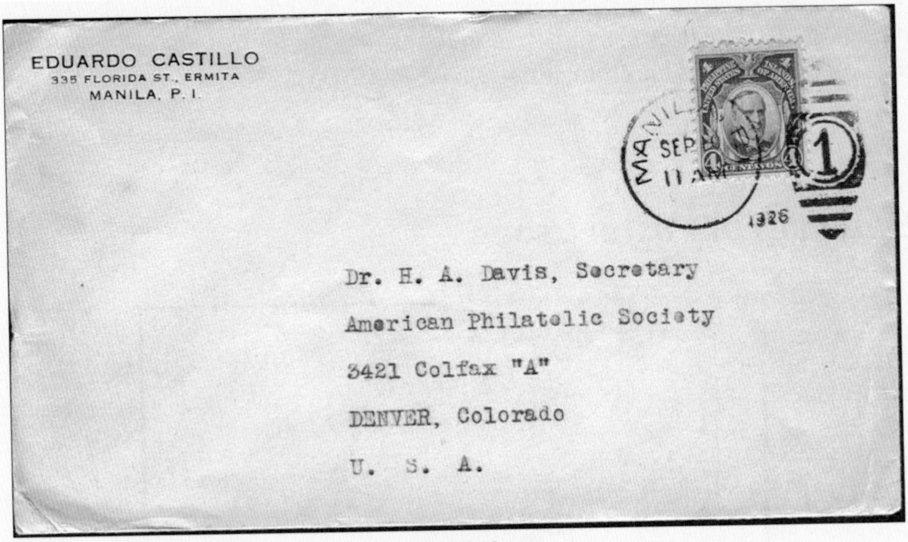

Figure 10

A 1926 double weight cover from Manila, Philippine Islands to the United States franked with BEP printed stamp honoring William McKinley. Domestic rates applied to and from the Philippine Islands, therefore 4¢ paid the correct postage.

Where to Find More Information

Canal Zone
- *Canal Zone Stamps* by Gilbert N. Plass, Geoffrey Brewster & Richard H Salz is considered to be the most comprehensive reference available on Canal Zone postage stamps.
- *Canal Zone Postage Stamps* by Edward Tatelman.

Cuba
- *A Handbook of the Stamps of Cuba/Handbook of Cuba*, Pt. II. The U.S. Administration, 1898-1902, by William M. Jones, is devoted to Cuba as a U.S. possession.

Danish West Indies/Virgin Islands
- *Postal History of the United States Virgin Islands (formerly the Danish West Indies)* by Alfred J. Birch.

Guam
- *A Postal History/Cancellation Study of the U.S. Pacific Islands* (including the Trust Territories) by Richard Murphy.

- *Guam Guard Mail*, by H. Bowker describes establishment of postal service and stamp production.

Hawaii

- *Hawaii, Its Stamps and Postal History* by Meyer, Harris, Davey & Bash is considered the most comprehensive reference on early Hawaiian stamps and postal history.

- *Plating the Hawaiian Numerals* by Joshua F. Westerberg is the standard work on plating the stamps and the most useful for detecting forgeries.

Philippines

- *Napp's Numbers*, Volume Two, by Joseph Napp is a study of the plate number combinations and of the quantities issued.

Ryukyu Islands

- *Ryukyu Islands: Lists of Post Offices under the Administration of the United States Government (1945-1961)* by Melvin H. Schoberlin is an introduction to the post offices by island, with opening and closing dates and various notes.

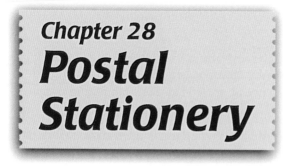
Envelopes of any kind were
uncommon in the mail prior
to the mid-1800s because
postage was generally based
on both the number of sheets
of paper and the distance
traveled. An envelope would
have counted as a second
sheet and thus doubled the
postage rate! Envelopes
became more common after 1845 when the United States began to charge postage
based not on the number of sheets of paper, but solely on weight and distance.

U.S. postal envelopes were authorized by the Postal Act of August 31, 1852.
The original purpose of these envelopes was primarily to obtain revenue
(postage) from mail carried by private express companies. The Postal Act
allowed for letters to be, "sent, conveyed and delivered otherwise than by post
or mail," provided
that the postage oth-
erwise due the
United States was
paid by the use of
stamped envelopes.
The act further pro-
vided that, "said
envelope shall be
duly sealed, or other-
wise firmly and
securely closed, so
that such letter can-
not be taken there-
from without tearing
or destroying such
envelope." The pur-

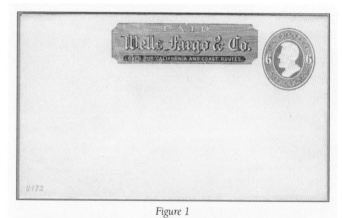

Figure 1

The law required letters carried by private companies be enclosed in
a Post Office envelope, even though the Post Office provided no
service. This envelope was used by Wells, Fargo & Co.

pose was to make sure the envelope could not be reused. Many companies
bought envelopes from the Post Office Department (POD), and had their own
frank printed on the envelopes for resale to their customers. The most common
were those issued by **Wells Fargo & Co.** (fig. 1). The requirement that letters
carried "out-of-the-mails" be enclosed in postal stationery continued until 1938.
It affected many businesses in addition to the 1860s express companies, including banks, railroads, and the Greyhound Bus Company. After 1938 postage was

still required on out-of-the-mails communications, but stamps could then be used as an alternative to postal stationery.

The first U.S. postal envelopes were issued by the USPOD on July 1, 1853 (fig. 2). The indicium design was modeled after the British Victoria envelope, a bust in an oval with

Figure 2

The first stamped envelope (U1) was issued in 1853. The Scott numbers of all stamped envelopes begin with the prefix "U".

the denomination in an outside collar. To make counterfeiting more difficult the USPOD required that all postal envelopes be made with **watermarked** paper and have an **embossed** indicium (stamp). The then current stamp printer, **Toppan, Carpenter, Casilear & Co.** was passed over for the contract, which the USPOD awarded to New York stationer **George F. Nesbitt**.

The British Victoria envelope sent as a **specimen** for bidders had a rose embossed on the back flap. George Nesbitt's contract bid was for envelopes "made of white paper which shall be equal in quality to the Sample herewith (Marked A) having a water mark impressed therein and having stamped on each envelope by means of steel **dies** engraved expressly for that purpose, Postage Stamps of such denominations as may be required and also an additional stamp on the flap, or where the envelope is usually sealed." Nesbitt designed a seal that had the lettering "G. F. Nesbitt N.Y." This raised such uproar from other businesses that, within a week after release of the envelopes, Nesbitt asked permission to make further envelopes without the seal. On July 7 the Postmaster General forbade its further use. Thus only early production of envelopes had the seal (fig. 3).

Figure 3

The earliest envelopes produced by George F. Nesbit contained his seal on the flap.

Most nineteenth century envelopes were made from paper with laid lines, which are visible when the envelope is held to the light. The first production had the laid lines horizontal and watermark perpendicular to them, but Nesbitt quickly found that if the envelopes were turned 30 degrees he could cut more envelopes from a sheet of paper. The paper manufacturer changed the watermark so that it was horizontal when the paper was cut on 30-degree bias. Early envelopes made of paper with horizontal laid lines are scarce. Beginning in July 1915, and continuing into the twenty-first century, stamped envelopes were manufactured with wove paper.

Figure 4

"Cut-square" from one of the "Star Die" envelopes first issued in 1860.

In 1860, the USPOD decided to change the design of all denominations of envelopes and the new "star die" envelopes, so called because of the stars at the sides of the design, as shown in figure 4 were issued from August through December 1860. With the opening of the Civil War, the USPOD did not want stamps and envelopes from southern post offices that came into Confederate possession brought north and resold. Therefore the USPOD *demonetized* the first issue of stamped envelopes and the 3¢, 6¢, and 10¢ of the second (star die) series. This has created some great rarities for usages of the 6¢ and 10¢ values of the second series.

Envelopes have always been manufactured by private companies. Each manufacturing company generally introduced a new watermark for its envelopes. Some manufacturing companies used more than one paper supplier, with different watermarks used by different paper suppliers. The result is that stamped envelopes exist with many different patterns of watermarks. Watermarks are usually visible if the envelope, lettersheet, wrapper, or postal card is placed in front of a strong light. All envelopes and wrappers have watermarks except the manila and kraft envelopes and wrappers of the twentieth century.

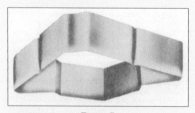

Figure 5

This metal form, known as a "knife", cut envelopes from large sheets of paper.

Most envelopes were issued in more than one size. A *knife* is the metal form with a sharp edge that was used to cut the envelope blanks (fig. 5). The term "knife" is also used to denote the specific shape and size of the blank and resulting envelope. Envelopes are categorized both by size and knife because each size is a different knife and the same size may have different knives. Sometimes manufacturers changed the shape of a particular envelope size, e.g. high back vs. low back.

The first commemorative stamped envelopes were issued for the American Centennial in 1876, but it was only beginning in the 1970s that a vast number of topics began to be commemorated on stamped envelopes (fig. 6).

Hyman L. Lipman, Philadelphia, Pennsylvania in 1861, first introduced post cards. These were cards that required a stamp to be affixed. *Postal cards* are cards produced under USPOD contract with an imprinted indicium (stamp) while *post cards* can be produced by anyone and do not have an imprinted stamp.

The USPOD was initially reluctant to produce postal cards, and did not do so until 1873 when it was required to do so by the impending U.S. entry into the General Postal Union (later called the Universal Postal Union). Prior to 1907 only the address could be placed on the front of the card (the side with the stamp or indicium). If any message was written on the address side of a post or postal card, it was charged the letter rate. After March 1, 1907, up to one half of the front could have a message on it.

Postal cards were produced for the USPOD by private companies (generally companies different than those producing other U.S. postal stationery) from 1873 to 1909, and then by the U.S. Government Printing Office from January 1, 1910 into the twenty-first century. Only the first two issues of U.S. postal cards were produced on watermarked paper. Beginning with the 1¢ Jefferson postal card in 1885, many postal cards were sold in sheets ranging from 18 to 48 so that commercial users

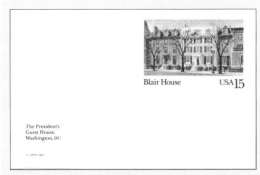

Figure 7

This 1988 postal card (UX121) honors Blair House in Washington, D.C. Many historic buildings have been honored with postal cards since the late 1970s, with special attention being given to historic buildings on college and university campuses. All Scott numbers for postal cards begin with the prefix "UX."

could more easily print a message on the back. These have frequently been cut to simulate errors with the indicium located other than in the upper right corner. Figure 7 illustrates a typical late twentieth century postal card.

In 1989 the USPS began selling picture postal cards, which sold at a premium over face value. The first ones (Scott UX143 and UX144) picture the White House and the Jefferson Memorial.

Paid Reply Postal Cards are sold in unsevered, unfolded condition, with sufficient postage for both original mailing and reply (fig. 8). They are normally perforated between the message and reply cards to facilitate separation and response. The card is mailed in folded condition and the intent is for the recipient to detach the reply portion and return it to the original sender. The first message reply card was issued in 1892 and the first international Paid Reply Postal Card was issued in 1893. Members of the Universal Postal Union agreed to return the reply side without additional postage, until July 1, 1971 when this arrangement was discontinued. This is one of the few historical opportunities to have U.S. postal items mailed in a foreign country.

The Act of February 27, 1861 authorized the Postmaster General to furnish **letter sheets** "with postage stamps impressed thereon, combining in one both a sheet and envelope." A number of designs and patents were considered. One was chosen and issued during August 1861 with the same 3¢ indicium used on contemporaneous envelopes. It was withdrawn from sale in April 1864 due to lack of interest by the public.

The letter sheet was again authorized by Congress in 1879 but Congress provided that no royalty or price be paid for any patent. This provision made it difficult for the Postmaster General to execute the contract, and another lettersheet was not issued until 1886 when the **American Bank Note Company**, using a patent issued to Lebbeus H. Rogers and owned by the United States Postal Card Company, produced the 2¢ Grant lettersheet (U293). Their manufacture was discontinued in 1894 and they were withdrawn from sale in 1902.

Lettersheets were not issued again until air letter sheets (**aerograms**) were issued in 1947. Because the cost of an aerogram was less than the postage on a one-ounce international air mail letter they continued to be popular into the twenty-first century.

Wrappers are rectangular sheets of paper printed with indicium and gummed at one end so that they can be wrapped around a newspaper, periodical, or other commercial mailing (fig. 9). They were first issued in 1861 with a 1¢ Franklin indicium. The first two issues were on both buff and manila paper but all issues thereafter have been on manila paper. Wrappers were discontinued in 1934. Usages of some issues are scarce since most were discarded as junk mail.

In 1920 many envelopes, postal cards, and message-reply cards were surcharged to revalue them when **First Class** postage was reduced following World War I.

Because the Post Office and public had large quantities of 3¢ envelopes and 2¢ postal cards on hand, revaluing them to 2¢ and 1¢ respectively allowed the existing supplies to be used. The revaluing was done not at the USPOD in Washington, but at central post offices throughout the country. Items were revalued by placing **slugs** in regular canceling machines and running postal stationery through those machines. Each slug differed slightly and imprints from them can be identified. Slugs were transferred at intervals to other post offices. "City" types are named for the first city of use. In addition to revaluing post office stocks, the Post Office allowed the public to bring in envelopes for revaluation in not less than full boxes. Many unintended envelopes were revalued, either by inclusion in a box without the knowledge of the post office, or as a "favor."

In 1925, another revaluing occurred when the third class postage rate rose from 1¢ to 1½¢ and the Post Office had many 1¢ envelopes on hand. The same procedure was used as in 1920, with special dies used in canceling machines. However in 1925 postmasters were specifically instructed not to revalue envelopes already in the hands of the public.

Notes on Collecting

United States Postal envelopes can be collected either as **cut squares** (**indicia** only) or the entire envelope. Many collect cut squares because there are fewer of them (only one for each die and paper type) and they are easy to mount in an album. Cut squares may be either mint or used and should have at least 1 cm of paper around the indicium. Some collect one example of each die and paper type as entire envelopes. Small envelopes are easier to store and have therefore been more popular with collectors than larger envelopes. Some collectors attempt to assemble each size and knife of each die and paper type. There are over 5,000 such items. Many collectors will specialize in a particular issue, collecting mint items and usages of the envelopes.

Postal cards and message-reply cards are collected as entires, either mint or used. Cut squares of postal cards are not collected. There is a great opportunity to specialize in die types and paper types as well as usages.

Letter sheets are collected either as cut squares or entires. The most common collection of airmail letter sheets is postal usages.

Some envelopes were overprinted with "Specimen" as favor items, for use as bidder samples for contract solicitations, and to promote envelope sales. A number of different specimen forms exist with or without advertising on a number of envelopes.

Almanac

1852 – A contract to manufacture the first stamped envelopes is issued to George F. Nesbitt & Company of New York City on October 25.

1853 – First stamped envelopes are issued July 1 in 3¢ and 6¢ denominations.

1861 – First stamped letter sheets (U36) are issued in August in blue, in two sizes.

1861 – First stamped newspaper wrapper, a "star die", (W18B) is issued in October.

1861 – All stamps and stamped envelopes issued through May 1861 are *demonetized* during the second half of the year.

1873 – First postal card (UX1), a 1¢ Liberty with large watermark, is issued May 13.

1876 – The first commemorative stamped envelopes, honoring the U.S. Centennial, are probably issued May 10.

1879 – First "PENALTY" overprinted stamped envelope is used by the War Department.

1892 – First Paid Reply (message/reply) Postal Card (UY1), a 1¢ + 1¢ Grant, is issued October 25.

1897 – First "PENALTY" clause stampless envelope is used.

1928 – The Post Office begins providing *precanceled* stamped envelopes. Local precanceled stamped envelopes and wrappers date from the late 1860s.

1929 – First air mail stamped envelope (UC1) is issued January 12.

1947 – First air letter sheet (UC16), featuring DC-4 Skymaster, is issued April 29.

1949 – First air mail postal card (UXC1), a 4¢ card featuring an eagle in flight, is issued January 10.

1956 – First commemorative postal card (UX44) is issued May 4, honoring the Fifth International Philatelic Exhibition.

1962 – Experimental precanceled 4¢ Lincoln postal card (UX48) is issued November 19.

1966 – First international air mail postal card (UXC5), the 11¢ "Visit the USA" card, is issued May 27.

1966 – The 4¢ Lincoln postal card (UX48a) is re-issued on June 25 as the first stamped envelope or postal card with *tagging*.

1977 – First envelope produced by *photogravure* and *embossing* (U583) is issued April 7, with a golf theme.

1977 – First stamped envelopes (U584 and 585) without embossing are issued October 20. They have an energy theme.

1989 – First picture postal card (UX143), featuring the White House, is issued November 30.

1989 – First hologram stamped envelope (U617), featuring a shuttle docking at space station, is issued December 3.

What Others Have Said

Reasons for Using Stamped Envelopes
"1st Cheapness
2nd Saving of Labor – The envelope being ready to mail, as soon as directed, without the trouble of applying a stamp.
3rd Safety – The stamp, being a part of the Envelope, is not liable to come off, like an adhesive stamp leaving your letter to appear unpaid.
4th It lessens fraud, the prevention of which is to the interest of every honest man. A stamped envelope can be used but once, while it is well known that a large business is carried on in our cities by boys who collect and sell cancelled stamps to parties, who after removing the cancel-marks, dispose of the same to be used a second time."

—from a USPOD flyer dated May 11, 1875.

There are commemorative postal cards, and then there are the workhorses....
"The long awaited 21¢ White Barn postal card will be issued in Washington, D.C. on Sept. 20. There will be no official first day ceremony, according to the United States Postal Service, which has an erratic history of celebrating the release of its workhorse postal cards....A workhorse card is a definitive, or regular issue, postal card that can be purchased at every post office in the land, as opposed to commemorative postal cards, which are issued regionally and are seldom seen in the general mailstream....The White Barn Card is being issued in four formats: individual postal cards, packs of five for vending machines, message-reply cards and sheets of 40. The sheets of 40 are purchased by businesses which have advertising printed on the cards."

—Rob Haeseler, "21¢ White Barn postal card will be new workhorse item," Linn's Stamp News, *2001.*

A Postal Card surprise for the USPS – 8 million copies of an error!

"The Stamp Management Branch of the U.S. Postal Service received an unwelcome surprise in mid-January 1981. The impossible and the unspeakable had occurred! A rejected design on postal stationery that had been ordered destroyed was instead issued. Moreover, the error was not known to Stamp Management officials for nine months...an acquaintance called my attention to the difference in the designs on the front and back of the Isaiah Thomas paid reply postal card (Scott No. UY33). The design on the front is 48½ mm wide and 24 mm high, the numerals are 4mm high. The design on the back is 46 mm wide and 22 mm high, with the numerals 2¼ mm. High...Linda Foster of the Stamp Management Branch....provided the following information. The Government Printing Office prepared plates of the 12¢ Isaiah Thomas Card (Scott UX89)... A test run was made and postal officials concluded that the design was too small. The plates and the cards that were printed were ordered destroyed. Somehow, unbeknownst to postal officials one plate prepared for the reply card was not destroyed....approximately eight million [reply] cards were produced...total production of the reply card was 18,306,000."

—John Gulka, "Isaiah Thomas Paid Reply Postal Card – Error," The United States Specialist, 1982.

Modern Albinos

"An EFOddity is the disdain that most people show toward albino envelopes and the modern missing all color rarities that Scott says cannot exist. The "old standard" albinos were created when two blanks (or sheets in a few issues) went through the press simultaneously so that the lower envelope got only the embossing. True, they are seen often on some issues but are scarce on many and may not exist on others. They tend to look much like plain envelopes...they can be quite fascinating if one really takes a good look at them, especially those inside of double envelopes, or those postally used with such postal markings as "returned for postage"....Since January 1, 1965, when U.S. envelopes began to be printed on web-fed presses...what should we call the new embossed only rarities that sometimes reach the public? Scott says such items cannot exist, and using the old criteria they may be right."

—Francis C. Pogue, "Modern Albinos are Something Else," Postal Stationery, 1989.

Examples of Postal Usage

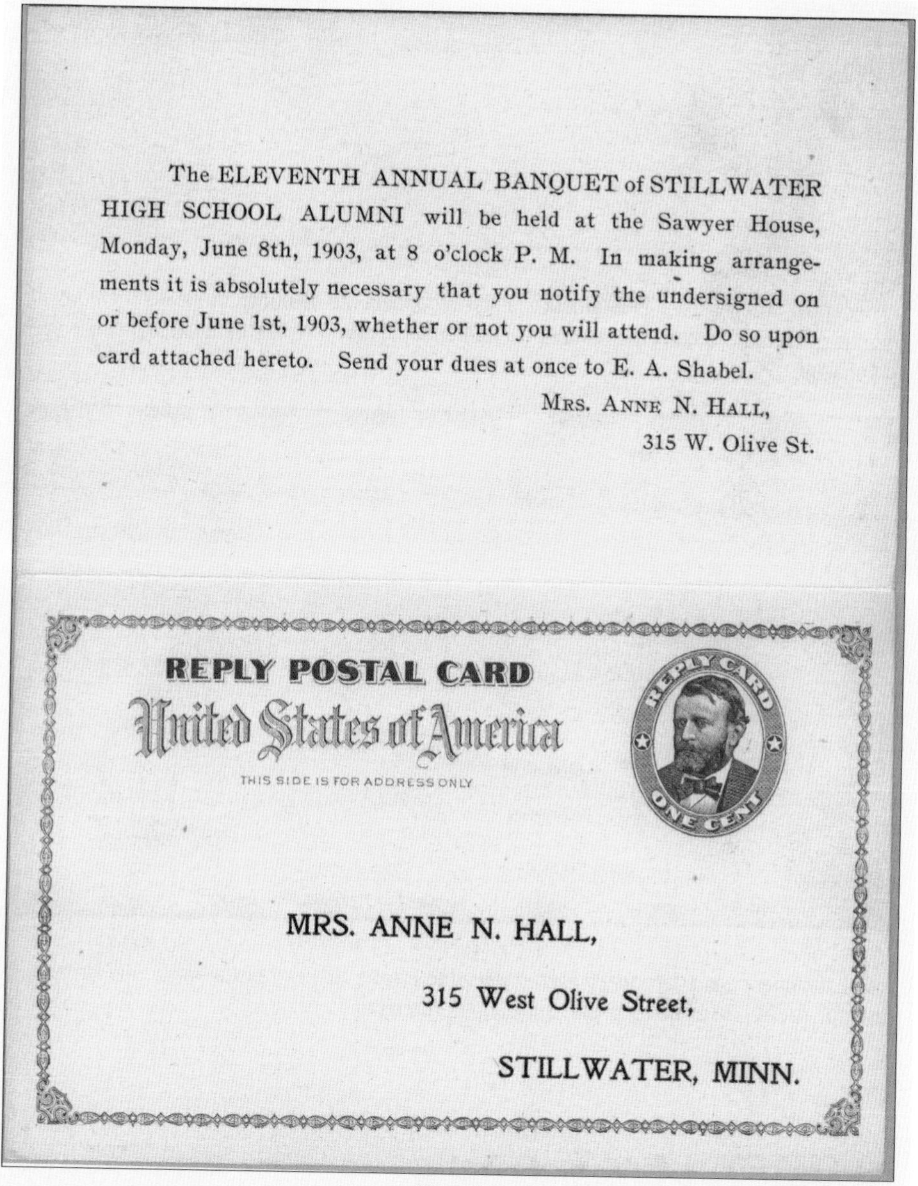

The ELEVENTH ANNUAL BANQUET of STILLWATER HIGH SCHOOL ALUMNI will be held at the Sawyer House, Monday, June 8th, 1903, at 8 o'clock P. M. In making arrangements it is absolutely necessary that you notify the undersigned on or before June 1st, 1903, whether or not you will attend. Do so upon card attached hereto. Send your dues at once to E. A. Shabel.

MRS. ANNE N. HALL,
315 W. Olive St.

REPLY POSTAL CARD
United States of America
THIS SIDE IS FOR ADDRESS ONLY

REPLY CARD
ONE CENT

MRS. ANNE N. HALL,
315 West Olive Street,
STILLWATER, MINN.

Figure 8

Scott numbers for Message-reply cards begin with the prefix "UY." This card (UY1), was issued in 1892. The recipient of this card never sent back the reply portion! Does this mean that he or she never attended the alumni banquet for Stillwater High School?

Figure 9

This wrapper still encloses its original contents! Wrappers are identified in the *Scott Catalogue* with the prefix "W." Stamped envelopes (U) and wrappers (W) are intermingled in a single section of Scott.

Figure 10

Postal stationery has occasionally been revalued to meet a changed postal rate. This air mail envelope (UC20), used in 1952 was surcharged, changing its value to 6¢.

Where to Find More Information

- The United Postal Stationery Society (UPSS) is devoted exclusively to postal stationery. Its website is: www.upss.org. The organization publishes a bimonthly journal, *Postal Stationery*.

- *United States Postal Card Catalog 2000*, John H. Beachboard, editor, is the definitive guide to U.S. postal cards, including varieties.

- *Catalog of the 19th Century Stamped Envelopes, Wrappers, Cut Squares and Full Corners of the United States*, Allen Mintz, editor, is the definitive guide to these items and their varieties.

- *Catalog of the 20th Century Stamped Envelopes, Wrappers, Cut Squares and Full Corners of the United States*, Jerry Summers, editor, is the definitive guide to these items and their varieties.

- *United States Commemorative Stamped Envelopes 1876–1965*, by F.L. Ellis and William H. Maisel.

- "The first United States stamped envelopes" by Ken Lawrence explores the history and varieties of the first Nesbitt produced envelopes.

Chapter 29
Precancels and Perfins

Precancel and perfin stamps are quite different and yet they are often linked together. This linkage is so strong, that the major collecting societies devoted to these specialties hold joint annual conventions. Upholding this tradition, precancels and perfins are treated together in this chapter.

Precanceled Stamps

A precancel is an adhesive postage (or revenue) stamp that has been canceled, under proper authority, before being affixed to mail (or taxable) matter. The exception to this generalization is certain pioneer precancels, the precancel being applied after affixing but before the item being mailed was submitted to the Post Office.

As the U.S. grew during the nineteenth century, commerce flourished. The mails were the basic form of business communication. Even with the introduction of the telephone, the mails continued to dominate commercial communication well into the twentieth century. The enormous growth in mail volume challenged the ability of the labor intensive Post Offices to receive, process, and deliver the mails in a timely fashion. This was a serious problem for expanding commercial enterprises, some of which might mail many thousands of pieces each day. By the late 1800s, several very large mailers were generating hundreds of thousands of pieces of mail. Everything from patent medicine to appliances and clothing were sold by mail as companies like Sears, Roebuck Co. and Montgomery Ward were changing the face of commerce through catalog mail sales. However, by far the most significant use of precancels was not on merchandise shipped, but on advertising material sent out at circular rate.

Throughout its history, the Post Office Department (POD) adopted methods to help speed the process of mail handling. Many changes were based on technology, others on innovation or adaptation. The concept of precancelation is an example of adaptation, illustrating how Post Office methods and practices evolved to meet the needs of commercial customers.

Precanceling stamps saved time and labor at the post office by reducing the number of times a piece of mail was handled. Some postmasters, upon receiving a large order for stamps, and anticipating the task of canceling each piece of mail, instead canceled the stamps before selling them to the user. The precanceled stamps would then be applied to the mail by the sender. Upon receipt at the post office, the precanceled mail could be dispatched with a minimum of further processing. Eliminating the hand or machine canceling of each mail piece was not the only advantage. Ordinary mail arriving at the post office was dumped on "facing" tables where clerks would have to arrange (face) them the same way, with the stamp in the corner, in preparation for canceling. Thereafter the mail went to sorting tables for sacking and further routing. When precanceled stamps were used the steps of facing and canceling were eliminated. Additionally, it was not uncommon for sacking to be accomplished by mailers who were interested in the prompt dispatch of their mail.

Post Office Precancel Regulations

The POD did not officially embrace the concept of precancelation until long after this practice had become widespread. *Mekeel's Weekly Stamp News*, reported in the August 1, 1901 issue: "Postmaster Bruce [Dwight H. Bruce, PM, Syracuse, N.Y.] has written the department and has received from Third Assistant Postmaster General Edwin C. Madden, an explanation of the system. Precancelation is not favored by the department, nor is it permitted except in rare cases, where the quantity of third or fourth class matter mailed by a particular firm or individual each day for a period of consecutive days is too large to be promptly handled in the ordinary way."

The POD was concerned about the potential loss of revenue that would occur if precanceled stamps were reused. After all, a "used" precancel stamp looks the same on an envelope as an "unused" one. The POD ran "by the book", and when the book was first written, it did not include precancelation.

Clearly however, there was an unofficial POD policy that recognized the value of precanceling. Eventually regulations were formulated and established in May 1903 when Third Assistant Postmaster General Edwin C. Madden issued the directive, "Conditions governing the use of Precanceled Postage Stamps." One interesting part of the regulations stipulated that Precanceled stamps were only valid for postage at the post office named on the face of the stamp. Since that time the regulations governing precancelation have undergone many changes, but generally have expanded the availability and use of precancelation.

Initially, the POD regulations of 1903 permitted precancels on only **Third** and **Fourth Class mail**. Eventually this practice was extended so that precancels could be used on any class of mail. Mailers using precancels on bulk mailings paid an annual fee to the post office for a bulk-mail permit.

Types of Precancels

There are two primary categories of precancels: Local (also known as City) pre-cancels and Bureau (BEP) precancels. Each of these categories can be further subdivided. Apparently between the late 1870s and the mid-1880s, precancel-ing became popular with a few local post offices. There exist a number of rea-sonably well identified (by city) precancels that are found on 1870s and 1880s issues. Early precancelation was accomplished by applying inked lines, or some identifiable pattern, or even a post-canceller on the stamps, while they were still in multiple pieces or panes. In some cases, where large numbers of stamps were needed, precanceling was done on a printing press. Precanceled stamps in this "class" of postal artifacts are known to collectors as "pioneer", "bars and lines", "mute", or "silent" precancels. Because the stamps by them-selves generally do not include any indication of their point of origin, they must be initially identified based on complete mailing pieces. Once this is accomplished, there are usually sufficient criteria to enable identification as to its origin for off cover examples.

Local or City Types

In the early 1890s, a gradual transition in the appearance of precanceled stamps began. Standardized patterns in which the city and state of origin were spelled out came into use. Sometimes, bars or lines were included. The 1903 regula-tions stipulated, "The name of the post-office and State, and, if mailed at a sta-tion, the proper designation of such station, as well as two parallel heavy black lines, one above and one below the name of the office must appear across the face of each stamp."

A few post offices continued to use their fanciful non-conforming patterns. Some of these imaginative designs have nicknames like the Jackson, Michigan "Oval," the Fort Wayne, Indiana "Tombstone," and the Lansing, Michigan "Railroad Spider" (fig. 1). Precancel devices used through the first decade of the twentieth century were produced by, or at the direction of, local postmasters. Printing and

Figure 1

Fancy Local Precancels.

plate-making resources available to postmasters varied widely, resulting in the use of handstamps, typeset forms and electroplates. These precanceled stamps are often referred to as "Classic" precancels. There is a class of early twentieth century precancels known as "classic-dated" which generally complied with the regulations, but were dated with the month and year of use. Classic-dated precancels are known from several cities, mostly issued during 1901 and 1902.

Local Devices

By the end of the first decade of the twentieth century precancel designs generally complied with POD regulations requiring the office (city) and state to appear between horizontal lines or bars. The devices for precanceling were made locally at the direction of individual post offices. The POD, desiring uniformity, issued a regulation on July 1, 1913 requiring that Handstamp and Electroplate precanceling devices be ordered through the Department, which then contracted with

Figure 2

Examples of Local Devices; from left to right: Electro, Handstamp, Typeset, Mimeograph.

manufacturers to produce devices within POD standards. Local precancel devices continued to be used at the beginning of the twenty-first century. Based on the kind of printing device used, there are four major types of local precancels (fig. 2). They are:

ELECTROS: Stamps precanceled by electroplates, usually of 100 subjects but sometimes less. Electroplates were furnished to post offices for use by a local printer, or to large post offices having their own printing equipment. Such devices were issued to post offices requiring large quantities of precancels.

HANDSTAMPS: Stamps precanceled by a handstamp. Hard rubber handstamps having 5- to 25-subjects were supplied to post offices until 1932. In 1932 the POD began providing 25-subject and later 10-subject metal "rocker" handstamps known as "hand-electros" to reduce the cost of frequent replacement due to the rapid degradation of the rubber handstamps. In 1958 these were in turn superceded by 10-subject hand stamps made from synthetic rubber, known as "vinyl" handstamps.

TYPESETS: Stamps precanceled with movable type set up in a printing form in a local print shop. Such precancels came from post offices requiring a moderately large quantity of precancels.

MIMEOGRAPHS: Stamps precanceled on a mimeograph machine. Mimeographs were used by offices needing a moderately large quantity of precancels.

Bureau Precancels

The Bureau Precancels, commonly known as Bureaus, were printed at the Bureau of Engraving and Printing (BEP) in Washington, D.C. The first attempt to produce precancels at the BEP involved *engraving* the precancel into the stamp design, but none of these stamps were ever issued. In 1916 the POD, in its continuing effort to reduce precancels printing costs, had the BEP produce experimental precancels for three cities: "Augusta, Maine", "Springfield, Mass.", and "New Orleans, La." Using electrotype plates mounted on a flat-bed press, the BEP produced 21 experimental precancel varieties. Because difficulties experienced during the production process resulted in significant additional costs, no further precanceling was done at the BEP until the advent of the Stickney Rotary press in 1923.

Figure 3

The first Stickney Press Bureau Precancel, from New York, N.Y.

When precanceling resumed at the BEP it was done on the Stickney Rotary Press (ch. 36), which printed stamps and applied the precancelation in a single operation. Stamps were printed from one set of curved plates, the precanceling from another. Sometime around May 2, 1923, 20 million precanceled 1¢ Franklin perf. 10 stamps (581) were sent to New York City (fig. 3).

The rotary press precanceling process was so successful that on August 20, 1923, the Third Assistant Postmaster General announced that 1¢ precanceled sheet stamps would be shipped to additional cities. By June 1927 this stamp had been precanceled for 64 different cities.

From 1923 until 1978 there were changes to the typeface, thickness of the lines, and spacing of the lines, however the basic design remained the same on all Bureau precancels during these years.

To enable cost efficient production of Bureau precancels, they were supplied only to cities that ordered a minimum quantity of 500,000 sheet stamps or 250,000 coil stamps. To accommodate longer (more economical) press runs, several different cities' precancels were sometimes printed simultaneously.

In 1938, the USPOD began requiring precanceled stamps denominated more than 6¢ to be marked with the initials of the user and the month and year of use. This was to preclude the possible reuse of the higher valued stamps. Post offices were required to disallow the use of any dated precancel used more than ten days into the month following the one shown on the stamp. A "Chicago, Ill.", precancel used by Sears, Roebuck and Co. (abbreviated "SRC") in March 1956 is shown in figure 4. These are known as *dateds*. Firms generally applied the date and initials to stamps that were already precanceled. An *integral* is a device that applied the initials, date, and the precancel simultaneously.

National Bureau Precancels
Beginning in 1978 the USPS made significant policy changes affecting precancels, resulting in stamps known as *National Bureau Precancels*. After September 1978, stamps intended for bulk mail no longer bore the city and state precancel. All BEP produced precancels were precanceled with two parallel lines only, and were valid for precanceled mail at any U.S. post office.

Stamps precanceled with words such as "Presorted First-Class" and "Bulk Rate" between the lines exist from as early as 1980 (see fig. 3 in chapter 16). These precancels were a transitional step between the "lines only" precancels and the *service inscribed* precancels that were to follow.

Figure 4

The 17¢ Presidential Series, with CHICAGO ILL. precancel showing required initials of user, Sears Roebuck and Co. (SRC), month and year.

Since 1986 the USPS has produced several varieties of service inscribed "nationals". The stamp design includes text that identifies the specific use for which the stamp is intended: Bulk Rate, Presorted First Class, Non-profit Org., etc. Some were issued without precancel lines, with only a service indicator as a basic part of the stamp design. Some of the service inscriptions are the same color as the stamp and some are a different color. Some nationals with a service indicator as a part of the design were overprinted with two parallel lines applied by a printing mat. Several examples of National Bureau Precancels are illustrated in figure 5.

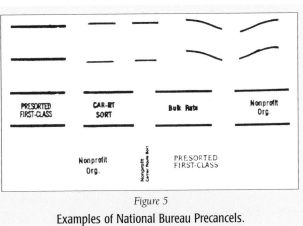

Figure 5

Examples of National Bureau Precancels.

Perfin Stamps
Perfin stamps were not created to improve the efficiency of the Post Office's ability to process or deliver mail. Rather they are a security measure used by busi-

nesses and commercial enterprises to prevent employee theft of stamps. Perfins are stamps that have small holes punched through the body of the stamps in patterns that usually form initials or insignias. The word "perfin" is a contraction of "perforated initials" or "perforated insignia" and is the term adopted by stamp collectors to describe these stamps.

Perfins were introduced in the United States in 1908. The use of perfins as a security measure in the U.S. was first authorized by a directive in the April 9, 1908 POD *Postal Bulletin* which read:

> "United States Postage stamps, to be acceptable for postage, must be absolutely without defacement: Provided that for the purpose of identification only, and not for advertising, it shall be permissible to puncture or perforate letters, numerals or other marks or devices in United States postage and special-delivery stamps. The punctures or perforations shall not exceed one sixty-fourth of an inch in diameter, and the whole space occupied by the identifying device shall not exceed one-third inch square. The puncturing or perforating must be done in such a manner as to leave the stamp easily recognizable as genuine and not previously used. The use of ink or other coloring matter in connection with such puncturing or perforation is prohibited."

These regulated dimensions were very restrictive and very few patterns with these extremely small holes were ever manufactured. The POD, receiving strong objections from the manufacturers of perforators that the extremely small hole-size were difficult to produce or that such small pins broke very easily, responded quickly. The *Postal Bulletin*, May 5, 1908, amended the initial authorization to read:

> "The punctures or perforations shall not exceed one thirty-second of an inch in diameter, and the whole space occupied by the identifying device shall not exceed one-half inch square."

This regulation has remained in force ever since. There has never been any provision for approving perfin patterns by the POD, or any provision for ensuring against unauthorized use. The Post Office's sole interest was that there be no further defacement of their stamps.

Perfin Machines
The perfin idea caught on rapidly. Within a few years thousands of machines were being used to create perfins. The largest manufacturer of U.S. perforators was the B. F. Cummins Company of Chicago, which had been in the perforating business for several decades before the advent of punching postage stamps.

There were several types of machines available in the market place. Many of the early perforators were probably made with a single die. These single die machines were labor intensive and soon the manufactures provided larger perforators that could punch five or ten stamps at once (fig. 6).

Perfin Patterns

There has been considerable creativity in the design of perfin patterns. Many perfin patterns uniquely identify thousands of commercial business that used them. A few companies, fortunate to have a business name small enough to fit within the half inch square, took full advantage of using the stamp as a method of self promotion. Since there was no official Post Office registry, the identification of patterns to their company origins has been left to collectors who obtained them from covers with printed *corner cards*. Patterns range from single letters and/or numbers, to multiple letters, usually the company initials, arranged in single or multiple rows. Often interesting geometric patterns were incorporated with the initials. Many are quite fancy, reminiscent of the fancy postmark cancels of the nineteenth century (fig. 7).

The number of perfin patterns in use shrank after World War I. Perfin stamps were used during the 1920s, but the growing use of postage meters during the

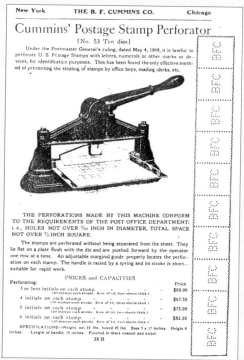

Figure 6

Advertisement for a B.F. Cummins 10 die, stroke stamp perforator. The text reads in part, "the stamps are perforated without being separated from the sheet. They lie flat on a plate flush with the die and are pushed forward by the operator one row at a time. An adjustable marginal guide properly locates the perforation on each stamp. The handle is raised by a spring and its stroke is short — suitable for rapid work."

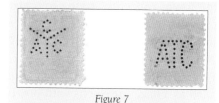

Figure 7

Examples of perfin designs from the Chicago Association of Commerce, Chicago, Illinois (left) and the American Tobacco Co., New York, N.Y. (right)

1930s and 1940s diminished the need for perfins as an office security device. The use of perfins continued to decline rapidly during the 1940s and 1950s. While the use of perfins is still permitted, few take advantage of this permission.

Control Perfins

A sub-category of the perfin is the "Schermack Coil Punches," often referred to as "*Control Perfins.*" The Schermack Company manufactured machines to affix stamps to envelopes. They made their own coils from imperforate sheet stamps issued by the Post Office (ch. 49). The "Control Perfins" were small holes punched into the privately made Schermack coil stamps, while in the affixing machine, as the stamps were dispensed, cut, and attached to envelopes. Different patterns were obtained by removing one or more pins from a basic 9- or 12-hole open square pattern (fig. 8). Like other perfins, Schermack control patterns were used as a security device. The missing pin hole patterns were a code that identified the company using the machine.

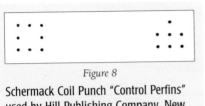

Figure 8

Schermack Coil Punch "Control Perfins" used by Hill Publishing Company, New York, N.Y. (left) and Cosmopolitan Magazine, New York, N.Y. (right).

Notes on Collecting

Precanceled Stamps

Collecting all varieties of precancels, other than dateds, is known as General Collecting. Although it is an extremely large field, many collectors enjoy it because they can easily add items to their collections. However there are many specialized precancel fields. Many collectors concentrate their interests on different "Towns and Types." Collectors have recorded over 21,000 different "Town" precancels and over 46,000 "Types." Generally, "T & T" enthusiasts, attempt to collect one example of each type from each town. Some engage only in "Town" collecting, trying to represent every town regardless of types. Others concentrate on towns from specific states or regions. Some collectors limit their interest to Bureau Precancels while others collect **Double Line Electros**. Some collect precancels on only one issue of U.S. stamps like the Washington Bicentennials or National Parks. Precancel collectors let their imagination run, such as, collecting towns with boy or girl names, biblical town names or just about any other topic.

The values of precancels vary greatly. While most are very modestly priced, a few are expensive rarities. The 1916 experimental Bureaus are not common, but several are well within the reach of almost every collector.

Perfin Stamps

Perfins, like precancels, had a checkered past as many early collectors regarded perfins as damaged and worthless stamps. There has been a renaissance as collectors realize that the stamps carry a unique history of American enterprise. They are usually found as used single stamps. On cover examples are also collected and highly prized, especially those used between 1908 and 1918, sometimes referred to as the "classic period" of perfins. Single stamps can be displayed from either the front or the back. Collectors interested in patterns only, usually mount their stamps "in reverse" against a dark background as the pattern is more clearly identifiable. Those that collect perfins as a sub-category of a stamp series or issue will usually display the front of the stamps.

Even though the security concept worked quite well, stamps were still stolen and collectors can find examples of a company's perfined stamps used on private letters and post cards. These illegally used stamps are termed "Illegal Usage Perfins." Perfin collecting today has acquired respectability and dealers acknowledge that perfins deserve a legitimate and valued place in their inventory.

Almanac

1903 – POD issues the first official directive in May covering the, "Conditions governing the use of Precanceled Postage Stamps."

1908 – On April 9 the POD permits, for purpose of identification only, private perforations in postage and special delivery stamps.

1908 – POD regulation on May 5 amends the allowable size of perfin holes and area permitted for perfins.

1911 – Precancels authorized on December 5 for use on Christmas parcels for the first time.

1913 – On July 1 the POD issues standard handstamps and electroplates for the production of local precancels.

1923 – On May 2 the first curved precanceling plates are made for New York and the initial shipment consists of 20 million 1¢ stamps.

1924 – On August 7 the POD authorizes the use of precanceled stamps on First Class matter under special conditions.

1928 – On August 7 the POD announces it will supply precanceled 1¢ stamped envelopes with and without printed return card.

1978 – USPS eliminates Bureau Precancels with individual post office names on September 21.

What Others Have Said

Precanceled Stamps

What a great idea: cancel the stamps ahead of time to save POD processing time

"The precancellation of stamps was put in effect at the Chicago post office Feb. 21st. This will facilitate the handling of mail matter from the large mail order houses. The first sheet of stamps was presented to Postmaster Gordon and the first order was for 410,000 stamps. Chicago did not want pre-cancelled stamps but was compelled to have them because of insufficient help at the POD."

—Weekly Philatelic ERA, *March 2, 1901.*

The idea of precancels has been around since our first stamps were issued

"You often hear the term 'Classic' precancels. There is no real set definition. It depends on the collector. Some include only 19th century items; others extend the time to 1910 or 1920. Regardless of the definition, there have been some very fine collections formed with the early precancels. The transition from the Classic to the modern precancel came gradually between 1890 and 1910 with a trend toward city and state names placed between lines or bars."

—G. William Schnall, *"A Precancel Primer – 3,"* The United States Specialist, *1985.*

Experimentation with precancels has been part of twentieth century Post Office history

"Collectors and the general public were advised of the plan [for precanceled Christmas stamps] through the Post Office Department's Philatelic Release No. 57, Friday, October 31, 1969, which stated: 'An experimental precanceled Christmas stamp, aimed at reducing costs and speeding holiday mail, will be issued November 4 in four pilot cities [Atlanta, Baltimore, Memphis and New Haven], Postmaster General Winton M. Blount announced today....These four cities will be the only areas which will have the new special 6-cent Christmas stamp precanceled with the city name in green ink. Elsewhere, this special stamp...will not be precanceled.'"

—William H. Bayless, *"The 1969 Baltimore MD Precanceled Christmas Stamp,"* The United States Specialist, *1970.*

One of the most famed collectors was the foremost precancel collector

"An inveterate stamp collector for eight decades, Mr. Boker began collecting United States precancels as a 10-year-old, when he acquired a box of stamps bearing mostly New York and New Jersey precancels. Years of careful study and determination, along with a discriminating eye, allowed him to assemble perhaps the most significant collection of U.S. precancels. By the mid-1990's, he had amassed several hundred thousand precancels, documenting better than 99 percent of all known types of precancels."

—*Charles R. Snee's obituary for John R. Boker Jr., Linn's Stamp News, 2003.*

Perfin Stamps

In the beginning perfins were thought to be nothing more than trash...
"Finding Perfins on the 1902 issue is difficult...as the bulk of perfins on the 1902 issue long ago were thrown into the wastebasket by accumulators and dealers who thought them defective."

—*William Corliss, "Perfins on the Bureau issue of 1902," The Perfins Bulletin, 1973.*

...but have since created a wonderful following among many collectors
"Perfin collecting is one of those common denominations of philately. The extreme specialist, the topical collector, the cover enthusiast all can find something of interest in perforated initial stamps. Perfins also form an interesting and integral part of postal history and for this reason alone belong in collections instead of wastebaskets. As a specialty in themselves or as a satellite collection perfins offer much in enjoyment and opportunities for original research."

—*William R. Corliss, "Railroading with Stuart Perfins," The Bureau Specialist, 1952.*

Perfins have their most treasured finds
"The most sought after perfin stamp of the classic 1902 Series is the 2-cent "Flag" design that was produced only for eleven months in 1902. I have seen only one 2-cent Flag perfin stamp properly used in the 1908 period."

—*Roger Brody, Collectors Club of New York presentation, February 1997.*

Examples of Postal Usage

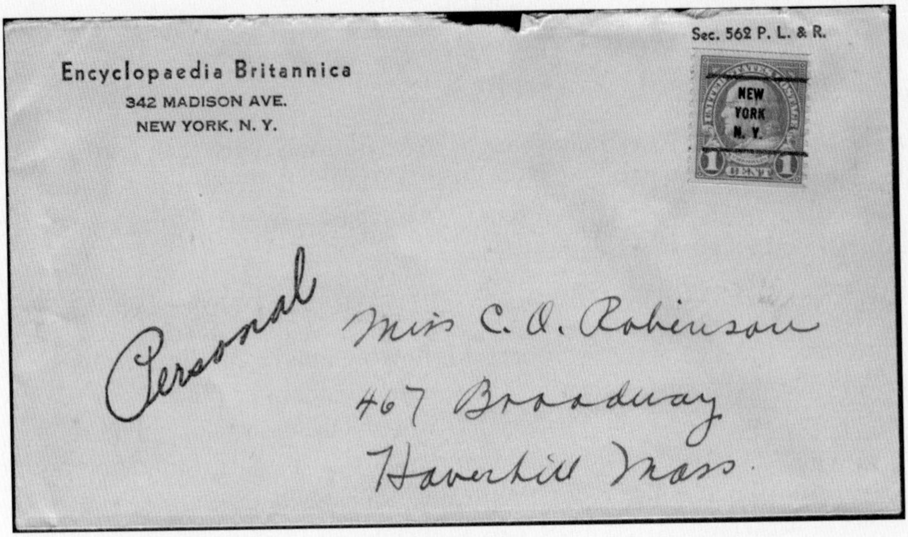

Figure 9

A "New York N.Y." Bureau precancel used on a Third Class mailing. Note the reference to "P. L. & R." (Postal Laws and Regulations) printed on the envelope.

Figure 10

Ford Motor Company perfin on cover.

Where to Find More Information

Precanceled Stamps

- G. William Schall, "A Precancel Primer."

- *U.S. Postage Precancel Primer* by Barbara R. Mueller is a detailed introduction to everything the beginning collector needs to know about collecting precancels.

- *Precancel Stamp Society Catalog of US Bureau Precancels*, edited by Dick Laetsch, is fully illustrated with an introduction explaining Bureau prints.

- *The Precancel Stamp Society Town and Type Catalog of the U.S. and Territories*, by Philp Cayford and Arnold H. Selengut, provides a complete listing of all recognized local precancels, alphabetically by state and town. All precancel styles are illustrated.

- *Precanceled Envelopes of the United States*, David W. Smith, editor, lists all known precanceled envelopes by state and United Postal Stationery Society catalog number.

- The Precancel Stamp Society Inc. publishes *The Precancel Forum* monthly containing information on every aspect of precancel collecting, as well as numerous catalogs for the many different precancel types. The Society's website (www.precancels.org) contains important historical precancel data and information about articles, publications, catalog information and materials for precancel collecting.

Perfin Stamps

- *Catalog of United States Perfins: a Catalog and Album of Security Punches on United States Postage Stamps, 1908-1998* by John M. Randall is a comprehensive loose-leaf catalogue listing thousands of perfins and includes a useful introduction and index.

- The Perfins Club official newsletter the *Perfins Bulletin* is published 10 times annually.

Chapter 30
Carriers' and Locals

From the Colonial era through the middle of the nineteenth century, and even later, intermediaries sometimes helped move mail. The stamps issued in connection with their activities are known as **Carriers'** and *Locals*.

Carriers' Stamps

Free delivery of mail to businesses and homes was instituted in selected cities in 1863. Prior to then, ordinary postage only paid for mail to be transported from one post office to another. Those desiring mail to be delivered to their home or business, or to have mail carried to the post office, could get that service, where it was available, for an extra fee, typically 1¢ or 2¢ for each piece. Local post offices employed or contracted with individuals (carriers) to provide this service in a number of cities. They were salaried by the post office, or compensated on a fee basis. Stamps issued for this service are called Carriers' Stamps, or simply, carriers.

Figure 1
The first official carrier stamps (LO1) were used in Philadelphia, New Orleans and New York in 1851.

There are two types of Carriers' Stamps, official and semi-official. The two official carrier stamps, depicting Benjamin Franklin (*Scott* LO1, fig. 1) and an eagle (LO2), were issued in 1851. These general issues are known to have been used in New York, Philadelphia, and New Orleans. The eagle carrier was also used in Wilmington, Delaware; Washington, D.C.; Cincinnati, Ohio; and Kensington, Pennsylvania. Both official carriers were printed by **Toppan, Carpenter, Casilear & Co.**, and, like all carriers, are imperforate.

Figure 2
A semi-official carrier stamp (1LB8) from Baltimore.

Semi-official carriers' stamps were issued in Baltimore, Maryland (fig. 2); Boston, Massachusetts; Charleston, South Carolina; Cincinnati, Ohio; Cleveland, Ohio; Louisville, Kentucky; New York, New York; Philadelphia, Pennsylvania; and St. Louis, Missouri. They were valid only in the city in which they were issued, and they were either issued directly by the postmaster, or at least sanctioned by him. These semi-official issues all have a "LB" in their *Scott* number.

Carrier service for a fee was made obsolete when free city delivery was available, beginning July 1, 1863. At that time all mail carriers became employees of the U.S. Post Office. The Postmaster General's report for 1863 indicates that 49 cities were providing carrier service, having each from one to 137 carriers.

Local Stamps

Local stamps were issued by private posts. Their *Scott* numbers contain an "L". As the term "local" implies, many private posts operated in a single locale (a particular city). However others, generally known as express companies, provided package delivery service to a much larger area. Sometimes private posts simply complemented the work of the Post Office, functioning much as the official carriers did, delivering mail to and from a local post office. However, private posts also competed with the official Post Office, offering an alternative mail system.

Figure 3

An 1846 local stamp (15L5) issued by D.O. Blood of Philadelphia.

Over 175 different local companies delivered mail in 37 cities during their golden age in the 1840s and 1850s. Some of the better-known companies were D.O. Blood & Co., which operated in Philadelphia and was one of the largest local posts (fig. 3), and three New York City companies: Boyd's City Express, a.k.a. Boyd's City Dispatch, a.k.a. Boyd's Dispatch; Hussey's Post; and City Despatch Post. City Despatch Post is of particular interest because it issued the first adhesive stamp used in the United States (40L1, fig. 4). It was begun on February 1, 1842, but was soon purchased by the U.S. Government and ceased to operate as a private post on August 15, 1842. The next day it reopened as "United States City Despatch Post", an official provider of carrier services! It is interesting to note that entrepreneur Alexander M. Greig, a founder of City Post Despatch, was now an official U.S. letter carrier, supervising the company he had sold to the government. Numerous local posts operated in the profitable New York market, but local posts also operated in other large cities such as Cleveland, Ohio; Brooklyn, New York; and Chicago, Illinois; as well as smaller towns like Millville, New Jersey; and Westtown, Pennsylvania.

Figure 4

This local stamp issued by the City Despatch Post in New York (40L1) was the first adhesive stamp used in the United States.

The acquisition of Greig's New York company by the government is indicative of the efforts of the U.S. Government to thwart private posts, and retain a postal monopoly. The Postal Law passed by Congress in 1845 suppressed inter-city mail routes by prohibiting the carrying of letters by private companies where the Post Office offered inter-city mail service, and an 1861 law put an end to most, but not all, local posts. Some survived because they carried bills, circulars, and notices. Hussey's and Boyd's, in New York, managed to stay a step ahead of the law and keep their local posts in business into the 1880s by serving the banking and insurance industries (fig. 5).

Figure 5

Local stamp of long-lived Hussey's Post (87L59) issued in 1877.

Some of the private posts maintained boxes for the deposit of letters at various locations around the cities they served. If a letter was to be delivered within that city by the local post, it required only that company's local stamp. If the letter was to be delivered to the official post office, it often bore a government postage stamp as well. After 1847 cancellation of the stamps was done in a variety of ways, including hand stamp, pen, pencil, or crayon. As is the case today, many covers went through the system without any cancellation at all.

Independent Mails

Some of the private posts were regional and handled the mail in several cities. These are known as independent mail companies. The American Letter Mail Company (fig. 6) had offices in New York City, Philadelphia, and Boston.

Figure 6

American Letter Mail Co., an independent mail company, issued this stamp (5L1), in 1844.

Overton and Company delivered mail between New York City and Boston as well as Albany. Brainard and Company serviced mail in New York, Albany and Troy, three cities in New York. Hale & Company served points in New England, New York State, Philadelphia, and Baltimore. The Letter Express Company served Western New York, Chicago, Detroit, and Duluth, Minnesota. The Hartford, Connecticut Mail Route operated to points south, west and east. Pomeroy operated in New York State. These seven independent mail companies connected with each other to carry the mail. Covers handled by more than one private post are known as conjunctive usage. The private carriage of inter-city mail, without the payment of U.S. postage, was prohibited after July 1, 1845.

While private posts complemented or competed with the Post Office in the eastern U.S., they were sometimes the only option in the mid-nineteenth century for the western part of the country. In the midst of the California Gold Rush, Adams & Co.'s Express was formed in September 1849, operating along the Pacific Coast. California Penny Post was established in 1855 and served cities in Northern California (San Francisco, Sacramento, Stockton, Marysville, and Benicia) as well as cities in the nearby Gold Country (Coloma, Nevada City, Grass Valley, and Mokelumne Hill). However, probably the most legendary private express company was **Wells, Fargo and Co.**, which began operating in the western U.S. in 1852. Acquiring other companies, it became the dominant express company in its territory. Wells, Fargo is perhaps best remembered for its connection with the legendary **Pony Express** (fig. 7). The Pony Express was begun by William Russell, Alexander Majors, and William Waddell. Wells, Fargo and Co. became its agent in April 1861, issuing distinctive Pony Express stamps and franked envelopes. The Pony Express operated between St. Joseph, Missouri and Sacramento, California, from April 3, 1860, until October 26, 1861 – two days after the completion of the transcontinental telegraph line. Pony Express service was not inexpensive. A ½ ounce letter carried by the heroic young men on horse back was initially charged $5, plus regular U.S. postage. Rates were later reduced, eventually to $1 per ½ ounce.

Figure 7

The 25¢ red Wells Fargo & Co. Pony Express stamp (143L9) carried mail on the Virginia City, Nevada Territory to San Francisco, California route. It is known to have been used from June 20, 1864 to March 17, 1865.

Although the golden age of the local post came to an end around 1861, local posts have never fully vanished from the scene. Some operated because the government was slow to begin service in remote areas. The Glen Haven Daily Mail was operated by the hotels and sanatoriums in Glen Haven, New York to carry mail to the post office in Home or Scott, New York. In 1898, during the Alaska Gold Rush, the McGreely's Express Company was formed in Alaska and carried mail between Skagway and Dyea by motorboat.

In June 1894, when the American Railway Union workers went on strike an enterprising individual, Arthur C. Banta, an agent for the Victor Bicycle Company, established bicycle mail service from Fresno to San Francisco (fig. 8). The service was conducted by a relay of eight bicycles traveling the 210 miles between the two cities. The most difficult leg of the trip was from Menlo Park,

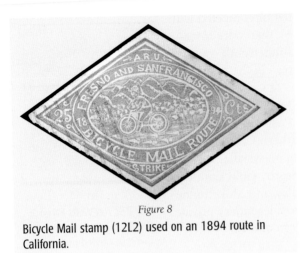

Figure 8

Bicycle Mail stamp (12L2) used on an 1894 route in California.

as the rider was required to deliver the mail to San Francisco, pick up mail bound for Fresno, and then immediately return to Menlo Park. This leg was effectively a 60-mile round trip. The Bicycle Mail Route lasted only thirteen days from July 6 to July 18, 1894. Only 380 covers are known to have made the trip between San Francisco and Fresno. Deliveries were made along the way as well.

As with the railway strike of 1894, other local posts were established due to circumstantial events. An example was Blizzard Mail, which serviced New York City from March 12–16, 1888. U. S. mail service was interrupted during a blizzard at that time. The New York Times of March 13, 1888, called it "The Worst Storm the City Has Ever Known."

Figure 9

Rattlesnake Island air mail local stamp, unlisted in Scott.

There has even been an air mail local post, operating from 1966 through 1989 between Rattlesnake Island, a resort island in Lake Erie, and the Ohio mainland at Port Clinton. The service resumed in 2005. A number of colorful stamps were issued, but none are listed in *Scott* (fig. 9).

Finally, one should note the ill-fated Independent Postal System of America, which attempted to compete with the United States Postal System in 1971, and even issued its own stamps. The courts required it to suspend operation.

Notes on Collecting

Most collectors of carriers and locals build a collection by acquiring individual stamps. This allows greater flexibility in acquisitions rather than the challenge of acquiring them on cover. There is one problem; forgeries have plagued collectors of U.S. locals since they were first collected in the 1860s. A good forgery reference is needed when collecting U.S. local and carrier stamps. An alternative to possessing forgery reference material is to have purchases *expertized*. Most forgeries were created by three men: John W. Scott, S. Allan Taylor, or George Hussey, many being made during the 1860s. These forgeries have become collectibles in their own right.

Almanac

1689 – The first known carrier service is operated by the postmaster of Boston.

1836 – On July 2, an Act of Congress, modified in 1851, establishes the basic law governing carrier service, providing a maximum carrier fee of 2¢.

1845 – Most Independent Mail Routes, operating in competition with the Post Office, are forced out of business by the Postal Reform Act on July 1.

1851 – Act passes Congress March 3 setting the charge for carrier service at 1¢ or 2¢.

1851 – The Franklin Official Carrier Stamp (LO1) is issued in September.

1851 – Eagle Official Carrier Stamp (LO2) is issued in November.

1860 – The transcontinental Pony Express begins operating on April 3 between St. Joseph, Missouri and Sacramento, California.

1861 – Last trip of the transcontinental Pony Express occurs October 26.

1861 – Nearly all Local Posts are forced out of business except two New York locals: Boyd's and Hussey.

1863 – Carrier service is discontinued June 30; all carriers become salaried employees of the Post Office.

1883 – The Government raids the offices of Boyd's and Hussey on May 4, effectively ending their existence as local posts.

1888 – Blizzard Mail operates in New York City March 12 through 16.

1894 – Bicycle Mail Route operates between Fresno and San Francisco from July 6 through 18.

1898 – McGreely Express Company is formed in Alaska to deliver mail for the miners participating in the Alaska Gold Rush.

What Others Have Said

Exact start up dates of many local carriers are often difficult to determine
"The commencement date for Greig's City Despatch Post established in New York February 1, 1842 has some controversy attached to it…Greig's own advertisement declared the post operational on February 7, 1842. Very few first week usages have survived to provide sufficient evidence to prove or disprove the declared start date…. The first cover [illustrated here has a] cds that ties the Greig's (40L1) stamp dated February 1, (1842) at 9 o'clock. The controversy with this cover is that it has a second cds dated February 25, (1842) at 9 o'clock. The second strike of the circular date stamp has led some students to speculate that certain letters, this among them, could not be delivered until much later than February 1st….[It is pretty certain] that [only] circulars were handled the first week and the carrying of patron mail began on February 7, (1842) as announced by Alexander M. Greig."

—*Larry Lyons, "First Day of Operation of Greig's City Despatch Post,"* The Penny Post, *2004.*

A quarter of a million Carrier Stamps disappear for six months
"On October 11, 1851 there were 250,000 one cent stamps noted as 'carriers' sent to New York City. For some reason which… the records of shipments and arrivals do not explain, this shipment was not received at the New York post office until April 15, 1852…Franklin carriers are known used in both New Orleans and Philadelphia but neither the Franklin nor Eagle could have been used extensively in New York – certainly nothing like the 250,000 of the Franklin were used in New York. Franklin or Eagle stamps bearing genuine New York cancellations or genuinely used on New York covers are excessively rare if they exist at all. What happened to the large supply of Franklin stamps between October 11, 1851 and April 15, 1852 and what became of them after they finally reached New York? I can only hazard a guess that…the package went astray…and most of the stamps, or all of them were not used."

—*Elliott Perry, "The Franklin Carrier,"* Collectors Club Philatelist, *1930.*

The Pony Express' 80th Anniversary is commemorated with a stamp on April 3, 1940
"More has been written about the Pony Express than any other episode in U.S. communications history….to refresh our readers interested in the 3¢ commemorative to be issued April 3rd, we have attempted in this article to cover the general history of the Express. The unusual feature, generally overlooked is that it was not a government conducted postal service, but started and ended as a com-

munication service conducted by a private organization…The route's rise and fall in the short space of 20 months entails a combination of elements that tend to make the story of the Pony Express sound more like a blood and thunder melodrama rather than a business venture which was a failure: the construction of the first transcontinental telegraph, the outbreak of the Civil War, Indian troubles so bad that troops had to be called out, a Senator so disloyal to the federal cause he was imprisoned…"

—*Bob Richardson, "The Pony Express Anniversary," Linn's Stamp Weekly, 1940.*

The Private Carriers are able to deliver newspapers faster than the USPOD
"Wells Fargo & Co. also issued six different stamps between the period of 1861–88 for the carrying of one newspaper over their routes in New York, in California and over any of their routes in the United States. The stamps are similar in appearance; some are imperforate, rouletted 10, and perforated 10, 11 and 12. One is black in color, the others are all blue. These are listed in Scott's Catalogue as 143LP1 to 143LP9…..Due to the large and profitable business developed by the Express companies, the Government tried to step in. The effort was not successful. The reason for the Government's failure to obtain the carriage of newspapers in large quantities was due to the fact that papers handled by the Post Office Department had to be delivered from the post office, whereas the Express companies delivered the papers direct from the train immediately on its arrival; thus, newsdealers were served by the private carriers at least a half-hour earlier than they could be by the Post Office."

—*J. Frank Braceland, "Newspapers and Periodicals," The United States Specialist, 1966.*

Example of Postal Usage

Figure 10

A (1¢) black Broadway Post Office local (26L2), tied together with a 3¢ cent stamp (11) by a New York postmark to an 1853 letter to Ithaca, New York. The Broadway Post Office in New York City was founded in 1848 by James C. Harriott.

Where to Find More Information

- *The Pony Express: A Postal History* by Frajola, Kramer, and Walske provides a colorful history of this fabled service, and a census of known covers.

- An authoritative source on fakes and forgeries of carriers and locals is Larry Lyon's, *The Identifier for Carriers, Locals, Fakes, Forgeries and Bogus Posts*.

- The Carriers and Locals Society maintains a useful website at www.pennypost.org.

Chapter 31
Confederate States of America

On December 20, 1860, South Carolina became the first state to secede from the Union. Other states followed quickly and on February 4, 1861 delegates from seceded states assembled in Montgomery, Alabama and formed the Confederate States of America (CSA). The CSA Post Office Department was created on February 21 of that year, but did not immediately begin operations. On March 6, John H. Reagan of Texas was appointed CSA Postmaster General. On April 12 Fort Sumter was attacked and the Civil War had begun. Yet through all of these events, U.S. mail service continued in the southern states, and mail moved freely between north and south! It was only on June 1, 1861 that the United States Post Office ceased to function in the South, and its stamps were no longer valid for postage in the Confederacy. It is interesting to note that all stamps available on that date were eventually *demonetized* in the North as well, in order to prevent supplies still existing in southern hands from being sold to help finance the Confederacy. At the same time that U.S. mail service in the South officially ended, the CSA post office began operations. The cost of mailing a half-ounce letter up to 500 miles was set at 5¢ (an increase from the prewar rate of 3¢). Letters traveling over 500 miles were charged 10¢. *Drop letters* were 2¢.

On March 27, PMG Reagan had advertised for bidders for a stamp contract, and he hoped to obtain high quality stamps, printed from *engraved* steel plates, such as were in use in the North. The attack on Ft. Sumter, and beginning of hostilities, ended that hope. Reagan eventually had to settle for lower quality stamps produced by *lithography*, and a contract was awarded to the firm of Hoyer & Ludwig in Richmond, Virginia.

Figure 1

A New Orleans Postmaster Provisional (62X1), issued in 1861.

The first CSA stamp was not available until October 16, 1861. Thus for a period of almost half a year there were no postage stamps to use in the CSA! During this period some postmasters reverted to the practice of marking letters **PAID** when payment was tendered by a customer. Other post-masters produced and sold adhesive stamps (fig. 1) and envelopes on a local basis, for use in their towns. Such "provisionals" exist from at least 150 southern towns, most of which are very rare. "Paid" markings are relatively common.

Before CSA presses were stilled in 1865, a total of 13 different stamps (*Scott* 1-13) were issued that actually saw postal use. Eight of them picture Jefferson Davis, CSA president. Two stamps feature Thomas Jefferson. Andrew Jackson appears on two and George Washington on one. A fourteenth stamp (14), a 1¢ John C. Calhoun, was printed and delivered, but never used. All CSA stamps are imperforate except for a small quantity of two of the 10¢ Jefferson Davis stamps (11e and 12f).

Figure 2

A margin copy of the 1862 "London" printing of the 5¢ Jefferson Davis (6). Subsequent stamps printed in Richmond (7) show a coarser impression.

The stamps we know as *Scott* 2, 11, and 12 were each printed by two different printers. Considering stamps from each printer as a different stamp raises from 14 to 17 the number of stamps required for a "complete" CSA collection.

The first five stamps issued by the CSA consisted of 5¢ and 10¢ stamps, and a 2¢ drop rate stamp (1-5). They were printed by lithography, which produced stamps of less than stellar quality. PMG Reagan dispatched an agent to England in an effort to obtain higher quality stamps. The prominent London printing firm of Thomas De La Rue & Co. produced printing plates and a supply of stamps for the CSA. However, they were intercepted by Union forces and never reached the CSA.

More were produced and a second delivery was successful. Light blue 5¢ Jefferson Davis stamps (6, fig. 2), and the plates from which they were printed, reached Richmond in 1862. Stamps subsequently printed from these plates in Richmond (7) are greatly inferior to their London printed counterparts.

In 1863, PMG Reagan was finally able to obtain the engraved stamps he desired (8-13) by awarding a contract to the firm of Archer & Daly. Two of these stamps (11, fig. 3 and 12) were printed by Archer &

Figure 3

A 10¢ Jefferson Davis (11).

Daly, and then, later, from the same plates, by Keatinge & Ball of Columbia, South Carolina. In 1865, as the war entered its final stages, the employees of Keatinge & Ball placed these plates in the Congaree River to prevent their fall into Union hands. There are no 5¢ values among these engraved stamps since the basic letter rate had been raised to 10¢ on July 1, 1862. These engraved stamps consist of four 10¢ stamps (9-12), a 2¢ stamp (8) to met the drop rate, and a 20¢ George Washington (13, fig. 4) to pay double the letter rate.

Figure 4

The 20¢ Washington (13) of 1863 was intended to pay for a double weight letter.

The exigencies of war created hardships that gave rise to some desirable covers. For example, "blockade" covers are those that managed to evade the Union blockade of the Atlantic and Gulf coasts. After the Union gained control of the Mississippi River in 1863 the CSA was divided, and mail did not pass easily between the two sections. A trans-Mississippi rate of 40¢ was established for these covers that were essentially "smuggled" across the river. Another interesting category of cover is the "adversity" cover. As paper became scarcer with the progression of the war, some people used any paper they could find for their correspondence, including wallpaper and previously used envelopes turned inside out! Prisoner of war covers and *patriotic covers* not only document the postal history of the era, but political and social history as well.

Notes on Collecting

Successfully collecting Confederate stamps and postal history requires a good working knowledge of many dates of civil war history.

Many fakes and forgeries exist of CSA stamps and covers. It is advisable to make purchases from a reputable dealer, and to secure an expert opinion on more valuable items.

There are hundreds of varieties of stampless covers, handstamp paid and manuscript covers, as well as provisional adhesive stamps and envelopes used before the Confederate government could issue regular stamps. In addition to the 17 major varieties of the 13 regular issue Confederate States stamps, there are also minor varieties and endless shades. There are Prisoner-of-War and Flag-of-Truce covers, Express Company markings, Blockade-Run covers to and from Europe, College covers, Official and Semi-Official envelopes, Packet and Steamboat covers, Patriotic covers with their war mottos, and covers showing use of United States stamps in the Confederacy. There are envelopes made of wallpaper, envelopes used twice over, and United States stamped envelopes seized and overprinted for the use of the Confederacy. Confederate stamp collecting epitomizes the thrill of the hunt.

Almanac

1860 – On December 20 South Carolina is the first state to secede.

1861 – John H. Reagan is appointed CSA Postmaster General on March 6.

1861 – Fort Sumter is attacked on April 12 and the Civil War begins.

1861 – On May 13 PMG Reagan announces the CSA postal service will begin operation on June 1.

1861 – On May 27 U.S. Postmaster General Montgomery Blair announces suspension of postal service in the Confederate States, effective May 31.

1861 – On June 1 the CSA postal service begins operation, with a letter rate of 5¢ for up to 500 miles, and 10¢ for over 500 miles.

1861 – First stamp, printed by Hoyer & Ludwig, is issued October 16.

1862 – Letter rate is increased to 10¢ on July 1.

1863 – The fall of Port Hudson, Louisiana on July 9 impedes Confederate mail service across the Mississippi River.

1865 – Four stamp printing plates are sunk in the Congaree River as Columbia, South Carolina falls to Union forces on February 17.

1865 – PMG Regan is captured at Irwinsville, Georgia on May 10.

What Others Have Said

Covers are needed to tell the Confederate story

"Covers are required for the greater portion of the collection. Postmarks, cancellations, backstamps, forwarded, dues, and a wide variety of other markings are in this way at our disposal and aid greatly in our studies. For the other part, to demonstrate papers, shades, minor varieties, imprints and so forth, large blocks and even panes or sheets of the unused are much to be desired...."

—Don Preston Peters, *"A comprehensive Confederate Collection,"* First American Philatelic Congress, *1935.*

He was a great postmaster general... for the rebels!

"John Henninger Reagan of Texas was appointed postmaster general [of the CSA]...Reagan was a masterful executive. Under his direction, the department actually made a profit. This was an incredible achievement, especially in view of conditions in the wartime South. Even the Union officials were impressed. In 1865, after the war had ended, Reagan was asked to assume responsibilities in the post-war U.S. Post Office Department. He declined."

—*Patricia A. Kaufmann, "The Rebel Post,"* Scott's Monthly Stamp Journal, *1976.*

Confederate covers are sought after...especially those of Robert E. Lee!

"The collecting of Confederate stamps is associated closely with the study of history of the great and tragic period ...our Civil War. No collector of them can fail to become a student of the Confederacy and its postal history, and as his studies progress his collection acquires more and more objects of historical interest. There are so many to be sought after,—The Prisoner-of-War and Flag-of-Truce covers, the Blockade and Express covers, the "turned" and home-made covers, the covers used with United States stamps after secession....those embellished and illuminated with Confederate flags and other patriotic designs. But, of them all, no single group or classification can quite equal...the covers addressed and autographed by the Confederacy's truly great and historic leader, General Robert E. Lee!"

—*Van Dyk Macbride, "The Autographed Field Letters of General Robert E. Lee,"* The Stamp Specialist – India Book, *1946.*

When there were no postage stamps available

"One of the most interesting emergency measures resorted to by Confederate Postmasters when (after June 1, 1861) they had no stamps, was the issuance of some of their own provisional adhesive stamps. These were usually recognized as having paid postage only when used by the issuing post office itself. They were generally withdrawn, or use terminated, after government stamps became available in 1861 or early 1862. A few postmasters west of the Mississippi River, principally in Texas, used such provisionals in 1863 and 1864 after Federal Forces had taken control of the river and supplies of stamps became exhausted."

—*Charles E. Kilbourne, "Confederate Philately,"* Collectors Club Philatelist, *1977.*

The Challenge of Confederate Collecting is knowing the many dates

"As the first of June approached, Montgomery Blair, Postmaster General of the United States, issued his order...on May 27, 1861, which read: 'All postal service in the States of Virginia, North Carolina, South Carolina, Georgia, Florida, Alabama, Mississippi, Louisiana, Arkansas and Texas, will be suspended from and after the 31st instant. Letters for offices temporarily closed by this order will be forwarded to the Dead Letter Office, except those for Western Virginia, which will be sent to Wheeling'....During the next four years service was discontinued and reinstated throughout the south and west with the fortunes of war...."

—John L. Kay, "U.S. Postal Operations and the Beginning of the Civil War," La Posta: A Journal of American Postal History, 1984.

Example of Postal Usage

Figure 5

A typical CSA cover, paying the single weight rate of 10¢ that went into effect July 1, 1862. A 10¢ Jefferson Davis (11) is used on this Dec. 16, 1864 cover from Cartersville, Ga. to Milledgeville, Ga.

Figure 6

A 5¢ Jefferson Davis (1), tied by a Carolina City, N.C., Mar. 12, 1862 postmark on an illustrated patriotic cover with a Jefferson Davis Medallion design with Confederate flags.

Figure 7

A 10¢ Thomas Jefferson (5) on a wallpaper cover, tied by a Corpus Christi, Texas postmark.

Where to Find More Information

- *Confederate Postal History, An Anthology from The Stamp Specialist* edited by Francis J. Crown, Jr.

- *The Postal Service of the Confederate States of America*, by August Dietz is considered the standard work in Confederate Philately.

- *The Confederate States Post-Office Department, Its Stamps & Stationery: A Record of Achievement*, by August Dietz.

- *The New Dietz Confederate States Catalog and Handbook*, by Skinner, Gunter, and Sanders.

- *Confederate States: How to tell the Genuine from the Counterfeit*, by Richard Krieger and Peter Powell.

- www.csalliance.org/ The Confederate Stamp Alliance.

- www.jlkstamps.com/ Confederate States of America Stamps and Postal History.

History, Production, and Technology

Chapter 32
United States Post Office Department

"Neither snow, nor rain, nor heat, nor gloom of night stays these couriers from the swift completion of their appointed rounds." These words, penned by the Greek historian Herodotus in the 6th Century BC/BCE, were inscribed atop the Main Post Office in New York City. Through the years they have come to represent the importance of getting the mail delivered, and may be considered the unofficial motto of the Post Office.

In 1639 a tavern in Boston was designated as the official repository for mail brought from or going overseas, and is regarded as the first post office. In the years that followed, many post offices, like that first one, were operated in commercial establishments. The first attempt at a postal organization came in 1692 at the order of the British crown.

Benjamin Franklin, regarded as the Father of the American postal system, was appointed deputy postmaster general by the British in 1753. By the time the British fired him in 1774, post roads operated from Maine to Georgia. In 1775 Franklin was reappointed Postmaster General, by the Continental Congress.

One might ask: "Who was the first Postmaster General (PMG) of the United States?" Most might answer Benjamin Franklin, but in fact it was Samuel Osgood. Osgood was PMG from 1789 to 1791. He had the distinction of being the first PMG appointed under the newly adopted Constitution.

President Andrew Jackson appointed PMG William Barry to his Cabinet in 1829. Barry dispensed partisan patronage at unprecedented levels. Until 1971 the PMG was frequently the president's chief dispenser of patronage, and a number of men were appointed PMG not because they had any skill or knowledge useful in managing the Department, but simply because they were members of the right political party at the right time.

Moving the mail in an ever-growing country was a major challenge in the nineteenth century. Steamboats began carrying the mail in 1811. Even before gold was discovered in California steamships carried mail to California. The

"Overland Mail" was a stagecoach line that carried mail to and from California for the Post Office beginning in 1858. Faster transportation of the mail was needed and three partners, William Russell, Alexander Majors, and William Waddell stepped up to the challenge. They organized the private **Pony Express**, which carried mail from St. Joseph, Missouri to Sacramento beginning April 3, 1860. The trip took ten days and required 75 horses. The cost of sending a letter was very expensive when the service began, $5 for each half-ounce. The rate was later reduced to $1. The fastest delivery was in March 1861, when President Lincoln's inaugural address was carried from St. Joseph to Sacramento in 7 days and 17 hours. On July 1, 1861 the Pony Express began operating under contract as a mail route. Less then four months later the Pony Express ended. It was made obsolete by completion of the transcontinental telegraph line.

The growing nation's railroads carried the mail as early as 1836, and in 1838 all railroads were designated as post roads. In 1864 the Post Office Department (POD) created the first **Railway Post Office** (RPO). In these specially designed rail cars, mail was sorted and transported simultaneously. RPO cars featured sorting bins and trays. Clerks would open sacks of mail and toss the letters into bins labeled by names of various cities and towns. In 1941, with rail service in inexorable decline, specially designed motor vehicles, with interiors similar to a RPO, were placed into service. Known as **Highway Post Offices** (HPO) they went places no longer served by trains.

Until 1863 postage only paid for mail to be carried from one post office to another. Getting it home was the citizen's problem. Some relief came in 1863 with the introduction of free delivery to individual homes and businesses in cities meeting certain requirements. But as one farmer asked in 1891, "Why should the cities have fancy mail service and the old colonial system still prevail in the country districts?" The answer to his complaint was **Rural Free Delivery** (RFD), established to bring mail deliveries to the farmer's door. After a period of experimentation, it became a permanent service in 1902.

As the nineteenth century came to a close the POD moved into a new building, servings as a headquarters, on Pennsylvania Avenue in Washington, D.C. (fig. 1). New postal services came rapidly in the new century. In 1911 a Postal Savings System was established at designated Post Offices. For the many people who could not afford to deposit a full dollar at one time, savings stamps were introduced, to allow small depositors to accumulate even dollar amounts. A "U.S. Postal Savings Card" was sold with ten spaces for the stamps. Ten-cent postal savings stamps were purchased and pasted onto a savings card. After being redeemed these cards were cancelled. For many years the system was considered the largest savings system in America. The POD stopped accepting deposits in April 1966.

In 1913 a domestic Parcel Post was introduced. This spurred the growth of the great mail-order companies, by making low-cost package delivery available to every household.

Scheduled air mail service began in 1918 with flights between New York and Washington, D.C. via Philadelphia. Through the 1920s air mail service expanded. A transcontinental route was established from New York to San Francisco, with a growing number of "feeder" routes. In the mid-1920s carrying air mail was privatized. It is not an exaggeration to say that commercial aviation in this country got off the ground, literally and figuratively, by carrying the mail. Trans-Pacific air mail service began in 1935 and in 1939 air mail was first carried across the Atlantic.

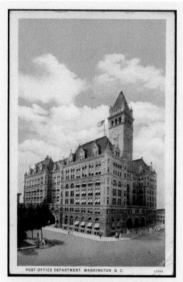

Figure 1

The Old Post Office Building in Washington, D.C.

PMG Will Hays left a lasting legacy to stamp collectors, even though his term of office was only from 1921 to 1922. At the urging of his Third Assistant PMG, W. Irving Glover, Hays created the Philatelic Sales Agency so that collectors could purchase stamps in choice condition (fig. 2). He announced in December 1921, "It is the purpose of the Philatelic Stamp Agency to keep on hand specimens of all future issues and all such discontinued issues…for sale to collectors and dealers…also a small stock of the current series of ordinary stamps, well-centered and perforated."

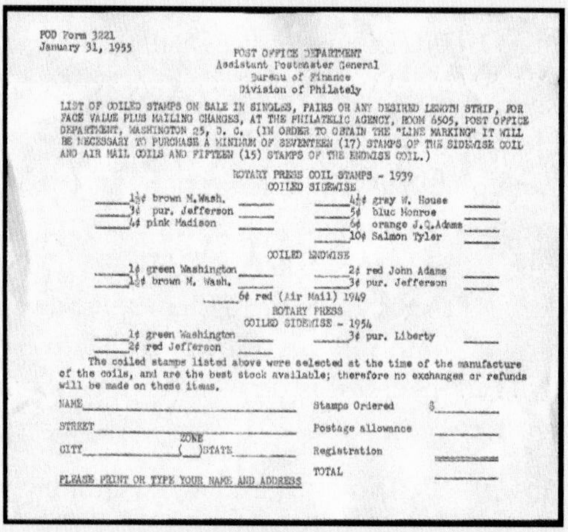

POD Form 3221
January 31, 1955

POST OFFICE DEPARTMENT
Assistant Postmaster General
Bureau of Finance
Division of Philately

LIST OF COILED STAMPS ON SALE IN SINGLES, PAIRS OR ANY DESIRED LENGTH STRIP, FOR FACE VALUE PLUS MAILING CHARGES, AT THE PHILATELIC AGENCY, ROOM 6505, POST OFFICE DEPARTMENT, WASHINGTON 25, D. C. (IN ORDER TO OBTAIN THE "LINE MARKING" IT WILL BE NECESSARY TO PURCHASE A MINIMUM OF SEVENTEEN (17) STAMPS OF THE SIDEWISE COIL AND AIR MAIL COILS AND FIFTEEN (15) STAMPS OF THE ENDWISE COIL.)

ROTARY PRESS COIL STAMPS - 1939
COILED SIDEWISE

_____ $1\frac{1}{2}$¢ brown M.Wash. _____   _____ $4\frac{1}{2}$¢ gray W. House _____
_____ 3¢ pur. Jefferson _____   _____ 5¢ bluc Monroe _____
_____ 4¢ pink Madison _____   _____ 6¢ orange J.Q.Adams _____
_____ 10¢ Salmon Tyler _____

COILED ENDWISE

_____ 1¢ green Washington _____   _____ 2¢ red John Adams _____
_____ $1\frac{1}{2}$¢ brown M. Wash. _____   _____ 3¢ pur. Jefferson _____
_____ 6¢ red (Air Mail) 1949

ROTARY PRESS
COILED SIDEWISE - 1954

_____ 1¢ green Washington _____   _____ 3¢ pur. Liberty _____
_____ 2¢ red Jefferson _____

The coiled stamps listed above were selected at the time of the manufacture of the coils, and are the best stock available; therefore no exchanges or refunds will be made on these items.

NAME_____   Stamps Ordered $_____
STREET_____   Postage allowance _____
CITY_____ ZONE (__) STATE_____   Registration _____
TOTAL _____

PLEASE PRINT OR TYPE YOUR NAME AND ADDRESS

Figure 2

A mimeographed order form for ordering stamps that were in stock at the Philatelic Agency in Washington in 1955.

C.E. Nickles, a famous stamp dealer, wrote in 1927, "You may credit W. Irving Glover, Third Assistant Postmaster General in 1921 and his associates in the Division of Stamps with being great benefactors of philately, for to their endeavors the Philatelic Agency owes its existence." Glover may have been motivated when he happened upon a letter the POD received from a collector complaining that when he asked for a well-centered block of four stamps at his local post office, the clerk informed him that he could not accommodate him, as he had no time to waste on "nuts." Glover was determined to correct this situation and the Philatelic Agency was born. For the first three decades of operation, customers received their purchases, as today, via registered mail. Unlike today, when *indicias* are used, all of the registered mail from the Philatelic Agency was *franked* with new issue stamps.

Glover changed the culture of stamp collecting in other ways too. In 1922 it was announced, "henceforth every new stamp issued will have a designated first day of issue." On July 12, 1922 the 10¢ Special Delivery stamp (*Scott E12*) debuted as the first stamp under this new policy. The 11¢ Rutherford B. Hayes stamp, issued at Hayes' birthplace of Fremont, Ohio on October 4, 1922, was the first stamp to have a first day of issue in a specific city. Until 1937, the First Day Cover (FDC) collector had to be very familiar with the date of issue for each stamp, as only the normal machines and handstamps were used to cancel FDCs. To recognize that a cover was indeed a first day cover, you had to know your dates. Beginning in 1937, the words "First Day of Issue" appeared in the cancel, making FDCs easier to recognize.

In 1934 the POD moved to a new building, serving as a headquarters, on Pennsylvania Avenue (fig. 3). Located adjacent to the old POD building, it served until 1973 when a new building was erected for the newly created United States Postal Service.

In 1943, a system of mail "zones" was introduced in 124 large post offices to help speed

Figure 3
The 1934 Post Office Department Building.

the sorting of the ever-increasing volume of mail by the POD. With the zone system, the address of "231 West 34th Street, New York, N.Y." became "New York 1, N.Y." In 1963, this address was updated to read "New York, NY 10001" when the **zip code** and **Sectional Center Facility** were introduced.

Postmaster General Arthur G. Summerfield created the ***Citizens' Stamp Advisory Committee*** (CSAC) in 1957. He noted that its primary purpose was to provide the POD with a "breadth of judgment and depth of experience in various areas, which influence the subject matter, character, and beauty of postage stamps." For much of the first half of the twentieth century, Congress involved itself with approving new stamp issues. For example, many of the 29 commemoratives issued in 1948, some with the most esoteric subjects, were issued because Congressmen lobbied to have stamps issued for various constituencies. The CSAC was intended to bring some order to the decision-making process. The CSAC developed guidelines and rules for how subjects were chosen for postage stamps.

In 1968, a report titled "The Report of the President's Commission on Postal Organization" was submitted to President Lyndon B. Johnson. In it, Commission Chair Frederic R. Kappel noted, "our basic ordinary executive departments of government are inappropriate for the post office. We recommend…that Congress charter a Government-owned corporation to operate the postal service…" Three years later, on July 1, 1971, the old Post Office Department went out of business, an act of Congress having created a new government-owned corporation, the United States Postal Service.

Notes on Collecting

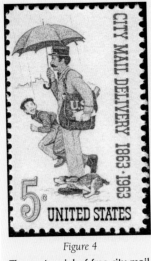

Figure 4

The centennial of free city mail delivery was celebrated on this 1963 stamp (1238) designed by Norman Rockwell.

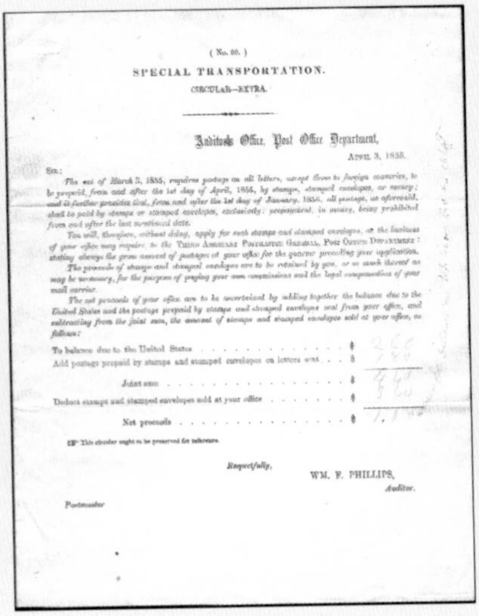

(No. 90.)

SPECIAL TRANSPORTATION.

CIRCULAR—EXTRA.

Auditor's Office, Post Office Department,
April 3, 1855.

Sir:

The act of March 3, 1855, requires postage on all letters, except those to foreign countries, to be prepaid, from and after the 1st day of April, 1855, by stamps, stamped envelopes, or money; and it further provides that, from and after the 1st day of January, 1856, all postage, as aforesaid, shall be paid by stamps or stamped envelopes, exclusively; prepayment, in money, being prohibited from and after the last mentioned date.

You will, therefore, without delay, apply for such stamps and stamped envelopes, as the business of your office may require, to the Third Assistant Postmaster General, Post Office Department; *stating always the gross amount of postages at your office for the quarter preceding your application.*

The proceeds of stamps and stamped envelopes are to be retained by you, or so much thereof as may be necessary, for the purpose of paying your own commissions and the legal compensation of your mail carrier.

The net proceeds of your office are to be ascertained by adding together the balance due to the United States and the postage prepaid by stamps and stamped envelopes sent from your office, and subtracting from the joint sum, the amount of stamps and stamped envelopes sold at your office, as follows:

To balance due to the United States . . . . $

Add postage prepaid by stamps and stamped envelopes on letters sent . . . $

Joint sum . . . . $

Deduct stamps and stamped envelopes sold at your office . . . . . $

Net proceeds . . . . $

☞ This circular ought to be preserved for reference.

Respectfully,

WM. F. PHILLIPS,
Auditor.

Postmaster

Figure 5

Circular Number 90 from the POD's Auditor's Office informing local postmasters of the phase-in dates of the requirement that all letters were to be prepaid starting April 1, 1855, and prepaid only with postage stamps starting January 1, 1856.

Collecting any stamps issued prior to July 1971 is one form of "collecting" the POD, since the POD issued all of these stamps. One can also "collect" the POD by forming a topical collection of stamps (fig. 4), which might include people who have in some way been connected to the POD, vehicles and methods of post office transportation, or a specific person such as Benjamin Franklin. Franklin's significant role in shaping the Post Office led to his portrait appearing on the first stamp, Scott #1. Some collect **collateral material** or **ephemera** (ch. 62) that helps tell the story of the POD (fig. 5).

The almanac below, suggests a number of collecting opportunities that feature the story of the POD. For example, one might choose to collect covers that show the use of zone numbers from the early 1940s all the way to the introduction of Zip codes in the early 1960s.

Almanac

1775 – Benjamin Franklin becomes the first PMG under the Continental Congress.

1789 – Samuel Osgood becomes the first PMG under the U.S. Constitution.

1792 – For the first time, newspapers are admitted to the mails at favorable rates.

1823 – Navigable waters are designated as post roads.

1825 – The **Dead Letter Office** is established.

1829 – Andrew Jackson includes the Postmaster General in the Presidential Cabinet.

1838 – Congress designates the railroads as post roads to carry the mails.

1845 – First Star Routes are established.

1847 – Adhesive postage stamps are introduced.

1852 – First stamped envelopes are introduced.

1855 – The Registered mail system begins.

1856 – Stamps are required to prepay postage beginning January 1.

1859 – The Postmaster General orders transcontinental mails be carried by overland mail coach instead of by steamship via Panama.

1863 – Free City Delivery is introduced.

1863 – Domestic mail is divided into three classes.

1864 – The first Railway Post Office is established.

1864 – Postal money order system created.

1873 – The Penny postal card is introduced.

1879 – Domestic mail is divided into four classes.

1885 – Special Delivery begins.

1887 – International Parcel Post begins.

1902 – Rural Free Delivery (RFD) is permanently established.

1911 – Postal Savings System begins operation.

1913 – Parcel Post Service begins.

1913 – Insurance is offered on mail for the first time.

1918 – After years of experiments, scheduled airmail service begins.

1920 – The first postage meter is authorized for franking mail.

1924 – Regular transcontinental airmail is introduced.

1925 – Special Handling is established.

1941 – Highway Post Office system is established.

1943 – Postal zone system is introduced.

1955 – Certified Mail is established.

1957 – The Citizens' Stamp Advisory Committee is created.

1963 – Zip Codes and the accompanying Sectional Center Facilities debut.

1966 – Postal Savings System ends.

1970 – Postal Reorganization Act is passed by Congress.

What Others Have Said

The Founding Fathers knew we needed it! Article I, Section 8, Clause 7
"The Congress shall have power…To establish Post Offices and post Roads."

—*The section of the United States Constitution creating federal authority to establish a post office system. Benjamin Franklin is credited with having paved the way for the Post Office, although he was never Postmaster General under the Constitution.*

Superseded and abrogated
"The accompanying revision of the regulations for the government of the Post Office Department and Postal Service, and the compilation of the acts of Congress relating to said department and service, which have been prepared in accordance with the act of Congress approved June 19, 1922, shall take effect on

July 1, 1924; and all previous regulations and rulings in conflict therewith are hereby superseded and abrogated…This new edition shall be known as the 'Postal Laws and Regulations of 1924'…Harry S. New, Postmaster General."

—Postal Laws and Regulations of the United States of America – 1924. *This is one example of a myriad of POD documents and publications that were produced to inform local clerks and carriers. While PL&R was published every few years, regular monthly publications announced changes and new regulations. Some PL&Rs are found preserved with many of these updates carefully pasted onto the appropriate page.*

Unprecedented in American postal history

"It is said that there are a half-million collectors in the United States, and probably that is a conservative estimate….Postmaster General Hays…has established…what the Third Assistant Postmaster General officially calls a 'Philatelic Stamp Agency'…This action is unprecedented in American postal history, and the philatelic world must wish Mr. Hays a prosperous New Year."

—Kent B. Stiles, "Of Topical Interest," *Scott's Monthly Stamp Journal, 1922. Stiles discusses the formation of the Philatelic Sales Agency to benefit stamp collectors, and salutes PMG Will Hays' decision to create the new Agency.*

Fifteen Million Stamp Collectors Pleased

"Robert E. Fellers has just been appointed by Postmaster General Donaldson to the post of Deputy Third Assistant Postmaster General…Mr. Fellers needs little introduction to stamp collectors, for his face is a familiar one at various first day sales and other philatelic events…in the past sixteen years when he has been Superintendent of the Division of Stamps….The fifteen million stamp collectors of the country will be very pleased with his appointment, for collectors always like to have a man in this post who is thoroughly familiar with and sympathetic towards collectors' needs and problems."

—Stamps Magazine, 1949. *An example of the on-going love-hate relationships that have always existed between the philatelic community and senior Post Office officials. Fellers' contributions to supporting philately are notable.*

The Post Office Department realizes its time to aggressively reach out to stamp collectors

"Under a reorganization of the Bureau of Finance of the Post Office Department, all functions pertaining to the Philatelic Agency, the Philatelic Exhibition Room and philatelic matters will be handled under a new Division of Philately. In commenting on this new facility to be devoted exclusively to philatelic matters in all its phases, Postmaster General Arthur E. Summerfield stated: 'Common business sense dictated that there be a Division to cater exclusively to the needs and desires of the millions of collectors throughout the United States. In past years, from $1,500,000 to $4,000,000 worth of business has been transacted annually at the Philatelic Agency, and estimates are that hundreds of thousands of dollars worth of stamps are purchased each year in post offices around the country by collectors'….the new Division of Philately will be headed by Robert E. Fellers, veteran postal official."

—"Division of Philately – A New Service," The Bureau Specialist, 1953.

Into a Man's Blood

"I found my seven and a half years as Postmaster General one of the most fascinating and rewarding periods of my life. Once the Post Office gets into a man's blood, it stays there…. After all, the Post Office touches more people, in a personal way, and more often than does any other agency of our government. It is essential to our way of life. Yet far too many Americans take it for granted."

—James A. Farley, PMG under Franklin D. Roosevelt, quoted by Gerald Cullinan, The Post Office Department, 1968.

Examples of Postal Usage

Figure 6

A special cacheted cover postmarked from the Benjamin Franklin Station in the new Post Office Building on its dedication day, June 11, 1934.

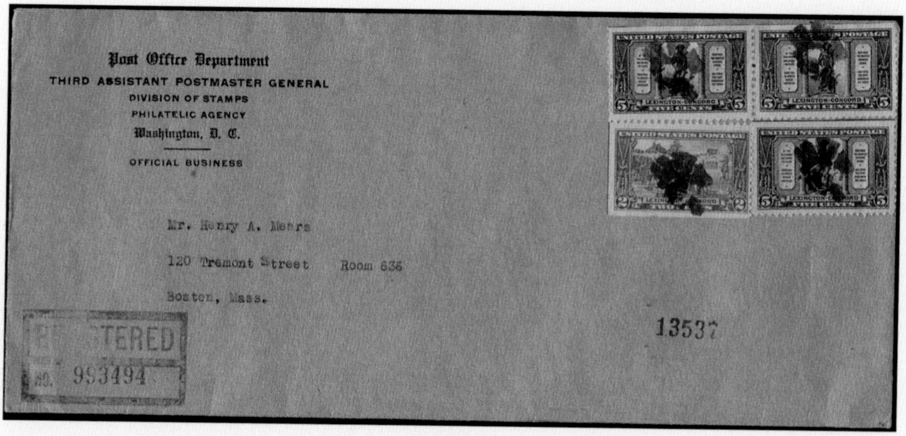

Figure 7

For many of its early years, the POD's Philatelic Agency, a department of the Division of Stamps, franked all of its outgoing mail to its customers, such as this 1925 registered order fulfillment, with current stamps on sale.

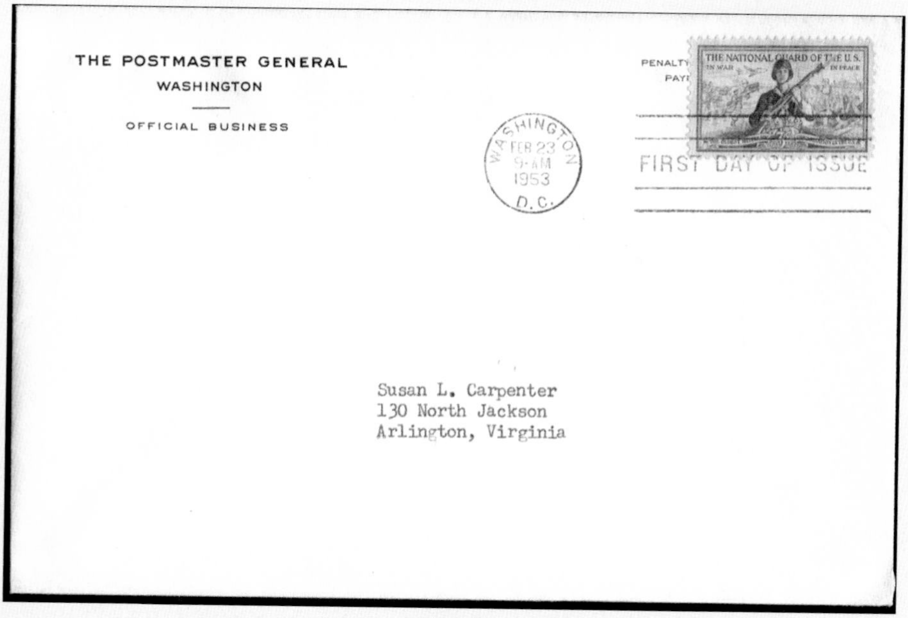

Figure 8

A FDC of the 1953 National Guard stamp (1017) on a Postmaster General corner card.

Where to Find More Information

- Marshall Cushing's *The Story of our Post Office* is the most detailed reference available on the development of the Post Office Department through the end of the nineteenth century.

- There is also Richard R. John's *Spreading the News: the American Postal System from Franklin to Morse* on the same subject.

- *The Post Office Department*, by Gerald Cullinan provides an overview through 1968.

- The Postmaster General's *Annual Report* has been published every year since the nineteenth century and forms a great "diary" of the development of the POD.

- Several autobiographies, such as those by PMGs James A. Farley, Arthur Summerfield and J. Edward Day are a must read for the serious student of the POD.

Chapter 33
United States
Postal Service

With the stroke of his pen on August 12, 1970, President Richard Nixon signed the Postal Reorganization Act, legislation that would dramatically reshape the postal service of our nation. When Americans awoke on the morning of July 1, 1971, they found that the Postal Reorganization Act had been implemented. No longer did the old familiar United States Post Office Department (POD) serve them. Instead they were served by a new "independent establishment of the executive branch of the government," the United States Postal Service (USPS). If an American waking up that morning had ventured to the local post office he or she could have obtained a special commemorative envelope honoring the inauguration of the USPS, available one to a customer. That postal patron could also have purchased one of the new stamps (*Scott* 1396, fig. 1) being issued simultaneously that day at all post offices across the county. If that stamp was then affixed to the commemorative cover and canceled, that customer had a *First Day Cover* (FDC). This is exactly what many customers did that July day. It has been estimated that over 16.3 million first day covers were created in over 22,000 post offices (fig. 2)! Collecting these FDCs has become a popular specialty.

Figure 1

This 1971 stamp (1396) honors the United States Postal Service.

Figure 2

A First Day Cover of the stamp issued 7-1-71 celebrating the birth of the USPS (1396). Notice the cachet on the cover superimposes the seal of the USPS over the seal of the old USPOD. The envelope (but not the stamp) was supplied free of charge to postal patrons. This cover was postmarked in "Brooklyn, NY".

There were some obvious differences between the new USPS and the old POD. Beside the new name there was a new seal, which depicts an eagle poised for flight. The seal appears on the stamp depicted in figure 1. Another obvious difference was that the Postmaster General was no longer a presidential appointee or a member of the president's cabinet. The Postmaster General under the USPS (Winston M. Blount in 1971) was appointed by an independent Board of Governors. The President, with the advice and consent of the Senate appointed Governors to nine-year terms. Even the head-

Figure 3

Headquarters of the USPS at L'Enfant Plaza, Washington, D.C.

quarters of the USPS was new. In 1973 the USPS moved from its old depression era headquarters on Pennsylvania Ave. in Washington, D.C. to a newly constructed building at L'Enfant Plaza (fig. 3).

Some other differences between the old POD and the new USPS were perhaps less obvious to the mailing public. The new USPS had new financing authority; it no longer operated under the old political "spoils" system; it could engage in collective bargaining with its employees; and its rates and classifications were determined through an independent Postal Rate Commission.

The change from POD to USPS was deemed necessary to fix what was viewed as an archaic and inefficient postal system, still doing business in much the same way it had for 100 years. Perhaps the event which triggered a widespread realization that the "system was broken" occurred in October 1966 when the Chicago Post Office ground to a virtual halt under a mountain of mail. A few months later Postmaster General Lawrence F. O'Brien described the POD as in a, "race with catastrophe." He explained that the breakdown in Chicago was not the result of any specific event, but the result of, "trying to move our mail through facilities largely unchanged since the days of Jim Farley." Jim Farley was Franklin Roosevelt's first Postmaster General, from 1933 to 1940.

The postal service in 1971 needed automation, mechanization, and new technologies. Although innovation certainly began before 1971, with letter sorters, facer-cancellers, automatic address readers, mail coding, and stamp tagging all in use, much more needed to be achieved in order to reduce the number of times a piece of mail was handled. Ironically a series of stamps issued in 1973 to salute USPS employees (1489–1498) depicts some of the very technology that was too labor intensive and antiquated to meet the needs of the Postal Service (fig. 4).

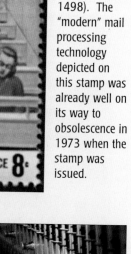

One of ten "Postal People" stamps (1489-1498). The "modern" mail processing technology depicted on this stamp was already well on its way to obsolescence in 1973 when the stamp was issued.

Figure 4

Several things were done to reduce the number of times a piece of mail was handled. Two traditional methods of sorting mail while in transit were eliminated: the **Highway Post Office** (HPO) and the **Railway Post Office** (RPO). This was perhaps a gain for postal efficiency, but a loss to collectors who treasure HPO and RPO covers. **Optical Character Readers** (OCRs) came into widespread use to "read" addresses. **ZIP+ 4** was also introduced. At the end of the twentieth century mail was processed at over 500 Processing and Distribution Centers (P&DC), generally located away from major urban centers. A typical scene from a P&DC is shown in Figure 5. The P&DC through which mail is processed can often be identified from the postmark. An example is the PALATINE (IL) P&DC postmark shown in Figure 6.

Figure 5

A scene inside a Processing & Distribution Center.

Figure 6

A postmark from the Processing and Distribution Center (P&DC) at Palatine, Illinois.

The USPS does not print its own stamps. Printing has always been contracted out. A variety of private firms print stamps for the USPS (ch. 38) while the

Bureau of Engraving and Printing (BEP) which had been the dominant printer of stamps during the twentieth century, no longer prints any.

One of the more infamous "goofs" in USPS history came when a picture of the wrong person was used for Bill Pickett on the 1994 "Legends of the West" **pane**. The mistake was caught before the panes were released, but a few had already been prematurely and inadvertently sold to the public. The panes with the wrong picture were recalled, and new ones printed with the correct picture (2869). But in a controversial lottery 150,000 panes with the wrong picture (2870) were sold to the public (fig. 7). The rest were destroyed. It should be noted that the use of the wrong picture on a stamp is an **oddity**, not an **error**, in the philatelic definition of that word.

Figure 7

Perhaps the most infamous design error in USPS history, this "Bill Picket" stamp (2870g), actually depicts his brother!

As the twenty-first century began the USPS was struggling with significantly decreasing volumes of **First Class Mail** and increasing competition. Competition came from private providers of delivery services and from the internet. In late 2002 a "Commission on the United States Postal Service" was established by President George W. Bush to consider the challenges faced by the USPS, and consider possible responses. The commission issued a report on July 31, 2003 titled, "Embracing the Future: Making the Tough Choices to Preserve Universal Mail Service." The title of the report reveals the key value of the Commission, universal service. In order to continue providing universal service (service for everyone) at affordable rates the Commission rejected the idea of privatizing the USPS. The commission also said, among other things, that the USPS must become more business-like, seek private sector partnerships, and have a restructured board of directors and a new regulator. The Commission predicted that the internet would not replace mail, that the future USPS would be smaller, with fewer distribution plants, and that there would be increases in automation, and changes in how mail is distributed. Of special interest to stamp collectors was the proposal to introduce personalized stamps. The Commission also called for standardization of procedures throughout the postal system and performance based pay.

The "War on Terrorism" at the beginning of the twenty-first century resulted in several initiatives that affected the Postal Service. "Intelligent Mail" was the name given to services offered by the USPS that allowed for improved tracking of mail as it moves through the mail stream. Its purpose is to improve the accuracy, timeliness, and convenience of mail delivery and services, while protecting the privacy and security of the mail. The creation of "smart stamps" was also proposed in order to track the identity of people who send mail.

To meet the competitive challenges of a dynamic environment of contemporary communications, the USPS has achieved service and cost improvements. For example, in 1971 the new USPS organization delivered 87 billion pieces of mail to 81 million homes and businesses. By 2002, it delivered 203 billion pieces of mail (43% of the world's mail volume) to 139 million delivery points. The remarkable success during this 31-year period has resulted in the delivery of 133% more mail to 72% more delivery points with only 17% more employees.

The USPS is a time-tested American institution serving every community. It has proved itself able to meet the changing needs of our demanding society. Perhaps the only future prediction regarding the USPS that can be made with any certainty is that its future will be dynamic. This one certainty will guarantee continued excitement and interest well into the twenty-first century for the fascinating hobby we fondly call, stamp collecting.

Notes on Collecting

A popular specialty is collecting First Day Covers of the USPS stamp (1396, fig. 2). These are sometimes affectionately known as "7-1-71" covers. Covers from some post offices are common, while rare or even non-existent from others.

The USPS partially funds the National Postal Museum, which opened in 1993. The museum is located on Capitol Hill, in the old Washington City Post Office, adjacent to Union Station. It serves as the custodian of priceless postal artifacts, which are accessible to researchers.

Stamp Fulfillment Services sells stamps and other philatelic material to the public from a climate controlled limestone cave beneath an amusement park in Kansas City, Missouri. Stamp Fulfillment Services traces its roots back to the Philatelic Agency founded in 1921 in the Washington City Post Office.

In 1996 the USPS changed some terminology that collectors and postal patrons had used for generations. Postal Cards became "Stamped Cards." **Second Class** Mail became **Periodicals Class**. **Third Class** Mail became **Standard Mail** (A) and **Fourth Class** Mail became Standard Mail (B).

Almanac

1971 – The USPS begins operation on July 1.

1974 – Highway Post Offices are abolished.

1974 – A pioneering self-adhesive stamp is introduced (1552).

1976 – Post Office "class" categories are eliminated.

1977 – Domestic Air Mail is abolished as a separate rate category.

1977 – Railway Post Offices are abolished.

1978 – Copyrighting of stamps begins.

1982 – USPS receives its last public subsidy.

1983 – Zip+4 method of sorting mail is instituted.

1990 – International business reply mail is offered for first time.

1993 – The National Postal Museum opens on July 30.

1994 – A lottery is held in October for the opportunity to purchase one of 150,000 recalled panes of "Legends of the West."

1996 – Classification Reform changes some traditional Post Office terminology.

1997 – *Special Delivery* is eliminated.

1998 – The first *semi-postal* stamp issued (B1) raises funds for breast cancer research.

2001 – Mail is irradiated due to the anthrax threat.

What Others Have Said

The 7-1-71 Affair: From Pony to the Eagle

"7-1-71 was the date of change from the old Post Office Department to the new Postal Service. Many big changes were planned. One thing to start was to encourage stamp collecting. Scott #1396 [fig. 1] was issued with first day cancels available at all 39,521 named facilities. A cacheted envelope was given free. For the price of the eight-cents stamp with any postmark, this became a first day cover. A limit of one envelope per person and one day only was imposed. This kept down the number of FDCs. Interest did not materialize as planned. The 'official' cachet combines the old with the new. The familiar Post Office Department's emblem of a post rider, which served to identify the mail service for nearly a century and a half, and the new postal emblem...a stylized eagle, perched atop red, white and blue bars."

—*Roy E. Mooney, introduction to* The 7-1-71 Affair, *2003.*

What is the USPS supposed to do?

"The Postal Service shall have as its basic function the obligation to provide postal services to bind the Nation together through the personal, educational, literary and business correspondence of the people. It shall provide prompt, reliable, and efficient services to patrons in all areas and shall render postal services to all communities."

—*The mission statement of the USPS.*

Embracing the Future: Making the Tough Choices to Preserve Universal Mail Service

"In appointing this Commission, you recognized that the Postal Service faces significant challenges to its fiscal health due largely to an outmoded and inflexible business model amid a rapidly changing postal landscape...We believe that the Postal Service has an extraordinary opportunity to usher in an exciting new era of greater efficiency and rising value to the mailing public. As a result, while the sustainability of the Postal Service's current business model is in serious doubt, with bold leadership today, the future of universal postal service can most certainly be secured."

—*July 31, 2003 letter to President Bush from the President's Commission on the United States Postal Service.*

The first stamp store in the United States

"On Aug. 11, 1986, the first stamp store in a United States Postal Service facility opened in Des Moines Iowa. This [was a] new concept in merchandising stamps and related products....This has evolved into today's Postal Store. These outlets are now being opened in many post offices throughout the country. This new retail store approach provides an opportunity for stamp collectors that is unparalleled in philately....Hopefully, when postal customers see the variety of stamps and related products on display, they will select additional items for purchase in addition to what they originally wanted to purchase."

—*Les Winick, "The spotlight is on the self-adhesive stamp store,"* Scott's Stamp Monthly, *1995.*

Does the USPS issue too many postage stamps?

"Another factor in stamp issuance needs to be mentioned—the issuing authority that resides in the Postmaster General. From 1950 to the time of writing this, we have had 12 different Postmasters General and a 13th may have come aboard by the time you read this. These people are individuals and they have had their impact on issuance, with PMG Wm. F. Bolger probably having added the most numerically during his roughly seven-year tenure (1978-1985)....So how many are too many stamps for our country to issue per year? Of course, a definite figure could not be in order because events worth noting and the incidence of postal rate changes don't schedule themselves by the year, but there could be an approximate figure....Based on what we have developed, our feelings are that the USPS should try to hold at around 15 commemorative-type issues per year and that they should also economize a bit by having more single-design issues and so hold the overall number of new designs to 20-25 per year instead of the 40 average of the last ten."

—*George W. Brett, "How many U.S. Postage Stamps per year are too many?"* The Congress Book 1986, *1986.*

Examples of Postal Usage

Figure 8

A homemade cover postmarked on May 28, 1978, the last day of the 13¢ First Class rate, which had gone into effect December 31, 1975. Note the use of a very small size stamp on the cover. Several stamps of this size were issued experimentally as an economy measure. The experiment failed. Postal rates have changed frequently since the USPS came into being in 1971, providing collectors many opportunities to obtain first and last day of rate covers.

Figure 9

The quest for postal efficiency caused the demise of the Railroad Post Office (RPO). This is a last trip cover from the last RPO, which operated on June 30, 1977 between Washington, D.C. and New York. The acronym "RMS" in the cancellation stands for "Railway Mail Service."

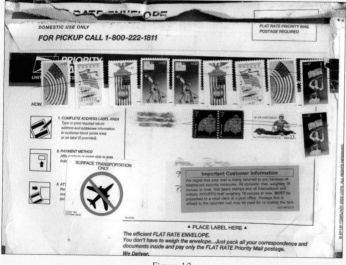

Figure 10

In the weeks following the terrorist attacks of September 11, 2001 the USPS increased security, resulting in interesting postal usages. This Priority Mail envelope was returned to sender because proper procedures were not followed. It bears a label prohibiting transportation by air, and a sticker informing the customer why the envelope was being returned.

The label reads, in part, "….your mail is being returned to you because of heightened security measures. All domestic mail, weighing 16 ounces or over, and that bears stamps and all international and military APO/FPO mail weighing 16 ounces or over, MUST be presented to a retail clerk at a post office." Note also the ballpoint pen cancellation. Such cancellations by postal workers are a legitimate means of revenue protection, but frustrate many collectors.

Where to Find More Information

- Original source material about the United States Postal service can be found in the following USPS publications: *Domestic Mail Manual, Postal Operations Manual,* and *Postal Bulletin* which have been published regularly since 1971.

- *The United States Postal Service: An American History 1775-2002,* published by the USPS, provides a nicely illustrated overview of the nation's postal service.

- The USPS maintains a web site at www.usps.com/ that includes a helpful section on the history of the Postal Service.

- The National Postal Museum maintains a web site at www.postalmuseum.si.edu.

- www.7-1-71-firstdaycovers.com is a site about "7-1-71" First Day Covers.

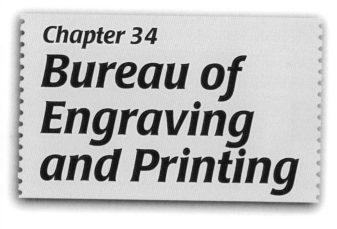

Chapter 34

Bureau of Engraving and Printing

The Bureau of Engraving and Printing (BEP), the Treasury Department's security printer, existed long before it first printed postage stamps in 1894, and continues to exist even after it printed its last postage stamp June 10, 2005. But for more than a century much of the romance of collecting U.S. stamps centered on this unique government agency in Washington, D.C.

For almost three quarters of a century, the BEP held a virtual monopoly on postage stamp production. The notable exception occurred in 1943 when the **American Bank Note Co.** produced the bi-colored **Overrun Countries** stamps for which the BEP did not have the necessary presses. But by the late 1960s the monopoly began to unravel when a few production contracts were awarded by the Post Office to non-BEP suppliers. This was the beginning of a trend that accelerated in the ensuing years. By 1997 the BEP's share of all postage stamps printed fell below 50%. When the end finally came in 2005, the BEP was producing only some coil stamps.

The BEP traces its origin back to the Civil War era, to August 29, 1862. In what has been called the "charter" of the BEP, an August 22, 1862 letter from Secretary of the Treasury Salmon P. Chase gives instructions for "the preparation for the issue of one and two dollar Treasury Notes." Those notes, the first federal paper money, were prepared in a basement room in the Treasury Department. While stamp collectors may think of the BEP primarily in terms of stamp production, the general public almost certainly thinks of the BEP primarily in terms of paper money.

The first stamps produced at the BEP were not postage stamps, but *revenue stamps*. Although private banknote firms printed the earliest revenue stamps issued to finance the Civil War, by 1866 the Note Printing Division of the Treasury Department (only later to be called the BEP) was printing beer and cigar revenue stamps. The once ubiquitous blue Cigarette revenue stamps, with their familiar portrait of DeWitt Clinton, began pouring from BEP presses in 1878.

Figure 1

This building in Washington, D.C. served as home to the BEP from 1880 to 1914.

Figure 2

This stamp (224), and the die used in its production, were made by The American Bank Note Co. In 1894 the dies and plates were transferred to the BEP.

Figure 3

Stamps were produced by the BEP using the same dies originally used by the American Bank Note Co., but only after those dies had been altered. Note the addition by the BEP of triangles in the upper right and left corners of these stamps. Also note that the BEP added its imprint and a unique plate number in the plate margin.

In 1880 a facility was built exclusively for the BEP, located adjacent to the Washington Monument (fig. 1). This building, though no longer serving the BEP, still stands in Washington, D.C.

The BEP began printing postage stamps for the Post Office Department on July 1, 1894. Prior to that date private banknote companies had produced postage stamps. The first postage stamps produced by the BEP, the Series of 1894, were produced from *dies* turned over to the BEP by the American Bank Note Company which had previously used them. Those dies were slightly altered by the BEP, and new plates were made from those dies. This was done in order to distinguish between the stamps produced by the BEP and the bank note company (fig.2 and 3). One immediate problem faced by the BEP in 1894 was that it had no gumming machines. By working with the recollections of an employee who had previous experience with gumming machines, the BEP was able to develop one of their own and have stamps available for the Post Office to sell on July 18, 1894. The first BEP stamps, like most subsequently produced, were perforated (fig. 4).

Eventually the BEP outgrew its 1880 facility and another building was constructed adjacent to the 1880 building. The new home of the BEP was formally opened on March 19, 1914 (fig. 5). The Engraving Division was initially located on the lower floor of the new building, but the *engravers* did not like the working conditions, so the entire Engraving Division was moved back to the old building in October 1925, where it remained until November 1938. On November 8, 1938 an annex was opened directly across the street from the "new" building and was happily occupied by the staff of the Engraving Division.

Figure 4

Post card showing stamps being perforated by a hand-fed, motor driven, sheet perforating machine, circa 1900s.

Late in the nineteenth and early twentieth centuries, all BEP postage stamps were produced from flat intaglio plates, on flat bed presses, using individual sheets of paper. But the need to produce more stamps more rapidly, especially coil stamps, drove the development of new technology. One of the most significant technological innovations in BEP history was the introduction of the **rotary press** – a press that could print on a continuous roll of paper from plates curved around a cylinder. First used in 1914, it is often called the **Stickney Press**, in honor of its

Figure 5

The "new" Bureau of Engraving and Printing building opened in 1914.

inventor, a BEP employee, Benjamin F. Stickney. The Stickney Press came to dominate BEP production during the mid-1920s, and though the flat bed press continued in limited use, the Stickney rotary press reigned supreme at the BEP for many years. The last one was decommissioned in 1962.

Henry Holtzclaw emerged as the BEP's preeminent inventor and mechanical expert in the 1930s. He developed the **electric-eye** perforator, supervised construction of the Annex which opened in 1938, and served as director of the BEP from 1953–1967.

Line-engraved stamps, whether produced on a flat or rotary press, dominated the BEP through most of its stamp production history. Producing a line-engraved intaglio stamp takes time and great skill. Other printing methods lack the fidelity of fine line engraving and the distinctive three-dimensional effect produced on the stamp. Besides being beautiful, such stamps are difficult to counterfeit! Taken together these two realities explain why line-engraved intaglio dominated production at the BEP. At the beginning of the twenty-first century BEP director Thomas A. Ferguson observed, "To those of us who grew up in the business, that's our image of what a stamp should be…To me that [engraved stamp] symbolizes strength, stability, integrity and quality."

But other printing methods beside line-engraved intaglio have been used by the BEP. From 1918 to 1920 the BEP, out of necessity, used **offset printing** to produce some **Washington-Franklin** stamps. This action resulted from supply shortages of high quality ink that made traditional intaglio printing impractical. Later in the twentieth century, printing methods such as **gravure** and offset were used by choice.

In the years following World War II interest grew in being able to produce full color stamps, which required new presses (ch. 37). A successor to the Stickney Press, the so-called **Huck press** was used to print the 3¢ International Red Cross stamp of 1952, the first bi-color stamp printed on a continuous web of paper.

Figure 6

The BEP's first truly full color stamp (1094), produced on the Giori Press. It was designed by Victor S. McCloskey and issued in 1957.

Another successor to the Stickney Press was the technologically related **Cottrell press**. But stamps from both presses were only bi-color, not full color. True full color production did not occur until the BEP acquired its first Giori Press, an intaglio sheet-fed rotary press. Its first assignment, and the BEP's first true full color stamp, was the 4¢ American flag stamp of 1957 (fig. 6).

In the following years a variety of others presses, with names like **Andreotti**, and more prosaic names like the **A, B, C, D**, and **F** presses came into service at the BEP, employing a full range of printing methods: line engraved intaglio, gravure, and offset.

The BEP was more than just a production plant. It was also a place of creative and artistic genius. For much of the twentieth century BEP artists designed stamps and BEP craftsmen engraved them.

Designers were the artists who conceived the stamps, sometimes making use of existing artwork as source material, and sometimes creating original artwork.

Several designers deserve special mention. R. Ostrander Smith was employed by the BEP from 1897 until 1902. He designed the Trans-Mississippi Issue, the Pan-American Exposition Issue, and most of the Series of 1902, also known as the Second Bureau Issue. Clair Aubrey Huston, who may be regarded as Smith's successor at the BEP, had an incredible tenure of 31 years, designing most stamps issued until his retirement in 1933. Alvin Meissner was a designer from 1925 through 1946. He and Victor McCloskey, who designed about 125 stamps during his tenure as a designer (1934–1965), may be considered as successors to Huston. Charles Chickering began as an engraver in 1947 and retired in 1962. He personally designed 66 stamps, beginning with the 1947 "Doctors" stamp, and collaborated on many others. His last stamp was the 1962 Homestead Act Centenary stamp. By the 1960s the Post Office began using the talent of non-BEP designers, and Chickering could be regarded as the last of the great, prolific, in-house BEP designers.

Designers produced the artwork for stamps. But it was other craftsmen at the BEP who took those designs and engraved them into steel dies, the first part of the stamp making process. Engravers tend to specialize in a particular kind of engraving: portrait, frame, or lettering. The BEP estimated it takes 125 hours to engrave a stamp. The names of engravers are not as well known as the designers, but a few stand out, such as George F.C. Smillie who worked at the BEP from 1894 until 1922, Marcus W. Baldwin, employed from 1897 to 1920, John Eissler (1911 to 1941), Charles Brooks, who engraved nearly 200 stamps between 1938 and 1966, Joachim Benzing who plied his craft from 1905 until 1943, and Matthew Fenton who engraved over 60 stamps. A prominent engraver of more recent times is Tom R. Hipschen, whose long career at the BEP began at age 17, and whose first stamp credit is the 15¢ "Progress in Electronics" issue of 1973. He also takes credit for engraving work on the "Large Portrait" currency first released in 1996.

Other employees of the BEP made the plates from which stamps were printed. Still others did the actual printing and processing of stamps. Some names of BEP workers are familiar to collectors because the initials of **siderographers** and **plate finishers** once appeared in the margins of printing plates.

An interesting event in the history of the BEP revolves around the Project Mercury stamp of 1962. This stamp was prepared, printed, and shipped in strict secrecy, in case John Glenn's flight did not end successfully and the stamps were not to be released. Once Glenn returned safely to earth on February 20, the stamps were placed on sale simultaneously all across the country. In order to ensure secrecy the stamp's designer, Charles Chickering, ostensibly took "leave" from work but was actually working at home. The engraver who did the lettering, Howard F. Sharpless, worked only on weekends when no one else was in the building. The picture engraver, Richard M. Bower, ostensibly on vacation, worked at night.

Significant failures of quality control at the BEP are both rare and notable. *Inverts* are perhaps the most well-known failures of BEP quality control. Inverts exist of three of the Pan-American Exposition stamps of 1901. The first air mail stamp exists as an invert (C3a). This so called *inverted Jenny* is perhaps the most recognized of all errors on stamps. The Dag Hammarskjöld invert of 1962 (fig. 2, ch. 52) is an invert anyone can own because after the original inverts were discovered the Postmaster General ordered more inverts produced in large quantities. The $1 Candle Stick invert (fig. 8, ch.14) in the Americana Series is sometimes known as the "CIA" invert, a nickname derived from the fact that the only known pane of this error was purchased by a CIA employee.

Notes on Collecting

One can "Collect the BEP" by obtaining anything produced by the BEP. But there are several items available to collectors at modest cost that have especially strong BEP connections. A souvenir sheet issued in 1994 (*Scott* 2875) honors the 100th anniversary of postage stamp production at the BEP (fig. 7).

Beautifully engraved souvenir cards, printed by the BEP, often reproducing classic stamps, have been distributed at selected philatelic and numismatic gathering since 1954. They are listed in *Scott* with the prefix SC or NCS (fig. 8). A fore-

Figure 7

Souvenir Sheet issued to commemorate the 100th anniversary of postage stamp production at the BEP (2875). Note the original BEP building at the top of the sheet. This sheet is known with a major double transfer (fig. 4, ch. 46)!

Figure 8

The BEP issued this Souvenir Card to compliment the 1973 Chicago stamp show known as COMPEX.

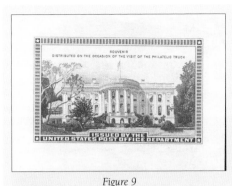

Figure 9

The "Philatelic Truck" was a philatelic museum in a bus-like vehicle that toured the U.S. between May 9, 1939 and December 31, 1941. These souvenirs were given to visitors.

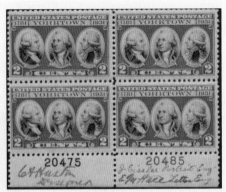

Figure 10

This plate block of the Yorktown Issue (703) is signed by its designer, C. Aubrey Huston, and its two engravers, J. Eissler, and E.M. Hall, all BEP employees.

runner of these cards is the 1939 Philatelic Truck souvenir sheet (fig. 9). None of these items are valid for postage.

Material signed by, or otherwise associated with BEP employees, can also be collected. Figure 10 shows the autographs of Clair Aubrey Huston, and of two engravers.

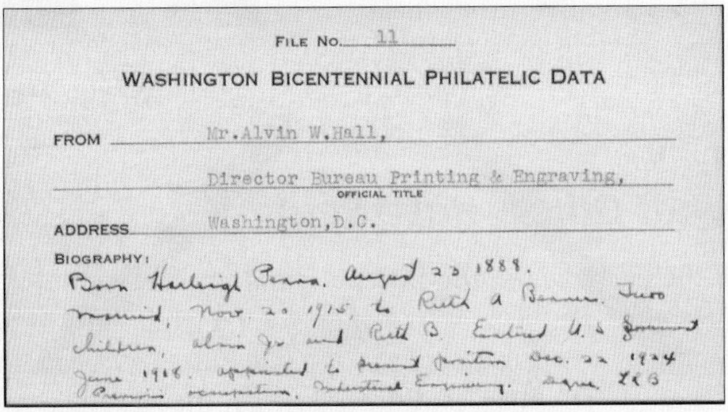
FILE NO. 11

WASHINGTON BICENTENNIAL PHILATELIC DATA

FROM Mr. Alvin W. Hall,

Director Bureau Printing & Engraving,

OFFICIAL TITLE

ADDRESS Washington, D.C.

BIOGRAPHY: Born Harleigh Penna. August 23 1888. Married, Nov. 20 1915, to Ruth A Benner. Two children, Alvin Jr and Ruth B.

Figure 11

This "Washington Bicentennial Philatelic Data" card was filled out by Mr. Hall, and mailed in the envelope shown in Figure 13.

Figure 11 shows a data card used by the Washington Bicentennial Commission for Alvin W. Hall, a Director of the BEP.

Almanac

1862 – The division of the Treasury, eventually named the BEP, begins operations in the basement of the Treasury Building.

1880 – The BEP moves into its own facility on July 1.

1894 – The BEP assumes responsibility for printing postage stamps on July 1.

1908 – The BEP produces its first coil stamps.

1914 – The BEP moves into its new building.

1914 – The BEP places a rotary press into production for the first time.

1930 – The BEP begins experimenting with electronic controls (electric eye) in the perforating process.

1938 – The BEP annex opens.

1957 – The Giori sheet-fed rotary press prints its first stamp for the BEP.

1962 – The last Stickney rotary press is decommissioned.

2005 – The BEP prints its last postage stamp June 10, the 37¢ Flag (3632), on the Andreotti press (fig. 12).

Figure 12
Coiling operation for the last BEP produced stamps.

What Others Have Said

In the early years, the Bureau had some personnel problems
"Personnel problems were a bother for a while. It was necessary to find and to train men and girls to operate the machines. Wages for women ranged from $390 to $470 a year, and the salaries of their brothers were not much higher. The temptations to the 'hired help' were disturbing. Mr. Johnson was obliged to admit that 'dishonest men stole some of the stamps,' but 'the theft was discovered and the criminals promptly apprehended, prosecuted and convicted with loss of but a few hundred dollars to the Government.'

—*James Waldo Fawcett, "50th Anniversary of the Bureau of Engraving and Printing,"* Mekeel's Weekly Stamp News, *1944.*

A hundred years of stamp production at the BEP: Missing parts of history
"This month marks a hundred years of postage stamp production by the Bureau of Engraving and Printing. On July 1, 1894, the beginning of the government's fiscal year, the Bureau took over the printing of the nation's stamps….As part of its commemoration on this centennial, the Bureau has prepared a philatelic exhibit of treasures from its files, concentrating on unique material that has

never before been displayed outside the Bureau. Among the items are original drawings, models, essay, die proofs, and other material related to the design and production of stamps from 1894 to the present. While the printed records of Bureau stamp production are generally quite complete, the same cannot be said of its design files. Before about 1930, much of the original artwork is missing, and has been presumably discarded. Before about 1920, even most of the approved models are gone. Surprisingly, the Bureau also has retained very little in the way of printed stamps before 1930."

—*Gary Griffiths, "The First Hundred Years: A Bureau Exhibit," The United States Specialist, 1994.*

The Bureau produces non-accountable paper to demonstrate its printing process

"[We] sought reports of demonstration plates used by the Bureau of Engraving and Printing in exhibition at numismatic and philatelic shows. A member reports a demonstration plate used by the Bureau at the A.S.D.A. [American Stamp Dealers Association] show in November 1977 that is new to me. The demonstration plate used was a block of nine in vertical format with the subject identified as 'Frigate.' The vignette depicted a sailing vessel under full canvas moving through moderate seas. The point of view was slightly left of head-on. Other than the designation of "Frigate" at the bottom of the design there were no other words or letters. The ink color reported in use at the demonstration was green.... I believe this is the first show demonstration plate I know about that doesn't reproduce an identifiable stamp or paper money. Those that I had the opportunity to see first hand have always been subjects existing as stamps or currency. Perhaps the Bureau is now using general subject matter in connection with the move to copyrighting of stamp designs by the Postal Service."

—*David E. McGuire, "Bureau Demonstration Pates," The Essay-Proof Journal, 1978.*

Why the BEP no longer prints postage stamps

"There are people out there who do it better than we do....They do it all the time. And they do it with equipment that, when it's not printing stamps is printing other products in that basic format...That's something the Bureau can't do."

—*Thomas A. Ferguson, director of the Bureau of Engraving and Printing, in a November 25, 2003 interview, explaining why the BEP no longer prints stamps.*

Examples of Postal Usage

Figure 13
A cover from Alvin W. Hall, director of the BEP from 1924 to 1954.

Figure 14

This First Day cover, with cachet by A.E. Gorham, of the Arbor Day issue of 1932 (717) has at least three BEP connections. It is signed by Alvin Meissner, the BEP employed designer of the stamp. It is addressed to Clyde De Binder, a BEP siderographer, and the two children depicted on the stamp are the children of BEP Director Alvin W. Hall!

Where to Find More Information

• *History of the Bureau of Engraving and Printing, 1862-1962.*

• Gene Hessler's *The Engraver's Line* is a most useful book that introduces readers to the BEP's designers and engravers.

• Several issues of *The United States Specialist* have been devoted to the Bureau, most notably July and October 1994.

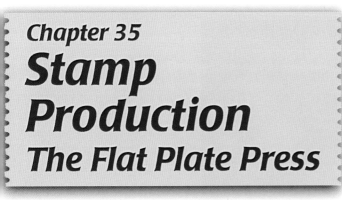

Chapter 35

Stamp Production

The Flat Plate Press

From the beginning of postage stamp production in 1847 until the second decade of the twentieth century, all stamps were printed on a flat plate press, sometimes called a flat bed press. Even after the **rotary press** (ch. 36) supplanted it in the late 1920s, the flat plate press was used occasionally until the early 1960s, when it was still printing the $5 Hamilton stamp in the Liberty Series.

The first type of flat plate press was relatively simple. It consisted of a flat bed, also called a plank, which held the flat printing plate. During the printing process the plate would be inked and a piece of paper placed on it. The plate would then pass under a heavy roller to impress the images onto the paper, which was then removed and set aside to dry. The press was manually operated by turning a large wheel with several radiating handles, and is sometimes known as a Spider Press or hand roller-press (fig. 1). Only a few thousand stamps could be printed each day on this press. The flat plate printing process was labor intensive. The printer had to manually ink, and then polish the plate between the printings of each sheet. The plate also had to be heated in order to make a good impression.

In 1876 James Milligan invented a steam powered four-plate flat bed press, which greatly increased the efficiency of flat plate printing. These presses were first used in production at the BEP, at least on a limited basis, by 1881. The politically powerful printers, fearful of automation, opposed the use of these presses, but ultimately could not prevent their use. Additional presses were acquired to fulfill the 1894 stamp contract, and by 1921 the BEP was using 243 power

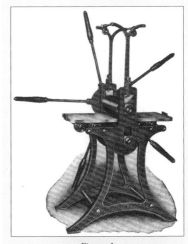

Figure 1

A single plate flat bed press, often called a Spider Press.

Figure 2

A four-plate flat bed press with its three operators.

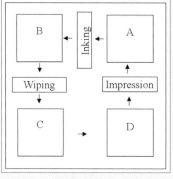

Figure 3

Schematic diagram of a four-plate flat bed press as illustrated in Figure 2. An empty plate is mechanically inked while moving from position A to position B. The plate then moves through the wiping mechanism to position C where the printer hand polishes it. The plate next moves to position D where a sheet of paper is placed on it. The plate then moves under the Impression roller where the sheet is printed. When the sheet emerges at position A it is removed from the press and the cycle begins again.

presses, though not all for printing stamps.

The four-plate power press (fig. 2) enabled the continuous movement of four plates within a square frame (fig. 3), and required three operators. A male printer would polish the plate with his bare hands after it had been inked and wiped. Polishing was done to remove any excess ink from the surface of the plate, as the plate was intended to print only from its recessed engraved lines. Then a female operator, known as a "putter-on-er" would place a single sheet of dampened paper on the inked plate, which would then travel under an impression roller, which would cause the ink on the plate to be transferred to the paper. The use of dampened paper enabled a better impression. Finally a second female operator, known as a "taker-off-er," would remove the printed sheet from the plate, and place it in a stack. The empty plate was then reinked and wiped and the cycle was ready to begin again.

When the power flat plate press was used to print stamps from typical 400 subject plates, a single press could produce approximately 1,600,000 stamps per day. Each impression was automatically recorded by a counter each time the impression roller rotated. At the close of each working day, the number of printed and unprinted sheets had to be reconciled with the counter before employees were permitted to leave the building. As printed stamps were stacked by the taker-off-er, sheets of tissue paper were placed between them in order to prevent the transfer of ink. After being allowed to dry overnight the tissue was removed from the stamps, and they were placed in a hydraulic press. This pressure resulted in some ink from one sheet being *set-off* on the back of the sheet stacked on top of it. This is characteristic of flat plate printed stamps (fig. 4).

The back of a flat plate printed stamp, showing a set-off picked up when printed sheets were stacked.

Figure 4

Notes on Collecting

Until 1914 only the flat plate press was used to print postage stamps, which means that a collection of stamps from prior to then is a collection of flat plate printed stamps and their varieties. The rotary press was introduced for the first time to print some of the Washington-Franklin series (ch. 9). This series offers the collector an opportunity to build a collection of face-same stamps that were produced on both presses. There are two conventional ways to determine whether a stamp was printed using the flat plate or rotary press method. The first is to measure the design with a ruler, and consult *Scott* for the size of the stamp design. *Scott* lists the millimeters of the length and width of the stamp design which is always slightly smaller on the flatbed version of the stamp. The problem is that it is difficult for most people to accurately use a ruler to measure such minute measurements.

Figure 5

This template was made from a common flat plate stamp. Placing it on top of another stamp will determine if the other stamp is flat plate or rotary printed. The design of any rotary stamp will be slightly larger than the design of the template stamp. Note that it is not the size of the stamps that are being compared, but the size of the printed designs.

Therefore, a better way to accurately sort flat plate and rotary press stamps is to make a pattern or template, as shown in figure 5. This is done by cutting a damaged common flat plate perf 12 Washington-Franklin stamp at the four corners. Perf 12 stamps are always flat plate press stamps and can then be used to measure all of the unknown stamps to determine if they are flat or rotary printed. Note that any flat plate definitive stamp may be used for the template; it does not have to be of the same denomination or color, only the size matters.

The 1934 Mother's day stamp (737 and 738) was produced by both flat and rotary presses; however, they are easily distinguishable as they have different perforations. The flat plate printing is perf 11 while the rotary press printing is perf 11 x 10½.

Flat plate press plate blocks are most often collected as a *plate number* block of six with the plate number centered in the margin next to the middle stamp, as opposed to rotary press plate blocks which are usually collected in blocks of four with the plate number in the corner margin.

Collectors should beware of fakes of the flat plate press coils, which are made from sheet stamps. *Expertization* of early flat plate coils is recommended.

Almanac

1876 – James Milligan invents a steam powered flat plate press.

1881 – The BEP acquires its first power four-plate power presses.

1894 – The BEP acquires additional power presses in order to print postage stamps.

1926 – Last year that majority of stamps are produced by flatbed press at the BEP.

What Others Have Said

Flat plate press printing of stamps was very labor intensive…
"An increasing amount of interest is being shown in the collecting of 'freak' printings….it may be more apt to refer to such printings as 'production varieties'. This group includes…paper-creases, wet and dry printings, etc.…Printing from engraved plates in this period [1861–1867] required manual inking as well as wiping and polishing by hand. This process forced the ink into all of the finest engraved lines as well as removed any excess amounts of ink. Correct polishing of the inked plate in order to produce fine, sharp impressions required considerable experience and great skill. Obviously an overzealous wiping of the plate or careless polishing by a workman with insufficient experience could remove too much ink from a portion of the plate leaving part of the image dry or free of ink."

—*C.W. Christian, "'Production Varieties' of Printing and Perforating, 1861-1867," The Chronicle of the U.S. Classic Postal Issues, 1974.*

…but as they were improved performed major service in stamp production
"The hand press should be well known to all…. After the hand-press, the 4-plate flatbed power press was developed in the early 1870's. At first powered by steam, they are now actuated by electricity…the 4-plate presses since 1894 have performed a very large amount of the postage and revenue stamp printing, and

today they are printing on dry paper instead of wet as they were originally made to do....These presses may be used with any number of plates on, from one to the full complement of four, so that they are relatively versatile....The operations of inking, rough wipe, polish, laying on of the printing paper, taking the impression and the removal of the printed sheet are performed in succession and roughly simultaneously."

—*George W. Brett, "The Manufacture of United States Stamp,"* The Congress Book 1958, *1958.*

The flatbed presses were mostly discontinued by the 1930s...
"The hand press has been used by the Bureau since 1862. With but little modification, principally the addition of an electric motor presses of this type were utilized for the printing of various issues of...stamps on diminishing basis until 1929, when they were discontinued as major production equipment....By July 1, 1926, all ordinary postage stamps of 10 cents and under were being produced on the rotary presses."

—*Sanford Durst,* Bureau of Engraving and Printing – The First Hundred Years 1862-1863, *1978.*

...but were in use until the 1960s creating varieties of United States stamps.
"The 8c Bicolor, 1954 Regular Issue...was printed by two different types of presses: rotary and flatbed. Both types of presses were sheet fed....in the case of the flatbed press...separate sets of flat press frame plates and flat press center [vignette] plates were used to make successive impressions on the sheets to print the flatbed press stamps. During the printing of the stamp, impressions were made from five different rotary frame plates and four different rotary center plates. In the flatbed press printings nine different frame and nine different center plates were used....By merely looking with the naked eye at the frame and center portions of any one of these stamps, no way is presently known of telling whether the stamp was printed by either the rotary press or by one of the flatbed presses. Of course, where the stamps are in full panes of 100 stamps, or in a portion thereof which contains the plate numbers in the attached margins, these stamps can...be...identified...by reference to such plate numbers."

—*Laurence S. Gifford, "The 8¢ Bicolor, 1954 Regular Issue Rotary and Flatbed Press Printing,"* The Bureau Specialist, *1962. There is also a difference in size of blue frames and difference in widths of horizontal gutters which distinguishes the rotary from the flatbed stamps.*

Example of Postal Usage

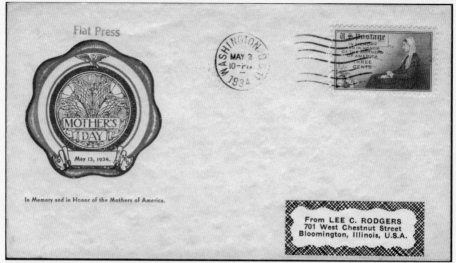

Figure 6

First Day Cover of the flat plate press printing of the 1934 Mothers of America Issue (738).

Where to Find More Information

- *Printing Postage Stamps by Line Engraving* by James A Baxter is the classic text describing in detail how the flatbed presses produced postage stamps.

- *Printing Methods and Techniques* by George W. Brett is the "textbook" used in teaching a course on printing and philately at Penn State.

- *Postage Stamps in the Making* by Fred J. Melville provides a detailed description of flatbed press operation.

Chapter 36
Stamp Production
The Stickney Rotary Press

In the early 1900s American businesses were generating record amounts of mail. Part of the explanation for this phenomenon was the availability and use of mechanical equipment, which rapidly affixed coil stamps to letters. The need for coil stamps was also increased by the growing number of stamp *vending machines*, which dispensed coil stamps in many public places. Unfortunately, the Bureau of Engraving and Printing (BEP) in the early 1900s did not have the capacity to meet the huge demand.

A *rotary printing press* that was conceived, designed and developed by Benjamin R. Stickney was the BEP's solution. This press represented a significant technological advance over the *flat plate presses*, for it enabled postage stamps to be printed on a continuous web (roll) of paper. Prior to the development of Stickney's press, stamps could only be printed one sheet at a time. The rotary presses that Stickney developed, which came to be known by his name, were the

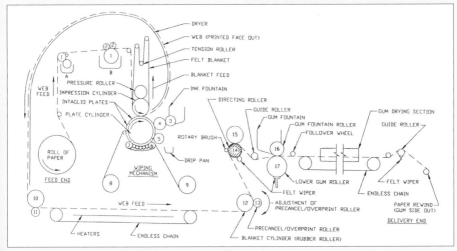

Figure 1

The legendary Stickney Rotary Press evolved over the years, but existed in two basic versions – large and small. This schematic summarizes its operation.

"work horses" of the BEP. Stickney presses produced stamps starting in 1914 and continued producing them until 1957. The last of the Stickney presses was decommissioned on March 15, 1962.

The Stickney Press actually came in two different sizes. The first model developed was the smaller of the two, and used smaller printing plates. It printed coil stamps from 150- and 170-subject plates. The second press was larger, printing regular sheet stamps and booklet pane stamps from wider 400- and 360-subject plates.

Figure 2

The Stickney Rotary Press

The Stickney was a manually controlled, single-color, web-fed printing press and gumming machine. The web was a 24-inch diameter roll of unprinted paper mounted at the feed end of the press. The paper was carried through a series of processes (stations) that produced a printed and gummed roll at the end of the press. The entire printing and gumming process is depicted in the schematic diagram of the press shown in Figure 1. The dashed line in the figure shows the paper path. A photograph of the press appears in Figure 2.

At the feed end of the press the unprinted paper was fed vertically from its housing to station "A" where the underside (good side) of the paper was moistened with warm water which would permit the ink to adhere to the paper.

At station "B" excess water was squeezed out. At this point the paper contained 15 to 30 percent moisture by weight. The paper then moved downward to the rotating intaglio printing plates, which were carefully fitted to the plate cylinder.

The paper, under pressure, passed between the continuous felt blanket and printing plates. Each printing plate is semi-circular with two companion plates joined to form a complete cylinder. The impression cylinder forced the felt blanket to press the moist paper into the inked recesses of the plate to pick up the stamp image.

The ink, at room temperature, was issued to the press in 50- to 70-pound pails and was manually transferred to the ink fountain by spatula. The printing plates received a regulated amount of ink from the fountain by a distributing roller (#3 in the schematic diagram), an integral part of the fountain, and an inking roller (#4). The ink covered both the recessed engraved lines and the non-printing areas. A cylinder (#5) redistributed the ink more evenly over the printing plate surfaces.

Efficient wiping and polishing of the printing plates was essential to producing a satisfactory stamp image. The adjustable wiping apparatus was located directly under the plate cylinder. The wiping material, a clean roll of absorbent crepe paper (#8), was automatically fed between an endless band that formed a wiping cradle designed to conform to the plate contour, and the inked plates. A roller (#6) applied heavy pressure to force the wiper paper to clean the bulk of the surplus ink from the face of the plates. The wiping paper and rollers move in the opposite direction of plate cylinder rotation. The cradle also vibrates, side-to-side, at an angle, across the width of the plate to remove excess ink and polish the non-printing plate surfaces.

After printing, the web emerged printed face out and traveled upward through a heated chute to dry the paper and "set" the ink, and maintain a continuous process. The web then traveled completely around, and then under the press, and over additional heaters. The unprinted side of the paper then passed around a blanket cylinder (#12), and the web was turned diagonally upward. As the web continued upward, the printed face came in contact with the directing roller (#14). The attitude of the printed web was reversed from a face-out position to the unprinted-side-out position. This was the first time the printed side of the web was allowed to contact any part of the press. As a safeguard, the middle portion of this roller was recessed to prevent pressure from being applied to the printed face by the upper roller (#15). Only the outer edges of these two rollers gripped the web margins to ensure paper feed. At this time the web was turned horizontally for the application of gum.

The gum, made from powdered dextrin, was prepared in large cookers and transferred to storage tanks. It was piped from the storage tanks to the gum fountain on the press. The web passed printed-face down between a pair of gumming rollers. The gum fountain roller (#16) revolved in the gum fountain and deposited a film of adhesive over the unprinted side of the web. This roller was shorter than the web width to prevent gum from being applied to the web edges and spilling under to the printed side.

The thickness of the gum was controlled by manually adjusting the space between a metering blade in the gum fountain and the gum fountain roller. Variations in air temperature and relative humidity in the pressroom would affect gum flow.

The web was held down by a series of follower wheels. A colorless line or trail was left in the web gum by these wheels and is a fundamental characteristic of Stickney rotary press stamps.

Spring clips mounted on endless chains at each side of the press gripped the web margins and guided the paper through the gum-drying section. The printed and gummed stamps, sufficiently dried to prevent sticking were wound gum side-out, usually into smaller more conveniently handled rolls at the delivery end of the press.

A major step in the development of **Bureau precancels** was precipitated by complaints the Stickney rotary press sheet stamp pane side margins were too narrow, and the panes had a tendency to curl, which made overprinting almost impossible. Several schemes to precancel full finished printed rolls of stamps were presented. The first plan was to run a finished printed and gummed roll of stamps through a second rotary press. This press would be fitted with a pair of precancel plates to accomplish the precancel task. An economic analysis indicated this process was too expensive to implement and was discarded.

A **letterpress** printing system was developed to precancel or overprint stamps on the Stickney press at the time the stamps were printed. The precancel/**overprint** printing unit (#13) was an afterthought. It was positioned as far away from the intaglio printing station as possible, and before the gumming unit. When the unit was in operation four relief style plates were used to overprint on the finished stamp face. Two plates were used to cover the web width, and two plates were used to complete the printing cylinder.

Late in April 1923, the letterpress printing unit was integrated with the Stickney rotary press, and the Stickney became, in effect, a two-color press. The 1¢ Franklin sheet stamp, series 1922, precanceled "NEW YORK/N.Y." in black and issued in early June 1923 was the first stamp produced by this set-up.

Notes on Collecting

The first stamp to be printed by the Stickney Press was a 2¢ **Washington-Franklin** coil (*Scott* 459) in 1914. The last postage stamp the BEP can document as having been printed on the Stickney Press is the 2¢ **Liberty** coil (1055d). The last commemorative that the BEP claims was printed on the Stickney Press is the 1956 Fifth International Philatelic Exhibition (FIPEX) issue (1076). Some advanced collectors might be interested in collecting the life and times of Benjamin R. Stickney by acquiring correspondence and related articles of interest.

Almanac

1914 – The BEP ships its first rotary printed postage stamps.

1920 – The first large Stickney presses are installed at the BEP.

1957 – Last documented use of a Stickney Press for printing postage stamps.

1962 – The last Stickney Press is decommissioned.

What Others Have Said

A revolution in stamp making
"…we have perfected a rotary printing press for the printing of postage stamps that will completely revolutionize stamp printing from intaglio plates."

—*BEP director Joseph E. Ralph, 1913.*

How did you get the idea for the press, Mr. Stickney?
"Mr. Stickney, the American expert on the printing of postage stamps by rotary presses, has been visiting London, and the Evening News has interviewed him on the subject of the machine with which his name is identified — the Intaglio Security machine. Mr. Stickney, by the way, received and asked for no royalties upon his invention. He turned the machine over voluntarily as a contribution to the Government. Asked whether it was the newspaper rotary press that gave him the idea, Mr. Stickney said, 'No, the principle of web presses does not apply in any sense. The idea struck when I was seeking ways of reducing the cost of printing stamps, which was very high. Also, there was a pressing demand for coiled stamps printed and rolled in continuous strips; for use in automatic stamp affixing and stamp vending machines. The output of stamps by the rotary machines has increased in the last four years from one million a day to seven millions. Under the old flat bed method it took from 7 to 9 days from the beginning of operations to produce the finished stamp. Now we can fill a requisition of this kind in a day.' About one-seventh of the total output of the United States stamps is now printed by rotary machines, and films showing the new machines have been shown in many parts of the country."

—*Percy C. Bishop, "At Home and Abroad,"* Mekeel's Weekly Stamp News, *1919.*

Mr. Stickney's perseverance prevents the system from crushing his idea
"The mechanical expert at the Bureau, Benjamin R. Stickney, brought his creative talents to bear on this problem. Encouraged by Joseph R. Ralph, director of the Bureau, Stickney conceived and developed the design for a rotary, roll-fed, single-color press. There were strong vibrations of action and reaction between the organized plate printers, the hierarchy at the Bureau, and the POD.

The phenomenon of 'technological unemployment,' the misconception by labor that a changing technology would cause unemployment, was a formidable concern. Unfortunately the then-current political structure at the Bureau dictated that appropriations for this project be terminated. Stickney, sensing a technological breakthrough, approached and pressed William C. Fitch, superintendent of the Stamps Division of the POD, to obtain funds to continue this work."

—Louis E. Repeta, "The Stickney Rotary Printing Press – Part I," The United States Specialist, 1996.

From Benjamin Rollin Stickney's Obituary – January 22, 1946
"He went to Washington in 1898 and was mechanical expert and designer at the Bureau of Engraving and Printing for thirty-four years. He is the only man ever to occupy that position, it is stated....Mr. Stickney developed the stamp press that bears his name during seven years of work by day and night. The battery of presses now used in the bureau stamp division was set up in 1914 and had been in almost continuous operation ever since. They are said to have cut the cost of stamp manufacturing between 60 and 70 percent. When the patents were given to the Government by the inventor, they were valued at approximately $1,000,000..."

—"Benjamin R. Stickney Dies – Inventor of Rotary Press for Stamps," Stamps, 1946.

Example of Postal Usage

Figure 3
First Day Cover of the rotary press printing of the 1934 Mothers of America Issue (737).

Where to Find More Information

- A detailed description of the stamp printing and gumming operations of the Stickney Press may be found in Louis Repeta's *The Stickney Rotary Printing Press*.

Chapter 37
Stamp Production
Modern Presses

In the mid-twentieth century, as mail volume increased, and with it the demand for increased numbers of stamps, the Bureau of Engraving and Printing (BEP) needed more efficient and cost-effective stamp printing presses. In 1948 two of the aging **Stickney presses** (ch. 36) were removed to the BEP's engineering facility for study and determination of the requirements for new equipment. Three things seemed certain, the new presses should be **intaglio**, **rotary**, and **web-fed**, as these were considered the most secure and efficient for stamp production. On April 27, 1948 the complete specifications were determined and the bidding process began.

Intaglio Presses

On June 23, 1948, a contract for an experimental bi-color rotary web-fed intaglio press was awarded to the Huck Co. of New York, N.Y. The press was designed to print one color on an initial pass through the press, have the web wound onto a roll at the end of the machine, and then run through the press again for application of a second color. The press included a **typographic** station that was used primarily for **precancels**. This press, commonly known as the Huck Press, was delivered to the BEP on June 27, 1950.

From August 1950 until October 1952 the Huck Press was only used experimentally. Many tests were required to fine-tune the press for stamp production. The most significant problem encountered was the

Figure 1

The first stamp printed on a Huck Press was the 1952 3¢ Red Cross commemorative (1016).

uneven drying of paper between printing runs. In order to produce a good image, the web was dampened prior to the first printing. Because of the uneven drying, the second pass through the press often produced images significantly out of alignment with the first. This was somewhat less of a problem when the second color was added on a single pass using the typographic station, as was done to produce the first stamp printed on this press, the 1952 3¢ Red Cross stamp (Scott 1016, fig. 1), on which the red crosses were applied at the typographic station. By 1954 the Huck Press was in regular use printing commemoratives, the newly designed 20¢ Special Delivery stamp (E20), and 2¢ (1033), and 5¢ (1038) sheet stamps of the Liberty Series.

Figure 2

The Huck-Cottrell Press.

In 1955 five presses of an improved version of the Huck Press were purchased from the Cottrell Co. of Westerly, R.I. While these latter presses are correctly termed Cottrell presses, they are frequently grouped with the earlier version and referred to as **Huck-Cottrell presses** (fig. 2). The BEP designated them Presses 801, 802, 803, 804, and 805.

The Cottrell presses were designed to print sheet, booklet, and coil stamps with little mechanical adjustment, using two plates bent onto the printing cylinder, as was the case with the Stickney Press. Initially gum was added to the back of the web as part of the printing process. By the late 1970s the BEP exclusively used pregummed paper that worked well on these presses.

These presses had significant advantages over the Stickney presses. Initially, less pre-dampening of the web was required, a process referred to as **dry printing**. They were faster than the Stickney presses. The typographic station designed for precanceling was later used for **tagging**. They eliminated the hand-coiling of stamps.

When first installed, the presses did not include their automated coiling equipment that would produce small perforation holes. The coiling equipment designed for the Stickney presses had to be used, producing large perforation holes. However by early 1958 the automated coiling equipment began producing 100-stamp coils. This equipment did not require the **leader strips** and **cores** necessitated by the manual assembly on old coiling tables. The strip of stamps was cut off cleanly at both ends, secured with a piece of tape, and wrapped in polyester.

Dry printing required increased impression pressures. This led to an increased incidence of **gripper-slot cracks** in the printing plates. When flat plates are curved to fit on a rotary press, they must be held in with clamps (grippers) since they tend to straighten out. Fourteen small grooves (slots) were cut into each end of the plates for the Huck-Cottrells. When this number was decreased to 12, there was a significant decrease in the number of stress cracks reported on the plates.

The 300°F drying ovens caused another problem, especially with sheet stamps. The heat made them brittle, readily breaking apart at their perforations, and the gum contracted more than the paper during the drying process. Decreasing the heat, applying thinner gum, using breaker bars in both directions, and printing on different paper helped alleviate these problems.

While the Huck-Cottrell presses never produced a satisfactory bi-color product, they did produce single-color stamps superior to those from the Stickney presses. By mid-1959 only four of the old Stickney presses were still printing stamps, primarily postage due stamps, playing card stamps, and due to problems with the typographic stations on the Huck-Cottrells, precanceled coil stamps. By 1968, the Huck-Cottrells' annual production reached 18.8 billion stamps, 60% of the BEP's production that year.

The Huck-Cottrell presses had long, productive lives printing stamps for some thirty years. Four lasted into the 1980s. Two were destroyed in a fire in the BEP Annex on March 5, 1982; the remaining two were taken out of service on November 20, 1985.

An important lesson was learned from the Huck-Cottrell Presses. Presses that used pre-dampened paper and multiple passes through the press did not produce good quality multi-colored stamps. What was needed was a press that did not require pre-dampened paper and printed all colors during a single pass through the press. While evaluating three **sheet-fed** rotary presses for printing currency, the BEP found one that would also be suitable for producing multi-color stamps. In 1956 the BEP obtained a **Giori Press** (fig. 3) that

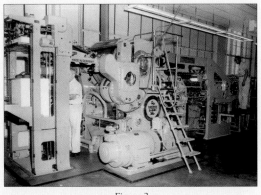

Figure 3
The Giori Press circa 1960.

printed in three colors from a single plate. A set of three inking rollers enabled a three-color stamp to be printed from a single impression of the plate. Each roller was cut out in such a way that it held a single color ink, which was deposited in only the precise locations on the plate that would print that color. Thus the plate could print in one, two, or three colors with a single impression.

The Giori used pre-gummed paper and did not require a drying unit. It did, however, require off-line perforating. Another Giori was purchased in 1959 and still another improved version in 1963. These presses continued to produce stamps through the 1970s.

In 1966 another web-fed Huck Co. press went into service at the BEP. Known as the Huck 9-Color or Huck Multicolor Press, it utilized two intaglio units with significant improvements. The first unit, containing two Giori-type stations, could print up to six colors, three directly onto the web and three more indirectly via a rubber roller. The second unit could print up to three additional colors directly onto the paper. Each unit was composed of 30 small plates with Giori-style inking rollers. When used to print nine colors, a total of 90 numbered plates were required. Since each pane contained seven or eight plate numbers, up to 27,000 plate number combinations were possible for each issue.

The press was designed to print sheet, booklet, and coil stamps and then perforate them online as the web was in motion. This was accomplished with a cylinder containing perforating pins in both directions. Where the horizontal and vertical *combs* crossed, they utilized a common pin. This created a single hole at each corner of the stamps, something the two-step **L-*perforator*** could not accomplish. This press was only economical to use for long runs like coil production and, although some three times faster than the Giori Presses, it proved to be less than satisfactory. After printing the 1968 Christmas stamp (1363) it produced only nine other sheet and coil stamps before being phased out in 1977.

In 1973 a new web-fed three-color intaglio press was purchased from Giori. Known as the B Press, or Press 701, it was specifically designed to produce coil stamps, although it was also used to print several booklet issues. Instead of utilizing the old style curved plates, the B Press utilized seamless *sleeves* on which 936 definitive sized stamps were engraved, 18 cross-web and 52 around the circumference of the cylinder. The stamp design was transferred directly to these sleeves; therefore, no bending of flat plates was required. Being seamless, these cylinders did not produce plate joint lines, which significantly changed the collecting of coil stamps. The press was specifically designed to use pre-gummed paper. It could print up to three colors from one of these sleeves, using inking-in rollers that had different areas removed with a pantograph machine. It had built-in tagging and precancel stations, but did not have an in-line perforator. Coils were finished on Goebel coiling equipment. The B Press produced stamps until 1993.

Giori continued to improve its sheet-fed intaglio presses. In 1976 the BEP purchased their Intaglio 8 Press, which contained four printing plates, each one of which could simultaneously print in three colors, using the specially designed inking rollers found on their other presses. This was also the first multi-color press that had an in-line tagging unit. Prior to this press, stamps were tagged by running them through an offset press after being printed. The Intaglio 8 Press did not, however, have an in-line perforator, so stamps had to be run through an L-type perforator. The first stamp printed on this press was the 1976 13¢ Interphil (1632). This press continued in use until 1985 when the BEP converted to all-web printing.

Another web-fed intaglio press was acquired from Goebel in 1982. Known as the C Press, or Press 901, it also used a sleeve that could accept up to three colors of ink. It was designed to produce 20 stamps across the web, which matched the capacity of the Goebel coiling equipment. The C Press had a very versatile printing format that allowed it to also produce sheet stamps in the traditional format of the Stickney and Huck-Cottrell presses, with margins on all four sides of panes, and normal size stamps for over-the-counter booklets. The C Press had a typographic unit that could be used for on-line tagging, using flexographic plates that were also used on the later D and F Presses. However, it required off-line perforating and sheeting. The C Press contained a major improvement on its unwinding roll stand. When one roll of paper was running out, the stand contained a mechanism that could make a "flying splice" and automatically change to another roll without stopping or even slowing down the press. The first stamp printed on this press was a version of the 20¢ Flag Over Supreme Court (1895) that had first been printed on the B Press in 1981. The C Press continued in operation until 1996.

Gravure Presses

Both the Post Office and the BEP were pleased with the stamps produced by the intaglio Huck-Cottrell and Giori Presses. However these presses could not produce the full-color stamps that the Postal Service began requesting, so full color stamps were out-sourced to private companies with gravure presses. However, the BEP did send employees to observe the *gravure* processes being used.

Gravure, basically a photographic and chemical transfer process, can produce a far wider variety of color shades than intaglio printing. It separates the colors of the original image and etches each one onto a separate sleeve via a series of dots. When the colored inks (yellow, red, blue, and black) that are held on the sleeves are transferred to the paper, a wide variety of shades are created due to the various sizes, closeness, and depth of the dots and overprinting of the various basic colors.

Figure 4

The Andreotti Press.

The BEP wanted to produce gravure stamps itself, but gravure printing was not considered secure enough for currency printing, and the expense of a press that could only be used for stamp production could not be justified. However, in 1969 the Post Office switched production of its aerograms from the U.S. Government Printing Office to the BEP. Since gravure was the appropriate printing method for these items, the BEP contracted with the Miehl Co. of Chicago for the necessary press. This press was designed and constructed by Andreotti S.P.A. of Ceprano, Italy, and is known as the Andreotti Press (fig. 4). It was scheduled to be installed in early 1970 and be ready to print that year's Christmas stamp. Unfortunately, it was not ready on time and that stamp was out-sourced to Guilford Gravure Corp, where it was printed on their Andreotti press. With the issuance of the Missouri Statehood stamps (1426, fig. 5) on May 8, 1971, however-

Figure 5

The Missouri Statehood commemorative (1426), the first printed in full color by the BEP, is a product of the Andreotti Press.

er, the BEP began modern full color printing. It was some time; however, before high quality gravure stamps were produced. It took time to learn the operation of this printing method, which was quite different from intaglio.

An innovative feature of the seven-color web-fed Andreotti Press, also known as Press 601, was that it could print on both sides of the paper during a single pass through the press. In 1973 this capability was used to produce the Postal

Service Employees issue (1489–1498), the first of many with information on the gum side of the stamps. The Andreotti Press could apply taggant to the entire web, but could only apply the spot gum needed for aerograms. It could operate either roll-to-roll for off-line perforating and sheeting, or roll-to-sheet with on-line perforating. After being refurbished in 1995–1996, this press produced self-adhesive coil stamps until June 2005 when all stamp production was switched to private contractors.

Offset Lithography Presses

Offset lithography is similar to intaglio, but the design is etched into a plate that holds ink in the design areas but not on the rest of the plate. The ink is then transferred from the plate to a rubber roller or blanket and from there to the paper.

In 1980 two offset lithographic presses were purchased from Goebel. Known as Optiforma Presses, or Presses 42 and 43, they could print in six colors and were primarily intended to produce aerograms, although they were also used to print a number of Official stamps. Attempts were made to use them in combination with several of the intaglio presses to produce stamps. However, the results were generally unsatisfactory due to registration problems, as illustrated by the 1988 Honey Bee coil (2281). Several offset lithograph presses not normally used for printing stamps were used in conjunction with intaglio and gravure presses for adding surface taggant. One such press, the Miller Press was used to print the American Bicentennial "mural" souvenir sheets (1686–1689) in 1976.

Combination Presses

The BEP obtained a number of presses that combined multiple printing methods. The first of these, acquired from Giori in 1973, known as the A Press, or Press 702, printed up to eight colors by five one-color gravure stations and a three-color intaglio station. The fifth gravure station (as on the Andreotti Press) could print on either side of the web. When it was installed however-er, the two types of printing were not used simultaneously. Thus it

Figure 6

The Touro Synagogue commemorative (2017) was the first to utilize both the intaglio and gravure capabilities of the A Press.

produced either intaglio or gravure stamps, until 1982 when it used both processes to print the Touro Synagogue issue (2017, fig. 6). It could produce either roll-to-roll (with off-line perforating and sheeting) or roll-to-sheet with on-line perforating.

The press produced sheets with 920 definitive subjects (or 460 commemorative subjects), that were cut into traditional sized 100 definitive stamp (or 50 commemorative stamp) panes. However, since the web was cut into sheets every ten stamps along the perforations, the panes lacked the usual horizontal or vertical gutters between the panes and only had selvedge along one edge. Thus the printed plate number advanced along the selvedge with each revolution, producing what collectors describe as floating plate numbers. For any given issue, there were 23 different plate number positions. In 1985 the cylinder layouts were adjusted to produce normal size sheets with plate numbers that remained in the corner.

The A Press was intended to print stamps in a combination of gravure and intaglio. However it never functioned smoothly, and was used mostly for printing intaglio sheet stamps until it was phased out in late 1993.

A more successful web-fed combination press was acquired from Goebel in 1984. Known as the D Press, or Press 902, it combined six single-color offset lithographic plates and a three-color intaglio sleeve. The D Press could only print roll-to-roll and required off-line perforating and sheeting. It primarily produced sheet stamps with four margins on each pane, but could also print booklets and coils. It produced the BEP's first issue to include both offset and intaglio in one pass. This stamp, the 1984 Smokey Bear (2096) was produced during the press's acceptance trial and, could be considered a "test stamp". The press continued in regular use until 1996.

In 1991 the BEP purchased another Goebel combined offset lithograph and intaglio press. The F Press had four single-color offset lithograph stations plus a three-color intaglio sleeve. The intaglio sleeve was interchangeable with both the C Press and D Press. Since each press used a different registration system, each intaglio sleeve had three different sets of register markings. The F press did not have the capacity for on-line perforating or coiling. It began production in early 1992 with the 29¢ World Columbian Stamp Expo commemorative (2616). It continued in use for postage stamps through 1998 and printed Duck Stamps until 2002 when private contractors took over their production.

Notes on Collecting

Many collectors build a collection that contains examples of face-same stamps that are considered unique from one another, and often have their own Scott number. Such distinguishing characteristics may include difference in type of separation, gauge of perforation, different papers used, different gums used, and different presses used. For example, some stamps were printed both **wet** on the

Stickney presses and dry on the Huck-Cottrells. Dry printings, according to *Scott*, show whiter paper, a higher sheen on the surface, feel thicker and stiffer, and the designs stand out more clearly then on wet printings.

No first days of issue were announced for dry printed stamps that had previously been printed wet on the Stickney presses. Potential *EKU*s are difficult to confirm if the stamp does not include a *marginal marking* (plate number or *electric eye dash/bar*) that is engraved with cross-hatching.

When an issue is printed on different presses (e.g., 20¢ Flag over Supreme Court), it is often difficult to determine the proper identity of an individual stamp. The presence of a plate number, however, makes this task is easy. If there is no plate number, the next best identifier is frequently the type of tagging used.

Modern press plate sizes and layouts differ greatly from the Stickney plates. This plays particular havoc with the collecting of sheet stamp plate blocks and coils. Plate blocks of four or six and coil pairs are frequently inadequate. Further, while plate numbers on the booklets produced on the Stickney and Huck-Cottrells Presses were designed to be removed from the finished product, many of the later machines intentionally printed the plate number on the pane tabs.

Almanac

1948 – BEP awards contract for new press on June 23 to the Huck Co. of New York, N.Y.

1950 – Huck Co. delivers its experimental press to the BEP on June 27.

1952 – First Huck printed stamp, the 3¢ International Red Cross (1016), is issued on October 13. This stamp was actually printed on a web dampened to 30% like the Stickney Press and is the only "wet-printing" Huck-Cottrell stamp.

Figure 7

The first Cottrell printed stamp, the 3¢ Wheatland (1081), honored President James Buchanan and his Lancaster, Pennsylvania home.

1954 – First truly dry printed stamp, the 3¢ Lewis and Clark (1063), is released on July 28.

1956 – First Cottrell Press stamp, the 3¢ Wheatland (1081, fig. 7), is issued on August 5. Some 2¢, 3¢, and 5¢ Liberty stamps were printed earlier that year, but their release dates are uncertain.

1956 – First Huck-Cottrell 384-subject coils, the 3¢ Statue of Liberty (1057) are released late in the year. (The "3C" on their leader strips indicates they were produced on Cottrell press #3, i.e., Press 803.)

1957 – First Giori Press stamp, the 4¢ American Flag (1094), is issued on July 4.

1959 – First shipments of Cottrell printed precancels, the 4½¢ Hermitage (1037) to Dallas, Texas and Cleveland, Ohio are made on June 26.

1968 – First stamp printed on Huck 9-Color Press, the Christmas Stamp (1363), is released November 1; also the first stamp with comb perforations.

1971 – First BEP printed gravure stamp, the 8¢ Missouri Statehood (1426), printed on the Andreotti Press, is released May 8.

1973 – First stamps printed on both sides, the 8¢ Postal Service Employees (1489-1498), printed on the Andreotti Press, are released April 30.

1975 – Released on November 15, the 13¢ Flag Over Independence Hall (1625) is the first stamp printed on the B Press, also the first coil stamp without a joint line.

1976 – Released on January 17, the 13¢ Interphil (1632) is the first stamp printed on the Intaglio 8 Press.

1976 – Released on October 27, the 13¢ "Winter Pastime" (1703) is the first stamp printed on the A Press and first with floating plate numbers. Other Christmas stamps (1701 and 1702) are printed on the Andreotti Press.

1981 – On April 24 the first booklet pane is released with the plate number intentionally printed on the tab, the 6¢ Star Circle (1892) and 18¢ Flag-Anthem/mountain (1893), printed on the B Press.

1982 – *EDU* for the first stamp printed on the C Press, the 20¢ Flag Over Supreme Court (1895a), is June 30, which had previously been printed on the B Press. The C Press stamps (plates 4, 6, 8, 9, 10, and 12) have plate numbers every 48 stamps and narrow block tagging (15.6 x 20.6 mm). The B Press stamps (plates 1, 2, 3, 5, 11, 13, and 14) have plate numbers every 52 stamps and wide block tagging (18.2 x 21.1 mm).

1982 – First stamp printed in gravure and intaglio in a single pass, on the A Press, the 20¢ Touro Synagogue (2017), is released on August 22.

1984 – On August 13 the first stamp printed on the D Press, the 20¢ Smokey Bear (2096) is released. It is the first stamp printed by BEP with both offset and intaglio in a single pass.

1985 – On October 30 is released the first stamp printed with the revised A Press gravure sleeve layout (four margin sheets with the plate number in the corners), the 22¢ Madonna and Child (2165).

1986 – The first stamp printed with the revised A Press intaglio cylinder layout (four margin sheets with the plate number in the corners), the 25¢ Jack London (2182), is released on January 11.

1988 – The first stamp printed using offset lithography only on the Optiforma Press, the E (non-denominated) Official coil (O140) is released on March 22.

1988 – Released on September 2, the 25¢ Honey Bee coil (2281) is the first stamp printed using offset lithography on the Optiforma Press and intaglio printing done on another press.

1992 – The first stamp printed on the F Press, the 29¢ World Columbian Stamp Expo (2616, fig. 8), is released January 24.

Figure 8

The first stamp printed on the F Press was the 29¢ World Columbian Stamp Expo (2616).

What Others Have Said

Old Glory, printed on a new press, captures the public's attention
"On July 4, 1957, the United States Post office department in Washington D.C. released a 4¢ commemorative stamp featuring the American flag....the stamp featured Old Glory, proudly unfurled in the breeze, and the legend 'Long May it Wave' (Scott 1094). The stamp prompted great interest in both the stamp collecting community and the general public....The interest in the new stamp was generated in part by the fact that the flag was depicted in the full, rich colors of dark blue, and dark carmine. These colors had for the first time on U.S. stamps, been printed simultaneously from a single printing plate! Prior multicolored stamps were printed, but required a separate pass through the press for each color. This remarkable method of printing was due to the new Giori Press....[which] worked on a very simple principle. A single printing plate with the flag stamp design was introduced into the press and separately inked with each color of which the stamp was to be printed. The inking-in rollers applied each color to the portion of the plate where it was needed."

—*Brian C. Baur, "The Giori Press forever changed U.S. Stamps," Scott Stamp Monthly, 1994.*

The Huck press performed an unprecedented number of simultaneous operations

"[On the Huck Press] in one continuous operation it is possible to wet the web of paper; to ink and wipe the engraved plates; to print the intaglio impression on paper; to dry the intaglio ink and paper; to ink the typographic plate; to print this latter plate in register with the intaglio impression; to dry this latter impression; to apply adhesive to the back of the web; to dry the adhesive; to determine the thickness of the gum; and to wind the finished product in a uniform, concentric coil. All of these operations…are performed while the web is in motion."

—James H. Baxter, "Experimental bi-color rotary web-fed press," The Bureau Specialist, 1955.

….but it produced stamps of questionable aesthetics

"Probably it is premature to comment significantly or with assurance on the movement toward gravure production of our postage stamps—the die is cast anyway. Neither should we draw conclusions based on gravure products thus far to reach our hands. This would be unfair to the Bureau of Engraving and Printing. Its new (Andreotti) gravure press has yet to go into production so evaluation of its capability must be deferred. But, based on the examples of gravure printing we have had thus far (all commercially produced) there sure is little to get excited about, favorably that is. One recent editorial comment compared the Anti-Pollution quartet to 'something out of a cereal box', and to that we say 'Amen'. Nor have the Eakins, the Disney or the 1970 Christmas issues been much better."

—Robert C. Masters, "The Editor's Corner: A New Day Dawning?" The United States Specialist, 1971.

The boldest experiment in the history of stamp printing is ultimately a failure

"Technicians began installing the massive Huck press at the main BEP building in Washington. It was almost 90 feet long, and weighed about that many tons. The first tests were run on April 23, 1966.…More than two years were spent working out the problems before actual stamp production began, delays that led the Post Office Department to adopt rival stamp printing technologies that the BEP had opposed. Both the 5¢ Thomas Eakins of 1967 (1335) and the 6¢ Walt Disney (1355) had been farmed out to private gravure printers by the time the first stamp went into production on the Huck press…The Huck Press remained in service for less than nine years, being finally retired early in 1977.…Although it was designed for production of sheet, booklet and coil stamps, no booklets were ever printed on the Huck. Both before and afterward, other BEP presses printed stamps with designs identical to those printed on the Huck press, but of higher quality and with less waste."

—*Ken Lawrence, "A grand failure: The nine-color webfed intaglio Huck Press," Scott's Stamp Monthly, 2002.*

Where to Find More Information

• George Brett's *The Giori Press* is the definitive, well-illustrated story of the Giori press.

• *Scott* identifies the presses used to print some stamps, but does not identify the presses used to print others. Detailed information on all stamps issued since 1983 is available in the relevant volumes of *Linn's U.S. Stamp Yearbook*, edited by Fred Boughner or George Amick.

Chapter 38
Stamp Production
Modern Private Printers

In 1894 the Bureau of Engraving and Printing (BEP) began the production of postage, which until then had been produced by private printing firms (ch. 3–6). For almost a century the BEP was the sole producer of postage stamps, with minor exceptions; however, as the twentieth century came to a close, private contractors were printing an ever increasing number of stamps. In 2005 private printers once again became the sole printers of postage stamps.

In 1943 the Post Office requested a series of stamps (*Scott* 909–921, fig. 1) honoring the countries occupied by Axis forces in World War II. The desired designs included the full-color flag of each of these nations; however, the BEP did not have the necessary printing equipment to produce multi-colored stamps. Therefore, the job was sub-contracted to a private security-printing firm, the ***American Bank Note Co.*** (American), one of the major producers of U.S. stamps prior to 1894. The stamps produced by American are the first modern stamps not printed by the BEP.

Figure 1

The American Bank Note Company, one of the private printers of stamps during the nineteenth century, printed the Overrun Countries stamps during World War II, including this one honoring Norway.

By the mid-1960s the Post Office was anxious to issue full color stamps. Unfortunately, the BEP's attempts to produce these on their *intaglio* presses were not satisfactory. *Gravure* presses were needed to produce the stamps requested by the Post Office; however, a gravure press could not be used for printing currency. As a result, purchasing a gravure press that could be used only for printing stamps could not be justified.

To satisfy the Post Office's needs, the BEP once again turned to private printing companies. The 5¢ Thomas Eakins (1335, fig. 2), was printed in 1967 by the Photogravure and Color Co. of Moonachie, New Jersey. In 1968, a second gravure stamp, the 6¢ Walt Disney (1355), was printed by the Achrovure Division of the Union Camp Corp. of Englewood, New Jersey. On both occasions, BEP staff members were present during the production in order to learn the techniques required to produce gravure stamps.

Figure 2

The 5¢ Thomas Eakins was printed in 1967 by the Photogravure and Color Co. It was a harbinger of the trend toward the production of stamps by private printers.

When the Post Office transferred its orders for **aerograms** from the U.S. Government Printing Office to the BEP in 1969, this increased the potential use of a gravure press. By then, staffs of both the BEP and Post Office were satisfied that a quality product could be printed by such a press, so the BEP ordered a gravure press from the Miehl Co. of Chicago. The press was not ready in time to produce the first scheduled stamps, so in 1970 the BEP leased the plant and equipment of Guilford Gravure Inc. in Guilford, Connecticut. BEP production staff then printed the 6¢ Anti-Pollution (1410–1413), 6¢ Madonna and Child (1414), and Christmas Toys issues (1415–1418) on Guilford's Andreotti press, which was quite similar to the one ordered for the BEP facility in Washington, D.C. These stamps printed in Connecticut were taken to the BEP for gumming and perforating.

With the installation of its Andreotti Press, the BEP was able to produce all of the requested gravure stamps until 1979. That year, USPS began soliciting bids directly from private printing firms. American and J.W. Fergusson & Sons combined their talents and resources to obtain the contract. In 1979 they produced John Paul Jones

Figure 3

In 1979 American Bank Note Co. printed the 15¢ John Paul Jones commemorative issue. It exists in three perforation varieties, including the very rare perf. 12. Shown here is the common perf. 11 x 12 variety (1789).

stamps (1789–1789B) with three perforation varieties (fig. 3), and the 10¢ Olympic Games (1790–1795); in 1980 they produced the 15¢ Benjamin Banneker (1804), 15¢ Veterans Administration (1825), and 15¢ Education (1833). In subsequent years they continued printing stamps, together and separately. American continued to produce an increasing number of stamps. From 1983 until 1990, they produced 46 issues (six of which were four-stamp setenants), which constituted the majority of stamps printed outside of the BEP.

In 1992, three printers produced 29¢ Eagle and Shield convertible booklets: Banknote Corporation of America (2595), Dittler Brothers, Inc. (2596), and Stamp Venturers (2597). Thus began the steadily increasing production and use of self-stick stamps, which were preferred by the majority of postal patrons.

A further self-stick experiment began in 1997, 32¢ Flag over Porch (3133) linerless coils. The production of these coils reveals how complex stamp procurement had become. Stamp Venturers printed them in Richmond, Virginia and shipped the entire rolled web to 3M Corp. in St. Paul, Minnesota. 3M coated the entire web with adhesive on the back and silicone on the front then shipped the entire roll back to Stamp Venturers for finishing into 100-stamp coils for sale.

Also in 1997, [25¢] Jukebox linerless coils (3132) were produced by Stamp Venturers for a **First Class Presorted** rate used by mass-mailers; however, they did not work well on existing automated stamp affixers. Consequently, few have been found on commercial covers.

In 2000, Guilford Gravure produced another linerless coil, the Fruit Berries (3404–3407). The die cuts on this issue were at the top and bottom of the design, rather than on the sides as previous linerless coils had been. Buyers criticized these stamps as being difficult to separate.

In 2002, 37¢ Snowmen setenants linerless coils (3680–3683) were produced by Guilford Gravure. A container for them was provided at a cost of one dollar. Linerless coils provided no significant savings in production, and required new or modified equipment for affixing stamps, making it doubtful that more linerless coils would be produced.

The Move to Exclusive Private Production
Even as the BEP acquired equipment to produce diverse types of stamps, other factors increased the use of private printers. In 1971 the Post Office Department was transformed into the U.S. Postal Service (USPS). As a largely autonomous organization, it was no longer required to have close ties to other government bodies such as the BEP. One of the Postal Service's goals was to be self-sustain-

ing, generating enough income from its operations that it would no longer require a subsidy from the federal government. Among others things the USPS needed to produce stamps at the lowest possible cost.

In open competition, the BEP had two problems offering the lowest bids. Their equipment tended to be older and less sophisticated than that of private firms. Private firms could use depreciation to write off much of their equipment expenses from their taxes, but the BEP relied on Congressional appropriations to purchase new equipment. Additionally, the BEP had higher labor costs than the private companies.

As the number of commemoratives increased, each requiring hundreds of millions of copies, the BEP did not have adequate production capacity. While many companies could produce the printed product, not all had the necessary equipment to finish them into the required stamp formats; however, when it became apparent that printing U.S. stamps would be an on-going and lucrative activity, the number of firms bidding on contracts increased. The printing and the various steps of finishing were often done by different companies.

By the late 1980s, there was increasing pressure on the USPS to break-even and perhaps even to earn a profit. Thus the cost of stamp production became more important than its previous close relationship with the BEP. This was countered by the quality product produced by the BEP compared to the often sub-standard stamps received from private firms. In order to keep their lucrative stamp contracts, private printers increased their quality controls and in 1997 produced 54% of that year's postage stamps. That percentage continued to increase until it reached 100% in 2006.

Notes on Collecting

As printers in the private sector produced more and more stamps, collectors seized this collecting opportunity, and began to collect the stamps of the many different modern private printers. Determining the printer of many modern issues is sometimes challenging. This is especially true of definitives that are often produced by several different companies. *Scott* generally identifies the companies that received the initial contract from the Post Office. However, *Scott* does not detail the various subcontractors. When a contracted firm has a stamp printed by two or more subcontractors, specialists attempt to identify the detectable differences between the printings.

The *plate number* is often a good clue in determining the printer (fig. 4). A prefix letter appears on the plate number of private printed stamps. For example, those numbers beginning with "S" were printed by Sennett, with "A" by Avery-

Figure 4

A plate number single of the 1998 Wisconsin Statehood commemorative, the first stamp printed by Sennett Security Products. The "S" prefix in the plate number identifies the stamp as a Sennett product.

Denison, with "V" by Stamp Venturers. Individual stamps, without a plate number attached, may often be identified as to printer by such factors as color variations, size, location of the printed year date, and/or the style of the perforations or die cuts.

A collection of modern stamps produced by private printers may be mounted simply in year order, by the name of the contractor, or by the types of stamps produced. Identifying commemoratives of the various printers is usually quite easy, as *Scott* identifies the name of the printer. With many of the definitives, when a number of printers were used to produce the identical face-same stamp, there may be a need for some research. Some professional stamp dealers sell sets of face same definitives in pre-packaged kits, which identify the different printers and varieties. Purchasing such a kit is a good way to start a collection of modern privately printed stamps.

Almanac

1943 – American Bank Note Co. prints its first twentieth century U.S. stamps (909–921).

1967 – Photogravure & Color Co. prints its first U.S. stamp (1335).

1968 – Achrovure Division of Union Camp Corp. prints its first U.S. stamp (1355).

1970 – BEP personnel produce U.S. stamps (1410–1413) using facilities of Guilford Gravure Inc.

1979 – American Bank Note Co. and J.W. Fergusson & Sons jointly produce their first U.S. stamps (1790).

1990 – U.S. Banknote Co. prints its first U.S. stamp (2440).

1990 – Avery International Corp. prints its first U.S. stamp (2475).

1991 – KCS Industries prints its first U.S. stamp (2520).

1991 – Avery Dennison Co. (Avery-Dennison Co.) prints its first U.S. stamp (2531A).

1991 – Jeffries Banknote Co. for American Bank Note Co. prints its first U.S. stamp (2542).

1991 – Stamp Venturers prints its first U.S. stamp (C128, fig. 5).

1991 – J. W. Fergusson prints its first U.S. stamp (2579), its first stamp for American Bank Note Co. (2538), its first U.S. stamp for KCS Industries Inc. (2485), and its first U.S. stamp for Stamp Venturers (2454).

1991 – Multi-Color Corp. prints its first U.S. stamp for American Bank Note Co. (2529).

Figure 5

The 1991 Harriet Quimby air mail stamp was the first stamp printed by Stamp Venturers.

1991 – Guilford Gravure for American Bank Note Co. prints its first U.S. stamp (2602).

1992 – The Press Inc. and J.W. Fergusson print a U.S. stamp for Stamp Venturers (2704).

1992 – Canadian Bank Note Co. for Stamp Venturers prints its first U.S. stamp (2184).

1992 – Banknote Corporation of America prints its first U.S. stamp (2595).

1992 – Dittler Brothers, Inc. prints its first U.S. stamp (2596).

1992 – Ashton-Potter America Inc. (Ashton-Potter, USA, Ltd. or Ashton-Potter) prints its first U.S. stamps (2647–2696).

1993 – Guilford Gravure Inc. prints its first U.S. stamp (2529a).

1993 – Multi-Color Corp. prints its first U.S. stamps (2731–2737).

1994 – National Label Co. prints its first U.S. stamp for 3M Corp. (2598).

1994 – Barton Press for Banknote Corp. of America prints its first U.S. stamps (2863–2866).

1995 – Sterling Sommer prints its first U.S. stamp for Ashton-Potter (USA) Ltd. (2968).

1997 – Stamp Venturers and 3M Corp. print their first U.S. stamp together (3133).

1997 – Stephens Security Press prints its first U.S. stamp for Ashton-Potter (USA) Ltd. (3141).

1998 – American Packaging Corp. for Sennett Security Products prints its first U.S. stamps (3212–3215).

1998 – Sennett Security Products (Sennett Security Printers) prints its first U.S. stamp (3206, fig. 4).

1998 – Guilford Gravure for Banknote Corp. of America prints its first U.S. stamps (3230–3234).

2000 – Sterling Sommer prints its first U.S. stamp (3370).

2001 – De La Rue Security Printing prints its first U.S. stamp (3504).

What Others Have Said

The first gravure stamp predates the 'outside printers' period by 25 years
"For the first time since the 1943-44 overrun countries issue [printed by the American Bank Note Co.]…the U.S. Post office Department will 'farm out' the printing of another commemorative stamp. In a startling announcement, that completely caught collectors by surprise, Postmaster Lawrence F. O'Brien stated the 1967 5-cent stamp in the continuing 'American Paintings' series will be printed by the Photogravure and Color Co. of Moonachie, NJ which was the low bidder when the Bureau of Engraving and Printing invited bids for gravure production. The 'farm-out' decision also creates a 'first' in printing technique. The painting stamp will become the first U.S. postage stamp adhesive to be printed by the gravure method….O'Brien was quick to emphasize the Bureau will continue to print almost all of the some 25 billion stamps used annually. However, he admitted, that 'if the gravure stamp is well received by postal patrons, gravure will be used from time to time in the future when a particular design lends itself to production by this method.'"

—*"U.S. to Release First Gravure Stamp,"* The American Philatelist, *1967.*

The first self-adhesive stamp pre-dates the 'self-adhesive period' by 20 years

"This issue [self-stick adhesive 1974 Christmas stamp] is a fairly new 'ball game' to most collectors and we shall present more details than otherwise. This may help in determining how it may be collected as well as enable collectors to be better prepared for possible future issues. Our feeling is that this kind of stamp will 'go,' whether we as collectors like it or not, and that the sooner it is understood the sooner decisions can be made."

—*George Brett, "Two Varieties of the Pressure-Sensitive (Self-Adhesive) Christmas Stamp,"* The United States Specialist, *1974.*

The USPS' linerless coils present problems for the consumer and collector

"The stamp surface appears to be too slick, a quality that seems necessary for the stamp to be linerless and to peel easily from other stamps in the roll....Is the surface stable? Is it chemically inert? In all likelihood, it's not. Collectors should think first before putting this new material in their albums or mounts. Like any of the other new self-adhesive stamps, the storage strip and the new linerless stamps have not stood the test of time. We collectors are the guinea pigs."

—*Michael Schreiber, "New linerless coils not ready for prime time,"* Linn's Stamp News, *1997.*

Private printers bring a whole new perspective to stamp production

"Richard Sennett tries not to let the slings and arrows of critics bother him...What life has dealt Mr. Sennett this year is a raft of charges and accusations that his role in stamp production was the result of, if not collusion, at least improprieties – charges that remain unsubstantiated. His company, Stamp Venturers, also caught flack for subcontracting the printing of two U.S. definitive stamps; one showing the late Sen. Dennis Chavez and the other showing the late U.S. Chief Justice Earl Warren - to a Canadian firm. That the deal was legal didn't seem to matter....'Stamp Venturers has an experience factor that no other company has,' he said....'Technology is changing the stamp printing business', Mr. Sennett said, including his work of converting stamp design art work to pre-print format....He claims credit for the first electronic pre-press work on a stamp, the Marianne Moore commemorative issued in 1990."

—*Mark A. Kellner, "Richard Sennett Seeks to Rise above Controversy,"* Stamp Collector, *1991.*

Example of Postal Usage

Figure 6

A 40¢ William T. Piper air mail stamp (C129), printed by J.W. Fergusson and Sons for American Bank Note Co., paying the international post card rate on August 4, 1991.

Where to Find More Information

• Detailed information on the modern private printers is found in the relevant volumes of *Linn's U.S. Stamp Yearbook*, edited by George Amick.

Chapter 39
Stamp Separation
1857-1980

Stamps have always been printed on sheets of paper. At the beginning, they had to be separated into individual stamps. The history of stamp separation is one of advancing technology, resulting in increased production efficiency and utility to the user. When postage stamps were first introduced in the United States, the stamps had to be separated using either a straight edge razor or a pair of scissors.

The U.S. began issuing perforated stamps in 1857. The first perforating machine used to perforate U.S. stamps, a rotary perforator, was invented by William and Henry Bemrose, and patented in England in 1854. The patent describes the mechanism as:

> "Our said Invention related to the punching or perforating of paper and other substances by means of circular perforators or punches, placed on a cylinder, which is made to rotate at a rate equal to that of the material being perforated or punched..."

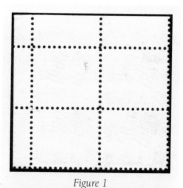

Figure 1

Line perforations are applied in one direction at a time, and cross each other at the corners of stamps in an irregular or imperfect manner.

The method of perforating employed by this machine is called *"line" perforating*. Perforations were applied in only one direction as the sheet went through the perforator. Then the sheet was rotated 90° and reinserted so that perforations would be applied in the other direction to finish the process. The key to distinguishing line perforations from *comb perforations* or *harrow perforations* is that the line perforations cross each other at the corners of stamps in an irregular or imperfect manner (fig. 1).

Toppan, Carpenter, Casilear & Co. of Philadelphia, the printers of the U.S. 1851 issue, secured a Bemrose rotary line perforator from England in 1856. The stamps resulting, perf. 15½ were issued in February 1857. The sheets, consisting of two adjoining 100-stamp panes, passed through this line perforator twice

– once for the vertical rows, and again, after adjustment of the pins, for the horizontal rows. In an hour, an experienced operator could perforate 250 sheets.

The first stamps to be perforated, the 3¢ Washington type I (*Scott* 25), were characterized by a lack of uniform spacing, and frame lines that made it difficult to keep the perforations holes from cutting into the design. In an attempt to solve this problem, new plates were laid down for the 3¢ and other stamps. With more uniform spacing between stamps, the designs were cut back to make more room for perforations. This modification, however, did not result in perfectly centered stamps, as two other problems remained. Machine operators could and did insert sheets incorrectly into the perforator, resulting in improperly aligned perforations. Additionally, printing stamps by line engraving required paper to be moistened so that it could be pressed into the recessed lines of the plate to pick up the ink. As the printed sheets dried prior to perforating, the paper would shrink unevenly, and unpredictably. Since time did not allow the row of perforating pins to be reset for each sheet, misperforations of varying degrees resulted, and were accepted as normal.

Not everyone waited patiently for the government to perforate stamps. The best-known forerunners of government-perforated stamps are the so-called **Chicago perfs** found on the 1¢ and 3¢ 1851s that were issued imperforate by the Post Office. The perforations are a coarse gauge 12½. Dr. Elijah W. Hadley, a Chicago dentist, invented a perforating machine, probably in 1854, which he offered, without success, to the Post Office Department. The few examples in existence seem to have been used from mid-1856 until early 1857. Other early unofficial perforations exist, for instance the 1¢ 1851, Type II, with rough sewing machine produced perforations.

Stamps of the Confederate States of America have unofficial perforations. All Confederate stamps were issued imperforate except for a very few that had test perforations. However, since perforations were the expected norm on U.S. stamps by 1861, many Confederate stamps had perforations and **roulettes** added by individuals, sometimes with the approval of local postmasters.

In August 1861 a new set a stamps was issued, prepared by the **National Bank Note Co.** (National), and the previously issued stamps were demonetized. The new stamps were perforated gauge 11.85 and 11.95 on American made machines similar to the Bemrose perforator. This perforation gauge is usually identified in catalogues as perf. 12, which became the standard gauge for the next fifty years. Misregistered perforations continued, but careful inspection resulted in relatively few **errors** or significant **freaks** reaching the public.

In 1894 the Bureau of Engraving and Printing (BEP) took over the printing of postage stamps from private companies. The first perforations applied by the BEP that year were rough, ragged and often were not punched out, leaving many *chads*. It is often possible to distinguish these stamps on **unwatermarked** paper from the 1895 printing on **watermarked** paper, because the later stamps have clean, crisp, sharply defined perforations. Specialists have theorized that in 1894 new equipment, combined with inexperienced operators, and perhaps an effort to perforate multiple sheets at one time, combined to cause the problem of ragged perforations.

When the BEP took over postage stamp production there was an increase in the amount of **error** and freak material reaching the public. The most likely cause was the increasing demand for stamps and the resulting negative impact on quality.

Beginning with the Series of 1902 (ch. 8), and continuing through the Series of 1922 (ch. 10), imperforate stamps were produced in large quantities. These were not intended for use by the public as imperforates. Rather, they were produced, beginning in 1906, in response to requests from manufacturers of stamp **vending and affixing machines**. These companies took imperforate sheets and pasted them together to form continuous rolls. To these they applied distinctive holes, slots, notches or roulette-like slits between the stamps, and then cut them apart into strips for use in their machines (ch. 49). The BEP began producing its own coil stamps in 1908.

Until 1910, coils were issued with the standard perf. 12 gauge. However these stamps separated too easily in the BEP's coiling machines, so the perforation gauge was changed to 8½. This gauge perforation, however, generated complaints that stamps could not be torn apart without damaging them! By 1914, a compromise perf. 10 was instituted for coils, a standard that continued until late in the twentieth century. The **Stickney rotary press** was inaugurated in 1914, which permitted printing of continuous lengths of stamps in **web** form, eliminating the need to paste sheets together to make coil rolls.

Developments in the perforation gauge of sheet stamps and booklet panes paralleled that of coil stamps. In 1908 perf. 12 was used, but changes resulted from various experiments, one of which was a series of efforts aimed at reducing paper shrinkage, or at least its negative effects on stamp centering.

The first attempt to control shrinkage took place during 1909 when a new paper was used, made of 65% wood pulp and 35% rag stock, instead of 100% pulp. The resulting stamps are known as **bluish paper** issues (357-366 and 369) identifiable by the grayish-blue paper color evenly distributed over the entire stamp. The experiment was unsuccessful.

The next attempt at controlling paper shrinkage was to change the 15-year-old double-line watermark to a smaller single-line version in hopes of strengthening the paper. While it made no appreciable difference, it created a number of unique stamp varieties.

Meanwhile the BEP was experimenting with variations in spacing between stamps in order to control the levels of waste. The standard horizontal spacing had been 2 mm. Since shrinkage was greatest at the outside edges of the 400-subject plates, the BEP in 1909 laid down the so-called star plates with 3 mm spacing between the six outer vertical rows, leaving the eight inner rows at 2 mm. While this did help reduce waste, it caused problems for the vending and affixing machine manufacturers, who could not set their machines to handle the variable spacing on these sheets. Therefore in 1912, "**A**" plates were created with uniform 2¾ mm spacing. These plates had an "A" placed adjacent to plate numbers and became known as "A" plates. The spacing on these plates became the standard for future plates.

Perforated 12 sheet stamps, like their perf. 12 coil counterparts were vulnerable to premature separation. They sometimes separated while still in post office drawers. This led to a 1914 change to perf. 10 for sheets and booklets – which gave rise to a new series of complaints that these stamps were too hard to sepa-rate! The change from perf. 12 to perf. 10 gave rise to a major variety that was only given major catalogue number status by *Scott* in 2003. Some 1¢, 2¢, and 5¢ Washington-Franklins are found perf. 10 x 12 and 12 x 10. (When two numbers are given for a stamp's perforation gauge, the first number is for the horizontal perforations, and the second is for the vertical perforations.) It appears that the change in perforating wheels was done gradually, one machine at a time. Some sheets were perforated in one direction using old wheels and in the other direction using new wheels. The result is **compound perforation** stamps.

In 1916, the use of watermarked paper was abandoned, and in 1917, an 11 gauge perforation became the standard for sheets and booklet panes printed on the flat plate press. Then, in 1919, in an experiment to increase production, an experimental **Rossback** perforator applied gauge 12½ perforations to 6,641 sheets 1¢ offset stamps (536), but the result was a failure, with only 3,466 being of sufficient quality to be cut into panes of 100 for sale.

Some interesting perforations varieties exist on Washington-Franklin and Series of 1922 stamps known as **Coil Waste** and **Sheet Waste**. Some of these stamps, which resulted from attempts to economize, are rarities, and none are commonly found. Sections of the rotary web, that were intended for production into coil or sheet stamps, but that were not long enough, or defective in some manner, were salvaged and perforated as if they had been flat plate press stamps.

Compound perforations, became standard as a result of experimentation with the Stickney rotary press. Since the web would strain and split too easily under tension when stamps were perforated gauge 11 across the web, the BEP tried gauge 10 x 11 on the 1¢ Washington in May 1920 (542). This did strengthen one side, but resulted in weakening the other side. The gum later predisposed the stamps to curl and separate along the perf. 11 side while still in post office drawers. The BEP began to apply **gum ridges** and **gum breakers** to combat this problem. They significantly reduced the curling that had contributed to the fragility of panes. Then, the BEP realized that paper has "grain", i.e., it is stronger in one direction than in the other. Thus, the need was recognized to use a smaller gauge perforation "with the grain." The BEP acquired equipment that would perforate rotary press upright (vertical) stamps 11x10½. On oblong (horizontal) stamps the perforation was 10½ x 11. This compound perforation style was used for definitive sized stamps through the Americana Series of 1975-1981.

When web printing became the method of choice, web perforating naturally followed. Using web perforation, productivity per operator increased from 3,000 sheets per day to 25,000 per day by the mid 1930s. However, waste due to misperforation ran as high as 15%.

In 1930, the BEP mechanical expert, Henry Holtzclaw, who was to become its Director in 1954, began working on photoelectric control of the perforation. In February 1935, production models were installed capable of producing 50,000 to 60,000 sheets per day with only 3% waste. Registration of perforations is controlled by **electric eye** (EE) markings in the sheet margins that are scanned by photoelectric cells. After

Figure 2

The Electric Eye Perforator perforating the 1948 Four Chaplains Issue.

many different markings and combinations of markings had been tested, the BEP settled on a standard set of markings early in the Presidential Series of 1938. Once established, the electric-eye web perforator became a workhorse that perforated almost all stamps into the late 1950s (fig. 2).

Change in perforation technology resulted from the introduction of the sheet fed Giori press in the mid-1950s, which was first used for the 1957 4¢ 48-Star Flag issue. Because the Giori press was sheet fed, it required a different type of perforator. The result was the **L-perforator**, designed to handle sheets rather than a web (fig. 3). The machine is named for its shape. A moving belt first carried sheets of printed stamps through perforating wheels that applied horizontal or vertical perforations as appropriate. Then the sheet fell onto a moving belt at a right angle to the first one,

Figure 3

L perforator on which stamps receive horizontal perforations on one leg of the L and vertical perforations on the other.

which carried the sheet through perforating wheels to apply the perforations in the remaining direction. Approximately 150 sheets per minute could be sent through the L-Perforator.

Harrow perforating arrived at the BEP in 1968 with the installation of the Huck Press, which had **in-line perforating** capability. An expanded Giori-type press with three 3-color printing stations, its first product was the 1968 Van Eyck Christmas stamp. The object of in-line perforating was to eliminate the need to rewind a web and feed it into a separate (off-line) perforator. This was accomplished by incorporating the perforating process into the printing process. Harrow perforating, unlike **Line** or **Comb perforating**, applied all perforations for a sheet in one impression. Thus there was no crossing of lines, or problem of lining up the combs. It featured perfect corners, with no overlapping of holes. A special feature of this equipment was its ability to perforate both regular issues and commemorative-sized stamps. This was accomplished by extending or retracting alternate rows of vertical perforation pins. This meant that the commemorative-sized Huck-press-printed stamps had to be precisely twice the length or height of definitives.

The next press to have an in-line perforator was the **Andreotti** web-fed gravure press acquired in 1970, although it was not equipped with its Harrow in-line perforator until 1975. Meanwhile, stamps not produced on the Huck press were perforated off-line on a Seybold EE-rotary web-fed perforator, or off-line on the L-perforator. These types of perforating machines were used through to the start of die-cut self stick stamps which began in earnest in 1989.

The perforating of the 1976 Bicentennial souvenir sheets created unique challenges. Each sheet contained five stamps, defined in the large mural design by the perforations. Without the perforations, the design concept would not have worked. Because of the layout of the perforations, they could not be placed by Line or Comb, so the Bureau adapted a letterpress normally used for overprinting currency to place the perforation grid in one impression. This process was used before it had been fully tested. Therefore many perforation freaks and errors were produced, including perforations that were high, low, missing and even inverted! The second use of this type of equipment was with the CAPEX '78 souvenir sheet (1757) and there were very few errors. This process was so reliable by the time the 1986 AMERIPEX Presidential souvenir sheets were produced that there has been only one imperforate sheet reported.

Unfortunately, comparatively slow in-line perforating proved to be unable to keep up with the more rapid printing process. Therefore the BEP opted to perforate off-press as much as possible and to explore faster off-line perforator technology. This led to the introduction in 1985 of what became the workhorse of off-line perforators: the **Bobst-Champlain Harrow perforator** used for definitives. This machine took a roll of printed stamps and perforated it – two adjoining panes across the web at a time, separated it into sheets four panes square, and sheeted out the product into stacks for further processing.

Because of the pressure to produce sufficient stock for post offices, the BEP has occasionally used two or more perforating methods for a single issue. An example is the 1975 (10¢) Louis Prang Christmas stamp. There is a version that is 11.2 x 11.2 done on the Andreotti in-Line harrow perforator with its "perfect" or **Bullseye** perforations (1580), an L-perforator 10.9 x 10.9 version (1580c), and an EE 10.5 x 11.3 version (1580B). The use of multiple perforation types on single issues continued through the 1980s. While it created a challenge for collectors, the BEP was simply using its available equipment efficiently, and did not look at these as "different" stamps.

Notes on Collecting

Acquiring a good perforation gauge is important to make accurate perforation measurements. A subtle difference in the perforation of a stamp can make the difference between a very common stamp, and a great rarity. A knowledgeable collector can still find rare and valuable stamps in mixtures or inexpensive cover boxes when knowing what to look for. Again, the measurement of the perforations can be a deciding factor in determining a rare stamp from an otherwise identical-looking common stamp.

Perforations on stamps can be more fully enjoyed and appreciated when one has a basic knowledge of the various perforating processes that have been used. This will make the difference between a "boring" page of almost identical stamps, and an album page that illustrates the dynamic history of ever changing stamp production.

Almanac

1856 – Bemrose rotary perforator is purchased from England.

1857 – First perforated stamp (25), with perf. gauge 15½, is released.

1861 – Perforation gauge changes to 12 with the new issue produced by the National Bank Note Co.

1906 – Imperforates are first produced for private vending and affixing machine companies.

1914 – Perforation 10 is introduced as the new standard for sheet stamps; leading to the first compound perforations.

1914 – Perforation 10 is introduced as the compromise standard for coils.

1917 – Perforation 11 is introduced as the new standard for sheet stamps.

1919-1923 – The era of *coil waste* production.

1923 – The use of gum breakers begins.

1926 – Perf. 11 x 10½ introduced for sheet stamps.

1935 – The Electric Eye perforator is placed in production.

1957 – The L-perforator is placed in production in connection with the introduction of the Giori press.

1968 – The Huck press is introduced, using in-line Harrow perforating.

1974 – First U.S. die cut stamp is released.

1976 – Converted currency press is used to apply Harrow perforations to a souvenir sheet.

1985 – Introduction of the Bobst-Champlain off-line Harrow perforator.

What Others Have Said

Before there were perforations, stamps had to be cut apart

"The earliest issues, such as the 1847 5¢ Franklin (Scott 1), did not have any means provided for separation. It was expected the stamps would be cut apart with scissors or folded and torn....Many stamps were first issued in imperforate formats and were later issued with perforations. Therefore, care must be observed in buying single imperforate stamps to be certain they were issued imperforate and are not perforated copies that have been altered by having the perforations trimmed away. Stamps issued imperforate usually are valued as singles. However, imperforate varieties of normally perforated stamps should be collected in pairs or larger pieces as indisputable evidence of their imperforate character."

—*Scott Specialized Catalogue of United States Stamps and Covers, 2005.*

Separating perforated stamps means always being careful

"It is rather difficult tearing apart stamps perforated 10, or separating coil stamps perforated 8, and so forth, and the utmost care is necessary in first folding them over the perforations several times to break down the resistance. Yet with care, perforations are very apt to break raggedly, to pull some of the teeth out entirely, and to rip unevenly. A simple device would be to cut along the perfs with a knife or scissors, but that will leave them too neatly and sharply cut, and the stamp then looks like a reperforation job, and consequently the cut-apart stamps lose [appeal] and desire in the eyes of collector. What to do? The answer seems to be to continue to tear them apart raggedly or the best way you can, and keep your fingers crossed. Acquire skill? You can experiment with cheap material and it will always separate neatly, but wait until you try it with a good item, and see what happens."

—*George B. Sloane, "Perforating – Idiosyncrasies of Stamp Collecting," 1936.*

Carefully measuring perforations can bring great reward

"New collectors may wonder why the gauge of a stamp's perforations is of any importance when it may have been produced on only one gauge. Generally speaking, in such a situation, it has no importance. However, it never does any harm to be curious, as it was only the curiosity of collectors that brought to light the two different perforations of the US $1 vending machine booklet pane of 1977."

—*Kenneth A. Wood, This is Philately, 1982.*

Perforations can vary in gauge by one thousandth of an inch
"The question of correct classification of our perforations was brought up by Harry B. Prest of Jenkintown, Pa, who found that the Bicentennials and other recent Rotary Press sheet stamps were perforated 11-1/4x10-3/4 instead of 11x10-1/2 as listed in the catalogs....Where the same stamp design is found in various perforations it is essential that the perforations be accurately checked as some are much more desirable than others....This is especially true where the stamp has also been issued imperf as these can easily be counterfeited to represent the scarce item."

—*Beverly S. King, "Notes on U.S. Stamps," Stamps, 1933.*

Kuisalas Perforation Gauge measures hole distance center to center in thousandths of an inch
"His gauge [The Kuisalas Gauge of 1965] – which is good for U.S. Stamps into the 1960's – is a great help in determining the genuineness of stamps on which perforations may have been added, slightly altered, fully reperforated, or totally counterfeited. It is also useful in distinguishing between production runs of certain stamps of very similar appearance."

—*John Hotchner, "The Hole Truth: The Perforating of United States Stamps," The United States Specialist, 1988.*

Where to find More Information

• *Early American Perforating Machines and Perforations 1857-1867* by Winthrop S. Boggs covers the early perforating machines used by the American Bank Note Co. and the stamps perforated by them, and teaches perforating basics.

• *Errors, Freaks and Oddities on U.S. Stamps: Question Marks in Philately* by Stanley B. Segal provides a detailed overview of the many varieties the perforating process has inadvertently created.

• "The Hole Truth: The Perforating of United States Postage Stamps" and "Major Perforation Varieties of the Early 20th Century" by John M. Hotchner.

Chapter 40
Stamp Separation Since 1980

The methods used to separate U.S. stamps have changed more since 1980 than in all the preceding years since U.S. stamps were first issued in 1847. Since 1980 stamp separation evolved from traditional *perforating* to grinding, slicing, and cutting - technology an earlier generation could only have imagined. As a result, these processes are now referred to as stamp separation, rather than just stamp perforation.

In 1980 the Bureau of Engraving and Printing (BEP) had almost exclusive responsibility for stamp production. A quarter of a century later it exited the stamp production business, as private contract printers gradually took over stamp production. Combined with the rise of *self-adhesive* stamps, this led to several new methods of stamp separation and an increase in the number of collectible varieties.

Regardless of classification or appearance, there are only two primary categories of stamp separation: those where paper is removed and those where it is not.

Stamp Separation by Removal of Paper
Perforations
Technically, perforation refers to any form of stamp separation that involves the removal of paper. Perforation holes are most frequently round, but they may appear in any shape, including oblong and star-shaped. Standard perforators, as they were used for almost 150 years on U.S. stamps, puncture (remove) paper through the use of matching male and female perforating pins and dies that remove bits of paper when they meet. The resulting scrap, tiny dots of paper, is known as **chads**. There are numerous ways that perforations can be applied to printed stamp paper, but only two basic methods – rotary and **stroke**.

The traditional rotary perforation process utilizes two cylinders (one with pins and one with dies) which continuously rotate while the printed stamp paper travels between them, resulting in holes being punched. The perforation holes are generally slightly oblong with one slightly rough inner edge which are characterized by protruding paper fibers. This method has been used on numerous sheet, booklet, and coil issues.

Stroke perforating is accomplished with a straight up-and-down action that results in perforation holes that are usually round and smooth. This method has been used to perforate numerous sheet, booklet, and coil issues. The basic types of stroke action perforating are **harrow** and guillotine. The harrow method perforates a number of stamps at a time from pins attached to a flat plate. The four-pane Eureka perforator, used to perforate most sheet stamps at the BEP since the late 1980s, is an example of a harrow perforator. Unlike harrow perforators, guillotine perforators apply perforations in only one direction. Most water-activated, typically by licking, coil stamps are perforated by a stroke-action guillotine perforator because they only need perforations vertically or horizontally. They are cut in the other direction, leaving natural straight edges on two opposite sides.

For many years rotary perforation was the standard. The most well-known rotary machine is the **L perforator** (ch 39, fig. 3), named for its shape, and used almost exclusively on sheet stamps. An L perforator perforates in only one direction at a time. Sheets of stamps travel along a belt and through a row of perforating pins, perforating the stamps either vertically or horizontally. After the first perforations are applied, the belt changes direction and leads to another row of perforating pins which perforate the stamps in the other direction.

During the late 1970s and early 1980s, perforators of several types were made integral parts of printing presses at the BEP. It was thought beneficial to have all phases of stamp production connected to the printing press. Unfortunately this was not the case. Processing (perforating and slitting) was slower than printing, and the on-press (also called on-line) perforators sometimes broke down. When that happened, the entire press was shut down while repairs were made, resulting in major losses of time and efficiency.

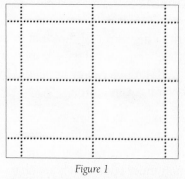

Figure 1

Bull's eye perforations meet perfectly at intersections.

One example comes from the production of the 1¢ Dorothea Dix (Scott 1844) of the Great Americans Issue. When it was released on September 23, 1983, the Dix stamp was touted as beginning a new era in printing. It was the first definitive prepared specifically for the BEP's **A press**, which featured continuous **sleeve** impressions, with no **gutters** between panes. The A press featured an online perforator. This perforator produced **bullseye** perforations that met perfectly at intersections (fig. 1). The A press printed, perforated and cut sheets into panes in an integrated process. This left naturally occurring straight edges on sheet stamps for the first time in nearly 60 years. However, as a result of problems encountered producing the Dix and other stamps, online perforating was abandoned after a relatively short period of time. In December 1983, press break-downs of the A press forced the BEP to move processing functions for the Dix stamp (and others) to the L perforator. Stamps produced on the L perforator have ragged, or overlapping, perforation intersections.

About a decade later, L perforators again came to the rescue of stamp printers. In the early 1990s, when the United States Banknote Co. (USBC) first began producing stamps under contract with the United States Postal Service (USPS), they planned to use an on-line *comb perforator*, producing perfectly aligned perforations. However, when the 29¢ Tulip sheet stamp was released on April 5, 1991, only stamps perf. 11 on the L-perforator were found (2524). When the comb perforator broke down early in the Tulip stamp press run, the majority of the stamps were printed, and then taken off-line to an L perforator. Later, the comb type (perf. 13 x 12¾) appeared (2524A).

Skiving

The other major paper-removal method of U.S. stamp separation is known as *skiving*. This method, based on leather processing technology, where thin layers of skin are removed from the hide, is actually a grinding rather than cutting or punching action. It was developed during the mid 1990s by Stamp Venturers (Sennett Enterprises) at its Unique Binders plant, a secured and refurbished Simmons mattress factory in Fredericksburg, Virginia. The units were known as APS grinding perforators, although there was nothing about their action that perforated. Unlike standard perforators, APS grinders leave no chad, only dust.

To accomplish this grinding, or skiving, a plastic perforation die, with the appropriate pattern for the stamp, pushes the printed stamp paper from the front, while sharp steel rotary blades resembling large pencil sharpener blades scrape the paper from the back. This action produces the appearance of perforation holes. The so-called perforation pins never puncture the paper. This is a highly precision action where the distance between the blades and the die is 4.5 thousandths of an inch.

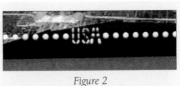

The nature of this process allows "perforations" to be produced in any desired shape. For example, star-shaped perforations were created on the 1995 Marilyn Monroe (2967) and 1996 James Dean (3082) issues, and

Figure 2

Detail from $3 Mars Lander Priority Mail stamp showing "perforations" created by skiving.

"USA" syncopated perforations were created on the 1997 $3 Mars Lander Priority Mail stamp (3178, fig. 2). This same skiving process was used to cut the Hitchcock profile into the 1998 Alfred Hitchcock commemorative (3226).

An unusual effect may be noted with this type of separation. As the **web** travels through the APS grinder occasionally there is slight web chatter or misalignment resulting in doubled perforation holes known as the "snowman effect." Depending on the degree of misalignment, the holes may show light doubling or complete duplication. This effect has been noted on sheet, booklet and coil stamps.

Stamp Separation without Paper Removal

The non-paper-removal methods of stamp separation, such as **rouletting** and **die-cutting** are less complex than stamp separation by removal of paper.

Rouletting

With this method of stamp separation dash-like cuts are made in the paper at regular intervals, but no paper is removed. This allows stamps to be separated easily without tearing or cutting. The most common form of rouletting, such as was done on the 1991 29¢ Tulip coil (2525, fig. 3), is a series of slits applied by a toothed wheel.

Figure 3
Detail from the 1991 29¢ Tulip coil showing rouletting.

Die Cutting

This is the most common method of separation found on self-adhesive stamps, which comprise the overwhelming majority of stamps produced since the mid-1990s. Die cutting may be accomplished in several ways, but all involve a sharp blade die making a precision cut through the stamp paper without cutting the backing paper (fig. 4). Die cutting can simulate almost any pattern or form of perforation, ranging from straight cuts to serpentine or serrated patterns. Most modern die cutting does not require the

Figure 4
Detail from a pane of die cut self-adhesive stamps, from which several stamps have been removed.

removal of any paper; however, some types, (used mostly for coils) require the removal of stamp paper surrounding each stamp, called waste material **matrix**.

Notes on Collecting

Since 1980 many face same stamps have been produced by a variety of printers. A chief differentiating characteristic of these stamps is the pattern of the die cuts. The companies use a variety of patterns (ch.38). Even within a single pane, one can find differences of die cut patterns from stamp to stamp.

Collectors interested in stamp separation since 1980 should consider acquiring and mounting these varieties on a black background which will show the various patterns of separation. With L-perforations and bullseye perforations the collector may chose a mint or used block because the identifying features are best observed at the intersections of the perforations.

Not since the Washington-Franklin issues (ch. 9) has stamp separation been the distinguishing factor of so many face-same stamps. The many varieties of stamp separation on contemporary face-same stamps create the possibility of forming a highly specialized collection at modest expense.

An interesting result of the use of L perforators is varying stamp size. Since the spaces between perforating wheels were set manually, workers did not always set them equidistant. As a result, it is possible to have stamps of differing sizes on the same pane. In a few cases these differences were so significant that they created jumbo or mini stamps. Jumbo stamps command a premium.

Almanac

1990 – The 25¢ Love stamps (2440 and 2441) issued January 18 are the first with true comb perforations and an unprecedented perf. gauge (12½ x 13).

1990 – The first self-adhesive "printed on plastic" die cut stamp (2475) is released May 18.

1995 – Star-shaped perforations first appear on June 1 on the Marilyn Monroe stamp (2967).

1997 – Priority Mail stamp (3178) issued December 10 has perforations that contain the letters "USA".

What Others Have Said

Nurse Dorothea Dix begins new era in stamp production
"With an eye toward the future...the Dix stamp was intentionally prepared for the "A" press, the combination gravure-intaglio press noted for its "floating" plate numbers and other marginal markings. As such, the Dix stamp becomes the

first monocolor U.S. definitive in recent years to go on a press other than the Cottrell. The "A" Press uses sleeve type printing cylinders that produce 46 intaglio rows of stamps per revolution. Panes with 10 rows (10 by 10) are then sliced apart through the perforation on a progressive basis. Markings – plate numbers, copyright notice and ZIP inscription – therefore float in the outer wide margin, and recur approximately every eight rows. Any marking can occur twice on any given pane."

—*Joe Brockert, "Dix definitive begins new era in printing," Linn's Stamp News, 1983.*

Many separation firsts on one stamp

"The 1990 Love sheet stamp will be remembered by collectors of United States stamps for a number of firsts. It is the first U.S. postage stamp produced by the United States Banknote Co.; it is the first true comb-perforated U.S. stamp; it is the first U.S. stamp to be perforated 12½ (horizontal) by 13; and it is the first U.S. stamp to be perforated in multiple sheets....After the Love stamp was released in January, the only item of interest to many collectors was the appearance of printing cylinder numbers in the selvage with the prefix letter "U"...only a handful of specialists measured the perforations to learn, surprisingly, that the stamps were perforated in a gauge different from all previous U.S. stamps."

—*Charles Yeager, "U.S. Banknote provides Love sheet stamp details," Linn's Stamp News, 1990.*

Sometimes new varieties happen by accident

"While the U.S. Postal Service has purposely produced different varieties and formats of some recent U.S. issues, two 1991 perforation varieties come about in a rather old-fashioned way: the equipment broke down and the manufacturer had to improvise. These varieties, although apparently not scarce, present some challenges for collectors, particularly in determining the earliest uses....When the first denominated Flower sheet stamps were released on April 5, 1991, they had the so called L-perfs, formed by an "L-Perforator" so named because of its shape. These perforations are quite easy to identify, particularly in multiples, because the perforations do not meet neatly at their intersections. The L Perforator runs in only one direction at a time, and the perforations it produces extend through the stamp selvedge. The perforations measure 11 x 11 and can also be identified with a standard perforation gauge. The L-perfs were the only ones known or anticipated on the Flower sheet stamps until....[stamps] 'perforated on 'Bull's eye' perforators' [were announced by the USPS which] measure approximately 12¾ x 13. Inquiries to the Postal Service and the contractor produced the information that the bull's eye perforations, although the second variety to be released, were actually applied first, and were the intended perforations...However, the Ormag bull's eye perforator broke down during the press run, when slightly fewer than half of the stamps had been printed."

—Wayne Youngblood, *"Perforation Varieties on 1991 United States Banknote Issues,"* The United States Specialist, *1992.*

Stamp Separation innovations abound in 1995

"Star-shaped, elliptical and simulated die-cut perforations are coming to the brave new world of United States stamps. The U.S. Postal Service announced March 10 that the 32¢ Marilyn Monroe commemorative to be issued June 1 will have perforations in the shape of small stars where the vertical and horizontal perforations intersect. In addition, the $3 Space Shuttle *Challenger* Priority Mail rate stamp and the $10.75 Space Shuttle Endeavor Express Mail rate stamp will have elliptical perforations along with the normal perforations of round holes....The perforation innovations are partly to please stamp collectors and partly for added security reasons, according to the Postal Service....The die-cut perforations are to please collectors, so that the stamps "look more like the traditional lick-and-stick stamps for serious collectors who prefer perforations over straight die cuts, said the press release....The star perforations are a marketing gimmick that the public should find amusing, and collectors probably will, too."

—Michael Schreiber, *"Monroe stamp will have star-perforations; elliptical and die-cut perfs on other stamps,"* Linn's Stamp News, *1995.*

Where to Find More Information

- The relevant volumes of *Linn's U.S. Stamp Yearbook*, edited by Fred Boughner or George Amick.

Chapter 41
Self-Adhesive Stamps

The majority of innovations in U.S. stamp production occurring during the twentieth century went largely unnoticed by the general public. The changeover from *flat plate* printing to the use of the *rotary press* was of no consequence and the introduction of phosphorescent *tagging* in 1963 was not a major news story. However, when postage stamps became available which customers were able to simply peel off a sheet of backing paper and stick on an envelope, the public noticed. In this respect, the introduction of self-adhesive postage stamps in the United States could be regarded as being the most important stamp production innovation of the past century.

The 1974 Dove Weather Vane Issue

The U.S. Postal Service (USPS) asked the Bureau of Engraving and Printing (BEP) to produce a stamp with pressure sensitive adhesive. The USPS issued a special Christmas stamp (*Scott* 1552) on November 15, 1974, in New York City. It featured the dove shaped weather vane atop Mount Vernon (fig. 1). The BEP did the production in-house on their Andreotti press, with additional equipment leased from two companies experienced with producing self-stick labels, Avery Label Systems and International Machine Products. They each finished part of the production on similar equipment that die-cut, stripped, rouletted, and cut the finished panes. A *precancel* feature was included to determine if it would speed the processing and delivery of holiday season mail. The stamp was produced with crossed center slits which were supposed to prevent the stamp from being removed from an envelope and reused on a second mailing.

Figure 1

The first self-adhesive, a 1974 Christmas stamp (1552).

As can be observed in figure 1, the stamps were issued on a piece of backing paper, also known as a liner, with 50 stamps on each pane. The stamps had rounded corners and were separated from each other by a blank section of the liner. The pane was **rouletted** both horizontally and vertically to facilitate the detaching of stamps and their portion of the liner from the pane. Each pane also had ten self adhesive tabs similar to the selvage paper found on regular stamp panes. These tabs contained the numbers of the plates used to print the stamps as well as various instructional remarks. Three of these were specifically for the self-adhesive stamps: "Self Sticking Stamps", "Remove From Backing", and "Do Not Moisten".

From the standpoint of both the USPS and stamp collectors, this first self-adhesive stamp was a failure. The USPS found that the stamps were too costly to produce and the cross cuts on the stamps did not prevent their reuse to the degree anticipated. For collectors the real problem came to light years later when they discovered that the rubber-based adhesive applied to the stamps had a tendency, over time, to cause the stamps to develop brownish spots. If the stamp was on cover, this adhesive could "migrate" from the stamp onto the cover and result in the staining of the cover itself. Because of these features of this adhesive, it is virtually impossible to find a pristine copy of this stamp today.

The 1989 Eagle and Shield Issue
In 1989, fifteen years after the failed Dove Weather Vane issue, the USPS again experimented with self-adhesive stamps, this time using an acrylic-based adhesive. On November 10, 1989, in Virginia Beach, Virginia, the 25¢ Eagle and Shield stamp (2431) was issued in an 18 stamp convertible booklet format as well as in strips of 18 with the stamps spaced for use in affixing machines (fig. 2). They were distributed in fifteen cities, for a thirty day test period. They were also sold through the Philatelic Sales Agency. Those who purchased the stamps were given a questionnaire containing nine questions asking how well they liked the new self-adhesive stamps and if they would purchase more in the future, if they were available. Although the stamps within each booklet had a face

Figure 2
Convertible booklet (2431) issued in 1989.

value of $4.50, a 50¢ premium was added to the price of each booklet to cover the increased cost of producing the self-adhesives. Again, the experiment was deemed to be a failure. However, this was probably due to the added fifty-cent premium rather than a lack of acceptance by the public.

Although the first day of issue ceremony for the Eagle and Shield self-adhesive was held in Virginia Beach, Virginia, this was not one of the fifteen test cities. Instead, this site for the stamp's release was chosen so that the annual VAPEX stamp show held in Virginia Beach would have a major philatelic event that year to attract collectors.

Figure 3

ATM pane (2522) printed on plastic.

The ATM Stamps

The following year, in 1990, the USPS partnered with Seafirst Bank for a new self-adhesive stamp experiment. This time, the stamps were printed on plastic instead of paper, and were sold via selected ATM machines. Each pane of the 25¢ Flag design stamp (2475) contained twelve stamps and was the exact size, shape, and thickness of U.S. paper currency. Unlike the 25¢ Eagle and Shield booklet the year before, there was no premium added and this 1990 pane sold for its face value of $4.50. The test period lasted six months during which the stamps were distributed through twenty-two ATM machines in the Seattle, Washington area. With a new first class domestic letter rate scheduled to go into effect on February 3, 1991, a non-denominated F-stamp version (2522 fig. 3) was issued on January 22, 1991 in the same plastic stamp ATM format.

Figure 4

ATM pane (2531A) printed on paper.

The Seattle experiment was deemed a success and gradually the ATM self-adhesive stamp distribution program was expanded. However, the next ATM self-adhesive stamp, the Liberty Torch stamp (2531A, fig. 4) was printed on paper rather than plastic due to complaints received from paper recyclers.

Nationwide Distribution

The beginning of the USPS's total commitment to self-adhesive postage stamps was marked in 1992. The 29¢ Eagle and Shield stamps (2595, 2596, and 2597) were the first nationally distributed self-adhesive stamps since the ill-fated 1974 Dove Weather Vane issue.

Since 1992, every type of U.S. stamp has been issued as a self-adhesive. In 1996, the first self-adhesive commemorative appeared, the 32¢ Tennessee Statehood (3070),

Figure 5
20¢ Blue Jay coil (3053).

along with the first post card rate stamps, the 20¢ Blue Jay, in both booklet and coil (fig. 5) format (3048 and 3053). The first U.S. *semi-postal* stamp was issued in 1998 as a self adhesive, the Breast Cancer Awareness stamp (B1). In 1999, the Sonoran Desert issue (3293) was the first self-adhesive *se-tenant* incorporating different designs into one overall larger illustrative scene.

Related Developments

As the public grew more enthusiastic about self-adhesives, or peel-n-stick, stamps, the USPS looked for new and more efficient ways to provide the product. One result was the development in 1997 of linerless coils, which have no backing paper and come in a Scotch tape type dispenser. Another innovation was the mounting of self-adhesives on both the front and back of the liner (backing paper).

"Perforations"

The advent of self-adhesive stamps required a new method to separate stamps from one another that left the backing paper (liner) intact (ch. 40). The result was the introduction of serpentine *die cuts*. These cuts are produced by a machine with a cutting die that cuts through both the stamp itself and the underlying adhesive layer, but not through the backing paper (liner). These die cuts are made in a serpentine pattern that resemble traditional perforations.

These "perforations" are described and measured in terms of "peaks" and "valleys". The "peak" is the part of the die cut that protrudes from the side of the stamp while the "valley" refers to the curved inward section next to each "peak". Just as traditionally perforated stamps are measured by the number of perforations found within a certain distance, die cut stamps are measured and described in the same manner.

Collectible Backing Paper

An increasing number of self-adhesive stamp issues have a brief description printed on the reverse side of the backing paper (liner). Figure 6 shows the brief biographical information added to the backing paper of the 2004 Henry Mancini commemorative (3839).

> Henry Mancini (1924-1994) was one of the most successful composers in the history of television and film and also a popular pianist and conductor. He won 20 Grammys and 4 Oscars; his albums have sold more than 30 million copies.

Figure 6

Some backing paper has a description printed on it, such as this backing paper from the 2004 Henry Mancini commemorative.

Notes on Collecting

Production anomalies have resulted in self-adhesive stamps that have other than the normal number of peaks. Such varieties are of great interest to those who study methods of stamp separation and can be worth significant premiums.

Some collectors retain examples of backing paper with printed descriptions. They may be placed in mounts, just as stamps are.

Anyone collecting post-1989 U.S. stamps should be familiar with some basic collecting techniques which are unique to self adhesive stamps:

Unused Self-Adhesive Stamps

The most popular way to collect unused self-adhesive stamps is to leave them attached to their backing paper (liner). If collecting full panes of these stamps, all that remains is to place the panes in protective mounts when adding them to your album.

If saving only a single stamp, or block of stamps, there are two approaches, depending on the specific issue. The easiest method is to use the unwanted stamps surrounding the desired stamp or block for postage, and then closely cut away the remaining backing paper around the stamp(s) to be saved. This will leave a thin border of backing paper around the stamp(s), which can then be placed in a protective mount. A second method may be utilized if the backing paper has been rouletted. This feature allows the collector to carefully separate individual stamps in much the same way as with traditionally perforated stamps. To make this task easier, it is advisable to remove any unwanted surrounding stamps first. To facilitate the separation of such individual stamps, one should fold the pane back to back several times along each side of the stamp, one side at a time, and separate the targeted stamp from its neighbors. Do not fold the panes front to front during this process since it may cause the die cut "perforation peaks" to bend and crease and result in an overall sloppy appearance.

Chapter 41 | Self-Adhesive Stamps

Self-adhesive coil stamps with backing paper (liners) will be found in two formats. The first has stamps adjacent to each other, with none of the liner showing between them. The second has the stamps separated from one another with a section of blank liner paper between them. The latter format allows the collector to easily cut off a strip of as many stamps as desired. The former requires that one remove one stamp at each end of the desired strip to expose the liner where the cut is to be made. The two removed stamps can then be used for postage.

The linerless coil stamps, as the name implies, have no backing paper and, therefore, the adhesive itself is exposed. The USPS has produced a specially treated backing strip on which collectors can mount these stamps. The mounted coils can then be inserted into protective mounts.

Although these are the safest ways to save unused self-adhesive stamps, they should be checked periodically for a condition known as "cold flow". This physical phenomena may, over time, cause some adhesive to "seep" out around the edges of the stamp. If this occurs, the stamps should be carefully removed from its mount and placed in a new one.

Caution should be exercised in collecting the ATM vended stamps printed on plastic during 1990 and 1991 (2475 and 2522). These stamps, because of their plastic composition, should be stored so that they do not come into contact with paper stamps.

Used Self-Adhesive Stamps
Used examples of self-adhesive stamps are best removed from the envelope or other material to which they are attached as soon as possible, unless there is a compelling postal history reason not to do so. This is due to the bond becoming stronger the longer the adhesive is in contact with the paper.

To separate a stamp from its envelope, cut off a section of envelope containing the stamp. Then soak the stamp and attached paper in hot water for thirty to forty-five minutes. Because a "primer layer" has been inserted between the stamp paper and the adhesive layer on all post-1989 self adhesives, the stamp *should* float free within this timeframe. If the stamp does not free itself from the attached paper, one may, using extreme caution, soak the item in either lighter fluid or turpentine. This will usually separate the most securely attached stamps from the paper. If, however, even this does not work, one will have to be content with trimming away as much of the envelope paper as possible and saving the used stamp "on piece".

A special word of caution is necessary regarding the original U.S. self-adhesive stamp, the Dove Weather Vane issue of 1974. Never attempt to soak this stamp under any circumstances! As noted in *Scott*, the stamp will separate into layers if soaked. This same "Do Not Soak" warning holds true for the U.S. hologram stamps issued during World Stamp Expo 2000 (3411–3413). Soaking these stamps in water will cause the holographic image to separate. The only safe method of preservation is to trim away the envelope from around the stamp and save it "on piece".

Almanac

1974 – The first U.S. self-adhesive postage stamp, the 10¢ Dove Weather Vane (1552), is issued November 15.

1989 – The 25¢ Eagle Shield stamp (2431) is issued November 10 for testing in fifteen cities.

1990 – The 25¢ Flag self adhesive stamp printed on plastic is issued (2475) May 18.

1991 – The 29¢ Liberty Torch stamp (2531A) is issued June 25 in the same ATM compatible format as the 25¢ Flag stamp but is printed on paper instead of plastic.

1992 – The Eagle and Shield stamp (2595) is issued September 25 for nation-wide distribution.

1993 – The first self-adhesive coil stamp with a plate number, the 29¢ Contemporary Christmas issue consisting of four designs (2799-2802), is issued October 28.

1996 – The five stamp Riverboat issue (3091-3095) is released August 22 in panes of 20 stamps. The serpentine die cuts on these panes go through the backing paper so that individual stamps can be separated easily.

What Others Have Said

An Accurate Prediction
"This issue is a fairly new 'ball game' to most collectors....Our feeling is that this kind of stamp will 'go', whether we as collectors like it or not..."

—*George W. Brett, "Two Varieties of the Pressure-Sensitive (Self-Adhesive) Christmas Stamp Issued December 15, 1974,"* The United States Specialist, *1975, from a detailed article about the Dove Weather Vane self adhesive, by the late "Dean of U.S. Stamp Production".*

The beginning of the self-adhesive revolution – 15 years after the first one failed

"The second United States self-adhesive postage stamp was released Nov. 10 at the Vapex stamp exhibition in Virginia Beach, Va...the new stamp is being test marketed in 15 cities for a period of 30 days between Nov. 11 and Dec 11. The U.S. Postal Service had dubbed the new 25¢ stamps, which feature an eagle and shield design, "EXTRAordinary" and has trademarked the name. The 25¢ Eagle and Shield self-adhesives come in panes of 18 stamps ($4.50 face value) and sell for $5 per pane. Coil strips of 18 are also being offered through the Philatelic Sales Division at the same price....the new stamps don't need to be torn or licked and they won't stick to each other in high humidity situations. USPS officials believe that these conveniences warrant the almost 3¢ per stamp cost over face value."

—*Wayne L. Youngblood, "United States 25¢ self-adhesive stamp being test-marketed in 15 cities for 30 days," Linn's Stamp News, 1989.*

Self-adhesives that stick to the heart

"Two United States self-adhesive postage stamps with edges that are die-cut to match the shape of the stamp design will debut on Jan. 28... The two stamps are the first issues from the United States Postal Service to feature irregular cut-to-shape edges... The new Love stamps represent an interesting step forward for United States postage..."

—*Michael Baadke, "Two new Victorian Heart Love stamps are first cut-to-shape self-adhesives," Linn's Stamp News, 1999.*

Self Adhesive Stamp Technology Prevents Potential Embarrassment

"The Postal Service first unveiled the 12-stamp [Chinese Lunar] Happy New Year design Dec. 29, 2003. At the time, it was planned as a single sided souvenir sheet of 12 different 37c stamps, which would have sold for $4.44. The unluckiest number in the Chinese culture is the number "4". To avoid ... the "death number", the Postal Service decided to issue the pane with 24 stamps instead of 12. The good news is that the total adds up to $8.88 and the number "8" is the luckiest number in the Chinese culture. Consultants [said] in the Chinese culture paying $4.44 for a pane of stamps would have been a real faux pas for the Postal Service."

—*Charles Snee, "12 Happy New Year designs return Jan 3 on pane of 24," Linn's Stamp News, 2005.*

Where to Find More Information

- *Pressure Sensitive Adhesive United States Stamps*, by Ken Lawrence is a comprehensive report about the history, production, and collecting of U.S. self adhesive stamps.

- *Catalog of United States Self-Adhesive Stamps* by Alan M. Malakoff provides lists of plate numbers and other detailed information, along with prices, for self-adhesive stamps.

- The relevant volumes of *Linn's U.S. Stamp Yearbook*, edited by Fred Boughner or George Amick.

Chapter 42
Watermarks

A watermark is a pattern embedded in paper during the production process, created by an intentional thinning of the paper. The presence of a watermark in the paper of a stamp creates a major variety of otherwise identical looking stamps. Contrary to its name; however, watermarks have little if anything to do with water. Stamps that appear otherwise identical receive different catalogue numbers based on the presence or absence of a watermark. Watermarked paper was used to print U.S. postage stamps for about 21 years, from 1895 until early 1917. As late as the 1950s, however, some stamps appeared, in error, on watermarked paper.

Watermarks appeared on some *revenue* stamps for a longer period of time – from the late 1870s until as late as the 1950s. *Postal cards* used watermarks briefly in their early years, while *stamped envelopes* used them continuously from their introduction in 1853 until late in the twentieth century.

The Bureau of Engraving and Printing (BEP) did not apply the watermark to paper, but purchased paper previously watermarked by the manufacturer. Paper used to print postage stamps was watermarked with one of two repeating patterns, each pattern a variation on the letters "USPS", which is presumed to stand for "United States Postage Stamp". Watermarked revenue stamps have a "USIR" design, while at least fifty different watermark designs were used on stamped envelopes! Early postal cards are known with two variations of the watermark "USPOD."

Watermarks are produced with the use of a device called a "dandy" roll. Pieces of metal forming the pattern of the desired watermark are attached to the dandy roll at the prescribed intervals. The dandy roll is then rolled over the still moist paper, impressing the mark.

When the BEP began producing postage stamps in 1894 it initially used a supply of unwatermarked paper that remained from the former postage stamp printer, the **American Bank Note Company**. These unwatermarked BEP produced stamps are *Scott* 246–263. However, since paper used to print stamps was viewed as "security paper," which required control and accountability, it was decided to use watermarked paper in the future. Since paper watermarked USIR (United States Internal Revenue) was already in use for revenue stamps, it must have seemed logical to use the letters USPS in a similar design as the watermark

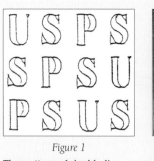

Figure 1

The pattern of double-line watermark.

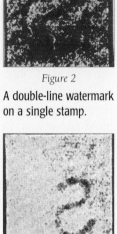

Figure 2

A double-line watermark on a single stamp.

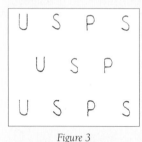

Figure 3

The pattern of single-line watermark.

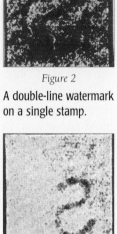

Figure 4

A single-line watermark, unusually-well centered on a single stamp.

for postage stamp paper. This first watermarked paper for postage stamps used a repeating pattern of "USPS" in double line Roman capital letters (fig. 1). One hundred letters appear on each pane of stamps. The actual size of each letter is ½ inch wide by ¹¹/₁₆ inch high. Stamps with these double line watermarks are generally readily identifiable. Each stamp exhibits either a single letter, reasonably well centered and fairly complete, or else portions of two, three, or even four different letters (fig. 2).

Watermarks are actually a thin spot on the paper. This thinning, some have concluded, offered an explanation for one of the major production problems the BEP had at the turn of the century. Before stamps could be printed, the paper had to be moistened. As the paper dried following printing it had a tendency to shrink unevenly, which made the subsequent accurate perforation of sheets more difficult. It was believed that watermarks (actually thins) contributed to the uneven shrinking of the paper, and so as early as 1898 suggestions were made to reduce the size of the watermarks in hopes of lessening or eliminating the problem of uneven paper shrinkage.

In 1910 the BEP changed from a double-line watermark to a single-line watermark (fig. 3), the letters of which were smaller in size than those used previously. Single-line letters are only ⁵/₁₆ inch high, and there were fewer of them on each sheet. These letters have no serifs. While this change in letter size may have helped with the problem of uneven paper shrinkage, it sometimes created severe difficulties in detecting watermarks. While one may encounter a stamp with a complete single-line letter watermark (fig. 4), it is more likely to encounter stamps with just portions of each of two or three letters.

Notes on Collecting

While some watermarks are easily viewed by simply holding stamps up to a light, most of the time the collector will have to use a watermark detector. This consists of a small black tray and a bottle of watermark fluid. The collector places the stamp, face down, in the black tray containing watermark fluid. If there is a watermark present, it will show up as dark outline in the fluid. The fast drying, quick penetrating fluid enables the watermark to become visible as the light penetrates the wet paper and is reflected back from the black surface. The fluid evaporates rapidly, and so inspection for signs of the watermark must be immediately and carefully made.

Many experts use lighter fluid to check for watermarks on their stamps. It is more readily available, and evaporates more slowly than watermark fluid. This allows maximum viewing time for finding difficult-to-see watermarks. Use of watermark or lighter fluid does not damage a stamp's gum.

On occasion, however, use of fluid may not be conclusive for watermark identification. Difficulty may arise, for example, if a cancellation covers a suspected watermark, or if the stamp is printed in light color ink such as yellow or orange. Collectors should view these brightly colored stamps through a colored filter, so that the stamp color is neutralized, and hence the glare is reduced, allowing for the watermark to be seen through the filter.

Sometimes the difference in value is significant between watermarked and unwatermarked stamps that are otherwise identical. If a watermark's presence or absence is not certain, provision should be made to have the stamp submitted for *expertization*.

When a stamp is viewed from the front, a watermark typically reads from left to right. When viewed from the back, the most typical way collectors examine stamps for watermarks, it will typically read backward. But if a sheet of paper is incorrectly placed on a press, the watermark will not have its intended appearance. To help the printer avoid the error of incorrect sheet placement, a small triangular piece was cut from the lower right-hand corner of each sheet. This aided the printer in properly orienting the sheet of paper on the press.

The change from double-line watermarks to single-line watermarks did not solve the problem of uneven paper shrinkage. Eventually the use of watermarked paper was discontinued.

Some $1 Wilson stamps in the Prexie Series (832b) were inadvertently printed on USIR watermarked paper.

Almanac

1853 – Stamped envelopes appear with watermarks.

1873 – Postal cards appear with watermarks.

1878 – The BEP begins printing revenue stamps on paper watermarked "USIR".

1895 – Double line "USPS" watermarked paper is first used for postage stamps.

1910 – The first stamps appear with a single line "USPS" watermark.

1917 – Use of watermarked paper for printing postage stamps is discontinued.

1958 – The last of the "USIR" watermarked *documentary* revenue stamps appear.

What Others Have Said

The change from double to single-line watermarks
"In April the Director of the Bureau of Engraving and Printing stated that a reduction of the size of the letters composing the watermark on our stamps would increase the strength of the paper and give it a more uniform thickness. He submitted a new design for the watermark, in which the letters, reduced in size, were to be placed that a portion of the watermark would appear on each stamp."

—*PMG Frank H. Hitchcock*, Annual Report of the Postmaster General, *1910*.

Watermarks make the difference in otherwise identical appearing stamps
"A watermark, initially called a 'wiremark' or 'papermark,' is an unpigmented distinguishing mark or pattern created in paper during or after its formation. It may be a numeral, a figure, a letter, a symbol, a geometric shape or any combination of these, and it may appear lighter or darker than the surrounding paper when held to a light source…The watermark design is an integral part of the sheet of paper and cannot be removed without destroying the paper itself. Watermarks, or their absence, aid on the classification of postage stamps from many countries. For example, the first U.S. Bureau series, the 1894 and 1895 issues are identical in design, color and perforation size. But the unwatermarked 1894 issue catalogues at a premium over the watermarked 1895 series."

—*Louis Repeta, "Watermarks in Postage Stamp Paper,"* American Philatelist, *1987*.

What does USPS stand for? 'Pat' Herst (as well as so many others) says…
"Revenue stamps…had been printed on paper watermarked 'U.S.I.R.' (United States Internal Revenue) for fifteen years. It was decided to institute a similar procedure for postage stamps and paper with large outline letters 'U.S.P.S.' (United States Postal Service) was ordered for stamp use….the first stamps on watermarked paper appeared on April 25, 1895…Thereafter, as each new issue

of postage stamps went to press, the new watermarked paper was used. It was not until 1917 that the use of watermarked paper was discontinued, although for some years thereafter examples of newer stamps printed on old stocks of watermarked kept appearing."

—Herman "Pat" Herst, Jr., "Postal Forgeries of 1895" The United States Specialist, 1978.

....But it's pretty certain that J. Murray Bartels is correct when he says....
"In his 'Washington Letter' of August 15, 1896, which appeared in Mekeel's for August 27th, he [prominent stamp dealer and scholar J. Murray Bartels] wrote: 'On a recent visit to the Bureau of Engraving and Printing I found out a few facts regarding the paper of our current issue....When the contract with the American Bank Note Co. ceased, they turned over the residue of the paper which they had been used for printing stamps, but refused to make the name of the manufacturer known to the officials. This small supply being soon used up other paper was resorted to, until the old source of supply became known sometime afterwards to the government. Immediately a contract was made and ever since this paper company has been supplying the Bureau for the manufacture of stamps. As the law requires government securities to be printed on a special kind of paper, and postage stamps came under this heading, it was decided to use in the future only watermarked paper, since which time only such has been supplied to the government. The watermarked letters U.S.P.S. stand for 'United States Postage Stamp' and not U.S. Postal Service as is generally supposed."

—Winthrop Boggs, 'U.S.P.S.' Notes on United States Watermarked Postage Stamps, 1958.

Where to Find More Information

- "Detecting Watermarks" by Larry S. Weiss is an excellent guide to the art of watermark detection.

- "U.S.P.S." Notes on United States Watermarked Postage Stamps by Winthrop Boggs is an essential pamphlet.

- U.S.P.S. Watermarks by H.A. Froom is a very useful pamphlet that includes four full size, quarter-pane illustrations for checking doubtful watermarks, and describes in detail how to overcome veiled watermarks on certain light colored stamps.

- The Stamp Collector's Guidebook of Worldwide Watermarks and Perforations from 1840 to Date by Ervin J. Felix covers watermarks worldwide, including useful information on USPS watermarks, paper, watermark detectors, and other collecting accessories.

Chapter 43
Plate Construction and Layout

A printing **plate** is the part of a printing press from which stamps are actually printed. The earliest plates were all flat. In the early twentieth century curved plates were introduced, for use on a **rotary press**. Late in the twentieth century cylindrical plates, often called **sleeves**, came into use. But regardless of a plate's shape - flat, curved or cylindrical - all plates have a layout, that is, a schematic arrangement of the subjects (stamps) and any other markings on the plate. There are two aspects of plates treated in this chapter: their production and their layouts.

Plate Production

The printing plates most commonly used to print stamps have historically been **intaglio** plates, that is, plates that print from recessed lines on a metal plate. These line-engraved intaglio plates dominated stamp production from the 1840s until late in the twentieth century.

Once a stamp's design was approved, a highly talented craftsman engraved the design, in reverse (mirror image), in actual size, on a small plate of soft metal. The final product is called a **die**.

Occasionally, one or more sample copies of the image were pulled (printed) from the die. This is known as a **die proof**. Some proofs were pulled to review the engraver's progress. Others, called **trial color proofs**, were pulled to try different color inks. When the engraver was finished producing the die, the managers of the printing process reviewed final die proofs and, if satisfied, they approved the die. Then the die was subjected to a hardening process.

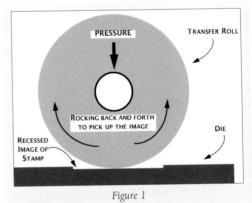

Figure 1

An engraved stamp's image is picked up by the transfer roll from the die. The transfer roll is then used to put images of the die onto the printing plate.

Once the die was certified for use and **hardened**, it was given to the **siderographer**, a craftsman who operated a device called a **transfer press**. The siderographer placed the die in the transfer press and rolled a soft metal cylinder back and forth over it (fig. 1). This transferred the stamp's image onto the cylinder, called a **transfer roll**. Once this process was completed, the roll was hardened. A roll was typically the width of the stamp and about three inches in diameter.

While the process of creating a die produced an engraved mirror image of the stamp, the transfer roll contained a true image of the stamp, called a **relief**. Often the siderographer would produce several reliefs on a transfer roll. If accomplished correctly, there are no visible differences between the different reliefs. However, if not accomplished correctly, reliefs can be created that are slightly different from each other, impacting any plate on which they are subsequently used!

In 1917, the Bureau experimented with wider transfer rolls containing ten reliefs. Rolls containing two subjects across and five around the circumference were made for the 2¢ and 3¢ Washingtons. The 2¢ roll was used to produce two plates, and yielded a scarce design variation known as Type Ia in *Scott*. The experiment was not repeated.

Once the transfer roll was hardened, the siderographer was ready to create the plate(s). The roll, with its reliefs, was locked into position and the plate on its sliding bed was raised to come in contact with it (fig. 2). This process was repeated for each subject on the plate. The subjects on the plate appear in reverse (mirror-image), just as they do on the die. Since each subject is entered on a plate individually, subjects sometimes differ from one other in minor ways. This was a common occurrence on nineteenth century stamps – and sometimes the basis for assigning different catalogue numbers to stamps printed from the same plate!

Figure 2

Siderographer Andrew Black using a transfer press to make a printing plate at the BEP.

The first plate created for the 10¢ Washington stamp in the issue of 1851 illustrates how subjects on a plate will differ when they are laid down on the plate by different reliefs. When the siderographer made his transfer roll (or rolls), he did not pick up all the details from the die on each of the reliefs. The three reliefs used to make the 10¢ Washington plate, arbitrarily called "A", "B", and "C" each lack small but different parts of the design (fig. 3). The result is stamps identified by *Scott* as Types I, II, and III, with Type IV arising from a subsequent **recutting**.

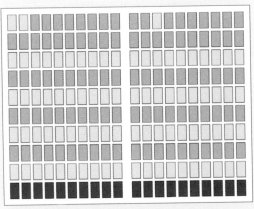

Figure 3

The plate created for the10¢ imperforate stamp in the Series of 1851 was made with three slightly different reliefs. As a result, it printed stamps that are also slightly different. This schematic diagram indicates the distribution of the subjects laid down by the three different reliefs. This plate layout is typical of the nineteenth century. It yielded a sheet of 200 stamps that was cut into two post office panes of 100.

In addition to placing the stamp images on the plate, the siderographer also placed on the plate any desired **marginal markings** (ch. 45). They helped workers in their tasks of accounting, and quality control, and the printing, cutting and perforating of stamps. Marginal markings also served to provide information to both the postal workers and public.

Once the plate was finished, the siderographer printed a **plate proof** to check the results. Once the printing managers approved the plate proof, the plate was hardened and was then ready to actually print stamps (fig. 4).

Figure 4

A detail from a plate proof, signed by BEP Director Joseph E. Ralph, approving the plate.

These line-engraved intaglio plates dominated stamp production until the last third of the twentieth century. Since the 1970s stamps have frequently been printed from photogravure plates, also called **gravure**, and from **lithographic** plates, also commonly known as offset.

Photogravure plates, like line engraved ones, actually print from recesses in the plate. Production of a gravure plate begins when the design to be printed is photographed through a fine screen. This breaks the image up into many fine dots, which are etched onto a plate. A photogravure plate was first used to print the Thomas Eakins (1335) stamp in 1967.

Lithographic plates, also known as offset plates, are smooth, without any recesses. A greasy inked image is applied to a plate, which is then transferred (offset) to a rubber blanket, and finally onto the stamp.

Plate Layout

Over the years, plates have varied in size, in the number of subjects they contain, and in the way those subjects are arranged. Plates vary in the spacing between subjects, the presence or absence of **gutters** between rows of stamps, and the nature and location of various markings, such as **guide lines**. All of these variables influence a plate's layout.

In considering plate layouts it is important to keep in mind that a printed **sheet** of stamps is a mirror image of the plate. When a plate's layout is described here, it is actually a description of the printed sheet! Thus, for example, a reference to the upper left **pane** on a sheet containing four panes is actually a description of that pane's location on a printed sheet of stamps, a location that corresponds to the upper right pane on the printing plate.

The starting point in plate layout is, of course, the size of the stamp. Since the 1890s U.S. regular (definitive) issues tend to be of a more-or-less uniform size. Commemoratives also tend to be of a uniform, but larger, size. There are, of course, notable exceptions. The size of the press naturally limits the size of the plate, which in turn limits the number and arrangement of stamps on the plate.

The first postage stamps (*Scott* 1 and 2) in 1847 were printed from plates of 200 subjects, as were most stamps until late in the nineteenth century. These sheets were then cut in half along a **guide line** and distributed to post offices in panes of 100. While "sheet" and "pane" are sometimes treated as synonymous terms, this is not the case. A sheet is a complete impression from a plate. Almost all U.S. stamps have been printed on sheets that required cutting into smaller units, called panes, for distribution to post offices.

By the beginning of the twentieth century, plates of 400 subjects became standard for definitive stamps, each printed sheet yielding four post office panes of 100 stamps. This format dominated definitive stamp plate layouts until late in the twentieth century (fig. 5). On the earliest of these 400 subject plates, all 400 subjects were equi-distant from each other, with only a guide line indicating the

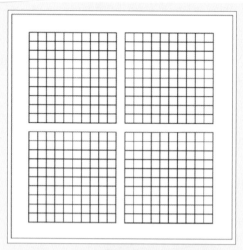

Figure 5

Most twentieth century definitive stamps were printed from plates of 400 subjects. Each such sheet of 400 stamps was divided into four post office panes of 100. This figure shows the spaces known as gutters, separating the four panes. This layout enabled perforations on all four sides of each stamp. Early plates, however, lacked these gutters and when the panes were cut apart, the result was stamps with straight-edges.

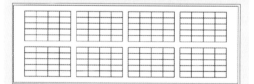

Figure 6

This plate layout of 160 commemorative sized subjects contains eight panes of twenty subjects each. Such plate layouts became common in the 1990s, replacing the traditional commemorative plate layout of 200 subjects divided into four panes of 50 subjects each.

division between panes. Such plates yield stamps with *straight edges*, because the guide line was cut, not perforated. Later, a space called a gutter was used to separate the four panes from each other. This made cutting sheets into panes easier, and produced stamps perforated on all four sides, that is, without straight edges.

Because commemorative stamps are generally larger than definitive stamps, commemorative plates generally contain fewer subjects, but otherwise their plates are very much analogous in layout to contemporaneous definitive plates. Through most of the twentieth century most commemoratives were printed from plates of 200 subjects, and divided into post office panes of fifty.

Plate size was limited by press size, but it could also be limited by the size of other equipment. For example, Brookman reports that studies of the 1857 series present evidence of a limitation in the width of paper that the perforation machines could handle. This in turn forced the plates to be laid out so that the subjects fit within the machine's width in the narrowest dimension.

The tradition of issuing definitive stamps in post office panes of 100 and commemoratives stamp in panes of 50 came to an end by the mid 1990s. Panes of twenty stamps then became the norm. These panes of 20 stamps were printed from plates that might contain 80, 100, 120, 160, 180, 200, 240, or 400 subjects (fig. 6). Perhaps in an effort to aid collectors, the Postal Service began printing a small marginal marking on the panes of many issues, indicating the plate layout employed. This marginal marking shows the number and arrangement of panes on the plate, and highlights the position on the sheet from which a given pane is cut (fig. 7).

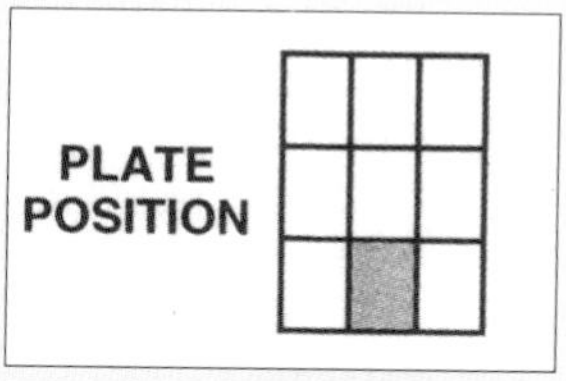

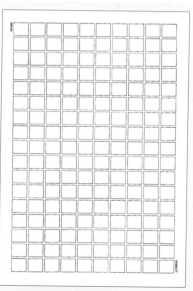

Figure 7

This marginal marking from a pane of the World War II Memorial issue, indicates the position of that pane on a plate of 9 panes (180 subjects.)

Plates of special sizes and layouts have been required for special purposes, such as souvenir sheets. In 1926, the Post Office Department issued its first "souvenir sheet" in honor of the international philatelic exhibition held in New York that year. The souvenir sheet, more accurately called a pane, consisted of a 25-subject pane of the 1926 Battle of White Planes commemorative (630). The souvenir sheet's margins carried a special message identifying the exhibition and its dates. The souvenir sheet required a special plate layout of 100 subjects arranged in four panes. To cite just two other examples, the souvenir sheets issued for the American Philatelic Society in 1933 were printed from plates of 225 subjects, each plate yielding nine panes (souvenir sheets) of 25 stamps, while the souvenir sheet issued for the Sixth International Philatelic Exposition in 1966 (1311) was printed from plates of 24 subjects.

The BEP introduced rotary press printing in 1914 to produce coil stamps. The earliest plates consisted of 150 or 170 subjects (fig. 8). The printing plates were laid out with subjects reaching to the two opposite edges of the plate so that the press produced a continuous web of stamps. Later, larger rotary presses accommodated larger plates for the printing of coil stamps.

Figure 8

Plates of 150 or 170 subjects were used to print coil stamps in the early days of the rotary press. Two such curved plates, mounted together, enabled coil stamps to be printed "by the mile."

By the beginning of the twenty-first century coil stamps were being printed from plates with an amazing diversity of layouts. For example, the New York Public Library coil produced by Sennett Security Products (3769) was printed from cylinders of 616 subjects (22 x 28) and the Sea Coast coil produced by Banknote Corp of America (3775) was printed from cylinders of 570 subjects (19 x 30).

In the early twentieth century, the BEP began producing stamps in a special booklet format for customer convenience. Booklets were pocket-sized, bound at one end with staples, and typically contained six stamps per page (pane). Each pane of a booklet had a *tab* along the top for the staples. The panes were perforated for stamp separation, but cut along the outer edges, giving each stamp in the pane at least one straight edge. To accommodate the assembling of panes into booklets, the plate layout incorporated gutters between every third row of stamps; this gutter provided the stapling tab for the booklet. The resulting plate yielded fewer stamps per plate. For example, if a stamp's normal plate layout contained 400 subjects, the booklet pane plate layout would contain 360 subjects. The additional stamps were sacrificed to make room for the stapling tab. These booklet plates, like plates for sheet stamps, contained marginal markings. After 1978 virtually every booklet had a different plate layout, and any generalization is difficult.

Notes on Collecting

Until the late 1950s, stamp paper had to be dampened before being printed. The paper had to dry before the stamps could be perforated, and the paper did not always shrink evenly. Occasionally the plate layout was modified to accommodate anticipated shrinkage. When laying out plates for one of the 2¢ Washington issues of the 1908 series, the BEP tried varying the spacing between columns of stamps to accommodate the shrinkage. Inner columns retained the usual separation of approximately 2 mm while the outer 8 columns had a wider spacing of approximately 3 mm. To distinguish these special plates, the BEP added a star adjacent to the plate numbers. When performing additional experiments with a different spacing in 1910, the BEP prefixed the plate number with the letter A. Stars were also used on some plates in the Series of 1922 to indicate wider spacing between subjects. Because they occurred less frequently, stars and A prefixes on plates are prized among plate number collectors.

Almanac

1847 – First postage stamps are printed from 200 subject plates.

1869 – First bicolor stamps (15¢ to 90¢ Pictorials) are printed from plates of 100. The single-color, lower value Pictorials are printed from plates of 300 subjects, separated into panes of 150.

1894 – Bureau takes over production of postage stamps, using plates of 200 and 400 subjects, for division into panes of 100.

1900 – Introduction of booklet panes, printed from flat plates of either 180 or 360 subjects.

1908 – Washington-Franklin stamps are issued, using standard plate layout of 400 subjects for sheet stamps.

1914 – Rotary press printing is introduced for coil stamps, using plates of 150 and 170 subjects.

1918 – Offset lithographic plates are introduced due to World War I ink shortages.

1920 – Rotary press printing is introduced for sheet stamps, using plates of 400 subjects.

1926 – Rotary press booklet panes are introduced and produced until 1978 from plates of 180, 320, 360, and 400 subjects.

1926 – First souvenir sheet is printed from plates of four panes of 25 subjects each.

1964 – Lithography is used for first modern stamp, Homemakers (1253).

1967 – First stamp is printed from photogravure plates, the Thomas Eakins (1335).

What Others Have Said

An organization for those who enjoy plate production and layout is founded
"Plate number collecting is a logical starting point for specialization of any issue, but it should lead to a systematic study of the entire issue. Paper, gum, marginal markings and guidelines, as well as methods of manufacture follow the plate number as a field of study and collection....It is the hope of the B.I.A. to develop these side lines under the direction of collectors specializing in these lines and to prepare where necessary detailed check lists of the various issues."

—*Hugh M. Southgate, "The P.P.N.A. Becomes the B.I.A.," 1930. From a special mimeographed letter dated March 29, 1930 from the President of the newly created Bureau Issues Association, now named The United States Stamp Society – the publisher of this Encyclopedia.*

Plating of stamps is fun says one of hobby's leading researchers
"Stamps are plated by studying the normal designs, noting and identifying variations from the normal on specimens that were intended to be identical, and finally by placing each of the specimens on a chart that is laid out to represent and correspond with the original plate, stone or electrotype from which the

stamps were printed. All this may sound rather difficult, but, in theory at least, plating much resembles the solution of a somewhat glorified jigsaw puzzle....The work – I should say fun – is interesting and apt to become extremely fascinating...."

—*Elliott Perry, "How Stamps are Plated," Scott's Monthly Stamp Journal, 1926.*

What a difference a dot makes – Susan B. Anthony Variety

"We are in receipt of an airmail letter from W.J. Stanton....calling attention to stamp #100 on the lower right pane of plate 21590. On the plate number stamp of this pane, there is no dot after the 'B'. Mr. Stanton has found this variety constant on 14 copies. We have checked this on our copy of this plate number position and also found the period to be missing. No other difference seems to be in evidence on a brief study of this position."

—*Max G. Johl, "Max Johl replies," Stamps Magazine, 1936. The discovery announcement of a now Scott listed plate variety.*

What happens when an engraved line may not be deep enough?

"...the one-cent value of the 1890 issue...sometimes showed a 'candle flame.'...the stamp was issued in various shades of blue. The white numerals lie against a field of blue within an ornamental oval and it here that the candle flame occurs, almost always originating at the bottom ball ornament on the right side of the figure '1.' The candle flames are not constant and come in all sorts of sizes and arrangement. Students of this stamp generally agree that candle flames are the result of 'scooped' color which resulted when the ink wiping process in printing removed all or too much ink from an area which should have been printed....It is conceivable that the engraved lines in the particular area were not deep enough to properly retain ink as portions of the plates wore...many variations of candle flames were created..."

—*Robert C. Ladd, "The Candle Flame Stamp," The United States Specialist, 1975.*

Where to Find More Information

- Max G. Johl's *United States Postage Stamps 1902-1935* contains a helpful and well-illustrated chapter on Plate Layouts.

- *Encyclopedia of Plate Varieties on U.S. Bureau Printed Stamps* by Loran C. French.

- The relevant volumes of *Linn's U.S. Stamp Yearbook*, edited by Fred Boughner or George Amick.

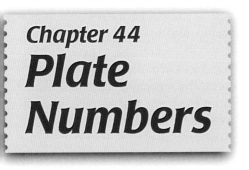
A plate number has traditionally been assigned to each printing plate. Placed one or more times on each plate, it has been used to track a plate's use and facilitate quality control. Plate numbers generally appear in the margins of sheets, often accompanied by other *marginal markings* (ch. 45). On occasion the plate number provides positive identification to a stamp without having to resort to perforation gauges, *watermark* fluids, or precise measurements of stamp images.

Until the Bureau of Engraving and Printing (BEP) began printing U.S. stamps in 1894, they were printed by several different private companies. Each followed its own internal rules for plate numbering.

First Printings The earliest U.S. postage stamps (*Scott* 1 and 2) were printed in 1847 by the New York City firm of *Rawdon, Wright, Hatch & Edson*. This firm did not use plate numbers. However, beginning with stamps printed in 1851 *Toppan, Carpenter, Casilear & Co.*, plates were typically numbered. The company apparently used number 1 on the first plate made for each different stamp, and successively higher numbers for each additional plate made for each denomination.

National Bank Note Company The *National Bank Note Company* of New York began printing U.S. stamps in 1861. Known as National, it began the practice of assigning plate numbers sequentially, as plates were made, at least within a particular series. The numbers 1, 2, and 3 were placed on plates made to print what are now considered *essays*. The next number, 4, was assigned to a plate used to print the 10¢ Washington. Numbers continued to be assigned, in sequence, as plates were produced. Figure 1 illustrates a plate number single from plate 34, used to print the 3¢ Washington (65). The highest plate number, 55, was also used to print the 3¢ Washington.

National also printed the 1869 pictorials (112–122). Numbers 1 and 2 were used on plates for the 1¢ Franklin stamp. Numbers 3, 4, 5, and 6 were used on plates for the 2¢ Post Horse and Rider stamp. Numbers 7 to12 were

Figure 1

A plate number single of the 3¢ Washington (65) from plate 34, produced in 1861 by the National Bank Note Company.

used on plates for the 3¢ Locomotive stamp. Numbers 13 and 14 were assigned to plates that printed the 6¢ Washington stamp, and so on, up to number 30, which was used for an additional plate for the 3¢ Locomotive. The 15¢, 24¢, 30¢, and 90¢ stamps in the 1869 series were bicolored. Each required two plates, one to print the *frame* and one to print the **vignette**. National assigned the same number both to a plate used to print the frame and to the correspon-ding plate that printed the vignette. For example, the two plates required to print the 90¢ Lincoln (122) were each assigned number 22.

National was awarded the contract for the series of stamps that began in 1870 (134–155). These are the first of what became known as the **Bank Note** issues. National again began to number plates beginning with 1. On this occasion number 1 was assigned to a plate used to print the 3¢ Washington, both **grilled** (136) and ungrilled (147). A total of 55 plate numbers were assigned to the plates used to print the eleven different denominations in this series, which ranged from the 1¢ Franklin to the 90¢ Perry.

Continental Bank Note Company The *Continental Bank Note Company* was awarded the printing contract for U.S. stamps from 1873 to 1879. Known as Continental, it began with number 1 on its first plate, and assigned sequentially higher numbers to plates as they were produced, regardless of denomination. Continental, however, did not make new plates for the 30¢ and 90¢ issues (165 and 166); it merely printed more stamps using the original National plates. Figure 2 shows a strip of Official stamps (O52) printed by Continental from plate 71.

Figure 2

A strip of the 12¢ Post Office Official Stamp of 1872, with plate number 71.

American Bank Note Company In 1879 the Continental Bank Note Company merged with American Bank Note, creating the new *American Bank Note Company*. American continued to use some existing Continental plates, but when creating new plates, it did not begin numbering them with 1. Rather it continued numbering plates where Continental had stopped, assigning new and ever higher numbers to the new plates.

Beginning with the 1883 2¢ red-brown Washington (210) American added a single or double letter prefix to plate numbers in groups of five. For example, the 2¢ Washington of 1883, printed from many plates, has an "A" associated with plate numbers 483 through 487, a "B" associated with plate numbers 490 through 494, and so on. Letters were added to sets of five plates because

American acquired
new presses that used
five plates at a time.
The letters allowed
printers to group the
set of five plates so
that they wore evenly.
American's practice of
associating a letter
with five plate num-
bers continued as long as American held the contract.

Figure 3

A Columbian Exposition plate number strip (230), printed by
American Bank Note, showing initials and plate number.

The final two series printed by American were the 1890
"*Small Bank Notes*" (219–229) and the 1893
Columbian Exposition Issue (230–245). American
broke the pattern of assigning ever-higher numbers to
plates, and again began numbering plates from 1, both
with the small Bank Notes, and again with the
Columbians (fig. 3).

Figure 4

A plate number single
from Plate 1, the first
plate for printing
postage stamps created
at the BEP.

In 1894, the BEP, a division of the U.S. Treasury
Department, began printing all U.S. postage stamps.
This began the era of "Bureau issues," and the BEP started the plate numbering scheme at 1 once again. Plate 1
(fig. 4) was used on one of the many plates used to print the 2¢ Washington in
the Series of 1894 (248, 249, and 250). The BEP assigned unique and sequentially higher numbers to each of the tens of thousands of printing plates it produced. These numbers appeared on printed sheets of stamps until 1980, when
the last traditional plate number, 41125, appeared on the $1 Candle Holder
(1610).

Occasionally a plate printed stamps that are sufficiently different to justify different *Scott* numbers, such as the previous example of the 2¢ Washington.
However, stamps printed from the same plate have different catalogue numbers
due to differences of color, perforation gauge, type of paper, or watermark – differences not related to the printing plate itself.

The BEP also placed plate numbers on plates used to print coil stamps and
booklet panes. Plate numbers do not appear on coils issued prior to 1980,
except those imperfectly cut (fig. 5). Plates created for use on the flat plate
press, to print booklet panes, most typically had a plate number located on the
plate so that it would appear on the tab of just one of the booklet panes printed

A 4¢ Lincoln coil stamp from the Liberty Series (1058), issued in 1958. The partial plate number 26150 is an EFO. It exists on the stamp only because the coil was miscut.

Figure 5

(fig. 6). However, since a sheet printed by a flat press plate could contain up to sixty booklet panes, with only one plate number per sheet, the vast majority of flat plate booklet panes contain no plate number at all.

When the BEP issued its first bi-colored postage stamps in 1901 (the Pan American issue), separate plates were required for the frames and the vignettes. This means that these stamps (294–299) are the first BEP postage stamps to show two different plate numbers on the same sheet.

A combination of historical and social factors early in the twentieth century, coupled with low postal rates, led to an increased demand for postage stamps. To meet this demand, the BEP produced many plates, especially of the commonly used 2¢ stamps. For example, the *Durland Catalog* reports that no less than 1,675 plates were made to print the 2¢ Washington "Shield" (319) in the Series of 1902 (ch. 8). These plates have a number between 1805 and 4776. However, not every plate made was used to print stamps. Additionally, some plates may have been used, but plate numbers from them are not known in collectors' hands, though they may be known on plate *proofs*.

Figure 6

A 2¢ Washington flat plate press booklet pane (554c) with a plate number. Only a single booklet pane, out of the 60 panes cut from a 360-subject sheet, shows a plate number.

While plate numbers appear at least once, they typically appear more than once on each plate. The vast majority of stamps produced by the BEP have a plate number appear at least once on each pane sold to a postal customer. Since most plates made until late in the twentieth century produced sheets of stamps that yielded four post office panes, each plate had to contain the plate number at least four times. The exact location of numbers on plates varied, but by the 1930s the location became standardized at the four corners of the plate. For more information on plates, their construction and layout, see chapter 43.

In 1970, the BEP began regular use of a separate five-digit plate number for each gravure plate. The gravure method requires one plate for each color needed to print the stamp. With so many multi-colored stamps being issued, panes of stamps had 4, 5, or 6 separate plate numbers, spread out over much of a pane's margin. While plate numbers had traditionally been saved on blocks of four or six stamps, depending on the plate layout, collectors now needed to collect blocks of 10, 12, or even 20 stamps to obtain a "plate block." This required a large investment on the part of collectors, and many stopped collecting them in protest over this practice. These large plate blocks of ten, twelve, or even twenty are sometimes referred to as "biggies" due to their large size (fig. 7).

Figure 7

A plate block of the Missouri Statehood stamp of 1971 (1426) with six plate numbers and twelve stamps.

After a decade of collector complaints, the Postal Service switched to "representative plate numbers." Beginning in 1981, a five-digit plate number was no longer printed for each color. Instead, a *representative plate number*, usually 1, was assigned to each actual plate used for each color. Thus, if six colors were used to print a particular stamp, and six plates were prepared, then a single plate number 111111 was printed. Each "1" was printed in a different color; for example, the first might be red, the next green and so on. Traditional plate numbers no longer appeared on stamps, although traditional numbers continued to be assigned for accounting and historical purposes. Since representative numbers could be printed next to a single stamp, "biggies" were no longer issued, and collectors were again able to collect the traditional four stamp plate block, though without the traditional plate number.

Beginning with the 1981 18¢ Flag and Anthem stamp (1891), a tiny representative plate number was included at regular intervals on the face of coil stamps. For the first time, the presence of a plate number actually altered the design of a stamp itself.

The BEP printed virtually all U.S. stamps issued from 1894 until late in the twentieth century. As printing contracts were awarded to private printers in the early 1980s, **prefix letters** were added to plate numbers in order to distinguish stamps printed by these private companies from those printed by the BEP. The list of private printing companies that have produced U.S. stamps continues to grow. (See sidebar.) It should be noted for the record that the "T" which appears on the BEP printed Flag Over Capitol test coil (2115b) is not a prefix. Neither is the "X", which is sometimes used to represent a plate number prefix on USPS images of projected stamps, an actual plate number prefix which has ever appeared on an issued stamp.

Figure 8

A few plates, like this American Kestrel (2476), use two-digit representative plate numbers.

Figure 9

A few plates, like this American Kestrel, plate number 5555B, have used letter suffixes instead of two-digit representative numbers.

Occasionally more than nine sets of plates were required to print a stamp, with the tenth plate for each color receiving number 10, the eleventh plate receiving number 11, etc. (fig. 8). At other times, particularly with coils, a letter suffix was used when a stamp required more than nine sets of plates. Then, 11111A would represent a tenth set of plates, 22222A would represent an eleventh set of plates, etc., until 99999A was used to represent an eighteenth set of plates. Then 11111B would be used to represent a nineteenth set of plates, and so on. The number 5555B, shown in Figure 9, represents the twenty-third series of plates made for that stamp. Suffix letters were first used on the 32c Flag Over Porch **die cut** coil (2915A).

Chapter 44 | Plate Numbers

By the late 1990s, the BEP was printing only huge quantities of coil stamps, with the private companies printing everything else. Finding that it could no longer compete in the changing stamp market, the BEP exited from stamp printing altogether in 2005.

Prefixes Used With Plate Numbers*

Prefix	Company Name	Dates
None	Bureau of Engraving and Printing	1894-2005
A	American Bank Note Company	Beginning 1980
B	Bank Note Corp. of America, Inc.	1994
D	Dittler Brothers Inc.	1993
G	Guilford Gravure, Inc.	Beginning 2000
K	KCS Industries	1991-1993
LT/LTB	Bank Note Corp. of America, Inc.	2000
M	National Label and Stamp Venturers for 3M	Beginning 1994
P	Ashton-Potter America	Beginning 1992
S	Stamp Venturers and Sennett Security Products	Beginning 1992
U	United States Bank Note Company	1990-1992
V	Avery Dennison Security Printing Division	Beginning 1993

*3M Company produced stamps in ATM booklet formats in 1990 and 1991, but there are no plate numbers on these issues, thus no need for any prefix.

Notes on Collecting

Plate numbers can be collected on selvage attached to a single stamp, or to a block. Generally, it is preferred not to remove a single stamp from a plate block in order to create a plate number single, as the plate block is more valuable when left intact. Such separation is acceptable when the value of a particular plate number and position, as valued in *Durland*, is less than five times the value of a single stamp as valued in *Scott*. Such a plate block carries no special premium and is easily replaced.

Plate number blocks, plate number strips, and plate number singles from the nineteenth and early twentieth centuries are often rare, as they were not commonly collected at the time. As a result, many are quite expensive.

Some plate block collectors attempt to acquire a complete matched set of plate blocks – one from each position of each plate used to print a particular stamp. For example, the 1960 Washington Credo commemorative (1139) was printed

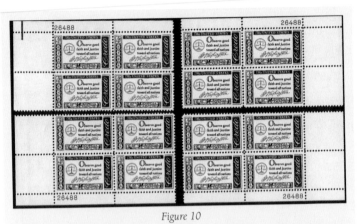

Figure 10

A matched set of plate blocks of the 4¢ Washington Credo (1139) from plate 26488. It contains blocks from the upper right (UR), lower right (LR), lower left (LL) and upper left (UL) corners of the plate.

#1139 4¢	WASHINGTON CREDO			
	UL	UR	LL	LR
26488	$.45 ☐	☐	☐	☐
26489	$1.00 ☐	☐	☐	☐
26494	$.45 ☐	☐	☐	☐
26495	$.45 ☐	☐	☐	☐
26508	$.45 ☐	☐	☐	☐

Figure 11

A representative listing from the Durland Catalog, for the 4¢ Washington Credo (1139).

from five plates: 26488, 26489, 26494, 26495, and 26508. Each plate produced four panes from which a plate block could be removed (fig. 10). Thus a complete matched set of this stamp would require 20 different plate blocks. Figure 11 illustrates the listing for these plate blocks in *Durland*.

Most non-collectors have little need to mail multiple-ounce letters, and might select to use the exact configuration of a plate block only by chance. Thus, virtually all used plate blocks are philatelically inspired – stamp collectors or stamp dealers using plate blocks on mailings amongst themselves. It is difficult to know how much to pay for a used plate block, as they are not listed in any catalog. Nor is there a large demand for them.

It is virtually impossible to collect used plate blocks or even used plate number singles of self-adhesive stamps. The act of removing the stamp from its backing paper typically separates it from its intended neighbors in a plate block, as well as from the selvage that would constitute a complete plate block or even a complete plate number single. On the rare occasion where separation from the backing paper and placement on an envelope are both successful, such stamps are generally saved "on cover" (on the complete envelope) or "on piece" (a neatly trimmed portion of the envelope paper). Soaking them off the envelope would undoubtedly also separate the stamp from its selvage, ruining the plate block or plate number single.

During World War II, a set of stamps was issued to honor the Overrun Countries (909–921). They were printed by American Banknote, not by the BEP. Instead of plate numbers, they carry the country name in the place where the plate number would normally be found.

Plate numbers exist not only on postage stamps, but also on many back of the book issues, both those printed by the private bank note companies, and the BEP. Plates for most revenue stamps, including **Duck stamps**, were assigned numbers from a "miscellaneous" series of numbers.

Almanac

1847 – United States issues its first stamps (1 and 2). Plate numbers are not known on these stamps.

1851 – Toppan, Carpenter, & Casilear begins numbering its plates, starting with 1 for each denomination.

1861 – National Bank Note Company numbers its plates beginning with 1.

1869 – National designates plate numbers, beginning with 1, for the pictorial series issued this year.

1870 – National designates plate numbers, beginning with 1, for the Bank Note issues.

1873 – Continental Bank Note Company receives the printing contract, and numbers its plates beginning with 1.

1879 – American Bank Note Company receives the printing contract, continues to use Continental's plates, and initially issues new plate numbers higher than those used by both National and Continental.

1883 – American adds prefix letters to plate numbers and continues this practice through Small Bank Note and Columbian issues.

1894 – The BEP begins printing all U.S. stamps and numbers plates beginning with number 1.

1901 – The BEP produces its first bicolor stamps, the Pan American issue (294-299) and assigns different plate numbers to the frames and vignettes.

1918 – 1920 – The BEP experiments with offset printing methods. Some plate numbers are entered by hand or with a rubber stamp.

1970 – "Biggie" plate block era begins.

1975 – 1980 – The Americana series uses the highest known plate number, 41125, on the $1 Rush Lamp and Candle Holder (1610).

1981 – The era of "biggie" plate blocks ends as the BEP moves to "representative" plate numbers, generally starting with 1 for each stamp. The actual sequential plate number is retained for accounting purposes but never appears on the issued stamps.

1981 – Private contractors begin printing stamps using plate numbers with prefix letters.

1981 – The BEP begins to include plate numbers on a separate selvage area of booklet issues.

What Others Have Said

Tracing the interest in plate numbers on U.S. Stamps

"While it might be supposed that stamps printed from plate number 1 would be the first to be issued by the Post Office Department, actually the 6¢ value, bearing Garfield's portrait printed in light maroon from plate number 28 was the first to be issued, on July 18, 1894. Stamp collectors of the 90's were much intrigued with the simplicity of the new series of plate numbers appearing in the margins of the sheets, and inasmuch as these began with 1 and ran in sequence upward, many more collectors in addition to those who had previously collected the numbers of the National, Continental, and American Bank Note Company now undertook to collect stamps, wither singly or in strips of 3 or more, showing these Bureau plate numbers and imprints. Thus was stimulated the collection of plate numbers…"

—*Walter A. McIntire, "The Bureau Issues Association,"* Weekly Philatelic Gossip, 1935.

The Bureau's Plate Numbering System (and cheap Columbian plate blocks!)

"Plate number collecting really began with the taking over of the contract for the printing of postage stamps of the 1894 issue by the Bureau of Engraving and Printing. There is little evidence that much was done prior to that time although the Columbian issue is not all difficult to find in strips and blocks with the plate number and imprint attached, and the previous issue, while scarce, exists in fair amounts….The Bureau opened up with Plate No. 1 on a two cent stamp and

Plate No. 2 on a one cent stamp. This was a change from the methods of the private companies who had a No. 1 plate block for each value and did not number them in sequence. Also, they would start all over again with a new issue. With the ballyhooing of the government that it was printing its own stamps and with the intriguing idea that starting with No. 1, the numbers might run into infinity, plate number collecting came into its own."

—W.R. McCoy, "A Few Rambling Remarks on Bureau Plate Numbers," Weekly Philatelic Gossip, 1931.

USPS Policy Regarding Plate Numbers

"Plate numbers are assigned to each plate made at the Bureau of Engraving and Printing for control over plates, and for identifying stamps printed from any plate. There are four different types of presses in use. Cottrell Press: stamps from this single cover press bear a single plate number. Giori Press: stamps are printed in a single pass through the press and have a single plate number, as only one plate is used, even though there may be as many as three different colors of ink applied to that single plate. If, because of the design a stamp requires two or three passes through the press, two or three plates would be used, and each plate is assigned an identifying number. Should lithography be used in connection with Giori printings, each lithographic plate has a separate number. However, lithography numbers are printed on the sheet edge and are trimmed off after final examination. Huck Press: The Huck Press has three separate printing stations. Each printing station has a cylinder on which thirty plates are mounted in a continuous manner around the circumference. Each plate contains eighty regular-sized stamps (4x20) or forty double sized stamps (2x20). Therefore each plate will have a number every fourth stamp for regular-size (Flag) or every second stamp for double size (1969 Christmas) stamps. If a second or third printing station is used, a second or third series of plate numbers would be added on the selvedge. Gravure Press (such as the Andreotti): Each color is printed from a separate cylinder, and each cylinder is numbered. On the 5¢ Thomas Eakins stamp, six cylinders were used, and six cylinder (or plate) numbers appear on the selvedge."

—"U.S.P.S. Policy Regarding Plate Numbers," Stamps Magazine, 1973.

Where to Find More Information

- A publication of interest is Hebert's Standard Plate Number Single Catalogue, published occasionally since 1952.

- The American Plate Number Single Society maintains a web-site at www.apnss.org.

The United States Stamp Society, publisher of this book, was founded in 1930 to help collectors study plate numbers. The Society's publications are the principal resources in the stamp collecting hobby for referencing plate numbers. They include:

- *Durland Standard Plate Number Catalog.* Published occasionally, this is the standard plate number reference for all United States and overprinted Possessions postage, revenue and back of the book stamps listed in *Scott.* It includes illustrations of marginal marking types and data on coil, sheet and booklets.

- *BIA Plate Number Checklist: Plates 1-20,000, Revised 1990* compiled by Wallace Cleland. This is a compact reference to all BEP produced plates, from 1 through 20,000, providing such information as dates plates were assigned, certified, at press, cancelled and melted. There is also information on imprints, initials, and number of impressions made.

- *BIA Plate Number Checklist: Plates 20,000-41,303, Revised 1990,* compiled by John Larson and Kim Johnson. Similar data as contained in checklist plates for 1-20,000.

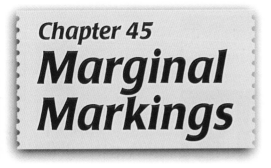

Chapter 45
Marginal Markings

It is often said that "one person's trash is another person's treasure!" In the case of most purchasers of postage stamps, they tear them off and throw them away. But for some collectors they are one of the great joys of the hobby. The technical term for this treasure is "marginal marking", which is defined as "any intentional marking found on a plate except for the stamp itself."

In addition to plate numbers (ch. 44), marginal markings may be divided into fifteen general categories:

Color Registration Marks	Lines
Design Elements	Pane-Position Diagrams
Imprints	Perforation Alignment Marks
Initials	Price Markings
Inventory Tracking	Stars
Labels	Words
Legal Notices	Zip Code Insignia
Letters	

Color Registration Marks. On May 14, 1918, William T. Robey walked into a Washington, D.C. post office to buy a pane of this country's first airmail stamps, which had been issued the previous day. He purchased the "***Inverted Jenny***" sheet of 100 (*Scott* C3a). The following day, an embarrassed Bureau of Engraving and Printing (BEP) began to add the word "TOP" to each plate used to print bi-color stamps, in an effort to prevent the printing of additional inverts. Bi-color stamps at that time were printed from two separate plates, requiring the paper be fed through the press twice. "TOP" was added to enable the pressman to more easily determine the correct plate orientation on the press. Figure 1a illustrates the dark blue and carmine 6¢ airmail issue of 1938 (C23) with the carmine word TOP in the margin, engraved on plate 21841; the dark blue word TOP also appears in the margin from plate 21837. The carmine and blue vertical lines on this piece allowed the press operator to determine whether the two designs (*frame* and **vignette**) were properly centered horizontally.

Color Registration Markings are known in various sizes and shapes, and they appear in each color used to print a particular stamp. When these colored markings are properly aligned with one another, it indicates that the color align-

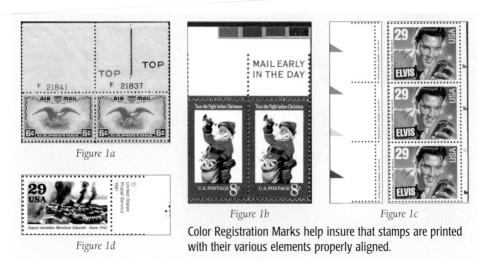

Figure 1a

Figure 1d

Figure 1b

Figure 1c

Color Registration Marks help insure that stamps are printed with their various elements properly aligned.

ment (registration) on the entire sheet is correct. Examples of color registration markings are the **Hurletron** triangular registration marks, illustrated in the left and right margins Figure 1c, and a video registration marking, (a cluster of 1 mm squares of different colors which enables inspection for both color and register variation), shown in Figure 1d. Figure 1b shows the characteristic color registration marks used on the Andreotti Press.

Design Elements. Occasionally a design spills out from the stamp into the surrounding selvage. A dramatic example of this is the souvenir sheet issued in 1976 showing Washington crossing the Delaware. A portion of that souvenir sheet is illustrated in Figure 2a. Note

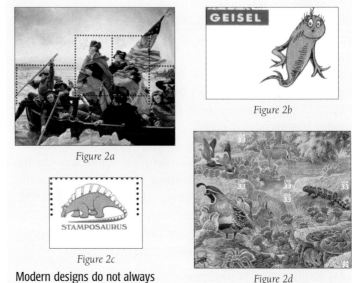

Figure 2a

Figure 2b

Figure 2c

Figure 2d

Modern designs do not always stop at the stamp. Some continue onto the selvage.

that the "USA 24¢" is barely visible on these stamps and that the stamp boundaries can be readily discerned only by the perforations! The design extends into the selvage, and that portion is classified as a marginal marking.

Figure 2d shows a portion of the Sonoran Desert stamp pane, which depicts 25 different plants and animals. Within this scene lurk ten different stamps – if you can find them. Six of these stamps are depicted in Figure 2d, each evident only by the printed "USA 33".

Figure 2b illustrates a fanciful creature from the selvage of the Theodor (Dr. Seuss) Geisel commemorative, while Figure 2c illustrates a "STAMPOSAURUS" from the selvage of the Prehistoric Creatures issue.

Imprints. From 1847 until 1894, all postage stamps were printed by private contractors. These printers identified (and advertised) themselves by placing their name on the stamp or in the margin. The *Durland Standard Plate Number Catalog* identifies 29 distinct **imprints** used by private printers. It also identified the 15 imprints used by the BEP from 1894 until 1911. All imprint references in this chapter refer to the imprint designations assigned in *Durland*.

Each stamp of the 1847 issue bore the initials of the printer, RWH & E (**Rawdon, Wright, Hatch & Edson**). The initials were printed inside the outer frame line of the design and, therefore, are not marginal markings.

In 1851 Toppan, Carpenter, Casilear & Company was awarded the printing contract. Durland designates their first imprint as A1. When Casilear left the firm a new imprint was created that omitted his name. The new imprint (known as A2) is shown in Figure 3a. An even later version of the Toppan Carpenter & Co. imprint (Imprint R3) was used on early revenue stamps and is illustrated in Figure 3c.

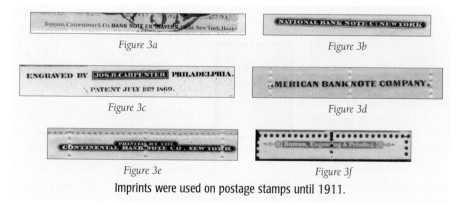

Figure 3a

Figure 3b

Figure 3c

Figure 3d

Figure 3e

Figure 3f

Imprints were used on postage stamps until 1911.

In 1861, the printing contract was awarded to the **National Bank Note Company**. Their imprints appeared in the top and bottom margins, as well as in the side margins. An example of a National Imprint (B2) is shown in Figure 3b. One of the three imprints used by The **Continental Bank Note Company** is shown in Figure 3e. National, Continental, and American were consolidated into the **American Bank Note Company** in 1878. One of the five imprints used by American is shown in Figure 3d.

In 1894 the BEP began producing postage stamps. One of the fifteen different BEP imprints (Imprint V) is shown in Figure 3f.

Initials. It was once customary for various BEP workers to place their initials on steel plates. Beginning in the 1890s, printers stamped their initials in the margin. In 1906 siderographers began adding their initials to plates and in 1908 plate finishers began including theirs.

"F" – This marginal marking was punched on flat plates, indicating that the plates had been hardened and approved. The F is usually located to the left of the upper right plate number. Frank Martie began this practice on May 9, 1919 when he stamped his single initial on plate 8168 (which printed several 1¢ green Washington issues). Figure 4e shows an orange F on the Grand Canyon issue of 1934. Figure 1a shows both a carmine F from plate 21841 and a dark blue F from plate 21837 from the 1938 air mail stamp.

Monograms – For a three month period in 1920, printers added their monogram to 31 offset plates used to print the 2¢ carmine Washington issues, 528 and 528A, and 534. Figure 4a shows the monograms of RSW (Ralph S. Wirsching) and OAM (Otto A. Myers).

Figure 4a

Figure 4b

Figure 4d

Figure 4c

Figure 4e

Figure 4f

Some workers put their initials on plates in the late nineteenth and early twentieth centuries.

Plate Finishers – The initials of *plate finishers* (also known as plate cleaners) can be found in different locations on plates, as shown by the four examples in Figure 4. Figures 4c and 4d have the initials A.C.N. and C.V., respectively, in the lower left corner of the sheet. In Figures 4b and 4f plate finisher initials J.M.B., A.L.C., and W.E.S. appear in the lower right corner of the sheet. The lower right margin eventually became the standardized location for such initials. Initials were punched using a hammer, often giving a shallow impression. These initials are known from 1908 until 1928.

Printers – The initials of printers were punched into a plate each time they printed from it, sometimes resulting in long strings of initials on a plate. An example, with the initials running vertically down the left side of the plate, is shown Figure 4c. The practice of punching *printers' initials* ended by 1912.

Siderographers – The initials of *siderographers* were normally placed in the lower left corner of the plate. Initials were engraved using a *transfer roll* and press leaving a deep, clear impression. This marginal marking first appeared in 1906. Examples include initials F.P.L. in Figure 4c and H.M.C. in Figure 4d.

Figure 5

Bar Codes and Item numbers are comparatively recent marginal markings.

Inventory Tracking. *Bar codes* and USPS item numbers were added to the selvage in 1998, starting with the Breast Cancer semi-postal (B1), shown in Figure 5. They are used to track inventory and sales.

Labels. What *Scott* describes as booklet pane "*labels*" are essentially advertisements or public service announcements. Since 1962, booklet panes have been issued with three to twenty stamps and, in order to control the pricing of booklets, many of them contain one or more labels of no postal value.

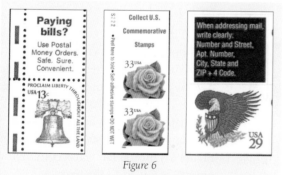

Figure 6

Labels began appearing on booklet panes in 1962.

In 1962, the 5¢ Washington was issued in booklet form (1213a) with labels printed with three different slogans: "YOUR MAILMAN DESERVES YOUR HELP KEEP HARMFUL OBJECTS OUT OF YOUR LETTERS", "ADD ZIP TO YOUR MAIL USE ZONE NUMBERS FOR ZIP CODE", and "ADD ZIP

Figure 7b

Figure 7c

Figure 7d

Legal notices began appearing as marginal markings during the last quarter of the twentieth century.

TO YOUR MAIL ALWAYS USE ZIP CODE". Three different booklet labels are illustrated in Figure 6.

Legal Notices. Legal notices protect USPS designs and slogans, as well as emblems of organizations and the names and images of individuals honored on stamps.

Copyright notices (©) first appeared in 1978 with the Indian Head Penny issue (1734). Examples of the copyright notices are shown in Figure 7b and 7c.

Various emblems have appeared in margins. Figure 7d shows the U.S. Bicentennial emblem in the margin of the Colonial American Craftsman Issue (1458) and Figure 7a shows the USPS Eagle with Olympic Rings in the margin of the Wildflowers Issue (2647-2696). Other emblems, or logos, that have appeared as marginal markings include WSE (World Stamp Expo) '89 logo (2410), American Music Stamp Festival logo (2982, 2983-2992, 3096-3099, and 3100-3103), and PUAS (Postal Union of the Americas and Spain) logo (2512).

W.C. Fields and Lou Gehrig were both honored with a commemorative stamp, and both estates insisted on royalties for the use of their name and image. As a result, the USPS now negotiates licenses in advance, and a licensing statement, such as the one in Figure 7b for the Dr. Seuss commemorative, is added to the margin.

The USPS first started registration of its slogans in 1978 with the Indian Head Penny Issue. The ® mark indicates that the slogan is registered. **Mr. Zip** became registered with the Captain Cook Issue (1732–1733). Figure 7a shows an example of a registered ZIP slogan plus a citation of the USC (United States Code). Figure 15 shows both registered (Fig. 15c) and unregistered (Fig. 15a) examples of Mr. Zip.

Trademarks first appeared in 1989 with the 25¢ Eagle & Shield (2431) pressure-sensitive stamp, marked "EXTRAordinary Stamps™" on unfolded panes.

Letters. Various letters have been used on plates through the years. Some were not meant to appear on finished sheets and were normally cut off in the trimming process, though occasionally such letters do appear on finished sheets. Others letters were meant to appear on the finished sheet.

The letter "*A*" was used on BEP flat plates indicating uniform spacing (2.75 mm) between vertical rows of stamps. The "A" marking was intended to assist operators of perforating equipment. It was included in the BEP imprint as shown in Figure 8e. The letter A has also been used in recent years as an integral part of plate numbers (ch. 44).

The letter "*C*" was first used on the Byrd Antarctic Issue (733) illustrated in Figure 8d. The mark indicates that the plate was chrome plated.

Figure 8a

Figure 8b

Figure 8c

Figure 8d

Letters have served several technological and production purposes.

Figure 8e

"**C.S.**" is a marginal marking for chrome steel, indicating that a plate has been chromium plated. The initials appear in the top margin on upper right panes. It can be found on Georgia Bicentennial Issue (Fig. 8c) and Kosciuszko Issue.

"***EI***" is an abbreviation for Electrolytic Iron, designating plates made by the electrolytic process. It can be found in the top margin of the 6¢ Airmail (Fig. 8a).

"GATF" can be found imbedded in the multicolor quality control strip on commemorative panes printed on the D Press, starting with the 22¢ Delaware Issue of 1987. GATF is an acronym printed on the sheet to credit the Graphic Arts Technical Foundation, which developed the strip.

The letter "R" is an abbreviation for Right and was used to aid in mounting a plate onto a cylinder. As far as is known, the marking is only on plates for the Cottrell press, placed high in the margin where it rarely survived the trimming process.

The marks *S20*, *S30*, and *S40* appear on certain rotary press plates of 150 and 170 subjects. These markings designate experimental variations in the depth and character of the frame line. The S30 mark is shown in Figure 8b.

Lines. *Arrows*, *feed lines*, and ***guide lines*** are used in the stamp production process.

Arrows, shaped like a "V", served both as a guide in the perforation process and for cutting sheets into smaller units. Arrow-shaped markings were used in the margins of stamp sheets, instead of guide lines, on the issues of 1870 through 1894. Since 1894, guide lines with arrows at both ends have characterized flat-plate printings. Figure 9b shows both an arrow-headed registration marker and

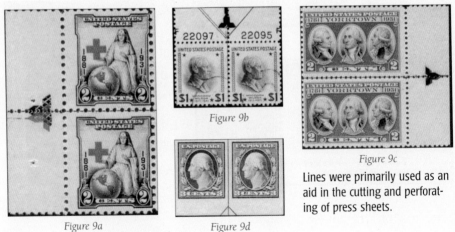

Figure 9b

Figure 9a   Figure 9d

Figure 9c

Lines were primarily used as an aid in the cutting and perforating of press sheets.

top arrows in both purple and black. The arrow-headed registration marker shown in Figure 9b was first used on the Pan-American Series of 1901. Figure 9d shows a bottom arrow on a 3¢ violet Washington.

Feed lines are lines placed upon certain flat plates as an aid to the proper placement of sheets of paper upon the plate. They are typically found as two horizontal lines in the margin of a sheet.

Guide lines are lines inscribed on a plate as an aid to perforating or cutting a sheet into panes. They divide the plate into four quadrants and were used by operators of the perforation machines. Vertical guide lines can be seen on the Wilson and Washington stamps in Figures 9b and 9d, while horizontal guide lines are shown on the 2¢ Red Cross Issue (Fig. 9a), and the 2¢ Yorktown Issue (Fig. 9c).

Pane-Position Diagrams. These were first used in 1992 on the Wildflowers Issue (2647-2696). This issue was the first to be printed on both a 200-subject plate of four panes and a 300-subject plate of six panes. The *pane diagram*, printed in the selvage of each pane next to the plate number, identifies from which position on which size sheet the pane came. Figure 10a from the Circus Issue (2752) shows a six-pane diagram and identifies the "TOP" of the pane. Figure 10b shows a ten-pane diagram appearing on the Niagara Falls (C133) airmail stamp.

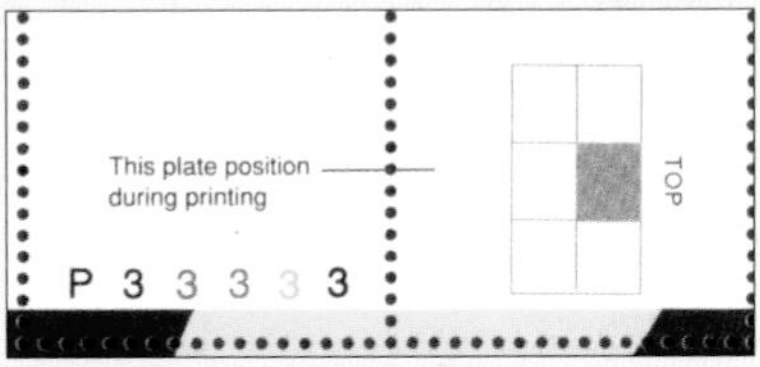

Figure 10a

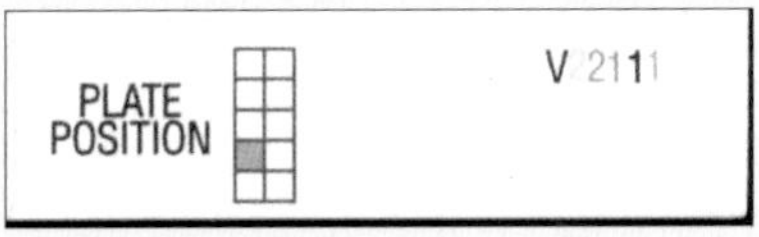

Figure 10b

Plate Position Diagrams, a comparatively recent innovation, identify a pane's place of origin on a sheet.

Perforation Alignment Marks. The *Electric Eye* is a device that employs a beam of light to facilitate more accurate perforation of stamps during the manufacturing process. **Electric Eye Frame Bars** (fig. 11a) are horizontal lines in the sheet

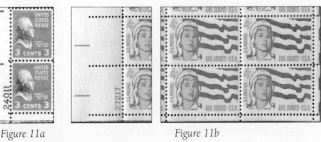

Figure 11a　　　　　*Figure 11b*

Perforation Alignment Marks were "read" by an electric eye to help guide the perforation process.

margin that were used by the electric eye in the perforating process. Perforation alignment marks were first used in 1939.

Electric Eye Gutter Dashes in the vertical ***gutter*** between the right and left panes and frame bars in the left and right margins were used in the perforating process in conjunction with the electric eye. Figure 11b shows both frame bars from the left margin and gutter dashes from the sheet's vertical gutter of the 1962 Girl Scout issue. Similar markings are used for die cutting.

Figure 12a   Figure 12b

Price Markings were included in the margin beginning in 1994.

Price Marking. The Edward R. Murrow commemorative (2812) was released on January 21, 1994 with a new marginal marking – a calculation of the price of the pane. An equation is used rather than just printing the face value of the pane. Figures 12a and 12b shows two different price marking formats used on the Dr. Seuss commemorative issue and on the Honoring Those Who Served.

Stars. Stars were used on some Washington-Franklin and Series of 1922 plates to indicate an increased spacing between stamps, when compared to earlier similar plates that had less space between stamps. The purpose of the star was to alert workers that adjustments needed to be made in perforating these sheets. On some Third Bureau flat plates, a star was added to the BEP imprint, as shown in Figure 13a. This imprint was first used in March 1909. Stars were also added to the rotary press plates such as the 2¢ carmine rose Washington (540) shown in Figure 13b. On the Fourth Bureau flat plates, a star was added in the selvage of the 2¢ carmine Washington (illustrated in Figure 13c), the 8¢ olive green Grant, and 12¢ brown violet Cleveland. While most of the Fourth Bureau flat plates have five-pointed stars, a few have a six-pointed star.

Figure 13a

Figure 13b   Figure 13c

Stars alerted BEP workers to make special provision for perforating sheets with this marking.

Words. There has been an increase of words used to supplement stamp designs and provide information to the public. Early usage of words was typically to assist postal employees.

"COIL STAMPS" is a marginal marking, shown in Figure 14g, found on the green 1¢ and rose red 2¢ Washington issues of 1914 (424 and 425). These sheets have increased spacing between the 10th and 11th vertical rows. While intended to be used to manufacture coil stamps, some became coil waste. This marginal inscription was trimmed off the sheet during coil production, but remained on the full panes sold as coil waste.

Figure 14a

Figure 14b

Figure 14c

Figure 14d

For more information about diabetes visit www.niddk.nih.gov

Figure 14e

Figure 14g

Ida M. Tarbell (1857–1944) wrote a landmark trust-busting exposé as well as serialized biographies for *McClure's Magazine*.

Nellie Bly (1864–1922), intrepid reporter for *The World*, won fame for circling the globe in just 72 days (Nov. 14, 1889–Jan. 25, 1890).

Women in Journalism

Figure 14f

Words have been used as marginal markings for a variety of purposes.

Commercial markings for USPS products can be found on several issues, including the 1992 World War II commemorative issue (2697) and Elvis Issue (2721) shown in Figure 14c and 14f. These markings were first used on the Prehistoric Animals Issue of 1989.

Decorative Banners are the illustrated margin on some modern commemorative panes. They have no postal value. An example of a decorative banner, The Legends of the West, is shown in Figure 14b.

Denominations in words (THREE, FIFTEEN, FIFTY, etc.) were added to parcel post stamps in 1913 after complaints from postal clerks that all the sheets looked alike, since they were all printed in carmine rose. Figure 14d shows an example of a parcel post stamp imprint, Imprint XIV, on the 25¢ issue (Q9).

Description/biography – Biographical data concerning individuals began in February 1990. Figure 14f illustrates descriptive biographical data on the Women in Journalism commemorative issue.

Mail Early slogans were used from 1968 to 1978. Postage stamps, airmail, special delivery, and officials all carried slogans. A couple of different styles of the slogan are illustrated in Figures 14a and 15d. Mail early blocks typically consist of four to six stamps.

Web site inscriptions began with the 34¢ Diabetes Awareness self-adhesive stamp issued in 2001, as shown in Figure 14e. Subsequently, the 37¢ Neuter or Spay self-adhesive sheet (3670-3671) was issued with a marginal web site inscription.

Zip Code Insignia. Zip code insignia includes an inscription urging the use of *ZIP Code*, and the "Mr. Zip" character. In the early 1960s, the Post Office Department was seeking more efficient ways to process and deliver growing volumes of mail. As a result, they developed a 5-digit number code for each address. Mr. ZIP®, is a unique brand icon who used a letter and satchel to encourage Americans to use ZIP Codes on their mail. The use of the ZIP (Zone Improvement Plan) Code system began on July 1, 1963 and within a year of this character's introduction, between a third and a half of the mail was using a ZIP Code. Zip Blocks appeared on the margins of many stamps between 1964 and 1994.

Mr. Zip – This marking was based on an original design by Harold Wilcox, son of a letter carrier, for use by a New York bank in a bank-by-mail campaign. Post Office Department artists retained the face of the original design but chose to sharpen the limbs and torso and add a mail bag. The new figure, dubbed Mr. Zip, was unveiled at a convention of postmasters in October 1962. Five different versions of the cartoon were used, three of which are shown in Figure 15a,

15b, and 15c. Typically ZIP blocks are collected as blocks of four. U.S. stamp blocks that include ZIP code messages are listed and valued in *Scott*.

Use Zip Code Slogans – Various Zip Code slogans were used from 1964 through 1994, including "Use Zip Code" (Figures 15a, 15b, and 15d), "Use Zip Codes" (Figure 15f), "It all depends on Zip Code", and

Figure 15a

Figure 15b

Figure 15c

Figure 15d

Figure 15e

The advent of the Zip Code gave birth to several marginal markings.

Figure 15f

"Use Correct Zip Code" (Figure 15c and 15e). The slogans were registered beginning in 1978.

Notes on Collecting

Some early marginal markings, such as the nineteenth century imprints, can be very expensive, costing thousands of dollars. While some early twentieth century material is expensive, many items can be purchased for fewer than ten dollars. More recent material will be relatively inexpensive. New items are sold at the Post Office for face value and current items on cover may show up in your mailbox.

Marginal markings can be collected in used or unused condition, on or off cover, and as singles, blocks, or sheets. One can collect for completeness or just collect examples of each type of marking.

By a little research it can be determined when a marginal marking was first issued and when it was discontinued, what varieties are available (i.e., five varieties of Mr. Zip), and on what type of postage stamp the marking can be found (i.e., commemorative, definitive, airmail, etc.).

Arrow blocks can be collected by position (top, bottom, right, left) and the four pieces for an issue can be arranged in an interesting display. Zip blocks on cover are difficult to find. They can be easily found on First Day Covers, but not on covers that are not philatelic usages. Many marginal markings are listed in *Scott*.

Almanac

1851 – Toppan, Carpenter, Casilear & Co. adds a company imprint to their printing plates.

1861 – On May 10 Postmaster General Blair awards a stamp-printing contract to National Bank Note Company, which puts their company imprint on plates.

1873 – Continental Bank Note Co. is awarded the contract to print stamps. The National plates, dies and transfer rolls were turned over to Continental, which made new plates of the lower denominations.

1879 – American Bank Note acquires Continental on February 4.

1906 – Charles Vermeule (C.V.) is the first siderographer to initial a plate, #3080.

1909 – John Reding (J.R.) is the first plate cleaner to initial a plate, #4959.

1909 – Both open and solid stars are added to the BEP imprint to indicate variations in separation between stamps.

1910 – The letter A is added to the BEP imprint to indicate uniform spacing of 2.75 mm between stamps.

1915 – The first experimental plates marked S20 go to press on December 31. They were followed in 1916 by plates marked S40, and by plates marked S30.

1918 – The letter F is first added to plate numbers 8377, 8388, and 8389 on March 20 to identify an approved hardened plate.

1918 – On May 14 William T. Robey purchases an "Inverted Jenny" pane of 100 (C3a).

1918 – On May 15 plates for bi-color stamps are marked TOP to reduce the possibility of a sheet being inverted on its second pass through the press.

1920 – In May printer Otto A. Myers is the first to inscribe his monogram in the margin of a plate, #11329.

1928 – Siderographers/Plate Finishers are instructed to stop putting their initials on the front of plates.

1933 – Georgia Bicentennial Issue is released February 12 with C.S., a marking that indicates that the plate had been chromium plated.

1933 – Electric Eye margin line and dashes are experimentally used.

1935 – First Electric Eye plates are made for 2¢ Washington (634).

1938 – Beginning in April, electrolytic plates for 6¢ Airmail issue (C23) are marked EI for electrolytic iron.

1939 – Electric Eye frame bars and gutter bars are first used.

1962 – Booklet pane (1213a) is issued November 23 with a label stating "YOUR MAILMAN DESERVES YOUR HELP KEEP HARMFUL OBJECTS OUT OF YOUR LETTERS."

1964 – Battle of the Wilderness (1181) issued May 4 with Mr. Zip and "Use Zip Code" insignia.

1968 – The 6¢ Hemisphere '68 (1340) is issued March 30 with "Mail Early in the Day" and "Use Zip Code." The Surrender at Saratoga American Bicentennial Issue (1728) was the last stamp issued with a "Mail Early" slogan.

1977 – USPS Philatelic Release No. 57 announces that the designs of all future postage stamps and postal stationary items would be copyrighted.

1978 – The Indian Head Penny issue (1734) appears January 11 with a registered slogan.

1978 – John Paul Jones U.S. Bicentennial (1789) is issued September 23 with a copyright notice.

1986 – USPS abruptly retires Mr. Zip after 22 years of dedicated service. Stamps with Zip slogans continue to be issued until 1994.

1990 – USPS prints biographical information "Luis Munoz Marin (1898-1980). First elected Governor of Puerto Rico, 1948. Founder of Puerto Rico Commonwealth." in the selvage of Scott 2173, the first stamp in the Great Americans series to contain such information, issued February 18.

1992 – The Wildflowers (2647-2696) pane of 50 is issued July 24 with a diagram, which identifies position, shaded in grey, on a sheet from which the pane was cut.

1994 – The Edward R. Murrow (2812) commemorative issued January 21 is the first to have a calculation of the price of the pane marking in the margin.

1998 – Breast Cancer Awareness semi-postal (B1) is issued July 29 with both bar codes and item number in the margin.

2001 – Diabetes Awareness stamp (3503) is issued March 16 with a web site address in the margin.

What Others Have Said

Initials in the margin were made by a number of people

"The chief task of a siderographer at the Bureau of Engraving and Printing is to operate a transfer press and transfer the design from a die to a roll and the enter impressions on a steel plate. Upon completion of a plate the siderographers used their presses to enter their initials in the margin of the plate....Since these initials were entered only once on the plate they are rarer than a plate number which frequently occurred eight times on a plate. After the plate was finished by the siderographer, it was turned over to a plate finisher or cleaner....Initials were entered on the margin of the plate by the finishers once they had finished their task. Not having a press to do this, they used a punch, which, with a blow of a hammer, gave an impression. Since the punch was hand held and would bounce when hit, plate finishers initials may show doubling of part of the initials and may not be parallel to the edge of the stamp margin."

—John S. Meek, "Initials of Siderographers and Plate Finishers," The United States Specialist, 1968.

On the Initials of Siderographers and Plate Finishers

"At present there does not seem to be a checklist in existence which lists all the initials for a given issue...From such a list one can soon get an idea which initials are rare and I feel it is going to be difficult to get an example of each worker. I wonder who worked on the rare 20¢ special delivery plates and who were the workers that handled the 5¢ error plate? The lure of the chase for such items is great. The series is closed and one does not have to go to the post office each week to seek new items. The specimens are not in great demand and one dealer said 'You are the first person to ever ask me for initials. I have been tearing them off for fifteen years.'"

—John S. Meek, "Initials of Siderographers and Plate Finishers," The United States Specialist, 1969. In the final installment of a five part series, 21 years before the first edition of the BIA Plate Number Checklist 1-20,000 was published, Meek incorporated a list of initials he had researched and compiled.

No more "huh?" stamps

"The postmaster general [Anthony M. Frank] started looking at the Great Americans series... and he said, if a stamp doesn't explain itself, if it leaves the customer saying 'Why is this person on this stamp I'm buying?' then the stamp design has failed. And even if we made it possible for a window clerk to answer that question, Mr. Frank said, it wouldn't help a person who received a letter with that stamp on it. He's not going to drive all the way down to his post office and ask a window clerk, and he's not going down to the library and look it up. Mr. Frank said to us: 'You've got to fix it.' In other words, there should be no more of what USPS staffers came to refer as "huh?" stamps. With the Munoz stamp, USPS began inserting identifying words into Great American designs."

—*Don McDowell, manager of the USPS Stamps Division, explaining why biographical material was printed in the selvage, quoted from* Linn's U.S. Stamp Yearbook, 1990.

The first "Coil Waste" stamps

"The vertical coils were produced from slightly modified plates which involved a minor change in the spacing...These new plates were redesigned completely in regard to their marginal imprints. Bold lettering had been added to denote their specific use, which simply could not be mis-understood since it read 'COIL STAMPS.' The plate numbers were removed from the top and bottom and placed in close proximity to the bold lettering on the sides of the plate. Naturally these markings are unobtainable since the side markings were always trimmed off during the coiling process. However, by a stroke of Philatelic luck, the rotary press assumed the total coil production during 1914 and the first 'Coil Waste' issue was released."

—*Martin Armstrong,* United States Coil Issues 1906–1938, 1977. *The markings that Armstrong describes here were never intended to be released to the public.*

Mr. Zip's Future

"Today, virtually everyone uses ZIP Codes, making Mr. ZIP one of the greatest salesmen in history. ZIP Codes are also embedded in the way businesses work and an integral part of the 911 emergency system that uses ZIP Codes as an aid in saving lives. As for Mr. ZIP, the cultural icon is back with a new look – and outlook – to promote stamp collecting and other topics of interest to kids. While there currently are no plans to include Mr. ZIP on the stamp selvage, this may be a possibility again sometime in the future."

—*Pamela York, USPS Manager, Licensing, 2004. Commenting on future plans for Mr. Zip.*

Examples of Postal Usage

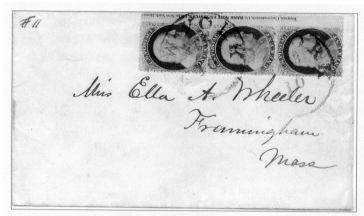

Figure 16a

Figure 16a shows a cover with three stamps (positions 50, 60, and 70) from the right pane of Plate 9 of the 1¢ Franklin (24) of the 1857 Toppan Carpenter perforated issue. Problems in the perforating process led to a wide "wing" margin at the right, which captured most of the first line of the imprint. Imprint A2 is enlarged in Figure 16b to show the "Carpenterar" imprint variety, caused by improper transfer of an old imprint in an attempt to omit the name "Casilear," traces of which can be seen on this plate.

Figure 16b

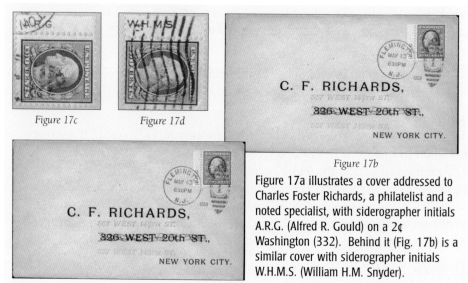

Figure 17c

Figure 17d

C. F. RICHARDS,
567 WEST 149TH ST.
326 WEST 20th ST.,
507 WEST 149TH ST.
NEW YORK CITY.

Figure 17b

Figure 17a illustrates a cover addressed to Charles Foster Richards, a philatelist and a noted specialist, with siderographer initials A.R.G. (Alfred R. Gould) on a 2¢ Washington (332). Behind it (Fig. 17b) is a similar cover with siderographer initials W.H.M.S. (William H.M. Snyder).

C. F. RICHARDS,
567 WEST 149TH ST.
326 WEST 20th ST.,
507 WEST 149TH ST.
NEW YORK CITY.

Figure 17a

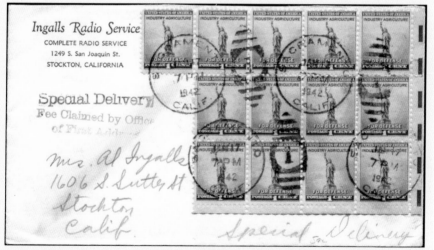

Figure 18a

Figure 18b

This cover from circa 1974 shows four different marginal markings! Figure 18a shows a cover with two 10¢ Expo '74 stamps (1527) from Steubenville, Ohio paying the international rate to Oakville, Ontario, Canada. The selvage contains Mr. Zip, a "MAIL EARLY IN THE DAY" slogan, electric eye markings, and a color registration marking. In spite of Mr. Zip's efforts, the cover is also stamped "RETURN TO SENDER."

Figure 19

A Special Delivery letter with a block of thirteen 1¢ stamps (899) tied by a "Sacramento, Calif." duplex cancel. The block shows electric eye markings in the selvage on the right. Note the joint line on the bottom. Joint lines were created where curved plates came together. They are not marginal markings.

Where to Find More Information

- BIA Plate Number Checklist 1-20000 compiled by Wallace Cleland and BIA Plate Number Checklist 20000-41303 compiled by John Larson and Kim Johnson provide data on marginal markings (existence/placement on the plate) starting with BEP plate number 1. The checklists cover stamps starting with Scott 246, as well as overprinted Possessions postage, revenue, and back of the book stamps.

- The relevant volumes of *Linn's U.S. Stamp Yearbook*, edited by Fred Boughner or George Amick, list marginal markings.

- Bruce Mosher's *Discovering U.S. Rotary Booklet Pane Varieties 1926-1978* illustrates different EE Bars, EE Dashes, and Process Marks.

- USSS Research Paper #2, Folded-style and Pressure Sensitive Booklet Checklist, by Michael Perry, includes a wealth of information about markings on booklets, beginning with those issued in 1977.

- The United States Stamp Society maintains a Marginal Markings Committee, a group comprised of enthusiastic collectors of marginal markings as well as those who have conducted research and published informative papers. It may be accessed at http://marginal-markings.usstamps.org.

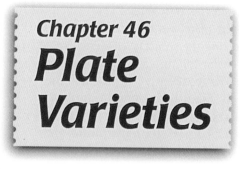

Chapter 46

Plate Varieties

Some stamps, at first glance may seem identical, but actually differ because of something on the printing *plate*. These stamps, which are easily overlooked by the casual observer, are called "plate varieties", and their study is sometimes called "flyspecking", referring to the fact that many plate varieties are the size of a "flyspeck".

Figure 1

This interesting freak was caused by an incomplete wiping of the printing plate. It is not a plate variety, because the aberration is not on the plate itself.

Stamps intended to be identical to each other sometimes differ for reasons other than the printing plate. For example, variations on stamps may occur because of some irregularity in the printing, gumming, or perforating process (fig. 1). But these randomly occurring varieties are not plate varieties. Plate varieties occur because of some irregularity on the printing plate itself. This means that plate varieties are consistent. In other words, every stamp printed from a given position on a specific plate will exhibit the same variety. And every sheet printed from a particular plate will be identical, assuming the plate remains unaltered throughout the period of its use.

"Plate variety" stamps exist because of an unusual occurrence to the plates from which they were printed. That occurrence may be accidental or intentional; however, the result is a collectible stamp that differs in some way from others that appear to be identical.

Plate varieties can be found on stamps printed by any printing method as well as on classic or modern stamps. For example, numerous plate varieties can be found on the *offset* printed Washington-Franklin Issues (Scott 525–536); however plate varieties are most typically associated with line engraved *intaglio* printed stamps.

The vast majority of plate varieties are not listed in *Scott*. *Scott* lists only the most dramatic and eye-catching plate varieties.

There is at least one dramatic plate variety not requiring a magnifying glass for easy identification. A printing plate of the 2¢ Washington-Franklin series, plate #7942, was originally made with three entries that were deemed unacceptable.

Figure 2

The central stamp on this block is a foreign transfer. The siderographer, presumably William A. McAleer who originally created the plate, inadvertently used a 5¢ transfer role instead of a 2¢ transfer role.

Figure 3

This is a drawing of a "foreign transfer" from plate 5299 found on Scott 332. The accented lines highlight the remnants of a 1¢ entry that was not completely erased.

Those entries were erased (burnished-out) from the plate, but then the **siderographer reentering** the subjects accidentally used a 5¢ transfer roll instead of a 2¢ **transfer roll**! The resulting 5¢ entries, and the printed stamps, are known as **foreign transfers** (fig. 2). Sheets from plate #7942 were issued perf. 10, **imperforate**, and perf. 11; therefore the foreign transfer errors are recognized in *Scott* with three major numbers, 467 (perf. 10), 485 (imperforate), and 505 (perf. 11).

Another classic foreign transfer is found on a 2¢ Washington-Franklin stamp (332, fig. 3). It was created by the reverse of the process previously described. On plate #5299 the siderographer creating the plate accidentally used the transfer roll for a 1¢ stamp at position #37 on the upper left pane. The error was discovered and removed, but the removal was incomplete. The remnants of the 1¢ entry remained even after the correct 2¢ transfer roll was used to enter a subject. This foreign transfer is extremely rare.

More frequently plate varieties occur, not because of the use of a wrong transfer role but, because of imperfect use of the correct one. This should not be surprising, for when a printing plate is created by entering subjects on a plate one subject at a time, some variation among the subjects is almost inevitable, and no matter how careful the transferrer (siderographer) might be. For example, if a siderographer is not careful when entering (rocking in) a subject from a transfer roll to a plate, some doubling of the image may result. This is called a **double transfer** (fig. 4). If a subject needs to be burnished-out, and if that removal is not completely successful, some trace of the original entry may remain on the plate. Even when a new entry is made, remnants of the original may still show.

Short transfers occur when the transfer roll is not rocked far enough back and forth to completely enter the subject, leaving one edge of the entry, or two opposite edges, incomplete. This has occurred both intentionally and unintentionally. Although short transfers are usually associated with nineteenth century stamps, a notable short transfer is found on the Brooklyn Bridge issue of 1983 (fig. 5).

Some plate varieties result not from the use of the wrong transfer roll, or even the imperfect use of the correct transfer roll, but from a defect on a transfer roll known as a **relief break**. A relief break occurs when a piece of steel breaks off a transfer roll containing the image of the stamp in relief (that is, raised up above the surface). The result is a stamp with an unprinted area where a bit of printing was intended to appear. The unprinted area on the stamp corresponds to the portion of the transfer roll that broke away. Perhaps the most well known example of a relief break is the so-called "broken circle" which appears on the 5¢ Huguenot-Walloon stamp (616, fig. 6, ch.19).

Most relief breaks are much less spectacular than the "broken circle." For example, copies of some 1¢ flat plate Washington-Franklin Issues (405 and 408) have little pieces of horizontal shading lines broken off (fig. 6). They are not listed in *Scott*.

Occasionally a plate variety is created by damage that occurs to a printing plate

Figure 4

Detail from a double transfer on the 1994 Bureau of Engraving and Printing Souvenir Sheet (2875, fig. 7, ch. 34). Note the especially prominent doubling in both the word, "DOLLARS" and in the dollar signs.

Figure 5

Detail from the Brooklyn Bridge (2041) short transfer. The insert is of the normal variety. Comparison of the two left edges illustrates how the siderographer failed to fully rock-in the design on the short transfer.

Detail from a 1¢ Washington (405) shows several minor relief breaks not listed in *Scott*. Note breaking away of some of the horizontal shading lines along the left side.

Figure 6

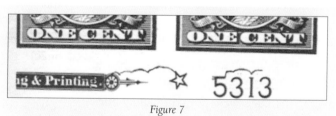

Figure 7

This detail from plate 5313 shows a crack above the plate number that later extended through the left side of the imprint.

Figure 8

Detail of a catalogue listed rosette plate crack on a 1¢ Washington (490).

Figure 9

A pair of 2¢ Washington stamps (634). The long ear variety is on the left and the insert is an enlargement of the "long ear."

after it is made. For example, sometimes plates crack. If the crack worsens while the plate is in use, it is known as a progressive crack (fig. 7). Sometimes plates are damaged by poor handling, scratches, or gouges. One rather spectacular example of a damaged plate is the **rosette crack**, which is *Scott* listed on 384 and 490 (fig. 8).

Plates can wear out from use. Among badly worn plates it may be possible to identify the "early" and "late" stages of a plate's use. For example, the 5¢ Grant stamp of 1895 (270) exists with the vertical lines in the background oval missing. They were literally worn off the plate by repeated use!

From time to time printing plates are **recut** (lines added or strengthened) for some aesthetic reason. The result can be a striking plate variety. One example is the so-called "Long Ear." A variety of the 2¢ Washington **compound perforation** stamp of 1926 (634), it is found only in position 34 (out of 100) on the upper right pane printed from plate 20342 (fig. 9). Because hundreds of different plates were used to print this stamp and the "long-ear" is found only on one position on one plate, it is indeed a rare stamp. Another significant *Scott* listed plate recutting (or retouching) is found on the 11¢ Hayes stamp of 1931 (692). There are actually two varieties of this recut, on the lower left pane from plate 20617, at positions 2 and 3 respectively.

Sometimes the lines and dots scribed on a blank plate by a siderographer to aid in producing the plate were not completely burnished out by the plate finisher. These also are plate varieties (fig. 10).

Figure 10

Detail showing a layout arc accidentally left behind between two stamps. Additionally, the bottom stamp on this piece is a triple transfer, which is especially noticeable above the frame line and in the letter "U".

One of the best-known, and perhaps mysterious, plate varieties is the so-called **broken hat** variety of the 2¢ Columbian stamp of 1893. There is a notch in the hat of the third figure to the left of Columbus (fig. 11). This plate variety was not discovered until the 1920s

Figure 11a   *Figure 11b*

Detail of both the 2¢ Columbian (231) normal hat (left) and "broken-hat" (right) varieties.

even though the broken hat appears on many different positions of many different plates. Part of the mystery of this variety is that not all of the broken hats are identical! One expert has identified 21 different broken hat varieties on at least 15 different plates. The cause(s) of the broken hat has still not been determined. About the only certainty is that it was caused by an abnormal relief on a transfer role.

Notes on Collecting

While many plate varieties have been extensively researched and documented, new discoveries can still be made, and more can be learned about those that are already known to exist. Specialists strive to identify the exact position on a plate from which a plate variety is printed. Sometimes this can be accomplished and other times not. The exact position of a plate variety can sometimes be determined by consulting a **plate proof**. Other times the position can only be determined by a labor intensive process of comparing multiples of attached stamps in order to reconstruct the plate in a process similar to assembling a jigsaw puzzle.

Most plate varieties are modestly priced, partly because they are not actively pursued. It is possible to find some low priced, but truly rare stamps by looking carefully through accumulations and dealers' stocks. For example, the 2¢ Columbian "broken hat" varieties in used condition can be purchased for less than a dollar. By expending some time, energy, and only a small amount of money, an impressive specialized collection of this stamp can be assembled.

Some of the rarest stamps, which are listed as major numbers in *Scott*, are actually plate varieties. For example the 1¢ Franklin design of 1851 has 15 major catalogue numbers. One of them, the very rare stamp known as *Scott* 5 is found on only a single plate position, known as 7R1E. Yet, this stamp is "only" a plate variety. It could be reasonably argued that *Scott* 5 and 9 (which come from the same plate) are just varieties of the same stamp despite the fact that *Scott* 9 in

Figure 12

Detail from the 6¢ 1972 Olympic Games (1460). Note the broken red circle on this photogravure printed stamp. Unlike the famous broken circle on the 5¢ Huguenot-Walloon (616), this plate variety was not caused by a faulty transfer roll.

used condition can be purchased for several hundred dollars or less, while *Scott* 5 will command many thousands of dollars. However for historical reasons these stamps, and other very early plate varieties, were given their own major catalogue numbers by *Scott*. The practice of assigning major catalogue listings to plate varieties was later abandoned. If the 1¢ Franklin stamps first issued in 1851 were to be issued today, even with the same plate varieties, it is likely they would be assigned only two major catalogue numbers (one each for the imperforate and perforated stamp respectively) instead of 15 different ones.

An interesting plate variety produced from a **gravure** plate is found on the 1972 6¢ Summer Olympics stamp (fig. 12). Located on plate 33313, position **UL**43, Cloudy French, an expert in plate varieties, explained the incomplete red circle as, "The left half of this circle was painted out while the plate was being prepared for etching."

Modern technology has given plate variety collectors a marvelous new tool. Scanning stamps at high resolution, and studying them on a computer screen is sure to provide many hours of pleasure.

What Others Have Said

Plate varieties give the collector many rewards

"One of the most fascinating and rewarding areas for the collector on a tight budget to get into is the pursuit and study of plate varieties....The term plate varieties is a catch-all phrase that also includes die and transfer flaws...Although every form of printing has its own peculiar flaws, those connected with line-engraved intaglio are the most interesting to U.S. collectors. To understand plate flaws, it is important to have at least a basic knowledge of the printing process and how these flaws occur...How can you begin? You'll first need at least a 10-power magnifying glass and access to large numbers of older cheap stamps. Then look for flaws. That's really all that is needed to begin.

—*Wayne Youngblood, "Plate Varieties Give Challenge, Rewards,"* Linn's Stamp News, *1992.*

The long awaited 'Cloudy French Book' makes its 1977 appearance

"Here is one of those intensely specialized, detailed, definitive guides to collecting and study that comes along at all too infrequent intervals. In this instance, it's an exhaustive listing (from over 150 handbooks, monographs, journals, auction catalogs, collections and individual researchers) of all the constant plate varieties on U.S. stamps printed by the BEP – in order of issue from the 1894 regulars to the 1978 Indianheads. Each variety is fully described and credited to the original source, and plate number and position specified where known. The majority of varieties are also illustrated in enlarged reproduction or sketch...The work is of obvious interest to those who, in Cloudy French's words 'seek out the rugged individual; the cracked, scratched or gouged; the erased and reentered, the multiple, extraneous, incomplete, or foreign transfer...[for those who] value character above conformity....' And for those who leave such pleasures to others, those 'others' in the person of French and his collaborators have now provided them with an invaluable reference to U.S. stamps."

—*C.J. Petersen, "Recent Philatelic Publications,"* Philatelic Literature Review, *1979. A review of Loren C. French's* Encyclopedia of Plate Varieties on U.S. Bureau-Printed Postage Stamps.

Plate varieties cause changes to the appearance of the printed stamp

"True plate varieties cause changes to the appearance of the printed stamp due to aberrations on the printing plate, and this is the only truism in their definition. A plate variety may be unique to a single pane position (plate damage, cracks, scratches, etc.), common to a few or many positions (relief breaks), or on every copy of a denomination (die flaws and engraver's errors). It is usually manifested by lines or areas of color where none was intended, but in the cases of relief breaks and short and damaged transfers just the opposite is true."

—*Loren C. "Cloudy" French, "The Plate Variety Specialist and His Language,"* The United States Specialist, *1977.*

A Sense of Proportion

"To the student of stamps each plate variety is of some importance but the collecting of 'ALL' plate varieties of one or all issues can be carried too far....We should be careful how far we go in collecting philatelic minutiae and try to retain a sense of proportion."

—*Max G. Johl,* United States Postage Stamps, 1902–1935, *1935.*

Where to Find More Information

- For a more complete understanding of how plate varieties come into existence, refer to James H. Baxter's *Printing Stamps by Line Engraving*.

- Loren C. (Cloudy) French is the acknowledged expert on plate varieties. His *Encyclopedia of Plate Varieties on U.S. Bureau-Printed Postage Stamps* is an indispensable reference for plate variety collectors.

- Max Johl's *United States Postage Stamps 1902-1935* is highly regarded for providing a wealth of information on plate varieties.

- For an analysis of the "Broken Hat" variety refer to Thomas Corette's "The 2-Cent Columbian 'Broken Hat,' Accidental or Deliberate?"

- To pursue the varieties of the 1¢ Franklin of 1851, consult Stanley B. Ashbrook's two-volume work *The United States One Cent Stamp of 1851-1857*.

- Carroll Chase wrote *The 3¢ Stamp of the United States 1851-1857 Issue*. Much of this book describes the plate varieties of those stamps.

Chapter 47
Stamps in Booklets
1900-1977

Stamps manufactured into booklet format can be divided into two major divisions. The "stapled era" from 1900 to 1977, which is presented here and the "folded era" from 1977 to date, which is presented in chapter 48.

The Bureau of Engraving and Printing (BEP) produced all stapled era booklets. Only six different plate layouts were used to print booklet panes in this 78-year period. There were only a small number of changes in the booklet manufacturing processes during this period.

Figure 1

Panes such as this one (279Be) were assembled, in 1900, into the first booklets issued.

The first booklets, issued in 1900, contained two, four, or eight panes of six 2¢ stamps (fig. 1). Booklet production was a labor-intensive operation. Stamps were printed one sheet at a time on a *flat plate press*. After the ink dried, the sheets were gummed and allowed to dry before individual sheets were fed into a perforator, once in each direction. Then, stacks of printed cover stock, waxed paper interleaving, and sheets of stamps were hand collated. Stacks of booklet "sandwiches" were then cut into strips, one booklet tall and ten booklets wide, on a guillotine cutter. Each strip was then inserted into a stapler that applied ten staples at a time. This operation was repeated to apply two staples per booklet. The strips were stacked up again and taken to a guillotine cutter where they were cut into stacks of individual booklets. The booklets were then packed into boxes for shipment to post offices. To help offset the added cost for manufacturing stamp booklets, the Post Office Department (POD) charged an extra 1¢ for each booklet sold.

Early booklet covers were filled with text providing information regarding postal rates and services (fig. 2). Over the years, many changes in the text occurred which most collectors ignored or overlooked. By 1910, the front cover of booklets had evolved to include various insignias (fig. 3), but the other three cover surfaces remained filled with information, sometimes so small that it was difficult to read without a magnifying glass. Changes on covers occurred frequently.

Figure 2

Outside front cover from 25¢ booklet (BIA Type I-e) used for 2¢ stamps.

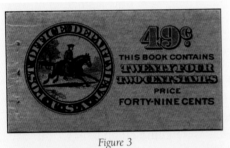

Figure 3

Outside front cover from 49¢ booklet with POD insignia (BIA Type II-a) used for 2¢ stamps.

In 1907, booklets with 1¢ stamps were issued (Scott BK10). A picture post card craze was sweeping the nation at that time, and these stamps paid their postage. In 1913, the first **combination booklets** were sold (BK34), containing equal numbers of 1¢ and 2¢ panes. During World War I, special booklets containing 300 stamps were made for the **American Expeditionary Force** (AEF) in France (BK64 and BK65). These booklets contained ten panes of 30 stamps (fig. 4). Few of the 1¢ and 2¢ booklet panes were saved, and it is doubtful if any complete 2¢ AEF booklets exist today. The letter rate was temporarily raised in 1917, so booklets with 3¢ stamps were issued.

Only two plate layouts were used for printing flat plate booklet panes during the first 25 years. Plates contained either 180-subjects (30 booklet panes) or 360-subjects (60 booklet panes). The smaller plates were used to help reduce wastage that resulted when the larger 360-subject sheets were processed. Horizontal and vertical **guide lines** divided each plate into quarters, so many of

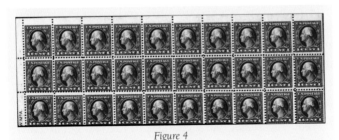

Figure 4

American Expeditionary Force (AEF) booklet pane (498f), position W-11, with initials of William A. McAleer (siderographer). Also shows the vertical guideline at the right.

the individual booklet panes show portions of those lines and thus allowed collectors to identify the plate positions (fig. 5). In addition, one pane from each plate impression contained a plate number in the stapling tab.

It was not until 1925 that booklet panes were produced on the **Stickney rotary presses** (ch. 36). By 1926, all booklet production, except for the 1928 Lindbergh air mail booklet (BKC1) had switched to the rotary press. While the plates were still 360-subjects like those used on the flat plate presses, the familiar guide lines were no longer needed and thus eliminated on all but the first two experimental plates. In addition, the plate number was no longer located in a stapling tab. Plate numbers were entered in the four corners of the plate and were intended to be removed in the trimming process. With this production change the only varieties left to collect were partial plate numbers on miscut panes (fig 6).

Figure 5

Examples of position panes from the flat bed press: 1¢ Washington (498e) position I (guideline at left), 2¢ Washington (499e) position B (split arrow and guideline at right, and 3¢ Washington (502b) position D (plate number in the tab).

Figure 6

Miscut partial plate number panes: 2¢ Washington (634d) position 1 with 100% of 19850 UL, and 3¢ Jefferson (807a), with a 3 mm wide vertical gutter, position 10 with 55% of 21996 UR.

Figure 7

Miscut 1¢ Washington panes (804b), with 2.5 mm gutter, showing EE dashes in gutter that runs down the middle of the web. Left pane is position 25, and right pane is position 26.

Figure 8

Miscut 3¢ Jefferson panes (807a). The left pane (3 mm gutter), printed before the BEP began using electric eye markings to control the on-line perforating, has a wide left margin without EE bars. The pane at the right (2.5 mm gutter) shows the complete EE bars in the left margin. Both panes are either position 11, 21, 31, or 41.

Figure 9

Set of six 2¢ Wright booklet panes (1280c) illustrating the different locations of the EE bars in the left margin. From left to right, positions 1, 11, 21, 31, 41, and 51.

In 1942, the BEP began making booklet plates with **electric eye bars** and **dashes** to improve the quality of perforating. These so-called EE markings were supposed to be trimmed off, but booklet collectors soon found examples on miscut panes. So, for the first time in 15 years, collectors again had something to seek besides plate numbers. There were twelve identifiable EE dash positions (fig. 7), but unlike the flat plate guide line positions, they were difficult to find, since they should have been trimmed off. The EE bars (fig. 8) were located in the same place until 1956, when the BEP began using the **dry printing** process on the new Huck press. While the dry-printed EE dash positions remained the same as on the earlier wet-printed panes, the EE bars were repositioned and thus appear in different places on each pane (fig. 9), making four collectible positions (six, if the two plate number positions are included).

The EE markings on the 360-subject plates remained constant from 1956 to 1976, so collectors continued to seek examples of miscut position panes, but they became harder to find as the BEP improved quality control.

Beginning in 1949, the BEP produced loose unstapled booklet panes for sale to collectors in order to allow first day covers to be prepared with panes that had the stapling tabs attached. Prior to 1949, panes were generally torn out of the booklets, greatly reducing the value of the first day covers. Many were unwilling to take the time to carefully remove the staples from a booklet in order to obtain complete booklet panes.

All booklets issued from 1900 until 1962 (except the two AEF booklets) were sold for 1¢ over face value to help defray the added cost of producing the booklets. However, with the advent of the 5¢ postage rate, the penny sur-charge was discontinued. This undoubtedly resulted in an increased demand for the booklets, so the BEP was continually seeking ways to increase production. At the same time, the POD was seeking to reduce costs by automating mail sorting operations. *Phosphor tagging* was applied to book-let stamps beginning in 1963 to allow new *facer*/canceller machinery to sort mail faster. Calcium silicate, which

Figure 10

Three different message labels used on 5¢ Washington panes (1213a/c). The 8¢ Jet Airliner Over Capital airmail panes (C64b/c) had similar filler labels, but since those panes contained horizontal format stamps, the arrangement of the words differs.

gives of a red-orange glow when exposed to shortwave ultraviolet light, was applied to air mail booklet panes. Regular booklet panes were tagged with zinc ortho-silicate, which glows yellow-green when exposed to UV light. The BEP also began using paper with optical brighteners in 1962; these panes are fluores-cent when viewed under longwave UV light (ch. 54).

In 1962 message *labels* were introduced on booklet panes. These filler labels were used to allow production of $1.00 booklets that could be sold in vending machines without the need to dispense change. Three different message labels (fig. 10), two of which promoted the new *Zip Code* system, were used during the next two years. A variety of other messages were used over the next 15 years. Information on the booklet cov-ers was also changed frequently.

While overlooked by many collectors, *Postal Insurance stamps*, issued between 1965 and 1985, only exist in booklet format (fig. 11). Insurance

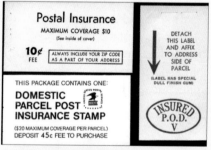

Figure 11

Front covers from the first (QI-1) and last (QI-5) Insurance booklets. At right is a complete booklet pane from the first Insurance booklet. The insurance stamp is at the bottom of the pane, with a row of roulettes just below the words "DULL FINISH GUM." Later insurance stamps had perforations rather than roulettes. Note that the 45¢ booklet cover has "vee" cuts at the left edge rather than staple holes.

booklets were only sold in vending machines as part of the POD's attempt to automate post offices in larger cities. Examples of insurance stamps used on cover are exceptionally difficult to find (fig. 12).

Figure 12

Insurance stamps were only valid for parcel post or airmail. This philatelic cover shows proper usage of an insurance stamp (QI-2).

In 1967, the BEP began making booklets with eight stamps per pane. Initial printings were made from 320-subject plates and no **marginal markings** are found unless the panes were miscut. However, the BEP soon switched to 400 subject plates and, for the first time, the EE bars and dashes were located in the stapling tabs of normally cut panes. This created seven new varieties (fig 13).

Figure 13

A set of 8¢ Eisenhower no-hole 400-subject panes showing all eight collectible positions. Panes without staple holes were made for use in preparing first day covers.

In addition, process marks, a series of ¾ inch long horizontal dashes printed in the gutter dividing the top and bottom halves of the sheet which may have served as a guide in the final bookbinding operation, could be found on miscut panes from both the 320- and 400-subject plates (fig. 14). Plate numbers were located in the four corners of the plates, but were rarely found on booklet panes (fig 15).

In 1971, experimental booklets were issued containing panes with a moisture-resistant dull gum. Dull gum had first been used in 1965 on the Postal Insurance booklet panes. The main benefit of dull gum was the elimination of the silicone interleaving required with the old shiny gum. The use of shiny gum was eliminated in 1972.

In 1975, the BEP discontinued the use of staples to hold booklets together. In their place, the BEP placed two "vee" notches into each booklet's selvage. Then the end of the unsevered, collated stack of covers and stamps was completely coated with a bookbinder's glue. This eliminated the need for the labor-intensive stapling operation, further reducing costs while increasing productivity. The special "no-hole" panes were still issued for first day cover servicing, so collectors must be careful when acquiring "no-hole" panes to be sure no "vee" cuts are located in the tab.

The end of the so-called stapled booklet era began in 1976 when the BEP started experimenting with the new *Goebel booklet forming machines*. These machines eliminated all the hand preparations that made booklet production so costly. By 1977, the first Goebel booklets were issued and a new era in booklet collecting began.

Figure 14

Miscut 320- and 400-subject booklet panes may show parts of one or two Process Marks at the top or bottom edges. Shown is 10¢ Jefferson Memorial (1510c) position 22 and "A" Non-denominated (1736a) position 27. Ten 400-subject Process Mark positions exist.

Figure 15

A 1¢ Jefferson pane (1278a), position 1, from a 400-subject plate, with fold-over showing 100% of plate 31775 at UL, and 13¢ Americana Issue (1595c) miscut position 5 with 40% of plate 37032 at UR. Such panes showing partial plate numbers are very scarce.

Notes on Collecting

Many collectors seek only a single example of each *Scott* numbered booklet pane, which have alpha suffixes in their catalogue numbers. Other collectors seek panes with plate numbers or the various marginal markings. A 1913 article by George Beans established a numbering system for flat plate booklet pane positions that is still used today, and the layout drawings of flat plates in *Scott* are based on Beans' work. Although they were in existence for more than two decades, booklet panes were not listed by *Scott* until 1923, when the first *U.S. Specialized Catalogue* debuted.

Still others collect **unexploded** booklets, which have catalogue numbers prefixed by a BK, or BKC for air mail. Prices of the early complete, unexploded, booklets are high. However, post World War II booklets are much more plentiful and less expensive. Still other collectors seek only booklet covers.

Once collectors were aware of all the booklet cover varieties, many began trying to obtain examples of every booklet variety. In 1917, C. K. B. Nevin proposed a cataloging system that applied to covers based on design and textual differences for each of the four booklet cover surfaces, not the complete booklet. His work became the basis for the Bureau Issues Association's (BIA) "Check List of the Postage Stamp Booklet Covers of the United States" initially published in 1955. For the first time, booklet collectors knew what to look for! Complete booklets were not listed in *Scott* until 1978. However even then *Scott* listings only told the reader how many booklet varieties existed for each *Scott*-listed booklet pane. Without the BIA checklists, collectors did not know what those varieties were. In 1995, Robert Furman published a comprehensive booklet catalog describing every complete booklet, with illustrations of the four cover surfaces.

While *Scott* illustrates outside front covers, the other three cover surfaces are ignored. The majority of booklets have differences on one or more surfaces, leading to confusion. In a footnote, *Scott* explains "when more than one combination of covers exists, the number of possible booklets is noted in parenthesis after the booklet listing." For example, BK14 is listed as existing in eleven different cover combinations. The only way to understand the cover differences was to use the "BIA/USSS Check List of the Postage Stamp Booklet Covers of the United States." While many people struggled to understand how to use the Checklists, they were the only way a person could determine for what to look. When Furman's booklet catalog was published, it became much easier since it listed the BIA Cover Types for each booklet, and contained reduced size images of all four booklet cover surfaces.

Attempts have been made to fake valuable booklets or booklet panes. The most dangerous fakes are the two AEF booklet panes, usually created from imperforate sheet stamps with fake perfs applied. Another common fake is BKC14, an untagged 8¢ air mail booklet with BIA Type AIR-IVb covers, usually made by reassembling parts from two different books.

It is possible to distinguish between single stamps from flat plate booklet panes and stamps from flat-plate sheets. Most, but not all, flat-plate booklet stamps have vertical watermarks, while sheet stamps have horizontal watermarks. Since most booklet panes were printed on paper with the grain running horizontally, while the grain is vertical on sheet stamps, and because of the manner in which paper dries, booklet stamps are slightly shorter and wider than sheet stamps. Distinguishing rotary press booklet stamps from rotary press sheet stamps is less complicated since all rotary booklet stamps will have one or two straight edges, while all rotary press sheet stamps, except coil waste issues, are perforated on all four sides.

Almanac

1900 – First booklets issued, containing 2¢ stamps.

1907 – First booklets containing 1¢ stamps.

1913 – First combination booklets, containing both 1¢ and 2¢ stamps.

1917 – Special booklets, with 30 stamps per pane, issued for use by American Expeditionary Forces in France during World War I.

1917 – First U.S. postage stamp booklet (BK62) is issued containing 3¢ stamps.

1926 – First booklets containing panes printed on the rotary press are issued.

1928 – First air mail booklets issued.

1942 – First use of electric eye markings on booklet plates.

1949 – First issuance of "no-hole" booklet panes for use on first day covers.

1956 – First "dry" printed booklet panes produced on the BEP's new Huck printing press.

1962 – One cent surcharge on selling price of booklets eliminated.

1962 – First use of a "filler" message label in a booklet pane.

1962 – First use of fluorescent paper for printing booklet panes.

1963 – First use of calcium silicate tagging on air mail booklet panes.

1963 – First use of zinc ortho-silicate tagging on regular postage booklet panes.

1965 – First booklet containing an Insurance stamp.

1967 – First booklets to contain eight stamps per pane, printed from 320 subject plates.

1969 – First use of 400 subject plates to print booklet panes containing eight stamps.

1971 – First use of dull gum on postage stamp booklet panes, eliminating interleaves.

1974 – First booklet containing both air mail and regular postage stamps.

1975 – First use of "vee" cuts and glue to hold collated booklet panes and covers together, eliminating the stapling process.

1977 – First booklets made on the BEP's new Goebel booklet forming machines (panes glued to single piece of cover stock which was then folded to create a booklet).

What Others Have Said

The "Department" will soon issue their first booklets
"The booklets containing stamps which the Department is soon to place in the hands of the public are making rapid progress. They are being turned out at the rate of 50,000 per day at present. The first order which calls for one million books will soon be completed and most of us think that this supply will last a very long time. The books are very neatly finished and contain a vast amount of information. The four pages of cover have been filled with valuable data regarding postal rates and information. The type used is so small that most people will require a magnifying glass to read it. One of the officials suggested to throw in a microscope with each purchase. Most of them believe that few people will take the time to read the entire volume. The sale of these books which is to begin May first, will probably be large at first, but as soon as the novelty wears off, there will be little demand for them, especially in the large cities, as the business men are rarely in the habit of carrying postage stamps in their pockets."

—*J. Murray Bartels, "Washington Notes," The Metropolitan Philatelist, 1900. A wonderfully inaccurate prediction about the new booklet panes and their future, by one of philately's leading dealers of the time.*

About the first official stamp books
"When the first official Bureau stamp books were issued two methods of stapling were used. One set of books has been seen with single staples, and the others with double staples. The single staples varied in length, some have been seen

with staples about one-half inch long, and others with a single staple nearly ³/₄"
long. The format on the cover of many of these specimen books reads the same.
The type appears to have been typewritten throughout with the exception of the
number of stamps contained in the book. That appears to be printed...Some of
the books had an improvement made in the covers in that the covers were
scored beneath the staples to form a hinge, and several different colors of waxed
interleaving was used."

—*Oliver J. Williams*, "Booklets and Booklet Panes," The United States Specialist,
1945.

The "A.E.F." booklet panes are the very rarest
"In September, 1917, the Post Office shipped to Europe special booklet panes
for use by personnel of the American Expeditionary Force and other Americans
involved in the war (Red Cross, YMCA, etc.). The initial shipment consisted of
3,000 each of one-cent and two-cent booklets, containing ten panes of 30
stamps. In October, Congress voted to allow active members of the armed
forces to send first class mail from Europe without payment of regular postage.
Thus the need for stamps by the A.E.F. was practically eliminated....Accordingly,
no more of the special booklets were prepared, and the few panes of the original
shipment which survived are now quite rare, especially the two-cent panes.
A.E.F. stamps used on cover are even rarer, as most such covers were likely to
have been discarded by the recipients."

—*Richard F. Larkin*, Determining the genuineness of United States 'A.E.F.' Booklet
Panes, *1984.*

The Presidential Booklets – at long last
"On the last day of November, the Post Office Department made its long awaited
announcement of first day sale arrangements for the coil and booklet pane varieties of the Presidential series. Of most importance the announcement settles
once and for all the recurring rumor that the P.O. would not service first day
covers. The Department has announced it will service covers, but states that it
cannot give assurance the stamps affixed to covers will be of the usual selected
centering. This reservation is due to the fact that...[with booklet panes] due to
the manner of manufacture, [they] are frequently not only off-center but cut
badly so that margins are not uniform....The booklet panes include 1¢, 2¢ and
3¢ denominations...All covers with booklet panes will bear the hand cancels
since machine cancellations are not practical on such large items."

—*"Presidential Coils and Booklets in January,"* Linn's Weekly Stamp News, *1938.*

Where to Find More Information

- *U.S. Booklets and Booklet Panes, 1900–1978, Volume 1: Flat Plate Regular Issues* by Donald B. Littlefield and Sam Frank treats flat plate booklets in the designated time period. Additional volumes were in preparation in 2006.

- *Discovering U. S. Rotary Booklet Pane Varieties 1926-1978* by Bruce Mosher provides exceptional information about rotary press booklet pane varieties.

- *An Illustrated Color Catalog of U.S. Postal and Non-Postal Booklet Covers Produced by the BEP from 1900-1978*, edited by Michael O. Perry is the definitive source of information for booklet cover varieties.

- *Research Paper #16 – Postal Insurance Booklets (1965 –1985)* by Alan Moll contains detailed information about the regular and revalued Insurance booklets.

Chapter 48

Stamps in Booklets

Since 1977

In 1977 a new era began in the story of U.S. stamp **booklets**. It is an era characterized by rapid innovation in the production of booklets, and by an explosive growth both in the number of booklets issued, and in their themes. These booklets have honored such diverse topics as Stamp Collecting (*Scott* BK153), Fishing Flies (BK 189) and Daffy Duck (3306).

Figure 1

This is the perf 10 version of the first booklet made on the Goebel booklet-forming machine (BK132). The pane (1623Bc) was attached to covers printed by the machine. The short vertical mark in the tab is called a Length Register Mark (LRM), while the line that runs across the tab is the Cross Reference Line (CRL). These electric-eye marks were used to control perforating during the manufacturing process.

Goebel Booklets

In 1977 the Bureau of Engraving and Printing (BEP) introduced revolutionary new booklets produced on booklet forming machines made by the West German firm of Goebel. These Flag and Capitol booklets (BK131 and BK132), were the first to have two different stamps on the same pane (1623a and 1623Bc, fig. 1). They also introduced the era of folded booklet panes, following 77 years of the booklets being stapled together.

The last stapled era postage stamp booklet was the 1978 "A" Rate issue (BK133). Those booklets had been produced prior to the introduction of the Goebel booklets, and had been stored for use when postage rates increased from 13¢ to 15¢. The last stapled era booklet, a 45¢ *Postal Insurance booklet* (Q15), was produced in 1981.

By the mid-1960s, as labor costs were rising, the BEP began considering new technology that would provide more efficient booklet production. The solution adopted in the 1970s was the Goebel booklet-forming machine. This machine eliminated all the time-consuming and expensive hand labor previously required to make booklets. The Goebel machine created a new kind of booklet, with panes that were

Figure 2

A 1978 Oliver Wendell Holmes pane (1288Bc) from a Goebel formed booklet (BK117A), exhibiting two joint lines as a result of miscutting.

glued to a single piece of cardboard cover that was then was folded and sealed shut.

The new Goebel booklet forming machines could do almost everything except print stamps! Stamps that had been printed on a **web** of pre-gummed paper were mounted on a Goebel machine. The machine then perforated the web, and slit it into strips to provide the number of panes needed for the booklet in production. The machine printed covers, and attached the panes to them. The machine was capable of making booklets with virtually any number of panes, in different pane sizes, and with different stamp sizes and orientations.

Unlike **plate layouts** during the previous 77 years, there were no standard plate layouts used for the stamps in the Goebel formed booklets. As a result, collectors often did not know what varieties of **marginal markings** might be available in each new booklet. Plate **joint lines** (fig. 2) were found in five Goebel booklets that contained panes printed using two rotary press plates: Oliver W. Holmes (BK117A), Windmills (BK135), "B" Non-denominated (BK136), American Wildlife (BK137), and Rocky Mountain Bighorn (BK142). However, by 1985, virtually all booklet panes were printed by seamless **cylinders**, making joint lines a thing of the past.

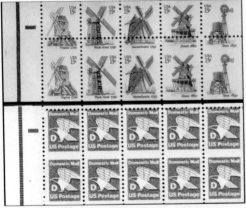

Figure 3

Misperforated panes such as these (1742a and 2113a), are the most common oddities found in Goebel booklets.

The BEP's Goebel booklet making machines did not create many **errors, freaks, and oddities**, but there were some. The most common was a misperforated pane. Occasionally a pane was so badly misperforated that the result was imperforate between pairs (fig. 3). An unusual perforation error occurred on some "G Rate" booklets (BK220) when perforations were mistakenly applied to

Chapter 48 | Stamps in Booklets, Since 1977

the bottom edge of the pane (fig. 4). A few *miscut* booklet panes have been found showing *electric eye* markings intended to be trimmed off (fig. 5). A few Roses booklets (BK134) were found with both panes imperforate.

In 1980, booklets began appearing with stamps that were not of traditional size. The Windmills booklet (BK135) was the first of several with small size stamps, made in an effort to reduce paper costs. However, the public disapproval of the tiny stamps resulted in the Postal Service returning to the traditional size. Commemorative size stamps soon appeared in Flag Over Capitol booklets (BK144 and BK145), and various stamp formats were sometimes found within the same booklet pane, such as the 1987 Special Occasions booklet (BK155).

Figure 4

This "G Rate" pane (2883a) with perforations along the bottom edge is from a $3.20 Goebel booklet (BK220). Whoever set up the perforating unit during one of the production runs forgot to retract that row of pins.

In 1981, the BEP began printing a *plate number* in the selvage *tab* of at least one pane in each booklet. It was discovered that the large plate numbers in the American Wildlife booklet (BK137), and the Flag and Anthem booklet (BK138), were confusing the electric eyes during the perforation process. The large numbers were replaced with tiny ones beginning with Flag Over Supreme Court booklet (BK139). These smaller numbers are similar to those found on modern plate number coils (ch. 50). Initially, only the top pane in multi-pane booklets contained a plate number, but some "reversed assembly" Bighorn Sheep and "D" Rate booklets (BK142 and BK143) were made with the plate number on the bottom pane. Beginning with the $2.20 Flag Over Capitol Dome booklet (BK145), the BEP printed a plate number on every pane in each booklet.

In 1983, an Express Mail booklet (BK140B) was issued containing three $9.35 stamps, having a $28.05 face value (fig. 6). When the rate increased to $10.75 in 1985, a $32.25 booklet (BK148) was issued. The $10.75 stamp was reissued in 1989, printed from new plates and in new covers (BK149).

Figure 5
A miscut 1978 Rose pane (1737a) showing EE dashes.

Figure 6

A $28.05 Express Mail booklet pane (1909a).

Beyond Goebel

By 1988, the BEP was unable to keep up with the demand for booklets. As a result it reverted to making some booklets the old fashioned way – by hand. The first handmade booklet (BK156) contained panes made from specially perforated Flag & Fireworks sheet stamp stock (2276). A special press run produced additional stamps for use in these booklets, and they contain a plate number found only in the booklets (as opposed to being found on sheet stamps). In 1988, in a further attempt to meet demand and to reduce costs, the USPS contracted with the **American Bank Note Company** to produce two 1988 Pheasant booklets (BK158 and BK159).

Beginning in 1991 booklets were being manufactured in many different ways as various private printers produced more of them. Meanwhile the BEP continued to make booklets both on the Goebel machines and by hand. Collectors discovered many miscut booklets, some showing marginal markings never seen on normal panes (fig. 7). Booklet panes were produced with selvage tabs at the right

Figure 7

An unusual 1989 Christmas pane (2429a) created when a strip of ten glued and folded booklets were cut at an angle.

side for the 1991 Honoring Those Who Served booklet (BK190) and down the middle for the 1988 Special Occasions booklet (BK165, fig. 8). Several booklets, such as the 1991 Fishing Flies booklet (BK189) produced by the American Banknote Company, had different plate numbers on each pane. To the frustration of collectors, the private printers refused to share any manufacturing information with them, so collectors did not know what was available to collect.

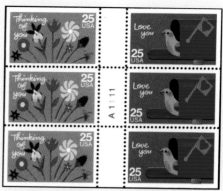

Figure 8

The 1988 Special Occasions booklet (BK165) is the only booklet made with the selvage in the center of the panes.

In 1989, the USPS addressed one of the major complaints collectors had voiced since the BEP started making booklets on the Goebel booklet forming machines. Beginning with the Steamboats pane (2409a) the USPS began selling mint, never-folded booklet panes for making first day covers, and for collectors who wanted intact (unfolded) booklet panes. Also in 1989, the BEP began placing *registration* marks in the tabs of some booklet issues (fig. 9), further increasing collector interest in unfolded panes.

Figure 9

Examples of marginal markings found on never-folded Garden Flowers panes (2764a). Many of the booklets produced by the BEP after 1989 contained panes with a wide variety of marginal markings in the selvage tab.

Convertible Booklets

Self-adhesive convertible booklets appeared in 1989 when the Eagle and Shield booklet was issued (2431a). Available in only a few cities, it was sold at a 50¢ premium over the face value. Believing there was a public demand for the new self-adhesive stamps (ch. 41), the USPS had three different contractors produce the next Eagle and Shield convertible booklets in 1992 (2595a, 2596a, and 2597a). However sales continued to lag even though the premium had been lowered to 7¢. Once the USPS eliminated the premium, sales increased dramatically.

In 1990, another new form of convertible booklet appeared – the Automatic Teller Machine (ATM) sheetlet. The first two ATM sheetlets, the 25¢ Flag (2475a) and "F" Non-denominated flag (2522a) were printed on plastic in order to meet the demanding specification that the thicknesses of each pane exactly match the thickness of U.S. currency. This was necessary in order for ATMs to successfully dispense the sheetlets. The plastic stamps presented a problem, for paper recyclers, since the plastic stamps clogged up their processes. A year later, ways were found to print ATM stamps on paper, saving money for the U.S.P.S., and satisfying the requirements of the recycling industry. The first two ATM panes did not have a peel strip, so there was no way to fold them in half. Beginning with the 1991 Liberty Torch pane (2531Ab), peel strips were added to panes, which when removed by the purchaser, facilitated folding the pane into a "booklet." By definition, all ATM sheetlets are now considered to be convertible booklets.

In 1991, the supply of booklets continued to lag behind demand, and the USPS continued to seek ways to reduce costs. This led to more and more booklets being produced by private contractors. In that year the USPS released two $2.90 "F" Rate booklets (BK182 and BK184) with the same stamp designs, made by two different printers, the BEP and KCS Industries.

Convertible booklets certainly did not seem like booklets in the traditional definition. They were simply small sheets of stamps with the potential to be folded into a "booklet" if the purchaser so desired. Nevertheless technology was fast making traditional booklets obsolete. By the end of the twentieth century traditional booklets, panes attached to a piece of cardboard cover, were things of the past. As the new century dawned, all booklets were self-adhesive convertible booklets. This included both ATM booklets, and self-adhesive vending booklets, the later being nothing more than small convertible booklets that have been folded and sealed shut by the manufacturer.

MDI Booklets

By 1996, a shortage of vending machine books resulted in the USPS contracting with Minnesota Diversified Industries (MDI) to make vending machine booklets by hand. While all MDI booklets appear to have identical blue covers (fig. 10), there are minor differences. The covers all have a canted square opening cut in the front cover, which allows portions of the enclosed stamps to be seen. The back cover of most MDI books contains text identifying the contents. Panes of stamps were folded by hand, one pane at a time, and glued to the inside of the covers.

Figure 10

The MDI booklets exist in countless variations. Initial $9.60 Pink Rose booklets (BK178A) contained a pane of 16 self-adhesive stamps, glued to the cover, along with a loose pane of 14 stamps. To keep everything together, each booklet was wrapped in cellophane, a time consuming and expensive process. Because they jammed the vending machines, a change was soon made and the booklets were all sealed shut with a round self-adhesive sticker. Many MDI books, like the American Dolls (BK266), contained panes made from surplus sheet stamp stock.

The first MDI books, released in March 1996, containing Pink Rose stamps (BK178A and BK178E), were made with one or two panes of self-adhesive stamps cut from rolls of stock originally intended for production into 20-stamp convertible booklets. This required special die-cutting mats and resulted in significant waste due to the incompatible plate layouts. In 1996, beginning with the Fulbright Scholarship stamps (BK246), MDI began making these makeshift vending machine booklets with panes made from surplus sheet stamps with regular gum. Since those sheets were torn apart in a variety of ways, numerous booklet varieties exist, based on the presence or absence of marginal markings. While MDI attempted to assemble each booklet issued the same way, most issues exist with non-standard assemblies. Some plate numbers were found on MDI booklet panes of 1995 Love stamps (BK244) and 1997 American Dolls stamps (BK266) that are unknown on the regularly issued sheet stamps. The last MDI booklets were issued in 1999, containing American Glass and Famous Trains stamps (BK277 and BK278).

An End and a Beginning

In 1996, the BEP made a Flag Over Porch booklet (BK228) with self-adhesive stamps attached to cardboard covers. Even though most postal customers preferred these BEP produced booklets to the privately printed large convertible booklets, the USPS had already decided to phase the BEP out of the stamp printing business. A similar Flag Over City booklet (BK276), issued in 1999, was the last booklet made by the BEP.

In 1999, the Tropical Flowers booklet (3313b) was the first double-sided convertible booklets issued. These booklets reduced the amount of backing paper required by 50%, thus answering one of the complaints the public had about self-adhesive stamps.

In 2000, the USPS released its first **Prestige** booklet (BK279). It contained two panes of Submarine stamps of various denominations, along with several pages of related information. It sold for face value. However, the 2004 Lewis & Clark prestige booklet (BK297) was sold for $1.55 over face value.

Notes on Collecting

The Goebel booklets created a challenge for collectors since the panes were glued to each other and then to the cardboard cover stock. It was impossible to remove a pane without damaging the gum in the selvage tab. Some collectors and dealers therefore simply tore the panes out of the booklet, but this left the panes without their all-important tabs, which greatly depreciated their value!

There are ways to remove Goebel panes with minimal damage to the tabs. Dull gum panes are the easiest since dry heat will soften the adhesive and allow the panes to be peeled away from the covers. While a steam iron will work, never use it with the steam setting on, or the pane will be damaged. Some collectors simply heat the tab area by holding the booklet up against an incandescent (tungsten) light bulb. Removing panes with shiny gum requires more care and patience since water must be used. Some have been successful with using steam to moisten and soften the glue holding the tabs to the cover. Another method is to insert toothpicks between each pane, as close as possible to the tabs, in order to keep them separated. Then, dip the tab end of the booklet into a glass of warm water, keeping the toothpicks above the water surface. Care must be taken to not allow water to wick up into the portion of the panes not attached to the covers or additional serious gum disturbance will result. Once water has soaked through the tab and softened the glue, the panes can be carefully peeled away. Removing an intact pane from a cardboard cover will always result in some gum disturbance on the tab, but that is preferable to a pane without any tab at all. Many collectors have chosen to collect the booklets intact to avoid the tedious process required to remove a pane.

Since almost all Goebel books were made by gluing one or more panes onto a single piece of cardboard cover stock, and then folded in half, the row of perforations where the pane was folded was weakened. As a result, many booklet panes have simply fallen apart due repeated opening and closing. A basic rule all collectors should follow is to either leave their Goebel booklets closed, or open them and never close them.

Many multi-pane booklets exist with marginal markings or plate numbers hidden on the bottom pane(s). Trying to lift the upper pane(s) to check for them will often result in damage to the booklet. A better method is to view the booklet when held in front of a high-intensity light. This may not work as well on books with four panes, or when the panes are printed on clay-coated paper, but it is the method to use first.

Scott lists the different plate numbers found in booklets, but it does not describe the marginal marking varieties. Information about marginal marking varieties is best obtained from *USSS Research Paper Number 2 – Folded Style Booklet Checklist*.

Because over 1,000 different varieties exist, it is unlikely that anyone can ever assemble a complete collection of varieties of MDI booklets. There will likely never be a definitive listing, although the *USSS Research Paper Number 2 – Folded Style Booklet Checklist* is the most comprehensive resource available.

Almanac

1977 – First booklets with two different values of stamps in same pane; also, the first multi-color stamps issued in booklet form (BK131 and BK132).

1978 – Last postage stamp booklet issued using the old manufacturing methods.

1980 – First booklet issued with non-standard size stamps (BK135).

1981 – First booklet with a plate number on at least one pane in every book (BK138).

1983 – First Express Mail stamps issued in booklet format (BK140B).

1985 – Postal Insurance booklets removed from sale.

1985 – First use of cover stock not printed on Goebel machine (BK146).

1987 – First booklet made with different format stamps (BK155).

1987 – First booklet made by hand using sheet stamp stock, Flag and Fireworks (BK156).

1988 – First booklet not made by BEP (BK158).

1988 – First booklet with selvage in the center of the panes (BK165).

1989 – First regular production of mint, never-folded booklet panes (2409a).

1989 – First self-adhesive convertible booklet is issued (2431a).

1990 – First ATM self-adhesive sheetlet printed on plastic (2475a).

1991 – First ATM self-adhesive sheetlet printed on paper (2531Ab).

1991 – First booklets with the same stamps are produced by different companies (BK182 and BK184).

1993 – First booklet with two different sizes of booklet panes (BK204).

1995 – First booklet with two plate numbers on each pane (BK233).

1996 – First booklet containing two panes of self-adhesive stamps (BK228).

1996 – First self-adhesive Vending Booklet (BK237).

1996 – First MDI vending booklets containing self-adhesive stamps (BK178A & BK178E).

1996 – First MDI vending booklet containing panes made from sheet stamps (BK246).

1997 – First booklet intentionally issued with an imperforate stamp (3138).

1998 – Last convertible booklet produced by the BEP (3244a).

1999 – First convertible booklet with custom die-cutting for stamps (3274a).

1999 – Last multi-pane booklet with cardboard covers (BK276).

1999 – First convertible booklet issued with stamps on both sides (3313b).

2000 – First Prestige Booklet issued (BK279).

What Others Have Said

Two Different Perforations on New $1 Booklet (Scott 1623a and 1623B)

"Boy, what a surprise this one has turned out to be! For starters, the final pane did not look much like the advance photos sent out by the USPS. Then the first day panes available at the INTERPEX post office were without tab! Next came the biggest surprise – the first day panes are perforated 10 x 10 while the regular panes issued in the booklet are perforated 11 x 10 ½! So in fact we have two different panes issued the same day. Now comes the question: Are the first day panes true booklet panes? After all, they were never issued in booklet form, but were rather a special for the first day ceremonies only."

—*Floyd L. Lickins, "Booklets and Booklet Panes," The United States Specialist, 1977. (The perf 10 x 10 booklets were eventually issued in smaller quantities to meet collector demand.)*

Removing Panes from Folded Era Booklets

"Collectors should be careful to obtain full pane specimens of all the current and future [post 1977] panes. Collectors must remove each pane's selvage from its booklet cover (or adjacent pane) by very carefully soaking, steaming or dry iron-ing it off. These removal techniques can be mastered after some experimental trial and error attempts but even the best attempts may leave the pane's selvage slightly wrinkled and/or gumless. But these minor flaws seem to be acceptable by today's dealers/collectors. Everyone is encouraged to make or buy the best selvage specimens obtainable as condition of these panes will be much more important in the future."

—*Bruce Mosher*, Discovering U.S. Rotary Press Booklet Pane Varieties, *1979.*

Many experiments tried in search of the best modern booklet format

"Less successful with the public were the $3.60 booklet of 18¢ wildlife stamps [BK137] issued in 1981 and the $4 booklet of 20¢ Bighorn Sheep stamps [BK142] issued in 1982. Their tiny monochrome designs did not appeal to the public, so the 10-subject pane format was abandoned. The next regularly book-let stamps intended for retail merchant sales was the most ambitious of all, the $4.40 booklet of 22¢ Seashells issued in 1985 [BK 146]. As originally issued on April 4 its covers consisted of bright, full color reproductions of seashells in a design that "floated". To collect the entire picture, seven booklets were required. As attractive as this was, it was expensive to produce, because the covers were printed on a separate offset press, and then loaded into the Goebel equipment for assembly. Before the year was out, a simpler two color cover design [BK 147], printed on the Goebel machine, replaced the original."

—*Ken Lawrence, "A closer look at collecting modern U.S. stamp booklets,"* Scott's Stamp Monthly, *2002.*

The secret is in making sure the tab is intact

"Most collectors praised USPS for issuing its first multicolor booklet stamps, but cursed the Goebel equipment designers for creating booklets with panes glued to the covers, and not easily removed from them. In bold type Scott says, "Booklet panes with tabs attached to the cover with adhesive instead of staples are valued on the basis of the tab being intact. Minor damage on the back of the tab due to removal from the booklet does not affect the value." Beginning in 1989 with the 25¢ Steamboats booklet pane [2409a], USPS provided unbound never-folded panes as separate products for collectors, putting an end to that problem. As with stapled booklets, those issued in the new format are more varied than Scott descriptions indicate. Besides perforation differences...[various color covers, changes in cover text, and a variety of marginal markings make for a special challenge in collecting all varieties]."

—*Ken Lawrence, "A closer look at collecting modern U.S. stamp booklets,"* Scott's Stamp Monthly, *2002.*

The first Prestige Booklet honors submarines and the U.S. Navy

"A century of pride, heroism and incredible technological achievement will be honored...with the release of five United States stamps honoring the submarine service of the U.S. Navy. The stamps will be issued as a so-called prestige booklet that includes two panes of five stamps, as well as photographs and supplementary text [16 pages] that trace the development and certain historical milestones of the U.S. submarine program... Each pane in the prestige booklet has a face value of $4.90....the booklet will be sold for the face value -- $9.80 – of the 10 stamps....It is likely that these colorful, historically inspired stamps will see little use on mail. The prestige book format seems tailor-made to appeal to anyone with an interest in submarines, whether military or civilian. Most of the booklets will probably be saved intact....[making] it difficult to find used examples of the...stamps, especially on cover."

—*Charles Snee, "Submarine prestige booklet due March 27; 33c stamp offered in booklet, panes of 20," Linn's Stamp News, 2000.*

Where to Find More Information

- *Folded Style Booklet Checklist* by Michael O. Perry contains detailed information about booklets from 1977 to date, including many plate layout drawings showing how the different booklets were made.

- *The 1999 Comprehensive Catalogue of United States Stamp Booklets* by Robert Furman.

- *Catalog of United States Self-Adhesive Stamps* by Alan M. Malakoff provides lists of plate numbers and other detailed information, along with prices, for every self-adhesive stamp issued between 1974 and 1999.

- "BIA Cover Numbers for Folded-style Booklets" by Michael O. Perry.

- The relevant volumes of *Linn's U.S. Stamp Yearbook*, edited by Fred Boughner or George Amick.

Chapter 49

Stamps in Coil Rolls

1907–1980

Stamps rolled into coils have been enormously popular with the mailing public through the years, especially with business mailers. This chapter deals with coil stamps produced by the Bureau of Engraving and Printing (BEP) from 1908 through 1980, and with the coil stamps - and the perforations applied to them - manufactured privately by the makers of stamp **vending and affixing** machines from imperforate sheets of BEP printed stamps.

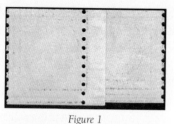

Figure 1
A "paste-up" pair of coil stamps.

BEP Coils: 1908–1980

While there were many different coil stamps produced between the years 1908–1980, there are only two noteworthy types. They are *flat plate* printed coils, first issued in 1908; and rotary press printed coils, first issued in 1914. Flat plate coils were printed one sheet at a time, with 400 stamps per sheet, from a flat printing plate, while rotary press stamps were printed on continuous rolls from rotating cylinders.

Pasting strips of stamps together created rolls of flat plate coil stamps. Rotary press coils were simply cut to the desired length after the **web** had been perforated and slit into strips. Despite numerous technological advances during the twentieth century, the basic process of producing rotary press coil stamps remained essentially unchanged until 1980.

The first BEP coil stamps to appear, in 1908, were created from imperforate sheets of 400 stamps. These sheets were first perforated 12 in one direction, then slit into strips of 20 stamps. These vertical or horizontal strips were then pasted together, using the margins at the top and bottom or sides of the sheets, to form coil rolls of 500 (25 strips) and 1,000 stamps (50 strips). The point where two sheets were joined together is known as a *paste-up* (fig. 1).

Both imperforate and perforated coil stamps appeared in either **endwise** (vertical strips) or **sidewise** (horizontal strips) coil rolls. Vertical strips have horizontal perforations while horizontal strips have vertical perforations.

At first coil stamps were assembled by hand, but within a year the BEP developed a machine to automate the process. The 1909 fiscal year report of the Third Assistant Postmaster General contained the following description of the machine: "[It] is of simple and effective construction and performs the work of about ten operatives....Under the old method of coiling the cost is from 6¢ to 12¢ per coil. During the past year the demand for coiled stamps grew to such an extant [sic] as to make this expense something of a burden and it became necessary to charge it to the users. With the new machine, however, the coiling is done at a cost of a fraction of a cent and the extra charge can probably be discontinued. If a sufficient number of the machines can be installed during the coming year it should be possible to supply coiled stamps for general purposes."

The first BEP coil stamps were endwise (*Scott* 316 and 321), sidewise (318 and 322) and imperforate (314V, 314H, 320V, and 320H) coil versions of the 1¢ Franklin and 2¢ Washington of the Series of 1902 (ch. 8), as well as an endwise-only version (317) of the 5¢ Lincoln design of the same series. These coils, released in February, July, and October 1908, were considered by the BEP to be experimental. All are extremely rare today because most collectors of the time neither knew of the existence of these coil stamps, nor were aware of their significance.

By 1914, coil stamps were quite popular with the stamp using public and with the help of the early coil-assembling machine, had become a regular part of BEP stamp production. Flat plate coils are known with perforations measuring 12, 8½, and 10. Flat plate production could not keep up with the demand for these enormously popular stamps, which led to the introduction of rotary press-printed stamps in 1914, which were printed in large rolls, also called webs, eliminating the need to paste strips together.

Before the Stickney rotary press began printing stamps in 1914, it underwent extensive testing and development. In 1912, while still in its testing phase, the third assistant postmaster general's report made the following note regarding the early success of the new Stickney rotary press: "The machine also gums the stamps as they are printed and an exceedingly rapid perforating device has been designed for use in connection with it..."

Both flat plate and rotary presses were used to print Washington-Franklin coils. Because of the basic differences between printing from a flat plate and a curved one, flat plate and rotary press stamp designs have different dimensions. Rotary press stamps will always be slightly wider or taller than their flat plate counterparts.

Perforations on rotary press coils of the Washington-Franklin Series are all gauge 10. Thus, all coil issues with size 8½ or 12 perforations are flat plate issues. Rotary press coils were not made with these gauge perforations. Coils with perf 10 measurements can originate from either flat plate or rotary press printings.

Coil production continued to be important as part of both the Series of 1922 and 1938 Presidential Series (fig. 2); however, there were no significant coil varieties during those years. However, the Liberty series, which was introduced in 1954, brought notable changes in coil production. There are the *wet* and *dry* paper types, significant color and plate varieties, ***phosphor tagging*** as well as shiny and dull gum varieties. The most significant Liberty Series coil types were created as a result of the switch from Stickney coilers to the Huck coiling equipment. There are **small-hole** varieties of several of the Liberty Series denominations that came from the Huck coilers, including the extremely scarce 2½¢ Bunker Hill type. Although both the

Figure 2

A Stickney coiler shown processing Presidential Series coil stamps, circa 1940.

large-hole and small-hole types measure 10 on a standard perforation gauge, the diameter of the holes is different, due to different size of perforation pins.

According to the BEP, the Huck coiling machines arrived at the BEP in early 1957, and were placed in regular production January 27, 1958, although coils with small holes did not appear until 1960. The arrival of the Huck coilers was fortuitous as the Post Office Department's (POD) effort to popularize coil stamps (with particular emphasis placed on a new 100-stamp size), as well as the much more extensive use of fractional-denominated coil stamps by large mailers, resulted in BEP coil-producing capabilities being taxed more than ever before.

The Huck coiler consisted of three functional components: a roll-to-roll examiner, a perforator/slitter/coiler, and a wrapper. The Huck coilers processed stamps, with the printed side down, from a full web, into individually wrapped coil rolls of 100, 500, or 3,000 stamps (and later 10,000-stamp rolls). First, the printed web was placed in the examining component where an employee examined it as it unwound. The machine had built-in provisions for detecting and removing imperfect work, as well as the automatic re-joining of the severed ends. The examined web was then placed in the actual coiler, which perforated the stamps with a guillotine action, slit the work by rows (usually 18) and formed the individual coils. Those coil rolls containing flags applied during the examining process were automatically diverted at this point into a separate bin. The non-flagged coils were conveyed to the third station that wrapped each coil in transparent plastic film and printed and applied a label indicating the contents and

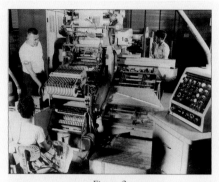

Figure 3

A Huck coiler shown processing 5¢ Washington coils of 1962.

sales price of the item. Virtually all coil stamps produced from the early 1960s through 1980 were processed on the Huck coilers (fig. 3).

Vending and Affixing Machine Perforations: 1907-1927

In the early part of the twentieth century, from approximately 1907 through 1927, a number of private companies produced coil stamps with proprietary perforations for use in their own stamp vending machines or stamp affixing machines. The elements which define these coil stamps are that they are all (1) made from regularly issued imperforate U.S. stamps, (2) with perforations applied by private companies, and (3) these perforations enabled the stamps to be used in either a stamp vending or stamp affixing machine. The third element is critical as perforations applied to stamps to facilitate their use in a vending or affixing machine distinguish them from all other perforations applied to imperforate stamps for any other reason. More than 240 collectable varieties exist in this large and complex category. They may be found listed in detail in *Scott* under "Vending and Affixing Machine Perforations."

Figure 4

A Schermack stamp affixing machine.

Although vending and affixing machine stamps are always grouped together, vending machines developed independently from affixing machines, served very different commercial purposes and required stamps with different kinds of perforations. The stamps are connected philatelically only because, in the early part of the twentieth century, both types of machines required stamps with special non-government perforations to work successfully.

The first stamp-affixing machine was patented in the U.S. in 1858. By 1906, patent applications for over 100 stamp-affixing machines had been filed. The tremendous growth in commercial mail during the late nineteenth century and early twentieth century made rapid methods of stamping and sealing letters a commercial necessity. An example of a stamp affixing machine, a Schermack, is shown is Figure 4.

Stamp vending machines developed later, with the first one patented in the U.S. in 1889. More than half of these early vending machines sold stamps from a roll made from regular perforated stamps. The rest of these vending machines sold stamps in folders or envelopes. In 1905 the POD became interested in selling stamps at face value in vending machines to serve the public in more places twenty-four hours a day. The POD encouraged the development of these machines and in 1907 selected six machines for extensive testing. Although the POD completed the tests and selected the United States Automatic Vending Company machine as the best, the POD never purchased any vending machines for general post office use for almost thirty years. An example of the United States Automatic Vending Company machine is shown in Figure 5.

Figure 5

A stamp vending machine of the U.S. Automatic Vending Company.

At the same time the Post Office was testing vending machines, it became sympathetic to the complaints of both vending and affixing machine manufacturers that the then current perf. 12 stamps were too fragile to be used by machines. In response, imperforate sheets of the current 1¢ and 2¢ regular issues (314 and 320) were issued to manufacturers on October 2, 1906. The first private vending and affixing machine coils were made in 1907 by the Detroit Mailing Machine Company (later called the Schermack Mailing Machine Company and then the Mailometer Company) and the International Vending Machine Company. The Post Office quickly recognized the utility of the coil format and issued its own coils on February 18, 1908. In response to the availability of coil stamps from the Post Office, most manufactures abandoned making their own coils. The period of private vending machine coils ended by 1915. Private affixing machine coils continued to be made much longer, until late 1927.

Vending Machine Perforations

Collectors recognize vending machine perforations from three companies. They are listed in *Scott*. The International Vending Machine Company was the first vending machine manufacturer to perforate imperforate sheets of stamps purchased from the Post Office to make its own stamps. After BEP coil stamps became available the company stopped making its own coil stamps and went out of business in 1909.

The next and most successful vending machine company to make its own coil stamps was the United States Automatic Vending Company of New York City. The company first tried using BEP coil stamps but began making its own coil stamps in late 1908. U.S. Automatic Vending developed three different types of perforations, known to collectors as Types I, II, and III (fig. 6). They also sold stamps in folded manila paper pockets from it vending machines (fig. 7). By late 1914, or early 1915, the company ceased production of its own perforated coils.

Figure 6

U.S. Automatic Vending Machine Company perforation type II.

Figure 7

A pocket of stamps sold from a U.S. Automatic Vending Machine.

The third and last vending machine company to make its own coil stamps was the Brinkerhoff Stamp Vending Machine Company, formed in 1909 with a manufacturing plant in Sedalia, Missouri. Around 1910 it relocated its plant to Lyons, Iowa. Brinkerhoff used two basic types of perforations, known as Types I and II, with three sub-varieties of Type II. The Brinkerhoff Company ceased perforating its own stamps about 1913.

Affixing Machine Companies

The story of coil stamps affixed by machine is almost entirely the story of stamps developed for use in the envelope sealing and stamp-affixing machine invented by Joseph J. Schermack. In 1906 Schermack assigned his rights to his machine to the Detroit Mailing Machine Company. In 1908 the company changed its name to the Schermack Mailing Machine Company in recognition of the Schermack Mailing Machine. When Schermack left the company, it changed its name to the Mail-om-eter Company. The name of the machine was likewise changed to the Mail-om-eter Mailing Machine. Sometime around 1917 or 1918 the company again changed the spelling of its name, this time to Mail-O-Meter. It is usually not important to distinguish between the two spellings of Mailometer. Most often the company name is simply spelled "Mailometer" and this spelling will be used in the rest of this chapter.

It is important to note that the three types of perforations developed before 1909 are identified as "Schermack" perforations while those developed after 1908 are called "Mailometer" perforations. *Scott* lists four basic types of Mailometer perforations, known as Types I, II, III, and IV. The most common Mailometer perforation is the Type IV, with five large holes 2.2 mm in diameter. It was used in the St. Louis office from 1911 to 1917, when they stopped perforating stamps in St. Louis (fig. 8). *Scott* lists three types of Schermack perforations, known as Types I, II, and III. The Schermack Type III hyphen-hole perforation is, by far, the best known private perforation. The Type III perforation is shown in Figure 9. It was first used commercially in early 1908 and was in use for twenty years. The

Figure 8

The most common Mailometer perforation, Type IV, with five large holes 2.2 mm in diameter.

Figure 9

The Schermack Type III hyphen-hole perforation is, by far, the best-known private perforation.

company efficiently produced tens of millions of these stamps by pasting twenty-five imperforate sheets of 200 stamps together and then stripping the sheets into coils of 500 stamps each.

In 1922 the Mailometer Company began making postage meters in competition with the Pitney-Bowes Company, which acquired Mailometer in 1924. Pitney-Bowes operated this business under the Mailometer name and perforated stamps for use in its machines until late 1927, or early 1928. At that time, the Post Office discontinued issuing imperforate stamps and the few Mailometer machines that still used private coil stamps were converted to use coil stamps produced by the BEP.

The John V. Farwell Company, a large Chicago, Illinois dry goods company, also produced coil stamps with private perforations for use in an affixing machine. Farwell was a large user of Schermack coil stamps. However, since Schermack charged a 50¢ premium for each roll of its coils, Farwell developed its own coils to avoid this fee. Farwell perforations are classified as Group 1, 2, 3, 4, and 5. The Farwell Company ceased perforating its own stamps in mid-1917.

For several months in 1909, the Attleboro Stamp Company of Attleboro, Massachusetts used an affixing machine to mail its newsletters and price lists. The machine made a distinctive perforation on the stamps as it affixed them on wrappers or envelopes. This machine was both a stamp perforating machine and a stamp-affixing machine. Although a "philatelic" creation in the sense that the perforation was made for a stamp dealer, it is validly recognized as an affixing machine perforation since the perforations were made to enable the stamps to be used in an affixing machine, and they were commercially used in the machine.

Notes on Collecting

Because coil stamps have always come in strips or rolls, collectors have generally preferred to save coil stamps in pairs or other multiples. There is a premium variety known as a joint **line pair**.

Flat plate imperforate coil stamps are listed in a separate section of *Scott*, and have a V or H as a suffix to their catalogue numbers. These coil stamps are difficult to distinguish from stamps cut from corresponding imperforate sheets, so expertization is recommended.

Because of the rarity (and corresponding value) of many of the early hand-created coils, numerous fakes have been created. It is extremely prudent to have these stamps expertized before purchase.

As with most coil stamps, it is usual to collect unused examples of vending and affixing machine perforations in pairs. This is possible because both vending and affixing machine manufacturers sold stamps to dealers and collectors. This practice also explains why genuine vending and affixing perforations exist on stamps for which there was no commercial use, or which could not fit a vending or affixing machine. Similarly blocks or larger multiples exist with either genuine vending or affixing machine perforations.

Rolls of coil stamps produced on the rotary press had a brown paper **leader** attached at the beginning of each roll and a brown paper **core** attached at the end. They were, in reality, portions of the splices introduced into the web to divide the web into desired lengths, and facilitate the processing of individual coil rolls (fig. 10).

There are many fakes of vending and affixing machine perforations. The inexperienced collector should utilize reliable dealers and other reliable sources in acquiring genuine varieties. **Expertizing** is advisable if acquiring the rare types.

In collecting vending and affixing machine stamps on cover, it is useful to keep in mind the very different purposes for vending and affixing machines. Vending machine stamps were used by individuals on post cards and other personal mail, and are rarely seen on commercial mail.

Conversely, affixing machine stamps were used on high volume commercial mail most often paying the First Class rate.

Almanac

1906 – On October 2 the Post Office issues the first imperforate 1¢ and 2¢ stamps for use by vending and affixing machine manufacturers.

1907 – Schermack Type I experimental perforations are first produced in October. They are the earliest U.S. coil stamps.

1907 – International Vending Machine Co. perforations appear late in the year.

1908 – Schermack Type III Hyphen-hole perforations are developed in January.

1908 – First BEP coil stamps (316 and 321) are issued February 18.

1908 – Imperforate BEP coils are issued in late February or March.

1908 – On November 8 the United States Automatic Vending Machine Co. files for a patent on its Type I perforation.

1908 – Brinkerhoff develops Type I perforations in December.

1909 – The International Vending Machine Co. goes out of business in mid-year.

1909 – Mailometer develops Type I and Type II perforations in August.

1911 – The Farwell Company begins to experiment with producing its own coil stamps in May.

1927 – Production of Schermack Type III coils is discontinued in December, ending the era of private vending and affixing machine coils.

What Others Have Said

Special Perforation on U.S. Stamps

"The Post Office Department of the United States, recognizing the utility of various patented devices for Vending Stamps and Machines for Rapid Mailing (sic) purposes, has issued stamps in special form for the convenience of users of these arrangements. Stamp collectors will recognize that we are entering a most interesting and important epoch of philatelic and postal history in the United States. These special issues may be classified under the three following heads: I. Part Perforated in Strips....II. Unperforated in Strips...III. Unperforated in Sheets....These stamps are put up neatly with oiled paper enclosing the rolls. Each roll is marked with the name of the employee who is responsible for the count and the whole endorsed with a printed label, of which the following is a sample: 500 1c Stamps Rolled Sidewise Perforated."

—C.H. Mekeel, "Special Perforations on U.S. Stamps – Issued for use in Patented Stamp Vending and mailing Machines," The Philatelic Journal of America, 1909. From one of the earliest detailed articles describing the new format of stamps in strips that were then made into rolls.

Description of Coil Manufacturing

"Coils of stamps are made from rolls printed on intaglio web presses… the printing and gumming of the rolls being accomplished at the same time. They are placed in special perforating machines, which perforate the rolls crosswise only, and wind them again into a roll. These perforated rolls are delivered to operatives at specially devised measuring tables, who unwind the rolls, measure them into lengths of 500, 1000, or 5000 stamps, according to the number of stamps to be in the finished coil, cut each length and insert labels denoting the class and denomination of the coil by pasting one edge to the margin of the cut off length and the opposite edge to the margin of the portion yet to be measured, thus joining the measured lengths with these labels. These lengths are rewound into rolls and the stamps are ready for the next operation-that of coiling. The spindle on which the stamps were wound during the preceding operation fits into the coiling machine. Eleven knives on the coiling machine slit apart the ten rows of stamps and trim the margin of the outside rows as the roll is then wound, and simultaneously each row is wound into coil form until the labels previously pasted on are reached. The operator at this point stops the machine, separates each coil from the roll by cutting the label, pastes the label as a binder for each coil, and places her initials or name on the binder. The coils are then carried to tables, counted and boxed ready for delivery to the vault from which they are shipped when ordered."

—History of the Bureau of Engraving and Printing 1862–1962.

Now there would be collectors' items!

"There lived in the same house with me a young man who was a bookkeeper for the Schermack Mailing Machine Co. Their shop was only a short distance away and I spent considerable time there. The machines and the method making up the stamps in coils for their machines was of little interest, but on many occasions I could have taken much of the spoiled stuff, such as miscuts, double or multiple perforations etc., and there were at times much that they would not even use on their own mail. Now those would be collectors items! For the customers only the good ones would be rolled up for delivery, the others just being waste."

—*Karl Koslowski, "The Story of the Finding of the 4¢ Schermack of 1902,"* Thirteenth American Philatelic Congress Book, 1947.

Coil Stamps are more Interesting if collected in Pairs

"Most coil stamps are more interesting if collected in pairs. Owing to the method of manufacture, all coils in U.S. stamps have pairs showing a colored line between the stamps at regular intervals. Such "line pairs" are of course choice items."

—*Stephen G. Rich, "Precanceled Coil Stamps,"* American Philatelist, 1934.

Two major varieties of the American 16¢ Horizontal Coil

"[The Bureau of Engraving and Printing wanted] to have more capability available for production of 16c stamps than the five web monocolor intaglio presses could provide….So additional production was cranked in by the use of the webfed 3-color intaglio press to do coils, its specialty…A detailed description of the two coil varieties follows: …Coil Variety 1 …Overall tagging, joint lines every 24 stamps…Coil variety 2 …Block tagging, no joint lines…"

—*George Brett, "The Two Major Varieties of the Americana 16c Horizontal Coil," The United States Specialist, 1980. From a detailed article on coil varieties that superficially look identical to one another.*

Examples of Postal Usage

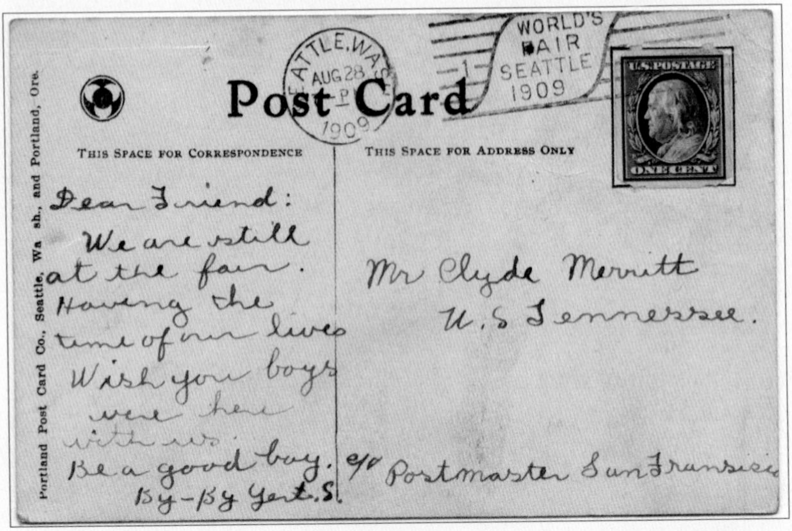

Figure 11

Among the vending machine companies, only the stamps made by the United States Vending Machine Co. had widespread use. The most typical use of their stamps was on post cards such as the one shown here, and to a lesser extent, on first class letters.

Figure 12

Affixing machine stamps are often found on covers from mass mailings. The most common are commercial uses of Schermack Type III stamps, such as the one on this cover. Insert shows enlargement of stamp.

Where to Find More Information

- *The Stamp Machines and Coiled Stamps* by George P. Howard is the classic account of privately perforated stamps, and the machines in which they were used.

- *United States Coil Issues 1906-1938* by Martin A. Armstrong.

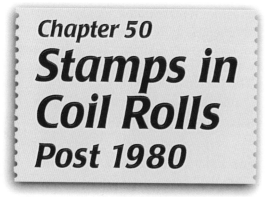

Chapter 50
Stamps in Coil Rolls
Post 1980

In 1981 a dramatic change took place in the printing and collecting of coil stamps. On April 24 of that year, a coil stamp was issued (*Scott* 1891), on which a plate number appeared at regular intervals on coil rolls. Previously, plate numbers only appeared in the selvage, not on the stamps themselves. In the case of coil stamps issued until 1981, the plate number was trimmed off before stamps reached the public, although occasionally, due to miscuts, partial plate numbers unintentionally appeared on finished coil stamps.

The first coils with plate numbers were printed on the **Cottrell presses**, which used a pair of curved plates that produced **joint lines**. Later stamps were printed on others presses, which used cylindrical plates known as **sleeves**, which produced no joint lines.

Stamps with a plate number are "face different" from the adjoining stamps that do not have a number. These plate-number-bearing stamps (fig. 1) are known as Plate Number Coils (or PNCs). Some PNCs have multiple numbers, due to the use of multiple printing cylinders (for different colors) or a large number of plate changes during the printing of the issue. For purposes of simplicity, this chapter will refer to the entire plate number sequence as "plate number".

The plate number is placed within the design of the stamps along the edge of the plate, thus appearing once in each row of stamps across the printing **web**. Plate numbers are therefore found intermittently on a coiled roll of stamps, usually one number per revolution of the printing plate. Some contract printers, however, included the plate number at intervals less than once per revolution.

Figure 1

This was the first Plate Number Coil (1891), issued in 1981. It differs from all previous coil stamps in that it shows a small plate number included in the design near the bottom of the stamp. The plate number appears on every 52nd stamp in the roll.

The "plate" number found on PNCs is actually a *representative number*. This means a one or two digit number is used to represent each plate used to print a stamp, with a different plate used to print each color. A single color stamp, such as those in the Transportation Series, has only a one or two digit plate number. Multi-color stamps will typically have a one or two digit number for each color plate used in printing. Some multi-color stamps have plate numbers of seven digits or more. Each digit (or pair of digits), printed in a different color represents a different printing plate.

Stamps printed by private contractors have a prefix letter in front of the plate number. The private contractor from whom the United States Postal Service (USPS) purchased the stamps is identifiable by the prefix letter (see ch. 43 – Plate Numbers). By the beginning of the twenty-first century the prefix letters A, B, G, M, P, and V had been assigned and used on coil stamps. The Bureau of Engraving and Printing (BEP) did not use a prefix, so a PNC having a number without a prefix letter can be identified as a product of the BEP.

Since PNCs were produced in large quantities, many different printing plates were frequently needed to print them. As a plate wore out from use it would be replaced with a new plate, one with a new plate number. For example, the first PNC (1891), the 18¢ Flag coil of 1981, eventually employed seven different plates, and so PNCs are found on this stamp with plate numbers 1 through 7. Each is technically a "face different" stamp.

Figure 2

This stamp from the Transportation Coil Series depicts a mail wagon common in the 1880s.

Interest in collecting PNCs was stimulated by the appearance of the Transportation Coil stamps, starting in 1981 (fig. 2). These strikingly attractive engraved stamps depict a wide array of obsolete transportation vehicles (ch. 16). Many plate numbers were used in the production of some of these stamps. This presented a challenge for collectors – to acquire a complete set of all known numbers.

In the years following 1980 there were many advances in stamp printing technology, which were often used on coil stamps first. Although the first *self-adhesive* stamp was not a coil, it was largely through coil stamps that the public was introduced to self-adhesive technology.

The introduction of self-adhesive stamps required a new method to separate them. The result is what is known as *die-cutting*. The finished stamp web (consisting of backing paper, water soluble adhesive assemblage and printed stamp) is processed through a machine that contains a cutting die, which cuts through the stamp and the adhesive layer, but not the backing paper. Die shapes are designed to simulate perforations and they take a serpentine form, resulting in "peaks" and "valleys" on each side of the stamp (figs. 3 and 4).

The 32¢ Flag over Porch issue (fig. 5) appeared in 1995 in both traditional "lick-'em" form, and as self-adhesives, and was the first coil to be produced in large quantities with self-adhesive construction. Many different PNCs with the Flag over Porch design were produced, resulting in many different *Scott* numbers, with different die cut varieties. Stamps with the same PNC number have been found with up to five different die cut varieties. In fact 33 different plate numbers are known to have produced 55 different plate number and die cut varieties. Some of these are quite rare. As late as 2005 three of these varieties were still not known in mint condition, and the number of known used copies was less than 20 for each.

In more than one case, a particular die cut variety was discovered only after the passage of some years. For example, the common variety of the self-adhesive 5¢ Mountain (10 peaks on each side) was released on January 24, 1997 (2904B). The scarce variety (9 peaks on the left side and 10 on the right) remained unreported until February 2003, when a used copy was discovered! Four mint examples of this stamp were reported in November of that year. The 32¢ Flag over Porch #88888 (2915A) was available for many years with two common die cut varieties, but a third (11 peaks on the left side and 12 on the right) was not

Figure 3

A self adhesive PNC on backing paper larger than stamp (3266). Note die cut peaks and valleys at sides resembling perforations.

Just like traditional perforations, serpentine die cuts come in different sizes. The stamp on the left has a gauge 9.8 serpentine die cut, while the one on the right has 11.2.

Figure 4

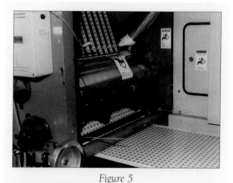

Figure 5

A Goebel coiling machine at the BEP processing 1995 "Flag Over Porch" coil stamps.

reported until March 2003! This discovery copy was a used stamp, and as late as 2005 no mint copy had been reported.

Self-adhesive non-denominated coil stamps, intended for use on bulk mailings, were first issued in 1991 (2602). They quickly became popular for use on so-called "junk" mail, which is sent at discounted rates. Mailing houses adapted to the new self-adhesive stamps, which were available in large roll sizes and did not require cutting at the perforations. Because there were so many different rates in existence, the Postal Service abandoned the practice of printing specific denominations on these stamps. Although these stamps are not imprinted with a specific denomination, they do have an assigned postage value. They carry a description of intended use, such as "non-profit" or "First Class Presort"

Figure 6

Photographically cropped from a piece of "junk mail", this stamp (3520) is known as a "Service Inscribed Stamp", because the words printed on it, "PRESORTED STD", indicate its intended use. Although no value is shown on this stamp, it has an assigned value of 10¢. Since it is a precancel, no further cancellation was applied by the Postal Service.

(fig. 6). The mailer pays the difference between the actual postal rate, and the value of the affixed stamp, at the time of entry into the mailstream. Many of these "service inscribed" stamps also have rare die-cut varieties.

Figure 7

Back Number on a coil stamp.

In order to facilitate inventory control, large size rolls of coils (printed in rolls as large as 10,000 stamps) have frequently been imprinted with **counting numbers** on the back of the stamps. The location of the stamp having a back number may vary with respect to the stamp having a plate number on the front. Back numbers may be printed in different colors, appearing at the top, middle or bottom of the stamp, and may consist of two, three, four, or five digits (fig. 7).

Figure 8

Computer Vended Coil (CVP32) strip of three with PNC.

In 1992, a new automated vending machine (ch. 61), called a Postage and Mailing Center (PMC), was introduced experimentally in a few locations around the country. A computer controlled the operation of the self-service PMC, and imprinted a customer-selected value on coil stamp stock stored inside the PMC. Computer Vended Postage Stamps (CVP31-33) could be imprinted with any monetary value from $.01 to $99.99 (fig. 8).

Notes on Collecting

The appearance of PNCs in 1981 changed the way coil stamps are collected. Previously, coil stamps were generally collected as pairs, or sometimes as strips of four or longer. Premiums were placed on pairs containing *joint lines*. With the advent of PNCs, the focus changed to the numbered stamp. As the specialty of PNC collecting evolved most specialist PNC collectors adopted the strip of five, with the PNC in the middle, as the standard collecting format (fig. 9), although other strip lengths are frequently encountered.

Figure 9

This strip of five of the 1981 Flag Over Supreme Court (1895) represents the most commonly collected format of PNCs.

Collecting PNCs can be as challenging a philatelic specialty as the collector desires. Most PNC collectors seek to acquire a single example of each number used for a given stamp. Some PNC collectors limit their pursuit to a single example, accepting any PNC number available for a particular issue. Others prefer to collect only used singles, attempting to find all numbers available for a given issue. Still others pursue more difficult challenges,

PNCs come of age
A look at the Scott Specialized Catalogues

It took many years for collectors to figure out what the rules were for collecting PNCs. The best way to illustrate this is to look at the *Scott Specialized Catalogue* listings for the very first PNC, the 18¢ Flag Stamp (Scott 1891).

Issued on April 24, 1981, this stamp was not listed in the 1981 catalogue, but appeared in the 1982 catalogue.

For five years (1982, 1983, 1984, 1985, and 1986), the only listings for 1891 are for a single copy in mint and used condition, and for a pair of coil stamps, the traditional way coil stamps had been collected since early in the twentieth century.

Then, the 1987, 1988, 1989, and 1990 catalogues added two more listings: the price of a plate number strip of three, and a used single. It was not until the 1991 catalogue that plate number strips of five were recognized.

looking for color errors, production **errors** and **freaks**, and other varieties. Subspecialties include: varieties in paper types, gum types, tagging, **precancel** gap locations, back numbering, **plate varieties** and imperforates. Among self-adhesive coils even more sub-specialties can be found: major and minor varieties in die cut, incision style and backing paper. There are hundreds of face different PNCs. The many different varieties and number of collectible examples produce thousands of varieties, enough to challenge even the most ardent collector.

One major reason that specialists have found PNC collecting so challenging is that some numbers are relatively scarce. One reason for the scarcity of some numbers is the early replacement of printing plates. Some die cut varieties are also extremely rare. More than a few PNC varieties have less than 50 known copies, and some are known only in used condition. This reality is reflected in the marketplace, with valuations of some PNCs in the three and four digit dollar range. The "key" 18¢ Flag (1891) plate #6 had a *Scott* value in 2005 of $3,750 as a mint plate strip of five.

PNCs are also collected on covers. Specialists seek both **commercial covers** and First Day Covers. Early First Day Covers bearing PNCs (those issued before PNC collecting became a popular specialty) can be elusive. Higher PNC numbers for a specific issue are not usually found on FDCs. This is because the stamps used on FDCs can only come from an initial printing, before higher numbered plates were usually created. Later press runs, which may have employed replacement plates (with higher numbers), typically occurred after the normal period in which First Day cancellations were available.

However, commercial covers can usually be found with all PNC numbers. The most commonly available commercial covers are those with **First Class** rate stamps. Less common are the bulk-rate covers using pre-canceled or **service inscribed stamps**. Far fewer of these covers are recovered, since they must usually be reclaimed from households. Many fractional rate Transportation Issue PNC covers, with stamps paying the correct rate at the time of mailing, are truly scarce.

Almanac

1981 – The first plate number coil stamp, the 18¢ Flag (1891) is issued April 24.

1985 – First Edition of the PNC catalog, *Catalog of Plate Number Coils* is published July 1.

1992 – Computer Vended Postage Coils are introduced at five test sites on August 20.

1993 – The first self-adhesive coil stamp, the 29¢ Pine Cone (2491) is issued on November 5.

What Others Have Said

It's always been difficult to price many of the coil varieties
"Prices of PNCs are unstable. Some prices, indicated in the catalog by italics, have been rising so steeply during the preparation of this catalog (1987) that they should be regarded as guesses, at best....The prices given for mint strips are

taken from dealers' price lists and advertisements through March, 1987 and were reviewed by a panel of the Plate Number Coil Study Group, but prices given in the catalog are the opinion of the editor."

—*Stephen G. Esrati*, Catalog of Plate Number Coils – Third Edition, *1987. When the plate number phenomenon hit the hobby, Esrati's were the first attempts to catalog this exciting market.*

PNC coil number First Day Covers came much later

"After a five-year gestation period, PNC first-day cover collecting has been born, to the delight of many collectors and some dealers, to the dismay of others. To a certain extent this was a logical development. Once the first generation of PNC collectors had nearly completed basic collections of mint strips, or used singles, or both it was natural that they would seek other PNC areas."

—*Ken Lawrence*, "FDC's with PNC Come of Age, The Plate Number, *1987. Lawrence explains why the first five years of PNCs are extremely hard to find on first day covers, because "first, there was the problem, of finding out what exists."*

There are so many varieties to seek for those who love "the thrill of the hunt"

"Specialists in coils have always had their eyes out for varieties, freaks, errors.... as the momentum continues with PNCs in general, there is a concurrent increased interest in variety material....Just what is the definition of a 'variety?'...something different from others of the same kind....As this is still an evolving area, the following should not be considered as all-inclusive....Plate Varieties...Mat Varieties...Chill Roller Offsets...Imperforates..."

—*A.S. Cibulskas*, "Introduction and Overview – Plate Number Coil Varieties," *The United States Specialist, 1988.*

Last in Transportation series-20¢ Cog Railway issued

"The transportation series rolled to a close June 9 with the issuance of the Cog Railway stamp at the TEXPEX '95 show in Dallas. The Transportation series has been the largest of American definitive series, with more than 50 subjects. The Transportation Series started with the 18¢ Surrey issued May, 18, 1981. Three new series will replace the Transportation series: American Transportation Series, American culture and American Scenes."

—Stamp Collector, 1995. *Subsequent to this article, the Great Americans became the largest American definitive series.*

Bureau coils to add letters

"Suffix letters soon will be printed on United States plate number coil stamps manufactured in very large quantities by the Bureau of Engraving and Printing. This change in how plate numbers are designated on Bureau coil stamps restores the covenant between the collector/dealer community and the stamp producers, the U.S. Postal Service and the Bureau. It means that the bond between the actual plates used to print stamps and the numbers printed on the stamps is being restored. The Postal Service and the Bureau have been discussing the situation for months. The change will be effective with the 32¢ Flag Over Porch self-adhesive coil stamps to be printed at the Bureau in early November."

—Linn's Stamp News, *October 20, 1997.*

In the beginning, PNCs were not understood and not catalogued....
"We began at the fringes of US stamp collecting, and we now have full catalog recognition, albums with annual supplements, and popular columns in the philatelic press."

—*Ken Lawrence,* Linn's Plate Number Coil Handbook, *1990. Commenting on how long it took the hobby to "catch on" to PNC collecting.*

Coil Plate No. Strips of Three
"Beginning with No. 2123, coil plate No. strips of 3 usually sell at the level of strips of 5 minus the face value of the two stamps."

—2004 Scott Specialized Catalogue of U.S. Stamps and Covers. *From the beginning it was very unclear if PNCs were to be collected in strips of three or five with the plate number in the center of the strip. Many of the earlier stamps were saved in strips of three, making strips of five on some of the issues much harder to find. This Scott listing first appeared in the 1999 Catalogue, and illustrates how long it took to "establish" the rules of PNC collecting.*

But now they are one of the most exciting parts of United States stamp collecting!
"It's great fun to look through ordinary used United States stamps and come upon one of the coil issues from 1981 to date with tiny numbers at the bottom..."

—*John Hotchner,* Linn's Stamp News, *1999.*

Example of Postal Usage

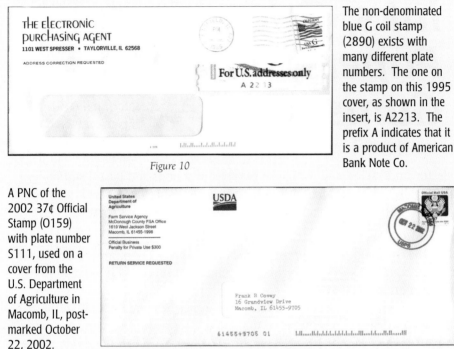

The non-denominated blue G coil stamp (2890) exists with many different plate numbers. The one on the stamp on this 1995 cover, as shown in the insert, is A2213. The prefix A indicates that it is a product of American Bank Note Co.

Figure 10

A PNC of the 2002 37¢ Official Stamp (O159) with plate number S111, used on a cover from the U.S. Department of Agriculture in Macomb, IL, postmarked October 22, 2002.

Figure 11

Where to Find More Information

- The Plate Number Coil Collectors Club maintains a website: www.pnc3.org.

- *An Introduction to Collecting Plate Number Coils*, by Ed Denson.

- *Linn's Plate Number Coil Handbook*, by Ken Lawrence.

- The *Transportation Coils and other Plate Number Coils*, by Joseph Agris.

- *1995 Plate Number Coil Catalog*, Richard Nazar, editor. Earlier editions of this work were published under the title *Catalog of Plate Number Coils* by Stephen G. Esrati. They contain much detailed information on PNCs.

- The relevant volumes of *Linn's U.S. Stamp Yearbook*, edited by Fred Boughner or George Amick.

- *Coil Line*, the journal of the Plate Number Coil Collectors Club, is published monthly.

Chapter 51
Inks, Colors, Papers, and Gums

Stated simply, the production of stamps has always involved applying ink onto paper. It has almost always involved applying gum to paper. An understanding of inks, their colors and shades, the papers on which they are applied, and application of gum will help a collector understand and recognize varieties of stamps and *postal stationery*. Additionally, ink is required in the application of cancellations and other postal markings, although a different type than those used to print stamps.

Inks and Colors

From 1847 through 1965 almost all postage stamps were produced by recess printing, commonly known as "line engraving", or *intaglio*. In intaglio printing a thick ink is applied to the surface of the printing plate. The plate is then wiped so that the ink is removed from the surface, leaving ink only in the recesses of the plate. The ink is so thick that it forms ridges, when deposited on the paper, which can be felt with sensitive fingertips. When too much ink is used, or not properly thinned, the press deposits too much on the paper, possibly obscuring portions of the stamp design. Inks used in printing from a surface, such as the plates used in **lithography** and *offset*, require a much thinner consistency, and do not leave raised ridges on paper.

In the last half of the twentieth century, stamps began to be produced by combining different printing techniques using different kinds of inks. For example, the Desert Plants issue of 1981 (*Scott* 1942–1945) was printed by lithography and intaglio.

Embossing has been used since the Colonial Period, but is most familiar to the contemporary collector for its use on *stamped envelopes*, first issued in 1853. These envelopes exhibit a raised-up, uninked portrait or image, surrounded by a surface-printed, colored background. The inscription "U.S. Postage" and the value are usually also embossed and uninked. Inks used to print stationery require a special consistency. If the required consistency is not maintained, areas of light or missing ink may result. Examples of this can be seen on some Heroes of the American Revolution postal cards (UX70 and 74).

The earliest inks used to print stamps contained natural pigments, often the same ones traditionally used in coloring oil paints. Pigments were ground from minerals and mixed with natural or hardened oils, which carried the pigments in suspension, with just enough moisture to help them moderately penetrate the paper and then dry on the paper leaving the raised ink typical of intaglio printing.

In the late 1880s, *aniline* red coloring agents became available in the U.S. from their German developers. These were bright colors created in the early days of modern chemistry and were not made with ground minerals. They were first used as canceling inks. Artificial aniline inks were first used for postage stamps on some of the bright rose red 2¢ stamps (267c and 279B) in the **Series of 1894**. Other aniline inks were used to create some of the brighter colors in the **Series of 1902** and the **Washington-Franklin** Heads. Only these artificial inks were used for the offset printed Washington-Franklin issues.

Most stamps since the late 1960s have been produced by surface printing methods using thin pigments mixed with solvents for fast drying. Virtually all inks used in modern surface printing are created artificially in the United States and Western Europe. However, mineral inks are generally still used for modern recess printing because their drier composition makes them appropriate for the thick inks needed.

Shades
Almost all stamps produced through the mid-1960s exist in different shades. A shade is a variant of the primary printing color caused by either differences in the inks or in their proportions mixed to create the intended color. For example, the first stamp, the 5¢ 1847 Franklin (1) is listed by *Scott* with shades of red brown, pale brown, brown, dark brown, grayish brown, blackish brown, orange brown, brown orange, and red orange, while the 50¢ Susan B. Anthony (1051a and 1051), issued more than 100 years later, although listed in *Scott* only as bright purple, can be found in shades of violet, purple, red-violet, and magenta (fig. 1). Interesting and inexpensive collections can be formed of the shades of the 3¢ stamp in the *Series of 1851* and **1857**, the 1¢ and 3¢ stamps in the **Series of 1861**, all the low values (1¢ through 6¢) of the Large and

Figure 1
Shades of the 50¢ Susan B. Anthony.

Figure 2

Copper red, red brown, and dark buff shades of the 12¢ Franklin (417, 474 and 512).

Figure 3

Shades of deep blue, blue, and ultramarine on the 1862 10¢ Contract revenue stamp (R34).

Small **Bank Notes**, the Series of 1894, Washington-Franklin issues (fig. 2), Series of 1922, Presidential Series, Liberty Series, and some selected definitives thereafter. Inexpensive shade studies can also be assembled on low value revenues (fig. 3).

Most shades are caused by mixing ink in different proportions prior to being placed in the ink troughs that feed the presses. However, occasionally unintended mixings of ink result from inadequate cleaning of ink troughs following the printing of other stamps. In this case, some stamps from the beginning of a press run have shade variations.

Some shades result from the use of the wrong ink. The 1932 Yorktown commemorative (703) was intended to be printed in carmine rose and black. However some stamps were printed in lake (703a) and dark lake (703b). Lake is a very dark red color made from a different pigment than the chemical ink used to make carmine rose. Another significant color error exists on the 4¢ Columbian of 1893. Intended to be printed in ultramarine (233), some stamps were printed in blue (233a). A variety unlisted in *Scott* is found on some singles and first day covers of the 1945 United Nations issue (928), which exists in colors ranging from light ultramarine to deep or dark ultramarine. However, a few can be found in a bright blue which resemble the 30¢ transport airmail (C30) then in production.

The **Giori Press** was introduced in 1957, making it possible to print engraved stamps with different areas, side by side, in different colors. This was made possible by using different inking rollers for parts of the design to be inked in different colors. For example, the 6¢ Flag Over White House stamp (1338) had inking rollers that applied green, carmine, and blue colors to different areas of each stamp. Sometimes colors became mixed on the plate, or spread too far. For example, the 25¢ Yosemite (2280) has a freak variety known as the "Forest Fire" where the red from the bottom stripes of the flag colored the green trees below (fig. 4).

Figure 4

"Forest Fire" and normal stamps in the same coil pair (2280).

Shades of certain stamps are highly prized by some collectors. For example, the 1861 3¢ Washington (65) is very common in its ordinary rose tones. However, in pink (64), pigeon blood pink (64a) or rose pink (64b), it is scarce. The $5 Coolidge of the 1938 Presidential series (834) is attractive with its carmine frame and black vignette, but is rarer in its red brown shade (834a).

Colors and Postal Markings

Up until the Civil War, many postal markings, especially from smaller towns, and almost all **auxiliary markings**, were in **manuscript**. The inks used were based on iron or oak gall and varied from black to black-brown, although tending to turn dark brown with the passage of time.

Postal markings from larger towns were generally applied in inks that were prepared for use on stamp pads or ink blocks. Black was most commonly used, but other colors include blue and red. The black inks contained charcoals or very finely ground iron and related compounds mixed with water, oils, or greases. Until 1890, blue and red canceling inks used the same pigments used for printing inks (fig. 5). Violet, purple, and magenta inks became more commonly used around 1890, especially for use with **registered** mail markings. Still later these colors were used for many other categories of auxiliary markings, from forwarding information blocks to the ubiquitous pointing hand "RETURN TO SENDER" markings.

Figure 5

The 1866 15¢ Lincoln stamps (77) with red, blue, and green cancels.

Almost every shade of green is known in postal markings, with a green cancel on a classic stamp or cover especially prized. Brown is very uncommon. What appears as brown is often seen under magnification to be a mix of black and red when a handstamp was used first on a black pad and then on a red one. Ultramarine and bright aniline reds are also quite scarce. Yellow and orange are very rare.

Since approximately 1970, there have been various experiments with pale violet inks as postmarks and wavy line machine cancels. Use of aniline inks for these markings has become common since 1970 (fig. 6).

Figure 6

Aniline magenta ink postmark on $2.00 Bobcat (2482).

Papers

All paper used in stamp production is a compound (composite) product made from natural or processed plant fibers held together with a "binder" which is often a plant starch. Papers also often include "fillers" which are animal, vegetable, mineral, or artificial substances added to both the fibers and the binder to give the paper greater body and firmness. Various additives may be used to color the paper, bleach to whiten it and pigments to give it specific coloration.

The names applied to different papers reflect the specific mixes used to produce them or to control shrinkage during drying. All stamp papers used until 1878 were rag papers. They generally contained rags or mill scraps of cotton or linen fabric, or discarded clothing which were shredded, boiled, processed, and bleached to create the raw material for stamp paper. Starting in early summer 1879, wood pulps processed with chemicals were introduced into U.S. stamp papers. By the time of the 1893 Columbian and Series of 1894, the transition to chemical wood pulp papers was complete. Various starches were added as a binder to both rag paper and chemical wood paper to provide better fiber and bending strength. The early rag papers are known as "hard white papers" because of their tightly woven fibers, significant amount of fill or binder and because they were bleached white.

Watermarks first appeared on postal stationery in 1853 and on postage stamps in 1895. Their creation is an integral part of the paper manufacturing process (ch. 42).

A very thin, heavily starched and brittle paper was used for grilled issues in late 1868 and early 1869 for stamps of the Series of 1861. It is a relatively scarce paper and almost always found impressed with the **F grill**.

Some **Large Bank Notes** of 1870–1876 are known on rag paper, sometimes inaccurately called "silk paper". Because some rags contained colored fibers, usually red or blue, they were fancifully thought to be silk fibers, which is how the paper got its name. A few of the rags may actually have been silk, but most have proved to be cotton. However, a true silk paper was used experimentally about 1869 for a number of revenue stamps.

Continental Bank Note Company printed some stamps on **double paper** as a security measure on an experimental basis. *Scott* lists these as minor varieties. The two-ply paper consisted of a hard white paper backing and a much thinner top layer of paper on which the stamp design was printed. Any attempt to clean and reuse the stamp would shred the almost tissue thin upper layer and leave the stamp unusable.

In late 1876 or early 1877, Continental began experimenting with intermediate and soft woven papers that contained more fiber and less binder and filler. There are challenges in identifying the many papers used by Continental. For example, specialists recognize 12 separately identifiable papers on the 6¢ Lincoln (159) alone, including hard, medium (intermediate), and soft with various degrees of strong to weak bleaching, false laid paper, ribbed paper, and "silk paper".

The challenge for the more casual collector is distinguishing stamps printed by Continental on soft paper from stamps printed later by **American Bank Note Co.** (American) on soft paper. Unless stamps are on cover with a readable postmark prior to February 5, 1879, or have an American **imprint** in attached selvedge, it is impossible to confidently distinguish between stamps printed by Continental from September 1978 through February 4, 1879 and those printed by American from February 5, 1879 until June or July 1879. This is because late on February 4, 1879 Continental was acquired lock, stock, and ink barrels by American, including printed stamps not yet gummed or perforated. This meant that tens of thousands of lower value stamps printed by Continental, on Continental bleached and lightly bleached soft paper, were still in stock at the plant and in the possession of the resident **stamp agent** when the takeover took place. American later issued them even though American did not print them.

In late June and July of 1879 American introduced virtually unbleached soft newsprint with lowered rag content as its basic paper for stamp production, which it continued to use until production was transferred to the Bureau of

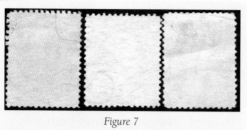

Figure 7

Contrasting 1870 hard paper, 1878 bleached soft paper, and 1882 unbleached newsprint soft paper.

Engraving and Printing (BEP) in 1894. Only stamps printed on this paper can be positively identified as a product of American (fig. 7).

When the Washington-Franklin issues were introduced in 1908 the BEP began experiments to control paper shrinkage. Unfortunately after the stamps had been printed, the moistened paper would shrink unevenly as it dried. This in turn made it difficult to properly perforate stamps.

One attempt to control shrinkage was the so-called **Bluish Paper** stamps (357–366 and 369) of 1909. Fillers were added to the paper mix in an attempt to minimize shrinkage in the drying process. Another experiment produced the

Figure 8

Examples of 2¢ Lincoln on regular paper (367) and on "blue" paper (369).

China Clay Papers which were intended to reduce shrinkage by the addition of finely powdered kaolin to the paper mix. Both of these papers are identifiable by their differing shades of gray (fig. 8). Scientific analysis has shown that their composition varied and did not necessarily always include the particular ingredient for which the series of experiments were named. These varieties are considerably rarer than the same stamps printed on regular paper.

Around 1927 or 1928 the BEP once more experimented to control shrinkage by changing the paper. After discovering that stamps were being miscut by the knives that cut printed sheets into booklet panes, the BEP ordered a horizontally laid paper in an effort to reduce shrinkage and thus give the knives more room in which to make their cuts. Originally ordered for the Lindbergh Airmail Booklet issue of 1928 (C10a), this paper has been discovered used on some *special delivery* stamps (E15 and early printings of E16) and the 1931 *rotary press* printings of the Series of 1922. Stamps printed on this paper are slightly larger than those printed on regular paper.

Another major category of paper varieties is also one of the easiest to detect, tinted or colored papers. These papers are colored all the way through, not just on one surface. The first stamps on tinted papers were the 1847 stamps. Although the paper stock was supposed to be white, the paper sometimes had a pale gray or pale blue appearance.

The intentional use of colored paper for postal stationery began with the first stamped envelopes in 1853. The colors used on the first envelopes included white, buff, manila, amber, and orange. An old ivory color called "cream" was introduced in the **Reay** issue of 1871 and blue (which became common thereafter) in the **Plimpton** issue of 1874–1886 (fig. 9).

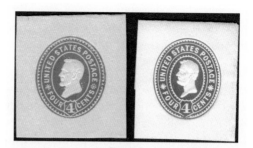

Figure 9

Four cent Lincoln brown on manila wrapper (W376) and brown on white envelope (U371).

Tinted paper became the norm for the Second Issue Documentary Stamps (R103–132). Using a specially patented "chameleon paper", the paper of these stamps appears in shades from pink through blue to violet, with colored fibers interspersed. Blue papers were used during 1875–1876 (fig. 10).

Despite its use in the nineteenth century, tinted paper was not used again until the 1961 Kansas Statehood issue (1183). This stamp, intaglio printed in brown, dark red, and green is on a bright yellow paper. There is a large sunflower on the left and the yellow paper gives the petals their color (fig. 11).

Figure 10

Two cent Liberty head revenue on blue paper (R152).

With the introduction of **photogravure** printing in 1967, an increasing number of stamps were printed on a medium to hard white paper with lots of fillers. This paper is calendared (polished) in the finishing process to create the very smooth surface needed for best results in photogravure printing. It is also a good paper for luminescent coatings (ch. 54).

Figure 11

Kansas Statehood stamp (1183) on bright yellow paper.

In 1989, the space station postal envelope (U617) used a hologram printed on metallic foil on top of paper. Eleven years later, holograms were again used on metallic foil for the stamp issue showing accomplishments in space (3411–3413).

Gum

With a few notable exceptions, virtually all postage stamps issued until the 1990s were coated with a water soluble gum which needed to be moistened in order to be affixed to a piece of mail. However, by the beginning of the twenty-first century almost all stamps were *self-adhesive* (ch. 41).

Until the end of World War II most gums were varieties of dextrin that were usually produced from cornstarch. The appearance of original gum on nineteenth century stamps can vary, depending upon how thin or thick it was applied, how dark the starch became due to the amount of humidity and heat applied in the gumming process, or the amount of heat and humidity the stamp experienced after it was issued.

Both white and amber colored gums are found on the 1847 stamps, white to brownish on the 1851 issues, and light amber to brownish on the 1857 issues. The issues of 1861 and 1867 usually show white gum but can sometimes tend toward brown and their color is affected by aging paper. Most of the older gums have various degrees of crackling, where the gum looks like windshield glass which was cracked but not broken out. The 1869 issues were mostly dark amber to brownish while the Bank Note issues tended toward white or light amber. From 1890 through the Washington-Franklin years there was an attempt to keep gum more toward the white to light amber range of colors.

Although different formulations for "winter gum" and "summer gum" were used at the BEP around the turn of the twentieth century, they have not created collectible varieties. Indeed, there were no significant gum varieties until the advent of the rotary press in 1914, and even then the varieties were not actually based on the gum, but on the method of application.

Because panes of stamps printed on the rotary press had a tendency to curl, the BEP applied "breakers" to the gum, beginning in 1919, in a somewhat successful attempt to reduce that curling. A breaker on the back of a stamp has a look and feel similar to a line of corrugated cardboard. Stamps are known with one to eight breakers, either horizontal or slightly sloping down to the left or right. Stamps produced experimentally with seven or eight breakers are very rare. Breakers were in general use until the early 1960s. With the notable exception of the 1926 1½¢ imperforate Harding (631), which *Scott* lists both with and without gum breakers, *Scott* does not include gum breaker varieties in its listings. During the 1920s another experiment with gum application was tried in response to complaints that stamps did not adhere well to mail. Gum was applied to the entire back of each stamp, but it was applied more thickly in numerous vertical lines called ridges. Resulting stamps have a very distinctive gum texture.

The apparent watering down of gum created problems during World War II. Some stamps, due to lack of adhesion, fell off their covers onto the floors of post offices and railway mail cars. After World War II, various polymer gums came into use based on polyvinyl alcohol and varieties of this gum continued into the beginning of the twenty-first century.

In the mid-1960s pre-gummed paper was introduced, the gum having a dull or matte appearance. These stamps appear to be ungummed until licked and placed on a cover. A number of Prominent Americans (ch. 13) exist with both shiny and dull gum varieties, which are listed in *Scott*.

Notes on Collecting

Many of the inks used from 1923 through 1965, especially magenta, purple, and violet, as well as shades of red and red orange are water soluble if allowed to soak in warm or hot water for too long a period of time. The ink will dissolve slightly and run into the paper. When soaking stamps to remove them from paper, these stamps should preferably be floated on top of the water just long enough to loosen the paper and then quickly removed from the water and separated from the paper and placed face down to dry. Any gum remaining can then later be washed off in lukewarm to cool water.

Stamps on brightly colored paper, especially red or green, should never be soaked. Instead, place them face up on a sponge until the gum is soft enough to remove the stamp from the paper, and then quickly wash off the gum before the color of the cover paper can damage the stamp.

Do not leave stamps or covers exposed in bright sunlight or artificial light. This will cause colors to bleach out.

If an intaglio printed stamp printed with orange, yellow, or light red brown ink has turned a darker brown color, it has oxidized. This can be reversed by barely moistening the face of the stamp with a highly diluted solution of hydrogen peroxide. Repeat two or three times if needed.

The easiest and cheapest way to obtain an understanding of the soft newsprint paper used for the later Large Bank Notes is to acquire and study some badly centered copies of the inexpensive 1881–1882 re-engraved or new design

American produced issues (206, 207, 210, 212, and 213). All of these stamps exist only on soft paper, and can be used as definitive reference material when examining Bank Notes that exist on both hard and soft paper.

Almanac

1853 – Nesbitt Co. manufactures the first stamped envelopes by embossing and surface printing. The first intentional use of tinted papers, they are also watermarked.

1877 – Continental Bank Note Company begins transitioning from "hard" paper to bleached "soft" paper in postage stamp printing.

1879 – American Bank Note Company introduces soft porous newsprint paper for postage stamps.

1894 – BEP takes over printing postage stamps, switches to whiter newsprint paper and whiter gums.

1899 – Aniline inks are introduced for 2¢ carmine rose stamps in the Series of 1894.

1943 – American Bank Note Company prints Overrun Countries Issue (909–921) with intaglio frames and lithographed central flags. This was the first combination printing process on a U.S. stamp.

1957 – The 48 star Flag Issue (1094) issued on July 4, a product of the Giori press, is the first stamp printed in a single pass through a press with multiple areas of color, side-by-side.

1967 – First stamp printed by photogravure is also first to use metallic ink (1335). Special hard white calendared (polished) paper is introduced.

What Others Have Said

The selection of the inks is one of the important first steps in stamp production
"Philatelists know that 19th century postage stamp manufacture did not end when the printer was handed the finished engraved plate, or lithographic plate or stone. Most collectors are aware of the successive skills required to reproduce postage stamps of quality. The selection and mixing of ink colorants, compounding the colors with oils and fillers, and choosing the papers most suitable for intaglio or lithographic printing very nearly equaled the importance of the plates."

—*R.H. White*, Encyclopedia of the Colors of United States Postage Stamps, *1981*.

Some colors of stamps come in a variety of shades of that color

"Speaking generally, the philatelist is interested in a variation in the normal color range only when that variation is significant, as indicating a new printing or a different ink...Shades or tints can result within a single printing from numerous possible causes, [such as] inconsistency of the ink, instability of the temperature or humidity control, uneven control of ink flow or uneven pressure on parts of the printing base - all of which can result in color of differing intensity or shade or tint of color within the compass of a single sheet."

—*L.N. Williams*, Fundamentals of Philately, *1990.*

Continental and American paper

"It is not too difficult to distinguish the somewhat porous paper used by Continental early in the life of the second contract but the soft paper used in the last months of the life of the Continental Bank Note Company makes it so difficult to distinguish these printings from those made by American that it is sensible to consider all such stamps as American printings....These soft paper Continentals can be proved to have been printed by Continental only when the date of their use can be shown and when such dates prove the stamp to have been used before the American printings were made [i.e. before February 5, 1879]."

—*Lester E. Brookman*, The United States Postage Stamps of the 19th Century, *1947.*

Stamp collectors also need to know about the gummed side of the stamp

"A previously unknown variety of gum breaker [see glossary] was recently discovered by the author at a bourse in Chicago....The 7 gum breaker configuration appears on a 1½¢ Harding compound perforation stamp (*Scott #633*) in the Series of 1922. Louis Fiset, the preeminent specialist in gum breakers, has described this 7 breaker configuration as a 'new gum breaker discovery,' which 'conforms to nothing in my own collection nor is it mentioned in any of the literature I have.' Gum breakers were first used in the early 1920s in an attempt to reduce the tendency of rotary press sheets to curl. Gum breakers have long been known with 8, 4, 2 and 1 breakers per stamp. Now, almost 80 years later, we must add a 7 breaker variety. The spring of 1928 was a time of much experimentation with gum breakers at the Bureau of Printing and Engraving, and this stamp may have been produced during that period. It has no discernible gum ridges and the gum is whiter than usual."

—*Rodney A. Juell, "New Variety of Gum Breaker Discovered,"* The United States Specialist, *2003.*

Where to Find More Information

- R.H. White's four-volume *Encyclopedia of the Colors of United States Postage Stamps* is the most comprehensive resource on inks and colors. Instead of color chips, this book uses actual U.S. stamps against a neutral gray background making it easy to match actual stamps against actual colors.

- R.H. White's *The Papers and Gums of United States Stamps, 1847–1909* is an excellent reference to gum and paper production.

- Several studies by Richard M. Morris explore the colors of several classic stamps.

- Louis Fiset writes about gum breakers in *Gum Breaker Experiments on BEP Definitives*.

- Rodney A. Juell's "Gum Ridges and Gum Breakers on Rotary Press Sheet Stamps of the Fourth Bureau Issue."

Chapter 52
Errors, Freaks, and Oddities

Stamps are not always produced perfectly. When a stamp varies in one or more ways from the intended norm, it falls into the category called Errors, Freaks, and Oddities (EFOs). These three terms are not synonyms, each having its own technical meaning.

Figure 1

The complete lack of intended perforations is an error, as illustrated on this 1981 Flag Over Supreme Court coil pair (1895d).

Errors are complete and major production mistakes, which are repeatable. For example, a stamp without any intended perforations (fig. 1), or with **tagging**, or a color that is completely missing is an error. An invert (fig. 2) is also an error. Errors are often listed in *Scott*.

Figure 2

The 1962 Dag Hammarskjöld issue exists as a very affordable error with the yellow background inverted, on the right (1204). The normal stamp is on the left (1203).

Freaks are partial production mistakes caused by some unusual circumstances and not likely to be exactly repeatable. For example, paper creases, misperforations (fig. 3), color shifts (fig. 4), and partially missing colors are freaks. Errors will sometimes be found within freak pieces. For example, a paper fold (freak) may result in a miscut booklet pane containing a pair of stamps which are **imperforate between** (error). Or perhaps an ink fountain on a press runs dry, depositing a minimal amount of ink on one row of stamps (freaks) and none on the adjoining row (errors).

Oddities are a broad category of unusual, often consistent, and curious variations that may arise from a variety of sources. For example, **plate varieties**, **private perforations**, design errors, and pre-first-day cancels are oddities.

Figure 3

A misperforation freak on the 1973 Jefferson Memorial stamp (1510).

Figure 4

A freak printing shift on a 1972 Family Planning Issue (1455) appears on the left. A normal stamp is on the right.

Errors

The unintentional use of the wrong paper is an error. For example, the 1¢ Franklin in the Series of 1857 exists on laid paper (*Scott* 24b). Since this stamp is a great rarity, the use of laid paper was probably unintentional, making it an error. An extremely rare error is a stamp printed on both sides of the paper, an example of which is the 1851 1¢ Franklin (9a). This should not be confused with a *set-off*, which is a freak (see fig. 4, ch. 35)

A new type of error appeared in 1895 when the Bureau of Engraving and Printing (BEP) printed postage stamps on paper intended for printing *revenue stamps*. Two stamps, the 6¢ Garfield (271a) and 8¢ Sherman (272a) were printed on paper *watermarked* "USIR" instead of paper watermarked "USPS".

Scott states, "Watermarks may be found normal, reversed, inverted, inverted reversed and sideways as seen from the back of the stamp." In some instances, watermark orientation is a clue to booklet or coil production, but if that is not the case, these orientation varieties are considered to be either freaks or oddities.

Four stamps in the Series of 1869 are bicolored. Three of them, the 15¢, 24¢, and 30¢ are known with the *vignette* inverted with respect to the *frame* (119b, 120b, and 121b), a phenomenon made possible because the vignette and frames were printed in separate operations. An invert is a classic example of an easily identifiable error. Others followed these early ones, the most famous being the *Inverted Jenny* (C3a).

An interesting perforation error appeared in 1917 during the printing of Washington-Franklin stamps, and continued into the first stamps of the Series of 1922. Some stamps, which were intended to be perforated 11, are perforated 10 at the top or bottom. These were created by a section of a damaged gauge 11 perforating wheel which was inadvertently replaced with a section having pins that produced gauge 10 perforations. This perforating wheel was used for some time, as the error has been discovered on seventeen different values.

Freak

The majority of stamps printed on "problem" paper are classified as freaks. Sometimes a *foldover* or *foldunder* is created at the corner of a sheet (fig. 5). If this happens, a part of the design or *marginal marking* may end up on the wrong side of the paper. Sometimes a crease is formed when paper is pinched or folded over on itself in the middle of a sheet. A paper crease, occurring before printing, will exhibit a blank area when subsequently pulled out and is sometimes called a pre-printing paper fold. With imperforate stamps, a crease or fold after printing simply becomes a defective stamp. However if a sheet is creased or folded after printing, but prior to perforating, the result will be prop-

Figure 5

These stamps were printed on paper that was folded prior to printing. The missing portion of the design appears on the back of the stamp.

Figure 6

The fold in this paper occurred between printing and perforating.

erly printed stamps with "crazy" perforations (fig. 6). A dramatic example of a corner fold occurs when the fold forms between the applications of two colors, as happened with the 1932 Red Cross Issue. A fold-over happened between the black print and the red print, in just such a way as to leave the red cross on the back of the margin, and no cross at all on the stamp (702a). *Scott* has assigned this stamp error status because of the completely missing color.

Sometimes too much ink is applied to the paper, generally resulting in a freak. Simply too much ink, or too little, can leave an impression that is dark, fuzzy, light, or even partially unprinted. Another problem is foreign matter on a plate or on paper that can leave gaps in the design. Foreign matter, covered by ink, may also be found on a stamp. String was at one time used to clean intaglio printing plates, with examples from the early twentieth century of pieces of string being found in stamp designs, and others with pieces of string leaving a white, snake-like line in the design (fig. 7). Sometimes even insects and spiders became embedded in a stamp or left a white space of their image! Freaks are also created when ink splatters or smears. A possible production problem with bicolor or multicolor stamps is the **misregistration** of one color in relation to another. This kind of freak is less common on modern stamps because of improved automated detection devices that identify poor **registration** products for destruction.

There is a great quantity of EFO material relating to perforations. For example, a stamp from which the intended perforations are completely absent is an error. Stamps with perforations missing in one direction (horizontal or vertical) but present in the other are errors that *Scott* often lists. Most perforation varieties however are freaks, and are not *Scott* listed. The perforations of freaks are not correctly placed, or are not com-

Figure 7

A piece of string on a printing plate caused this freak.

Figure 8

The gutter pair in the bottom row of this piece was caused by a paper fold.

plete, or are doubled, or even tripled. The more the perforation placement deviates from the intended norm, the more interesting the freak is. Significant freak perforations are somewhat scarce on early stamps but are more common on modern stamps, especially coils.

Most nineteenth century stamps were produced by plates of 200 side-by-side subjects. After printing, the sheets were slit into two panes of 100. There was typically a line between the panes used as a guide for slicing them apart. When the slicing deviated significantly left or right, the result is a freak called a "straddle pane" miscut. Later there were margins, also called gutters, separating panes on a sheet. When a sheet is miscut in such a way that a gutter separates two complete stamps, the resulting freak is called a gutter pair (fig. 8); the known varieties are listed in *Scott*. A related freak is a **gutter snipe**.

Occasionally what was once considered an error, is not. In 1914 several Washington-Franklin stamps were issued with **compound perforations** 12 x 10 or 10 x 12. These resulted from gauge 12 perforating wheels being replaced by gauge 10 perforating wheels. For ninety years these stamps were considered by *Scott* to be errors, the presumed result of inattentive workmen. However research has concluded that the perforating wheels were replaced as a normal and intentional part of the BEP's changeover from the use of perf. 12 to perf. 10. These rare stamps (423A, B, C, D, and E) are now considered normal production varieties and carry their own major *Scott* numbers.

Grills were introduced in 1867. They can be found inverted, doubled, tripled, split between two stamps, and even quartered among four stamps. All are classified as freaks. However, if a grill is entirely missing, the result is an error.

During the Series of 1922 era, some coil stamps and rotary press printed booklet panes began appearing with part of their plate numbers, which are typically trimmed off in the production process. The more of this number that is present, the more interesting and desirable this freak is. Also during the Series of 1922 brown kraft paper was introduced to repair tears in flat plate-printed sheets (fig. 9). Apparently this would allow partially ruined sheets to be completed so that the properly produced panes could be salvaged, with the torn one(s) removed

and destroyed. Repaired panes were sometimes inadvertently released to the public. If the repaired pane had
perforations missing in one direction, the result is an
error within a freak.

Repairs to a rotary press produced **web** are called
splices (fig. 10). Sometimes the web tore and needed
to be spliced together, often with a piece of paper.
Splices were also needed between rolls of paper in
order to maintain continuous production. Splices were
also made by the paper manufacturer. Splices are
freaks rarely seen before the years of the Presidential
Series. Splices have sometimes been made with red
plastic tape.

Double-paper web splices are common freaks from the
Presidential Series. They are often associated with
black or red grease-pencil markings on the printed side
of the web, indicating that the piece was to be removed
and destroyed. After the Presidential Series there are
about 12 different kinds of rejection markings and
splices that have been identified.
They were not common until the
First Class letter rate was raised
to 32¢ in 1995. Presumably as a
cost cutting measure, the USPS
decided to allow splices on coil
stamps to go through the production process and be released with
normal stamps.

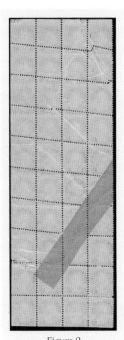

Figure 9

A block of forty from a
flat plate sheet that
jammed while horizon-
tal perforations were
being applied, result-
ing in freak perfora-
tions. It was repaired
with kraft tape after
which vertical perfora-
tions were applied
uneventfully.

Figure 10

A splice between
two rolls of pre-
gummed paper. The
design is printed on
top of the red tape.

The Overrun Countries Issue of
1943–1944 exhibits many minor freaks and oddities.
Printed by the American Bank Note Co., because the BEP
did not have the capability to print the multicolor flag
vignettes, stamps exist with color misregistrations, mis-
shapen letters, and double impressions of the country
names. The Korea stamp (921) exists with an oddity due
to a plate flaw resulting in the word "KOREA" appearing to read "KORPA."
Another variety of these stamps is caused by the order in which the vignettes
were printed. Most of these stamps seem to have been printed with the basic
flag colors printed first, with the shading lines added on top. However, close

inspection reveals that many examples have the basic colors printed over the shading lines. Whether this was done experimentally or through inadvertence has not been established.

In 1947, 1956, and 1966 in honor of the U.S. Philatelic Exhibitions, souvenir sheets were issued (948, 1075, and 1311). Each of these exists as miscut varieties, usually due to paper folds. The result is the presence of marginal paper that should have been trimmed off. Marginal markings are known on these striking freaks. While no plate numbers are known on the first two souvenir sheets, six different plate numbers have been reported on the 1966 sheet.

The American Bicentennial souvenir sheets of 1976 (1686-1689) were produced during a time of experimentation. This resulted in a number of sheets containing errors (missing values and tagging) and freaks (shifted, inverted, and missing perforations, and miscuts).

The introduction of the Giori press in the mid 1950s used three inking-in rollers, each applying a single color to specific areas of a plate. One problem encountered was wiping of excess ink from the plate often resulted in one color bleeding into an adjoining one on the final product, usually a minor freak. Another problem was dripping ink. The three ink troughs were located one above the other. Ink could spill from one trough into the trough below. A small spill that did not have time to be mixed into the different color ink would result in a spot of an incompatible color somewhere in the design. More serious was the larger ink spill, which as it was mixed in resulted in unexpected colors on the final products.

Backprints were introduced with the Postal People Issue of 1973 (1489–1498). Wide cutting of the panes left parts of the green ink plate number visible on the gummed side of the stamp, creating freaks on the backside of the stamp. There are missing backprint errors on the 1975 Contributors to the Cause (1559–1562). There are also the anticipated misregistrations of backprints on stamps that are classified as freaks.

Another freak created from the late 1950s into the early 1980s was a **set-off** of ink on the back of a stamp resulting from the use of two different sheet fed printing presses to produce the stamp. In this case, two or more colors were applied to sheets by one press then the sheet was sent through another press to receive the remaining color ink(s). This was a rapid and automated process, with metal "fingers" picking up each sheet and sending it through the press. However, if a skip occurred, the press did not recognize the absence of a sheet of paper and printed the color not on a sheet of paper, but on the impression roller that pressed the paper into the recesses of the intaglio plate.

The next sheets through the press would receive that wet ink from the impression roller on the backside of the sheet, even as the press was applying the same color(s) to the front. These freaks can be recognized by the clear image in reverse on the back.

Oddities

Plate varieties (ch. 46) found on many nineteenth and early twentieth century stamps are usually classified as oddities. However, some of the more extreme plate varieties, such as the 5¢ carmine Washington-Franklin *foreign transfers* (467, 485, and 505) are errors.

Color shade varieties (see fig. 1, 2, and 3, ch. 51) are classified as oddities. Stamps produced over a long period of time often show different shades for a variety of reasons. Sometimes *Scott* assigns major number status to such varieties, especially on mid-nineteenth century stamps. In other instances *Scott* simply lists shades without assigning catalogue numbers. Subtle and unlisted shade variations can be found on many stamps.

EFOs can also occur on precancels. While fairly rare on **Bureau Precancels**, they are common on **Local Precancels**, including inverts, misspellings, and doubled prints.

There is a category of unintended stamp material known as printers' waste (fig. 11) that is not error, freak, nor oddity. Printers' waste is created by a variety of causes which include stopping or starting a press, and the interruption of ink.

Figure 11

A piece of printer's waste, intended for destruction, picked up on the street outside the BEP, where it had fallen from a waste container.

Printers' waste is supposed to be removed from production and destroyed. On rare occasions printers' waste has been accidentally or criminally removed from the production or waste destruction facility. It then makes its way into the philatelic market, often misidentified as error material. Since printers waste is never intended to reach public hands, these items should be regarded with suspicion by collectors. Printers' waste is generally shunned by collectors. Items are not listed in *Scott*, and when known to exist, warnings about them do appear. Printers' waste in philatelic hands is known as early as the **Large Bank Notes**.

Notes on Collecting

EFO collecting is an unusual challenge. There is no single reference or catalog that describes all the varieties. No catalog lists every issue on which each variety occurs. *Scott* lists errors but does not include freaks. Complicating this situation, one cannot order a specific stamp to fill a space in an album for most categories of EFO. The EFO collector must always be alert for both useful information and interesting material.

Most EFOs exist in very small quantities, yet are often relatively inexpensive when compared to their quantity. For example, a unique pane of 50 significantly misperforated commemoratives may sell for only $10 to $15 per stamp. If a collector desires that particular misperfed commemorative, it is best purchased when offered, for the opportunity may not be presented again.

EFOs are sometimes used to enhance a collection of normal stamps. Other times EFOs are used as the basis of a specialized collection, perhaps of missing colors, misperfs, or folds and creases.

Most collectors will never discover an EFO despite the billions of stamps produced each year. The material is simply not common. Furthermore, what does exist is largely of minor significance. While most definitives will have some flawed material, there are many commemoratives with no known flawed material at all.

Almanac

1869 – Printing the first bicolored stamps results in the first inverts.

1918 – The 24¢ Curtiss Jenny air mail invert (C3a) is printed.

1978 – The EFO Collectors' Club formed.

What Others Have Said

First you have to know what's normal…
"An EFO collector's most important possession may be philatelic literature. The pages of books and periodicals contain a vast treasure of knowledge produced by collectors of all persuasions. It's available with relatively little cost compared to the benefit one may receive!…The EFO Collector is a seeker of a *deviant* stamp – one that did not turn out exactly as intended. To tell the deviant from the normal, one must first have a basic foundation of knowledge of what may be considered normal and how it is produced."

—*Larry S. Weiss, "Literature for the EFO Collector," EFO Collector, 1978.*

...and then you have to know about stamp production methods.

"A freak and error collection is in reality a study of the types of printing and perforating methods, along with the equipment being utilized to achieve normal stamp manufacture at any given time. An error, freak, and oddity collection certainly shows the evolution and modernization of our production techniques that at the present time have enabled the Bureau of Engraving and Printing to produce literally billions of multicolor stamps on mammoth presses."

—*Stanley B. Segal, 1979.*

How much is a freak really worth? It depends...

"Visual appeal and topical appeal are most often the key elements in pricing freaks. The element of scarcity comes more into play in pricing non-unique freaks, where a definite quantity is known. The best way to get a handle on the prices of freaks is to check retail price lists for comparables, sturdy prices realized from public auctions, and talk to dealers and collectors."

—*Stephen R. Datz*, Errors, Freaks and Oddities on U.S. Stamps – Question Marks in Philately, *2005.*

...and then there's the challenge of mounting those freaks!

"A collector of freaks can seldom plan an album page in advance unless the item is of such nature as to warrant a page of its own. He has no way of knowing what freak may be found in the future and often has no knowledge of those already discovered by others unless they have been reported....As my collection grew larger I began placing the stamps into various categories, such as misperfs, printing shifts, double papers, pre-printing folds, preprinting paper creases, printing varieties, inking varieties...and so on....It has always been my opinion that misperfs are more attractive as singles then as blocks. I feel blocks emphasize the over-all design of the stamp to such an extent that the focus on the misperforations is diminished."

—*E. Ellsworth Post, "Many are the problems of Mounting a Freak Collection,"* The United States Specialist, *1967.*

Example of Postal Usage

Figure 12

A stamp with freak perforations used on an 1861 cover.

Where to Find More Information

- The latest edition of Stephen R. Datz' *Catalogue of Errors on U.S. Postage Stamps* is a comprehensive guide to invert, color, and perforation errors.

- *Errors, Freaks and Oddities on U.S. Stamps – Question Marks in Philately* by Dr. Stanley B. Segal gives a detailed background on EFOs.

- The Errors, Freaks, Oddities Collectors Club maintains a very informative web site at www.efoers.org.

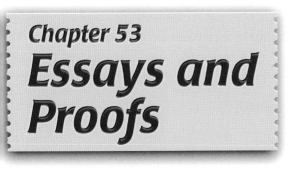

Chapter 53
Essays and Proofs

Essays and **proofs** are artifacts of the earliest stages of stamp production. Occasionally unique, and often scarce, these items hold a fascination for collectors because of their historical significance. Additionally, their special beauty, the beauty of a **designer's** artwork or the beauty of a crisp, bright print made directly from the **engraver's** die makes them desirable. Essays and proofs are often referenced and collected together. However they are very different kinds of collectibles, their commonality being that they are not stamps, but are indispensable to the stamp production process.

In United States philately, the terms essay and proof include an overwhelming variety of material, much of which is more dissimilar than it is alike. Consequently, generalities in this area of collecting are difficult, and some scholars may disagree on certain definitions.

Essays

The word essay is used to denote a trial, preliminary, or attempted item. Essays can be divided into two basic categories, "design essays" which are an artist's suggestion for a proposed stamp and "production essays", which are suggestions which are printed in some fashion. In order for an item to be classified in either essay category, it must meet certain requirements. It must have some official connection or sanction and vary in some degree, no matter how minute, from an issued stamp. The definition of essay, crafted by Clarence W. Brazer, the foremost student of essays of United States stamps is, "any design, or part of a design, essayed to or produced by a government (or established mail carrier) for a stamp and differing in design in any particular [manner] from an officially issued stamp."

Artwork produced by staff artists (designers) at bank note engraving and printing companies and at the Bureau of Engraving and Printing (BEP), is by defi-

Figure 1

A wash drawing essay (372-E2) of the frame design for the 1909 Hudson-Fulton Celebration Issue.

Figure 2

A photo-essay of the 1932 Arbor Day Issue, unlisted in *Scott*.

Figure 3

A production essay (11-E7).

nition, essay material. Artwork prepared as a design for a stamp by a private individual, and submitted for consideration would only qualify as an essay if solicited or if subsequent to its unsolicited submission, it was accepted as the basis for a stamp that was ultimately issued.

An essay includes: preliminary sketches, **wash drawings**, photographic composites, and the like, for the proposed stamp, as well as for any portion of the proposed stamp, (fig. 1). Drawings are usually done at four to five times the size of the stamp. When drawings are submitted for review, they are often accompanied by a photographically-reduced **photo-essay** (fig. 2), so the security printer or postal authority can see what the stamp is intended to look like in its intended size. The final approved drawing is known as the **model**. The engraver uses the full-sized model and the smaller photo-essay of the model to engrave the **die** from which the stamp will be produced.

The second category of essays, the production essay, consists of stamp-like items that have actually been printed in whole or in part from dies, plates, or even the flat stones used in **lithographic** printing (fig. 3). Production essays are examples of printers' work, most commonly from the nineteenth century. They were often produced for submission to the Post Office Department as part of an attempt to obtain a stamp production contract. Since thrifty printers made regular use of dies they had in stock, production essays often appear to be incomplete versions of actually issued stamps. That is, they have a familiar **vignette**, but a different frame.

Production essays include proposals to prevent the fraudulent reuse of stamps. These include essays printed with special inks, on special papers, with

Figure 4

A production essay, the so-called Bowlsby patent coupon (63-E13f).

experimental grills and with underprintings or **overprintings**. In order to prevent the reuse of stamps George W. Bowlsby proposed a stamp that would not be valid without its attached coupon, which was to be removed by the post office in lieu of canceling. Bowlsby patented his concept, and an essay was printed by the National Bank Note Company, using the design of their 1¢ stamp (fig. 4).

Proofs

Proofs are impressions **pulled** from a die or a plate to "prove" (in the sense of confirming or establishing) the condition of the die or plate either during or at the completion of the die-engraving or plate-making process. Although essays can exist for a stamp printed by any process, proofs exist only for stamps printed in whole, or in part, by an **intaglio** process.

A die is a block of steel which has been softened, onto which the engraver engraves the design of the stamp. A print made from a die before it is completely engraved is known as a **die essay**, since it is printed from a die that varies in some way from the stamp ultimately issued. Such prints are also known as **progressive die proofs** (fig. 5), because they show progress in the engraving of the die.

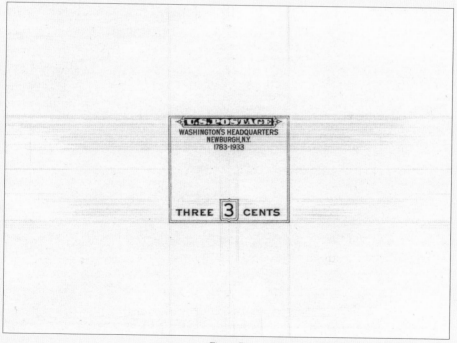

Figure 5

This progressive die proof, unlisted in *Scott*, shows progress in completing work on the die for the 1933 Peace Issue (727). It was once in Franklin D. Roosevelt's collection.

Prints made to prove dies are called *die proofs*, and prints made to prove plates are known as *plate proofs*. Die proofs are further characterized as *large die proofs* or *small die proofs*, based solely upon the size of the paper upon which the print has been made.

Die proofs are printed on special hand-operated proving presses that hold the die in place and produce one print at a time. Proofs often are printed on a special paper known as *india paper*, a thin, soft, and absorbent paper used to enhance the detail being impressed, which may be placed on a larger piece of card to withstand the pressure applied by the proving press. Proofs are also commonly printed directly onto card. The pressure of the proving press causes india paper to adhere to the card backing. On a large die proof, the full shape of the die block, known as the *die sinkage*, is impressed onto the card, providing the basis for one definition of a large die proof, a proof large enough to show the full die sinkage. The size of the card varies by printer, but most large die proofs that were printed at the BEP are approximately 6 by 9 inches in size (fig. 6).

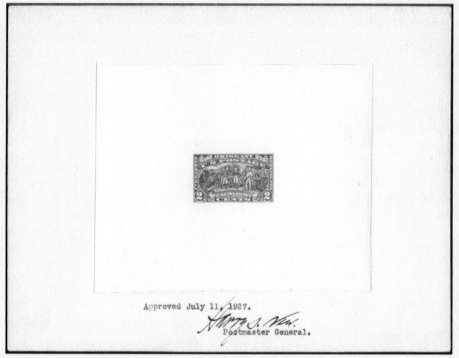

Figure 6

A large die proof (644P1) of the 1927 Burgoyne Campaign Issue, signed by Postmaster General Harry S. New.

The sources of large die proofs for collectors are varied and limited. In addition to being used to check and approve the quality of engraving, large die proofs were submitted as samples for the approval by the postal authorities. During the *banknote era*, salesmen carried sample books whose pages consisted of large die proofs. Some large die proofs were prepared by the BEP for the collection of President Franklin Roosevelt long after the stamps prepared from those dies had been issued. Until the mid-1950s, engravers at the BEP were allowed to keep a proof of each of the stamps that they engraved, and these copies have trickled onto the market from the engravers' estates.

Small die proofs, in contrast, do not show die sinkage and have been trimmed to produce items that look more like *imperforate* stamps. Some were produced years later to provide examples of the printers' work rather than to prove the engraver's work, so it may be argued that they are not really "proofs" at all, but rather "die prints".

There are two categories of small die proofs, Roosevelt and Panama-Pacific. Small die proofs are found in 85 **Roosevelt Presentation Albums** prepared by the BEP in 1903, during President Theodore Roosevelt's administration, for various dignitaries. Each album contained 308 small die proofs mounted in sets on stiff grey cardboard pages (fig. 7).

Figure 7
Page from a Roosevelt Presentation Album of small die proofs.

Panama-Pacific small die proofs were prepared in 1914 and 1915 by the BEP for an exhibition at the Panama-Pacific Exposition. Panama-Pacific small die proofs exist for 413 different stamps, generally in very small quantities of four or five per issue. The two Roosevelt and Panama-Pacific proofs can be distinguished by their paper (white wove for the Roosevelt, and yellow wove for the Panama-Pacific proofs) and by the size of their margins (4 to 5 mm for the Roosevelt, and 3 mm or less for the Panama-Pacific proofs). Many of the Roosevelt small die proofs are found still affixed to their gray card backing.

None of this nomenclature is exact. Small die proofs described as Roosevelt proofs exist for stamps issued after 1903, and small die proofs described as Panama-Pacific proofs exist for stamps issued after 1915. Current research suggests that additional sets probably were produced for the BEP's own records, as well as for other displays, such as the Post Office Department's **Philatelic Truck** that toured the country from 1939 to 1941.

After a die has been approved and **hardened**, its design is picked up on a **transfer roll**, which is thereafter used to transfer the design repeatedly onto the printing plate. After the plate has been prepared, it is necessary to prove the plate in order to determine if it is ready to print stamps, or if additional touch-up or transferring work is required. Prints made to prove a plate are **plate proofs**. Plate proofs are prints of full sheets made from complete finished plates. They exist either on India paper or on card and can exist as multiples on either (fig. 8).

Figure 8
Portion of a plate proof (150P3).

Trial color proofs are either die or plate proofs of an issued stamp printed in a color other than the final color, to determine the suitability of one or more proposed colors of ink for a specific stamp, or to see a range of colors for a series, or to test how the mixed inks print. For twentieth-century material, these are generally found only as large die proofs.

Specimens

Specimens are related to essays and proofs. They are actual stamps that have been overprinted or handstamped by the printer with the words, "specimen" or "sample." They had various uses for submissions to the Post Office, as examples held in the printer's stock, and for distribution to member countries of the *Universal Postal Union* as examples of the country's stamps.

Notes on Collecting

Large die proofs are relatively scarce items, particularly twentieth century large die proofs. Only limited numbers are available for collectors. Plate proofs on India or card are typically more affordable.

Although Brazer's handbook was the standard reference for essays for many years, the main catalog of U.S. essays and proofs now is *Scott*. *Scott* describes and prices essays of postage stamps and back-of-the-book stamps (but not revenues), and die, plate, and trial color proofs of these stamps (including revenues).

Proofs, being prints of issued stamps, are catalogued in a straight forward way. *Scott* uses the catalogue number of the stamp, followed by a suffix "P," which is followed by a numerical suffix: 1 for a large die proof of the issue, 2 for a Roosevelt small die proof, 2a for a Panama-Pacific small die proof, 3 for a plate proof on india paper, and 4 for a plate proof on card. For example, C1P1 would describe a large die proof of the 6¢ airmail stamp of 1918, while 330P2a would be a Panama-Pacific small die proof of the 5¢ Jamestown issue of 1907, and 245P3 would be a plate proof, on india, of the $5 Columbian issue of 1893.

Essays are more problematic, since many do not resemble issued stamps and could be subject to a haphazard numbering system. Instead, the cataloguers try to relate essays to issued stamps. They are catalogued first by the period in which they were produced, and then are grouped by printer. This system can take some getting used to, since similar-looking essays may appear in several places in *Scott* depending upon their time of production.

For example, all 3¢ essays attributed to the 1851 period begin with the number 11, being the *Scott* number assigned to the standard 3¢ stamp of that era, even though the essays may bear no resemblance whatsoever to that stamp. The number is followed by the suffix "-E" (for "essay"), which in turn is followed by another number representing the catalogue number assigned to that essay. Varieties – whether printed from a die or plate, type of paper or card, se-tenants or multiples – are given further small letter suffixes. Colors are listed but generally not further numbered.

When the BEP took over production of all U.S. stamps, there were few non-Bureau essays. For the era of BEP production, essays consist of artists' work, die prints of vignettes or frames, and progressive proofs, and they are easily catalogued by reference to the catalogue number of the issued stamp. For example, essays for the Alaska-Yukon-Pacific Exposition stamp of 1909 are 370-E1, 370-E2, 370-E3, etc.

Essays of United States revenue stamps have been catalogued by George T. Turner, using a numbering system he devised. Essays and proofs also exist of postal stationery (fig. 9).

New discoveries of essays and proofs are often reported in the *Chronicle of the U.S. Classic Postal Issues.*

Figure 9
Essay for a paid reply postal card from the 1877 to 1879 period.

Almanac

1889 – John K. Tiffany publishes the first list of U.S. essays in the *American Journal of Philately*.

1911 – Edward H. Mason presents his list of U.S. essays in the form of a handbook issued by the American Philatelic Society.

1941 – Clarence W. Brazer's handbook, *Essays for U.S. Adhesive Postage Stamps*, is published by the American Philatelic Society.

1944 – The Essay-Proof Society is formed. It publishes a quarterly journal, *The Essay-Proof Journal*, for fifty years, until the Society disbands in 1993.

What Others Have Said

Why Collect Proofs and Essays?

"Of what interest and value are proofs and essays to a philatelist?....proofs and essays show part of the history of a stamp and also reveal some things about the methods used in its production which otherwise might not be known or determinable. What can proofs and essays tell us about the origin and history of the stamp?

1. The character of the die, its shape and size, the technique of the engraver, and the methods of pulling proofs; effects of different papers and inks on the impression, etc.

2. In comparing proofs with the corresponding stamps, one can deduce the changes in the impression resulting from: the process of copying dies and making the plate; from the retouches, re-entries (double transfers)....wear in printing, surfacing and cleaning of plates, makeready, etc.

3. In comparing proofs with essays and stamps, modification of designs, of dies or complete re-engravings, are revealed.

4. Whether numerals were engraved on the original (master) die or on secondary dies, etc.

5. Whether rotogravure printing plates were made from a photo, a painting, or an engraving.

6. Proof sheets or blocks (plate proofs) may assist in plating studies.

....Many collectors include a few proofs in their collection merely because they think it contributes to completeness and will add points or prestige to the collection in exhibition (and they are so right!)....Then there are those who 'specialize' in proofs, some as an object of research, but more likely because proofs are generally beautiful (more beautiful that the stamps) and even as an investment or speculation."

—*Robert G. Stone, "Why Collect Proofs and Essays?" The Essay-Proof Journal, 1969.*

More about "progress proofs"
"...there can be no such thing philatelically as a 'progress proof' of incomplete states of a stamp design. Any incomplete design is not exactly like the completed and finally approved design of the issued stamp, and being incomplete it cannot be a proof but is a progress essay design which may be changed, and frequently is, prior to final approval of the completed design. The incorrect use of 'progress proof' for 'progress print (or impression)' has led to much confusion. Of course there cannot be any such thing philatelically as a 'die proof of an essay'; it must be either a 'die essay' or a 'die proof.'"

—*Clarence W. Brazer, "Essays versus Proofs," The Essay-Proof Journal, 1949. Engravers often prove their dies as they are engraving, thus producing proofs of stamps that ultimately will be issued, but incomplete to varying degrees. Most collectors have no difficulty accepting these prints – as long as they are part of the evolutionary process of an issued stamp -- as progress proofs or progressive die proofs. Brazer however was adamant that such terminology was improper.*

On-going research on essay and proofs continually reveals new information
"One of the attractions of essay/proof collecting is the detective work involved in determining the true status of a specific item and the ensuing collaboration with other collectors who can add to the store of information. Readers of these [essay-proof] committee reports will recall the initial article about the mystery 15¢ 'parcels post' design featuring Grover Cleveland in our February, 2001 issue. This was followed in the May issue with more information from Bill Weiss about how the 'essay' reached his firm, through a 'Smillie estate'.....The May article was subtitled 'The Rest of the Story', but that was premature in view of the additional details made available..."

—*Barbara R. Mueller, "The Parcels Post 'Essay' – The Story Has Not Ended," The United States Specialist, 2001.*

Project Mercury Large Die Proof Discovered in a 2004 internet auction
"A large die proof of the 1962 Project Mercury issue, currently unlisted in *Scott*, has recently come to light, over forty years after it was pulled (printed) at the Bureau of Engraving and Printing (BEP). No other proof of this stamp is known to exist in private hands, and it is the most recently produced large die proof of

any commemorative or definitive stamp currently known in private hands. James Kloetzel, editor of *Scott*, has confirmed that this large die proof will be listed in future editions of the Catalogue."

—*Rodney A. Juell, "Project Mercury Large Die Proof," The United States Specialist, 2005.*

Where to Find More Information

- *Scott* is the best guide for information on essays and proofs of U.S. adhesive stamps.

- Clarence W. Brazer's *Essays for U.S. Adhesive Stamps* first published in 1941 remains an essential classic reference. The 1977 Quarterman Publications reprint includes Brazer's addenda.

- The 50-year run of *The Essay-Proof Journal*, which has ceased publication, contains a wealth of articles about all aspects of design and engraving, as well as collecting essays and proofs.

- Ronald A. Burns has carefully reviewed small die proofs in *Study of the Production Records for the 1903 and 1914-15 Printings of the "Roosevelt" and "Panama-Pacific" Small Die Proofs.*

- James H. Patterson's *Small Die Proofs of the 20th Century's Second Quarter* is useful for those who wish to study the proofs of this period.

- For essays and proofs of U.S. revenue stamps, see George T. Turner's handbook, *Essays and Proofs of United States Internal Revenue Stamps.* This is the best source of information about these interesting items.

- Postal Stationery essays and proofs are handled beautifully in Dan Undersander's *Catalog of United States Stamped Envelope Essays and Proofs,* which includes a full-color CD-ROM.

Chapter 54
Luminescence

Some stamps glow if they are subjected to ultraviolet (UV) light. This glowing effect is known as "*luminescence*".

A stamp will exhibit luminescence for one of two reasons: either because a stamp's paper or ink contains *fluorescent* brighteners, or because a phosphorescent tagging has been applied to a printed stamp, or to a stamp's paper prior to printing, or mixed in with the ink used to print a stamp.

Fluorescence is best viewed under long wave UV light, but it also glows to a lesser extent under short wave UV light. To see tagging however (which is what stamp collectors call stamps with phosphorescence) the item must be viewed under short wave UV light.

Luminescence stamp collecting began when the "Jet Airliner over Capitol" air mail stamp of 1962 (*Scott* C64) was issued on August 1, 1963 in Dayton, Ohio with phosphorescent tagging (C64a). John Stark, Alfred "Tag" Boerger, and William Bayless were among the early pioneers who recognized the significance of luminescence for stamps collectors and who, by their study and writing, introduced stamp collectors to this new dimension of their hobby.

Stamps with Fluorescent Brighteners
The sole purpose for adding fluorescent brighteners to stamp paper is to increase the paper's apparent whiteness under normal lighting. We now know that fluorescent brighteners were added to stamp paper as early as 1938. But stamps with fluorescent brighteners went unnoticed until collectors started searching their collections for phosphor tagged stamps in the 1960s. At the beginning of the twenty-first century, the earliest known stamp exhibiting a noticeable degree of fluorescence was the 4¢ Bolivar (1110) issued on July 24, 1958.

Fluorescent stamps have optical brighteners added to their paper pulp during manufacturing. This causes the paper to glow, or "fluoresce" a bluish white under short or long wave UV light. The paper also appears whiter to the eye under natural light. Fluorescent stamps glow only while being exposed to UV light; there is no after glow.

The degree of brightness under UV light depends on the amount of brightener added to the paper pulp. It varies from a dull glow, to a dazzling brilliance. Prior to 1964, the Post Office Department (USPOD) was unaware of, and therefore exercised no control over, the degree of brightness that existed in the paper used for stamp production. After 1964 all paper vendors were advised by the Bureau of Engraving and Printing (BEP) to keep the brightness of the paper below a dull level. This was done both in the interest of uniformity and to avoid complicating the emerging use of phosphor tagging on stamps to expedite mail sorting. Since quality control was not always perfect, occasional bright paper items slipped through. The limit on adding brighteners to stamp paper was removed by the Postal Service (USPS) around 1980. Stamps now commonly appear printed on "hi-bright" paper. The State Birds and Flowers issue (1953-2002) and the 20¢ U.S.-Sweden stamp (2036) were among the first stamps purposely printed on hi-bright paper.

Stamps with Phosphorescent Tagging

Tagged (phosphorescent) stamps were created to effect a method of automating the "facing" of letters for canceling. A method was needed for the automatic canceler to be able to locate the stamp on a letter, which would then mechanically turn the envelope correctly so that the stamp would receive a cancel. The first field tests of this automated mail handling equipment were conducted in Dayton, Ohio, following the 1963 release of the first tagged stamp.

To enable the mail handling equipment to "find" a stamp, stamps were coated with an invisible phosphorescent **taggant** ink after they were printed. This is known as **Overall Tagging**. The coating glows green when exposed to short wave UV light; or, in the case of early tagged airmails, it glows red. After the UV light source is removed, the tagged ink continues to glow for a fraction of a second. It is this after-glow that allows the automatic letter facer to locate the stamp, and correctly face (position) the letter so that the stamp receives the cancel.

The green tagging colors (reddish-orange in the case of airmail) seen under UV light are affected by any fluorescent brightness in the paper. Short wave UV light also reveals some, but not all, of the fluorescent brightness. Since most fluorescent paper has a bluish-white glow, this changes the perceived green tagging color to various shades of bluish-green. The brighter the paper, the more the tagging tends toward a blue shade. Reddish-orange airmail tagging color also is affected by bright paper. Bright paper changes the red tagging color to an iridescent pinkish-red.

Many different methods for applying "overall" phosphorescent tagged coating have been used since 1963. This results in an interesting, but challenging variety of tagged stamps. The first "overall" tagged stamps had taggant ink applied by four rubber mats mounted on a printing **cylinder**. This produced **tagging - type I**. The entire pane of 50 stamps was completely tagged except for the four sheet margins that were outside of the tagging mat's perimeter (fig. 1). The use of these same mats caused untagged gaps to appear randomly both in early tagged coils and booklets.

Figure 1

Type I tagging, seen here on the 4¢ Liberty (1036b), is a type of "overall tagging" because the entire stamp is tagged, even though some of the margin (gray areas) are untagged. Type I tagging was used on the first tagged stamp – the 8¢ Jet Airliner over Capitol airmail (C64a).

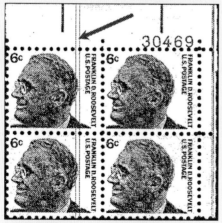

Figure 2

Type III tagging on a 6¢ Roosevelt (1284a). The entire piece is tagged except for the "gap". This is classified as "overall tagging".

Tagging mats were replaced by rollers that applied a continuous coating. Initially this eliminated all untagged sheet margins except for the large plate block selvage at the sides of the press sheets. Since the coating on the cylinder was not as wide as the paper web, the large plate block selvage margins on both outside edges of the paper web were left untagged. This is known as *tagging - type II*, introduced in 1964. Subsequently, tagging rollers were increased in width to eliminate all untagged selvage margins. This produced *tagging - type IIA*.

Two metal plates butted together and mounted on a printing cylinder were used for applying taggant for a very short period in 1966. They produced embossed lines very similar in appearance to the *joint lines* found on coil stamps of the period, and can be seen under normal light with a standard 2x magnifying glass. These embossed lines either lacked tagging, or in some cases had heavier, brighter, tagging where the taggant ink collected in the gap between the two plates. This produced *tagging – type III* (fig. 2).

Not all tagging is "overall". Several other methods have been used to apply tagging. One very common variation, **Block Tagging**, places a block of phosphor tagged coating in approximately the center of each stamp, leaving the areas adjoining the perforations untagged (fig. 3). **Band Tagging** is a continuous narrow band of phosphor tagged coating that extends across a pane. This tagging method was first used on the Postal Service Employees Issue of 1973 (1489-1498). Block tagging was developed in response to the BEP's discovery that overall tagging, applied prior to the perforating operation, accelerated wear of the perforating pins. **Image Tagging**, first used on the 1975 Eagle and Shield stamp (1596), tags only a stamp's image, or portion of its image.

Figure 3

"Block tagging" on a 1985 Walter Lippmann stamp (1849). The gray area is not tagged.

The phosphor tagging that causes a stamp to glow can also be imparted in ways other than applying it over the printed stamp. Phosphor taggant can be added to ink. Occasionally stamps are printed on a pre-phosphored paper. Pre-phosphored paper exists in two varieties, coated and uncoated. Taggant applied to uncoated paper will have a somewhat mottled appearance, while taggant applied to coated paper will have a more uniform appearance.

Bureau precanceled stamps were generally not tagged. Since there was no need for equipment to "find" and cancel these stamps, tagging was unnecessary.

Stamps with face values below 8¢ have not been tagged since January 1, 1991. In an attempt to avoid payment of postage, some placed a tagged, but low denomination stamp, on an envelope in the hope that the short payment would not be detected (fig. 4). The Postal Service eliminated tagging from low denomination stamps to attempt to avoid this loss of revenue.

Almanac

1958 – The first stamps with a notable degree of fluorescence are issued July 24.

1963 – Tagged stamps are officially introduced on August 1 with the issuance of the 8¢ airmail stamp (C64a).

1963 - The entire printing of the City Mail Delivery stamp (1238) is issued tagged on October 26. It is the first stamp issued only in a tagged version.

1964 – In June the USPOD orders all 8¢ air mail stamps tagged for general distribution.

1967 – Most stamps issued beginning January 1, including all commemoratives, are ordered to be tagged.

Notes on Collecting

Collecting luminescent stamps has some unique challenges. The most obvious is the purchase of an ultraviolet (UV) lamp. While no recommendations are made in these pages, the Raytech Company has long been a pioneer and producer of these lamps. In 2005 dollars, an UV lamp could cost as little as $50 and as much as $350. It is likely that a smaller lamp will lack the power to see small tagging differences, and will disappoint when attempting to distinguish between more difficult tagging types. Collectors of tagged stamps must have a portable UV lamp to look through dealer's stock at stamp shows and in stamp shops to be successful at their hunt.

Protecting the eyes is an important consideration when using an UV lamp. Do not look directly into the lamp when it is turned on. It would be similar to lookig into the sun which may damage the eyes. Limit exposure time when using an UV lamp.

There are unique mounting and storing concerns for luminescent stamps. It is strongly recommend that the early tagged stamps on cover (through 1967), never be removed from their covers. A theme throughout this *Encyclopedia* is, when in doubt, leave a stamp on its cover. This is particularly important here, so that the cover, with its destination and postal markings, shows the distribution and use of these stamps in their early period of use.

Remove a used stamp from its cover only after determining there is no particular value to retaining the stamp on its cover. Do not soak the stamp! Neatly cut it off, leaving a small paper border around the stamp. There is the possibility that soaking the stamp will wash off or dull some of the collectible phosphorescence!

Whether choosing to collect tagged stamps in mint or used condition, they pose a unique problem in mounting. Most better album pages have been brightened during the production process, so they will glow when using a UV lamp! Use non-brightened paper for album pages, or use the philatelic black pages which are available. Be aware that most polystyrene mounts will serve as a protective filter for UV light, and therefore the tagging on stamps cannot be viewed through the safety shield that these "see-through" mounts provide.

What Others Have Said

The Dean of luminescence defines the subject for clarity

"Since luminescent postal issues of the United States have been various, and issued both intentionally and inadvertently, the following philatelic definitions are offered in order that the reader...[may understand] the circumstances which brought them about:

Luminescent: Postal issues that glow when exposed to ultraviolet either during or after exposure.

Phosphorescent: Postal issues that exhibit some glow after exposure to ultraviolet regardless of how brief the time.

Fluorescent: Postal Issues that glow only when exposed to ultraviolet.

Tagged: Postal issues intentionally treated to glow when exposed to ultraviolet sources used in conjunction with automatic mail sorting equipment."

—*William H. Bayless, "Luminescent U.S. Postal Issues," American Philatelic Congress Book, 1968. It is easy to see that many collectors intertwine the use of these four words.*

Announcing ultra-violet light's entry into the USPOD mailstream

"Ultra-violet light has teamed up with photo electric eyes for high-speed mail sorting. Postmaster General J. Edward Day announced today the beginning of field tests August 1, in Dayton Ohio, in which envelopes bearing airmail stamps printed with special luminescent ink will be separated from untreated mail at an overall rate of 30,000 per hour. If the tests are successful eventually all stamps will be phosphor-tagged. A small, black box added to the Mark II facer-canceling machine will 'recognize' and separate specially treated airmail stamps in the field tests. Engineers said the modification is relatively inexpensive."

—*"Information Service – Post Office Department," Philatelic Release No. 51, July 7, 1963. The news release reports the completion of three years of planning, and the beginning of field-testing.*

Modern stamp papers vary greatly from one to the other

"An interesting thing often observed when examining stamps under ultra-violet is the variations in fluorescence of the paper on which the stamps are printed. Very old papers show for the most part little if any fluorescence...while modern papers vary from non-fluorescent to brilliant blue-white fluorescence which is best observed in longwave ultraviolet. It is common for the same issue of stamps to appear printed both on fluorescent and non-fluorescent paper....the U.S. 4¢ Lincoln stamp not only appears as a tagged stamp, but also in untagged varieties both on fluorescent and non-fluorescent papers."

—*The Story of Fluorescence, 1965 edition. The first edition of this book, commenting on the early tagged U.S. stamps being printed in many formats. Today all stamps over the 8¢ rate are tagged, and are printed on the same stock of paper.*

Early recognition of luminescent cover collecting

"An article in Linn's Stamp News of May 26, 1973, advises that the 1973-1974 edition of the 'United States Catalog of First Day Covers' has been published by the Washington Press of Maplewood, N.J....Part of the article states: 'In the 1960s many commemoratives were issued in phosphorescent varieties as well in untagged condition. The revised listings of tagged covers include prices for the first time. Though these covers are relatively scarce, demand for them has not yet boosted their prices to the heights probably warranted by their scarcity.'"

—William H. Bayless, "Luminescence," The United States Specialist, 1973. *Giving a perspective on how some aspects of U.S. stamp collecting take time to develop.*

The Look Magazine Liberty coil is one of the most famous tagged stamps

"Look Magazine, whose corporate offices were located [in] Des Moines, used combinations of low denomination stamps as a promotional gimmick on advertising mail....The earliest documented use of a tagged coil on a Look magazine envelope is canceled December 29, 1966. Alfred Boerger's 1974 *Handbook on Luminescent U.S. Stamps* illustrates the stamp and cancellation....The book refers to [this illustration as a cover], but in a 1982 article, Boerger refers to the Dec. 29 item as an 'on-piece' clipping."

—Ken Lawrence, "The 3¢ Statue of Liberty Coil Stamps," Scott's Stamp Monthly, 2003. *Lawrence describes the important discovery of one of the most famous tagged stamps, the "Look magazine coil" which was never announced to the public, but discovered by stamp collectors after its distribution and use.*

U.S. stamps below 8¢ face value being issued without tagging

"Don McDowell...told Linn's that effective on a certain date shortly after the first of the year...all new stamps with face values of less than 8¢ will be produced untagged only. The current stamps that go back to press...also will be produced untagged. This will create varieties for collectors to pursue. McDowell also told Linn's that the recent change is primarily related to revenue protection [since] the presence of a single tagged stamp is enough to send underpaid mail through highly automated equipment without detection....Why 8¢? [it] was decided upon in cooperation with the USPS' Postal Inspection Service. The 8c breakpoint will help assure that fewer shortpaid mailpieces are processed."

—Wayne Youngblood, "U.S. stamps below 8¢ face value being issued without tagging," Linn's Stamp News, 1991.

Example of Postal Usage

Figure 4

This 1988 cover, bearing only a tagged 1¢ stamp, successfully went through the mailstream. In order to reduce incidents of this nature, the tagging of low denomination stamps was ended in 1991.

For More Information

- *Handbook on U.S. Luminescent Stamps*, by Alfred G. Boerger.

- "Luminescent U.S. Stamps" by John S. Stark and Alfred G. Boerger is a reprint from a series in the SPA (Society of Philatelic Americans) Journal.

- *Stamps that Glow* by Wayne Youngblood.

- *The Story of Fluourescence* by Raytech Industries is a comprehensive guide to the topic with several pages devoted to stamp collecting.

Chapter 55
Test Stamps

Test stamps, sometimes called "Dummy Stamps", have been printed by the Bureau of Engraving and Printing (BEP) and used both by it and the Post Office. Test stamps have also been produced and used by private companies. They have served four purposes:

1. Develop and test stamp production equipment including printing presses and stamp and booklet manufacturing equipment.

2. Test and adjust stamp vending equipment at dispensing sites by the Postal Service and private companies.

3. Test and adjust stamp-affixing equipment used by commercial vendors.

4. Demonstrate and promote stamp dispensing equipment.

Test stamps clearly show the steps in the technological development of stamps through the years.

Figure 1

Test stamps like these were used early in the twentieth century at the BEP as the Stickney Rotary Press was being developed.

The first test stamps produced by the BEP resulted from an order placed on October 26, 1907 for "500 sheets of postage stamp paper, perforated and gummed, but not printed." These "stamps" were apparently for distribution to companies developing stamp vending machines for the Post Office.

A test stamp with a printed design was prepared by the BEP for experimental use when the first **Stickney rotary press** was acquired, and test runs made to develop that press. This test stamp was a simple, stamp-size adhesive, whose **vignette** consisted of an Alexander Hamilton portrait in an oval **frame** flanked with the numerals "1", "2", "3", and "4" (fig. 1). The first version of this test stamp was created in **proof** form on April 25, 1910. It exists in both **offset** printed and **engraved** varieties.

A second test stamp, similar in design to the 2¢ shield issue of 1903, but 50% larger and with "Minerva" in the center, was produced by offset lithography (fig.

2) at the BEP. These stamps also exist as "design reversed", that is, a mirror image. Experimental printings were made when the first Harris offset press, manufactured by Harris Automatic Press Company, arrived at the BEP on June 14, 1910. Stamps were printed on paper watermarked "HAMPDEN" which is the logo used by the American Writing Paper Co. of Holyoke, Massachusetts.

Through the 1920s and 1930s the BEP produced blank, perforated, gummed test stamps. Both coils and booklets were produced with these blank stamps.

The BEP produced test stamps that had a vertical rectangle with cross hatch lines inside (initially in purple, later carmine, and lastly in red violet color) from 1938 through the early 1960s (fig. 3). These were produced as coil, sheet, and booklet stamps for internal BEP use. In addition, Post Office personnel, to test and adjust coil stamp vending machines around the country, used coil rolls of 500, 1,000, and 3,000. The items were also produced in rolls of 100 to test and adjust coil vending machines that dispensed cellophane wrapped coil rolls of 100 to the public. Similarly these stamps were produced in booklet form to test and adjust booklet vending equipment.

Beginning in 1962 the BEP printed stamps with scrollwork and the words "FOR TESTING PURPOSES ONLY" (fig. 4). These are known as FTPO issues and were produced in many varieties and colors. They were used internally by the BEP for testing and adjusting printing, coiling, and booklet making equipment. Some of these stamps were printed in green with shiny gum and sent to Germany to develop and test Goebel coil making equipment in 1980. There was a need to test the press with dull gum stamps, so a second printing of

Figure 2

Test stamps like these were used to test an offset press at the BEP in 1910, about the same time the stamps in fig. 1 were being used to develop a rotary press.

Figure 3

Test stamps like these were used for about 20 years in the middle of the twentieth century. They were used internally at the BEP, and out in the field by postal workers to test vending equipment.

Figure 4

Test Stamps like these were used for about 30 years in the second half of the twentieth century for testing a variety of equipment.

green FTPO stamps, with dull gum, was made in 1981 and sent to Germany. FTPO stamps were also given to Post Office personnel for adjusting vending equipment. Still others went to mass mailers to test their affixing machines. Self-adhesive test stamps on **liners** with a **plate number** appeared in 1996.

Figure 5

This test booklet was used by a technician to adjust a vending machine. He drew the lines to indicate how far out the vending machine pushed the booklet.

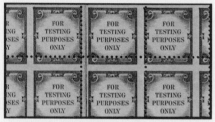

Figure 6

A miscut pane of stamps from a test booklet. Miscut panes are typical in test booklets.

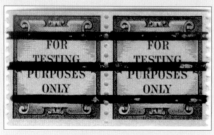

Figure 7

The precanceling of "tagged" test stamps helped insure that they would not be used in the mailstream.

Testing stamps were made into booklets of several types, showing the development of booklets through stapled, glued, and folded types. Post Office personnel used the booklets to adjust booklet vending machines. Test booklets with marks on the cover (fig. 5) are common. These occurred when a technician marked how far a booklet was pushed out of the vending machine; an adjustment was made and the booklet was put through the machine and marked again until it dispensed properly. Panes in these booklets are normally **miscut** since the panes were cut from sheets printed for coil stamps (fig. 6).

In the mid-1960s, the BEP produced some test stamps that had tagging. Since these would activate canceling devices, the Post Office required that users cancel the stamps so they could not be used for postage. These "precanceled" stamps (fig. 7) appear with several different types of precancel lines.

It should be noted that while test stamps produced by the BEP were not accountable paper (i.e. postage stamps), they were generally not made available to the public, and many are exceedingly scarce.

A number of private engraving companies have produced stamps to demonstrate their ability to engrave and produce gummed, perforated stamps. The first known example of this is the stamp shown in Figure 8, which is believed to have been produced by the American Banknote Company in 1865. Banknote companies printed a number of such test stamps when vying for stamp printing business of Central and South American countries and of U.S. businesses.

Figure 8

This test stamp was likely produced by the American Bank Note Co. in 1865.

A number of companies developed stamp *affixing machines* in the early 1900s. As equipment improved, these growing companies convinced the Post Office to issue stamps in imperforate sheets so they could make them into coil stamps for their affixing machines (ch. 49). These companies, beginning in about 1908, issued test stamps to demonstrate their affixing machines and, in some cases, to use as leader stamps for the rolls of coil stamps they manufactured from imperforate sheet stamps. The most common examples of these test stamps are from the **Schermack Company**, which produced varying forms for over 20 years (fig. 9).

Figure 9

Some test stamps were issued by private companies to demonstrate their affixing machines. These Mail-O-Meter stamps were produced by the Shermack Company, and exhibit what are known as Shermack type III perforations.

Companies were also competing in the stamp vending machine business. The **U.S. Automatic Vending Company** is perhaps the best known of the early companies that produced vending machines. The test stamps they produced, and perforated with their distinctive separations, were used to demonstrate their affixing machines (fig. 10).

Figure 10

Manufacturers of stamp vending machines used test stamps to demonstrate their products. These test stamps were used by the U.S. Automatic Vending Company.

In the early 1970s experimentation began with self-adhesive stamps. The first known self-adhesive test stamp (fig. 11) was produced by the Avery

Figure 11

This test stamp was used to develop self-adhesive stamps in the early 1970s.

Figure 12

Black test stamp for developing die cutting procedures for the 1973 self-adhesive Christmas stamp.

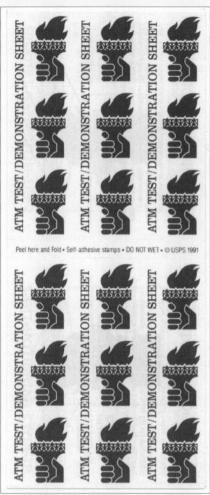

Figure 13

These Green Torch ATM test sheetlets, issued in 1990, were used to adjust stamp dispensing ATM machines.

Products Corporation. Shortly after this the Postal Service decided to experiment by producing a self-adhesive Christmas stamp in 1973. In preparation for this Christmas stamp a black test stamp (fig. 12) was printed by the BEP and sent to the Avery Products Corporation for die cutting and removal of the excess paper from around the stamp.

Another major type of test item developed was the automatic teller machine (ATM) sheetlet. In the late 1980s the Postal Service began experimenting with developing sheetlets of stamps that could be dispensed through ATMs. A number of ATM test sheetlets have been produced, for example the Green Torch sheetlet (fig. 13), to adjust ATMs for dispensing stamp sheetlets.

Notes on Collecting

Test stamps have been used for numerous purposes since the mid-1800s. They provide an interesting study in the development of stamps, stamp production equipment, and stamp vending equipment. It is possible to acquire many of the later test coils used on cover. However, while they may be considered very valuable postal history items, since they were carried through the mail system undetected, and made it to their destination, they may also be considered simply postal history oddities, which, much like any other label or cinderella, escaped detection and passed through the mail - an everyday occurrence. This is one example of how an item is truly worth only as much as the collector is willing to pay for it. Let the buyer beware when deciding to purchase test stamps or test stamps on cover for their collection.

Almanac

1865 – First known test stamp is printed by American Bank Note Company.

1907 – First test stamp is produced by BEP (blank, gummed, perforated stamps).

1908 – First test stamp with image is printed by BEP.

1927 – First U.S. test booklet.

1938 – BEP begins producing test stamps with rectangle and crosshatch design.

1962 – BEP begins producing test stamps with "FOR TESTING PURPOSES ONLY."

1970 – First self- adhesive test stamp.

1989 – First U.S. test sheetlet.

What Others Have Said About Test Stamps

They are not only curiosities any more!
"The Post Office Department has obtained appropriations in recent years for developing new machines and for modernizing their operations. In pursuing these objectives they have used a certain amount of sample or dummy stamped paper to facilitate testing and development....It has been customary for years for the Bureau of Engraving and Printing to supply manufacturers of coil handling equipment (particularly vending machines) with dummy coils...in appropriate sizes of 500, 1,000 and 3,000....We should again like to make it clear that this material is not considered as security paper by the government, and the items should be looked upon only as curiosities by the philatelic fraternity."

—*George W. Brett, "Those Test Samples Again," The Bureau Specialist, 1960. Brett, the Dean of U.S. stamp production and technology, did not realize at that time what a major collecting area test stamps would become.*

Member Urges Public Sale of Test Coils
"George J. Fiore (BIA 1234)...has proposed that the government make available the popular blank coil stamp-like labels inscribed 'For Testing Purposes Only' and requests reaction to the following statement: 'The USPS sale of 'For Testing Purposes Only' engraved coils to selected individuals, namely vending machine manufacturers, has resulted in the creation of a 'black market' situation. These attractive and desirable issues are being sold to the unwary philatelist at prices up to $1.00 each...and that's $500.00 for a roll of 500 which originally cost only twenty-seven cents! A most logical method of eliminating this practice is for the

USPS to sell the testing coil rolls to all, via the Washington, DC Philatelic Sales Unit. The U.S. philatelist, whose desires are a representative collection of his country's postal emissions and an understanding of its postal service, would find this a welcome opportunity to make these attractive additions to his collection.'"

—*The United States Specialist, 1973. Fiore requested all members to write to the Philatelic Sales Unit urging the sale of the test coils to the general public, an event that never came to pass.*

Test stamps are never officially made available to collectors, but...
"...the U.S. Postal Service will not make the test coils available to collectors. However, like most other versions of test coils, the new ones have gotten out through commercial channels and are on the market for sale to collectors by several dealers. You see, test coils are not used only by the USPS. Years ago, when the U.S. Post Office Dept. first began using test coils, the labels were used to test new printing and processing equipment at the BEP. Later, the use of test coils spread to post offices, where they were used to test vending machines and adjust tension chocks. The distribution of such items was still very tightly controlled and possession of test material was considered unlawful. By the late 1970's, however, there were many bulk mailers using coil stamps and distribution of test coils spread to include those firms so that their stamp-affixing machines could be adjusted without using actual stamps. Collectors have been able to easily access most issues since."

—*Wayne Youngblood, "Second self-stick U.S. test coil surfaces in coil rolls of 3,000," Stamp Collector, 1996.*

Test stamps are also called dummy stamps, but collecting them is not for dummies
"Dummy coil stamps make a good starting point for collectors who are just getting started in this area, because many varieties are available inexpensively from coil stamps dealers. Studying these will smooth the transition to a more advanced stage of specialized collecting, for which scarce and elusive varieties may be purchased at auction."

—*Ken Lawrence, Scott's Stamp Monthly, 1997.*

The body of knowledge on test stamps is constantly growing.
"There are other formats and designs of official U.S. test stamps than those currently listed here, including sheets and booklets. The editors are assembling data to correct, clarify and expand these listings, and they would welcome information and examples of stamps from interested individuals."

—*2004 Scott Specialized Catalogue of United States Stamps and Covers. Far from being static, Scott is always a work in progress.*

Examples of Postal Usage

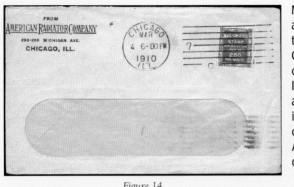

Mail-om-eter test stamp affixed to an envelope of the American Radiator Company. It has been cancelled. This envelope was obviously from a demonstration of affixing equipment for this company, using American Radiator's own envelopes.

Figure 14

BEP test stamp affixed to envelope and cancelled by the U.S. Post Office for publicity purposes during the Postal Parade of Progress on Oct. 17, 1959.

Figure 15

Where to Find More Information

- "A new section is added for an increasingly popular collecting area" by Wayne Youngblood is an article accompanying the first listings of test stamps in the 1994 *Scott*.

- "More on coil stamps, forerunners, and assorted mailing machines" by Ken Lawrence.

- "The Spotlight is on U.S. sheet and booklet format dummy stamps" by Ken Lawrence.

- *Dummy Stamp Booklets*, USSS Research Report #3.

- *Test Stamps*, by Steven R. Unkrich.

Expanding the Collector's Scope

Chapter 56
United States Stamp Society

The United States Stamp Society (USSS) is the preeminent organization devoted to the study of United States stamps. It is, "a non-profit, volunteer-run association of collectors to promote the study of the philatelic output of the Bureau of Engraving and Printing and of postage and revenue stamped paper produced by others for use in the United States and U.S. administered areas." Once concerned exclusively with the production of the Bureau of Engraving and Printing, the USSS has expanded its coverage to include all United States issues, both classic and modern, regardless of printer.

Figure 1

Hugh M. Southgate, a founding leader of what is now known as the United States Stamp Society, was the first president of the Bureau Issues Association.

The organization began in 1926 as the Philatelic Plate Number Association (PPNA). About 1929, R.A. Bryant, PPNA Publicity Manager, and PPNA President Hugh M. Southgate (fig. 1) recognized the membership's interest in expanding the scope of the organization beyond plate numbers. In March 1930, the name of the Association was changed to the Bureau Issues Association (BIA) and in 1938, the BIA incorporated as a non-profit organization.

R.A. Bryant published a three page organization *Bulletin #1*, February 19, 1930. The *Bulletin* formally became *The Bureau Specialist* with the third issue in April 1930 and its name was retained until 1966 (volume 37), when it changed to *The United States Specialist*, to better express the society's widening interest (fig. 2). The award-winning monthly journal is a membership benefit and continues to provide informational updates, features, and original research. For the first 50 years of the Association, *The Specialist* had but four editors: R.A. Bryant, Robert C. Masters, Barbara R. Mueller, and Sol Koved – a remarkable record for any philatelic organization.

Starting in 1962, the scope of the organization was expanded to cover the entire U.S. scene as well as all the U.S. administration issues. In 1986, the BIA became affiliate #150 of the *American Philatelic Society*. In 2000 the organization was renamed the United States Stamp Society, reflecting the diminishing role of the BEP in printing stamps and the increasing reliance on private contractors.

The Society promotes research through numerous committees and study groups, including Booklets and Booklet Panes, Washington-Franklin Series, Presidential Issue, Revenue Issues, Marginal Markings, and Registered Mail. These committees serve as sources of information for members and also provide members with opportunities to join in their activities. A convention is held each year in conjuction with a national stamp show. The annual convention features a membership meeting, seminars and exhibits, and both formal and informal fellowship (fig. 3).

The most prestigious awards presented by the Society are the Walter W. Hopkinson Trophy, presented for the best exhibit of twentieth century material at an annual meeting show, and the Hugh M. Southgate Memorial Trophy, presented for the best nineteenth century exhibit at the annual show. The Walter W. Hopkinson Memorial Literature Award is given annually for the best article or series of articles published in *The United States Specialist*. The Statue of

Figure 2
"The United States Specialist" is the monthly journal of The United States Stamp Society.

Figure 3
George Brett, known to generations of collectors as "Mr. BIA," was for many years, a prolific researcher, writer, exhibiter and arguably the most knowledgable expert on the Bureau of Engraving and Printing. He is shown here enjoying the exhibits at the USSS annual meeting held at NAPEX in 2000.

Freedom medal is presented for the best exhibit of U.S. material at a National World Series of Philately show, while the President's Award is given at regional and local shows. The Century of Service Award is awarded for service to the Society. The Society's highest honor is the Hall of Fame. Over the past eight decades only ten members have been inducted to the Hall in recognition of their outstanding contributions to the Society.

The USSS has contributed to philatelic research by publishing articles in *The United States Specialist*. Many books and research papers have been produced under USSS auspices, including this book and the *Durland Plate Number Catalogue*. Other books published by the Society cover such topics as Booklets Panes, The Prexies, Plate Varieties, the commemorative and air mail stamps of 1945–1952, the Transport air mail stamps, a collection of the philatelic writings of Elliott Perry, and a collection of the columns written by George B. Sloane for *STAMPS* magazine.

The Society emblem, based on the $5 "America" in the Series of 1922, designed by Alvin R. Meissner of the BEP, was introduced in January 1936. After the Society's name was changed to United States Stamp Society the emblem was updated, and a new die was engraved by Tom Hipschen of the BEP.

The USSS sponsors a dedicated room in the American Philatelic Center in Bellefonte, Pennsylvania. This room contains records and archival material of the society, its publications, and plaques honoring the service of members and significant award winners.

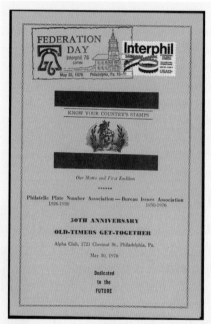

Figure 4

A franked program from a BIA event at Interphil '76, which was called a "50th Anniversary Old-Timers Get-Together".

Notes on Collecting

The BIA-USSS may be collected in so many fun and challenging ways. One of the primary "collections" to build is a complete run *The Bureau Specialist* and *The United States Specialist*, which has been published monthly since 1930. There was a predecessor publication to *The Bureau Specialist*, which was published monthly and printed on a mimeograph machine. Called the *Shift-Hunter Newsletter*, it was published by a group of collectors known as "Shift Hunters". They called themselves "an unorganized group of specialists who exchange information regarding U.S. double transfers, through the medium of these letters." While there are various reprints available, the originals were printed in purple and red ink by the rexograph process so that the illustrations of the various shifts, plate cracks and other deviants would be clearly illustrated.

There is a rich postal history that can be acquired with some patience. The address of the central office of the BIA/USSS has changed numerous times over the years, and building up a **corner card** collection of these covers would not only help tell the story, but will also contain some great **frankings**! Ephemera collectors can search for a treasure of BIA-USSS artifacts, including annual meeting programs, invitations, banquet invitations, and banquet programs, which were produced for various special events over the years. Shown in Figure 4 is a franked program from Interphil 1976, which was called a "50th Anniversary Old-Timers Get-Together".

Almanac

1926 – Philatelic Plate Number Association is formed.

1930 – Association name changed to Bureau Issues Association.

1930 – BIA Bulletin #1 is published in February.

1930 – The BIA Bulletin becomes *The Bureau Specialist* with the third issue in April.

1938 – The BIA incorporates as a non-profit organization.

1966 – *The Bureau Specialist* becomes *The United States Specialist* with Volume 37.

1986 – The BIA becomes affiliate #150 of the American Philatelic Society.

2000 – The BIA is renamed the United States Stamp Society.

What Others Have Said

Clear and concise words from the First President of the BIA

"Frequent inquiries from correspondents and occasional remarks in the philatelic press indicate that many are not familiar with the purpose or scope of the Bureau Issues Association. A few words of explanation may be of general interest….The study of the philatelic output of the Bureau is the duty of a group of technical committees, each headed by a hard-working, well known individual who is especially interested and versed in his particular group…A further outlet for the Association to serve the philatelic public is their cooperation with the publishers of philatelic catalogues and journals. A special committee will supply the listing of Bureau Issues for Scott's 'United States Stamp Catalogue.' A similar service will be available for any other company desiring it. Many of the columnists writing for the various philatelic publications are B.I.A. members and they often use – with the Association's authorization – data appearing in its publications. Essentially the Bureau Issues Association is an organization for advanced collectors and students, but its desire to promote, as well, the development of those wishing to learn about our postal emissions, or in the words of the B.I.A. motto, 'Know Your Country's Stamps'".

—*Hugh M. Southgate, "The Bureau Issues Association – An outline of its activities,"* Weekly Philatelic Gossip, 1937.

A conversation begun in 1974 as a Letter to the Editor about a name change…

"Dear Editor: I feel that we have outgrown 'BIA' as our name – Bureau Issues Association. We really are United States specialists as our magazine is now named. Why not update our association name to more fully clarify our purpose? [Signed] Warren R. Bower….Editor's Note:….In my correspondence with non-members, even informed philatelists, I still find the old 'Bureau issues only' tag hung on us. I feel our name, hallowed as it may be, is hindering our growth; at the very least it causes identity problems. The press has been most cooperative about publicizing our activities and the Specialist, but in spite of that the old 'Bureau Specialist' mentality remains. As Editor and without prior consultation with our officers, I am asking readers to comment on this issue and suggest new names. Hopefully, we can come up with a name that includes a sub-title reference to BIA and which can be incorporated into our famous seal. Adoption, of course, would have to be accomplished through the orderly means laid down in our constitution and through our elected officials."

—Letter to the editor of *The United States Specialist*, and response by Barbara R. Mueller, 1974.

…ended 26 years later when the BIA became The United States Stamp Society!

"Members of the Bureau Issues Association have voted overwhelmingly to change the name of their organization to the United States Stamp Society. A by-law change is required. No formal action will be taken on the vote until the BIA Convention at Napex 2000 in Tyson's Corner, VA. June 2-4, for its annual convention and to celebrate its 70th Anniversary. The BIA has approximately 2,000 members. About half of them mailed in ballots that were sent out in October 1999 with the annual dues-renewal notice. The vote, as reported in the February issue of The United States Specialist, was 719 in favor and 126 opposed. One ballot was void. The organization has outgrown its name, which was derived from the United States Bureau of Engraving and Printing. For many years the Bureau printed all United States stamps. Starting in the mid-1990s, it has printed less than half."

—*Rob Haesler, "BIA members approve name change,"* Linn's Stamp News, *2000.*

Example of Postal Usage

Figure 5
The BIA-USSS 70th anniversary cachet and special cancellation from 2000.

Where to Find More Information

- A complete run of *The Bureau Specialist* (1930-1966) and *The United States Specialist* (1966 to date) offers the most detailed and up to date account possible of the Society.

- The Society maintains a website at www.usstamps.org.

Chapter 57
United States Stamp Research

Stamp collectors may hear the declaration that "there is a great deal more to the little postage stamp than meets the eye!" Any rather simple looking stamp or **cover** has a story to tell. There are many ways to discover them.

Taking the time to learn about a stamp or cover is the mark of a true **philatelist**.

Stamp research is an adventure with many possibilities for discovery, utilizing a variety of methods. Examples of selected methods of research are illustrated below using three pieces; a plate block, stamp, and cover.

Figure 1

Plate block of the Jane Addams stamp (878) in the Famous Americans Series.

Researching a Plate Block

The first piece is a 10¢ Jane Addams **plate block** (fig. 1) of four with plate number 22588. The first research step is consulting *Scott*, in this case the Subject Index, which indicates the stamp is *Scott* number 878. Then, turning to the entry for *Scott* 878 several important things are learned. It is one of thirty-five stamps in the Famous Americans Series (859–893), the highest denomination stamp in a group of five entitled American Scientists. It is a rotary press printing using electric eye-plates of 280 subjects yielding four panes of 70. It was issued on April 26, 1940, with a color classified by *Scott* as dark brown. The current retail value of the plate block is listed. Turning to the First Day Covers section in *Scott* one learns that 132,375 covers were cancelled on its first day of issue in Chicago, Illinois. This basic information provides a variety of opportunities to proceed, depending on the objectives of the researcher.

The next step is to locate the most general resource available. A good place to begin is the on-line catalog of the American Philatelic Research Library (APRL). Here, a search of "Famous Americans" yields a number of text resources. After considering available texts one might chose to investigate George C. Hahn's *United States Famous Americans Series of 1940*. In that volume it can be gleaned that President Franklin D. Roosevelt conceived the original idea for this series in 1934. This finding leads us to investigate literature of the time, including such dependable sources as *Linn's Stamp Weekly, STAMPS, Western Stamp Collector, Mekeel's*, and *Weekly Philatelic Gossip*. In this example one discovers that the October 5 and 12, 1935 issues of *STAMPS* have an article entitled "A Stamp Program for Patriotic Progress, Postal Designs to Advance American Culture." From this, one learns that the Famous Americans Series was conceived in 1935, and that soon afterwards, legislative representatives in various states passed resolutions requesting the issuance of a stamp to honor famous individuals from their respective states. The National Federation of Stamp Clubs began soliciting suggestions for honorees from stamp collectors. Numerous other articles about the series have appeared in a variety of stamp publications.

Stamp production details for the Addams stamp can be found by turning to chapter 4, "U.S Postage Stamps" in *Linn's World Almanac*, which identifies that W. A. Roach designed the stamp, that J.T. Vail and C.T. Arlt engraved the vignette, and that W.B. Wells engraved the lettering. *The Engraver's Line* by Gene Hessler, presents the information more fully and precisely, identifying Carl T. Arlt as the vignette engraver and James T. Vail as the frame engraver. Hessler's book also provides brief biographical sketches of Arlt, Roach, Vail, and Wells.

The *Linn's World Almanac* also provides the following basic data about this stamp: where it was issued (Chicago), how many stamps were issued (15,112,580) and how many first day covers were canceled (132,375). Much of this information may also be available in other places, such as in *Franklin D. Roosevelt and the Stamps of the United States 1933-45*, by Brian C. Baur or *Scott*.

To obtain fundamental information on plate blocks, the *Durland Standard Plate Number Catalog* is utilized. *Durland* lists and prices plate blocks by plate number and position. This catalog reveals that two **plates**, numbers 22558 and 22560, were used to print this stamp. Another, more detailed technical plate number resource, is the *BIA Plate Number Checklist: Plates 20000-41303* which reveals three 280 subject **rotary** plates were actually made for this stamp, but **plate number** 22559 was never used. Both of the plates used were certified on February 21, 1940, while the unused plate was certified on March 4. Both of those plates were used on press beginning March 8, 1940, then all three plates were cancelled on November 28, 1940. Each plate printed 28025 units, which produced 15,694,000 stamps. This number is less than the number reported issued by *Linn's Almanac*. This discrepancy could be investigated by contacting the BEP Historical Resource Center in Washington, D.C.

All stamps are educational and this is certainly true for the collector who does more than stick stamps in an album! Many Americans are probably unaware of who Jane Addams was, or what contributions she made to our country. The collector researching this stamp does! To obtain this general information on the subject matter of a stamp, one might consult general encyclopedic resources which includes the internet. A philatelic source of biographic information originates from the cachets of first day covers, which often provide basic information. For example, the Jane Addams Artcraft **cachet** characterizes Addams as "Sociologist, co-founder of Hull House, and winner of the Nobel Peace Prize" and provides her dates of birth and death. Another source may be the information in first day ceremony programs. Illustrations of first day ceremony programs are found in the *Specialized Catalogue of First Day Ceremony Programs & Events* by Scott Pelcyger. Yet another source of biographic information is new issue announcements by the Post Office which have been published in the philatelic press since 1923.

For the researcher wanting detailed information regarding **plate varieties**, an invaluable resource is Loran French's *Encyclopedia of Plate Varieties on U.S. Bureau-Printed Postage Stamps*. This reference indicates the Addams plates had no reported plate varieties.

Researching a Stamp

Another opportunity for research is provided by the stamp in figure 2. By consulting the Identifier in *Scott* it is determined that this is a Washington-Franklin Head Issue (ch. 9), a series known for its many different **perforations**, *watermarks*, printing methods, and fakes. This stamp might be overlooked because, at first glance, it is unappealing due to its poor centering and heavy, dark **cancel**. Referring to *Scott* it is determined that the cancel is a precancel. Since Washington-Franklin stamps have many different perforations, they must be verified. Using a perforation gauge it is determined the stamp is perf. 14. This is surprising since there are no perf. 14 stamps listed in *Scott* or in *The Expert's Book: Washington-Franklin Issues of 1908 to 1923* by Paul Schmid. Further resources such as *United States Coil Issues: 1906 to 1938* and *Washington-Franklins: 1908 to 1923*, both written by Martin A. Armstrong also have no references to perf. 14.

Figure 2

Unwatermarked 1¢ Washington stamp (481) perforated privately with gauge 14 perforations by the Boy Scouts of America executive council in 1922.

The *Precancel Stamp Society Bureau Precancel Catalog* indicates that this stamp is not a **Bureau precancel**. The stamp is listed in *The Precancel Stamp Society's Town and Type Catalog of the United States and Territories*, valued in excess of $150. In an effort to further identify this stamp additional philatelic literature or auction catalogs must be searched. In the August 1997 issue of *American Philatelist* there is an article by Ken Lawrence with the intriguing title "VAMPing - The Use of Truly Private Perfs". The article describes how our "ugly little stamp" was privately perforated 14 by the Boy Scouts of America using the unwatermarked 1¢ Washington (481). This could be verified by using a watermark detector to determine the presence or absence of a watermark. Lawrence also expresses the opinion that the stamp should be *Scott* listed as privately perforated. Searching on-line, the Siegel encyclopedia and prices realized links at www.siegelauctions.com leads to the conclusion that the "ugly little stamp" is a very desirable item.

Researching a Cover

The final research item is the cover shown in figures 3a and 3b, a ***penalty envelope*** mailed by the Treasury Department on official business from New Orleans in 1941, franked with 27¢ postage and stamped on the front with two auxiliary markings, "Air Mail" and "Registered". These auxiliary markings provide significant clues to the researcher. On the back of the cover are two identical magenta circular ***registered*** markings from New Orleans and two different registered markings from New York, one magenta and one black. There are ***mute*** cancels on the front, but no postmarks. This cover raises numerous challenges for the researcher.

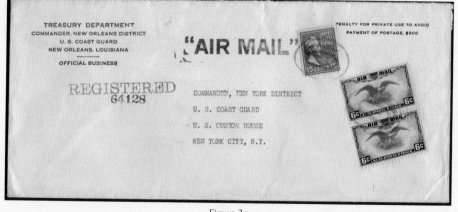

Figure 3a

1941 Air Mail cover.

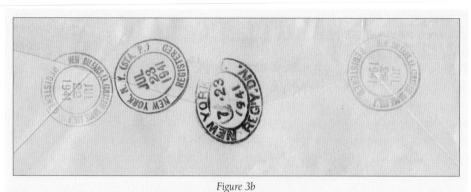

Figure 3b
Detail from the back of the cover in Figure 3a

To research this cover one can turn to a primary resource, the *Postal Laws & Regulations* (*PL&R*) issued by the POD in 1940. Editions of *PL&R* were also issued in 1832, 1843, 1847, 1852, 1866, 1879, 1887, 1902, 1907, 1913, 1924, and 1948. The contemporary *Domestic Mail Manual* (*DMM*) provides similar information to the researcher. However the information obtained in primary sources can often be found more easily in secondary resources. For example, the rate books by Beecher and Wawrukiewicz are often the most helpful. By consulting the chapter on Free Mail in the *Domestic* book it is learned that the penalty envelope paid the First Class surface rate for official mail and therefore could not be used to pay air mail or registration fees, which explains the otherwise puzzling presence of stamps on this cover.

Next, the registry markings lead the researcher to the Registry Service chapter in the *Domestic* rate book which explains what registry service is and that the basic registry fee in 1941 was 15¢. However, in addition to this basic information, the chapter explains the purpose of the registry postal markings and why the postmark is found only on the back of the cover.

The "AIR MAIL" auxiliary marking leads the researcher to the Airmail chapter in the *Domestic* rate book, which states the 1941 air mail rate was 6¢ per ounce. Since the envelope is franked with two 6¢ stamps, it is inferred to have weighed up to two ounces. This finding provides an accounting for the 27¢ postage placed on the cover.

The above illustrates how to begin research on both stamps and postal history; however these are only beginnings. The possibilities for further work and learning more are almost endless.

Notes on Collecting

While philatelic research is facilitated by the internet, a personal philatelic library will greatly increase the joys of researching. The foreword presents a short list of some basic books that every collector of U.S. stamps should consider owning. The annual *Scott Specialized Catalogue of U.S. Stamps and Covers* tops this list. It is the most comprehensive and detailed listing available for U.S. stamps. It is possible to purchase older editions at a relatively low cost and, with the exception of values and newer issues, they provide the collector with the basic information needed.

Collectors should consider joining one or more of the specialized societies that focus on the collector's interest. A list of these societies is found at www.stamps.org. Many produce journals of specialized information.

When in doubt, especially when working with a potentially valuable item, seek assistance from experts! Figure 4 illustrates a certificate from an *expertizing* service warning that this stamp submitted to them had a fake cancellation.

Figure 4

Philatelic Foundation Certificate, warning of an altered or counterfeit item.

Almanac

1863 – *Catalogue of Postage Stamps, American and Foreign, and U.S. Revenue Stamps* is published by Sever and Francis. It is the second earliest catalog published in the United States and the first to include *revenue stamps* (fig 5).

1864 – The first United States stamp journal, *The Stamp Collector's Record*, is published in Albany, New York.

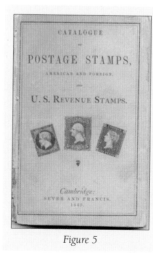

Figure 5

Catalogue of Postage Stamps, American and Foreign and U.S. Revenue Stamps is a 78 page catalog authored by George Dexter in 1863. Originally 1,000 copies were issued, with copies presently included in the Harvard Library (Houghton Treasures Room) and the American Philatelic Research Library (Rare Book Case).

1886 – The largest philatelic organization in the United States, the American Philatelic Society is organized on September 13 as the American Philatelic Association.

1968 – The American Philatelic Research Library is organized on October 28 with the motto "Knowledge through Research".

What Others Have Said

Philatelic Research has many benefits for the collector

"Philatelic research is in another category. Its devotees are all too few and the range of their combined research is too restricted, considering the many projects that are available and the benefits to be derived by the philatelic researcher and eventually by a group having similar interests. [There have been] outstanding contributions made by well-known philatelists who have minutely and comprehensively investigated selected fields. It may be emphasized, however, that not only the details of designing, engraving and printing of stamps are worthy of research but that the designs themselves merit far more studious inquiry than generally has been given them. It is only by including them in our philatelic research that the "complete story behind the stamp" can ever become known….Other values of philatelic research…are obvious."

—*Arthur Bevan, "Philatelic Research on Stamp Designs,"* Fourth American Philatelic Congress Book, 1938.

It is important to own your own reference material

"Reference philatelic material is essential for all stamp collectors. Whether it be merely a *Scott* Catalogue or a more extensive library consisting of classic philatelic works with complete runs of every major society's journals depends on the individual and the degrees of his specialization. Everyone needs basic information for identifying the more troublesome issues; however some desire more detail and background then others. There are several major philatelic libraries in the United States with several others associated with or maintained by specialized philatelic societies….Their services are available to all serious philatelic researchers and most individuals can obtain access through their local public library using the Interlibrary Loan System."

—*David G. Lee, "Q and A Corner,"* The United States Specialist, *1987*.

Where to Find More Information

Each chapter in this *Encyclopedia* includes a section entitled "Where to Find More Information." References identified in this section, coupled with the basic resources named in the foreword, will help a collector become a true student of U.S. stamps. In addition to the resources named in the foreword and the various chapters, the following may be useful in researching stamps and covers.

- The National Postal Museum, Smithsonian Institution, Washington, D.C. has a website at www.postalmuseum.si.edu. For those able to visit in person many research opportunities will present themselves. It is estimated that there are approximately 16 million postal-related items including stamps in the collection. There is a library open to the public by appointment, and a photograph collection of some 10,000 items. The files of the Post Office Department, housed at the museum, are particularly strong for the period 1920 to 1970. Postal publications and various microfilm collections of material are available to the researcher. Currently publications in the library are searchable at http://www.sil.si.edu/libraries/npm-hp.htm and most are available for interlibrary loan.

- The website maintained by the American Philatelic Society (APS) at www.stamps.org contains a link to the American Philatelic Research Library, where one can search the library's card catalog, article index and journal holdings. Members of the APS may borrow most of the library's holdings via the U.S. mail. The APRL publishes Philatelic Literature Review, a quarterly journal which contains a listing of philatelic literature dealers. Many of them maintain websites which are invaluable to the researcher.

- The AskPhil website sponsored by the Collectors Club of Chicago at www.askphil.org contains a number of helpful links to "how to" articles and "questions and answers". If a question is not answered, the site allows the user to ask their "own" question which is often answered within a few days.

- Other wonderful research material may be found on websites maintained by the various specialty societies such as those maintained by the **United States Stamp Society** (ch. 56) at www.usstamps.org, the U.S. Philatelic Classics Society at www.uspcs.org, and the Precancel Stamp Society at www.precancels.com.

Chapter 58
Postal History
Markings

The first known use of a United States postal marking had the words "Post Payd" in manuscript (hand written) form which was applied to a letter sent on January 22, 1673. Manuscript markings may indicate the city of origin of the mail and the rate, which is expressed, for example, as "5" or "10". An *auxiliary marking* such as "MISSENT" may also be applied in manuscript. Manuscript markings on mail continue to this day, although manuscript was used predominantly in the stampless period from 1672 to 1855.

The first *handstamp* was used in 1756 on mail originating in New York bound for Falmouth, England. It bore the words "NEW" and "YORK" which appeared on two separate lines. This marking, and others like it where the city name and date appear in a linear arrangement, are referred to as "straight line" markings. Another Colonial era handstamp postal marking is known as a "Franklin Mark", named after Benjamin Franklin. These markings, also called "American Bishop Marks" after their English counterpart, were comprised of a circle in which a date numeral was placed above an abbreviation for the month.

Figure 1

Circular Date Stamps (CDS) were first used in the eighteenth century and were still in use at the beginning of the twenty-first century. This example was used in "Chicago, III." on October 20, 1856.

Of all the canceling devices used in America, we are most familiar with "circular" handstamps in which the letters of the town and state are positioned inside the rim of a circle, while the month, day, and year are in stacked straight lines in the center of the circle (fig. 1). These Circular Dates Stamps (CDSs) are used for *postmarking*. They were first introduced in Charleston, South Carolina in 1778. Major variations include "oval" handstamps and "rimless" handstamps. During much of the nineteenth century, the year was not included in many CDSs. However sometimes the year can be determined from *docketing*, an enclosure in the envelope, distinguishing characteristics of the cancellation, or the stamps used.

Another group of early handstamps was comprised of numbers that represented the postal rates charged for delivery of pieces of mail. The earliest rate handstamps were used in Albany, New York in 1789. Rate handstamps were used extensively from the 1830s until January 1, 1856 when it became mandatory for the sender to prepay the cost of postage through the use of postage stamps. The most common rate markings are the "5" and "10" denominations. Other handstamps used during this period included "**PAID**" and "DUE" which indicate whether the sender had prepaid the cost of postage or whether it had to be collected before the letter was delivered.

With the issuance of the first postage stamps on July 1, 1847 came the need to ensure that postage stamps were not removed from folded letters or envelopes and reused. Postal clerks often accomplished this by marking stamps with ink from a pen. Handstamps were soon devised to obliterate or "cancel" postage stamps. While some of the larger post offices were issued obliterators by the government, postmasters of smaller offices procured their own canceling devices from private sources.

Some nineteenth century canceling devices made by private companies for use by postal officials were fitted with obliterators in standard formats, such as bars, grids, ellipses, or bulls-eyes. Some of these standard devices also included sharp points as part of their design. When applied to stamps, these devices deposited ink on the surface and also cut slits, punched holes, or scraped the stamp to prevent reuse.

On July 23, 1860, Postmaster General Joseph Holt issued an order forbidding the use of CDSs to cancel stamps. A separate handstamp, which canceled, or obliterated, the stamp, was to be used. Creative postmasters in some cities responded to the order by attaching a CDS and an obliterator, also called a killer, to a common base. These devices are known as **duplexes**. An envelope could be postmarked with the town of origin and the stamp canceled with a single strike.

Some duplex handstamps deserve special mention. Duplex devices that used an ellipse shape for an obliterator normally included a **slug** for the year date inside the circular date stamp, along with the slugs for the name of the month and the numerals for the date (fig. 2). However, some handstamps were designed with the year date slug positioned outside of the circular date stamp, between it and

Figure 2

A duplex cancel with a barrel-shaped obliterator used in New Orleans on May 20, 1938. Note the year is printed inside the postmark.

the ellipse. These devices are sometimes referred to as **triplex** handstamps and YOD or "Year Outside Dial" handstamps (fig. 3).

Figure 3

A duplex cancel with a barrel-shaped obliterator used in Philadelphia on May 24, 1935. Note the year is printed between the postmark and the obliterator.

Figure 4

The date on this Wesson Time-On-Bottom duplex handstamp from "Worcester, Mass." is December 27, 1881.

Another style of duplex handstamp is referred to as Wesson "Time-On-Bottom" or TOB devices after its inventor, Walter Wesson. TOB devices incorporated slugs for the time of day into the bottom section of the CDS. The date was displayed numerically in a MM-DD-YY, or pseudo-Quaker, configuration. The Quakers would display the months in numerical fashion rather than using their written names, which they believed referred to pagan gods. In true Quaker fashion, March was considered month "1", April was month "2" and so on. TOB devices, however, used "1" for January, "2" for February and so on up to "12" for December (fig. 4).

Other devices imparted a cancel from a piece of wood or cork. The design of the obliteration was essentially left to the imagination and carving ability of the postal clerks in the cities using them. These hand-carved cancels belong to a category of cancels known as "fancy cancels". Their designs are often quite artistic.

Because of the local nature of many fancy cancels, specific towns and cities are associated with some of the more striking examples of fancy cancels. Waterbury, Connecticut is noted for its fancy cancels, such as the "Running Chicken", Brattleboro, Vermont its "Devil And Pitchfork", and Worcester, Massachusetts its two "North-South Shaking Hands" fancy cancels.

Between 1870 and 1878, a group of approximately 250 fancy cancels, consisting of geometric designs, wheels, flowers, swirls, and the like, were used only in New York City on outgoing foreign mail. These New York Foreign Mail (NYFM) cancels are a specialized area of interest.

In order to increase the legibility of postmarks on mail, and thus to speed its processing and delivery, the Post Office Department (POD) began issuing rubber handstamps in 1903. The first group of devices, of which there are three distinct types, are the **Doane** cancels, named after Edith R. Doane, a postal historian, who first researched them in the 1950s. The issuance of Doane devices was discontin-

ued in the fall of 1906. A total of approximately 31,000 different Doane devices were produced (fig. 5).

There are a variety of other specialty types of
handstamp cancels which are collected and
studied. Examples include **Rural Free
Delivery** cancels (fig. 6), roller-type cancels
that are used to produce long markings on
large envelopes or flats, temporary postal station cancels used to highlight special events or
philatelic shows, and Mailer Permit Postmarks
which individuals may use to cancel their own
outgoing mail.

Figure 5

Detail of a cover with a Doane cancellation from Cornish, N.J. The
number "1" in the killer bars is a
code representing the annual compensation of the postmaster. This
Doane, known as a type I, was used
in Cornish from April 19, 1904 until
August 25, 1909.

Toward the end of the nineteenth
century, the volume of mail
increased to the point where manually canceling the mail with
handstamp devices alone was
becoming expensive and cumber-
some. The need for faster mail
handling led to the development
of machine-driven canceling
devices. Rather than pounding
each piece of mail with a hand-

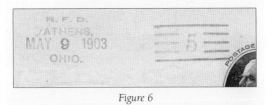

Figure 6

Detail of a postal card showing a Rural Free Delivery
(RFD) cancel from Athens, Ohio, Route 5, applied on
May 9, 1903.

stamp, the canceling machine allowed postal employees to load several dozen
pieces of mail into a hopper. Then, with the turn of a crank, and later through the
use of an electric motor, cancels were rapidly applied to mail.

The origin of machines to cancel mail is somewhat obscure. A few small companies experimented with machine canceling devices in the early 1870s. It is generally accepted that the first canceling machine to gain widespread regular usage was
developed by Thomas Leavitt. The first regular **Leavitt** machine cancel was applied
in Boston on January 6, 1876. Prototype cancels, also from Boston, dated
November 15, 1875, are also thought to have been produced by a Leavitt machine.

Besides Leavitt, other makers of machine canceling equipment included **American
Postal Machines Co.**, **International Postal Supply Co.**, **Universal Stamping
Machine Co.**, **Doremus Machine Co.**, Barr Fyke, Constantine, Hampden, and
Columbia Postal Supply Co. The machine cancels most commonly seen at the
beginning of the twenty-first century are the direct descendents of those early

machines, and have two parts, a "*dial*" and a "*killer*". The dial is a metal *die* that contains information about the location of the post office, the date and time at which the mail was cancelled, and sometimes a number which designates the

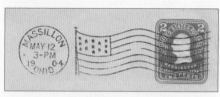

Figure 7

This waving flag cancel was used in Massillon, Ohio on May 12, 1904. Cancels also exist with an involute (folded) style of flag.

Figure 8

This "Air Mail Saves Time" slogan cancel was used in Detroit for about 11 months in 1940. There are literally thousands of different slogan cancels. Some have been used in only a single post office, while others such as "Pray for Peace" and "Mail Early for Christmas" have been used in many post offices nationwide.

Figure 9

This "sprayed-on" meter-date correction was accidentally applied at 12:07 AM on December 23, 1996 in Lafayette, IN. Note the slogan used to promote the city.

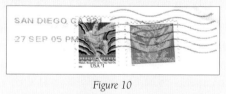

Figure 10

A sprayed-on postmark from "SAN DIEGO CA".

machine doing the canceling. The killer is a metal die that is usually composed of a series of wavy lines that actually cancels the stamp. However, killers may also be straight lines, waving flags (fig. 7), *involute flags*, or slogans (fig. 8).

In 1989 automated equipment was first used that "ink-sprayed" markings on mail. This technology was used to show the correct date on *metered mail* with "stale" dates. Sometimes this marking was accidentally applied to stamped mail (fig.9). *Optical Character Reader* (OCR) equipment could "read" addresses and print bar codes for sorters to use. This computer-driven technology greatly increased the Postal Service's ability to move the mails. In the fall of 2003 the Postal Service began testing inkjet postmarks in selected locations. In 2005 San Diego, California became the first postal facility to use only sprayed-on postmarks instead of traditional postmarks applied by a metal die (fig. 10).

While the vast majority of mail passes through the postal system without much trouble or delay, sometimes pieces of mail need special attention by postal workers, either clerks or carriers, to get them to their destination or, if that is not possible, back to the sender. In order to inform the recipient or sender (or other postal workers) of the type of special processing given to a piece of mail, auxiliary markings are usually applied. The study and collecting of mail with such auxiliary markings is a favorite topic of postal historians. For example, markings applied to **Registered** mail are considered particularly fascinating. An "R" marking for early local registered mail was introduced in Philadelphia in 1845, ten years before the official introduction of a nationwide registry system by the POD. "R" markings continued on registered mail into the twenty-first century.

In the nineteenth century, before mail was delivered to customer homes, sometimes a letter was not picked up at the post office by its intended recipient. The Postmaster might then take out an advertisement in the local paper informing the recipient that mail was waiting for him and that upon paying the postage and fees, the letter could be picked up. Letters handled in this fashion often bore an auxiliary marking such as "Adv. 1 Cent." If a letter was not picked up at the post office, it was returned, often with an auxiliary marking such as "Not Called For" applied to it.

Occasionally in the nineteenth century a letter was handed to a mail carrier who was transporting mail between post offices. Upon delivering this letter to the next post office on his route, the receiving postmaster would ascertain from the carrier where along the route the letter was received, and determine the amount of postage to the destination based on the full distance. The postmaster would indicate this by adding an auxiliary **Way** marking to the letter. The mail carrier in this instance could be anyone under contract to carry mail, such as a stage line, a post rider, a steamboat, or a railroad without its own **Route Agent**. If a private ship, one without a mail contract, was entrusted with letters to be delivered to a post office upon arrival in port, they received a "Ship" or "Steamship" auxiliary marking.

Probably the most-well known auxiliary marking is the one made famous by Elvis Presley in his song "Return To Sender". This type of marking is often accompanied by the graphic "Pointing Finger" symbol (fig. 11). Other auxiliary markings include variations of the words "Missent", or "Received", or "Transit". When mail is sent on from one destination post office to another, the cover is marked "Forwarded".

Figure 11

"Pointing Finger, Return to Sender" auxiliary markings such as this one are known in a variety of styles.

Auxiliary markings are not limited to handstamps. The American Postal Machines Co., for example, produced a number of dies for use in its machine cancellers. Markings include such phrases as "Train Late – Mail Delayed" and "Received Station A".

The first contract to carry mail by train was issued by the POD on November 30, 1832. The POD appointed

Figure 12

Detail from a cover postmarked April 29, 1914 on the Aberdeen (S.D.) & Sioux City (Iowa) Railroad Post Office. This RPO operated from 1890 until 1955. RPOs took their names from the terminal cities they served, not the railroad lines on which they operated.

the first Route Agent, John Kendall, in 1837 to accompany mail on a train. An Act of Congress of July 7, 1838, made all railroads **post roads**. In June 1840, route agents on the Boston, Massachusetts to Springfield, Massachusetts route originated the idea of sorting mail on moving rail cars. On August 28, 1864, the first United States **Railway Post Office** (RPO) route was established. Railway markings, including those of route agents, RPOs, and transfer clerks, are another fascinating aspect of postal history (fig. 12).

The mid-twentieth century witnessed a decline in railroad traffic. Motor vehicles began to replace trains as the primary means of transportation. Just as the RPO system allowed mail to be sorted en route in railroad cars, the **Highway Post Office** (HPO) system used bus-like vehicles traveling on highways to transport and sort mail between cities. Their interiors were patterned from the RPO cars they were intended to replace. The first HPO went into service on February 10, 1941 on the 149-mile route between Washington, D.C. and Harrisonburg, Virginia. The HPO system flourished from the end of World War II until the early 1970s when the USPS initiated the **sectional center** concept for processing mail. The last HPO

Figure 13

The Charlotte (N.C.) & Florence (S.C.) Highway Post Office (HPO) operated from 1949 until 1963. This commercially used cover was carried on April 25, 1951. Commercially used covers are generally more elusive than the philatelically inspired covers prepared for the "First Trip" of an HPO.

ran from Cincinnati to Cleveland, Ohio on June 30, 1974 (fig. 13).

The POD began scheduled domestic air mail service on May 15, 1918 between Washington, D.C. and New York via Philadelphia. This service expanded rapidly beginning in the mid-1920s. Unfortunately for the pilots, but fortunately for collectors, a lot of **crash mail** is known from those early years. Such crash covers, with their cancellations and markings are a specialty in postal history.

The U.S. entered World War I on April 6, 1917. The War Revenue Act of October 3, 1917 allowed servicemen assigned to duty in foreign countries to mail letters to the U.S. free of postage. This provision, effective October 20, 1917, required the envelope be marked with the words "Soldier's Mail" and be endorsed by an officer. Surviving examples of postal history from this era suggest that not many servicemen took advantage of this privilege.

The first U.S. **Army Post Office** (APO) was established in France on July 10, 1917. The civilian POD initially operated APOs. However, in May 1918, the Army's Military Express Service assumed operation of APOs. Postal markings of these early APO stations included code numbers instead of names of locations so as not to provide information to the enemy. Some of the most sought after examples of early APO postal history include Censor Markings and auxiliary markings associated with the perils of war. APOs were also used during World War II and are still in use today. Fleet Post Office (FPO) markings are used for overseas based naval and marine personnel.

Many U.S. Navy ships were outfitted with postal facilities, beginning in 1908, to handle mail for sailors. The study of naval ship cancellations and markings used aboard naval vessels is another specialized area of postal markings.

Postal History

Each year the United States Postal Service (USPS) handles billions of pieces of mail. The vast majority of these mailed items reach their destinations only to be promptly discarded by their recipients. But some are saved and become the raw material of "postal history."

Philatelic scholars have discussed the precise definition of postal history for decades. Here "Postal History" is defined as the study and collection of covers that chronicle the movement of the mails. The most desirable covers will have a combination of significant frankings, postal markings, rates, routes, usages, origins, and destinations which document the various functions and activities of the postal service, including collection, transportation, and delivery of the mail.

Notes on Collecting

Postal markings offer the collector many opportunities to define and build a collection. Many collectors of U.S. postal markings limit their collections to a specific topic or a group of related topics. Examples include the postal markings used in a particular city, the study of markings applied to a single stamp or a series of stamps, the study of mail from a particular period in history, hand-carved fancy cancels, and markings applied to mail while in transit, for example on a railroad.

Some collectors study the different machine cancels used to postmark stamps. One group, the Postmark Collector's Club, advocates collecting twentieth century postmarks as 2"x 4" cutouts from their covers; however, since most covers have a greater value when they are full and intact, collectors should ensure that covers to be cut down in order to create these cutouts have no greater value as intact covers. Most postal marking collections should be created by acquiring full, intact covers of the postal marking and franking.

Almanac

1639 – Fairbank's Tavern in Boston is named a repository for overseas mail.

1823 – Navigable waters are designated as post roads by Congress.

1838 – Railroads are designated as post roads by Congress.

1842 – The first private postage stamp (40L1) is issued for local mail delivery.

1845 – Postal Reform Act on July 1 sets guidelines for issuance of postage stamps.

1847 – Postage stamps are introduced on July 1, but their use is optional.

1855 – Pre-payment of postage becomes mandatory on April 1.

1856 – Use of stamps to prepay postage becomes mandatory on January 1.

1860 – The use of postmarks (CDSs) to cancel stamps is prohibited on July 23.

1863 – City Mail Delivery is introduced.

1863 – Postage rates are made uniform regardless of delivery distance.

1864 – Railway Post Offices are introduced on August 28 to facilitate mail sorting en route.

1876 – Regular machine canceling begins on January 6 with the introduction of Leavitt machines.

1881 – Wesson "Time-On-Bottom" cancels are introduced.

1884 – American Postal Machines Co. postmarks are used for the first time.

1888 – The first International Postal Supply Co. canceling machines are used.

1894 – First Barry Postal Supply Company canceling machines are used.

1899 – Doremus canceling machines are first used.

1899 – First slogans are used in machine cancels

1900 – Columbia Postal Supply Co. canceling machines are first used.

1902 – Rural Free Delivery system is established on a permanent basis.

1903 – Rubber handstamps, later called Doanes, are first issued on August 8 to post offices.

1909 – The first Universal Stamping Machine Co. canceling machines are used.

1917 – APO/FPO system is established on July 10.

1920 – First postage meter strip is used in lieu of postage stamp.

1941 – Highway Post Offices are established.

1943 – Zone system is introduced.

1963 – Zone Improvement Plan (**ZIP**) is introduced.

1982 – Automation is introduced with **OCR** equipment installation.

1983 – The ZIP+4 system is introduced.

1989 – Spray markings are first used.

What Others Have Said

The earliest attempts to cancel mail with machines in the U.S.
"Although the late 1850s saw the introduction of mechanical canceling devices in England, and other machines to cancel letters started to be used in Germany in 1866, it wasn't until 1876 that any machines were in regular use in more than one city in the United States. These were the Leavitt machines used to cancel postal cards….The idea of machines being used to cancel stamps on letters rapidly and legibly was always a target for inventors long before the Leavitt machines, however, the U.S. Post Office Department had interest in the development of such machines as early as the 1860s if not before. This is shown by an item in U.S. Mail & Post Office Assistant for February 1863….This told of a mechanical contrivance being tested without much success, at the New York Post Office."

—*Richard B. Graham, "Banknote Era Gaston Patent and ??? Machine Cancels," The Chronicle of the U.S. Classics, 1991.*

A hundred years of postmarking policy
"The recent rollover of our Western Calendar year digits provides an opportunity to review U.S. mail operations today and a century ago. In the days when William McKinley was President, the U.S. Post Office operated essentially every day, including Sundays and holidays. One can occasionally find covers postmarked on such dates as the Fourth of July in the 19th century, which adds interest to postal history collections….Today, a century later, the U.S. Postal Service operates on a different schedule. The USPS no longer 'processes' mail on Sundays

and holidays, i.e., mail is not cancelled, sorted and barcoded on those days as a matter of policy. Finding mail postmarked on a Sunday or a holiday is essentially impossible, if one is looking for a machine cancel, though hand cancels can be obtained….Post offices open on Sundays or holidays are generally those located at major airports (AMFs, AMCs, branches and stations)."

—*Leonard Piszkiewicz, "Y1.9K – Y2K," The United States Specialist, 2000.*

Collectors who build a postmark collection by town and city need to know dates

"The actual closing dates of post offices are different about 98% of the time from closing dates given by the USPS in the Postal Bulletin mainly because of the USPS definition of 'closed'. USPS considers a PO closed when the books are closed on the operation. For example, upon closing its doors June 30, a PO's postmaster may have earned a month's accumulated vacation. To keep the postmaster on the books and authorize pay, the closing date is given as July 31. A second discrepancy in dates occurs when USPS temporarily suspends operations at a PO. Perhaps a postmaster retired or a lease ended, and USPS thinks it might find a new postmaster or a new location. In the meantime, the PO is closed, possibly to reopen. But if in the future USPS decides not to resume operation, the closing of the PO is made official and permanent. Alas for collectors, the date given is that of the final decision not to reopen, not the date the PO actually closed its doors. The time between actual closing and official closing could be as much as 15 years."

—*"How Do I know when a Post Office Closed?" PMCC Bulletin, 1994.*

Many postmark collectors do not understand the basics of barcoding

"Barcoding is just what the name implies – a technique for coding information using lines or "bars" of various lengths or in particular positions or combinations….Barcoding as used by the United States mail processing refers to the black bars sprayed, usually below the address, and used to identify the destination zip code. Once a piece of mail is barcoded, automation can process the letter or mail piece at fast speeds. The purpose of the barcoding was part of an upgrade by the Postal Service to process more mail through less labor-intensive machines…..The use of OCR, or Optical Code Reading, machines to read barcodes was announced in the September-October issue of Postal Life, the magazine put out by the USPS for its employees. But experiments date back many years. The first machine was tested in the Detroit Post Office in 1965. In 1969 testing expanded to Boston and New York."

—*A. J. Savakis, "Barcoding in the U.S.A. – The A-B-C's," Machine Cancel Forum, 1998.*

Where to Find More Information

- A good introduction to postal history is Richard B Graham's *United States Postal History Sampler*.

- *A Primer of U.S. Postal Machine Markings* by Bart Billings, Reg Morris, and Robert Payne describes machine markings from the earliest machines to modern facer/cancellers.

- *A Collector's Guide to U.S. Machine Postmarks: 1871-1925*, by Russell F. Hanmer, provides essential information on machine cancels.

- Richard W. Helbock's second edition of *Postmarks on Postcards: An Illustrated Guide to Early 20th Century U.S. Postmarks* is an invaluable resource for any postal historian of the first quarter of the twentieth century.

- The Machine Cancel Society publishes a large number of excellent works on machine cancels. A good introduction to the subject is *A Handbook: US Postal Markings Impressed by Machines* by Bart Billings. Additionally, the Machine Cancel Society publishes *The Machine Cancel Forum Quarterly*. A web site is maintained at www.machinecancel.org.

- *United States Promotional Slogan Cancellations 1899 - 1940*, by Robert J. Payne is the definitive listing of the slogan cancels of the period.

- For flag cancels, Frederick Langford's *Standard Flag Cancel Encyclopedia* is the definitive resource.

- There are two works considered the standard references for the study of nineteenth century cancels: *United States Cancellations 1845-1869* by Huber C. Skinner and Amos Eno; and James M. Cole's *Cancellations and Killers of the Banknote Era 1870-1894*.

- Another fine work on nineteenth century cancels is Tracy Simpson's book *US Postal Markings and Related Mail Services 1851-1861*.

- For collectors of the postal history of mail transit, transfer, and distribution by rail, water, highway, or streetcar, there are the many excellent publications of the Mobile Post Office Society. They publish the quarterly *Transit Postmark Collector*, and maintain a website: www.eskimo.com/~rkunz/mposhome.html.

- *Auxiliary Markings* is the publication of The Auxiliary Markings Club. www.postal-markings.org.

- The major study of Doane cancels is *United States Doanes*, by Richard W. Helbock and Gary Anderson, Revised, Second Edition, 2002.

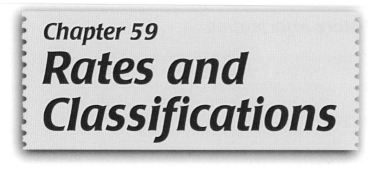

Chapter 59
Rates and Classifications

With a few notable exceptions, the Post Office has always charged for its services. Patrons have been required to pay postage on mailed items, as well as fees for ancillary services such as **registration**. Until the mid-nineteenth century postage was paid almost exclusively by recipients. Since the 1850s most postage has been paid by senders.

Over the years various factors have been used to calculate postage rates, including the number of sheets of paper in a letter, weight, distance sent, method of transport, as well as size and shape of the mailed matter. Postage rates, which were rather complex during the eighteenth and early nineteenth centuries, were simplified in the mid-nineteenth century and continued to be simplified through the twentieth century. Postage rates have reflected the values and priorities of American society. For example, newspapers and magazines have always moved through the mail at discounted rates, sometimes even for free. These low postage rates grew out of the long and widely held conviction that the public interest is served by encouraging the transmission of information.

While the Post Office has carried many different kinds of mail, letters remain the most prominent. However, the mails have also carried newspapers, periodicals, advertisements, packages, livestock, and produce. The Post Office has long distinguished between different kinds of mails, especially between letters and newspapers, which constituted the bulk of the mail through the mid-nineteenth century. In 1863 the Post Office Department (POD) formally established categories of mail known as "classes". Both the kinds of mailable matter embraced by the various classes and the names of the classes have changed over the years.

Letter Mail
Letters were the first type of mail to be carried. Early letters were written on sheets of paper then folded and mailed without envelopes (ch. 1). Postage was based on the number of sheets of paper used and the distance traveled. Rates prior to June 1, 1792 were paid in pennyweights and grains of silver. For example, from 1782 to 1787, a single sheet letter mailed 60 miles or less was charged 1 pennyweight 8 grains. The rates were doubled for letters with two sheets of paper. Rates also increased for longer distances.

Effective June 1, 1792, postage was charged in dollars and cents but continued to be based on the number of sheets contained in a letter and on distance. The rate for a single letter on June 1, 1792 was 6¢ for up to 31 miles, 8¢ for 31–60 miles, 10¢ for 61–100 miles, 12½¢ for 101–150 miles, 15¢ for 151–200 miles, 17¢ for 201–250 miles, 20¢ for 251–350 miles, 22¢ for 351–400 miles, and 25¢ for over 400 miles. Double weight letters were charged double, triple weight letters triple, etc. For approximately the next fifty years rates were adjusted both up and down, but the basic pattern of postage based on the number of pages and distance remained in tact. All of the letters in this era were **stampless**.

Various ship carriage charges were applicable during the late eighteenth and early nineteenth centuries. Effective in 1799, the fee for letters brought into the U.S. or transported from one port to another by private ship was 6¢, if the final port was also the post office of final delivery. If not, then another 2¢ was collectable for the additional conveyance. Effective May 1, 1825 until 1861, a ship's charge of 1¢ between U.S. ports was implemented.

On July 1, 1845, letter rates were greatly reduced and simplified. Half-ounce letters cost 5¢ for distances of up to 300 miles, and 10¢ for those sent over 300 miles. Rates were increased incrementally, by the same amount, for each additional half-ounce. The U.S. issued its first postage stamps (*Scott* 1 and 2) in 1847 to meet these rates (ch. 3). Use of these stamps was not mandatory as letters could still be sent "collect". It was not until April 1, 1855 that prepayment of postage was compulsory for domestic mail and it was not until January 1, 1856 that the use of postage stamps was required.

Westward expansion of the United States in the 1840s prompted an anomaly in the trend of reducing and simplifying postage rates. For mail to or from places within territories of the U.S. on the West Coast, the charge was set at 40¢ in 1847. In early 1861 it was reduced to 10¢. Also, a 12½¢ rate was established in 1848 for items mailed between points along the west coast.

By the time the use of postage stamps was mandatory in 1856, the rates of 1845 had been reduced even further. On July 1, 1851 a pre-paid half ounce letter could be mailed up to 3,000 miles for only 3¢, and over 3,000 miles for only 6¢. If not prepaid, the rates were 5¢ and 10¢ respectively. When prepayment of postage became compulsory on April 1, 1855, the rate for over 3,000 miles was raised to 10¢.

Postal rates were further simplified on July 1, 1863, the same day that free city delivery of mail was instituted in some cities. Distance was eliminated as a factor in letter postage, with weight alone determining the rate. This method of calculating postage on letters remained virtually unchanged into the twenty-first century. The domestic letter rate of 3¢ effective July 1, 1863 was reduced to 2¢ on October 1, 1883. On July 1, 1885, the weight that could be mailed for 2¢ was increased from one-half ounce to one ounce, an effective reduction in rates.

The 2¢ per ounce domestic letter rate lasted almost fifty years, from 1885 until increased to 3¢ on July 6, 1932. From November 2, 1917 until the end of June 1919 each domestic letter was charged an additional 1¢ per ounce as a war tax. The revenue raised by this tax was transferred monthly to the general fund of the Treasury.

After the rise of the letter rate to 3¢ in 1932 it was more than a quarter of a century for the next increase, to 4¢, in 1958. By the end of the twentieth century, letter rates increased 13 more times, to 33¢.

Carrier Letters

Prior to July 1, 1863, there was no free delivery of mail to homes or business. Patrons had to go to the post office to pick up their mail. Although free home delivery began in selected cities on July 1, 1863, and while the numbers of customers receiving free mail delivery expanded rapidly during the nineteenth century, there were still some customers without free home delivery at the end of the twentieth century. The lack of early universal free mail delivery gave rise to *carrier service* (ch. 30) in some cities. By 1794, mail carriers could deliver letters and collect 2¢ for the service. Patrons were not required to accept this service. If they declined, the letter presumably went back to the local post office where the addressee could retrieve it later and not be charged the delivery fee. Conversely, the Act of July 2, 1836, allowed carriers to charge an amount not to exceed 2¢ for picking up a letter from a mailer and depositing it into the postal system. Carrier service for a fee was made obsolete where free city delivery was available.

Drop Letters

The absence of free mail delivery also helps explain the origin of *drop letters*, also called local letters. A drop letter was one mailed or "dropped" at a post office for retrieval by the addressee at that same post office. The postal clerk simply stored the letter until such time as the addressee came in to pick up mail. A drop letter fee of 1¢ was introduced in 1794. This was a real bargain compared to the lowest possible rate at the time for a letter carried in the mailstream. The drop letter fee alternated between 1¢ and 2¢ until the implementation of free city delivery on July 1, 1863.

The drop letter charge was set at 2¢ per half ounce effective July 1, 1863. Also effective that date drop letters were classified as either originating from post offices that provided free carrier service, or from post offices that did not. Effective March 3, 1865 the fee for a drop letter at a post office without carrier service was reduced to 1¢, while the charge for a drop letter at a post office with carrier service remained 2¢. Rates for drop letters mailed at carrier post offices and non-carrier post offices varied until the service was abolished at carrier post offices in 1944 and at non-carrier post offices in 1963. By 1963 few letters were sent by drop rate since the vast majority of the population was served by post offices providing free carrier service.

International Letters

The most complex U.S. letter postage rates were those for letters mailed to foreign destinations prior to July 1, 1875. This was due to the confusing array of bilateral **treaty rates**, sometimes called conventions rates, which governed the exchange of mail between the U.S. and foreign destinations. Postage on a letter would be determined by the terms of a treaty, weight, surcharges, mail handling procedures, routings, and final destination. This method of handling mail required elaborate accounting systems, with debits and credits generated by each piece of mail. On July 1, 1875, the mailing of a letter to most foreign destination became simpler due to an international agreement governing international mail service known as the General Postal Union (later the **Universal Postal Union** [UPU]).

These complex pre-1875 rates can be illustrated by considering some rates available from the U.S. to one of the more common destinations, France. Effective March 1848, mail went directly by American packet ships to France. A basic weight letter was charged 24¢ for passage from New York to France. U.S. domestic postage was extra. Effective July 1851, the surcharge for sea transit was reduced to 20¢. This rate structure ended in April 1857.

Mail to France could also be sent via Great Britain, beginning in July 1849. Surcharges via Great Britain were 21¢ if by open mail on an American packet ship or 5¢ if by open mail on a British packet. Effective January 1853, the rates were identical by either American or British packets, being 21¢. A month later the rates returned to 21¢ and 5¢ respectively, lasting until April 1857.

Effective in April 1857 a letter to France was charged 15¢. Payment could be made by the sender or collected from the recipient. This rate lasted until January 1870 when it was replaced by three options: 4¢ by American packet ship via Britain, 12¢ by via British packet, or 10¢ via American or French packet direct to France. These rates were replaced by a 9¢ rate effective August 1, 1874.

Finally, on January 1, 1876, under terms of the General Postal Union, the postage on a letter to France, as to most countries, was 5¢ per half ounce. The 5¢ UPU basic letter rate remained in effect until November 1, 1953 when it was increased to 8¢. The rate increased in the following years, to 11¢ in 1961, 13¢

in 1967, and so on until it reached 70¢ on February 3, 1991. This surface (ship) rate ended July 9, 1995, resulting in all international letter mail moving by air at air mail rates.

The U.S. established special bilateral agreements with both Canada and Mexico from the mid-nineteenth century through April 3, 1988. These applied U.S. domestic letter and registry rates for mail to these countries. From the first decade of the twentieth century until the outbreak of World War I, "most favored nation rates", of 3¢ for the first ounce and 2¢ for each additional ounce were in effect for Great Britain, France, and Germany.

Domestic Air Mail Letters
The airplane made a significant impact during World War I and the POD took notice. Air mail service was established between New York City, Philadelphia, and Washington, D.C. on May 15, 1918. The rate was 24¢ per ounce, which included special delivery service (ch. 24). Effective July 15, the Postmaster General (PMG) reduced the rate to 16¢ for the first ounce, still including special delivery service (fig. 1). On December 15 the rate was reduced to 6¢, but without special delivery service.

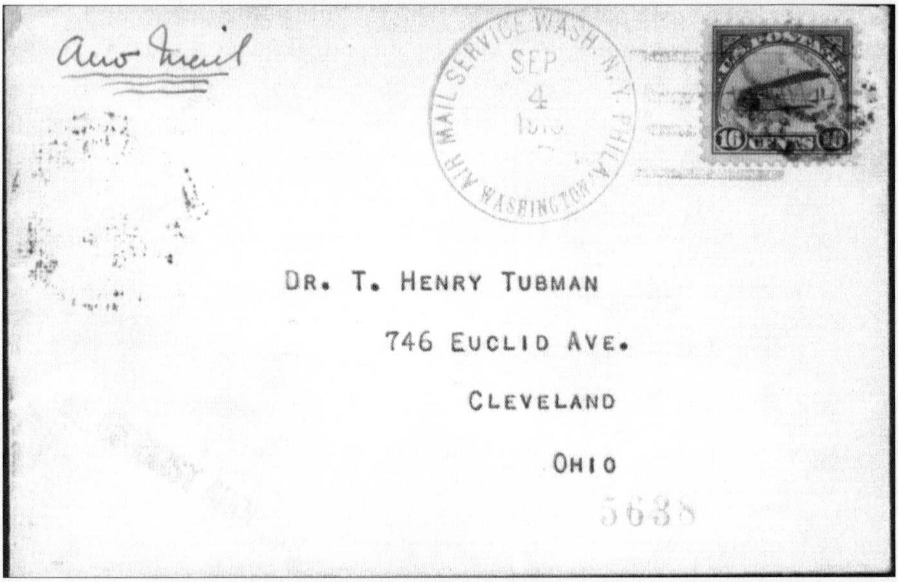

Figure 1

A cover mailed at the 16¢ airmail rate on September 4, 1918. It traveled from Washington to Philadelphia where it was placed on a train for Cleveland. Special Delivery was provided at 5:30 PM in Cleveland the next day according to the backstamp.

Between July 18, 1919 and June 30, 1924, there was no established air mail rate. Mail continued to be flown by air mail during this period, but all letters were charged 2¢ postage, the rate for ground transportation. The POD continued to develop routes, improve equipment, and prepare landing strips throughout this period.

On June 30, 1924, the transcontinental air mail route began operation with a new set of air mail rates. The country was divided into three air mail zones (New York to Chicago, Chicago to Cheyenne, and Cheyenne to San Francisco). For each zone, the rate was 8¢ per ounce. For example, a one ounce letter from San Francisco to Cleveland cost 24¢ because it traversed the western and central zones and a portion of the eastern zone. A two ounce letter from Minneapolis to New York City cost 16¢ because it was carried by train to Chicago then was flown across the eastern zone to New York City at the 8¢ per ounce rate. Night service between New York City and Chicago was introduced July on 1, 1925 at the rate of 10¢ per ounce.

Beginning February 15, 1926 various **contract air mail** (CAM) routes were established, primarily as feeder routes to the transcontinental route. The charge was 10¢ per ounce per CAM route up to 1,000 miles. Longer CAM routes (1,001–1,500 miles) were 15¢. Routes over 1,500 miles, though none were ever actually established, cost 20¢. The rate per zone on the government operated transcontinental route was reduced from 8¢ to 5¢ per ounce if the letter also traveled on a CAM route. When letters traveled on multiple routes the rate structure was very complex. This rate structure proved very difficult for postal clerks and the mailing public, so a simplified rate system was instituted. Effective February 1, 1927, the rate charged was 10¢ per half ounce, regardless of the distance or number of routes traveled.

On August 1, 1928, the basic air mail rate was lowered to 5¢ for the first ounce, but to discourage heavier items, each additional ounce was charged 10¢. On July 6, 1932, postage on the first ounce of air mail was increased to 8¢ and each additional ounce was charged 13¢. The domestic air

The Universal Postal Union

Twenty-one nations signed the Treaty of Bern on October 9, 1874, establishing the General Postal Union. The treaty took affect July 1, 1875. At the Paris convention in 1878, the name was changed to the Universal Postal Union (UPU).

A chief benefit of the UPU was lower postage rates between member nations. The old complicated accounting systems were eliminated and the country of origin kept the proceeds collected when postage was paid. The premise of accepting the simplification was that each letter would prompt a reply and both countries would benefit financially.

mail rate was reduced to 6¢ per ounce on July 1, 1934, then increased to 8¢ per ounce on March 26, 1944, then reduced to 5¢ per ounce on October 1, 1946. The rate was adjusted six more times by October 11, 1975, after which any letter that could benefit from air transportation was given air transportation. For most practical purposes, this ended domestic air mail rates; although the domestic air mail rate structure was not formally abolished until May 1, 1977.

International Air Mail Letters
Prior to November 1, 1946 international letter air mail rates were complicated, and can be grouped into four broad categories:

- those receiving domestic air mail service in the U.S. with surface transport beyond (fig. 2)

- those receiving surface transport domestically, but air mail service somewhere overseas

- those receiving air mail service in the U.S. and in one or more other countries, but with surface transport between

- those flown on *foreign air mail routes* (FAMS).

Figure 2.

A cover mailed from Pocatello, Idaho to Austria on November 2, 1931. Domestic air mail was 5¢. The envelope was endorsed "Via Air Mail" by rubber stamp. Upon arrival in New York City, the "Via Air Mail" marking nullified with a double bar strike. This indicated to the Europeans that there was not enough postage affixed for further airmail service on that continent. The surcharge for surface transport to Europe at this time was 4¢, so this cover is properly franked with a 9¢ stamp.

International mail receiving domestic air mail service is the oldest of these categories. Beginning in 1924 a patron paid the domestic air mail rate, plus a 3¢ surcharge if the letter was going to a country, such as France, with a UPU letter rate of 5¢, effectively giving the sender a 2¢ discount. However, if the letter was going to a country, such as Great Britain, which had a preferential rate of 2¢, no surcharge was applicable. Surcharges varied until the rate simplification in 1946.

For example, a one-ounce letter flown in 1924 from San Francisco to New York on the transcontinental air mail route, and then by sea to France, was charged 24¢ for domestic air mail service plus a 3¢ surcharge, for a total of 27¢. Similarly, a one ounce letter from Chicago to London in 1924 would be carried from Chicago to New York by air and then by sea to England. The postage would be 8¢ for its travel on the transcontinental air mail route, with no additional charge for sea transport to England.

The second category of pre-1946 letters is those provided only overseas air mail service. The sender paid the UPU surface rate (5¢ for the first ounce and 3¢ for additional ounces) or a special lower surface treaty rate if one existed, plus a surcharge for the air mail service to be received overseas. For example, a letter originating in New York City bound for Denmark in 1927 was charged the UPU letter rate of 5¢, which included ocean liner carriage to Europe. Air passage from England to Denmark was available if the cover was endorsed "By air mail from London" and the 6¢ per ounce air mail rate was paid, a total of 11¢ postage.

Letters in the third category, those receiving air mail services on more than one continent had high postage rates. The rate consisted of U.S. domestic air mail, the surcharge for surface transportation abroad, and the rate for foreign air mail. For example, a letter sent from Denver to Malaysia in early 1932 would likely have traveled by air from Denver to New York, costing 5¢. The surcharge for steamer service from New York to Amsterdam was 4¢. Finally, air mail service via KLM (Royal Dutch Airline) to Malaysia was 32¢ per half ounce, making the total charge 41¢.

The fourth type is mail flown on FAMs. These routes were operated by private carriers such as Pan American Airlines. Pan Am pioneered FAM routes throughout the Western Hemisphere as well as across the Pacific and Atlantic oceans. Each FAM route was assigned a number, and rates were established that provided surface transport on both ends of the flight. For example, FAM Route #8 was a comparatively short route from Brownsville, Texas to El Salvador. Starting service in March 1929, rates varied but in the mid-1930s, air mail to Mexico cost 10¢ per half ounce and air mail to Guatemala and El Salvador cost 15¢ per half ounce. FAM Route #18, air service across the Atlantic, was instituted in

May 1939 and cost 30¢ per half ounce, including additional surface transport as required, or air mail transport as available.

Simplification of international air mail letter rates occurred on November 1, 1946 when the world was divided into three destination areas. Mail destined for most of the Western Hemisphere was charged 10¢ per half ounce. Mail for Europe, Turkey, and Mediterranean Africa was charged 15¢ per half ounce, while mail for the rest of the world was charged 25¢, per half ounce. Air mail rates since 1946 have followed a modified zone approach. For example, effective July 1, 1961, rates were 13¢ for Central America and the Caribbean, 15¢ to South America and Europe, and 25¢ for the rest of the world. Then, effective April 3, 1988, a basic air mail letter could be sent anywhere in the world, except Canada and Mexico, for 45¢.

Classes of Mail

The growing diversity in the types of mail handled by the POD led to the Act of March 3, 1863, which divided mail into three classes. Carrying letters was regarded as the primary business of the Department, and therefore the most important. Letters became known as First Class mail, a designation they still carry today. *First Class* mail includes letters, *post cards*, *postal cards*, and *priority mail*. Any matter that is wholly or partly in writing, except book manuscripts and corrected proof sheets, is defined as First Class mail. Postal cards were introduced in May 1873 with a rate of 1¢. Post cards could also be mailed at this rate beginning July 1, 1898. Since then, postal cards and post cards have paid the same rate of postage, except from April 15, 1925 to July 1, 1928, when post cards were charged 2¢. The 1¢ rate for postal cards lasted over a quarter of a century, giving rise to the term "penny post card". The rate was finally raised to 2¢ on July 1, 1958. The rate was raised fourteen more times by the end of the twentieth century.

Second Class mail was comprised of publications exclusively in print, issued at stated intervals, including newspapers and magazines. Most postage on Second Class mail was paid in cash or from a prepaid account, although *Newspaper and Periodical stamps* (ch. 24) were used from January 1, 1875 until June 30, 1898. As part of the classification reform enacted in 1996 Second Class mail was renamed Periodicals Class mail.

Prior to 1863 newspapers and magazines had designated rates. Once based on the number of sheets, in 1845 the criteria was changed to weight. By 1851, the rate basis was per copy, a response to growing variety in sizes and dimensions of newspapers and magazines. Distance was a factor until eliminated in 1852. The Act of 1852 eliminated any distinctions between magazines and newspapers, setting the stage for the introduction of Second Class mail in 1863.

Third Class mail in 1863 was designated to include nearly all mailable matter not of the First or Second Class. At the time, circulars, handbills, and flyers were part of this category. Between 1863 and 1879, Third Class mail had become a catch-all category.

In 1879, modifications were made to the mail classes. Third Class was limited to printed matter other than regular magazines, periodicals, and newspapers. Postage rates were fixed on each individual piece of mail, with a basic rate of 1¢ (fig. 3). This mail is typically characterized by a mute cancellation containing no date. Because Third Class mail was of a low priority, the absence of a date

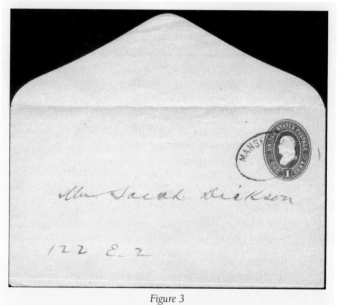

Figure 3

A Third Class mailing, exhibiting two characteristics of a Third Class item: a cancel that is devoid of a mailing date, and un unsealed flap.

meant recipients could not be certain how long delivery of their mail had taken. Another characteristic of this mail was the unsealed flap, a requirement that allowed postal employees to check for illegal First Class material, such as a personal note. Bulk rate, a sub-category of Third Class mail was introduced in 1928. Rates were based on the weight of the entire mailing, with per piece minimums. In 1952 special Third Class bulk rates were established for non-profit organizations, again with rates based on bulk weight with per piece minimums. As part of the classification reform of 1996 Third Class mail became **Standard Mail** (A).

Fourth Class was established May 1, 1879 and included all matter not embraced by First, Second, and Third Classes. The rate was 1¢ per ounce. Mailed items generally had to weigh four pounds or less, and most Fourth Class mail can be best described as merchandise.

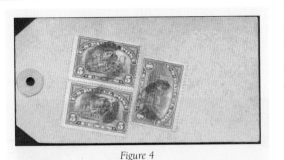
Figure 4

The back of a tag attached to a parcel and bearing the special Parcel Post stamps of 1913. The parcel was mailed from Carrabelle, Florida, to Louisville, Kentucky. This was a two-pound parcel mailed to the fourth zone. The charge was 8¢ for the first pound and 6¢ for each additional pound.

In one of the great postal and social reforms of the twentieth century, Fourth Class mail was expanded and renamed **Parcel Post** (fig. 4) on January 1, 1913. It provided for mailing items up to 11 pounds, with a combined length and girth of 72 inches or less. Parcels weighing not more than four ounces were charged 1¢ per ounce. Heavier packages were charged by the pound and the distance mailed. Eight zones were established based on quadrangles defined by latitude and longitude. Special stamps (Q1–12) were issued to accommodate the Parcel Post system, although they were used only briefly (ch. 24). Parcel Post rates were subject to the War Tax imposed in 1917. While that tax was removed from First Class mail in 1919, it continued on Parcel Post until 1922. Through the years both weight limitations and rates rose. On July 1, 1996, as part of the mail classification reform, Parcel Post became Standard Mail (B).

Service Fees

The POD and its successor, the United States Postal Service (USPS), have provided special services for a fee to help postal patrons secure their mailings and to expedite or enhance the basic classes of mail.

Registry has four purposes: 1) to provide security for valuable and important mail, 2) to provide proof of mailing, 3) to provide proof of receipt, and 4) to pay an indemnity or insurance for registered mail that is lost or stolen. Some efforts at the first two were made informally by some postmasters before 1845. Starting October 30, 1845 Philadelphia, and then other large cities, started registering mail on a semi-official local basis. The Post Office Department formalized the Registry system nationally in 1855. A limited indemnity was introduced in 1908 and a full multi-tiered rate system based on value was started in 1923. Its purpose was to provide greater security for valuable letters. The original fee was 5¢ per letter, applicable only to First Class mail. There was no insurance provided in case of loss. Later changes included the extension of the registry service to all classes of mail. In 1898, indemnification of up to $10 was provided. In 1923 graduated registry fees were introduced, based on the amount of indemnification. Registry service cost 10¢ for valuables up to $50, and 20¢ for valuables between $50 and $100. Fees increased in the following years and by the end of the twentieth century the cost of basic registration had risen to $6.00, without any insurance.

Insured mail was introduced in conjunction with the Parcel Post system in 1913. Officials believed the registry system would be over-burdened by both First Class and parcel post mail. Insured mail covered the loss, rifling, or damage to parcels within specific indemnity limits. Although both services include indemnity, one major difference existed between registered mail and insured mail. Registered mail is handled with special safeguards during transit while insured mail is handled in the normal mail stream.

Figure 5

A 1961 cover to which the mailer applied a 30¢ Special Delivery stamp, but neglected to add 4¢ First Class postage. Consequently, the letter arrived with postage due stamps added.

Special Delivery service (fig. 5) was introduced October 1, 1885 with a fee of 10¢. The POD described this service as extraordinary dispatch and delivery of the mail. In general, as soon as a Special Delivery item reached the addressee's local post office, a messenger delivered it immediately to the recipient. In 1925 weight became a consideration in determining the Special Delivery fee. The basic 10¢ fee for a letter in 1885 lasted almost sixty years, until 1944. The fee was raised modestly seven times until April 18, 1976, when it reached 80¢. The fee was then raised seven more times, until it reached $9.95 on January 1, 1995. Special Delivery service was discontinued on June 7, 1997, having been effectively replaced by **Express** and Priority mail.

Special Handling began in 1925. This service provided Fourth Class parcels the same expeditious handling, transportation, and delivery given to First Class mail. The fee originally was 25¢ per piece. Beginning in 1928, the per piece fee was determined by weight. Items less than 2 pounds were charged 10¢, those weighing 2 to 10 pounds cost 15¢, and heavier items were charged 20¢. By 1931, the definition of special handling changed to the most expeditious handling and transportation practical. By the end of the twentieth century the basic fee had risen to $5.40.

Collect on Delivery (COD) service was first offered on July 1, 1913 as a means of supporting and promoting the parcel post service. For a fee, the POD delivered the package and collected the appropriate fee and cost of the merchandise on delivery from the recipient. This was attractive to customers because they did not have to pay for merchandise in advance and then wait for the mail system to deliver it. Merchants also liked it because they did not risk the extension of credit to their customers. The basic fee in 1913 was 10¢. Beginning in 1929 registered mail could be sent COD. The total amount of the fee depended on the amount of money to be collected and the indemnity provided. By the end of the twentieth century the minimum fee had risen to $4.00.

A number of other services requiring a fee have been initiated to serve postal patrons. They include **return receipts, certified mail, certificates of mailing,** and **restricted delivery**.

Notes on Collecting

Changing rates and classifications over time provide challenges to collectors who wish to acquire examples of the many different rates and time periods. Many collectors choose to acquire covers illustrating these rates. Almost all definitive, air mail, and commemorative stamps have been issued to pay specific rates. One could form a collection of covers utilizing a chosen stamp that shows different rates to both domestic and international destinations. A collector could specialize by choosing a particular rate and form a collection of covers utilizing this rate.

Covers can also be collected to tell the story of a specific class of postal service. Examples include special services such as registered mail, special delivery, domestic air mail, international air mail, insured mail, and certified mail. For example, one could search for covers which show the July 6, 1932–June 30, 1984 6¢ air mail letter rate and build a collection based on this rate. One could find many different covers showing different frankings, destinations, and routes.

Solo usage covers are those which bear a single stamp to pay the total rate for all fees (e.g., first class plus registry). Many collectors enjoy the challenge of searching for solo usages. Some collectors prefer regimented frankings, which are covers bearing separate stamps for each service, an example being a stamp paying the First Class rate, another paying the certified mail rate, and a third to pay for the return receipt. Other collectors specialize in rates on postal stationery items such as envelopes, postal cards, or wrappers. Rates may also be collected on metered mail.

Almanac

1792 – On June 1 postage is first calculated in dollars and cents.

1845 – Letter rates are reduced and simplified July 1 as part of a postal reform.

1863 – An Act of Congress on March 3 divides mail into three classes, First, Second, and Third.

1863 – Distance ceases to be a factor in the calculation of letter rates effective July 1.

1873 – A rate is established for postal cards on May 1.

1875 – Effective January 1 publishers are required to pay postage on newspapers and magazines. Prior to this date postage was paid by subscribers upon delivery.

1875 – International letter rates are simplified on July 1 as the terms of the General Postal Union (later the Universal Postal Union) take effect for most countries.

1879 – Fourth Class mail is established on May 1.

1883 – First Class letter rate is reduced to 2¢ on October 1, a rate that remains in effect until 1932.

1885 – Special Delivery begins October 1.

1913 – Parcel Post service begins January 1, an expansion of Fourth Class mail.

1917 – War tax goes into effect November 2 on First Class mail and Parcel Post.

1918 – First regularly scheduled air mail service begins on May 15.

1919 – War tax on First Class mail ends on July 1.

1927 – Domestic air mail rates are simplified beginning February 1.

1928 – Third Class bulk mail rates go into effect on July 1 and **Business Reply Mail** service instituted.

1946 – International air mail letter rates are simplified on November 1.

1949 – Air mail rate is established on January 1 for postal and post cards.

1952 – Third Class non-profit bulk rates are instituted on July 1.

1996 – Classification reform goes into effect on July 1 with all prior Second Class mail renamed Periodicals, Third Class mail renamed Standard Mail (A), and Fourth Class Mail renamed Standard Mail (B).

1997 – Special Delivery is discontinued on June 7.

What Others Have Said

Only four rate scales from 1700 until twentieth century

"… we had four and only four scales of postage in this country, though on each basal scale the rates varied:

1. 1711 to 1845 by zones or distances and number of sheets of paper.

2. 1845 to 1849 and revived 1851 to 1885: unit rate per half-ounce.

3. 1849–1851: unit rate per half ounce only within the first ounce weight; by double unit rate per full ounce on multiples above one ounce.

4. 1885 – on: 2¢ per ounce regardless of weight."

—*"The Clubhouse – Boston Philatelic Society Night,"* The Collectors Club Philatelist, *1955.*

New Rates but familiar artists and portraits

"Congress will undoubtedly pass legislation increasing the first class postal rate from two to three cents. This will have results for the collectors in some new stamps probably [sic]. The Post Office has always had a Stuart or Houdon, Washington, on the single first class rate stamps and there is no reason to expect they will fail to run true to form now, especially when it's a fine excuse for another first day issue….As the 3 cent rate will run for two years presumably, next year they will have to have a Washington 3 cent in place of Lincoln on the permanent issue."

—*Hugh M. Southgate, "New Stamps,"* The Bureau Specialist, *1932.*

Campaigning for a Parcel Post System in the U.S.

"The system now in operation [Fourth Class] allows the express companies to bid under postal rates and get the short hauls, while the long and expensive hauls are left to the Department, whose rates are fixed irrespective of long or short distances."

—*Postmaster General John Wanamaker, Annual Report of the PMG, 1892. It would be another twenty years before the U.S. initiated a Parcel Post system of rating packages by distance carried.*

New rates means many new stamps

"Collectors of modern United States stamps should plan to add several more pages to their albums to accommodate an avalanche of new stamps and postal stationery items coming in the months ahead. The U.S. Postal Service plans to issue the new stamps in conjunction with its June 30 rate increase...To have enough stamps on hand to meet the new 37¢ first class domestic letter rate. The Postal Service plans to release...a non-denominated (37¢) U.S. Flag stamp and four non-denominated (37¢) stamps depicting antique toys. Nine different formats between the two issues are expected to be issued."

—*Charles Snee, "Upcoming stamps, stationery for June 20 rate increase could mean more than 50 distinct, collectible varieties," Linn's Stamp News, 2002.*

Where to Find More Information

- The definitive works on postal rates are the two volumes by Anthony Wawrukiewicz and Henry Beecher: *U.S. Domestic Postal Rates, 1872-1999 and U.S. International Postal Rates, 1872-1996.*

- Charles Starnes' *United States Letter Rates to Foreign Destinations 1847-1876.*

- Richard Graham's *United States Postal History Sampler* contains much useful rate information.

- The USPOD's *United States Domestic Postage Rates 1789-1956* is still useful.

- Several specialized handbooks on various postal rates and services exist, including *Via Airmail* by Simine Short and Cheryl Ganz; *United States Registered Mail 1845-1870* by James W. Milgram; and *U.S. Parcel Post* and *The Speedy: A History of the U.S. Special Delivery Service*, both by Henry Gobie.

Chapter 60
First Day Covers

When a new postage stamp is issued, collectors may obtain a souvenir of that event known as a First Day Cover (FDC). A FDC is a plain or *cacheted* envelope affixed with the new stamp cancelled on the day it is issued, in the city (issuance city) in which it is released. This date often has a special significance with the subject depicted on the stamp. The United States Postal Service (USPS) usually selects one issuance city, often related in some way to the subject matter of the stamp, as the place for the official first day issuance. A formal ceremony is also planned where the new stamp is first released to the public.

Prior to 1922, the Post Office Department (POD) did not regularly designate a date of issue for new stamps. Only a few pre-1922 stamps had a designated first day of issue, and most that did were *commemoratives*. For example, all of the 1893 Columbians (except the 8¢ stamp) were issued on January 1, and the 2¢ Lincoln centennial stamps of 1909 were issued on February 12. While first day covers exist for stamps as early as 1851, these early covers generally were not prepared specifically as FDCs as they are known today.

On July 12, 1922, the POD issued a new *Special Delivery* stamp with a considerable amount of promotional activity. A press release to major newspapers announcing this Special Delivery stamp was made on July 8. A separate official new stamp announcement was sent to postmasters on the first day of sale, July 12. This represents the first time that the POD notified collectors of the date and location of a new issue, giving birth to the "modern" first day cover.

The first regular stamp issued for the Series of 1922, the 11¢ Hayes (*Scott* 563), was released on October 4. This stamp was the first regular issue to be released on a designated day in a specific location. Both Washington, D.C. and Fremont, Ohio were designated as first day cities. The stamp also had the first public first day ceremony, with a mimeographed program.

During the 1920s, FDCs were prepared by such pioneers in the field as Adam K. Bert, H.F. Colman, Henry Hammelman, C.E. Nickles, Howard A. Robinette, Hugh M. Southgate, Phillip H. Ward, Jr., and Edward Worden. These servicers used plain envelopes of different sizes and quality. They, or their friends, usually had some connections with the POD, which enabled them to learn of upcoming new issues in time to prepare FDCs. Eventually, the POD began providing collectors the opportunity to submit addressed envelopes along with payment for the new stamps to be affixed. The POD then added the new stamps and cancelled them on the announced first day date. In 1929 the POD limited the number of covers serviced to 25 per person. Beginning January 1, 1961, the POD required that requests for first day cancellations be postmarked at least five days before the designated first day date.

On July 13, 1937, the POD began using machine cancellations on FDCs with a special slogan reading "First Day of Issue". The slogan appeared in a seven bar **killer** and was used on the Northwest Territory issue (fig. 1). Prior to this issue, FDCs were cancelled with the machine or **hand canceling** devices used on everyday mail. Beginning with the Virginia Dare stamp issued on August 18, 1937, the "First Day of Issue" slogan appeared in a five-bar cancellation. On January 29, 1940 when the 1¢ Washington Irving (859) and 2¢ James Fennimore Cooper (860) issues of the Famous American series appeared, the POD began using the same slogan in hand cancellations. A four-bar machine cancel containing the slogan was adopted beginning with the Progress of Women issue (959) of July 19, 1948.

Figure 1

Detail from the first FDC (795) to use the slogan "First Day of Issue".

Occasionally, the POD established a special sub-station post office for a first day event. This station usually was assigned a distinctive cancellation for that day (fig. 2). On March 15, 1958, the POD introduced a pictorial first day of issue cancellation for the Gardening and Horticulture issue (1100, fig. 3). These pictorial cancellations continued through the Louisiana Statehood stamp (1197) issued on April 30, 1962. The first day cancel for the Charles M. Russell stamp (1243) on March 19, 1964 was the first not to include the time of day in the dial. On April 9, 1965 for the Appomattox issue (1182), the **Zip Code** was included in the dial. Many modern first day of issue (FDOI) cancels contain slo-

Figure 2

FDC showing cancel from the sub-station established for the International Philatelic Exhibition of 1926.

Figure 3

FDC showing pictorial cancel as part of the first day of issue cancellation for the Gardening and Horticulture Issue (1100).

Figure 4

FDC of Bogart issue (3152) with cancel containing a related slogan.

gans relating to the subject of the stamp (fig. 4). A hand cancel with short bars was introduced in the 1940s. This cancel eventually evolved into a "bullseye" without killer bars.

Beginning with the Washington at Princeton issue (1704) on January 3, 1977, the USPS instituted a 15 day grace period. Collectors could buy stamps at their local post offices, affix them to envelopes, and mail them to the postmaster in the designated first day city for cancellation. Alternatively, money sufficient to cover the cost of the stamps could be sent and the post office would affix the stamps and cancel them. Effective with the Robert Morris postal card (UX93) issued on November 10, 1981, the grace period was extended to 30 days. After August 1, 1993, the USPS no longer affixed stamps to envelopes submitted by customers, effectively ending an era.

During the 1990s, unofficial cancellations became popular. Unofficial FDCs are produced when a collector purchases new stamps at the post office officially issuing them and takes them to other post offices to obtain a postmark on the same day. Such cancels must be obtained during regular post office hours on the first day. Most unofficial FDCs are not listed by *Scott*.

Unofficial FDCs exist from the 1920s on. A famous and *Scott* listed example of an unofficial FDC is the 13¢ Harrison stamp (622) postmarked at North Bend, Ohio. Issued on January 11, 1926, pioneer servicer Edward Worden purchased 500 stamps in Indianapolis,

Figure 5

Unofficial FDC of the 13¢ Harrison (622), canceled in North Bend, Ohio.

Indiana, an official first day city, and transported them to North Bend, Ohio, Harrison's home town. Worden had them cancelled in North Bend on the first day of issue (fig. 5).

Stamps are sometimes issued in more than one city. An example is the Sullivan Expedition issue (657) of June 17, 1929. It was issued in 15 cities in New York State, all of which could claim some connection to John Sullivan. Occasionally, the USPS issues stamps on a nationwide basis. In this case, all post offices are authorized to sell the new stamp on its first day of issue. Frequently, just one post office uses the official FDOI cancellation. A popular example is the stamp marking the beginning of the USPS (1396), issued on July 1, 1971. Only Washington D.C. used the official FDOI cancellation. This marked the first time that a stamp was issued at every post office on its first day.

In 1982, the USPS permitted two large FDC producers to cancel covers on their premises. When cancels of non-standard size appeared from these locations, the USPS rescinded this permission.

While small sized notices of new issues were sent out as early as 1922, page-size new issue announcement posters were sent to post offices beginning in 1959. Collectors could subscribe to these through the Government Printing Office. Many collectors affixed stamps to these posters and obtained FDOI cancels. The posters were discontinued in the 1970s. Since 1972 the USPS has issued souvenir pages. These describe the new stamp and bear the new stamp with a FDOI cancellation. They are sold by subscription by the USPS.

First day cancellations were applied where the stamp was issued until 1974. Then cancels were provided for larger servicers of FDCs at a central facility. By 1985, all **machine cancelled** FDCs were canceled at the Merrifield, Virginia processing facility. By 1990, this function was transferred to the Kansas City, Missouri philatelic facility. Hand cancels still are available at the first day of issue location.

On August 2, 1923, President Warren G. Harding died unexpectedly in San Francisco. The POD issued a memorial stamp on September 1, 1923 in Marion, Ohio, Harding's birthplace, and in Washington, D.C. George Linn, who later founded *Linn's Stamp News*, was a Harding admirer. He decided to print a black five-line cachet to honor the stamp. He printed the cachet on a variety of envelopes and drove to Marion to have his covers serviced (canceled). Enroute home to Columbus, Ohio, Linn had a number of covers serviced in others towns, resulting in unofficial FDCs. Linn's cachet is considered the first FDC cachet produced on a commercial basis.

The use of cachets on FDCs became popular during the mid-1920s. Early cachet makers included: G.A. Jackson, A.C. Roessler, C.E. Nickles, James H. Baxter, Herbert H. Griffin, Albert E. Gorham, Milton T. Mauck, and Harry Ioor. Color was first used in a cachet for the Norse-American issue (620 and 621) of May 18, 1925. This cachet was produced by Ernest J. Weschcke. The first known pictorial cachet was produced by C.E. Nickles for the 17¢ Woodrow Wilson issue (623) on December 28, 1925. Most cachets for FDCs in the 1920s have no identification of the cachet maker or artist. This sometimes makes it difficult to identify the originator of the cachet. By the early 1930s, most FDCs were cacheted.

Early cachets usually were either rubber-stamped or printed. Often several colors were used and descriptive text was added. Examples include those by C. Stephen Anderson. In some cases, the cachet was thermographed, a process by which the ink is heated, but not hot enough to damage the envelope. In 1932, Henry Grimsland began producing engraved cachets. Other servicers of FDCs such as Artcraft, Artmaster, Fleetwood, and Fulton followed in the late 1930s and 1940s. Cachetcraft and Fluegel are examples of printed cachets that began in the 1930s and 1940s. During the 1940s cachets appeared which were lithographed, silk screened, hand drawn or painted, air brushed, and pasted-on. All of these methods of producing cachets continue in use today. Since the mid-1960s, hand painted cachets have become more popular and common.

Beginning with the 2005 Happy New Year stamps, the USPS offered special color FDC cancellations for selected new issues. These cancels were available only on covers purchased from the USPS at a premium price and were not used to service covers submitted by the public or cachet makers.

Errors, freaks, and oddities (EFOs) have occurred on FDCs since the 1920s. An EFO designation can be based on the cachet, the stamp (or lack of a stamp), or the cancellation.

First Day Ceremony Programs

In 1922, a ceremony was held marking the issuance of the 11¢ Hayes issue (563). In following years, subsequent stamps were accorded similar ceremonies when issued. The earliest reported first day ceremony that distributed a specially printed program was the one for the Samuel L. Clemens (863) Famous American commemorative in 1940 (fig. 6). In the following years it became customary to provide a program containing the newly issued stamp with a first day cancellation to those attending the program. Many of these programs are highly attractive and attendees occasionally have them autographed by the dignitaries present the ceremony (fig. 7). As a cost cutting move, in 2001 the USPS substituted generic programs for the specially designed programs previously used. The first generic program was used for the 20¢ University of South Carolina stamped card (UX362) on April 26, 2001.

Figure 6

Program for the first day ceremony of the 10¢ Samuel Clemens (863).

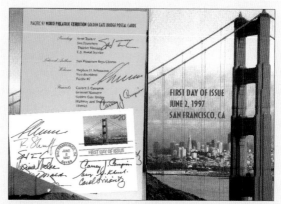

Figure 7

Program for the first day ceremony of the 1997 San Francisco Golden Gate postal card (UX282), signed by dignitaries.

Notes on Collecting

Generally the earliest possible date on which a stamp can be postmarked is its designated FDOI; however there are numerous exceptions. For example, stamps are mistakenly sold prior to the official FDOI. This may occur due to ignorance or carelessness on the part of window clerks, the confusion resulting from simi-

Figure 8

A pre-date of the 10¢ Jane Addams (878), canceled on April 22, 1940, although the stamp was not officially released until April 26.

lar stamp designs for different issues, or stamps in a set issued on different dates. Sometimes, postal clerks have improperly post-marked covers with an earlier date as a favor to collectors (fig. 8).

For some stamps, mostly those issued prior to 1922, there are no des-ignated FDOIs. Of those pre-1922 stamps with a designated FDOI, not all are known to exist on a FDC. Collectors have long sought covers with the earliest postmark date for a given stamp. Such a record holding cover, when recognized by expert opinion, is known as an **Earliest Documented Use** (EDU). An EDU cover is always in danger of losing its record to a new discovery, which happens frequently.

While not common, fakes and forgeries of FDCs do exist. One telltale sign of a fake FDC is the use of a type of envelope that did not exist at the time the stamp was issued. Counterfeit cachets exist that imitate engraved cachets. Many examples of bogus older FDCs exist on which a stamp has been added at a later date. Sometimes stamps have been added to stampless covers with authentic postmarks in order to make them appear as earliest known uses (EKUs). Stamps also have been altered to simulate a more valuable issue. In some cases, the mis-spelling of an addressee's name or an incorrect address identifies the FDC as a fake. Fake FDCs can also be identified by a genuine cancellation that has been altered, use of the wrong ink, use of a counterfeit cancellation device, or use of the incorrect type of cancellation for the period in which the stamp was issued.

FDCs can be collected a various ways depending on personal preference. One popular way is to collect by cachet maker, attempting to obtain as many FDC cachets as possible produced by one cachet maker. Other collectors specialize in one or more stamp issues, seeking all possible FDC cachets for those issues. The collection of the first FDC cachet made by a variety of cachet makers also is popular. One can also collect FDCs by topic. Some FDC collectors specialize in a certain time period such as the 1930s, while others collect one FDC for each issue.

Some collectors create combination FDCs (combos) by affixing a previously issued but topically related stamp to a cover before a newly issued stamp is affixed and canceled. Others collect dual FDCs, combining two or more FDOI cancellations, for different issues on related subjects, on a single cover. The collecting of stamps on FDCs issued jointly by the U.S. and another country is another possibility. The first of these joint issues was the St. Lawrence Seaway Issue of June 26, 1959. Both Canada and the U. S. issued a commemorative with the same design. Only the country designation and denomination were different. Other specialized areas include autographed FDCs, philatelic-numismatic combinations, first day ceremony programs, maximum cards, **plate blocks** on FDCs, **plate number coils** on FDCs, and USPS souvenir pages. Some collectors prefer to begin with current issues and work backwards to include earlier stamps.

There are several subscription services that will provide FDCs when a deposit is made. The USPS offers uncacheted FDCs from its Stamp Fulfillment Services. For those who wish to be more directly involved, collectors can prepare their own envelopes, affix the new stamps purchased at their post offices or philatelic windows, and submit them to the postmaster at the designated first day city. The envelopes may have cachets, either purchased commercially or made by the sender. With the advent of computers and suitable software, homemade cachets have become increasingly popular.

For protection and display purposes, FDCs should be sleeved, preferably in clear Mylar sleeves, and stored upright in sturdy containers. Alternatively, they may be placed in albums made of acid free archival material.

Many hand drawn/hand painted cachets are miniature works of art. They often command premium prices in the market.

Most modern FDCs are not processed in the mailstream. They are either cancelled on a **handback** basis in the first day city, or are cancelled by the USPS in Kansas City with the correct FDOI of cancel and shipped under separate cover. Many collectors prefer unaddressed FDCs because they are cleaner and neater. Others prefer addressed FDCs that have gone through the mailstream and demonstrate genuine postal usage.

Almanac

1922 – The first official announcement by the POD of a new stamp is made on July 12 for the new 10¢ Special Delivery stamp.

1922 – A regular stamp, the 11¢ Hayes, is issued both on a designated date and in a designated city for the first time on October 4. A public first day ceremony is also held for the first time.

1923 – On September 1 George Linn produces the first commercial cachet for FDCs of the 2¢ black Harding Memorial issue.

1925 – The first colored cachet is used for a FDC on May 18 by Ernest J. Weschcke.

1925 – The first known pictorial cachet is used for a FDC by C.E. Nickles on December 28.

1937 – On July 13 the phrase "First Day of Issue" is used for the first time in the killer bars of the official FDC cancellation of the Northwest Territory Issue.

1940 – On January 29 the phrase "First Day of Issue" is used for the first time in the killer bars of a hand cancel.

1977 – On January 3 the USPS establishes a grace period for FDC servicing.

1977 - Publication of the *Photo Encyclopedia of Cacheted First Day Covers*, by Earl Planty and Michael Mellone is announced on October 31.

What Others Have Said

A new issue
"The new special delivery stamps will not be issued to the postmasters until the present supply is exhausted. However, the first issue of the new stamp was placed on sale July 12, 1922 at the Philatelic Stamp Agency for the benefit of stamp collectors and dealers. All inquires from stamp collectors should be referred to the Philatelic Stamp Agency."

—*First official USPOD stamp announcement for a new issue, 1922.*

If Only We Had Known
"Our first advertisement offered the set of C4-6 on FDCs for $5... We hoped that we would sell a few covers, but the results were zilch-nil--blank-zip-nothing....When a year or so passed and our cost price had not even been returned to us, we took the desperation course that was needed; we started tearing the stamps off the covers and soaking them, including the 1923 airs....When we

advertised the stamps off cover they began to sell and to sell well...We were not the only one soaking stamps off FDCs in those days. Criminal as it may seem now, there was no way to avoid it. Unless we sold our stamps, we would not have eaten."

—*Herman Herst, Jr.*, More Stories to Collect Stamps By.

The First Modern Cacheted FDC was produced by the founder of Linn's

"George Linn never could have had an inkling of what he was starting that day in 1923. He motored the 40 miles from Columbus north to Marion, Ohio with a small packet of freshly printed cacheted envelopes. September 1 was the first day of the black stamp (610) memorializing the sudden death of President Warren G. Harding. Linn was swept by the wave of emotion which gripped our nation; 'Our President is dead. Let us mourn our loss.' Linn's simple design on a black bordered mourning envelope was the first commercially produced First Day cachet. This simple envelope started the hobby which we follow today. The Linn cachet is a classic."

—*Allison W. Cusick*, "50th Anniversary of Modern FDC's Remembered," First Days, 1998.

First Day cover collecting has a very wide audience

"What are the three most popular ways to collect United States stamps? ....collecting unused (mint) stamps, collecting used (canceled) stamps, and collecting stamps on first day covers. But in some respects the first day cover collecting casts a wider net than ordinary stamp collecting....Most first day covers of modern stamps exist in enormous quantities. I believe the champion of all time is the 10¢ Moon Landing airmail stamp (C76) with more than 8.7 million canceled on Sept. 9, 1969, at Washington. In contrast to that, a mere 5,956 FDCs of the 45¢ Official Mail passport stamped envelope (UO79) were canceled on March 17, 1990. Despite the great disparity in numbers, neither is rare. Perhaps surprisingly, a cacheted, unaddressed FDC of *Scott* C76 has a catalog value of $4.50, while a FDC of *Scott* UO79 is valued at $2. Obviously the former is more popular with collectors."

—*Ken Lawrence*, "Specialized First Day Cover Collecting," Scott Stamp's Monthly, 2003.

The collector and the Postal Service sometimes disagree on "What is a new issue?"

"One of the peripheral problems is the fact that the Postal Service's 'definition' of a new issue or a different stamp does not always agree with what the collector considers a new issue or different stamp. For example the production of a certain design on different presses, or with different paper, or with a different perforation, the collector considers a different stamp, if he can distinguish same. There will never be total agreement on this basic factor...The Postal Service can be helpful, but it is our view that it is not their job to police the hobby. USPS has leaned over backward to make collectors happy with such things as leeway in time to prepare 'covers' and also to return them in 'ambulance' containers. The latter certainly emphasizes that they are souvenirs and not pieces of mail."

—*George W. Brett, "What is a First-Day Cover?" The United States Specialist, 1989.*

Examples of Postal Usage

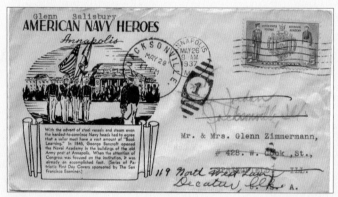

Figure 9

FDC that required multiple forwarding to reach the addressee. If the address is illegible or addressed to a discontinued or unknown post office, a directory section may endeavor to correct the address and forward the FDC. Sometimes the post office itself missends a cover, which requires a redirection.

Figure 10

FDC that was refused by the addressee and returned to the sender. Undeliverable mail includes FDCs that are unclaimed, refused, addressed to someone who is deceased, or unforwardable. FDCs sent special delivery, registered, certified, or insured, usually exhibit various auxiliary markings showing evidence that they passed through the mailstream. FDCs with stamps that underpay the correct rates can be assessed postage due.

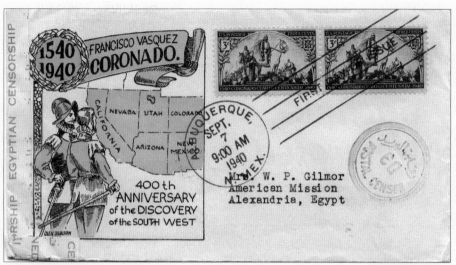

Figure 11

FDC cleared by an Egyptian censor. This cover is also very desirable because of its foreign destination.

Where to Find More Information

- There are numerous FDC catalogs available; the most comprehensive are the cachet catalogs published by Michael A. Mellone, *Planty's Photo Encyclopedia of Cacheted First Day Covers*.

- Each year *Scott* publishes a new edition of its *First Day Cover Catalogue & Checklist* that includes updated EDUs. *The Brookman Guide* is an annual catalogue that includes a section on FDCs.

- Comprehensive studies on FDCs can be found in *First Days*, published by the American First Day Cover Society. They also publish handbooks on various aspects of FDC collecting, and maintain a useful website at www.afdcs.org.

- *Mellone's Specialized Catalogue of First Day Ceremony Programs and Events* by Scott Pelcyger, and The American Ceremony Program Society's web site, www.webacps.org. are sources of information on ceremony programs.

- Jack V. Harvey provides an introduction to modern First Day Cover collecting in his *First Day Covers of the Regular Issue of 1922–1935*.

Chapter 61

Meters and Machine Generated Postage

Postage stamps were introduced in 1847 (ch. 3) in an America that was constantly exploring and expanding. The period near the turn-of-the-century was known as the Progressive era, when men and machines helped move America forward into the twentieth century. Among those who helped propel the country's mails into the twentieth century was Arthur H. Pitney, and his partner, Walter H. Bowes, who established Pitney Bowes Postage Meter Company on April 23, 1920. Pitney developed a postage stamp *meter* machine, which earned his first patent in 1902. Using this machine, a customer could conveniently pre-pay postage, and efficiently affix postage to mail. Although Elmer E. Wolf patented the first meter machine in the United States in 1898, his machine never saw postal use.

A meter, or more precisely a postage stamp meter machine, is a device that imprints an **indicium** and town mark on an envelope, post card, or label. **Indicia** are the imprints made by the meter machine to represent the postage paid. The indicium and town mark are imprinted on gummed strips of security paper and these printed meter tapes are then affixed to packages or letters.

Figure 1

Meter used by the City of Buffalo, New York in 1967 with a slogan proclaiming, "City of Good Neighbors". The streamlined eagle Pitney Bowes design, introduced in 1940, was the longest-lived meter design.

Alternately, they may be imprinted directly on letters as they pass through the machines. There have been many different styles of meters.

There were many meter machines tested from 1903 through 1920. However it was not until 1920 that the Post Office Department (POD) authorized their use. Slogans, a possible third element on meters, appearing to the left of the town mark and indicia, were first used in 1929 (fig. 1). The use of advertisements as slogans became popular and by mid-century there were tens of thousands in use. The slogan **die** (sometimes called the slug) is the metal die which imprints words or pictures to the left of the indicium and town mark.

To prevent fraudulent use of meters, machines are built with safeguards. Each has two registers. An ascending register provides a cumulative total of all postage ever printed by the machine and is not accessible by the machine's user or a postal employee. A second, descending register, originally set by a postal employee in a local post office, reflects the amount of postage prepaid by the customer. By viewing this register a customer knew the value of postage remaining to be dispensed. At the turn of the twenty-first century, meter companies began to establish procedures for meters to be set (add postage) via a series of touch-tone telephone entries, or on-line, and most meters are now replenished without the visit to the post office that was required for more than half a century.

As the use of meters by businesses increased, the POD established rules that allowed bundled metered mail to bypass the cancellation process. This enabled machine manufacturers to claim that metered mail sped the handling of the mails.

In 1939, Pitney Bowes introduced the Mailomat, a coin operated, self-service machine that imprinted a meter and retained mail for collection. It was popular for several years in the early 1940s (fig. 2).

Pitney Bowes held the monopoly on postage meter machines for more than 50 years before others began entering the market, including National Cash Register, Multipost Company, and Friden, Inc. At the beginning of the twenty-first century there were four firms producing meter machines which were approved by the United States Postal Service (USPS): Francotyp-Postalia Inc. of Addison, Illinois; Hasler, Inc. of Shelton, Connecticut; Neopost of Hayward, California; and Pitney Bowes of Stamford, Connecticut. In order to use a postage meter machine, a license must first be obtained from the local post office. The meter machine itself may be rented from any approved company and the serial number of the machine must be registered with the local post office. Pursuant to USPS regulations, only authorized postal machine manufacturers and the USPS may hold title to postage meters.

Figure 2

One version of an "instructional post card" provided by "Pitney-Bowes, Inc.", promoting the use of Mailomat.

Essays and proofs (ch. 53) of meters exist. Meter essays are imprints of indicia produced solely for submission to the Post Office for its approval. Meter proofs are impressions taken from machines prior to the time they are shipped to the user. Some collectors also classify all impressions which are run on both tapes and envelopes with a "00¢" denomination as meter proofs.

Writing in 1977, George W. Brett, the Dean of American Philately, asked, "For how long will postage stamps continue to be issued?" In an amazingly accurate foreshadowing he answers his own question: "This will depend upon communication technology but we can't imagine the postage stamp system continuing forever even if it has been with us for 140 years. Especially is this so today when we consider that a number of different new communication methods have been sampled in recent years. Ultimately one of them will click and that will be it...." Brett predicted the arrival of e-mail to replace traditional mail and of machine and computer generated stamps long before most could imagine them. As the twentieth century came to a close, the USPS tested a number of innovative postage generating machines, some more successful than others.

Computer Vended Postage Stamps

In the late 1980s, the Postal Service experimented with "computer-vended postage". These pioneer computer vended stamps were dubbed Autopost stamps (*Scott* CVP1–30), generated from Autopost machines. They were hailed as a complete mailing system, which included a scale, and made their much-heralded debut at World Stamp Expo '89. Several machines were placed into service in the Washington, D.C. area in 1989; however, most were removed in 1990. The Autopost experiment was deemed a short-lived failure.

There are two basic types of Autopost stamps. The first has stamps with a "USA" with stars in the design that were used for First Class, Third Class, Priority, and Express Mail. The second type has a bar code for the Zip Code of destination replacing the "USA" logo of the first type.

In 1992 the ECA GARD Postage and Mailing Center (PMC) machines were introduced, which dispensed three different styles of coil stamps with a flag and shield design (CVP31–33, ch. 50, fig. 8) which featured a computer printed denomination. Initially a customer could have stamps of any denomination printed, but eventually machines were set to print only denominations of 19¢ or more.

Experimental vending machines produced by IBM and NCR were installed in selected central Florida locations in 1999. They dispensed stamps with a barcode (CVP 34–35) until 2000 or 2001.

Postal Buddy "Postal Buddies" were machines introduced in 1992 as computerized service centers where a customer could enter a change of address and purchase **postal cards** (CVUX1–3). Thirty-one prototype Postal Buddy machines were field-tested beginning July 1990. They were replaced with a more modern version of the machine in November 1992. Less than a year later, the USPS cancelled the entire project due to low sales. The plan to install 10,000 Postal Buddies never materialized.

PVI Labels In 1992, the USPS introduced, in the San Diego area, a new label called the PVI, (Postage Validation Imprint). "With no advance notice, the United States Postal Service has put a new type of meter label into service." wrote Gary Griffith in *Linn's* on May 4 1992. "…the new labels were first used April 16. The Postal Service did not distribute notice to the stamp collecting press until the following day." There were three different types of PVIs, as the new labels were quickly dubbed. One without any bar-coding was for letter size mail; the second with a standard **Postnet** barcode was for use on flats; and the third for use on parcels utilizes a bar code which looked very much like the Universal Product Code (UPC) seen on retail products. PVI labels (fig. 3) can be printed in denominations from 1¢ to $999.99. Since USPS personnel affix them, they are generally not available for sale directly to collectors and are not listed in *Scott*.

Figure 3

A PVI paying First Class postage on a two-ounce letter in 2005.

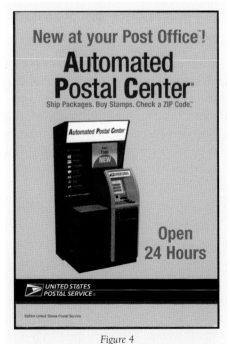

Figure 4

A promotional post card for the Automated Postal Center.

Automated Postal Center (APC)
Fifteen years after the failure of the proto-type Autopost machines, APCs began appearing in post office lobbies in April 2004. The APC is touch-screen activated, accepting debit and credit cards, but not cash. By December 2004

a total of 2,500 machines, at least one in each state, were in place throughout the nation (fig. 4). Testing of the APC system, manufactured by IBM, had begun in 1999. Features of the APC include allowing customers to purchase self-adhesive stamps individually or by booklet (fig. 5); weigh, calculate, and purchase postage in any amount for items weighing up to 70 pounds; send items via Express Mail, Priority Mail, First-Class Mail, and Parcel Post services, look up ZIP Codes, and obtain Postal Service mailing information. The APC accepts packages measuring up to 12 inches by 14 inches by 20 inches.

Figure 5

Postage dispensed by an Automated Postal Center (CVP57).

Personal Computer Postage

On March 31, 1998, with a double click on an oversized computer mouse, Postmaster General Marvin T. Runyon proclaimed the beginning of a new form of postage: computer-generated stamps. Dubbed "mouse mail" by some, the high-tech procedure would revolutionize the way many small businesses handle their letters. It was "postage without licking or sticking – just clicking." Runyon proclaimed. The USPS noted that it was the first major change in U.S. postage since the introduction of postage meters.

With the phenomenal growth of personal and small business computers, the USPS approved a relationship with Stamps.com, a private enterprise, which enabled customers to generate and print postage directly from their home computer and printer. Stamps.com became a leading innovator and major provider of internet-based postage. Two other providers of internet postage in 2005 were Pitney Works, the small business division of Pitney Bowes which offered Clickstamp® and Neopost which offered SimplyPostage. *Scott* lists Personal Computer Postage using numbers prefixed by 1CVP.

Personalized Postage

Stamps.com introduced what the USPS termed "customized postage" in which personal images could be incorporated into a computer generated adhesive postage stamp, although the USPS does not call them stamps. Customized postage was test marketed in 2004 (fig. 6). After a successful market test and a

Figure 6

A PhotoStamp with the seal of the United States Stamp Society (2CVP8).

thorough evaluation by the USPS, sale of the PhotoStamps™, as Stamps.com called them, was temporarily suspended when several customers ordered postage featuring objectionable photos. PhotoStamps™ were re-introduced in May 2005 for a one year test period. They featured a new design and a system which checked the appropriateness of photos being used. In an indication that customized postage would be a competitive business, the internet postage service provider Endica™ announced on June 2, 2005 that it would market customized postage under the trade name PictureItPostage™ (fig. 7). and Pitney Bowes and Zazzle entered the competition on July 18 with a product called ZazzleStamps. *Scott* lists customized postage as Personalized Postage using numbers prefixed by 2CVP.

Figure 7

PictureItPostage with an image of George Brett (2CVP16). Note the freak die cutting.

Notes on Collecting

Some modern fractional cent postage rates cannot be paid with stamps because no stamps exist to pay them. The collector who desires to document and collect such postal history will of necessity be a meter collector (fig. 8).

Like postage stamps, there are many ways to collect meters and machine generated postage. State, town, and city collecting attracts those who wish to build a collection from many different locations. The search for meters of towns no longer in existence, of post offices closed and combined with other post offices and of towns with exotic-sounding names all offer challenges to

Figure 8

Some postage rates, including Standard Presorted rates, cannot be exactly paid with postage stamps. However these rates can be collected on metered mail, such as this 18.2¢ meter.

the meter collector. Some attempt to obtain examples of each meter used in a town. Topical meter collecting is of interest to some, meters being collected based on the design or content of their slogans. Many topical stamp collectors supplement their collections with topical meters. Some assemble a collection of covers showing the combined usage of a meter with one or more postage stamps. Though metered mail was intended to bypass the normal cancellation process, it is possible to build a collection of canceled/postmarked metered mail.

During the early days of meter collecting, there was almost no consensus among collectors regarding the proper size of the piece containing the meter imprint cut from an envelope. Eventually, uniform strips 2 inches wide by 5 or 6 inches long became the standard. However, as greater interest in modern postal history continues to develop, more people collect meters on *entires*. This provides the advantage of being able to refer to any *auxiliary markings* on the front or back of the cover and is consistent with collecting modern postage stamps on cover.

Collecting modern machine generated postage offers many opportunities and challenges. AUTOPOST stamps are listed in *Scott* and are more readily available in mint condition than on covers. Finding some of them on cover is a formidable challenge. Collecting the Postal Buddy postal cards may be considered necessary for those who wish to attempt a complete USPS postal card collection. Since PVI labels are only supposed to be affixed to letters and packages, not sold individually to customers, they are extremely difficult to find off cover. The collection of PVI labels in their several varieties and many denominations is best achieved by finding them on cover and wrapper.

Almanac

1898 – First meter machine to print and apply postage to letters is patented.

1920 – Pitney Bowes receives Post Office Department approval for meter machines on September 1.

1920 – The first authorized commercial mailing using a meter occurs December 10.

1929 – First advertising slogans are used in meter machines.

1934 – Postage meters are first used in post offices.

1939 – Mailomat is introduced.

1940 – Pitney Bowes introduces its long-lived streamlined eagle design meter in January (fig. 1).

1989 – AUTOPOST machines debut, but are short lived.

1992 – Postal Buddy machines are installed.

1992 – PVI labels are introduced on April 16.

1993 – The USPS cancels the Postal Buddy Machine contract.

1994 – USPS begins to decertify more than 10,000 older Pitney Bowes machines.

1998 – USPS signs an agreement to allow postage to be generated by personal computer.

2004 – Customized (Personalized) Postage is introduced.

What Others Have Said

Meters are stamps!

"Are postal meters postage stamps?...yes. While meter stamps do not resemble most adhesive postage stamps, they are both authorized and accepted for the prepayment of mail....To their credit, meters have seldom been produced with the purpose of 'printing money' as some contrived philatelic items regularly are. Meters exist for their postal and advertising functions."

—*Howard Lucas, "Meters are Stamps,"* Stamp Collector, *1991.*

The first meters were printed in UPU colors

"Third Assistant Postmaster General W.J. Barrows formally approved the postage meter in a letter dated September 20, 1920. Barrows authorized the first use of metered mail under the provision of Section 459 of the PL&R. The first postage meters were single denomination machines. Only 69 machines and five different denominations were used. Dies included 11 1¢, 51 2¢, five 4¢...one 5¢ and one 10¢...each meter stamp die was hand engraved. Meter imprints were in colors corresponding to adhesive stamps currently in use: 1¢ green, 2¢ red 4¢ brown or bistre, 5¢ blue and 10¢ yellow....Not counting the first two meters used in Pitney Bowes' Stamford offices in December, 1920, the first meter stamps had a short commercial life of only eight months, from August 1921 to April 1922."

—*Doug Kelsey, "The first postage meters and their stamps,"* Linn's Stamp News, *1992.*

Making meters equal to postage stamps when it come to fluorescence

"Postal Forum III, held in Washington, D.C. September 8th and 9th [had a] group of displays of equipment used to expedite mail handling. Among these was a Mark II Facer-Canceler, equipped with the ultra-violet sensor....This equipment was well explained, with emphasis on the fact that the principal function was to face the mail, with canceling a secondary operation. We noticed that some of the sample letters being used were metered items that were channeled into the proper slots. Questioning revealed that these meters had been printed with an experimental fluorescent ink now being tested by Pitney-Bowes. The meter ink fluoresces a bright red that activates the facer-canceler on the on-cycle of the ultra violet sensor. Tests, for toxic or other harmful effects, are being conducted by the Food and Drug Administration prior to the final approval of the ink for general use."

—*William H. Bayless, "Luminescence,"* The United States Specialist, *1969.*

"We understand that, after much experimenting, Pitney-Bowes, Inc. has been authorized to sell a red-glowing fluorescent ink for use with postage meters. This ink will activate the ultraviolet sensor on the Mark II Facer Canceler used for facing mail. This will be an innovation for meter collectors."

—*William H. Bayless, "Luminescence,"* The United States Specialist, *1970.*

The first meter slogans are pioneers for thousands to follow
"In November 1927, Pitney-Bowes brought out another type of meter designated as Type F in Steiger's Handbook… Since this company had manufactured slogan postmark dies, the possibility of a slogan or meter ad arose and this led to one of the most interesting sections of meter collecting. The first slogan from Pitney-Bowes appeared in 1929 and read 'X Adhesive Stamps Are out of date' and was followed closely by 'Metered Mail Saves Time and Gets Attention.'…This was the impetus required to make meter ads popular.…Slogans have covered every topic, and more recently the patriotics have attracted wide attention of philatelists everywhere."

—*Althea Harvey, "Silver Anniversary of Metered Mail,"* Eleventh American Philatelic Congress Book, *1945.*

Unlike meters, AUTOPOST stamps maybe used on any date from any post office.
"In a letter to this writer dated August 17, 1990 from Frank Thomas, USPS Philatelic and Retail Services Department, I was told that 'use of AUTOPOST postage strips is not limited to the postal station where purchased nor is it restricted to the date of purchase. It is possible to use previously purchased AUTOPOST postage strips as domestic postage. The U.S. Postal Service policy on use of AUTOPOST postage strips allows the mailing public to utilize them…for letters and packages throughout the United States. They are not valid on international mail.'"

—*Richard Stambaugh, "More on the Autopost Experiment,"* The United States Specialist, *1991.*

PVIs are generally not available to collectors except on incoming mail
"Unfortunately for collectors, the Philatelic Release stated, 'PVI labels are not sold to customers for later use and thus cannot be sold for collector purposes.' This restriction was added to the Domestic Mail Manual…as 163.525: 'Postage validator imprinter [sic] (PVI) strips are not meter stamps and may not be sold.' Thus the only way collectors can get examples is on incoming mail.…One last item of interest are PVI test labels. When the clerk initially sets up each day he repeatedly presses the mode switch, until the label appears on the PVI display.

Few of these labels exist in collectors' hands, as the clerks must account for them. The clerk then presses the paper feed switch once. The PVI then ejects one blank and four test labels [containing cumulative information required by the clerks for record keeping.]"

—*Richard Schulman, "Postage validation imprinter [sic]," Scott Stamp Monthly, 1993.*

Examples of Postal Usage

Figure 9

An early Pitney Bowes meter, used by Sears, Roebuck and Co., in Philadelphia, on December 7, 1922.

Figure 10

The Holland, Michigan post office used a meter label for postage due on this 1974 air mail letter.

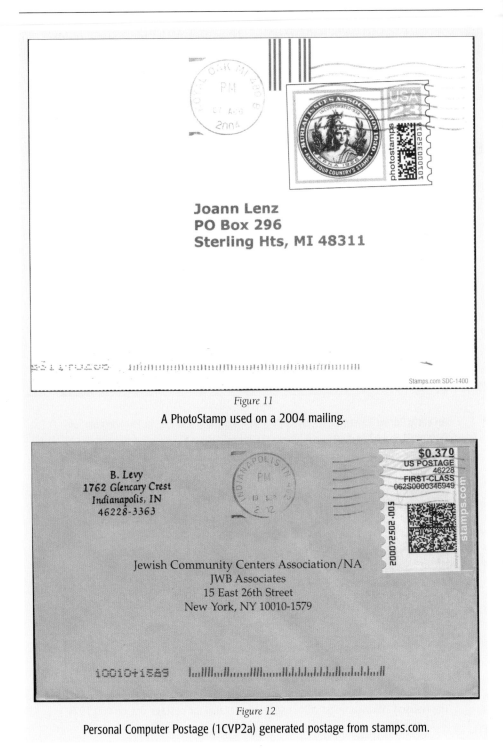

Figure 11

A PhotoStamp used on a 2004 mailing.

Figure 12

Personal Computer Postage (1CVP2a) generated postage from stamps.com.

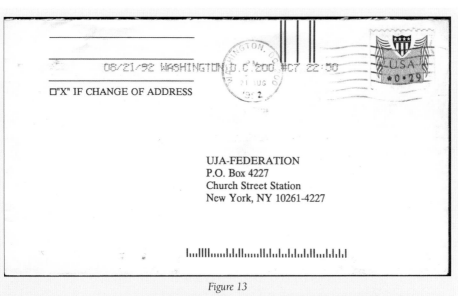

Figure 13

First Class cover franked with a 29¢ stamp (CVP31) dispensed by an ECA GARD Postage and Mailing Center machine and postmarked on the second day of the stamp's availability, August 21, 1992.

Where to Find More Information

- The very interesting story of the postage stamp meter's development can be found in William K. Thomas' *History and Evolution of Metered Postage*, and Doug Kelsey's *Pictorial Meter Stamps of the United States*.

- *The Story of Pitney Bowes* by William Cahn.

- Doug Kelsey also wrote *United States Meter Stamps: First Days and Earliest-known Uses*.

- The earliest significant meter catalog, still pertinent, *A Handbook of United States Postage Meters, Including Meter Slogans* was published by William Steiger in 1940.

- *An Illustrated Guide to Meter Stamp Collecting with Valuations Quoted on Most Basic Types* by Walter M. Swan.

- The 1994 *United States Postage Meter Stamp Catalog* by Joel A. Hawkins and Werner Simon is the most comprehensive resource currently available on meters.

- As this *Encyclopedia* went to press the field of Personalized Postage was rapidly evolving. Collectors interested in this dynamic area should check the philatelic press regularly for updates.

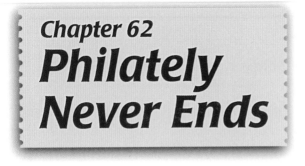

Chapter 62
Philately Never Ends

This final chapter introduces an aspect of collecting that offers almost unlimited opportunities. Alternative philately refers to any stamp, label, or related item other than regular stamps or covers – collectibles known as *ephemera* or *collateral* material. Ephemera literally means "printed material of a transient nature", an item not intended to be stored, filed, or kept. Collateral material refers to any item which is related to stamps and covers being collected, and helps tell their story. Many such items may be referred to interchangeably by these two terms, and they provide an alternative or addition to a stamp collection. They can form a broad, diverse, complex, and almost endless category of collectibles related to stamp collecting that enhances its pleasure. While some ephemera are listed in *Scott*, most are not.

Figure 1

This Cinderella was issued by the National One Cent Letter Postage Association, which was formed in 1912 to lobby for the elimination of the postal subsidy given to magazine and newspaper publishers. The seals were made for members to use on their correspondence.

Figure 2

A philatelic seal used in 1930 to promote the convention of the American Philatelic Society.

Cinderellas

Cinderellas are labels that look like stamps, generally issued for a promotional, advertising, or fund raising purpose. (The name comes from the fact that Cinderella looked like a princess when she was really not!) They may originate with private individuals or organizations. There are literally uncounted thousands of Cinderellas. Figure 1 illustrates a Cinderella label issued by the "National One Cent Letter Postage Association" (NOCLPA) of Cleveland, Ohio. Early in the twentieth century, NOCLPA was organized to encourage businessmen and farmers to lobby for lower postage rates, from 2¢ to 1¢. They used their red labels on all of their outgoing correspondence, but not on the envelopes themselves. Their campaign was not successful!

Philatelic Seals have been used for promotional purposes by stamp clubs and stamp shows since late in the nineteenth century, although their golden age was the middle of the twentieth century. Figure 2 illustrates a seal used to promote the 1930 convention of the American Philatelic Society held in Boston.

Christmas Seals

Christmas Seals are a sub-category of Cinderellas. Seals issued annually from 1907 through 1978 are listed in *Scott* with the prefix WX. The first seals were issued in 1907 by the Delaware chapter of the American Red Cross under the leadership of Emily P. Bissell. Bissell was honored on a commemorative stamp (*Scott* 1823) in 1980. From 1907 through 1919 the American Red Cross sold seals, with proceeds used for tuberculosis treatment and research. In 1911 the Red Cross requested the National Association for the Study and Prevention of Tuberculosis to manage the annual campaign. In 1920 The National Tuberculosis Association became the sole sponsor of U.S. Christmas Seals. Seals using the Red Cross emblem (fig. 3) were issued through 1919. In 1919 the double barred Lorraine Cross was also included on the seal. The Lorraine Cross, the international emblem of tuberculosis associations, was used without the Red Cross emblem, beginning with the 1920 seal (fig. 4).

Figure 3
1908 Christmas Seal.

Figure 4
1954 Christmas Seals.

Telegraph Stamps

Telegraph stamps were issued by telegraph companies for use on their telegrams (fig. 5). They were issued by at least 26 telegraph or wireless companies, including Western Union Telegraph

Figure 5

This Telegraph stamp (1T11) was issued by American Rapid Telegraph Company in 1881. It was for use on a "collect" telegram. The punch indicates that this stamp was part of an obsolete surplus stock purchased by a New York dealer.

Company. Sixteen companies have stamps listed in *Scott*, with a T in their catalogue number. Company personnel used some of these stamps while others were sold to the public.

Figure 6

Sanitary Fair stamp (WV14) from the Springfield, Massachusetts Soldiers' Fair held December 19-24, 1864.

Figure 7

A limited edition card promoting Washington 2006, given to those who financially supported that international show.

Sanitary Fair Stamps

The United States Sanitary Commission was a federally sanctioned Civil War era organization that promoted the health and welfare of Union troops. A number of "Sanitary Fairs" were held around the country to raise funds for the Commission. Some fairs had post offices and issued their own stamps (fig. 6). These "sanitary fair stamps" were not valid for postage but were sold at fair post offices, with the cooperation of the local postmasters. Sanitary Fair stamps are *Scott* listed with a WV prefix.

Philatelic Souvenir Cards

Privately printed souvenir cards became more popular as the popularity of seals waned. A souvenir card is one whose only purpose is to be a souvenir, and not created for use as postal correspondence. Souvenir cards are usually single flat sheets or single folded sheets, with printing on one or both sides. Figure 7 illustrates a card promoting World Philatelic Exposition Washington 2006, which was given to financial patrons of that event. There have been Souvenir Cards issued by the United States Postal Service that are listed in *Scott*. Starting in 1975, local post offices were permitted to produce their own souvenir cards to commemorate local events. The first known example of a local card is one issued by the Charlestown, Massachusetts post office to commemorate the Battle of Bunker Hill and the two hundredth anniversary of the postal service.

Post Cards

Picture ***post cards*** are perhaps the most popular form of ephemera, especially cards with front sides picturing stamp related themes, such as post office buildings. A post card is primarily valued by a stamp collector for its back, that is, for its address side. These are often excellent examples of postal history, especially post cards from the early twentieth century when picture post cards were very popular with the public. However when a post card is collected primarily for its picture side it is categorized as ephemera. Deltiology is the term used for the collection and study of post cards. Government issued **postal cards** (ch. 28) are not post cards.

Post Office Ephemera

In the course of doing its business the Post Office has produced many items of interest to collectors beside postage stamps or other items with postage value. Like any bureaucracy, it has generated many forms (fig. 8 and 9). Various publications, such as the *U.S. Postal Guide* (fig. 10) are collectibles and sources of valuable information. One popular Post Office collectible is the new issue announcement. These announcements of new issues were initially printed on cards (fig. 11), but by 1960 had evolved into 8½ x 11 inch posters. If a stamp is affixed with a first day of issue cancel they are Unofficial Souvenir Pages. By 1970 these new issue announcement posters further evolved into Official Souvenir Pages, to which newly issued stamp were attached and canceled. Souvenir Pages are *Scott* listed with the prefix SP.

Figure 8

A 1974 USPS "Receipt For Domestic Insured Parcel", Form 3813.

Figure 9

An informational card used on a mail chute.

Figure 10

The U.S. Official Postal Guide was published annually from 1874 to 1954. The monthly supplement for May 1923 is illustrated here.

Still More

Some stamp auction catalogs are valued either for their research information or as collectibles. Catalogs for "named" sales, which auction the collections of famed collectors, are especially popular.

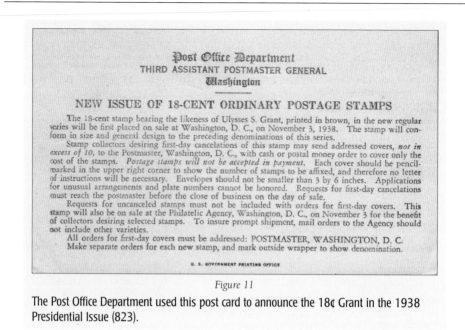

Figure 11

The Post Office Department used this post card to announce the 18¢ Grant in the 1938 Presidential Issue (823).

Other collateral material collected includes items as diverse as antique stamp boxes, mailboxes, refrigerator magnets, telephone calling cards, ties, buttons, pins, mouse pads, stamp games, jewelry, posters, and Christmas ornaments. Any item that can be decorated with a stamp design or philatelic theme is fair game – and someone will collect it.

Notes on Collecting

In 2001, collateral material and ephemera went mainstream, when the American Philatelic Society created a new category of stamp exhibits, the "Display Division". For the first time, it was permissible to include non-philatelic items in exhibition frames, if those items helped to tell the story of the exhibit. These collateral items could not, in the opinion of the judges, dominate or overwhelm the philatelic aspects of the exhibit. Items such as maps, time schedules, promotional flyers, and other ephemera can be legitimately used to enhance a stamp collection or exhibit. Collecting collateral material and ephemera opens a collection to almost unlimited possibilities. The discovery of new items is always on the horizon. Pricing collateral material and ephemera can sometimes be a problem, since there is no comprehensive reference catalog. It takes some time to become familiar with price trends, but most collateral material and ephemera is reasonably priced. One can build a collection to stand on its own, or to supplement a stamp or postal history collection.

652   *Chapter 62 | Philately Never Ends*

Almanac

1864 – First Sanitary Fair stamps issued.

1881 – First Telegraph stamps issued.

1907 – First Christmas Seals are issued.

1913 – *American Bank Note Company* produces the first promotional stamp show seals for the International Philatelic Exhibition in NYC.

1954 – First USPOD Souvenir Card issued (SC1).

1975 – First local souvenir card issued in Charlestown, Massachusetts.

What Other Have Said

Cinderella collecting can add unlimited collecting potential...
"It is quite natural and reasonable to reach a state in one's collecting activities where they become...a bit disinterested in their efforts. A few years back when this started happening to me, I began to search about for the solution, which in my case, turned out to be the labels, seals, vignettes, locals, private posts, strike posts, Christmas seals etc as long as they were either of a sports or Olympic theme. The amount of effort to start this type of a highly specialized collection is enormous, but eventually this time and effort is well paid, as the results are most gratifying, as not only does the Cinderella collecting revive one's entire interest in philately, it also leads you into your own specialties, much deeper that you ever thought possible."

—*Joe Schirmer, "What Cinderella Collecting can do for you,"* The S. Allan Taylor Society Journal, *1978.*

....and has the same challenges and rewards as collecting postage stamps.
"For some time the Post Offices have distributed, free of charge, labels for First Class, Air Mail and Special Delivery. We have recently been told that labels for First Class and Special Delivery have been discontinued but will be distributed as long as remaining stocks last. Upon examination, under long wave U.V., of samples picked up from various Post Offices, it was found that many color variances exist including several degrees of fluorescence on each type."

—*William H. Bayless, "Fluorescent Paper,"* The Bureau Specialist, *1965.*

A first for Christmas Seal Collectors
"For the first time, philatelists will need six 'key seals' to make a complete set. The 1954 Christmas Seals were printed by six lithographers and each sheet bears the printers mark of identification on the fifty-sixth, or key seal, the sixth

from the left in the sixth horizontal row. The lithographers and their identifying marks are: Edwards and Deutch Lithographing Co., 'D'; Eureka Specialty Printing, 'E', Fleming-Potter Co. - 'F' Strobridge Lithographing Co. – 'S', United States Printing and Lithographing – 'U', and Western Lithograph – 'W'. Eureka....uses a comb perforation of 12³/₄ by 12³/₄. The other five use a rotary perforation of 12¹/₂ by 12¹/₂."

—*"The 1954 Christmas Seals," The American Philatelist, 1954.*

A label is used in place of a stamp or meter
"The U.S. Postal Service started what is known as an Express Mail Corporate Account in 1984. With such an account all that appears on the Express Mail envelope or package are the Post Office to Addressee Label 11-B, which has space for the corporate account number, and in place of an Express Mail stamp or meter indicium, a Corporate Account Express Mail Postage and Fees Paid label. The current label is No. 108, dated January 1986. The label is self-adhesive and comes in pads of 50. The label measures 3⁵/₈ by 2 inches. Another label, also self-adhesive but smaller (2¹/₂ by 1³/₁₄ inches), comes in rolls."

—*Richard Schulman, "Express Mail Corporate Account Labels," The United States Specialist, 1989.*

Where to Find More Information

There are no comprehensive or universal guides to alternative philately. Some useful resources on specific topics include:

- Dick Green's *Catalog of the Tuberculosis Seals of the World.*

- Stanley Wasson and Sandy Dolin's *Catalogue of U.S. and Canadian Philatelic Exhibition Seals*, a useful 1946 publication that unfortunately was never revised to include later issues.

- George Kramer's *Telegraph Stamps.*

- Bob and Marjory Kantor's *Sanitary Fairs: A Philatelic and Historical Study of Civil War Benevolences.*

- The Christmas Seal & Charity Stamp Society publishes a journal and maintains a website at: www.cscss.home.att.net/.

- The American Society for Philatelic Pages and Panels publishes a journal and maintains a website at: www.asppp.org.

- *The Fields-Picklo Catalog of Philatelic Show Seals, Labels & Souvenirs*, an on-line catalogue produced by Sandy Fields and Ken Picklo over a 20 year period, available at: www.rigastamps.com.

Appendices

Appendix A

Glossary

Throughout the Encyclopedia a number of terms are used which may be unfamiliar to the reader. Therefore the first time they appear in a chapter they may be printed in this *type face*, indicating their presence in this glossary. Additionally, terms printed in this *type face* in this glossary have their own listing for additional clarification.

Definitions provided in this glossary are intended only for application to United States stamps and covers. Their application to foreign stamps could result in error or misunderstanding.

Updates to this glossary can be found at http://glossary.usstamps.org.

A

A – 1) a *marginal marking* used on *flat plates* indicating uniform vertical spacing between columns of *stamps*. This marking was intended to assist operators of *perforating* equipment. 2) the prefix letter used by the *American Bank Note Co.* in front of the *plate number* on its modern *stamp* production.

"A" (Combination) Press – a *web-fed*, eight color press (three *intaglio* colors and five *gravure* colors) in use at the *BEP* from 1973 to 1993. It created *panes* with *floating plate numbers*.

"A" Grill – one of several types of *grills* used in the nineteenth century, which covers the entire *stamp*. Example: *Scott 79*.

"A" Stamps – *nondenominated stamps* issued in 1978 with an assigned *postage* value of 15¢.

AC Tagging - Added to Color tagging. See also *Phosphored Ink*.

AEF – see *American Expeditionary Force*.

AMF – see *Air Mail Field*.

AMG – see *Allied Military Government*.

AMSD – see *Air Mail Special Delivery*.

APC – see *Automated Postal Center*.

APEX – see *American Philatelic Expertizing Service*.

APO – see *Army and Air Force Post Office*.

APRL – see *American Philatelic Research Library*.

APS – see *American Philatelic Society*.

A.R. – a *postal marking* used on *registered* mail to foreign countries; an abbreviation of "Avis de reception," indicating *return receipt* service is requested.

Abroad – see *Offices Abroad*.

Achrovure Division of Union-Camp, Corp. – private printer of the 1968 6¢ Walt Disney *Commemorative* (1355).

Acknowledgement of Receipt Service – *Return Receipt*.

Add-on – a *cachet* added to a *first day cover* subsequent to its *cancellation*.

Advertised Letter – a letter which was advertised in a newspaper by the post office in an attempt to induce the addressee to claim it. Advertising of letters ended in the early 1920s.

Advertising Cover – a *cover* with an inscription or illustration advertising some product or service of the sender.

Aerogram – a sheet of paper with a strategically placed stamp-like *indicium* that prepays *air mail postage*. After the message and the name and address of the recipient are written, the sheet is folded, sealed, and mailed. No enclosures are permitted. See also *Private Aerogram*. *Scott* numbers for aerograms and *air mail stamped envelopes* are prefixed UC.

Affixing Machine – a machine that affixes *stamps* to an envelope, card, or *wrapper*. The first affixing machines appeared in the 1850s but were not widely used until the early twentieth century.

Air Letter Sheet – see *Aerogram*.

Airlift – see *Parcel Airlift*.

Air Mail – the carrying of mail by airplane or other airship. This service, provided for a fee, originated in 1918. Since 1977 no separate fee has been charged for *domestic air mail* service.

Air Mail Field – a postal facility located at an air field. Frequently the abbreviation AMF appears in *postmarks* applied at such facilities.

Air Mail Postal Card – a *postal card* intended to be sent by *air mail*. *Scott* numbers are prefixed with UXC.

Air Mail Semi-Official Stamps – privately printed stamps issued for a balloon flight in 1877 and an airplane flight in 1911. See *Buffalo Balloon* and *Rodgers Aerial Post*. *Scott* numbers are prefixed with CL.

Air Mail Special Delivery Stamp – a *stamp* that pays the fee both for *air mail* and *special delivery*. Although the first two air mail stamps of 1918 also provided for *special delivery* service, they are not generally included in the category of Air Mail Special Delivery Stamps. *Scott* numbers for air mail special delivery stamps are prefixed with CE.

Air Mail Stamp – a *stamp* paying the *postage* for *air mail*. Since 1977 Air Mail stamps are issued only for international air mail. *Scott* numbers for air mail stamps are prefixed with C.

Air Mail Stamped Envelope – a *stamped envelope* intended for *air mail* service. *Scott* numbers for air mail stamped envelopes and *aerograms* are prefixed with UC.

Air Post Semi-Official Stamps – see *Buffalo Balloon* and *Rodgers Aerial Post*.

Air Post Stamp – see *Air Mail Stamp*.

Albino Stationery – a *stamped envelope* on which the embossed stamp-like *indicium* is entirely lacking in its intended color.

Allied Military Government Stamps – *postage stamps* issued following World War II by the Allied Military Government for use in Italy, France, Germany, and Austria. Most of these stamps were printed by the *BEP*. They are not listed in the *Scott Specialized Catalogue* but are regarded by many collectors as belonging within the family of U.S. stamps.

Ambulance Bag – a nickname for the plastic bags used by the *USPS* to deliver mail that has been damaged. Paper envelopes serving a similar purpose were used by the Post Office as long ago as the mid-nineteenth century.

American Bank Note Company – a contractor which printed *postage stamps* from 1879 to 1894, the Overrun Nations stamps of 1943-1944, and various issues since 1979.

American Design Series – series of *definitive postage stamps* that began in 2002 with the 5¢ American Toleware *coil postage stamp* (3612).

American Expeditionary Force – the American forces in Europe during World War I for which two different *booklets* of *stamps* were produced. The booklets contained *panes* of 30 stamps each, sometimes called AEF panes (498f & 499f).

American Packaging Corporation – subcontractor to *Sennett Security Products* for *stamp* printing. Example: *Scott* 3052, the 1999 33¢ Rose stamp.

American Philatelic Center – home of the *American Philatelic Society* and the *American Philatelic Research Library* in Bellefonte, Pennsylvania.

American Philatelic Expertizing Service – service of the *APS* that renders authoritative opinions on the genuineness of stamps and covers.

American Philatelic Research Library – largest private philatelic library in the United States, with extensive resources for researchers and collectors.

American Philatelic Society – largest *philatelic* organization in the United States.

American Postal Machines Company – major manufacturer of *canceling machines* in use from the 1880s to the 1940s. This company is known for its *flag cancels*.

Americana Issue – series of *definitive stamps* that began in 1975. The first *Scott* number is 1581.

Ameripex '86 – one in a series of international stamp shows hosted once every decade in the U.S. Ameripex '86 was held in Chicago in 1986. A *stamp* (2145), *souvenir sheets* (2216-2219) and an *Air Mail Postal Card* (UXC23) were issued in conjunction with this show.

Andreotti Press – a seven color *gravure* press installed at the *BEP* in 1970. The first *stamp* printed by this press was the 1971 Missouri Statehood Issue (1426). In addition to stamps this press also produced *aerograms*.

Aniline Ink – a *fugitive* ink made with synthetic organic pigments produced as derivatives of nitrobenzene. Aniline ink was used in the production of stamp ink from before the *Washington-Franklin* era until its importation from Germany became impossible during World War I. When inferior quality aniline ink was used, bleeding of pigment resulted in stamps known as *pink backs*. Aniline ink was also used to *surcharge* some *revenue* stamps.

Army and Air Force Post Office – (formerly Army Post Office) a U.S. post office established for military units overseas. APOs, as it is called, are designated by a number.

Army Flights – 1) *air mail* flights flown by army pilots from May 15 to August 11, 1918. Beginning August 12, 1918 the mail was flown by civilian pilots. 2) air mail flights flown by army air corp pilots during a short, disastrous "emergency" period in 1934 when President Roosevelt cancelled *CAM* contracts.

Arrow – a *marginal marking*, shaped like a "V" which served as a guide for cutting *sheets* into smaller units, and as a guide in the perforation process.

Arrow Block – *margin block* with a "V" shaped *marginal marking*.

Ashton-Potter (USA) Ltd. - private printer of *postage stamps* since in 1991. Printer of the first *commemoratives* produced exclusively by *offset lithography*, the 1992 Wildflowers Stamps *pane* (2647-2696).

Atherton Shift – a striking *double transfer* on the 1861 2¢ black Andrew Jackson *postage stamp*.

Attleboro Perforations – *perforations* privately applied to *imperforate flat plate* stamps by the *Attleboro Stamp Co.* for use in an *affixing machine*.

Attleboro Stamp Company – a stamp company in Massachusetts that produced *private coils* for use in its own *affixing machine*.

August Issues – nickname for a group of *essays* and *trial color proofs* once erroneously given catalogue status as *postage stamps*. The nickname derives from the belief that they were printed in August 1861. Example: *Scott* 63-Elle.

Austrian Occupation Issues – see *Allied Military Government Stamps*.

Automated Postal Center – a machine introduced by the *USPS* in 2004 allowing customers to use a debit or credit card to purchase computer-generated *postage* stamps and also mail items.

Automatic Canceling Machines – *canceling* machines introduced in 1963 when *phosphor tagging* was introduced. These machines replaced manual canceling machines.

Auto-wound – 1) the semi-automatic, mechanical process of creating *coil stamps* introduced at the *BEP* in 1910. 2) a phrase printed on the *coil leader* of some stamps.

Auxiliary Marking – *postal marking* applied to *covers* indicating that the covers were given special attention due to some special circumstance. Examples: "Postage Due", "Return to Sender", and "Refused". Auxiliary markings are sometimes known as Instructional Markings.

Avery Dennison – private printer of *postage stamps* beginning in 1991 with the 29¢ Liberty Torch (2531A).

Avery International – private printer of *postage stamps* beginning in 1990 with the 25¢ Flag self-adhesive stamp (2475). Previously Avery International provided pressure sensitive materials for other stamps, including the first self-adhesive stamp, the 1974 10¢ Dove Weathervane (1552).

AVSEC Clearance Stamp – AVSEC is *USPS* shorthand for "Aviation Security". This *auxiliary marking* was introduced in 2002 as a security feature.

B

B – prefix letter used by *Banknote Corporation of America* in front of the *plate number* on its modern *postage stamp* production.

B Grill – one of several types of *grills* used in the nineteenth century, about 18 x 15 mm in size. Example: *Scott* 82.

"B" Press – *web-fed*, three-color, *intaglio* press used exclusively to print *coils* and *booklet panes* from seamless *cylindrical sleeves*. Used at the *BEP* from 1973 to 1993.

"B" Stamps – *nondenominated stamps* issued in March 1981 with an assigned *postage* value of 18¢.

BEP – see *Bureau of Engraving and Printing*.

BIA – see *Bureau Issues Association*.

BOB – see *Back-of-the-Book*.

Baby Zepp – a nickname for 1933 50¢ Century of Progress Flight *air mail postage stamp*, (C18) which portrays the Graf Zeppelin.

Back-of-the Book – items listed in *Scott* following *Postage Stamps*, which begin their *Scott* numbers with a letter prefix. For example, catalogue numbers for *Air Mail Stamps* are prefixed with C and those for *revenue stamps* are prefixed with R.

Backprint – printing which intentionally appears on the back of a stamp.

Backstamp – a *postal marking*, usually applied to the back of a *cover*, evidencing either the arrival of a cover at its destination post office or the handling of a cover while in transit. Applying a backstamp to *First Class Mail* upon arrival at the destination post office was mandatory from 1879 until 1913. The backstamping of ordinary *air mail* was discontinued in 1929. See *Receiving Mark* and *Transit Mark*.

Band Tagging – a continuous narrow band of horizontal or vertical *tagging* that extends across a *pane* of *stamps*. Example: 1973 8¢ Postal Service Employees stamps (1489-1498).

Banknote Corporation of America – private printer of modern *stamps*, beginning with the 1992 29¢ Eagle & Shield, (2595).

Bank Notes – nickname for the *stamps* of 1870-1894 produced by the *National Bank Note Co.*, *Continental Bank Note Co.*, and *American Bank Note Co.* The Bank Notes are sub-divided into *Large*

Bank Notes and **Small Bank Notes**. Begins with **Scott** 134.

Barcode – 1) a machine-readable code typically in the form of parallel lines of variable height or spacing sprayed in a row on the front or back of a *cover* by the *U.S. Postal Service* or mailer. The *POSTNET* barcode is used to expedite the sorting and delivery of mail. Other barcodes are used for tracing and tracking mail and are used in *indicia* for security purposes. 2) a machine-readable code used by the *BEP* as part of their Electronic Stamp Inspection process. Barcodes are sprayed onto the margins of all *coil* and *booklet stamps* to facilitate the identification and removal of defective stamps. While these bar codes are usually trimmed off in the manufacturing process, booklet panes do exist with a barcode on the *tab*.

Barrel Duplex – 1) a *duplex handstamp* in which the *cancel* has a central section shaped like a barrel, usually containing a number or letter. 2) the impression left by a barrel duplex cancel handstamp on a *cover*.

Barry Postal Supply Company – major manufacturer of *cancelling machines* in use from the 1890s to the 1910s.

Barton Press – a subcontractor to *Banknote Corporation of America* for printing the 1994 Wonders of the Sea *stamps* (2863-2866).

Battleships – nickname for the *documentary* and *proprietary revenue stamps* of 1898 depicting the U. S. Navy battleship Maine (R161-172 and RB20-31).

Bear Stamps – nickname for the St. Louis, Missouri *postmasters provisional* stamps of 1845.

Beecher-Wawrukiewicz – authors of *postage* rate studies. Their definitive works are *U.S. Domestic Postal Rates, 1872-1999* and *U.S. International Postal Rates, 1872-1996*. Both works have updates available.

Beer Stamps – *revenue stamps* (*Scott* REA) issued 1866-1951 to pay the federal tax on beer.

Bisect – see *Fractional Usages*.

Black Hardings – black *stamps* issued in 1923 to mourn the death of President Warren Harding (610-613).

Black Heritage Series – series of *commemorative postage stamps* honoring Black Americans; begun in 1978 with the Harriet Tubman stamp (1744).

Black Jack – nickname for the black 2¢ Andrew Jackson *stamps* and *postal envelopes* first issued in 1863. Examples: *Scott* 73 and U46.

Blind Perforations – an impression made by *perforating* pins in a location where perforations were intended, but from which *chads* were not removed. These interesting varieties are not *imperforate* stamps. Blind perforations are considered *freaks*, not *errors*.

Block – a unit of *stamps*, generally four or more in number.

Block Tagging – a rectangle of clear *phosphor taggant ink* applied over a *stamp*'s *design*, as opposed to taggant covering the entire stamp.

Bluish Paper – paper with 35% rag content (instead of all wood pulp) and a blue mineral colorant, used to print certain *postage stamps* issued in 1909. The resulting stamp papers have a pale bluish color. Examples: *Scott* 357-366.

Boating Stamp – *revenue stamp* used on applications for motorboats. *Scott* RVB.

Bobst-Champlain Perforator – work-horse perforator at the BEP for definitive sheet stamps during the late 1980s and beyond. Introduced in February 1985, this machine used a Eureka *bullseye perforation* die to perforate two adjoining panes across a printed web at one time. It also separated the web into sheets four panes square then stacked them.

Body Bag – see *Ambulance bag.*

Booklet – a unit of *stamps*, sold by the post office, comprising one or **more booklet panes**. Traditional booklets used cardboard covers stapled or glued together to protect the enclosed booklet panes. With a few exceptions, traditional booklet panes used water-activated gum. Contemporary booklets (both **convertible booklets** and **vending booklets**) contain self-adhesive stamps and are sold as single panes. Contemporary booklets do not have separate covers. The backing paper serves as the cover.

Booklet Pane – 1) a unit of *stamps* produced for use in traditional booklets (those with cardboard covers). Such booklet panes usually, but not always, have **water-activated gum**. Panes in a traditional booklet usually (but not always) have six stamps. 2) a unit of **self-adhesive** stamps sold by the post office as a complete **booklet** that may be folded for convenience to form a **convertible booklet**. 3) a unit of stamps sold as a booklet from a **vending** machine.

Branch – a retail postal facility that is subordinate to a primary (main) post office.

(The) Brinkerhoff Company – a manufacturer of **vending machines** and **private coils** once located in Sedalia, Missouri, and Clinton, Iowa.

Brinkerhoff Perforations – *perforations* privately applied to **imperforate flat plate postage stamps** by The **Brinkerhoff Company** for use in its **vending machines**.

Broken Hat – nickname for a **plate variety** on the 2¢ **Columbian** of 1893 (231).

Brunswick Printings – *AMG stamps* printed in 1945 in Brunswick, Germany.

Buffalo Balloon – an 1877 balloon flight in Tennessee that carried mail for which a privately printed *stamp* was issued (CL1).

Bulk Mail – *quantity* mail that is *rated* by bulk (aggregate weight), rather than by the piece, although minimum per-piece rates apply.

Bullseye – a *stamp* on which the *postmark* is struck directly onto the center of the *stamp*. Also known as "*socked-on-the-nose.*"

Bullseye Perforations – perforations that meet perfectly in the corners of stamps.

Bureau Issue – a product of the *Bureau of Engraving and Printing*.

Bureau Issues Association – former name of the *United States Stamp Society*.

Bureau of Engraving and Printing – a division of the U.S. Treasury Department with facilities in Washington, D.C. producing almost all *stamps* from 1894 through the 1960s. Since 1967 the BEP shared the production of stamps with a wide variety of private companies. Production of stamps by the BEP ended in 2005.

Bureau Precancel – a *stamp* with the *precancel* applied by the *BEP*.

Bureau Print – see *Bureau Issue*.

(The) Bureau Specialist – the monthly journal of the *Bureau Issues Association* (*USSS*) from 1930 to 1966 when the journal was renamed *The United States Specialist*.

Burnish – the process of removing unwanted entries from an *engraved* printing *plate*, which is performed by a *plate finisher*.

Business Reply Mail – a postal service that allows a mailer to receive mail back from customers on which the customer has not paid *postage*. The mailer pays the postage and fees when the mailed item is returned to the mailer.

Butler & Carpenter – printers of the *revenue stamps* issued from 1862-1871.

C

"C" Grill – one of several types of *grills* used in the nineteenth century, about 13 x 16mm in size. Example: *Scott* 83.

"C" Press – *web-fed*, three-color, *intaglio* press used exclusively to print *coils* and *booklet panes* from seamless *cylindrical sleeves*. Used at the *BEP* from 1982 to 1996.

"C" Stamps – *nondenominated stamps* issued in October, 1981 with an assigned *postage* value of 20¢.

CAM – see *Contract Air Mail*.

CDS – see *Circular Date Stamp*.

CIPEX – see *Centenary International Philatelic Exhibition*.

COD – see *Collect on Delivery*.

"CS" – *marginal marking* meaning "Chromed Steel" indicating that a *plate* has been *chromium* plated. Example: Georgia Bicentennial Issue (726). See also *Chrome Plating and Chrome Stain*.

CSAC – see *Citizens Stamp Advisory Committee*.

Cachet – 1) any text or graphic applied to an envelope for a commemorative purpose. Cachets are frequently found on *First Day Covers*, *Patriotic Covers*, and *Event Covers*. 2) any advertisement, censor marking, or commercial handstamp applied to a cover.

Canadian Bank Note Company – subcontractor to *Stamp Venturers*. Example: 1992 29¢ Earl Warren *definitive postage stamp* (2184).

Canal Zone – a territory leased to the U.S. from 1904 to 1979 and for which *stamps* were issued. Those stamps include *overprinted* issues of Panama and the U.S., and stamps designed and printed specifically for the Canal Zone by the *Bureau of Engraving and Printing*.

Cancel – see *Cancellation*.

Cancellation – any *postal marking* applied to a *stamp* to prevent its reuse. Cancellation is not synonymous with *postmark*, although the two terms are frequently confused and used interchangeably. Cancellations have been applied by *handstamps*, *machine*, including *sprayed on*, and pen or marker.

Cancelling Machines – machines that *cancel stamps* and *postmark* envelopes in a single operation. Many different makes and models of cancelling machines have been used by post offices.

Carmine Error – nickname for *Scott* 467, 485, and 505. The *transfer roll* for a 5¢ *stamp*, normally printed in blue, was mistakenly used on a *plate* of 2¢ stamps printed in carmine, thus creating a color *error* for the 5¢ stamp.

Carpenter, Jos. R. – printer of nineteenth century *revenue stamps*.

Carrier Service – the pick-up of mail by an official letter carrier from collection boxes and residences along his route, and the delivery of that mail to the local post office, or directly to an addressee in the same city. Sometimes carrier service included delivery of mail from the post office to an addressee. The fee for this service (prior to the elimination of the fee on June 30, 1863 and establishment of free city delivery) was either 1¢ or 2¢. Special *Carrier Stamps* were issued to pay for this service. Prior to July 1, 1863 the payment of regular postage only paid for transportation of mail between post offices.

Carriers' Stamps – *stamps* that paid for *carrier service*. Carriers' stamps for national use were issued beginning in 1851 and are called Official Issues or general issues (*Scott* LO). Other carriers' stamps were used locally in Baltimore, Boston, Charleston, Cincinnati, Cleveland, Louisville, New York, and Philadelphia, and St. Louis (*Scott* LB). They were issued by or under the authority of the local postmaster. They are called semi-official issues, and were issued as early as 1842.

Catapult Mail – mail carried by air, for a fee, from a ship at sea to land. This obsolete service was intended to shorten the length of time it took mail to cross the Atlantic Ocean.

Censored Mail – a *cover* that has had its contents examined by civilian or military censors and bears a marking evidencing the examination.

Centenary International Philatelic Exhibition – one in a series of international stamp shows hosted once a decade in the U.S. Held in New York City in 1947. A *stamp* (947) and *souvenir sheet* (948) were issued in conjunction with the show.

Center Line Block – a *block* of stamps from the very center of certain *sheets*, that is, a block on which two *guidelines* intersect each other.

Century of Progress Issues – *Scott* 728-731 and an *air mail stamp* (C18) issued in conjunction with the 1933 Century of Progress Exposition in Chicago. The air mail stamp also marks an October 1933 flight of the Graf Zeppelin to the Century of Progress Exposition.

Ceremony Programs – programs issued in conjunction with *First Day* events. While formerly individualized for each new issue, generic programs are now used.

Certificate of Authenticity – a certificate from a recognized authority attesting to the genuineness of a philatelic item. See also *expertization*.

Certificate of Mailing – service for a fee that provides evidence of mailing. Certificates of Mailing were first made available in 1915.

Certified Mail – service for a fee that provides a mailing receipt and maintenance by the *USPS* of a delivery record. Certified Mail requires the signature of the recipient. First offered in 1955.

Certified Mail Stamp – a *stamp* issued in 1955 to pay the fee for *Certified Mail* (FA1).

Chads – the bits of paper removed in the *perforating* process.

Champions of Liberty – a series of *commemorative postage stamps* (late 1950s to early 1960s) honoring foreign nationals who sought freedom in their homelands. Example: *Scott* 1125.

Changeling – a *stamp* on which the color has been changed as the result of a chemical reaction.

Charity Stamp – see *Semi-postal*.

Chicago Perfs – nickname for the first *perforated stamps* produced by a machine. These unofficial perforations were privately applied to 3¢ imperforate stamps (11) by a Chicago businessman.

China Clay Paper – a paper with a 15 to 20% mineral content, used to print a small quantity of stamps in 1909. Example: *Scott* 331b.

China Clipper – the seaplane depicted on the three "China Clipper" *air mail stamps* of 1935 and 1937 (C20-22), and the 1985 *Air Mail Postal Card* (UXC22), which carried mail across the Pacific to and from San Francisco, with inaugural service to Manila on November 22, 1935, on *FAM* 14.

Christmas Seals – privately produced, fund raising *labels* intended for use on mail during the Christmas season. First issued in 1907. *Scott* numbers are prefixed with WX.

Chrome Plating – technique of covering engraved steel *plates* with a thin layer of chromium to make them last longer. See also *CS*.

Chrome Stain – a printing *variety* on a *stamp* that is the result of chrome plating stripping off a printing *plate*. See *CS*

Cigarette Tubes Stamps – *revenue stamps* used to pay a tax on cigarette paper. *Scott* numbers are prefixed with RH.

Cinderella – a nickname frequently used for fantasy *labels* with no postal validity.

Circular Date Stamp – circular *postmark*, which generally contains the city and state of mailing as well as the date and time the postmark was applied.

Citizens' Stamp Advisory Committee – advisory committee to the Postmaster

General, formed in 1957 to recommend new *postage stamp* issues.

City Despatch Post – a private **local post** established in New York City in 1841. The first **local stamp** it issued (40L1) was the first adhesive stamp used in the United States. This organization was purchased by the Post Office and reorganized as United States City Despatch Post.

Clay Paper – see *China Clay Paper*.

Clipper – generic name for the planes flown by Pan American on its trans-oceanic routes. See also *China Clipper*.

Closed Mail – mid-nineteenth century mail moved by ship in sealed bags from an *exchange office* to an exchange office in another country, containing mail for that country.

Closed Transit Dispatches – closed bags of international mail that pass through an intermediate country without being opened.

Closing of the Mail – the time after which mail will no longer be accepted by a local post office for dispatch by a specific train or ship. See *Supplementary Mail*.

Clothes-line Stamp – nickname for the 1939 *commemorative* (858) marking the 50th anniversary of statehood for North and South Dakota, Montana, and Washington.

Coated Paper – paper that has a smooth surface when viewed under magnification. The "hills and valleys" visible on **uncoated paper** will either be filled in or have rounded edges. Coated paper has a range of smoothness. See *Uncoated Papers* and *Prephosphored Papers*.

Coil Core – see *Core*.

Coil Counting Number – see *Counting Number*.

Coil Leader – see *Leader*.

Coil Line Pair – see *Joint Line Pair*.

Coil Paste-up – see *Paste-up Pair*.

Coil Plate Numbers – 1) numbers that appear at regular intervals at the bottom of modern *coil stamps*. 2) numbers used on coil stamp *plates* prior to 1981. These numbers were normally trimmed off the *sheet* as a part of the production process and did not normally reach the public. See also *Partial Plate Numbers*.

Coil Stamps – *stamps* produced in a long strip, either vertically or horizontally. Some were once issued **imperforate**. More commonly coil stamps have been issued with **perforations**, **die cuts**, or **roulette**s between the stamps. Coil stamps have been produced by the **BEP** and by private printers under contract to the Post Office. Coil stamps were once produced by private manufacturers from **imperforate sheets** provided by the Post Office. Coil stamps are sold by the Postal Service in rolls of 100, 3,000, and 10,000. Historically they have also been sold in rolls of 500.

"Coil Stamps" – a **marginal marking** found on certain **flat plate sheets**. These sheets have increased spacing between the 10th and 11th vertical rows. These sheets were intended to become **coil stamps**, but some became sheet stamps known as **coil waste**. This marginal inscription was trimmed off the sheet during coil production, but remained on the **panes** sold as coil waste.

Coil Waste – **sheet stamps** created from left-over pieces that were intended to become coil stamps, but that were too short for **coil stamp** production. Coil waste was released in sheet format as an economy measure. Example: *Scott* 578.

Collateral material – material that is not intrinsically **philatelic** but that is related to philatelic material which enhances appreciation for and understanding of philatelic material. Examples: photographs and maps.

Collect on Delivery – service for a fee in which the post office collects money from a mail recipient and forwards the money to the sender.

Collection and Distribution Wagons – horse drawn vehicles used briefly by the post office in four cities at the turn of the twentieth century for collecting, sorting, *postmarking*, and distributing mail.

Color Changeling – see *Changeling*.

Color Missing – an *error* resulting from color transferred from a press not appearing on a *stamp*.

Color Omitted – an *error* resulting from the complete failure of a press to transfer a color to a *stamp*.

Color Registration Markings – *marginal markings* of various sizes and shapes, in each color used to print a *stamp*. When these colored markings are properly aligned with one another, it indicates that the color alignment (*registration*) on the entire *sheet* is correct.

Color Trials – see *Trial Color Proofs*.

Columbia Postal Supply Company – major manufacturer of *cancelling machines* in use from the 1900s to the 1950s.

Columbians – nickname for the first *commemorative* series of *postage stamps*, issued in 1893 to commemorate Christopher Columbus and the World's Columbian Exposition held in Chicago. *Stamped envelopes* (230-245 and U348-351) were also issued.

Comb Perforator – a rotary perforator with one long horizontal row of pins and numerous short vertical columns of pins. This pin format resembles a typical comb. A single rotation perforates three sides of each of the stamps in a single row.

Combination Booklet – a *booklet* containing *panes* of *stamps* of more than one *denomination*. Example: BK68.

Combo – (combination) a *First Day Cover* combining a new issue with related *stamps* or *postal stationery*.

Commemorative – a *stamp*, generally larger in size than a *definitive*, on sale in limited quantities for a limited period of time, honoring a person, place, event, etc.

Commemorative Panel – a product of the

USPS, sold in conjunction with *commemorative postage stamps*. Each panel has the commemorative stamp affixed and contains background information and illustrations.

Commercial Cover – a *cover* of commercial (as opposed to *philatelic*) origin.

Complete Matched Set – a set of *plate number blocks* representing every number *and pane position* possible for a given *stamp*.

Compound Perforation – two different *gauges* (sizes) of *perforations* used on the same *stamp*. Most frequently one gauge is used for the vertical perforations, and another for the horizontal perforations. Example: Printing Tercentenary Issue (857). See also *Perforation* and *Perforation Gauge*.

Computer Generated Postage – *postage* generated by a computer.

Computer Vended Postage – *stamps* dispensed by a *vending machine* on which the *face value* of the *postage* is imprinted at the time of sale. See also *Denominated Postal Cards*.

Concession Rate – see *Convention Rate*.

Constant Variety – a *plate variety* that appears on a *plate* and on every *sheet* printed from it. All sheets printed from a plate will show the variety from the time the trait is entered on the plate until the time it is removed from the plate. Sheets printed from the same plate before the trait appeared on the plate, or after it was removed, will not exhibit the constant variety.

Consular Service Fee Stamp – a *revenue stamp* paying a fee (not a tax) for certain documents issued by American diplomats at consular offices in foreign countries. *Scott* RK.

Continental Bank Note Company – a contractor which printed *postage stamps* (156-179) from 1873 to 1879.

Contract Air Mail (CAM) – system of carrying *air mail* over established routes, by private contractors, as opposed to air mail carried by government-employed pilots.

Contract Station – a subunit of a larger post office, operated by a private individual or firm; frequently operated in a private business.

Control Number – see *Counting Number*.

Control Perfin – a *perforation* composed of a square pattern of up to nine holes arranged in three rows of three, made by an affixing machine through the *face* of a *Schermack* or Mailometer *coil*. See *Perfin*.

Convention Rate – see *Treaty rate*.

Convertible Booklet – a small *pane* of modern *self-adhesive postage stamps*, sold flat, but designed to be folded into *booklet* form when the peelable strip(s) is removed. These booklets do not have separate covers. The backing paper serves as the cover. The complete unfolded convertible booklet is considered to be a *booklet pane*, and the *liner* paper to which the stamps are attached is the booklet cover.

Copyright Block – a *margin block* of *stamps* containing a copyright notice. Copyright notices first appeared in 1978.

Cordials, Wines, etc. Stamps – *revenue stamps* paying the federal tax on wines. Issued from 1914 to 1954. *Scott* RE.

Core – a strip of brown kraft paper attached to the innermost (last) stamp on a roll of *coil* stamps.

Cork Cancel – a nineteenth century *cancelling* device, made out of cork, usually carved with an image, produced by or at the direction of a local *postmaster*.

Corner Card – the printed address of a sender in the upper left corner of an envelope.

Corrosion Stain – a printing *variety* resulting from corrosion on a metal *plate*.

Cotton Order Stamps – *stamps* produced by the *BEP* as part of a subsidy program that enabled low income families to purchase goods made with cotton.

Cottrell Press – see *Huck-Cottrell Presses*.

Counting Number – 1) a number printed on the back of the *liner* of some *self-adhesive coil* stamps. This number is an accounting device. 2) number printed in the trimmed off margin of some earlier coils. This number aided *BEP* employees who cut the *web* of coil stamps into specified lengths (100, 500, or 3,000 stamps), spliced together by a piece of kraft paper. After such splicing the web was cut and processed into individual coil rolls. See also *Leader* and *Core*.

Covel Coils – privately perforated *Second Bureau Issue coil stamps* made by the Covel Manufacturing Company of Benton Harbor, Michigan using a *Rossback* perforator.

Cover(s) – 1) any intact envelope, *postal card*, *wrapper*, or similar mailed item. 2) the printed pieces of cardboard used for the front and back of traditional *booklets*. The *Scott* numbers identifying such booklet covers are prefixed with BC.

Cracked Plate – a crack in a printing *plate* that shows up on the corresponding stamps. Cracks can be progressive, that is, they can become worse with time and use.

Crash Cover – a *cover* rescued from the crash site of the plane or other vehicle in which the cover was being carried. Such covers generally bear some *postal marking* explaining their delay and possibly damaged condition.

Cross Gutter Block – a *block* of *stamps* containing the intersection of the vertical and horizontal *gutters*.

Cuba – island under U.S. administration from 1899 to 1902, and for which *overprinted* U.S. *stamps* were issued.

Curvature Crack – see *Gripper Crack*.

Customized Postage – postage sold by authorized private vendors containing images supplied by purchasers.

Customs Fee Stamps – *revenue stamps* used to pay certain customs fees (not duties). *Scott* RL.

Cut Cancel – a *cancellation* that slices into the *stamp* paper. Most commonly found on *revenue stamps*. Stamps with cut cancellations are generally considered less desirable.

Cut Square – a section of *postal stationery*, cut from the *entire*, which contains the stamp-like *indicium*. Cut squares are considered less desirable than entires. While cut squares from *stamped envelopes* are considered collectible, cut squares from *postal cards* are not.

Cut-to-shape – the stamp-like *indicium* from a *stamped envelope* that has been cut from the *entire* and trimmed to the size of the indicium. A cut-to-shape piece is generally less desirable than a *cut square*.

Cylinder – 1) the drum-like part of a rotary printing press, also called a mandrel, to which curved printing plates are attached. 2) the seamless curved *plate* used on a press to print *gravure* stamps.

D

D – prefix letter used by *Dittler Brothers, Inc.* in front of the *plate number* on its modern *stamp* production.

D Grill – one of several types of *grills* used in the nineteenth century, about 12 x 14mm in size. Example: *Scott* 84.

"D" Press – *web-fed* press with both *offset* and *intaglio* capacities in use at *BEP* 1984-1996.

"D" Stamps – *nondenominated stamps* issued in 1985 with an assigned *postage* value of 22¢.

DPO – see *Discontinued Post Office*.

Danish West Indies – territory purchased by U.S. from Denmark and renamed U.S. Virgin Islands.

Dated Precancel – a *precancel* stamp marked by the user with the month and year of use.

Dead Letter Office – unit of the post office which receives undeliverable mail with no return address, and attempts to return it to the sender. Until 1917 the Dead Letter Office was located in Washington, D.C. In 1917 its work was decentralized, with branches in various cities.

Decorative Banner – the illustrated *margin* on the top of some modern *commemorative panes*. It has no postal value. Example: 1996 Summer Olympics (3068).

Definitive – *postage stamp* intended for routine postal use, issued for an indefinite period of time in indefinite quantities. Also called *ordinary* stamps.

De La Rue Security Printing – private printer of *postage stamps*. Example: 34¢ Nobel Prize (3504).

Delivery Confirmation – service for a fee that provides the sender with the date and time of delivery of a piece of mail.

Demonetized Stamp (or Stamped Envelope) – a *stamp* or *stamped envelope* that is no longer valid for *postage*. Those issued prior to the Civil War have been demonetized. Most pre-1979 postal cards have been effectively demonetized because they do not meet current minimum size requirements. Likewise *Special Delivery stamps* and *Newspaper and Periodical stamps* have been effectively demonetized.

Denominated Postal Cards – *postal cards* printed by *vending machines* in selected locations during the early 1990s. *Scott* CVUX.

Denomination – the *face value* of a *stamp*, as printed on the stamp, normally in numerals. Compare: *Nondenominated Stamps*.

Departmental Stamp – see *Official Stamps*.

Design – the image on a *stamp*.

Designer – the person who creates the artwork which is the basis for a *stamp*. Most stamps were once designed by employees of the *BEP* (e.g. Smith, Huston, Meissner, McCloskey, and Chickering). More recently the Postal Service has relied on private designers.

Diagonal Half – a *fractional usage* – a *stamp bisected* diagonally.

Dial – circular *postmarking die*, used to impress a postmark on an envelope, generally containing the following information: city and state of mailing, and the date and time the postmark was applied.

Die – 1) the piece of steel on which a *design* is engraved. A die has the stamp image engraved in reverse (mirror-image). The creation of the die is the first step in the production of engraved stamps. 2) the printing surface, found in a *cancelling machine*, from which a *cancellation* and *postmark* are printed on an envelope. 3) the metal form used for the *embossing* process.

Die Cut – a modern method of separating *self-adhesive stamps*. A cut completely penetrates the paper all around the stamp, making it possible to remove individual stamps from the *liner* located underneath. Die cuts can have a variety of shapes, including straight lines and wavy lines that simulate traditional *perforations*.

Die Cut Gauge – 1) a number that equals the total quantity of serpentine peaks (or valleys) within the space of 20 mm on die cut stamps. 2) a tool that measures the total quantity of serpentine peaks (or valleys) within the space of 20 mm on die cut stamps. Compare: *Perforation Gauge*.

Die Essay – a print made from a *die* that has not yet been completely engraved, generally made to check the phases of engraving, also known as a *progressive die proof*.

Die Flaw – an imperfection that existed on the surface of a blank *die* before the die was engraved. This imperfection can appear on the printed *stamps*.

Die Proof – a printed impression made directly from a *die*. See also **Large Die Proof** and **Small Die Proof**.

Die Sinkage – on a *large die proof*, the impression or indentation in the card made by the *die*.

Directory Markings – *postal markings* applied to a *cover* indicating *forwarding* for delivery, or a failed attempt to deliver mail such as "Address Unknown" or "Forwarding Time Expired".

Discontinued Post Office – a post office no longer in operation, or in operation with a different name.

Disinfected Mail – mail that has been treated to prevent the spread of a contagion. See also **Irradiated Mail**.

Distilled Spirits Stamp – *revenue stamp* for payment of taxes on distilled spirits. Used from 1950 to 1959. *Scott* RX.

Distinguished Americans – series of *definitive stamps* begun in 2000 with the 10¢ Joseph Stilwell (3420).

Dittler Brothers, Inc. – private printer of *postage stamps*. Their first stamp was the green denominated 29¢ Eagle and Shield of 1992, (2596).

Doane Cancel – a *duplex handstamp*, common in the early twentieth century, containing a numeral as a part of the *cancel*. The numeral indicates the annual compensation of the *postmaster*. For example, a number 5 in the cancel indicates that for the year prior to the issuing of the handstamp, the postmaster's annual compensation was between $400 and $499.

Docketing – notation written on a *cover* by the recipient. Docketing sometimes helps establish the date of a cover.

Documentary Stamps – *revenue stamps* used to pay a federal tax on certain transactions that are documented on paper. The stamps were attached to the documents. They were first used in 1862 to help pay for the Civil War. *Scott* numbers are prefixed with R. Some documentary stamps have been *overprinted* to serve other purposes.

Domestic Mail – mail that never leaves the mailstream of the United States, as opposed to **International Mail**.

Doremus Machine Company – major manufacturer of *cancelling machines* in use from the 1890s to the 1930s.

Double Grill – a *stamp grilled* twice.

Double Impression – a stamp on which the *design*, or a portion of the design, is doubled. This occurs when a sheet slips against an *offset* blanket, or when the press is stopped, relaxing the tension on the *web*. Double impressions are *freaks*. A double impression is not the same as a *double printing* or *double transfer*.

Double Joint Line – a *joint line* on *rotary press stamps* that appears to be two parallel lines. It is caused by a gap between the two rotary *plates* that is wider than normal.

Double Line Electros – *precancels* produced from an electro printing plate with the city and state designation between double lines above and below.

Double Line Watermark – a *watermark* in which the initials *USPS* have double lines. In other words, the initials USPS are outlined and hollow. Example: *Scott* 264.

Double Paper – a *stamp* printed on two layers of paper. There are two distinct causes of double paper: 1) a double paper was intentionally used on some stamps by the *Continental Bank Note Co.* in printing the *Large Bank Note* stamps of 1873. 2) double paper resulted on some *rotary press* stamps when a tear or cut in the *web* was repaired with a *splice*. Splicing required some overlapping of the *web*, hence creating a double paper variety. Double paper varieties were also created when two webs were attached to each other.

Double Perforation – a *stamp* or multiple stamps with an extraneous row of *perforations*. These are *freaks*, not *errors*.

Double Printing – a *stamp* that has passed through the press twice.

Double Transfer – a *plate variety* in which a portion of the *design* is doubled, that is, it appears twice. A double transfer occurs on *engraved* stamps when a design is "*rocked*" into a *plate* from a *transfer roll* in such a way that the rocked images are out of alignment. Thus, if the *siderographer* is not careful, the rocking in of the design will cause a part of the design to appear more than once. Sometimes a double transfer on a *plate* is discovered and is *burnished* out. But if this process is not totally successful, some amount of doubling of the design may remain. All sheets printed from a plate with a double transfer will show the double transfer. Thus, the double transfer will be a *constant variety*.

Drop Letter – a letter deposited at a post office for delivery to another patron at the same office. Drop letters were sometimes charged less than letters requiring dispatch to a different post office. See also *Local Letter*.

Dropped Mail – mail intentionally dropped from an aircraft in flight for forwarding to its destination.

Dropped Transfer – 1) an impression on an *engraved* printing *plate* caused when a *transfer roll* accidentally touches the blank plate before being properly positioned. This results in a narrow band of doubling across the *design*. 2) one or more entries on a plate that are lower than intended and lower than the other entries on the plate.

Dry Printing – the printing of *intaglio stamps* on paper with low moisture content. Dry printing was first used at the *BEP* in 1953. All *Bureau Issues* have been dry printed since the late 1950s. Compare: *Wet Printing*.

Duck Stamps – *revenue stamps*, officially known as "United States Migratory Bird Hunting and Conservation" stamps, issued annually, and required to be signed by hunters and affixed to their hunting licenses. Collected both on- and off license. *Scott* RW.

Dumb Cancel – see *Mute Cancel*.

Dummy Booklet – see *Dummy Stamps*.

Dummy Coil – see *Dummy Stamps*.

Dummy Stamps – stamp-like *labels* either without *denomination* or with a value shown that has a defacement line through it. These stamps were used for training and testing purposes. Produced in *sheet*, *coil*, and *booklet* format. These "stamps" have no postal value or validity.

Duplex Cancel – 1) a single unit *handstamp* uniting both a *postmark* and *cancel*. First introduced in the 1860s, it was used through the 1940s. 2) the impression left by a duplex cancel handstamp on a *cover*.

Durland – abbreviated term for *Durland Standard Plate Number Catalog*, the authoritative catalog of *plate numbers* originally published by Clarence Durland beginning in 1950, and now edited and published by the *United States Stamp Society*.

E

1847s – nickname for the first two *postage stamps* (1 and 2), issued in 1847, and *demonetized* in 1851.

E-COM – (Electronic Computer-Originated Mail) a service of the *USPS* begun in 1982 enabling a customer to send a *bulk* mail message from a computer terminal. The Post Office delivered the messages in special blue and white envelopes. The service ended in 1985.

EDU – see *Earliest Documented Use*.

EFO – see *Errors, Freaks, and Oddities*.

EMU – see *Early Matching Use*.

E Grill – one of several types of *grills* used in the nineteenth century, about 11 x 13 mm in size. Example: *Scott 86*.

"E" Stamps – *nondenominated stamps* issued in 1988 with an assigned *postage* value of 25¢.

EKU – see *Earliest Known Use*.

Earliest Documented Use – the earliest date on which a *stamp* or item of *postal stationery* is known to have been used, as documented by expert opinion. Generally

applied to items issued in the nineteenth and early twentieth centuries that did not have formal *first days of issue* and that might have arrived at different post offices at different times.

Earliest Known Use – the earliest known date on which a stamp is used, even if prior to the official *first day of issue*. Generally applied to contemporary stamps.

Early Impression – a *stamp* produced in the first phase of a *plate's* life, before the plate shows any indication of wear.

Early Matching Use – a term applied to a *First Issue Revenue stamp* used in the last few days of 1862 or early 1863 when the stamp is used on the type of document for which it was intended.

Electric Eye – 1) a device employing a beam of light to facilitate more accurate *perforation* of *stamps* during the manufacturing process. 2) the markings (see also *Electric Eye Dashes*, *Electric Eye Margin Line*, *Electric Eye Gutter Bar*, and *Electric Eye Frame Bars*) in the *margins* and *gutters* of *sheets* of stamps that enable the electric eye device to accomplish its purpose of more accurately perforating stamps. Stamps with electric eye markings were first sold in 1935.

Electric Eye Dashes – vertical dashes in the vertical *gutter* between the right and left *panes* used by the *electric eye* in the *perforating* process. First used experimentally in 1933.

Electric Eye Frame Bars – horizontal lines in the *sheet* margin used by the *electric eye* in the *perforating* process. This marking was first used in 1939.

Electric Eye Gutter Bar – horizontal line in the left *sheet* margin at the end of the horizontal sheet *gutter* that was used by the *electric* eye in the *perforating* process. This marking replaced the *Electric Eye Margin Line* on some plates in 1939.

Electric Eye Margin Line – horizontal line in the right *margin* of a *sheet* at the end of the horizontal sheet *gutter* that was used by the *electric eye* in the *perforating* process. First used experimentally in 1933.

Electronic Computer-Originated Mail – see *E-COM*.

Embossed Double Impression – a *stamped envelope* on which the *embossed* stamp-like *indicium* is doubled. Such doubling usually involves some overlapping. An *error*.

Embossed Envelope – a *stamped envelope* produced by the *embossing* process. Example: New York World's Fair Issue (U546).

Embossing – the process of impressing a *design* into paper with a *die* so that the design is raised up on the paper; similar to a rotary seal. The embossing process was used for most *stamped envelopes* of the nineteenth and twentieth centuries.

Encased Postage – a *postage stamp* encased in a coin-like container that was treated as if it were a coin with a *face value* equivalent to that printed on the stamp. Encased postage was used in the Civil War period. *Scott* numbers are prefixed with EP.

Endwise Coil – *coil stamps* with *perforations* along the top and bottom, as opposed to a *sidewise coil*.

Engraver – a skilled craftsperson who engraves a *die*.

Engraving – a process by which a stamp's *design* is cut into a metal *die*. The design is then transferred to a *transfer roll* and from there to a printing *plate*. The recesses created by transferring the design to the plate are filled with ink in the printing process. Paper that is forced under pressure into these recesses picks up ink, thus reproducing the design on the paper. A distinguishing characteristic of the engraving process is that the dried ink on the printed sheet has texture that can be felt by lightly touching the surface with a fingernail or a pair of stamp tongs. Although few modern stamps are printed by the engrav-

ing method, it was the dominant method of stamp production until well into the middle of the twentieth century.

Entire – 1) an intact piece of *postal stationery*, that is, a piece of postal stationery that has not been reduced in size. Not a *cut square*. 2) any intact *cover*.

Entry – the image of a *stamp* on a printing *plate*.

Ephemera – printed material of a transient nature, not intended to be stored, filed, or kept.

Error – a major and total production mistake, often defined as a mistake that can be identically repeated. Examples: Inverts (such as *Scott* C3a), imperforate stamps that were intended to be *perforated*, use of the wrong perforation *gauge*, and totally missing colors or *tagging*.

Errors, Freaks and Oddities – a collective term for *philatelic* material that deviates in some manner from an intended norm. An *error* may be considered to have a greater deviation from the intended norm than a *freak*. *Oddities* encompass a wide range of unusual *variations*.

Essay – artwork officially proposed as the *design* for a *stamp*. An essay is artwork that was not adopted for the design; hence it differs from the design that was issued. A *Progressive Die Proof* is a special type of essay sometimes referred to as a "die essay". *Scott* numbers contain an E preceded by a number.

Etiquette – a gummed *label* placed on an envelope indicating a desired postal service. *Air mail* etiquettes are the most common.

Europe-Pan America Round Flight – 1930 flight of the Graf Zeppelin from Germany to South America to Lakehurst, New Jersey and then back to Germany. The U.S. issued three high value *air mail stamps*, the *Zepps*, for this flight.

Even Tagging – *tagging* that appears smooth or even when viewed under short wave *ultraviolet light*, as opposed to *mottled* or *grainy tagging*. An example is the 1995 Milton Hershey stamp, (2933).

Event Cover – a *cover*, usually with a *cachet*, marking an event. Examples of event covers include: first flight covers, airport dedication covers, and stamp show covers.

Exchange Label – gummed labels used by post offices designated as *exchange offices* to distinguish and account for international *registered* mail during the period from 1883 to 1911. They are known from at least 25 post offices, with New York being the most common.

Exchange Office – a postal facility, typically in a large port city, which handled the "exchange" of mail between the U.S. and foreign countries.

Expertization – the process by which an expertizing service renders an authoritative opinion on the genuineness of *stamps* and *covers*. Most authoritative opinions are provided by the American Philatelic Expertizing Service (a service of the *APS*), and by The *Philatelic Foundation*.

Exploded Booklet – a *booklet* that has been disassembled, usually to facilitate the display of the individual components: covers, *panes*, *interleaving,* and staple.

Express Mail – 1) an expedited delivery service provided by the Postal Service to the general public since 1971. 2) a premium priced government service in the early (pre-stamp) nineteenth century. 3) a private service provided since the mid-nineteenth century by companies such as *Wells, Fargo and Co.*, which operated "The *Pony Express*". An 1845 law prohibited private express companies from carrying letter mail unless regular *postage* was paid in addition to the express company charges.

F

F – a *marginal marking* punched on *flat plates*, usually to the left of the **UR** *plate number*, indicating that the plates were hardened and approved for use. Most commonly used in the 1920s and 1930s.

F Grill – one of several types of *grills* used in the nineteenth century, about 9 x 13 mm in size. Example: *Scott* 92.

"F" Press – *web-fed offset-intaglio press* (four color offset, three color intaglio) obtained by the *BEP* in 1991. The first *stamp* printed on this press was the 1992 World Columbian Stamp Expo, (2616).

"F" Stamps – *nondenominated stamps* issued in 1991 with an assigned *postage* value of 29¢.

FAM – see *Foreign Air Mail Route*.

FDOI – see *First Day of Issue*.

FIPEX – see *Fifth International Philatelic Exhibition*.

FPO – see *Fleet Post Office*.

Face – the front of a *stamp*, that is, the side bearing the printed *design*. Compare *Face Value*.

Face Value – the *postage* value of a *stamp*, generally indicated in numerals printed on the face of the stamp.

Facing – the orienting of envelopes by the Postal Service in a consistent manner for subsequent sorting or mail processing operations.

Facing Slip – a piece of paper placed by a postal employee on the top of a bundle of mail as a part of the sorting and distribution process. It was usually *postmarked*.

Facsimile Mail Service – a service provided briefly by the *USPS* beginning in 1971 that enabled customers to send fax messages which were then delivered by the post office in specially designed envelopes.

False Franking – use of a *stamp*, generally on *bulk-rate* mail, which pays only a portion of the actual cost of mailing the item.

Famous Americans – series of *commemorative postage stamps* honoring authors, poets, educators, scientists, composers, and artists appearing in 1940. Begins with *Scott* 859.

Fancy Cancel – a *cancel* that is pictorial or geometric in nature, produced by a local post office.

Farley's Follies – a nickname given to a 1935 *special printing* of *stamps* (752-771). Postmaster General James Farley had given selected individuals **imperforate**, ungummed, uncut **sheets** of 1933-1934 *commemoratives*. After protests from collectors similar imperforate sheets were made available to the public at *face value*.

(The) Farwell Company – a Chicago firm that produced its own *private coils* for use in *Schermack affixing machines*.

Farwell Perforations – *perforations* privately applied to *imperforate flat plate postage stamps* by the **Farwell Co.** for use in *Schermack affixing machines*.

Feed Lines – lines placed upon certain *flat plates* as an aid to the proper placement of sheets of paper upon the plate.

Fergusson & Sons (J.W.) – private printer of postage stamps. Example: **Scott** 2454, which is one of the 5¢ Canoe stamps.

Fermented Fruit Juice Stamps – *revenue stamps,* used in 1933 pending the repeal of prohibition, to pay the federal tax on certain wines and fermented juice products legalized by Congress effective April 7, 1933. *Scott* numbers are prefixed with REF.

Fifth Bureau Issue – see *Presidential Series*.

Fifth International Philatelic Exhibition – one in a series of international stamp shows hosted in the U.S. once every ten years. It was held in New York City in 1956. A *stamp* (1075) and *souvenir sheet* (1076) were issued in conjunction with this show.

Finisher Initials – see *Plate Finisher Initials*.

Finishing – the processing of a *web* of printed *stamps* into units ready for sale to customers.

First Bureau Issue – see *Series of 1894*.

First Class Mail – the class of mail required for sending letters, *post cards*, *postal cards*, invoices, statements, and payments. First Class Mail is sealed against inspection, a feature that permits private messages. *Priority Mail* is a form of First Class mail.

First Day Cover – a *cover cancelled* on the day a *stamp* is issued, in the city in which it is released. Modern First Day Covers may actually be cancelled up to 30 days after the date of issue, and not necessarily in the city whose *postmarks* they bear. First Day Covers may be addressed or unaddressed, and with or without *cachets*. See also *Unofficial First Day Cover* and *Second Day Cover*.

First Day of Issue – the date on which a *stamp* is issued.

First Flight Cover – a *cover* flown on a flight marking the inauguration of a new air mail route, or a new stop on an existing air mail route, or the initial flight of an airline.

First Issue Revenue Stamps – *revenue stamps* (R1-R102) issued from 1862-1871 to help finance the Civil War.

Flag Cancel – a *cancel* (generally a *machine cancel*) that features a flag as part of its *design*. Flag cancels were common in the late nineteenth and early twentieth century, most of them produced by *American Postal Machine Co.* machines. See also *Involute flag cancel*.

Flat Plate Press – a press that prints from a flat *plate* (as opposed to a curved or *cylindrical* plate). Prior to 1915 only the Flat Plate Press was used to print *stamps*.

Flats – Post Office term for large envelopes in the *mailstream*.

Fleet Post Office (FPO) – a military post office for Navy and Marine personnel. APOs and FPOs are often referenced together.

Flexography – *Letterpress* printing that employs a resilient synthetic or rubber composition *plate*.

Flier – the most enduring *cancelling machine* ever used by the Post Office; manufactured by **International Postal Supply Company**. Introduced in 1888, some later versions of the machine were still in service at the beginning of the 21st century.

Floating Plate Numbers – numbers on a **plate block** whose positions vary from **pane** to pane, thus creating a large number of possible combinations. Example: 1976 13¢ Currier & Ives Christmas stamp (1702). Plate numbers on most **stamp panes** do not float.

Flora & Fauna Series – *definitive* series of *postage stamps* begun in 1990. Begins with **Scott** 2476.

Flown Cover – a *cover* that has been carried by *air mail*, and bears evidence of having been flown.

Fluorescence – stamp paper or inks containing fluorescent brighteners that glow brighter while exposed to short or long wave *ultraviolet light*. There is no afterglow, and fluorescent papers usually glow a bluish-white. Stamp inks containing fluorescent brighteners can glow in a variety of colors.

Flyspecking – the act of seeking, examining, studying, or collecting **stamps** with minor variations.

Folded Letter – a sheet of paper with a message written on one side, and folded in such a way that the name and address of the recipient could be written on the exposed blank side of the paper. Folded letters were gradually made obsolete by the introduction of envelopes.

Foldover (under) – *stamps* affected during the printing or *perforating* process by a paperfold, often producing spectacular *freaks*.

Food Order Stamps – *stamps* produced by the **BEP** as part of a subsidy program that enabled low income families to purchase food at grocery stores.

Foreign Air Mail Route – *air mail* service provided by contract carriers, on established routes, to foreign countries.

Foreign Entry – see *Foreign Transfer*.

Foreign Transfer – 1) the appearance on a *plate* (and resulting *stamp*) of the remnants of a wrong *design*. This occurs when an incorrect *transfer roll* is used to enter a design on a plate, and when, upon discovery of the mistake, the incorrect impression is not completely *burnished* out before the correct one is entered in its place. 2) the intact appearance of an incorrect design on a plate (and resulting stamp), caused by the undetected use of a wrong transfer roll by a *siderographer*. Classic example: 5¢ rose stamps of 1917 (467, 485, and 505).

Forwarding – the service of sending a piece of mail to an address other than the one originally on the *cover* in order to deliver it to the person to whom it is addressed. This service has, at various times, been provided both with and without additional charge.

Forwarding Agent – a person or entity, usually in a foreign city, who sends a piece of mail entrusted to him on to an addressee in the most expeditious manner. This service was made obsolete by the formation of the **Universal Postal Union**.

Four Bar Cancel – a *duplex handstamp* consisting of a circular *postmark* and four parallel bars as a *cancel*.

Fourth Bureau Issue – see *Series of 1922*.

Fourth Class Mail – obsolete mail classification for packages, also known as *parcel post*.

Fractional Usages – use of a portion of a *stamp*. Stamps were sometimes cut in half (or some other fraction) and placed on an envelope in an attempt to pay *postage* equal to one half (or other fraction) of the *face value* of the whole stamp. Occasionally an approved practice, sometimes tolerated, especially when there was a shortage of stamps in a needed *denomination*. Fractional usages are generally collected *tied* on cover. One half of a stamp is known as a bisect.

Frame – the outer portion of a stamp *design*, which encloses the central portion (*vignette*) of the design.

Frank(ing) – an indication on an envelope (e.g. *stamp*, *meter*, *PVI*, signature, or printed message) of *postage* being paid or that the envelope is to be carried without payment of postage.

Franklin-Washington Series – see *Washington-Franklin Head Issues*.

Freak – a mistake in production caused by an unusual circumstance not likely to be identically repeated, such as a color shift, *perforation* shift, inking irregularity or paper fold. A freak is a less severe and less valuable mistake than an *error*.

"Free" – *handstamp* marking sometimes used on *free franked* mail.

Free Frank – the right to send mail without payment of *postage*. Usually indicated by a signature where a *stamp* is usually affixed. This privilege has been extended to various individuals at different times, including government officials and military personnel.

French Occupation Issues – see *Allied Military Government Stamps*.

Front – the front (face) of a *cover* from which the back panels have been removed. A front is less desirable than an *entire*.

Fugitive Ink – soluble ink that tends to dissolve when placed in water or watermark fluid. See also *Aniline Ink* and *Pink Backs*.

Future Delivery Stamp – *revenue stamp* issued to pay the tax on a future delivery instrument. All Future Delivery Stamps are *overprints* of the *Documentary Stamps* of 1917. *Scott* numbers are prefixed with RC.

G

G – prefix letter used by *Guilford Gravure, Inc.* in front of the *plate number* on its modern *stamp* production.

"G" Stamps – *nondenominated stamps* issued in 1995 with assigned *postage* values of 5¢, 20¢, 25¢, and 32¢.

GPO – see *1) General Post Office. 2) Government Printing Office.*

Gaps in Tagging – *tagging* gaps and bright lines as observed under *ultraviolet light*. They can be caused by: the gap where tagging *plates* butt together; screws and clips used to hold tagging mats to their cylinders; the scraping action of perforating wheels and guides; scratches and foreign matter on the tagging plates or rollers; cleaning solvent residue on the tagging rollers; etc.

Gauge – see *Perforation.*

General Delivery – the delivery of mail over the post office counter to customers in a community without local delivery or post office boxes, or to other persons, such as travelers, who lack an address in the community.

General Post Office – typically the main post office in a city.

German Occupation Issues – see *Allied Military Government Stamps*.

Ghost Tagging Images - portions of a *stamp's* image, or more commonly the *plate number* from the just previously printed *plate*, *setoff* on the following printed stamp. Ghosts occur during offset tagging, are usually faint, and slightly off center.

Giori Press – *sheet-fed*, multicolor, *intaglio*, *rotary* presses that were first used to print the 4¢ American Flag stamp of 1957 (1094). This press could print in three colors and is best known for the bright, multicolored *commemorative postage stamps* of the late 1950s through the 1970s.

Glow-Bar Tagging – vertical bar of *tagging* used on some *Postal Stationery* issues. Size varies, and the bar is usually to the left of the *indicium*. Examples: 1982 20¢ Purple Heart *stamped envelope* (U603); 1987 14¢ Plow *postal card* (UX115).

Goebel Booklet Forming Machine – machine introduced at the *BEP* in 1977 for the manufacture of booklets.

Government Coil – *coil stamps* produced by the *BEP*, or by a private manufacturer working under contract to the Post Office, as opposed to coil stamps produced by a private company from *BEP* sheets for its own proprietary purpose.

Government Flight – *air mail* flight on which the pilot was a federal employee, as opposed to *Contract Air Mail Flights*.

Government Printing Office – federal agency that has printed all *postal cards* since 1910 and many *aerograms*.

Grainy Tagging – *tagging* with an uneven, grainy appearance when viewed using *ultraviolet light*, as opposed to *even* or *mottled tagging*.

Gravure – a printing process utilizing *cylinders* (a separate one for each color) upon which the *design* has been recessed in dots by photographic and chemical means. The *web* is printed directly from these cylinders. The first *stamp* to be produced by gravure was the 1967 5¢ Eakins (1335).

Great Americans Issue – the longest running *definitive stamp* series, issued between 1980 and 1999. Its 63 *face-different* stamps give it more face-different stamps than any other series. The first *Scott* number is 1844.

Gridiron Cancels – common nineteenth century *cancellations* consisting of rows of parallel lines enclosed in a circle.

Grill – 1) a device with a waffle-like pattern of parallel rows of raised points that is used to break the paper fiber of *stamps* 2) the waffle-like pattern of raised, broken points on a stamp, created by a grilling device. Stamps were grilled from 1867-1871 by the *National Bank Note Co.* as a security device. By breaking the fibers of paper it was hoped to make the ink used in *cancellations* more completely absorbed and thus harder to wash out.

Gripper Cracks – cracks formed in a curved *rotary press plate* at the spot where clamps hold the plate to the press.

Guam – a U.S. territory for which *overprinted stamps* were used from 1899-1901.

Guide Dot – a dot placed upon an engraved *plate* as a guide to the *siderographer* in properly placing subjects upon the plate.

Guide Line Block – a *block* of *stamps* that is divided in half, either vertically or horizontally, by a *guide line*. See also *Center Line Block*

Guide Line Pair – a pair of *flat plate stamps* with a segment of a *guide line* between them. This term is most commonly used in association with *coil stamps*.

Guide Lines – lines inscribed on a *plate* as an aid to *perforating* or cutting a *sheet* into *panes*. Guide lines are not the same as *Joint Lines*.

Guilford Gravure Incorporated – private printer of *postage stamps*. Their association with stamp production began when their plant and presses were used by *BEP* employees to print the 1970 Anti-Pollution Issue (1410-1413) and 1970 Christmas stamps (1414-1418).

Gum – the adhesive substance applied to the back of *stamps* that enables them to be affixed to an envelope. See also *Water-activated Gum* and *Self-Adhesive Stamp*

Gum Breakers – the horizontal or slightly diagonal impressions created on the *gum* of *rotary sheet stamps* by physically "breaking" the gum. Breakers look something like speed-bumps, and were created as part of the *perforating* process. The intended purpose of breakers was to reduce the tendency of *panes* to curl. Gum breakers are known in several configurations, and were used from about 1920 until as late as 1970.

Gum Crease – a naturally occurring crease found on *flat plate stamps*, usually caused by handling during production.

Gum Ridges – vertical ridges of **gum** on the backs of **rotary sheet stamps**, created as a part of the printing process when gum was applied to stamps using rollers that had ridges engraved on them. Ridges are known in two varieties: 1/16 and 1/32 of an inch apart. The intended purpose of ridges was to make stamps adhere better. They were used in the 1920s and 1930s.

Gum Skip – a generally small area on a **stamp** to which no **gum** adhered during production. Gum skips are most commonly encountered on **flat plate** stamps from the first part of the twentieth century.

Gutter – the margin between the **panes** of a **sheet** of **stamps**. The gutters of mid-twentieth century sheets may contain markings such as dashes or crosses that aid in **perforation**. The gutters of modern sheets, containing more than the traditional four panes, may contain other **marginal markings**, including **plate numbers**. The **margin** around the outside edge of the sheet is not a gutter. Gutters are located only between panes.

Gutter Block – a **block** of **stamps** that includes complete **stamps** from two or four adjacent **panes**, and the **gutter or gutters** between them. Gutter blocks are generally not available to collectors when the stamps are sold only in **pane** form. They are available to collectors when stamps are sold in **sheet** form.

Gutter Pair – a **pair** of complete **stamps** separated by a **gutter**. A gutter pair is of more value than a corresponding **guttersnipe**.

Guttersnipe – a **stamp** or stamps to which is attached the full adjacent **gutter**, including **perforations**, and sometimes including portions of the stamp(s) on the other side of the gutter. A guttersnipe is a **freak** that may be caused by a paper fold or a misregistration in the production process.

H

"H" Stamps – *nondenominated stamps* issued in 1998 with an assigned *postage* value of 33¢.

HPO – see *Highway Post Office*.

Hammarskjöld Special Printing (1204) – a printing of the 1962 Hammarskjöld Issue with the yellow background *inverted*. When several *panes* of the Hammarskjöld *stamp* unintentionally reached the public with the background inverted, the Postmaster General intentionally printed a large quantity of this *error* for sale to collectors.

Handback – a *cover* that is *cancelled* at a post office window and returned to the person presenting it. A handback cover is never carried in the *mailstream*.

Hand Cancel – a *cancellation* applied with a hand-held device, as opposed to a cancellation applied by *machine*.

Handstamp – 1) a hand-held device used by a postal worker to *cancel* a *stamp* or apply a *postal marking*. 2) the impression left by a handstamp on a *cover*.

Handwound – the labor-intensive process of making the earliest *coils* before the introduction of a mechanical process. See also *autowound*.

Hardening – the process of taking a soft *die*, *transfer roll*, or *plate* and making it metallurgically hard. In the process of producing *engraved stamps*, the *design* can only be worked into soft steel, but is generally only transferred from hard steel. The hardening process can be reversed. That is, a hardened die, roll or plate can be made metallurgically soft again.

Harrow Perforator – a plate with pins that perforates a complete sheet or pane of stamps with a single stroke. Its name comes from its resemblance to the farming implement of the same name.

Hartford Manufacturing Company – manufacturer of *stamped envelopes and wrappers from 1903-1907*.

Helicopter Mail – mail transported by helicopter between an airfield and a post office. Instituted in 1946.

Hidden Images – obscured images, placed on certain modern *postage stamps,* which can be viewed with a *Stamp Decoder.*

Highway Post Office – a motorized bus-like vehicle used by the Post Office. As it traveled along a route connecting a number of post offices, mail would be picked up, sorted and delivered (to post offices, not individual customers). The first HPO began service in 1941, the last was discontinued in 1974. *Postmarks* usually contain the initials H.P.O.

Hologram – an image which, viewed at an angle, appears to be three-dimensional. Holograms are used on selected modern *postage stamps* and *postal envelopes.*

Hopkinson Memorial Award – prestigious award, given annually by the *United States Stamp Society,* for the best article published in *The United States Specialist.*

Hopkinson Trophy – prestigious award given at the annual meeting of the *United States Stamp Society* for the best exhibit of twentieth century material by a USSS member.

Horizontal Half – a *fractional* use of a *stamp;* a horizontal *bisect;* a stamp cut in half horizontally.

Huck Multicolor Press – a nine-color, *web-fed,* *intaglio* press used by the *BEP* from 1968 to 1976. The Huck Press could print, *tag,* gum, and *perforate stamps* in one continuous operation. The first stamp printed from this press was the 1968 Christmas stamp (1363).

Huck-Cottrell Presses – a group of high speed, *intaglio,* *web-fed* presses first used to print the bi-color International Red Cross *stamp* of 1952 (1016). These presses were similar to a *Stickney press,* but faster. The last Huck-Cottrell presses were decommissioned in 1985.

Hunting Permit Stamps – see *Duck Stamps*

Hurletron marks – solid right-angle triangular *electric-eye* markings for use with the eight-color *intaglio-gravure* press. First used on the Civilian Conservation Corp issue (2037).

Hybrid Proof – generally, a nineteenth century *plate proof* cut close and typically mounted on *India paper* which is then mounted on a larger piece of cardboard. It may also show die *sinkage.* Some hybrid proofs were made from *die proofs.* Hybrid proofs resemble *Large Die Proofs.*

Hyphen-Hole Perforations – *perforations* in the shape of comparatively large rectangles, applied to *imperforate stamps* by *Schermack Mailing Company,* for use in *affixing machines.*

I

IBI – see *Identification Based Indicia.*

IRC – see *International Reply Coupon.*

IRT – see *Integrated Retail Terminals.*

Identification Based Indicia – a commercial product which is a computer generated, *postage* paying, stamp-like imprint authorized by the *USPS.*

Illegal Use – an illegal use of a *stamp,* such as a *revenue* stamp used in an attempt to pay *postage.*

Image Tagging – the *tagging* of only the image (*design*) or a portion of the image on a *stamp.* Examples: 1988 25¢ Classic Autos (2381-2385); 1999 33¢ American Glass (3325-3328).

Imperforate – *stamps* without *perforations.* The earliest stamps were issued in *imperforate* form. Imperforate stamps that were intended to be *perforated* are *errors.*

Imprint – design containing the name of the producer of the stamps, which appears on the sheet margin, usually near the *plate number.*

Imprint Block – a *margin block* of *stamps,* analogous to a *plate block,* which contains an *imprint* instead of a *plate number.*

India Paper – a thin, tough, translucent paper used for making *die proofs*.

Indicia – plural of *indicium*.

Indicium – 1) the stamp-like impression on *postal stationery*. 2) the imprint of postage made by a postage *meter*.

Ink-Jet Cancel – a dot matrix *cancel* also known as a *Sprayed-on Cancel*.

In-line Perforator – a perforating device included in the mechanized portion of a printing press, automatically activated as the printed *web* or *sheets* pass through the station.

Instructional Marking – see *Auxiliary Marking*.

Insured Mail – mailed articles insured for a fee by the Postal Service.

Intaglio – a process of printing from the recessed portion of a printing *plate*. See also *Engraving*.

Intagliocolor 8 Press – high-speed, three-color, *sheet-fed intaglio* press used at the *BEP* from 1976 to 1985.

Integral – a device that applied initials, date and precancel simultaneously.

Integrated Retail Terminals – Computers in post offices that weigh items, calculate *postage*, print receipts, and maintain records.

Interleaves – sheetlets of glassine paper placed between *panes* in stamp *booklets*.

International Envelope Corporation – manufacturer of early and mid-twentieth century *stamped envelopes* and *wrappers*.

International Mail – mail sent from the United States to a foreign nation or sent from a foreign nation to the United States, as opposed to *Domestic Mail*.

International Philatelic Exhibition – one in a series of international stamp shows hosted once every decade in the U.S. Held in New York City in 1926, the Battle of White Plains *stamp* and *souvenir sheet* (629, 630) were issued in conjunction with this show.

International Postal Supply Company – major manufacturer of *cancelling machines* in use from the 1880s into the 21st century.

International Reply Coupon – a coupon sold by the post office that is redeemable by its recipient in a foreign country for return *postage*. *Scott* numbers are prefixed with IRC.

International Vending Machine Company – Baltimore-based manufacturer of *vending machines* and *private coils*.

International Vending Machine Company Perforations – *perforations* privately applied to *imperforate flat plate stamps* by the International Vending Machine Company for use in its *vending machines*.

Interphil '76 – one in a series of international stamp shows hosted once every decade in the U.S. Held in Philadelphia in 1976, a *stamp* (1632) was issued to honor Interphil '76.

Interrupted Mail – mail that has been delayed by some external event such as a plane or train crash, war, fire, etc.

Invert – a *stamp* or item of *postal stationery* on which one portion of the *design* is upside down in relation to the rest of the design. Inverts can only be produced when the production process requires at least two independent passes through a press. Inverts are *errors*.

Inverted Jenny – nickname for the 24¢ *air mail error stamp* of 1918 on which the airplane (*vignette*) was printed upside down in relation to the *frame* (C3a).

Involute Flag Cancel – a *flag cancel* in which the flag is folded.

Irradiated Mail – mail irradiated by the *U.S. Postal Service* during the anthrax terrorism of 2001-2002.

Italian Occupation Issues – see *Allied Military Government Stamps*.

J

Jeffries Banknote Company – subcontractor to *American Bank Note Co*. for the 1991 $14 *postage stamp* (2542).

Jenny – see *Inverted Jenny*.

Joint Issue – *stamps* issued by two or more countries simultaneously, with similar *designs*, honoring the same person or event. Example: 1975 Apollo-Soyuz Space Issue (1569–1570).

Joint Line – the printed line produced on the *web* by the *rotary press* at the point where two *plates* met. Two plates were used in combination with each other on the classic *rotary press*. Each plate would fit over half of the printing *cylinder*. Ink would gather in the joints between the plates, leaving an impression (a joint line) on the web. One complete revolution of the press cylinder created two joint lines on the web. Joint lines were produced on both *sheet* and *coil stamps*, but only those produced on the coil stamps are commonly collected. A joint line is not the same as a *Guide Line*.

Joint Line Gap Pair – A *joint line pair* of *precancelled coil stamps* that shows the gap between the auxiliary *plates* used to print the precancel.

Joint Line Pair – a pair of *coil stamps* produced from the *rotary press* with a *joint line* between them. A joint line pair will contain one stamp from each of two different plates. See also *Joint Line*.

Junk Mail – nickname for advertisements send by *bulk rate mail*.

K

K – prefix letter used by *KCS Industries* in front of the *plate number* on its modern *stamp* production.

KCS Industries – private printer and finisher of *postage stamps*. Example: *non-denominated* Tulip booklet of 1991 (2520).

Kansas City Roulettes – improvised *perforations* applied by *roulette* to *imperforate* 1¢ and 2¢ *postage stamps* (408, 409) by the *postmaster* of Kansas City in 1914 and 1915.

Kansas-Nebraska Overprints – *Series of 1922 postage stamps* overprinted "Kans." or "Nebr." in 1929 for sale in those states, but valid in all states (658-679).

Killer Cancel – a *cancellation* that is very heavy, obliterating most of the *design* of a *stamp*.

Knife – 1) the pattern used to cut an envelope from a sheet of paper. 2) the device that cuts *stamps* apart as they are fed through an *affixing machine*.

L

LL – Lower left. Refers to the lower left *pane* from a traditional *sheet* of four panes. These initials are also used to describe *plate blocks* taken from the lower left corner of the sheets.

LR – Lower right. Refers to the lower right *pane* from a traditional *sheet* of four panes. These initials are also used to describe *plate blocks* taken from the lower right corner of the sheets.

L perforator – an L-shaped manually fed *perforating* machine on which stamps receive horizontal perforations on one leg of the L and vertical perforations on the other.

Label – a stamp-like adhesive of no postal value, often used for promotional purposes. *Christmas Seals* are examples of labels. "Label" may also be used to describe the stamp-like units that bear messages that occasionally appear in *stamp booklets*.

Large Bank Notes – *postage stamps* produced from 1870-1888 by the *National, Continental* and *American Bank Note Companies* (134-218). See also *Small Bank Notes*.

Large Die Proof – a *die proof* printed on card stock that is considerably larger than the image created by the die, as opposed to a **Small Die Proof**. The die print on a Large Die Proof is located in a recess on the card known as a **sinkage**.

Large Holes – *perforation* holes that are larger than other perforations holes of the same gauge. For example, **Scott** 1055 in the **Liberty Issue** exists with perforation holes of two different sizes (large and small) even though all are perforation gauge 10. Compare: **Small Holes**.

Last Day of Sale – 1) the day a **stamp** is removed from sale by the **Postal Service**. 2) a **slogan cancellation** applied to stamps on the last day of sale. A "Last Day of Sale" cancellation was used for the first time on March 16, 1997.

Late Fee – 1) payment required for mail accepted for dispatch (usually on a particular ship) after the **closing of the mails**. 2) a **Supplementary Mail Marking** applied to **Supplementary Mail**.

Laundry Tags – two-sided address cards used on suitcase-like containers (mostly by college students) to mail dirty laundry home to be cleaned and returned.

Layout Marks – dots, lines, and arcs that are scribed by a **siderographer** on a blank **plate** to determine the precise location for each entry to be made from the **transfer roll**.

Leader – a strip of brown kraft paper (white paper beginning in 1948) attached to the leading (first) **stamp** on a roll of **coil stamps**.

Leavitt, Thomas – major manufacturer of **cancelling machines** in use from the 1870s to the 1890s. Leavitt cancelling machines were the first to receive extensive use.

Legends of Hollywood – series of **commemorative stamps** honoring famous Hollywood personalities. The first stamp in this series is the 1995 Marilyn Monroe (2967).

Legends of the West – a **pane** of twenty **stamps** that was recalled because an incorrect picture appeared on the stamp honoring Bill Pickett (2870). A limited number of recalled panes was sold by public lottery. The corrected version (2869) was then printed and issued.

Letterpress – a process of printing which is the exact opposite of **intaglio**, that is, the inked portion of the **plate** is raised above the surface of the plate, as opposed to be being recessed below it. Letterpress (see also **typography**) has been used to produce **overprints** on U.S. **stamps**. It is also used in perfecting (back printing) inscriptions on the gum of many stamps and to print most modern **stamped envelopes**.

Letter Sheet – an item of **postal stationery** similar in format to an **aerogram**. Example: **Scott** U293. Privately produced letter sheets exist.

Liberty Series – **definitive** series of **postage stamps** appearing in 1954, consisting of **sheet stamps**, **coils**, and **booklets**. Also known as Sixth Bureau Issue. First **Scott** number is 1030a.

Library Mail Rate – special rate for mailing certain materials to or from certain non-profit organizations, a sub-category of Package Service. Commercial libraries could also use this rate if the contents were appropriate (books, motion pictures, etc.).

Line Engraving – see **Engraving**.

Line Gaps – the gap between **plates** printing **precancels** that appears on **coil stamps** at regular intervals.

Line Pair – see **Joint Line Pair**.

Line Perforator – A **perforator** that applies lines of perforation holes in only one direction.

Liner – slick paper used as peelable backing for **self-adhesive stamps**.

Linerless Coil – **self-adhesive coil stamps** sold in a roll without a **liner**. Example: 1997 32¢ Flag over Porch stamp (3133).

Literary Arts Series – series of **commemorative stamps** honoring important American writers, begun with the John Steinbeck stamp of 1979 (1773).

Lithography – printing from a smooth surface on which the area not to be printed repels the ink. One form of lithography is direct lithography, in which printing occurs without the use of an intermediate roller or blanket. Some early Post Office *Seals* were printed from such direct lithography. Indirect lithography uses an intermediate roller or blanket, and is called *offset*. See also *Offset Lithography*.

Little America – the Antarctic base of Admiral Richard Byrd that was home to a special post office, for which the "Little America Issue" (733) was released in 1933. *Covers* bear a "Little America" *postmark*.

Local Letter – a letter mailed within a city at a *rate* sometimes less than the regular *first class* rate. Such local letters are of two types: those mailed in cities with *carrier service* and those mailed in cities without carrier service. Some form of local letter rate was in existence from 1863 to 1968. See also *Drop Letter*.

Local Post – a private postal system operating in a limited area, usually a major city. Example: Hussey's Post, New York, N.Y. Local posts once played a significant role in mail delivery.

Local Precancel – a precancel applied to *stamps* locally, as opposed to being applied at the *Bureau of Engraving and Printing*. See also *Bureau Precancel*.

Local Stamps – *stamps* issued by private companies operating in limited service areas. Most of these stamps were issued by companies operating in a single city, but local stamps were also issued by independent mail routes and *express* companies. *Scott* numbers contain an L.

LOOK Coil – *phosphor tagged* version of the 3-cent Statue of Liberty *coil* in the 1954 *Liberty Series*, issued without advance notice in October 1966 for use on LOOK Magazine promotional mailings. Use by LOOK Magazine was limited to about a six month period, after which the *stamps* were recalled, marking the first time the *U.S. Post Office Department* bought stamps back from the private sector for distribution to collectors. *Tagging* applied by rubber mats and glows brightly under *ultraviolet light*. See also *LOOK Coil Reprint*.

LOOK Coil Reprint – a *special printing* of the *LOOK Coil* produced to satisfy collector demand. The reprint became a new *variety* because the *BEP* applied the *tagging* by metal plates. The tagging on the reprint glows duller and grainier under *ultraviolet light* than the tagging on the original LOOK Coil.

Louisiana Purchase Exposition Stamps – *commemorative postage stamps* issued for the St. Louis Exposition of 1904 (323-327).

Lozenges – the bi-colored border frequently found on *air mail postal stationery*.

Luminescence – the light given off by *fluorescent* brighteners and *phosphorescent tagging* in paper and ink when activated by *ultraviolet light*.

Lunar New Year Series – series of twelve *postage stamps* honoring the Chinese New Year. The first of the series is *Scott* 2720, issued in 1992.

M

M – prefix letter used by *3M Corporation* in front of the *plate number* on its modern *stamp* production.

MDI Booklets – hand made *booklets* produced by Minnesota Diversified Industries. Most contained 15 *water-activated gum sheet stamps* placed within blue cardboard covers having a rectangular opening through which the stamps could be seen. By comparison, other MDI booklets contained *self-adhesive stamps* that were produced from pieces of *web* originally intended to be processed into *convertible booklets*. With these booklets, special die cut mats were used to create booklet panes of

14, 15, or 16 stamps that were glued into the blue covers.

MOB – see *Money Order Business Cancellation*.

MPO – see *Mobile Post Office*.

MPP – see *Mailer's Permit Postmark*.

Machine Cancel – a *cancellation* applied by a machine, as opposed to one applied by a hand-held device. Machine cancels were first used in the 1870s.

"Mail Early in the Day" – a slogan used as a *marginal marking* from 1966 to 1978.

Mailer's Permit Postmark – a *postmark* applied to mail by a mailer prior to being submitted to the Postal Service. Such private postmarks were first authorized in 1925.

Mailgram – a joint effort between Western Union and the *USPS* in which Western Union handled electronic transmission with hard copies delivered by the Postal Service. The service is known to have been provided from 1972 to 1992.

Mailomat – a coin operated, self-service *Pitney Bowes* machine that imprinted a *meter* and retained mail for collection. It was primarily used in the 1940s.

Mailometer Company – successor corporation to The *Schermack Co.*

Mailometer Perforations – see *Schermack Perforations*.

Mail Stream – the movement of mail from the moment it is entrusted into the care of the Postal Service until it is delivered to its recipient.

Main Post Office – the primary post office of a city that has secondary post office facilities. Formerly known as *General Post Office*.

Make-shift booklets – see *MDI booklets*.

Make-up Rate Stamp – a *nondenominated postage stamp*, intended for use on *first class* mail, printed in anticipation of an increase in postal rates. The stamp is equivalent in value to the amount of the increase. Example: Weathervane stamp of 1998 (3257).

Manhardt-Alexander – subcontractor to *Ashton-Potter (USA) LTD* for the printing of the 1994 *lithographed* American Music Series *postage stamps* (2854-2861).

Manila Paper – a coarse, light brown paper used in the manufacture of *stamped envelopes*.

Manuscript Cancel – *cancellation* of a *stamp* by pen or marker. Some early manuscript cancellations were applied by post offices with no cancelling device. Modern manuscript cancellations are often applied in the field to stamps that escaped normal cancellation. Stamps with manuscript cancellations are considered by some to be less desirable than stamps with other types of cancellations.

Maps – nickname for *airmail stamps* of 1926-1927 (C7-C9) that include a map in their *design*.

Margin – any printed or unprinted paper on a *sheet* or *pane* of *stamps* that does not contain a *stamp*. *Marginal markings* are found in the margin.

Margin Block – any *block* of *stamps* with a *margin* attached. Frequently, but not necessarily, a *marginal marking* will be found on a margin block.

Marginal Marking – any intentional marking found on a *plate* except for the stamp itself. Such markings will also appear on the printed *sheet*. Examples of marginal markings include *plate numbers*, *siderographer initials*, *Mr. ZIP*, and *copyright notices*.

Match and Medicine Stamps – see *Private Die Proprietary Stamps*.

Matrix – the waste produced by the process of die cutting.

MeadWestvaco – Williamsburg, Pennsylvania based manufacturer of *stamped envelopes*.

Mercantile Corporation – manufacturer of early twentieth century *stamped envelopes* and *wrappers*.

Merry Widow – nickname for the 1908 green *Special Delivery stamp* (E7).

Meter – 1) a machine that imprints evidence of payment of *postage*. 2) the imprint of such a machine.

Micro-printing – extremely small words, or acronyms printed on some modern *stamps* as a security measure.

Middle West Supply Company – manufacturer of early twentieth century *stamped envelopes* and *wrappers*.

Miehle Press – 1) *flat plate press* first used at the *BEP* in 1894. 2) *offset* press used at the *BEP* in 1970s.

Minnesota Diversified Industries – manufacturer of *MDI booklets*.

Mint – a *stamp* in the original unused condition in which it came from the post office. Sometimes this term is also applied to unused stamps that have been previously hinged.

Miscut – a *freak* that is created when a *stamp* or *pane* is not cut in the normal manner during the production process.

Misregistration – see *Registration*.

Missionaries – a nickname for the 1851-1852 *stamps* of Hawaii.

Mixed Franking – 1) a *cover* bearing the *stamps* of two or more nations. 2) a *cover* with any other unusual combination of *stamps* used together, such as an *Official* and a *definitive*.

Mobile Post Office – post office facility that sorts and distributes mail while in transit, whether by rail (including street car), water, or highway.

Model – the final, approved illustration of a *stamp*. It can be in the form of a drawing, a sketch, a photograph, a print or engraving, or any combination, or composite, of layers.

Money Order Business Cancellation – a circular *handstamp cancellation* containing the initials MOB; intended for use only on money orders but occasionally used on *cover*.

Morgan Envelope Company – manufacturer of nineteenth century *stamped envelopes* and *wrappers*.

Motor Vehicle Use Revenue Stamp – a *revenue stamp* paying the tax on the use of a motor vehicle. *Scott* RV.

Mottled Tagging – *tagging* with an uneven, rough, or dappled appearance when viewed under *ultraviolet light*, as opposed to *even* or *grainy tagging*. Some causes of mottled tagging are uncoated paper, worn tagging rollers, and offsetting of wet *taggant* ink when *sheets* are stacked. Example: 1991 Dennis Chavez stamp (2186).

Mourning Cover – a *cover* with a black border, conveying news of a death.

Mr. ZIP – a cartoon-like character used as a *marginal marking* from 1964 to 1986 promoting the use of *ZIP Code*.

Multi-Color Corporation – private printer of modern *postage stamps*. Example: 19¢ Fishing Boat (2529).

Multiple – a unit of two or more unseparated *stamps*.

Mute Cancel – a *cancel* that does not include a date or time. Generally used on *Registered Mail* and mail other than *First Class*.

N

Name Block – a block of *stamps* from the 1943-1944 Overrun Countries Issue (909-921) with a country name in the location where a *plate number* is customarily located.

Narcotic Tax Stamps – *revenue stamps* paying the federal tax on opium, coca leaves and their derivatives. The tax was in effect from 1917 through 1971. *Scott* RJA

National Air Mail Week – a campaign by the *Post Office Department* to promote *air mail*, conducted May 15–21, 1938, the twentieth anniversary of regularly scheduled air mail service. A large variety of *cachets* and special flights were used in this observance.

National Bank Note Company – contractor for printing *postage stamps* from 1861 to 1873.

National Bureau Precancels – *BEP* produced *precancels* with two parallel lines only and valid for precanceled mail at any U.S. post office.

National Defense Issue – set of three *postage stamps* promoting national defense in 1940 (899-901).

National Label Company – subcontractor to *3M* for printing the 1994 Eagle stamp (2598).

National Parks Issue – *commemorative postage stamp* set of 1934 honoring various National Parks (740-749). See also *Farleys Follies*.

National Postal Museum – a museum of the Smithsonian Institution, located in the old Washington City Post Office, housing the national *postage stamp* collection.

Nesbitt, George F. & Company – printer of *stamped envelopes* and *wrappers* from 1853 to 1870.

Newspaper and Periodical Stamps – *stamps* issued to document payment of *postage* on newspapers and periodicals. From their release in 1865 until 1869 the stamps were affixed to wrappers on bundles, not to individual newspapers. Beginning in 1875 stamps were placed in a receipt book. Their use was discontinued in 1898. *Scott* numbers are prefixed with PR.

Nixie Clerk – a post office clerk responsible for handling items not readily deliverable because of a deficiency in address.

Non-denominated Stamp – a *stamp* that does not have a value printed on its *face*, but does have a value assigned. Such stamps often have a letter of the alphabet as part of their *design* that represents the assigned value. Example: 1978 "A" stamp

(1735) has an assigned value of 15¢.

Nonstandard Mail – *First Class mail* weighing less than one ounce, and also of nonstandard size or thickness. An additional charge is imposed for nonstandard mail.

O

OCR – see *Optical Character Reader*.

Obliterator – a device that *cancels* a *stamp*; may also be called a "*killer*".

Occupation Stamps – see *Allied Military Government Stamps*.

Oddity – a broad category of unusual *variations*. Examples: *stamps* used before their first day of issue, errors in *postmarks*, and semi-official separations such as the *Kansas City roulettes*.

Off Center – a *stamp* whose *design* is not centered in relation to the edges of the stamp.

Offices Abroad – a post office maintained on the soil of a foreign county. Between 1919 and 1922 the U.S. Postal Agency in Shanghai, China was provided with *surcharged postage stamps* for use by that agency.

Offices in China – U.S. *postage stamps surcharged* for use by the U.S. Postal Agency in Shanghai, China. Issued in 1919 and 1922. *Scott* numbers are prefixed with K.

Official Mail – mail sent by a government agency, using *official stamps* or a *penalty envelope*.

Official Postal Cards – *postal cards* issued for use by federal government departments. *Scott* numbers are prefixed with UZ.

Official Stamped Envelopes – envelopes (and *wrappers*) used by federal government departments in the 1870s and early 1880s, and again beginning in 1983. *Scott* numbers are prefixed with UO for envelopes and WO for wrappers.

Official Stamps – *stamps* used by federal

government departments in the 1870s and early 1880s, and again beginning in 1983. *Scott* numbers are prefixed with O. See also *Postal Savings Mail*.

Officially Sealed Label – See *Seal*.

Off-line Perforator – a perforating device that is an independent machine; not an integral portion of a printing press.

Offset Lithography – see *Offset Printing*.

Offset Printing – a method of printing in which the inked image is first transferred from the printing *plate* to a rubber roller or blanket. The inked image is then transferred from the roller to paper. *Postage stamps* were first printed from offset lithography in 1918-1920. More recent stamps have been produced by a combination of offset and *intaglio* printing. Offset printing is usually *lithography*, but not always. For example, the *Overrun Countries* stamps were printed by offset letterpress, sometimes called dry offset or letterset. The background colors on the 1968 and 1969 Christmas stamps (1363 and 1384) were printed by offset *intaglio*.

Open Mail – mid-nineteenth century mail sent from an *exchange office* to an exchange office in another country for further processing and subsequent transmittal to another exchange office.

Optical Character Reader – postal equipment that "reads" the address on an envelope. Sometimes this term is also used for the entire system, including the device that sprays the address on the envelope as a *barcode*.

Optiforma Press – six-color offset lithographic presses purchased from Goebel primarily intended to produce aerograms.

Orangeburg Coil – nickname for the rare 3¢ *Washington-Franklin coil* with a vertical *perforation gauge* of 12 (389). Used only by a drug company in Orangeburg, New York briefly in 1911.

Ordinary Stamps – see *Definitives*.

Original Gum – *gum* on a *stamp* as issued by the post office.

Overall Tagging – *Phosphor tagging* that completely covers a *stamp*, as opposed to *block tagging*. The clear *taggant* ink is applied on top of the stamp, as opposed to *prephosphored paper* tagging in which the taggant is in the paper itself.

Overland Mail – mid-nineteenth century mail that traveled across the U.S. by land.

Overprint – printing placed on top of a *stamps face* for some special purpose. Overprints have been used for *precancelling*, *service inscription*, *surcharging*, *commemorative* and security purposes, and on *AMGs*. Example: Hawaii Sesquicentennial stamps (647-648).

Overrun Countries – set issued in 1943-1944 honoring countries overrun during World War II (909-921).

P

P – prefix letter used by *Ashton-Potter (USA) LTD.*, in front of the *plate number* on its modern *stamp* production.

PAL – see *Parcel Airlift*.

PNC – abbreviation for *Plate Number Coil*. See *Coil Plate Number*.

POD – see *United States Post Office Department*.

POSTNET – *U.S. Postal Service* term for *ZIP Code barcode* (acronym of POSTal Numeric Encoding Technique).

PMG – see *Postmaster General*.

PTS – see *Postal Transportation Service*.

PVI – see *Postage Validation Imprints*.

Pacific '97 – one in a series of international stamp shows hosted once every decade in the U.S. Held in San Francisco in 1997. *Stamps* (3130-3131) and *souvenir sheets* (3139-3140) were issued in conjunction with this show.

Packet Letter – a letter carried by a ship operating on a regular schedule and under contract to the Post Office.

PAID – a marking applied to a *stampless letter* to indicate that *postage* had been paid in cash.

Paid Reply Postal Cards – two *postal cards* that are attached to each other and sold by the post office as a single unit. One card is for sending a message. The other is for the recipient to detach and send a reply. *Scott* numbers are prefixed with UY.

Pair – two unseparated *stamps*.

Pan-American Issue – *commemorative postage stamps* issued for the Pan-American Exposition in Buffalo in 1901 (294-299).

Panama Canal Zone – see *Canal Zone*.

Pane – a unit of *stamps* cut from a full *sheet*, either for assembly into *booklets*, or for individual sale at post offices. Sheets intended to be cut into *panes* for assembly into booklets will each produce a large number of relatively small panes, typically 30, 40, or 60. Sheets intended for division into panes to be sold individually are divided into fewer but larger panes. Many early sheets consisted of only two panes. Most twentieth century sheets consisted of four panes. Modern sheets consist of six or more panes. Panes are commonly, but inaccurately, referred to by the public as sheets.

Pane-Position Diagrams – *marginal marking* first used in 1992. This diagram identifies the *position* on a *sheet* from which the *pane* was cut.

Pantone Matching System – A popular color matching system used by the printing industry to print spot colors. Most applications that support color printing allow specification of colors by indicating the Pantone name or number.

Paquebot – see *Packet Letter*.

Parcel Airlift – service for a fee that provides for air transportation, on a space available basis for mail on which the normal *postage* is paid, to or from military post offices out-side the contiguous 48 states. This service was popular during the Viet Nam conflict. One special *stamp* was issued in connection with this service, *Scott* 1341.

Parcel Post – the traditional name for the service for mailing most domestic packages, which began in 1913. International Parcel Post was introduced in 1887. Parcel Post is now a sub-category of Package Service, formerly *Fourth Class Mail*.

Parcel Post Postage Due Stamps – *stamps* used to account for *postage due* on *parcel post mail*, issued in 1913. *Scott* numbers are prefixed with JQ.

Parcel Post Stamps – *stamps* issued for use on *Parcel Post*, beginning January 1, 1913. Only these stamps could be used on Parcel Post until July 1, 1913, when any stamps could be used for Parcel Post, and Parcel Post stamps could be used as regular stamps. *Scott* numbers are prefixed with Q.

Part Perforate – *stamps* on which at least one side is *perforated* as intended and on which one or more sides are lacking any intended perforations. Note: This term originally referred to properly perforated *coil stamps* that were not perforated on the two edges perpendicular to the perforations. Such stamps were thus distinguished from *imperforate* coils.

Partial Plate Number – a less than complete *plate number* appearing on a traditional *coil stamp* or on certain *booklet panes*. These are freaks. Plate numbers on these coils and booklet panes were generally trimmed off in the production process and were not regularly available.

Paste-up – the location on a *flat plate coil stamp* (or more commonly on a pair or more of such stamps) where two sheets of flat plate stamps were pasted together. Rolls of coil stamps were made from lengths of flat plate *sheets* that were 20 stamps long. Thus a paste-up is normally found at 20 stamp intervals.

Paste-up Pair – a pair of *coil stamps* joined together by a *paste-up*.

Patent Cancellation – a *cancelling* device patented by the inventor. These were popular in the period of the 1860s to 1880s. In general, these devices operated by destroying, in some way, a portion of a *stamp's* paper.

Patent Lines – lines printed on the inside of a *stamped envelope* to guide writers in aligning the addressee's name and address.

Patriotic Cover – a *cover* with a patriotic *cachet*, which was especially popular during the Civil War.

Peak – the portion of a simulated *perforation* on a *self-adhesive stamp* that protrudes from the side of the stamp.

Pen Cancel – see *Manuscript Cancel*.

Penalty Envelope – an envelope sent free of *postage* by a government agency that contains a printed inscription, usually in the place where a *stamp* is customarily affixed, warning of a penalty for unauthorized use of the envelope. Authorized in 1877. Penalty envelopes are still used by the *U.S. Postal Service* but are obsolete for the executive departments of the federal government.

Perf. – see *Perforation*.

Perfecting – the process of printing inscriptions on the *gum* of some modern *stamps* by *letterpress*.

Perfin – (shortened form of "perforated initials" or "perforated insignia") a *stamp* with privately produced *perforations* through its *face*. The perforations are generally in the form of initials or a symbol that identify the owner of the stamp. Perfins are produced by businesses or organizations to discourage theft or misuse of their stamps. Perfins were first made in 1908, and were most popular through the 1950s. See *Control Perfin*.

Perforated Initials – see *Perfin*.

Perforated Insignia – see *Perfin*.

Perforation – 1) the rows of holes between *stamps* that enable easy separation of stamps. The gauge (perforation size) has frequently changed. For example, perf. 15 was introduced in 1857, perf. 12 in 1861, perf. 10 in 1913, and perf 11. in 1917. Other perfs have also been used. "Perf" is a commonly used contraction for perforation. 2) holes that were privately added by some private companies to help *coil stamps* pass through a *vending* or *affixing machine*.

Perforation Gauge – 1) a number that equals the total quantity of *perforation* holes (or *teeth*) within the space of 20 mm. For example, the Wildlife Conservation Issue of 1970 (1392) is said to have a perforation gauge of 11 x 10½. When referencing perforations, the horizontal perforation gauge is given first, and then the vertical. 2) a tool that measures the total quantity of perforation holes (or *teeth*) within the space of 20 mm.

Periodicals-Class Mail – the mailing classification for newspapers, magazines, and other periodicals. This classification was previously known as *Second Class Mail*.

Permit Mail Indicium – an imprint in the upper right hand corner of a *cover* indicating the authority, under permit, of a mailer to make large (*bulk*) mailings at a special (*quantity*) rate.

Persian Rug – nickname for the $200 and $500 *revenue stamps* of 1871 (R132, R133).

Personalized Computer Postage – postage purchased from an internet vendor and printed at a customer's convenience.

Personalized Postage – see *Customized Postage*.

Phantom Numbers – unintended, lightly printed *plate numbers* found in varying locations in the *margins* of *sheets* produced on the *rotary press*. These are *freaks* caused by a *set-off* that occurs when the dryer on the press is not operating at a warm enough temperature.

Philatelic – pertaining to the hobby of collecting *stamps*, *postal stationery*, *postal history*, and related materials.

Philatelic Cover – a *cover* that is *philatelic* in origin, as opposed to a cover produced in the normal course of commercial or personal correspondence.

Philatelic Foundation, The – a leading organization in the *expertization* of *stamps*.

Philatelic Plate Number Association - predecessor organization to the *United States Stamp Society*.

Philatelic Truck Souvenir Sheet – a souvenir *label*, with no postal value, distributed by a post office truck that toured the nation from 1939 to 1941.

Philatelist – a *stamp*, *postal stationery*, or *postal history* collector.

Philippines – now independent country over which the U.S. exercised sovereignty from 1898 to 1946. *Overprinted* U.S. *stamps* were used there beginning in 1899. Beginning in 1906 the *BEP* printed stamps for use in the Philippines.

Phosphor Tagging – a clear phosphor colloidal solution (*taggant* ink) applied over a *stamp*, or to its paper, or mixed with stamp printers' ink. Tagging glows bluish-green or reddish when exposed to short wave *ultraviolet light*. Reddish tagging was only used for *air mail stamps* from 1963 to 1978. Beginning with the 1978 31¢ Wright Brothers (C91-C92), bluish-green tagging was used for all subsequent air mail stamps. Tagging has a brief afterglow that is used by *automatic cancelling machines* to find, face, and *cancel* an envelope's stamp.

Phosphored Ink – ink to which a clear *taggant* compound has been added. Phosphored ink is infrequently used on *stamps*, but is frequently used for *postal stationery*. Example of use of phospho-

red ink: Leif Erikson stamp of 1968 (1359), and the Bicentennial envelope of 1976 (U582).

Photo essay – an *essay* in the form of a photograph.

Photogravure – see *Gravure*.

Photogravure and Color Company - private printer of the 1967 5¢ Thomas Eakins (1335).

PhotoStamps™ – *Personalized postage* produced by *Stamps.com*.

(Bill) Pickett Stamp – see *Legends of the West*.

Pictorial Cancel – a *cancellation* that contains an illustration.

PictureItPostage – *Personalized postage* produced by Endicia.

Pigeon Blood Pink – a color found on a rare variety of the 3¢ 1861 *stamp* (64a).

Pink Backs – nickname for those *Washington-Franklin stamps* that "bleed" a pink coloration into the paper when placed in water. This condition results from the use of inferior quality *aniline ink*.

Pioneer Flights – *air mail* flights flown prior to the establishment of regularly scheduled air mail service. The Pioneer Flight period is 1910-1916.

Pitney Bowes – the oldest supplier of *postage meters* (since 1920); manufacturer of mailing machines, inserters, *cancelling machines*, sorters and other postal equipment; bought out *Mailometer* in 1924.

Plate – the unit of a printing press from which *stamps* are actually printed. Nineteenth and early twentieth century stamps were produced from *flat plates*. Beginning in the mid-1920s most stamps were produced from curved (180°) plates that were used in pairs on a *rotary press*. Still more recently, many stamps have been printed from *cylindrical* plates. A plate is sometimes also known as a printing base.

Plate Arrangement – see *Plate Layout*.

Plate Block – a block of *stamps*, traditionally four in number, but sometimes more, which has a *plate number* printed on the attached margin. Most collectors of plate blocks collect them in sizes as standardized by *Scott*.

Plate Cleaner – see *Plate Finisher*.

Plate Finisher – a *BEP* employee who removes extraneous lines or dots from an engraved *plate* after the *siderographer* has completed his job.

Plate Finisher Initials – *marginal marking* consisting of the initials of a *plate finisher*, punched into the *plate*, found in different locations on various *plates* before the location for them was standardized as the lower right corner. These initials were placed on plates from 1909 until 1928.

Plate Flaw – a flaw in a printing *plate* that shows up on the corresponding *sheet* of *stamps*. A plate flaw may be a crack or other defect that develops in a plate, or damage inflicted on a plate, such as an accidental dropping.

Plate Layout – the layout of a *plate*; that is, the relationship of the elements on a plate, especially of the *panes*, to each other.

Plate Marking – any marking on a *plate* that is printed on the corresponding *sheet*.

Plate Number – the numbers that appear on a printing *plate*. These numbers are a part of the *plate layout* and most typically appear one or more times on each printed *pane*. Numbers were most commonly assigned to plates sequentially, in ever ascending order, with the same number never being assigned twice. Plate numbers appeared on *sheets* printed at the *BEP* from 1894 through 1980, when the practice was discontinued. Today's plate numbers are *Representative Numbers*. The first plate of each type (i.e. *intaglio*, *gravure*, and *offset*) prepared for a given stamp is given number 1. Subsequent plates of the same type are given consecutive numbers.

Plate Number Block – see *Plate Block*.

Plate Number Coil – see *Coil Plate Number*.

Plate Number Single – an individual *stamp*, mint or used, with a *plate number* attached.

Plate Printer Initials – see *Printer's Initials*.

Plate Proof – a *proof* printed (*pulled*) from a *plate*, as opposed to one pulled from a *die*.

Plate Varieties – minor variations between apparently identical *stamps* that were printed from different *plates*. Plate varieties can result from a damaged plate, or when there is some irregularity in the way a plate is made. Plate varieties are *constant*, that is, as long as the variety appears on the plate, it will appear on every *sheet* produced from that plate. More information about Plate Varieties may be obtained by referring to *Encyclopedia of Plate Varieties on U.S. Bureau-Printed Postage Stamps*.

Plating – 1) the art of reconstructing a *pane* by determining the position of any given *stamp* on a pane. Each position is assigned a consecutive number, beginning with the upper left corner and concluding with the lower right. Plating is only done on early stamps where each stamp on a pane is unique due to minor variation. 2) the art of reconstructing a production-size sheet of certain booklet panes.

Playing Cards Stamps – *revenue stamps* issued from 1894 to 1940 to pay the federal tax on playing cards. *Scott* numbers are prefixed with RF.

Plimpton Manufacturing Company – manufacturer of nineteenth century *stamped envelopes* and *wrappers*.

Pneumatic Mail – mail moved between post offices and railroad stations by pneumatic tubes in certain large cities beginning with Philadelphia in 1893. Pneumatic tube service was discontinued June 30, 1918.

Points down – the *grill* of a *stamp*, which, when viewed from the *face*, has the points of the grill directed downward. Example: *Scott* 84.

Points up – the *grill* of a *stamp*, which, when viewed from the *face*, has the points of the grill directed upward. Example: *Scott* 79.

Pony Express – mail service operated in 1860 and 1861 between St. Joseph, Missouri and Sacramento, California. *Local stamps* were issued for this service by *Wells, Fargo and Co.*

Position – the place (location) on a printing *plate* from which a given *stamp* or *pane* was printed.

Position Blocks – *blocks* taken from various places on a *sheet* which show *guide lines*, *arrows*, or other *marginal markings*.

Possessions and Administered Areas – foreign territories owned or administered by the United States, and for which the U.S. issued stamps, including: *Canal Zone*, *Cuba*, *Guam*, the *Philippines*, *Puerto Rico*, and Ryukyu Islands.

Post Card – a privately produced mailing card, as opposed to a Post Office produced *postal card*. A post card does not have an *indicium*.

Post Office Department – see *United States Post Office Department*.

Post Office Seal – see *Seal*.

Post Road – a road, airway, waterway, or railway officially designated for the carrying of mail.

Postage – the fee charged for sending an item through the mail.

Postage Currency – *postage stamps* affixed to or printed on treasury paper during the Civil War as a way of making stamps negotiable. *Scott* numbers are prefixed with PC.

Postage Due Bill – a government generated form to which *postage due stamps* are attached. It represents the amount of money owed by a postal customer and frequently represents many individual pieces of *business reply mail*.

Postage Due Stamp – a *stamp* indicating a deficiency in *postage* paid by the recipient.

First used in 1879. *Scott* numbers are prefixed with J.

Postage Rate – the amount of money charged for *postage*. See also *Postal Fee*.

Postage Stamp – a piece of printed security paper, usually *gummed*, produced by the *BEP* or other authorized printer under controlled and secure conditions, sold by the Post Office, to be used by a mailer to document payment of *postage*.

Postage Validation Imprints – labels generated in post offices in conjunction with *Integrated Retail Terminals* (IRTs). Postage Validation Imprints, which evidence payment of *postage*, replaced *meters* in post offices and first appeared in 1993.

Postal Buddy Machine – see *Denominated Postal cards*.

Postal Card – a mailing card produced by the post office, as opposed to a privately produced *post card*. A postal card has a stamp-like *indicium*. Postal Cards were first issued in 1873. Since 1999 Postal Cards have been sold for 1¢ over *face value*. *Scott* numbers are prefixed with UX. See also *Denominated Postal Cards* and *Stamped Card*.

Postal Convention – see *Convention Rate*.

Postal Envelope – see *Stamped Envelope*.

Postal Fee – the amount of money charged for a postal service, such as *registered mail*.

Postal History – the study and collection of *covers* that chronicle the movement of the mails. Desirable covers will have significant *postal markings*, *rates*, routes, usages, origins, and destinations.

Postal Insurance Stamps – *stamps* sold in a *booklet* of one stamp, from *vending machines*, to provide insurance on parcels. *Scott* numbers are prefixed with QI.

Postal Marking – any impression (whether by *machine*, *handstamp*, or *pen*), placed on mail by an employee of the Post Office in the course of handling mail.

Postal Note Stamp – *stamps* used on Postal Money Orders. *Scott* numbers are prefixed with PN.

Postal Savings Mail – *official stamps* issued in 1910 for use by the *Postal Savings System*.

Postal Savings Stamps – *stamps* issued by the *Post Office Department*, beginning in 1911, redeemable in the form of credits to Postal Savings Accounts. *Scott* numbers begin with PS.

Postal Savings System – an interest paying savings system operated by the *Post Office Department* from 1910-1966.

Postal Service – see *United States Postal Service*.

Postal Stationery – a category of products which includes *Postal Envelopes*, *Postal Cards, aerograms, wrappers*, and *international reply coupons*.

Postal Transportation Service – successor to the *Railway Mail Service* in 1949 with responsibility for the transportation of mail by land, sea, and air.

Postal Treaty – see *Convention Rate*.

Postmark – the impression made by the post office or authorized mailer on a *cover*, typically indicating the date, time, and place of mailing. Postmarks may be made by *machine* or *handstamp*. Postmarks are most commonly circular, but are also found as ovals, boxes, straight lines, and *spray ons*. While postmarks are not *cancels*, they are sometimes used for that purpose, and the two terms are often and incorrectly used interchangeably.

Postmaster – the postal official in charge of a post office in a given locality.

Postmaster General – the chief executive officer of the old *United States Post Office Department*, and now of its successor, the *United States Postal Service*.

Postmasters' Provisionals – *stamps* and envelopes issued unilaterally by *postmasters* to meet local needs. *Scott* numbers are prefixed with X (XU for envelopes).

Potato Tax Exempt Stamp – *stamp* documenting exemption from the tax under the Agricultural Adjustment Act. *Scott* numbers are prefixed with RI. See also *Potato Tax Paid Stamp*.

Potato Tax Paid Stamp – *revenue stamp* required by the Potato Act of 1935. Because the Supreme Court quickly declared the act unconstitutional, these stamps were never used. *Scott* numbers are prefixed with RI. See also *Potato Tax Exempt Stamp*.

Precancel – a *postage* or *revenue stamp* that has been canceled, under proper postal authority, before being affixed to mail (or taxable) matter. Precancels are either *Bureau Precancels* or *Local Precancels*. Some *postal stationery* has also been precanceled.

Predates – *stamps* or *postal stationery postmarked* with dates prior to the official *first day of issue*. These are not *First Day Covers*.

Prefix Letter – the letter preceding *plate numbers* on *plates* produced since the 1980s by private printers. Each letter designates a specific private printer. *BEP* plate numbers do not use a prefix letter.

Premiere Gravures – see *August Issues*.

Prephosphored Paper – paper that has *taggant* added during its production. There are two types of prephosphored paper: *Uncoated Paper* and *Coated Paper*. Uncoated paper tagging will be *mottled*. Coated paper tagging may be *grainy*, mottled, or *even*.

Preprinting Paper Crease – a *stamp* printed on paper that was creased prior to printing. When this crease is eventually opened up, an unprinted area becomes visible. Preprinting paper creases are *freaks*.

Presentation Album – an album presented by postal authorities to a dignitary. Examples are albums containing panes of newly released stamps presented at First

Day Ceremonies, and the so-called *"Roosevelt Albums"* of *small die proofs*.

Presidential Series – a series of *sheet, coil* and *booklet stamps*, also known as Fifth Bureau Issue. Most of the Presidential Series stamps were issued in 1938-1939. *Scott* numbers begin at 803.

Presort Stamp – a *postage stamp* that documents the payment of postage on mail that is presorted, that is, mail bundled and prepared by the mailer in conformity with *USPS* standards.

Press (The) – private printer of modern *postage stamps*. Example: 45¢ Pumpkinseed Sunfish (2481).

Press Sheet – see *Sheet*.

Prestige Booklet – a *booklet* containing several *face-different stamps*, descriptive text, and illustrations. The first Prestige Booklet (BK279) was issued in 2000 and honored U.S. Navy Submarines.

Prexies – see *Presidential Series*.

Printer's Initials – a *marginal marking* consisting of printer's initials, punched into an engraved *plate* by printers each time a printer printed from a plate. The practice probably began in 1894. It was discontinued in 1911 or 1912. Printer's initials were again used briefly in 1920 on some *Washington-Franklin offset* plates.

Printer's Waste – waste paper generated in the production of *stamps*. Printer's waste is not a genuine error or freak. It is simply waste paper intended for destruction which can usually only reach the public through the illegal activity of an employee. Some infamous printer's waste was stolen from the printer during the production of the 1995 Nixon commemorative.

Printing Plate – see *Plate*.

Priority Mail – a subclass of *first class mail*, begun in 1968, providing a *postage* savings for items weighing 13 ounces or more. The first *stamp* specifically intended for use on priority mail was the 1989 $2.40 Moon Landing stamp (2419). The first stamped (prepaid) Priority Mail envelope was issued in 2003.

Private Aerogram – an *aerogram* (air letter sheet) privately printed, under permit, by a non-postal entity. The air rate is correctly prepaid by *postage stamp*(s) as opposed to a stamp-like *indicium*. While private aerograms are scarce, they are known from the *Prexie* and *Liberty* eras.

Private Coil – *coil stamps* produced by a private company from *BEP* printed *imperforate sheets*, as opposed to those produced by the *BEP*.

Private Die Proprietary Stamp – a *revenue stamp* produced from a *die* and *plate* created at the expense of a private company and used exclusively by that private company. The stamp was used to pay the tax on products sold by the company, and the stamps were generally affixed to the products sold. The dies and plates were controlled by the *BEP*. The categories of products that required these stamps were: medicines (*Scott* RS), matches (*Scott* RO), perfumes and cosmetics (*Scott* RT), playing cards (*Scott* RU), and canned goods (*Scott* RP). See also *Proprietary Stamps*.

Private Mailing Card – official term, used from 1898 until 1901, for what are now known as *post cards*.

Private Perforations – see *Vending and Affixing Machine Perforations*.

Progressive Die Proof – a *proof* made from a *die* that is not complete. Such die proofs illustrate how work on a die progressed. A progressive die proof is a special type of *essay* sometimes called a *die essay* or a "progressive essay".

Progressive Essay – see *Progressive Die Proof*.

Progressive Relief Break – see *Relief Break*.

Project Mercury – the *postage stamp* honoring the 1962 orbital flight of John Glenn (1193). The stamp was printed and shipped in secrecy, and released simultaneously at many post offices in the country upon Glenn's safe return to earth.

Prominent Americans – *definitive* series of *postage stamps* appearing 1965-1981. *Scott* numbers begin with 1278.

Proof – an impression printed (*pulled*) directly from a *die* or a *plate*, usually done before *stamp* production begins. A proof is made to "prove" (approve) the engraving of the die, or the transfer to the plate. Proofs are also pulled to enable engravers to determine how their work on a die is progressing. See *Progressive Proof*. Proofs have been made as philatelic favors for dignitaries, sometimes years after the stamp was issued. The *BEP* kept accurate records of all proofs that were made. Proofs tend to have sharper images than the corresponding stamps. *Scott* numbers for proofs contain a P.

Proprietary Stamp – a *revenue stamp* documenting payment of federal tax on a commodity. The federal government sold these stamps to many companies. The categories of products requiring a proprietary stamp were: medicines, matches, perfumes and cosmetics, playing cards, and photographs. See also *Private Die Proprietary Stamps,* which were produced exclusively for a single user. *Scott* numbers are generally prefixed with RB although some are prefixed with R.

Provenance – the ownership history of a *philatelic* item.

Provisional Meter – a *meter* with a *surcharge slug* inserted to meet a temporary need.

Provisional Stamp – a *stamp* produced as an interim (temporary) measure to meet an immediate need. Such stamps are often made by *overprinting* existing stamps. Example: the first *Cigarette Tubes Stamp* (RH1), which is an overprint on a *Documentary Stamp*.

Puerto Rico – U.S. commonwealth that used *provisional* issues and *overprinted* U.S.

stamps, stamped envelopes, wrappers, postal cards, and *revenue stamps*.

Pulling – the process of printing a *proof* or other print from a *die* or a *plate*, as in the expression, "to pull a proof".

Punch Cancel – *cancellation* of a *stamp* by means of punching a hole. Such cancels are generally found only on *revenue* stamps, although *proofs* are also found with punch cancels.

Punch Marks – marks made on an *engraved plate* using a punch tool. Examples of these marks include *printer's initials*, *plate finisher's initials*, "F", and stars.

Purvis Printing Company – *overprinter* of a small quantity of *revenue stamps* in 1898.

Putter-On-er – nickname for employees of the *BEP* who placed unprinted sheets of paper on the *flat plate* press.

Q

Quantity Mail – bundled business mail that is discounted from the equivalent single-piece rates. This is an incentive to the mailer to precancel, presort, barcode, or otherwise reduce the required processing by the Postal Service. *First Class* quantity mailings are discounted at reduced per-piece rates. *Third Class* (*Standard Mail*) quantity mailings are discounted at *bulk rates*.

R

R.F. – a *postal marking* placed on a U.S. stamp, authorized by the U.S. Fleet Post Office during World War II for use on correspondence to the United States and Canada from French naval personnel. *Scott* numbers are prefixed with CM.

RFD – see *Rural Free Delivery*.

RMS – see *Railway Mail Service*.

RMU – see *Required Matching Usage*.

RPO – see *Railway Post Office*.

Railway Mail Service – a division of the Post Office established in 1882. In 1949 the

Railway Mail Service was consolidated into the *Postal Transportation Service*, which was itself discontinued in 1977. The initials R.M.S. (or P.T.S. after 1949) generally appear in *cancellations* applied by a *Railway Post Office*.

Railway Post Office – a postal facility on trains, steamships, and *street cars* for processing mail in transit. The initials R.P.O. generally appear in *postmarks* applied by a Railway Post Office.

Rate – see *Postage Rate*.

Rate Mark – a numeral placed on a *stampless letter* at its place of origin indicating the amount to be collected from the addressee.

Rawdon, Wright, Hatch & Edson – printers of the first *postage stamps*, issued in 1847 (1 and 2).

Reay, George H. – manufacturer of *stamped envelopes* and *wrappers* from 1870 to 1874.

Receiving Mark – a *postmark* applied to a *cover* (generally on the back), by the receiving post office as opposed to the originating post office. The requirement for such *backstamping* of *first class* mail was in effect from 1879 to 1913.

Rectification Tax Stamps – *revenue stamps* issued in 1946 to pay the tax on distilled spirits that were condensed and purified for additional blending through repeated distillations. *Scott* numbers are prefixed with RZ.

Recut – see *re-engraved*.

Recycled Paper – paper used in the manufacture of *stamped envelopes*. Recycled paper replaced *watermarked* paper beginning in 1992.

Redrawn – a *stamp* whose *design* is based on the design of an existing stamp, but which has been altered in some way, thus producing a new *face*-different stamp. For example, Scott 1283B is a redrawn version of 1283.

Reds – a nickname for 1) the red *commemorative postage stamps* of the late 1920s and early 1930s. 2) the red *documentary revenue stamps* of 1940-1958.

Re-engraved – a *transfer roll* or *plate* on which the original *design* is altered. *Stamps* produced from such re-engraving are distinguishable from stamps printed before the re-engraving.

Re-entry – a second entry on a *plate* position, made by carefully re-*rocking* the *transfer roll* over the initial impression. If not done carefully, a *double transfer* may result. This procedure was used to fix defective entries or to extend the lives of worn plates.

Registered Mail – the most secure service provided by the Postal Service, which closely controls and records the movement of mail given this service. First offered in 1855.

Registration – 1) the alignment of colors on a *stamp*. A stamp's colors can be described as properly registered or misregistered. 2) see also *Registered Mail*.

Registration Stamp – a *stamp*, issued in 1911, to pay the fee for *registered mail* (F1).

Regressive Die Essay – an *essay pulled* from a *transfer roll* that has been partially cut way to remove unwanted elements of a *design*.

Regular Stamp – see *Definitive*.

Re-issue – an official reprinting of an obsolete *stamp*.

Relief – the *design* of a stamp raised up (as opposed to recessed) on a *transfer roll*.

Relief Break – the breaking away of portions of the *relief* on a *transfer roll*. This results in *stamps* with a blank space where an engraved line was intended. Relief breaks can be progressive, that is, can become worse as the transfer roll continues in use. Progressive relief breaks can result in stamps that show the progressive deterioration of the transfer roll. A classic example of this is found on the 5¢ Huguenot-Walloon of 1924 (616).

Relief Printing – see *Letterpress*.

Reply Postal Card – see *Paid Reply Postal Card*.

Representative Number – see *Plate Number*.

Reprint – an additional printing of a *stamp* that is still in stock by the Post Office, generally done to meet public demand.

Reproductions – official imitations. Examples: *Scott* 3 and 4.

Required Matching Usage – term that applies to a *First Issue Revenue stamp* used from October 1 through December 25, 1862 when the matching of the stamp and the document was required.

Restricted Delivery – service for a fee, which provides for the delivery of an item of mail only to the addressee or addressee's agent.

Retouch – a repair of a damaged *die* or *plate* made in such a way that a minor variation results.

Return Receipt – service for fee (though once provided at no fee) that provides the sender with evidence of delivery.

Return Receipt Demanded – see *Return Receipt*.

Return Receipt Requested – see *Return Receipt*.

Revenue Stamp – a piece of printed security paper, usually *gummed*, produced by the *BEP* or other authorized printer under controlled and secure conditions, sold to document payment of a tax, duty, or a fee other than *postage*. Revenue stamps can be divided into numerous categories, which include *documentary* and *proprietary*.

Revenue Stamped Paper – a taxable document such as a stock certificate or check, with a *revenue* stamp-like design printed directly on the document. There are twenty-four major designs for revenue stamped paper. *Scott* numbers are prefixed with RN.

Rocking – the process of using a *transfer roll* to create a printing *plate* for the production of *engraved* stamps.

Rodgers Aerial Post – a 1911 cross-country airplane flight that carried mail and for which a privately printed stamp was issued (CL2).

Roller Cancel – a device that applies a continuous *cancellation* and repeating circular *postmark* from its cylindrical roller. Often used to cancel large pieces of *flat* mail. Roller cancels are applied both by *machine* and *hand*.

Roosevelt Presentation Albums – albums presented to dignitaries in 1903 containing *small die proofs* of *stamps* issued through 1902.

Rosette Crack – a cluster of fine cracks on an *engraved plate*, radiating from a central point.

Rossback Perforation – a 12½ *gauge perforation* used by the *BEP* in 1919 on offset printed 1¢ stamps (536).

Rotary Plate – the curved *plate* used on a *rotary press*.

Rotary Press – a press that prints from curved *plates* fastened around a *cylinder*. First used in 1914 to print an *imperforate coil* stamp (459).

Roughly Opened Envelope – a *cover* opened in such a way that the top or side is torn in an uneven or jagged pattern. Such a cover is less desirable than one that is neatly opened.

Roulette – the slitting of paper between *stamps* to make their separation easier. No paper is actually removed in the rouletting process.

Round The World Flight – flight of the Graf Zeppelin around the world, starting from and ending at Lakehurst, New Jersey, August 8 – September 1, 1929. The flight was made with the cooperation of a number of postal administrations, including that of the United States.

Route Agent – a postal agent who accompanied and processed mail in transit. This position became obsolete in 1882 with the establishment of the *Railway Post Office*.

Rural Free Delivery – service of the post office, begun October 1, 1896 that provides mail delivery to rural customers. In the early years, mail was *postmarked* on the route by the carrier.

Rural Route – a route, usually numbered, traveled by a *Rural Free Delivery* carrier from the parent post office.

S

S – prefix letter used by Stamp Venturers (until 1998) in front of the *plate number* on its modern *postage stamp* production. Since 1998 the S prefix has been used by Sennett Security Products.

SIPEX – see *Sixth International Philatelic Exhibition*.

S20 – *marginal marking* on certain *rotary* press *plates* indicating the plate was made from a *die* with an experimental variation in the depth of the *frame* line.

S30 – *marginal marking* on certain *rotary* press *plates* indicating the plate was made from a *die* with an experimental variation in the depth of the *frame* line.

S40 – *marginal marking* on certain *rotary* press *plates* indicating the plate was made from a *die* with an experimental variation in the depth of the *frame* line.

Saint Louis Bears – see *Bear Stamps*.

Sanitary Fair Stamps – *labels* sold at post offices stations located at fairs held to raise money for the medical care of soldiers in the Civil War. The labels were issued by the government-chartered United States Sanitary Commission, but were not valid for *postage*. *Scott* numbers are prefixed with WV.

Savings Stamps – *stamps* issued by the *Post Office Department* that were redeemable in the form of U.S. Savings Bonds. Sale of Savings Stamps was discontinued in 1970. *Scott* numbers are prefixed with S or PS.

(The) Schermack Mailing Machine Company – a Detroit, Michigan based manufacturer of stamp *affixing machines,* *vending machines,* and *private coils*. Became *Mailometer Co.* in 1909.

Schermack Perforations – *perforations* privately applied to *imperforate flat plate stamps* by the *Schermack Mailing Machine Company*, which later became the *Mailometer Co.*, for use in its *affixing machines*. See also *Hyphen-Hole Perforations*.

Scott Specialized Catalogue of U.S. Stamps & Covers – the most widely accepted and comprehensive catalogue of United States *philatelic* material, generally abbreviated as *Scott* in this book

Scrambled Indicia – *hidden images* on *stamps* that can be viewed through a special lens available from the *USPS*.

Scratchboard – a *stamp* production technique that resembles traditional line *engraving*.

Screened Tagging – *tagging* that is made up of thin lines, or dot patterns that appear as lines, when viewed with low magnification. Example: 1998 32¢ Remember the Maine (3192).

Sea Post Office – a post office operated on a ship plying one of several sea routes. Sea Post Offices were full post offices and operated from 1891 into the 1930s.

Seal – 1) a *label* applied by the Post Office to "seal" mail, which was opened either intentionally, or by accident. Post Office Seals were supplied to larger post offices and have *Scott* numbers prefixed with OX. Typeset Seals were privately printed for sale to Fourth Class post offices and have Scott numbers prefixed with LOX. 2) a *label* such as a *Christmas Seal*.

Second Bureau Issue – see *Series of 1902*.

Second Class Mail – class of mail for newspapers, magazines, and other periodicals. This class of mail is now known as *Periodicals-Class Mail*.

Second Day Cover – a *cover postmarked* on the day following the official release of a stamp. Such covers were popular from the 1920s through the 1940s when stamps were placed on sale at the Philatelic Agency in Washington on the day after being issued elsewhere.

Second Issue Documentary Stamps – *revenue stamps* issued in 1871 (R103-133) printed by *Jos. R. Carpenter* on paper with *silk fibers*.

Secret Mark – marks added to *dies* by the *Continental Bank Note Co.* in order to distinguish their *stamps* from stamps previously produced from the same dies by the *National Bank Note Co.*

Sectional Center Facility – place where mail is processed for post offices in a specified geographic area.

Self Adhesive Stamp – a *stamp* that employs pressure-sensitive adhesive, as opposed to *water-activated gum.*

Selvage – see *margin.*

Semi-Postal – a *postage stamp* sold for more than its *face value*, with a portion of the difference between face value and sale price donated to a specified charitable activity. The first semi-postal (Breast Cancer Awareness) appeared in 1998. *Scott* numbers are prefixed with B.

Sennett Security Products – private printer of modern *postage stamps.* Example: 1998 Wisconsin Statehood (3206).

Separated Perforations – *perforations* between *stamps* in a block or other multiple that are no longer intact.

Separating Offices – a post office that processes mail in transit. See also *Transit Mark.*

Series of 1894 – the first set of *definitive postage stamps* to be printed by the *BEP.* Issued beginning in 1894. These stamps were prepared from *dies* received from the private company that previously used them to print stamps for the Post Office. The dies were altered, however, before their use by the *BEP.* Begins with *Scott* 246.

Series of 1902 – the second set of *definitive postage stamps* issued by the *BEP.* These stamps appeared in 1902. *Scott* numbers begin with 300.

Series of 1908 – see *Washington-Franklins.*

Series of 1922 – the *definitive* series of *postage stamps* issued beginning in 1922. Includes sheet *stamps*, *coils*, and *booklets.* Begins with *Scott* 551.

Series of 1938 – see *Presidential Series.*

Service Indicators – see *Service Inscribed Stamps.*

Service Inscribed Stamps – *stamps* that include wording in their *design* indicating the mail handling service for which the stamps were issued, as, for example, "Presorted First-Class". Stamps inscribed *Air Mail*, *Special Delivery*, etc. may also be considered Service Inscribed Stamps.

Se-Tenant – two or more *stamps* of different *designs* printed adjacent to one another on a *pane.* Earliest example: 1964 Christmas issue (1254-1257).

Set-off – 1) the result of ink from a newly printed *sheet* leaving an impression on the back of the sheet stacked on top of it. 2) the result of ink accidentally applied to the roller of a printing press being picked up by the next *sheet* to be printed. These *freaks* are sometimes misleadingly called offsets. See also *Phantom Numbers.*

7-1-71 – the date of issue for the 1971 *U.S. Postal Service stamp* (1396). This stamp was issued at every post office in the country, thus creating a specialty in the field of *First Day Cover* collecting.

Shade – a minor variation in color.

Shanghai – see *Offices in China.*

Sheet – a unit of *sheet stamps* produced on a printing press subdivided into *panes.* A sheet typically contains two or more panes. Early sheets contained two panes. Most twentieth century sheets contained four panes. Modern sheets may contain six or more panes. Although there are exceptions, sheet stamps are generally sold to the public only in pane format, not in sheet format. In popular usage the term "sheet" is incorrectly used for a "pane".

Sheet-fed – the process of printing on individual sheets of paper, as opposed to printing on a continuous *web* of paper.

Sheet Stamp – a *stamp* produced in *sheet* format and intended for sale in individual panes, as opposed to a stamp issued in *coil* or *booklet pane* format.

Sheet Waste – odd-sized remnants of the *web* of *rotary press sheet stamps* that were salvaged and *perforated gauge* 11, an economy measure creating very rare stamps. Example: *Scott* 596. Not to be confused with *Coil Waste*.

Shifted Transfer – a faulty impression created on an *engraved plate* when too much pressure is applied to a *transfer roll*, causing the *plate* to move slightly forward in the *transfer press*. As a result, the subsequent *rocking-in* of the transfer roll will not match exactly with the first impression and the lines are doubled at the forward edge of the *design*.

Ship Letter – a letter carried on a private ship that is not under government contract to carry mail. Such letters were delivered to the post office at the ship's port of entry.

Short Paid – see *Underfranked*.

Short Transfer – an impression on an *engraved plate* on which one edge, or two opposite edges, are weak, incomplete, or missing because the *siderographer* did not rock the *transfer roll* far enough in one or both directions. Example: 1983 Brooklyn Bridge, *UL2* (*position* 2 of the upper left *pane*).

Show Cancel – a *cancel*, unusually decorative and commemorative in nature, applied to *covers* at a stamp show.

Siderographer – an employee of the *BEP* who created *engraved* printing *plates* from a *transfer roll*.

Siderographer Initials – a *marginal marking*; the initials of the *siderographer* who created the *plate*, located in the lower left corner of the *plate*. This marginal marking first appeared in 1906 and was last used in 1928.

Siderography – the process of creating an *engraved plate* from a *transfer roll*.

Sidewise Coil – coil stamps with perforations at the sides, as opposed to *endwise coils*.

Silk Paper – paper containing silk threads, used to produce some *revenue* stamps. Example: *Scott* R135.

Silkote Paper – a special paper, very white and smooth, used experimentally by the *BEP* to produce a small number of the 2¢ Jefferson *sheet stamps* in the *Liberty Series* (1033a).

Silver Tax Stamp – *revenue stamp* used to pay a tax on profits from transactions in silver. Some older *documentary* stamps were *overprinted* "Silver Tax" prior to stamps being printed that were designed specifically for payment of the silver tax. *Scott* numbers are prefixed with RG.

Single Line Watermark – a *watermark* in which the initials USPS are composed with a single line. Example: *Scott* 374.

Sinkage – the outline, or impression, created by a *die*, found on most *large die proofs*.

Sixth Bureau Issue – see *Liberty Series*.

Sixth International Philatelic Exhibition – one in a series of international stamp shows hosted once every decade in the U.S. Held in Washington, D.C. in 1966. A *stamp* (1310) and *souvenir sheet* (1311) were issued in conjunction with this show.

Skiving – a method of stamp separation in which thin layers of paper are removed by grinding instead of cutting or punching. The result resembles perforations.

Sleeve – a seamless cylindrical *plate* used to print *intaglio* stamps on a *rotary* press.

Slogan Cancellation – a *cancellation* that contains words or graphics that promote or celebrate some cause or event.

Slogan Die – *die* in a *meter* machine which imprints words or pictures to the left of the *indicium* and town mark.

Slug – a removable piece of metal, used in the *postmark die* or *cancellation die* of a *cancelling machine*. The slug contains changeable information, such as date and time.

Small Bank Notes – nickname for the series of *postage stamps* produced in 1890-1893 by the *American Bank Note Co*. (219-229). This nickname helps distinguish these stamps from the *Large Bank Notes* that preceded them.

Small Die Proof – a *die proof*, often printed on a piece of *India paper*, which is significantly smaller than a *large die proof*.

Small Holes – *perforation* holes that are smaller than other perforations holes of the same *gauge*. For example, *Scott* 1055 in the *Liberty Series* exists with perforation holes of two different sizes (large and small) even though all are perforation gauge 10. Compare: *Large Holes*.

Socked-on-the-nose – see *Bullseye*.

Solid Tagging – see *Even Tagging*.

Solo Usage – a *cover franked* with only one *stamp*.

Southgate Memorial Trophy – prestigious award given at the annual meeting of the *United States Stamp Society*, for the best exhibit of nineteenth century material by a *USSS* member.

Souvenir Card – a *philatelic* card, not valid for *postage*, often depicting the *design* of one or more *stamps*. *Scott* numbers are prefixed with SC.

Souvenir Pages – post office announcement bulletins of new *postage stamps* that include text and an illustration of the postage stamp to be issued. Prior to the first souvenir pages in 1960 new issues were for a time announced to customers by postal card. *Scott* numbers are prefixed with SP.

Souvenir Sheet – a small *sheet* of one or more *stamps*, valid for *postage*, usually issued in conjunction with a *philatelic* exposition.

Special Delivery – service for a fee that provided for delivery of an item of mail to an addressee immediately upon its arrival at the addressee's post office. Begun in 1885, it was discontinued in 1997.

Special Delivery Stamps – *stamps* issued for use on *Special Delivery* mail. *Scott* numbers are prefixed with E.

Special Handling – service for a fee that expedites *parcel post* mail as though it were *First Class mail*. Such mail does not have the protection against examination given to First Class mail. When this service was first offered in 1925, mailers of live animals such as bees, chicks, and alligators were required to use it.

Special Handling Stamps – *stamps* issued to pay the *Special Handling* fee. *Scott* numbers are prefixed with QE.

Special Printing – re-issue of a *stamp* for a special purpose. This term applies particularly to stamps provided by the *Post Office Department* for (and subsequent to) the Centennial Exposition of 1876 (Examples: 2-3, 40-47, 102-111, and 123-132), and "*Farleys Follies*" (752-771).

Special Usage Stamps – *stamps* that are intended for just one specific function, for example, *Special Delivery*, *Special Handling*, and *Postage Due*.

Specimen – a sample *stamp* or *stamped envelope*, not valid for *postage*, generally overprinted "Specimen".

Speed Mail – a *USPOD* service that lasted for six weeks in 1960. It was a "fax" service for inter-agency mail, which the Post Office delivered in specially designed envelopes.

Speedy – a nickname for a *Special Delivery* letter.

Splice – a repair made to the *web* where it has been torn or cut. The web is reconnected, often with a piece of paper. On older rotary stamps this will usually result in a **double paper** variety.

Split Grill – a *stamp* showing portions of two or more **grills**.

Sprayed-on marking – *cancellation* or other marking sprayed-on a *cover* by the **Postal Service** in a dot-matrix pattern.

Squash-effect doubling – a *freak* created when a printing plate contacts the paper with too much pressure, creating a doubling effect of the *design*. This is not a *double impression*.

Stamp – a piece of printed security paper, usually gummed and perforated, printed under controlled and secure conditions, generally sold to the public to represent payment of a fee-for-service or a tax. See also *Postage Stamp, Local Stamp, Telegraph Stamp, and Revenue Stamp*.

Stamp agent – *USPOD* employee responsible for receiving and accounting for deliveries of completed *stamps* from nineteenth century private security printers and sending them to post offices as needed.

Stamp Decoder – a device marketed by *USPS*; used to observe **hidden images** on certain modern *postage stamps*.

Stamp Venturers – private contractor for *postage stamps* in partnership with other companies. An example of its work is the 29¢ Desert Shield/Desert Storm **sheet stamp** (2551).

Stamped Card – the current *USPS* term for what was formerly known as a *postal card*.

Stamped Envelope – an envelope with a stamp-like **indicium** documenting payment of *postage*. Stamped envelopes were introduced in 1853.

Stampless Letter – a letter that does not have a *postage stamp* affixed. Generally used to refer to letters from before the introduction of postage stamps, or from the time when prepayment of postage by stamps was not required.

Stamps.com – first company approved by the *USPS* to sell *postage* online.

Standard Mail (A) – *bulk-rate* mail known as **Third Class Mail** prior to July 1, 1996.

Standard Mail (B) – mail known *as Fourth Class Mail* prior to July 1, 1996.

Star Plates – *flat press plates* containing a star in the *margin*. Stars were used on some **Washington-Franklin** and **Fourth Bureau** plates to indicate a slightly wider spacing in the vertical margins between *stamps* (when compared to earlier similar plates that had less space between stamps). The purpose of the star was to alert workers that adjustments needed to be made in *perforating* these *sheets*. Star plates were produced in an attempt to manufacture better centered stamps.

Star Route – a route along which a contractor carries mail, as opposed to a route along which a postal employee carries mail. Sometimes mail was also collected and delivered along a star route.

State Revenue Stamp – a *revenue stamp* issued by a state, municipality, or other local jurisdiction.

Station Cancel – a *cancellation* that identifies the post office branch where the canceling was done.

Sterling Sommer – private printer of modern postage stamps. Example: the 1995 Carousel Horses (2976-2979).

Stevens Security Press – subcontractor to *Ashton-Potter (USA) LTD* for printing the 1997 Marshall Plan Anniversary *stamps* (3141).

Stickney Press – an *intaglio*, *web-fed*, *rotary press* developed by *BEP* employee Benjamin Stickney. The first one became operational in 1914. The last was decommissioned in 1962.

Stock Transfer Stamp – a *revenue stamp* used to pay a federal tax on transfers of stock ownership. *Scott* numbers are prefixed with RD.

Straight Edge – a *sheet stamp* on which one side (edge), or two adjacent sides (edges), are without *perforations*. This is the manner in which many early and some recent stamps were issued. A straight edge is a normal result of the production process.

Straight Line Perforator – a machine once used at the *BEP* that had a set of *perforating* pins and a center cutting wheel. In one pass through this machine either horizontal or vertical perforations were produced and the *sheet* was cut in half.

Street Car R.P.O. – a specialized type of *Railway Post Office* operated in a street car in one of fourteen cities in the years between 1891 and 1929.

Strike – 1) the *postal marking* made on a *cover* by a *cancellation* or *postmarking* device, sometimes described with words such as, "clear" or "illegible". 2) the action of making a mark on a cover, usually with a hand-held device.

Strip – three or more *stamps* in a vertical or horizontal format.

Stripe Tagging – see *Band Tagging*.

Stripper marks – small marks of ink between the *perforation* holes of *stamps* caused by the accumulation of ink on *strippers*.

Strippers – "fingers" used in the *perforating* process to free the perforated *sheets* from the perforating pins.

Stroke Perforating – perforating accomplished with a straight up and down action of the perforating pins.

Stuffer – a piece of card placed in a *cover* of *philatelic* origin in an attempt to enable the cover to go through the *mailstream* without damage and to improve the quality of any postal markings placed on the face of the cover.

Sub Station – designation used from 1890-1902 for certain retail postal units that operated under the supervision of a full station or main post office; they frequently used *postal markings* containing "SUB".

Summer gum – name given to the comparatively hard *gum* applied to *stamps* at the *BEP* during the summer season during the first decades of the twentieth century.

Supplementary Mail – mail dispatched to a particular ship or train after the normal *Closing of the Mail*. An extra fee was usually charged for this service.

Supplementary Mail Marking – *auxiliary marking* indicating a *cover* received *Supplementary Mail* service.

Surcharge – an *overprint* that changes the *face value* of a *stamp* or item of *postal stationery*. Example: *Postal Cards* of 1917 surcharged in 1952 (UX31-UX35).

Surface Mail – *international* mail that does not travel by air.

Surface Printing – see *Lithography*.

Survey Flight – a flight made to determine a new *air mail* route, or to acquaint a crew with a new air mail route.

T

T – a *UPU* auxiliary marking indicating *postage due*, typically applied by the Post Office at an *exchange office*.

3M Corporation – private printer of modern *stamps*, beginning with the 1994 29¢ Eagle self-adhesive (2598). *National Label Co.* actually printed this stamp for 3M.

Tab – the piece of paper selvedge, with or without *marginal marking*, attached to a *booklet pane*. In traditional *booklets*, panes were either glued by the tabs into cardboard covers, or stapled between the covers through the tab.

Taggant – the phosphor compound used in the *tagging* of *stamps*.

Tagging – see *Phosphor Tagging*.

Tagging - Type I – *overall tagging* where all four *margins* on a *pane* of 100 *stamps* are only partially tagged. The stamps are all fully tagged. This, the first type of tagging used, appears on seven stamps. Example: *Liberty* issue 4¢ Lincoln (1036a).

Tagging - Type II – *overall tagging* where the large *margin* on a *pane* of 100 *stamps* is only partially tagged. The other three margins and all stamps are fully tagged. Examples are many **Prominent American** issue stamps and a few **Liberty** issues.

Tagging - Type IIA – *overall tagging* where all four *margins*, as well as all *stamps* on a *pane* of 100 are fully tagged. Examples are many **Prominent American** issue stamps.

Tagging - Type III – *tagging* similar to Type IIA, but characterized by gaps in tagging or bright lines resembling coil *joint lines* that cross the narrow axis of one row of *stamps* in a *pane* of 100. The lines were produced by the gap where two metal tagging plates butted together. Examples: 3¢ Statue of Liberty in the **Liberty** series (1035b).

Tagging - Type OP – Tagging applied by an *offset* press. Example: 1966 5¢ Women's Clubs *stamp* (1316).

Taker-Off-er – nickname for employees of the **BEP** who removed printed *sheets* from the *flat plate press*.

TAP Tagging – *stamps* that were Tagged After being **Perforated**. This was only done to the 1966 6¢ National Park Service (1314), and 1969 6¢ Beautification of America (1365-1368) stamps.

Taxpaid Revenue Stamp – a *revenue stamp* that is not denominated in money, but in some other measurement, generally a quantity or unit size, for example: one pint, 1/8 barrel, ten cigarettes.

Teeth – the tooth-like projections of paper on the edges of *perforated stamps*.

Telegraph Stamps – *stamps* issued by private telegraph companies for use on their own telegrams. *Scott* numbers contain a T.

Tenebrescent – a chemical agent that when added to stamp papers or printers ink causes them to appear darker when viewed under long wave **ultra-violet light**. This is the opposite of a fluorescent agent that causes paper or inks to glow brighter under long wave ultra-violet light. Example of tenebrescent ink: 2001 34¢ Flag over Farm, water activated gum, plate P2222.

Territorial Cover – a *cover* posted in what was a territory at the time of its mailing.

Test Stamp – see **Dummy Stamp**.

Third Bureau Issue – see **Washington-Franklins**.

Third Class Mail – category of mail that has evolved over the years, providing for the mailing of both single-piece items and, since 1928, **bulk** mailings. Items mailed by Third Class have included printed mater, catalogs, seed, samples of merchandise, and advertising. This category has been used for bulk mailings both by commercial and non-profit users. Now known as **Standard Mail**.

Third International Philatelic Exhibition – one in a series of international stamp shows hosted once every decade in the U.S. Held in New York City in 1936. A **Souvenir sheet** (778) was issued in conjunction with this show.

Third Issue Documentary Stamps – *revenue stamps* (R134-R150) issued in 1871-1874, printed by Jos. R. Carpenter.

Tied – a *stamp* that is connected (tied) to a cover by a *cancellation* or *postmark*.

TIPEX – see **Third International Philatelic Exhibition**.

Tobacco Sale Tax Stamp – *overprinted documentary revenue stamps* issued to pay a federal tax on tobacco sales. The Supreme Court declared the tax unconstitutional. *Scott* RJ.

Toning – the undesirable discoloration of a *cover* or a *stamp*; also sometimes known as "foxing".

TOP – a *marginal inscription* appearing on some bicolored *flat press* stamps. The purpose of the inscription was to reduce of the possibility of a *sheet* being inverted on its second pass through the press, and thus also to reduce the possibility of creating *invert stamps*.

Toppan, Carpenter & Company – contractor for *postage stamps* from 1857-1861.

Toppan, Carpenter, Casilear & Company – contractor for *postage stamps* from 1851-1857.

Track Tagging Lines – two or more continuous horizontal *tagging* lines that resemble "train tracks" that are sometimes found on *coils*. Under *ultraviolet light* the lines can appear brighter or untagged. The cause is the wearing of the tagging ink transfer roller that was previously used for precancelling coil stamps with two lines on the *Cottrell* 803 press. Track tagging is more commonly found on the Cottrell Press 1983 2¢ Locomotive coil (1897).

Trailer Permit Stamps – *revenue stamps* issued by the National Park Service. These stamps were required to bring a house trailer into a national park or monument. Issued in 1939. *Scott* numbers are prefixed with RVT.

Transfer Press – a special press on which a *siderographer* creates *transfer rolls and printing plates*.

Transfer Roll – a roll of steel used in the production of a *plate* that prints *engraved* stamps. The shape of the roll is not unlike a slice of a modest sized tree branch. Once a *die* has been completed, a soft, blank transfer roll is pressed into it. In this way the design from the die is transferred to the roll in *relief*. Several such designs are usually transferred onto each roll. After being *hardened*, the transfer roll is used to create a *plate* by *rocking* the *design* into each position on the unhardened steel plate where a subject is to appear.

Transit Mark(ings) – a *postmark* applied to a *cover* by a *separating post office* while in transit between an originating and destination post office. A separating post office was one at which mail was received for dispatch to other post offices. Transit postmarks generally contain the word "transit" and were applied to the back of covers.

Used in the late nineteenth and early twentieth centuries. See also *Receiving Mark*.

Transitional Perforations – *perforations* on one side of a *stamp* that begin as perf. 11 and end as perf. 10. These transitional perforations were produced during the early 1920s on some *flat plate* stamps. The cause was the use of a gauge 11 perforating wheel on which a small section of pins was replaced by a section of gauge 10 pins.

Trans-Mississippi Issue – *commemorative postage stamps* issued for the Omaha Exposition of 1898 (285-293).

Transportation Coils – an extensive series of *definitive postage stamps*, which began appearing in 1981. *Scott* numbers begin with 1897.

Transports – a series of *air mail stamps*, all with the same *design*, first appearing in 1941 (C25-C31).

Treasury Savings Stamp – *stamp* issued by the Treasury Department, redeemable in the form of **War Savings Stamps** or Treasury Savings Certificates. *Scott* numbers are prefixed with TS.

Treaty Rate – 1) an international *postage* rate established by one of several bilateral agreements between the U.S. and other nations prior to establishment of the **Universal Postal Union**. 2) a special postal rate, less than the standard *UPU* rate, negotiated between the U.S. and a foreign country. Also called **Convention Rate**.

Trial Color Proof – a *proof*, typically a *die proof* (but sometimes a *plate proof*), printed in a test color, as part of the process of determining the color in which a *stamp* will be issued.

Trieste Occupation Issues – see **Allied Military Government Stamps**.

Triple Transfer – a *plate variety* in which a portion of the *design* is tripled. For further explanation see **Double Transfer**.

Triplex Cancel – *cancel* similar to a *duplex*, except that the year is located between the *dial* and the *killer*.

Twisted Double Transfer – two impressions of a *double transfer* that are not oriented clockwise.

Type Number – a number assigned by the *Scott Catalogue* to all *stamps* of a common *design*.

Typeset Seals – see *Seal*.

Typography – see *Letterpress*.

U

U – prefix letter used by *U.S. Bank Note Company* in front of the *plate number* on its modern *stamp* production.

UGAI – see *Ungummed As Issued*.

UL – Upper left. Refers to the upper left *pane* from a traditional *sheet* of four *panes*. These initials are also used to describe *plate blocks* taken from the upper left corner of such sheets.

UPU – see *Universal Postal Union*.

UR – Upper right. Refers to the upper right *pane* from a traditional *sheet* of four *panes*. These initials are also used to describe *plate blocks* taken from the upper right corner of such sheets.

U.S. Automatic Vending Co. – New York based manufacturer of *vending machines* and *private coils*.

U.S. Automatic Vending Perforations – *perforations* privately applied to *imperforate stamps* by the U.S. Automatic Vending Company for use in its *vending machines*.

U.S. Bank Note Co. – contractor for *postage stamps* beginning in 1989.

U.S. Official Postal Guide – primary resource for information on post office listings, domestic and foreign *postage rates*, policy, orders and regulations. Published from 1890 to 1953.

USIR – a *watermark* found on some *revenue stamps* and, by *error*, on a printing of the $1 Woodrow Wilson stamp in the *Presidential Issue* (832b). USIR is an acronym for United States Internal Revenue.

USPOD – see *United States Post Office Department*.

USPS – 1) the *watermark* used on almost all watermarked *postage stamps*. Some authorities believe these initials stood for United States Postage Stamp. See *Single Line Watermark* and *Double Line Watermark*. 2) see *United States Postal Service*.

USSS – see *United States Stamp Society*.

Ultraviolet Light – light beyond the visible spectrum used to detect *luminescence*. Long wave ultraviolet light is commonly used to detect *fluorescent* brighteners, while short wave is commonly used to detect *phosphor tagging*.

Uncoated Paper – Paper with a rough surface, with many jagged "hills and valleys" when looked at under magnification. See also *Coated Paper* and *Prephosphored Paper*.

Underfranked – an item of mail bearing insufficient *postage*.

Unexploded – a *stamp booklet* that is intact, that is, not taken apart.

Ungummed As Issued – stamps issued without *gum*, as opposed to stamps from which the gum has been removed. *Farleys Follies* were issued without gum.

United States Envelope Company – manufacturer of modern *stamped envelopes*.

United States Post Office Department – the branch of government that operated the Post Office prior to its reorganization in 1971.

United States Postal Service – the government corporation formed to operate the Post Office in 1971.

The United States Specialist – monthly journal of the *United States Stamp Society*.

United States Stamp Society – leading organization of collectors of U.S. *stamps*, formerly known as the BIA (Bureau Issues Association).

Universal Postal Union – an international organization, tracing its origin to 1863, which facilitates the transmission of mail between member countries.

Universal Stamping Machine Co. – major manufacturer of *cancelling machines* in use from the 1900s to the 1990s.

Unlisted – a stamp or other philatelic item not recognized by a catalog publisher.

Unofficial First Day Cover – a *stamp* on *cover cancelled* on the first day of issue, but from a city other than the one(s) in which the stamp was officially released.

Unwatermarked – *stamp* or *postal stationery* with no *watermark*.

V

V – prefix letter used by *Avery Dennison* in front of the *plate number* on its modern *postage stamp* production.

Valley – the portion of a simulated *perforation* on a *self-adhesive stamp* that curves inward next to each *peak*.

VAMP – see *Vending and Affixing Machine Perforations*.

V-Mail – a mail system used during World War II, from 1942 to 1945, to expedite messages to and from active duty military personnel overseas. Messages were written on standard forms, mailed to processing centers, photographed in quantity on microfilm, and sent by air to or from the U.S. The microfilm was then processed, printed, and dispatched to the addressee by ordinary mail. V-Mail letters were sent free of postage by members of the Armed Forces.

Variety – a *stamp* or other *philatelic* item that differs in some way from the norm. Example: the second type of the 1970 Christmas stamp (1414d).

Vending and Affixing Machine Perforations – *perforations* privately applied to *imperforate stamps* by *The Attleboro Stamp Company, The Brinkerhoff Company, The Farwell Company, International Vending Machine Co., The Mailometer Co., The Schermack Co.,* and *U.S. Automatic Vending Co.* These privately *perforated* stamps were sold in *coil* format for use in *vending machines* and *affixing machines*.

Vending Booklet – 1) traditional *booklet* of *stamps* (one or more *panes* attached to a set of cardboard covers) intended to be sold from a *vending machine*. 2) contemporary booklet of *self-adhesive stamps* folded and sealed to form a booklet intended to be sold in a vending machine.

Vending Machine – a machine that sells *stamps* or other postal material to the public.

Vignette – the central portion of a stamp *design*, often surrounded by a border or *frame*.

W

War Emergency Rate – a tax, levied in the form of increased *postage* rates, to help pay for World War I. The war emergency rate was in effect from November 2, 1917 until restoration of the pre-war rates on July 1, 1919.

War Savings Stamps – *stamps* issued by the Treasury Department during World War I and World War II that were redeemable during WWI for War Certificates and during WWII for Defense Bonds or War Bonds. *Scott* numbers begin with WS.

Wash Drawing – a painting or drawing in which thin layers, or washes, of watercolors or India ink are used.

Washington 2006 – one of a series of international stamp shows hosted once every decade in the U.S.; held in Washington, D.C. in 2006.

Washington Bicentennials – *commemorative stamps* (704-715) and *stamped envelopes* (U523-U528) issued in 1932 for the bicentennial of Washington's birth.

Washington-Franklin Head Issue – the Third Bureau Issue; a series of about 350 *definitive postage stamps* issued between 1908 and 1922. Found between *Scott* 331 and 547, and K1-18.

Washington Views – series of high *face-value Priority Mail* and *Express Mail stamps* begun with the 2001 $3.50 Capitol Dome (3472).

Water-activated gum – *gum* on a *stamp* that must be moistened in order to affix the stamp to an envelope.

Waterbury Cancels – *fancy cancels* used in Waterbury, Connecticut that were created by its *postmaster*.

Watermark – a pattern embedded in paper during the production process, created by an intentional thinning of the paper. Watermarked paper has been used for *stamps*, *stamped envelopes*, and *postal cards*. The design of the watermark on stamps generally consists of the letters USPS. Watermarks on postal stationery vary, but generally contain the letters "US".

Way Letter – a loose letter handed to an official mail carrier (stage, horseback, boat or railroad) in the absence of a *route agent*. A way letter could not be added to sacks of mail being transported because they were locked and the mail carrier did not have a key to them. The way letter was delivered to the first post office reached for dispatch to its destination. A fee was charged for this service. The word "Way" was written or stamped on such letters as an accounting device.

Web – a continuous roll of paper used on a printing press or *off-line perforator*.

Web-fed – the process of printing from continuous paper on a roll (a *web*), as opposed to printing from individual sheets of paper.

Wells, Fargo and Company – An *express mail* company formed in 1852 that provided service in the West; agents for the operators of *the Pony Express*; issuers of *local stamps*.

Wesson "Time-On-Bottom" handstamp – duplex handstamp that displays date numerically as DD MM YY, with the time of day at the bottom of the dial.

Wet Printing – *intaglio* printing on paper that has been dampened to facilitate the transfer of the ink. Wet printing of *Bureau Issues* ended in the late 1950s. See also *Dry Printing*.

Window Envelope – envelope with a transparent window for displaying the name and address of the recipient.

Wine Stamps – see *Cordials, Wine, etc. Stamps*.

Winter gum – name given to the comparatively soft *gum* applied to *stamps* during the winter at the *BEP* during the early decades of the twentieth century.

Wiper marks – streaks of ink left on an *intaglio* printed *stamp* due to the failure of the wiper to completely remove ink from the surface of the *plate*. A stamp with wiper marks is a *freak*.

Wrapper – a sheet of paper imprinted with a stamp-like *indicium* that can be folded and sealed around a newspaper or periodical for mailing. A wrapper is an item of *postal stationery*.

Wrinkled Tagging – Short bright or untagged lines overlying a stamp's tagging that resemble "chicken wire" when viewed under *ultraviolet light*. Caused by tagging roller surfaces that became wrinkled from pressure and age.

Z

Z Grill – 1) one of several types of *grills* used in the nineteenth century, about 11 x 14 mm in size. 2) a nickname for *Scott* 85A, of which only one copy is known to exist in private ownership.

ZazzleStamps – *Personalized Postage* produced by *Pitney Bowes*.

Zepps – nickname for the high *face value air mail stamps* of 1930 issued for mail carried on the dirigible Graf Zeppelin (C13-C15).

ZIP Block – a *margin block* with inscription urging the use of *ZIP code*, or depicting the "Mr. Zip" character. ZIP Blocks appeared between 1964 and 1994.

ZIP Code – originally an acronym for "Zone Improvement Plan", this five digit number, now an essential part of every address, helps facilitate the sorting of mail. Instituted in 1963.

ZIP+4 – the nine digit *ZIP Code* which includes the basic five digit ZIP Code plus four additional digits representing the sector or segment of the address. The ZIP+4 encodes an address to a block face (one side of a city block).

Zone – a number that was part of addresses, introduced in Boston in the 1920s, and used in many large cities from 1943 until the institution of the *ZIP Code* in 1963. The Zone number was placed between the name of the city and state. Example: "Brooklyn 32, N.Y." The zone number helped facilitate the sorting and distribution of mail. A prototype of postal zones was attempted without notable success in Chicago in the 1890s.

Appendix B
Print Resources

Agris, Joseph. *The Transportation Coils and other Plate Number Coil Issues*. Houston, Texas: Eclectic Publishing Co., 1987.

Alexander, Thomas J. *United States 1847 Issue: A Cover Census*. Austin, Texas: U.S. Philatelic Classics Society, Inc., 2001.

Amick, George. *The Inverted Jenny: Money, Mystery, Mania*. Sidney, Ohio: Amos Press Inc., 1986.

—— *Linn's U.S. Stamp Yearbook 1988*. Sidney, Ohio: Linn's Stamp News, 1989.

—— *Linn's U.S. Stamp Yearbook 1989*. Sidney, Ohio: Linn's Stamp News, 1990.

—— *Linn's U.S. Stamp Yearbook 1990*. Sidney, Ohio: Linn's Stamp News, 1991.

—— *Linn's U.S. Stamp Yearbook 1991*. Sidney, Ohio: Linn's Stamp News, 1992.

—— *Linn's U.S. Stamp Yearbook 1992*. Sidney, Ohio: Linn's Stamp News, 1993.

—— *Linn's U.S. Stamp Yearbook 1993*. Sidney, Ohio: Linn's Stamp News, 1994.

—— *Linn's U.S. Stamp Yearbook 1994*. Sidney, Ohio: Linn's Stamp News, 1995.

—— *Linn's U.S. Stamp Yearbook 1995*. Sidney, Ohio: Linn's Stamp News, 1996.

—— *Linn's U.S. Stamp Yearbook 1996*. Sidney, Ohio: Linn's Stamp News, 1997.

—— *Linn's U.S. Stamp Yearbook 1997*. Sidney, Ohio: Linn's Stamp News, 1998.

—— *Linn's U.S. Stamp Yearbook 1998*. Sidney, Ohio: Linn's Stamp News, 1999.

—— *Linn's U.S. Stamp Yearbook 1999*. Sidney, Ohio: Linn's Stamp News, 2000.

—— *Linn's U.S. Stamp Yearbook 2000*. Sidney, Ohio: Linn's Stamp News, 2002.

—— *Linn's U.S. Stamp Yearbook 2001*. Sidney, Ohio: Linn's Stamp News, 2002.

—— *Linn's U.S. Stamp Yearbook 2002*. Sidney, Ohio: Linn's Stamp News, 2003.

—— *Linn's U.S. Stamp Yearbook 2003*. Sidney, Ohio: Linn's Stamp News, 2004.

Anonymous. *Report of the Postmaster General for the Year Ending June 30, 1870*. Washington, D.C.: United States Post Office, November 15, 1870.

—— *Mekeel's Weekly* 16(9):1.1902.

—— "Chronicle – United States," *The Metropolitan Philatelist* 31(24):193.1913.

—— *Postal Laws and Regulations of the United States of America – 1924*. Washington, D.C., Post Office Department, 1924.

—— "U.S. Notes," *Linn's Weekly Stamp News*, September 24, 1938.

—— "Benjamin R. Stickney Dies – Inventor of Rotary Press for Stamps," *STAMPS* 54(5):199.1946.

—— "Robert E. Fellers Becomes Deputy Third Assistant Postmaster General," *STAMPS* 66(12):509.1949.

—— "1954 Christmas Seals," *American Philatelist* 68(2):146.1954.

—— "The Clubhouse – Boston Philatelic Society Night," *The Collectors Club Philatelist* 34(4)198.1955.

—— "Certified Mail to Start About June 1st," *STAMPS* 91(6):236.1955.

—— "Additional Liberties Revealed – Series of Eighteen To Have 6 Presidents, 6 Historical Shrines, 6 Famous Americans," *Linn's Stamp News* p. 1. June 20, 1955.

—— *The Story of Fluorescence*. Raytech Industries: Middletown, Connecticut. 1965.

—— "The Initial Step to Photogravure in U.S. Stamp Production," *The United States Specialist* 38(7):257–258.1967.

—— "U.S. to Release First Gravure Stamp," *American Philatelist* 80(10):726–728.1967.

—— *History of the Bureau of Engraving and*

Printing 1862–1962. 18th ed. New York: Sanford J. Durst, 1978.

—— "U.S.P.S. to Issue Sequoyah Stamp Dec. 27, 1980 – News, Views and Comments," *STAMPS* 193(12):802.1980.

—— "Americana Definitive to Debut in Dallas," *Linn's Stamp News* p. 11. April 6, 1981.

—— "World Stamp Expo '89 Will be an Historic Event," *American Philatelist* 103(10):944–946.1989.

—— "How Do I Know When a Post Office Closed?" *PMCC Bulletin* 47(6):17.1994.

—— *Catalog of United States Perfins.* Long Beach, New York: Perfins Club of the United States. 1998.

—— *Precancel Stamp Society Bureau Precancel Catalog.* Wichita, Kansas; Framingham, Massachusetts; Missoula, Montana: Dilmond D. Postlewait. 1997.

Armstrong, Martin A. *United States Coil Issues 1906–1938.* Lawrenceville, New Jersey: Martin A. Armstrong Enterprises, 1977.

—— *The Washington Franklins, 1908–1921.* Lawrenceville, New Jersey: Trenton Publishing Co., 1979.

Ashbrook, Stanley. "An Analysis of the Types of the U.S. One Cent 1851 and 1857," *American Philatelist* 35(5):203.1922.

—— *The United States One Cent Stamp of 1851–1857,* 2 vols. New York: Lindquist Publishing Inc., 1938.

Ashbrook, Stanley and Mortimer Neinken. *The United States One Cent Stamp of 1851 to 1861.* United States: U.S. Philatelic Classics Society, 1972

Baadke, Michael. "Two new Victorian Heart Love stamps are first cut-to-shape self adhesives," *Linn's Stamp News,* p. 1. January 18, 1999.

Barlett, J. Delano and Walter W. Norton. *Handbook and Checklist of United States Internal Revenue Stamps, Hydrometers, Lock Seals.* Springfield, Massachusetts: United States Revenue Society. 1912.

Bauman, Fred. "The American Artists Series of 1961–1975," *Stamp Collector* p. 18–19. December 15, 1997.

Baur, Brian C. *Franklin D. Roosevelt and the Stamps of the United States 1933–45.* Sidney, Ohio: Linn's Stamp News, 1993.

—— "The Giori Press Forever Changed U.S. Stamps," *Scott Stamp Monthly* 12(9):14–15.1994.

—— *Franklin D. Roosevelt: The Stamp Collecting President.* Sidney, Ohio: Linn's Stamp News, 1999.

Baxter, James H. "Experimental Bi-Color Rotary Web-Fed Press," *The Bureau Specialist* 26(6):163–170.1955; 26(7):200–205.1955; 26(8):228–234.1955.

Baxter, James A. *Printing Postage Stamps by Line Engraving.* Lawrence, Massachusetts: Quarterman Publications, 1981.

Bayless, William H. "Fluorescent Papers," *The Bureau Specialist* 36(6):212–213.1965.

—— "Luminescent U.S. Postal Issues," *American Philatelic Congress Book* vol. 34. Baltimore, Maryland: American Philatelic Congress, 1968.

—— "Luminescence," *The United States Specialist* 40(11):482–483.1969.

—— "The 1969 Baltimore, MD., Precanceled Christmas Stamp," *The United States Specialist* 41(4):141–148.1970.

—— "Luminescence," *The United States Specialist* 41(12):464–466.1970.

—— "Luminescence," *The United States Specialist* 44(7):338–342.1973.

Beachboard, John H. *United States Postal Card Catalog.* Thousand Oaks, California: United Postal Stationary Society, 2000.

Beecher, Henry W., and Anthony S. Wawrukiewicz. *U. S. International Postal Rates, 1872–1996.* Portland, Oregon: CAMA Publishing Company, 1996.

—— *U.S. Domestic Postal Rates, 1872–1999.* Portland, Oregon: CAMA Publishing Company, 1999.

Bennett, David M. "Unique Marginal Markings on the U.S. Offset Printing Issue of 1918–20," *The 1965 Congress Book, Thirty-First Philatelic Congress.* Phoenix, Arizona: American Philatelic Congress, 1965.

Bevan, Arthur. "Philatelic Research on Stamp Designs," *Fourth American Philatelic Congress Book,* Hartford, Connecticut: American Philatelic Congress, 1938.

Billings, Bart A. *A Handbook: U.S. Postal Markings Impressed by Machines.* Tampa, Florida: The Machine Cancel Society, 1992.

Birch, Alfred J. *Postal history of the United States Virgin Islands formerly the Danish West Indies* State College, Pennsylvania: American Philatelic Society, c. 1966.

Bishop, Percy C. "At Home and Abroad," *Mekeel's Weekly Stamp News* 33(52):494.1919.

Blessington, John J. and Arthur Thomas. *The Postal Stationary of the Philippines under United States Administration 1898–1946.* Redlands, California: United Postal Stationary Society, 1983.

Boerger, Alfred G. *Handbook on U.S. Luminescent Stamps.* Ft. Lauderdale, Florida: A. Boerger, 1974.

Boggs, Winthrop S. "U.S.P.S.," *Notes on United States Watermarked Postage Stamps.* London: Unwin Brothers Ltd, 1958.

—— *Early American Perforating Machines and Perforations 1857–1867.* Toronto, Canada: Unitrade Press, 1982.

Boughner, Fred et al. *Linn's U. S. Stamp Yearbook 1983.* Sidney, Ohio: Linn's Stamp News, 1984.

Boughner, Fred. *Linn's U. S. Stamp Yearbook 1984.* Sidney, Ohio: Linn's Stamp News, 1985.

—— *Linn's U. S. Stamp Yearbook 1985.* Sidney, Ohio: Linn's Stamp News, 1986.

—— *Linn's U. S. Stamp Yearbook 1986.* Sidney, Ohio: Linn's Stamp News, 1987.

—— *Linn's U. S. Stamp Yearbook 1987.* Sidney, Ohio: Linn's Stamp News, 1988.

—— *Airmail Antics.* Sidney, Ohio: Amos Press, 1988.

Bourke, Paul. "Exploring the Washington-Franklin Era," *The United States Specialist* 74(1):27–34.2003; 74(2):59–66.2003; 74(3):123–128.2003; 74(4):171–174.2003; 74(5):219–229.2003; 74(6):267–276.2003; 74(7):315–323.2003; 74(8):363–371.2003; 74(9):411–420.2003; 74(10):459–467.2003; 74(11):507–518.2003; 74(12):555–560.2003; 75(1):27–32.2004; 75(2):55–61.2004; 75(3):123–128.2004; 4(4):171–179.2004; 75(5):207–214.2004; 75(6):267–274.2004; 75(7):315–320.2004.

Bowker, H. *Guam Guard Mail.* Privately Printed, 1939.

—— *Philately: Printing Methods and Techniques.* State College, Pennsylvania: Pennsylvania State University, 1985.

Braceland, Jr., J. Frank. "Newspapers and Periodicals," *United States Specialist* 37(9):365–369.1966; 37(10):413–415.1966; 38(1):15–18.1967; 38(2):68–69.1967; 38(4):144.1967; 38(5):177–179.1967; 38(10):382–383.1967; 38(11):429–431.1967; 38(12):460–463.1967; 39(2):70–72.1968; 39(4):150–153.1968; 39(8):288–291.1968; 39(9):312–315.1968; 40(1):30–32.1969; 40(2):62–65.1969; 40(4):156–161.1969; 40(6):248–251.1968; 40(10):428–431.1969; 41(2)48.1970; 41(6):229–232.1970; 42(2):48–53.1970; 42(5):148–152.1971; 43(4):164–172.1972; 44(7):321–327.1973; 45(7):338–341.1974; 45(9):410–413.1974.

Brazer, Clarence W. "Essays versus Proofs," *The Essay-Proof Journal* 6(1):32.1949.

—— "New York Postmaster's Miniature Plate of Nine," *Twentieth American Philatelic Congress Book*. St. Louis, Missouri: American Philatelic Congress, 1954.

Brett, George W. "The Recognition and Differentiation of Dry and Wet Intaglio Engraved Stamps Produced at the Bureau of Printing and Engraving" *STAMPS* pp. 50–51. October 8, 1955.

—— *The Manufacture of United States Postage Stamps*. New York: American Philatelic Congress, 1958.

—— "Those Test Samples Again," *The Bureau Specialist* 31(3):64–65.1960.

—— *The Giori Press*. West Somerville, Massachusetts: Bureau Issues Association, Inc., 1961.

—— "The U.S. Postage Stamp Plates of the Banknote Companies," *The Bureau Specialist* 35(5):163–164,167.1964.

—— "Two Varieties of the Pressure-Sensitive (Self-Adhesive) Christmas Stamp, Issued November 15, 1974," *The United States Specialist* 46(4):159–163.1975; 46(5):203–212.1975.

—— "Two Major Varieties of the Americana 16¢ Horizontal Coil," *The United States Specialist* 51(1):5–10.1980; 51(2):72–76.1980.

—— *Printing Methods and Techniques*. University Park, Pennsylvania: The Pennsylvania State University, 1985.

—— "How many U.S. Postage Stamps per year are too many?" *The Congress Book 1986: Fifty-Second American Philatelic Congress*. Los Angeles, California: American Philatelic Congress, 1986.

—— "What is a First-Day Cover?" *The United States Specialist* 60(12):635–637.1989.

—— "The Two-Cent 1894 Type IV: An Uncatalogued Major Variety," *The United States Specialist* 64(9):390–395.1993.

—— "Updating the U.S. 1847's on Their 150th Anniversary: Beginning, Production, Ending," *The Congress Book 1997*. San Francisco, California: The American Philatelic Congress, Inc., 1997.

Brockert, Joe. "Dix definitive begins new era in printing," *Linn's Stamp News* p. 8. September 26, 1983.

Brookman, Lester G. *The United States Postage Stamps of the 19th Century*, 3 vols. North Miami, Florida: David G. Phillips Publishing Co. Inc., 1989.

—— *The Bank Note Issues of United States Stamps 1870–1893*. Weston, Massachusetts: Triad Publications, 1981.

Bruns, Weimer, and Maisel. *Specimens of Stamped Envelopes and Wrappers of the United States*. Redlands, California: United Postal Stationary Society, c. 1991.

Burcham Carl. "Quadrant Printing; BEP Groups 4 Different Panes in Sheet," *The United States Specialist* 55(3):131–133.1984.

Burleson, Albert. *Postmaster General's Annual Report for fiscal 1919 (year ending June 30, 1919)*. Washington, D.C.: U.S. Government Printing Office, 1919.

Burns, Ronald A. *Study of the Production Records for the 1903 and 1914–15 Printings of the "Roosevelt" and "Panama-Pacific" Small Die Proofs*. Bureau Issues Association Research Paper #7. Madison, Wisconsin: Private Press. 1994.

—— *A Type Written Transcription of the U.S. Post Office Dept. Stamp Bill Book Numbers for the Issue of 1870 Ordinaries, 1870-1879. Part One: The National & Continental Issues*. USSS Research Paper #19. Columbus, Ohio: United States Stamp Society. 2005.

Cabot, George D. "The Story of the Discovery of the Trout and Game Stamp," *Fourteenth Philatelic Congress Book*.

Reading, Pennsylvania: American Philatelic Congress, 1948.

Cahn, William H. *The Story of Pitney Bowes.* New York: Harper and Brothers, 1961.

Carver, Fred. E. "State Fruit Tax Stamps Paid for Promoting Sales," *The American Philatelist* 74(9):658.1961.

Castenholz, Bill J. *An Introduction to Revenue Stamps.* Pacific Palisades, California: Castenholz & Sons, c. 1994.

Cayford, Philip and Arnold Selengut. *The Precancel Stamp Society's Town and Type Catalog of the United States and Territories.* Framingham, Massachusetts: The Precancel Stamp Society, 1998.

Chase, Carroll. "The United States 1847 Issue," *The Philatelic Gazette* 6(5):129–138.1916; (6):165–172.1916; 6(7):197–206.1916; 6(8):225–233.1916; 6(9):257–265.1916; 6(10):292–299.1916; 6(11):332–336.1916; 6(12):269–373.1916; 7(1):1–6.1917.

—— *The 3¢ Stamp of the United States 1851–1857 Issue.* Lawrence, Massachusetts: Quarterman Publications Inc., 1975.

Chemi, James M. "Timely Observations," *The American Philatelist* 82(4):273–278.1968.

Christian, C.W. "'Production Varieties' of Printing and Perforating, 1861–1867," *The Chronicle of the U.S. Classic Postal Issues* 26(1): 25–30.1974.

Clark, Hugh M. *Postmasters' Provisional Stamps* rev. ed. New York, N.Y.: Scott Stamp and Coin Company, 1937.

Clarke, Tom. "Free Franks and Official Mail – A Cross Section of History," *La Posta: A Journal of American Postal History* 27(2):37.1996.

Clarence W. Brazer. *Essays for U.S. Adhesive Postage Stamps.* Lawrence, Massachusetts: Quarterman Publications, 1977.

Cleland, Wallace. *BIA Plate Number Checklist: Plates 1-20,000, Revised 1990.* Belleville, Illinois: Bureau Issues Association, 1990.

—— *Printing History of Postage Dues, Series of 1894 and 1930 Flat Plates.* Bureau Issues Association Research Paper #1. Madison, Wisconsin: Private Printing, December 1992.

—— *Printing History of Washington-Franklin 3¢–$5 Denominations.* Bureau Issues Association Research Paper #5. Madison, Wisconsin: Private Printing. 1994.

—— *Printing History of Special Delivery, Parcel Post, Parcel Post Due, Special Handling, Registration, Official Mail and Postal Savings Flat Plates.* Bureau Issues Association Research Paper #6. Madison, Wisconsin: Private Printing, March, 1994.

—— *Printing History of Booklet Pane Plates, 1900–1954.* Bureau Issues Association Research Paper #8. Madison, Wisconsin: Private Printing, September 1994.

—— *Printing History of Plates used for Production of the First Bureau Issue, 1894-1903.* Bureau Issues Association Research Paper #9. Madison, Wisconsin: Private Printing. 1995.

—— "Plate Manufacture and Printing by the Bureau, 1894," *The United States Specialist* 66(1):4–10.1995.

—— *Printing History of Second Bureau Issue Plates Used for Sheet Stamps.* Bureau Issues Association Research Paper #11. Madison, Wisconsin: Private Printing. 1996.

—— *Printing History of Rotary Sheet Plates, Series of 1922.* Bureau Issues Association Research Paper #13. Madison, Wisconsin: Private Printing, May 1997.

—— *Printing History of Coil Plates, Series of 1922.* Bureau Issues Association Research Paper #14. Madison, Wisconsin: Private Printing, May 1997.

—— *Printing History of Series 1922 Flat Plates Used for Sheet Stamps, Except the 2¢ Value.* Bureau Issues Association Research Paper #15. Madison, Wisconsin: Private Printing, September 1997.

—— *Printing History of 3¢ Stuart Coil Plates Series 1932.* Bureau Issues Association Research Paper #17. Madison, Wisconsin: Private Printing. 1999.

—— *Printing History of Series 1922 Flat Plates Used for 2¢ Washington and Harding Memorial Sheet Stamps.* Bureau Issues Association Research Paper #18. Madison, Wisconsin: Private Printing, June 1999.

Cleland, Wallace and Kent Johnston. *Printing History of Washington-Franklin Flat 1¢ and 2¢ Plates and Rotary Sheet and Coil Plates.* USSS Research Paper #10. Columbus, Ohio: United States Stamp Society. 1995.

Cole, Clifford C. "United States Gossip – 20th Century – The Issue of 1902–03," *Weekly Philatelic Gossip* 45(2):42.1947.

Cole, James M. *Cancellations and Killers of the Banknote Era 1870–1894.* Columbus, Ohio: U.S. Philatelic Classics Society, Inc., 1995.

Corette, Thomas. "The 2-Cent Columbian 'Broken Hat': Accidental or Deliberate?" *American Philatelic Congress Book* 58:29–40.1992.

Corliss, William. "Perfins on the Bureau issue of 1902," *The Perfins Bulletin* January 1973.

Crown, Francis J. ed. *Confederate Postal History: An Anthology from The Stamp Specialist.* Lawrence, Massachusetts: Quarterman Publications, 1976.

Cullinan, Gerald. *The Post Office Department.* New York: Frederick A. Praeger, 1968.

Cushing, Marshall. *The Story of our Post Office: "The Greatest Government Department in all its Phases."* Boston, Massachusetts: A.M. Thayer and Company, 1893.

Cusick, Allison W. "50th Anniversary of Modern FDC's Remembered," *First Days* 43(6):452–453.1998.

Datz, Stephen R. *Catalogue of Errors on U.S. Postage Stamps.* 13th ed. Iola, Wisconsin: Krause Publications, 2005.

Davidson, Charles and Lincoln Diamant. *Stamping Our History –– The Story of the United States Portrayed on Its Postage Stamps.* New York: Carol Publishing Group, 1990.

Davis, G. H. *The Transports.* Reston, Virginia: Bureau Issues Association, 1999.

Davis, Henry F. "The Stamp of Approval," *The United States Specialist* 38(10):390–394.1967; 38(11):418–421.1967; 38(12):465–469,479.1967; 39(1):20–23.1968; 39(2):63–67.1968; 39(3):101–106.1968; 39(4):139–141.1968; 39(5):183–187.1968; 39(6):219–225.1968; 39(8):280–283.1968; 39(9):329–333.1968; 39(10):372–373.1968; 39(11):414–415.1968; 39(12):450–453.1968; 40(1):25–29.1969; 40(2):74–77.1969; 40(3):121–126.1969; 40(4):172–174.1969; 40(5):211–213.1969; 40(6):271–274.1969; 40(7):314–317.1969; 40(8):364–367.1969; 40(9):404–406.1969; 40(10):436–440.1969; 40(11):470–472.1969; 40(12):514–519.1969; 41(2):72–73.1970; 41(3):109–111.1970; 41(5):206–209.1970; 41(7):283–287; 41(8):314–318.1970; 41(11):421–425.1970.

Day, J. Edward. *My Appointed Round: 929 Days as Postmaster General.* New York: Holt, Rinehart, and Winston, c. 1965.

Denson, Ed. "The 2¢ Plate Proofs on Card: Distinguishing the Emissions," *The United States Specialist* 41(10):382–383.1970.

—— *An Introduction to Collecting Plate Number Coils.* Alderpoint, California: E. Dennson, 1986.

DeVoss, James A. "U.S. 6-cent Eisenhower Counterfeit," *American Philatelist* 85(8):692–693.1971.

Diehl, Kenneth. "The 2¢ Stamps of the First Bureau Issue, Series of 1894–1898," *The United States Specialist* 65(12):532–541.1994.

Dietz, August. *Postal Service of the Confederate States of America*. Richmond, Virginia: Dietz Printing Co., 1929.

—— *The Confederate States Post-Office Department, its Stamps & Stationery: A Record of Achievement*. Richmond, Virginia: The Dietz Press, Inc., 1948.

Durst, Sanford. *Bureau of Engraving and Printing – The First Hundred Years 1862–1962*. New York: Numismatic Publications, 1978.

Ellis, F.L. and William Maisel. *United States Commemorative and Special Printed Envelopes: 1876–1965*. State College, Pennsylvania: American Philatelic Society, 1974.

Esrati, Stephen G. *The Great Americans*. Shaker Heights, Ohio: S.G. Esrati, 1999.

Evans, Don L. *The United States 1¢ Franklin 1861–67*. Sidney, Ohio: Linn's Stamp News, 1997.

Farley, James A. *Behind the Ballots, The Personal History of a Politician*. New York: Harcourt, Brace and Company, 1938.

Farley, James A. *Jim Farley's Story, The Roosevelt Years*. New York: McGraw Hill, 1948.

Fawcett, James Waldo. "50th Anniversary of the Bureau of Engraving and Printing," *Mekeel's Weekly Stamp News* 48(3):35–39.1944.

Felix, Ervin J. *The stamp collector's guidebook of worldwide watermarks and perforations from 1840 to date*. Racine, Wisconsin: Whitman Publishing Co., 1966.

Fernald, Paul R. "Hydrometer Labels," *The Bureau Specialist* 18(8):176.1947.

Fiore, George J. "Member Urges Public Sale of Test Coils," *The United States Specialist* 44(5):230.1973.

Fiset, Louis. "Gum Breaker Experiments on BEP Definitives, 1919–31," *United States Specialist* 60(6):277–287.1989; 60(7):357–365.1989.

Frajola, Richard C., George J. Kramer, and Steven Walske. *The Pony Express, A Postal History*. New York: The Philatelic Foundation, 2005.

Frajola, Richard C., Frederick R. Mayer. *The United States Five Cent Stamp of 1856*. New York: The Collectors Club. 2005.

French, Cloudy. "The Plate Variety Specialist and His Language," *The United States Specialist* 44(8):187–197.1977.

French, Loran C. *Encyclopedia of Plate Varieties on U.S. Bureau Printed Stamps*. Arlington, Massachusetts: Bureau Issues Association, 1979.

Friedberg, Richard. "Cigarette Tubes and Tobacco Sale Tax Stamps," *Linn's Stamp News* p. 12. June 12, 1989

—— *Introduction to United States Revenue Stamps*. Sidney, Ohio: Linn's Stamp News, c. 1994.

Froom, H. A. *U.S.P.S. Watermarks*. San Diego, California: H.A. Froom, 1941.

Furman, Robert. *The 1999 Comprehensive Catalogue of United States Stamp Booklets*. Iola, Wisconsin: Krause Publications, 1999.

Gibbs, Irwin J. *The Postal Stationery of the Canal Zone*. Norfolk, Virginia: United Postal Stationary Society, 2003.

Gifford, Laurence S. "The 8¢ Bicolor, 1954 Regular Issue Rotary and Flatbed Press Printing," *The Bureau Specialist* 33(1):6–11.1962; 33(2):42–47, 52.1962

Glass, Sol. *United States Postage Stamps 1945–1952*. West Somerville, Massachusetts: Bureau Issues Association, Inc., 1954.

Gobie, Henry M. *The Speedy: A History of United States Special Delivery Service*. North Miami, Florida: Wilhelmina Gobie, 1976.

—— *US Parcel Post: A Postal History*. North Miami, Florida: Wilhelmina Gobie, 1979.

Godin, George V.H. and D. Postlewait. *Bureau Precancel Plate Numbers [of the 1/2¢ Presidential]*. USSS Research Paper #4. Columbus, Ohio: Private Press. 1994.

Goodwin, Frank E. *Goodwin's Specialized United States*. Portland, Maine: Severn-Wylie-Jewett Co. 1919.

Gouled, Paul. "The Parenthood of the Bicentennial Series," *STAMPS* 1(12):413–415.1932.

Graham, Richard B. "Banknote Era Gaston Patent and ??? Machine Cancels," *The Chronicle of the U.S. Classics* 43(2):109–113.1991.

—— *United States Postal History Sampler*. Sidney, Ohio: Linn's Stamp News, 1992.

Green, Dick. *Dick Green's Catalog of the Tuberculosis Seals of the World*. Corona: California: The Christmas Seal and Charity Stamp Society, c. 1995–1997.

Griffith, Gary. "New Earliest Documented Covers for Type II Varieties of the 2¢ Washington 1922," *The United States Specialist* 60(7):327–331.1989.

—— "The First Hundred Years: A Bureau Exhibit," *The United States Specialist* 65(7):292–310.1994.

—— *United States Stamps 1922–26*. Sidney, Ohio: Linn's Stamp News, 1997.

—— *United States Stamps 1927–32*. Sidney, Ohio: Linn's Stamp News, 2001.

Gulka, John. "Isaiah Thomas Paid Reply Postal Card – Error," *The United States Specialist* 53(3):113.1982.

Haeseler, Rob. "BIA Members Approve Name Change," *Linn's Stamp News*, p. 9. February 28, 2000.

—— "21¢ White Barn Postal Card Will Be New Workhorse Item," *Linn's Stamp News* p. 1. September 17, 2001.

Hahn, Calvet M. "Reexamining the 1847 Colors," *Collectors Club Philatelist* 65(3):195–218.1986; 65(4):271–294.1986; 65(5):367–390.1986.

Hahn, George H. *United States Famous Americans Series of 1940*. State College, Pennsylvania: American Philatelic Society, 1950.

Hanmer, Russell F. *A Collector's Guide to U.S. Machine Postmarks 1871–1925*. North Miamai, Flordia: David G. Phillips Publishing Co., 1989.

Harmer, H.R. *Postmasters Stamps of St. Louis – The Charnley and Whelen Find*, H.R. Harmer Auction Sale Catalog, December 13, 1948. H.R. Harmer, New York, N.Y.

Harvey, Althea. "Silver Anniversary of Metered Mail," *Eleventh American Philatelic Congress Book*. Cleveland, Ohio: American Philatelic Congress, 1945.

Harvey, Jack V. *First Day Covers of the Regular Postage Issue of 1922–1935*. Silver Spring, Maryland: American First Day Cover Society, 1985.

Hatcher, Robert S. "Note For U.S. Philatelists," *American Philatelist* 2(7):142–144.1888.

Haverbeck, H.D.S. "The Grill and Other Patents of Charles F. Steele Relating to Postage Stamp Production 1867–1875," *Collectors Club Philatelist* 35(2)67–85, 148.1956.

Hawkins, Joel A. and Werner Simon. *United States Postage Meter Stamp Catalog*. Phoenix, Arizona: The Authors, c.1994.

Hayes, Muriel Bemis. "1845 Provisional Postage Stamps of James M. Buchanan," *The Collectors Club Philatelist* 49(1):19–35.1970; 49(2):83–97.1970; 49(3):157–170.1970.

Helbock, Richard W. and Gary Anderson. *United States Doanes: A Catalog of Doane Cancellations Used in United States Post Offices*. 2nd ed. Scappoose, Oregon: La Posta Publications, 2002.

Helbock, Richard W. "Introduction," *Prexie Postal History*. Lake Oswego, Oregon: LaPosta Publications. p. 5. 1988.

—— *Postmarks on Postcards: An Illustrated Guide to early 20th Century U.S. Postmarks*. 2nd ed. Scappoose, Oregon: La Posta Publications, 2002.

—— ed. *Prexie Postal History*, 2nd ed. Lake Oswego, Oregon: La Posta Publications, 2003.

Heizmann, Louis J. "Wanamaker's Columbians," *Thirty-Fourth American Philatelic Congress Book*. Baltimore, Maryland: American Philatelic Congress, 1968.

Hennan, Clarence. "Stampless Covers of Chicago," *STAMPS* 45(4):126.1943.

Herst Jr., Herman. "The Postal Forgeries of 1895," *The United States Specialist* 49(10):449–450.1978.

—— *More Stories to Collect Stamps By*. Florham Park, New Jersey: The Washington Press, 1982.

Hessler, Gene. *The Engraver's Line*. Port Clinton, Ohio: BNR Press, 1993.

Hicks, John Alan. "History of the American Postal Service in Cuba," *The Collectors Club Philatelist* 16(1):4.1937.

—— *United States Internal Revenue Tax-Paid Stamps Printed on Tin-Foil and Paper Tobacco Wrappers*. New York: Hicks Philatelic Company, 1988.

Hill, George S. "History of the American Postal Service in Cuba," *The Collectors Club Philatelist* 16(1):4.1937.

Hotchner, John M. "Major Perforation Varieties of the Early 20th Century," *The United States Specialist* 53(11):515–518.1982; 53(12):543–547.1982; 54(1):15–19.1983; 54(3):133–135.1983; 54(4):177–182.1983; 54(6):270–276.1983.

—— "The Hole Truth: The Perforating of United States Postage Stamps," *The United States Specialist* 59(8):343–348.1988; 59(9):411–418.1988; 59(11):495–499.1988; 59(12):539–545.1988; 60(2):83–88.1988; 60(5):231–238.1988; 60(6):288–294.1988; 60(8):428–434.1988; 60(9):475–477.1988; 60(10):545–549.1988; 60(11):571–577.1988; 60(12):661–662.1989.

—— "Errors, Freaks, & Oddities on U.S. Stamps," *U.S. Stamps and Postal History* 1(2):35–38.1992; 1(3):35–38.1992; 2(1):35–38.1993; 3(1):35–38.1994; 3(2):27–30.1994; 3(4):27–30.1994; 3(5):27–30.1994; 4(1):27–30.1995; 5(2):27–30.1995; 5(3):27–30.1995; *U.S. Stamp News* 1(1):25–26.1995; 1(2):25–26.1996; 2(2):25–26.1996; 3(1):25–26.1997.

—— "Errors, Freaks and Oddities," in *Linn's World Stamp Almanac Millennium Edition*, Sidney, Ohio: Linn's Stamp News, 2000.

Howard, George P. *The Stamp Machines and Coiled Stamps*. New York: H.L. Lindquist Publications, 1943.

—— "Cover Collecting," *The United States Specialist* 26(3):70–73, 81.1955.

Hubbard, Elbert S. *State Revenue Catalog*. San Jose, California: Private Press, 1990.

Huff, Henry. "C3 – The 24¢ Air Mail Stamp of 1918," *The Bureau Specialist* 19(12):286–287, 302.1948.

Jaffer, Azeezaly S. ed. *USA Philatelic: The Official Source for Stamp Enthusiasts* 4(1):2.1999.

Johl, Max G . "Max G. Johl Replies," *STAMPS* 16(13):446.1936.

—— *United States Postage Stamps 1902–1935*. Lawrence, Massachusetts: Quarterman Publications, 1976.

—— *The United States Commemorative Stamps of the Twentieth Century* 2 vol. New York, N.Y.: H.L. Lindquist, 1947.

John, Richard R. *Spreading the News: The American Postal System From Franklin to Morse*. Cambridge, Massachusetts: Harvard University Press, 1995.

Johnson, Kim D. and W. Cleland. ed. *Durland Standard Plate Number Catalog*. Katy, Texas: United States Stamp Society, 2005.

Jones, William M. *A Handbook of the Stamps of Cuba* 2 vols. Winter Park, Florida: The Authors [sic], c. 1982–1988.

Juell, Rodney A. "New Variety of Gum Breaker Discovered," *The United States Specialist* 74(6):245.2003.

——— "Gum Ridges and Gum Breakers on Rotary Press Sheet Stamps of the Fourth Bureau Issue," *The United States Specialist* 74(6):246–257.2003.

——— "Project Mercury Large Die Proof," *The United States Specialist* 76(1):7–8.2005.

Kantor, Alvin Robert and Marjorie Kantor. *Sanitary Fairs: A Philatelic and Historical Study of Civil Was Benevolences*. Glencoe, Illinois: SF Publishing, 1992.

Kaufmann, Patricia A. "The Rebel Post," *Scott's Monthly Stamp Journal* 57(5):8–14.1976.

Kay, John L. "U.S. Postal Operations and the Beginning of the Civil War," *La Posta: A Journal of American Postal History* 15(2):53–55.1984.

Kellner, Mark A. "Richard Sennett Seeks to Rise above Controversy," *Stamp Collector* p. 1. August 10, 1991.

Kelsey, Douglas A. *Pictorial Meter Stamps of the United States*. Fishkill, New York: Meter Stamp Associates, c. 1993.

——— *United States Meter Stamps: First Days and Earliest-Known Uses*. Tucson, Arizona: American First Day Cover Society, c. 1996.

Kilbourne, Charles E. "Confederate Philately," *Collectors Club Philatelist*

56(1):43–47.1977.

King, Beverly S. "Notes on U.S. Stamps," *STAMPS* 2(11):372.1933.

King, Beverly S. and Max G. Johl, *The United States Postage Stamps of the Twentieth Century*. Vol 1 rev. (1901–1922), New York: H. L. Lindquist, 1937.

Kloetzel, James E. *2006 Specialized Catalogue of United States Stamps & Covers*. Scott Publishing Co.: Sidney, Ohio.2005.

Konwiser, Harry M. "'Way' Postal Markings," *Scott's Monthly Journal* 15(11):286.1935.

Koslowski, Karl. "The Story of the Finding of the 4¢ Schermack of 1902," *Thirteenth American Philatelic Congress Book*. American Philatelic Congress: Detroit, Michigan, 1947.

Kramer, George Jay. *United States Telegraph Stamps and Franks*. 2 vol. New York: Collectors Club, 1992.

Krieger, Richard and Peter Powell. *Confederate States: How To Tell the Genuine From the Counterfeit*. Ord, Nebraska: Confederate Stamp Alliance, 1994.

Kunze, Albert F. *Stamp Romances: The Lore and Legend Associated with the 1934 National Parks Series of Stamps*. Washington, D.C.: The Washington Stamp Club of the Air, 1934.

Ladd, Robert C. "The Candle Flame Stamp," *The United States Specialist* 46(3):112–113.1975.

Landau, Eliot A. ed. *Linn's U.S. Stamp Facts 19th Century*. Sidney, Ohio: Linn's Stamp News. 1999.

Langford, Frederick. *Standard Flag Cancel Encyclopedia*. Pasadena, California: by the compiler [sic], 1986.

Larkin, Richard. "Booklet Stamps On Cover," *The United States Specialist* 56(2):69–70.1985.

Larson, John L. and Kim Johnson. *Bureau Issues Association Plate Number Checklist: Plates 20,000–41,303* rev. ed. Belleville, Illinois: Bureau Issues Association, 1990.

Laurence, Michael. "Transportation Series Highly Collectible," *Linn's Stamp News* p. 3. May 6, 1985.

Lawrence, Ken. *Linn's Plate Number Coil Handbook*. Sidney, Ohio: Linn's Stamp News, 1990.

—— "A Tribute to the Transportation Coils," *American Philatelist* 105(6):530–541.1991.

—— "Collecting the Liberty Series," *The United States Specialist* 63(8):405–411.1992.

—— "The Great Americans Series," *American Philatelist* 107(4):324–343.1993.

—— "Who shaved George Washington's Face?" *American Philatelist* 107(8):732–736.1993.

—— "Americana Series 1975–83," *American Philatelist* 109(5):438–468.1995.

—— "Alphabet Soup: U.S. Non-denominated Stamps and Postal Stationery," *Scott's Stamp Monthly* 13(11):16–18.1995.

—— "The Culture of Presidential Series Collectors," *American Philatelist* 109(12):1121.1995.

—— "More on Coil Stamps, Forerunners, and Assorted Mailing Machines," *American Philatelist* 110(5):402–408.1996.

—— "The Spotlight is on U.S. Sheet and Booklet Format Dummy Stamps," *Scott Stamp Monthly*, August 1997.

—— "VAMPing – The Use of Truly Private Perfs," *American Philatelist* 111(8):702–708.1997.

—— *Pressure Sensitive Adhesive United States Stamps*. Salm Report Number 5. Chicago, Illinois: Collectors Club of Chicago, 1999. Re-published in the July 1999 issue of *American Philatelist*, pp. 700–705.

—— "A Grand Failure: The Nine-color Webfed Intaglio Huck Press," *Scott's Stamp Monthly* 20(11):22.2002.

—— "The 3¢ Statue of Liberty Coil Stamps," *Scott's Stamp Monthly* 21(27):19–20.2003.

—— "Specialized First Day Cover collecting," *Scott Stamp's Monthly* 21(9):32–33.2003.

—— "The First United States Stamped Envelopes," *Scott Stamp's Monthly* 23(9):32–38, 95–99.2005.

Lee, David G. "Q and A Corner" *The United States Specialist* 58(1):42.1987.

Linn's Stamp News. *Linn's World Stamp Almanac*, 6th ed. Sidney, Ohio: Linn's Stamp News, 2000.

Litchfield, Carter. *History of Oleomargarine Tax Stamps and Licenses in the United States*. Kemblesville, Pennsylvania: Olearisus Editions, 1968.

Littlefield, Donald B. and Sam Frank. *U.S. Booklets and Booklet Panes, 1900–1978, Volume 1: Flat Plate Regular Issues*. Katy, Texas: United States Stamp Society, 2004.

Lorenzen, Robert C. and Walter A. McIntire. "The Trans-Mississippi Series – The One-Dollar Trans-Mississippi Issue," *The United States Specialist* 43(6):265–269.1972.

Luff, John L. *The Postage Stamps of the United States*. New York: Scott Stamp & Coin Co. LTD, 1902.

—— *The Postage Stamps of the United States: 19th Century Issues. Part 1. Postmasters' Provisional Stamps*. New York: Scott Stamp & Coin Co., Ltd., 1937.

Lyons, Larry. *The Identifier for Carriers, Locals, Fakes, Forgeries and Bogus Posts of the United States*. 3 vols. Westport, Connecticut, 1998.

—— "First Day of Operation of Greig's City Despatch Post," *The Penny Post* 12(4):34–36.2004.

Macbride, Van Dyk. "The Autographed Field Letters of General Robert E. Lee," *The Stamp Specialist – India Book*. New York: H.L. Lindquist, 1946.

MacLellan, George. "New Data on the...1958 Ryukyu Provisionals," *S.P.A. Journal* 33(3):169–190.1970.

Mahler, Michael. *Catalog of United States*

Revenue-Stamped Documents of the Civil War Era by Type and Tax Rate. Rockford, Iowa: American Revenue Association, 1999.

Malakoff, Alan M. *Catalog of United States Self-Adhesive Stamps*, 4th ed. Highland Park, New Jersey: The Editor, 1999.

Maniker, Art. *The "Americana" Series Reference Manual Depicted in the "at-a-glance System"*. Lathrup Village, Michigan: A. Mann Publishing, 1999.

Markovits, Robert L. "United States: The 10¢ Registry Stamp of 1911," *Collectors Club Philatelist*, 50(2):279–289.1971; 50(6):348–354.1971; 51(1):39–48.1972.

Masters, Robert C. "The Editor's Corner," *The United States Specialist* 37(4):132.1966.

—— "A New Day Dawning?" *The United States Specialist* 42(1):18.1971.

McAfee, Earl. *Dummy Stamp Booklets*, 3rd ed. USSS Research Paper #3. Columbus, Ohio: Private Press. 1998.

McAllister, Bill. "It Looks Important but it's Slow," *Linn's Stamp News* p. 14. June 23, 1997.

—— "After 111 Years, Postage Stamps Go Private," *The Washington Post*. June 13, 2005.

McGuire, David. "Bureau Demonstration Plates," *The Essay-Proof Journal* 35(1):40.1978.

Meek, John S. "Initials of Sideographers and Plate Finishers," *The United States Specialist* 39(10):354–355,369.1968; 39(11):406–408.1968; 39(12):447–449.1968; 40(1):40–41.1969; 40(2):66–68.1969; 44(9):431–437.1973; 44(11):514–520.1973; 45(2):88–90.1974; 45(10):460–461.1974.

Mekeel, Charles H. "Special Perforations on U.S. Stamps – Issued for Use in Patented Stamp Vending and Mailing Machines," *The Philatelic Journal of America* 20(1):17–27.1909.

—— "U.S. Parcels Post," *The Philatelic Journal of America* 23(9):252.1913.

Mellone, Michael A. *Mellone's Planty Photo Encyclopedia of Cacheted First Day Covers*. 15 vols. Stewartsville, New Jersey: F.D.C. Publishing Co., 1994.

Melville, Fred J. *Postage Stamps in the Making*. London: Stanley Gibbons, Ltd., 1916.

Meyer, Henry A. et al. *Hawaii, Its Stamps and Postal History*. New York: The Philatelic Foundation, 1948.

Micarelli, Charles N. *The Micarelli Identification Guide to U.S. Stamps - Regular Issues 1847–1934*. Sidney Ohio: Scott Publishing Company, 2001.

Miers, Lewis A. "Shades of the Regular Issue of 1898," *The Bureau Specialist* 32(9):217.1961.

—— "The Two and Five Dollar Stamps of the Bureau Issues," *The United States Specialist* 35(8):309–310.1964.

Milgram, James W. "Early Railway Postmarks," *The United States Specialist* 43(5):205–211.1972.

—— *United States Registered Mail 1845–1870*. North Miami, Florida: David G. Phillips Publishing Co. Inc., 1998.

Miller, Rick. "Collectors Bullish on Faiman's St. Louis Bears; Many Lots Hit Record Multiples of Catalog Value," *Linn's Stamp News* 76(3918):1.2003.

Mintz, Allen. *Catalog of the 19th Century Stamped Envelopes, Wrappers, Cut Squares and Full Corners of the United States*. Norfolk, Virginia: United Postal Stationary Society, Inc., 2001.

Moll, Alan L. *Postal Insurance Booklets, 1965–1985*. Bureau Issues Association Research Paper #16. Madison, Wisconsin: Private Press. 1998.

Mooney, Roy E. "The 7-1-71 Affair." *Postal Service Day: Handbook and catalog for July 1, 1971 FDC Issue*. Cleveland, Georgia: R.E. Mooney, 2003.

Mosher, Bruce H.. *Discovering U. S. Rotary Booklet Pane Varieties 1926–1978*. Indialantic, Florida: Mosher Philatelics,

1979.

—— "Discovering U.S. Rotary Printed Booklet Pane Varieties (Part 9)," *The United States Specialist* 53(6):248–255.1982.

Moser, Howard A. "Notes on Aspects of the $1 Rush Lamp Americana Stamp Normal and Invert," *The United States Specialist* 66(10–12):415–430.1995.

Mueller, Barbara R. "U.S. Registry Fees, 1855–1955 – Their Philatelic and Postal Significance," *Twenty-First American Philatelic Congress Book*. Washington, D.C.: American Philatelic Congress, 1955.

—— *U.S. Postage Precancel Primer*. Cincinnati, Ohio: B.F. Deitzer, 1961.

—— "The Members Speak Up" *The United States Specialist* 45(3):98.1974.

—— "Realistic Goals for the New American Series," *The United States Specialist* 46(12):563, 584.1975.

—— "The Parcels Post 'Essay' – The Story Has Not Ended," *The United States Specialist* 72(9):393–395.2001.

Murphy, Robert T. *A Postal History/Cancellation Study of the U.S. Pacific Islands* (including the Trust Territories). State College, Pennsylvania: American Philatelic Society, 1983.

Napp, Joseph. *Napp's Numbers* 2 vols. West Orange, New Jersey: Grounds for Divorce Publications, 2001.

Nazar, Richard J. *Catalog of Plate Number Coils*. 8th ed. Somerset, New Jersey: Nazar Publications, 1995.

Neil, Randy, L. *The Trans-Mississippi Issue of 1898*. Danbury, Connecticut: Andrew Levitt, 1997.

Neill, Fred A. *The B.I.A. Check List of the Postage Stamp Booklet Covers of the United States*. USA: Bureau Issues Association 1975.

Neinken, Mortimer L. and Stanley Ashbrook. *The 1851–57 Twelve Cent Stamp*. New York: Collectors Club, 1961.

Owens, Mary Ann. "U.S. Transportation Series Coils from a Thematic Viewpoint," *The United States Specialist* 63(6):317–319.1992.

Patterson, James H. *Small Die Proofs of the 20th Century's Second Quarter*. Reston, Virginia: Bureau Issues Association, Inc., 1998.

Payne, Robert J. *United States Promotional Slogan Cancellations 1899–1940*. North Las Vegas, Nevada: Bart Billings, 2005.

Pelcyger, Scott. *Mellone's Specialized Catalogue of First Day Ceremony Programs and Events*. Stewartsville, New Jersey: FDC Publishing Co., 1989.

Petersen, C.J. "Recent Philatelic Publications – Reviewed by C.J. Petersen," *Philatelic Literature Review* 28(2):117.1979.

Perry, Elliot. "The Franklin Carrier," *Mekeel's Weekly August 23, 1919*.

—— "How Stamps are Plated," *Scott's Monthly Journal* 7(10):302–304.1926.

—— "Plating the 10¢ 1847," *Collectors Club Philatelist* 3(2):43–51.1924; 3(2):91–95.1924; 4(1):5–7.1925; 4(2):53–58.1925; 4(3):95–104.1925; 4(4):149–155.1925; 4(4):149–155.1925; 5(1):13–24.1926; 5(2):69–76.1926; 5(3):117–124.1926.

Perry, Michael O. *Folded-Style Booklet Checklist: Includes Booklets and Self-adhesive Sheetlets from 1977 to 2006*. Bureau Issues Association Research Paper #2. Katy, Texas: Private Press, 2006.

—— *An Illustrated Color Catalog of U.S. Postal and Non-Postal Booklet Covers Produced by the BEP from 1900–1978*. Katy, Texas: United States Stamp Society, 2006.

Peters, Don Preston. "A Comprehensive Confederate Collection," *First American Philatelic Congress*. Philadelphia, Pennsylvania: American Philatelic Congress. 1935.

Phillips, David G. ed. *American Stampless Cover Catalog*. 3 vols. North Miami, Florida: David G. Phillips Co. Inc., Vol. 1

published 1985; Vol. 2 published 1987; and Vol. 3 published 1993.

Piller, Stanley M. *The New York Postmaster's Provisional.* Wayne, New Jersey: Robert G. Kaufman Publishing Company, 1991.

Piszkiewicz, Leonard. "Y1.9K – Y2K," *The United States Specialist* 71(2):59–60.2000.

Piszkiewicz, Leonard et al. "Presidential Issue Usages," *United States Specialist* 70(7):317–322.1999;
70(8):363–368.1999;
70(9):415–420.1999;
70(10):459–466.1999;
70(11):487–501.1999;
70(12):544–550.1999; 71(1):17–22.2000;
71(2):75–82.2000; 71(3):131–138.2000;
71(4):173–178.2000;
71(5):221–229.2000;
71(6):267–273.2000;
71(7):313–325.2000;
71(8):369–376.2000;
71(9):411–418.2000;
71(10):465–471.2000;
71(11):507–513.2000;
71(12):557–564.2000; 72(1):27–34.2001;
72(2):63–69.2001; 72(3):123–130.2001;
72(4):171–176.2001;
72(5):219–226.2001;
72(6):266–274.2001;
72(7):314–321.2001;
72(8):363–369.2001;
72(9):411–418.2001;
72(10):459–466.2001;
72(11):507–518.2001;
72(12):555–565.2001; 73(1):27–35.2002;
73(2):63–70.2002.

Plass, Gilbert N. *Canal Zone Stamps.* Atlantic City, New Jersey: The Canal Study Group, 1986.

Pogue, Francis C. "Modern Albinos are Something Else," *Postal Stationery* 31(3):78–80.1989.

Randall, John M. *Catalog of United States Perfins: A Catalog and Album of Security Punches on United States Postage Stamps, 1908–1998.* Long Beach, New York: The Perfins Club, 1998.

Repeta, Louis E. "Watermarks in Postage Stamp Paper," *American Philatelist* 101(2):131.1987.

—— *The Stickney Rotary Printing Press.* Charleston, South Carolina: L.E. Repeta, 1996.

—— "The Stickney Rotary Printing Press – Part I," *The United States Specialist* 67(2):52–67.1996.

Reynolds, J.H. Davis and John L. Steele, Jr. "Guide Line and Other Plate Markings," *The United States Specialist* 41(7):298–299.1970.

Rich, Stephen G. "Precancelled Coil Stamps," *The American Philatelist* 47(9):485–486.1934

Richardson, Bob. "The Pony Express Anniversary," *Linn's Weekly Stamp News* p. 323. March 23, 1940.

Roper, Daniel C. *The United States Post Office.* New York: Funk and Wagnalls, 1917.

Rose, Jon. *Classic United States Imperforate Stamps.* Sidney, Ohio: Linn's Stamp News, 1990.

—— *United States Postage Stamps of 1869.* Sidney, Ohio: Linn's Stamp News, 1990.

Rosen, Steven. "The Events Leading up to the Postmaster Provisionals," *The United States Specialist* 50(8):399–401.1979.

—— *United States Postage Stamps of 1869.* Sidney, Ohio: Linn's Stamp News, 1996.

Rustad, Roland E. *The Prexies.* Belleville, Illinois: Bureau Issues Association, Inc., 1994.

Rybalka, Michel. "Remarks on Some Recent Issues," *The United States Specialist* 59(3):123–126.1988.

Saadi, Wade E. "The 5¢ and 10¢ General Issue of 1847," *American Philatelist* 111(3):226–230.1997;
111(4):330–335.1997;
111(5):442–451.1997.

Savakis, A.J. "Barcoding in the U.S.A. – The A - B - C's," *Machine Cancel Forum* (198):2345. July 1998.

Schirmer, Joe. "What Cinderella Collecting Can Do For You," *The S. Allan Taylor Society Journal* (Second Series) 1(6):7–8.1978.

Schmid, Paul W. *The Expert's Book: A Practical Guide to the Authentication of United States Stamps; Washington/Franklin Issues 1908–1923.* Huntington, New York: Palm Press, 1990.

Schnall, G. William. "A Precancel Primer," *The United States Specialist,* 55(11):495–499.1984; 55(12):551–552.1984; 56(1):27–28.1985; 56(2):57–59.1985; 56(3):105–107.1985; 56(4):173–175.1985.

Schoberlin, Melvin H. *Ryukyu Islands: Lists of Post Offices under the Administration of the United States Government (1945–1961).* Yokoska, Kanagawa, Japan: Mogollon Press, 1962.

Schreiber, Michael. "Great Americans to Continue with Hershey," *Linn's Stamp News* pp. 1, 25. November 21, 1994.

—— "New Linerless Coils Not Ready for Prime Time," *Linn's Stamp News* p. 8. April 7, 1997.

Schulman, Richard C. "Express Mail Corporate Account Labels," *The United States Specialist* 50(2):93–94.1989.

—— "Postage Validation Imprinter," *Scott Stamp Monthly* 12(2)16–18.1993.

Scott, J. Walter. "Washington Notes," *The Metropolitan Philatelist* 18(3):19.1902.

Scott Publishing Company. *Scott Specialized Catalogue of United States Stamps and Covers.* Sidney, Ohio: Amos Press, 2005.

Segal, Stanley B. *Errors, Freaks and Oddities on U.S. Stamps: Question Marks in Philately.* White Plains, New York: Bureau Issues Association, 1979.

Shively, Jr., Frank. "Transportation Coils – 'Small Number' Varieties," *The United States Specialist* 57(6):266–269.1986.

Short, Simine ed. *Via Airmail, An Aerophilatelic Survey of Events, Routes, and Rates.* Chicago, Illinois: The American Air Mail Society, 1992.

Shreiber, Michael. "Monroe Stamp Will Have Star-perforations; Elliptical and Die-cut Perfs on Other Stamps," *Linn's Stamp News* p. 1. March 27, 1995.

Silver, Philip. "Random Thoughts on U.S. Air Mails," *The Aero Philatelist Annals* 20(2):59–62.1977.

Simpson, Tracy W. *U.S. Postal Markings 1851–'61 and Related Mail Services.* Berkley, California: T.W. Simpson. 1959.

Skinner, Huber C. and Amos Eno. *United States Cancellations 1845–1869.* New Orleans, Louisiana: Heritage Press, 1980.

Skinner, Hubert C., Erin Gunter, and Warren Sanders. *The New Dietz Confederate States Catalog and Handbook.* Miami, Florida: Blogg & Laurence Publishing Co. Inc., 1986.

Slater, A.B. *The Stamps of the Providence, R.I. Postmaster, 1846–1847.* Providence, Rhode Island: A.B. Slater, 1930.

Sloane, George B. "Topical Notes on United States Stamps," *Collectors Club Philatelist* 1(2):59.1922.

—— "The Trans-Mississippi Issue of 1898 (The So-Called Omaha Issue)," *The Green Book* 9:3–31. New York, New York: H. L. Lindquist, 1943.

—— "Perforating – Idiosyncrasies of Stamp Collecting," *Sloane's Column.* West Summerville, Massachusetts: Bureau Issues Association. 1961.

—— *New York Postmaster's Stamp Used From Washington.* Somerville, Massachusetts: The Bureau Issues Association, 1961.

Sloat, Ralph L. *Farley's Follies.* Federalsburg, Maryland: Bureau Issues Association Inc., 1979.

Smith, David W. ed. *Precancelled Envelopes of the United States* 3rd ed. Missoula, Montana: Precancel Stamp Society, 2003.

Snee, Charles R. "Upcoming Stamps, Stationery for June 20 Rate Increase Could

Mean More Than 50 Distinct, Collectible Varieties," *Linn's Stamp News* p. 1. April 29, 2002.

—— "New Heroes Stamp to be Issued June 7 in New York, Nation's Second Semipostal Remembers Sept 11," *Linn's Stamp News* p. 37. June 3, 2002.

—— "Obituary, John R. Boker Jr. 1913–2003," *Linn's Stamp News*, May 12, 2003.

—— "12 Happy New Year Designs Return Jan 6 on Pane of 24," *Linn's Stamp News*, pp. 1, 18. January 3, 2005.

Southgate, Hugh M. "The P.P.N.A. Becomes the B.I.A.," *Correspondence*. March 29, 1930.

—— "New Stamps," *The Bureau Specialist* 3(4):28.1932.

—— "District of Columbia Beverage Tax Paids," *The Bureau Specialist* 8(5):56–57. 1937.

—— "The Bureau Issues Association – An Outline of its Activities," *Weekly Philatelic Gossip* 23(22):783.1937.

—— "The Presidential Series," *The Bureau Specialist* 9(4):37–38.1938.

Springer, Sherwood. *Springer's Handbook of North American Cinderella Stamps Including Taxpaid Revenues*. Hawthorne, California: Sherwood Springer, 1975.

Stambaugh, Richard. "More on the Autopost Experiment," *The United States Specialist* 62(10):548.1991.

Stark, John S. and Alfred Boerger. *Luminescent U.S. Stamps*. Ord, Nebraska: Quiz Graphic Arts, Inc., 1965.

Starnes, Charles J. *United States Letter Rates to Foreign Destinations 1847–1876*. rev. ed. Louisville, Kentucky: Leonard H. Hartmann, 1989.

Steiger, William C. *A Handbook of United States Postage Meters, Including Meter Sloans*. Verona, New Jersey: Stephen G. Rich, 1940.

Stein, E. P. *Flight of the Vin Fiz*. New York: Arbor House, 1985.

Stern, Edward. *History of the "Free Franking" of Mail in the United States*. New York: H.L. Lindquist, 1936.

Stiles, Kent B. "Of Topical Interest," *Scott's Monthly Journal* 2(11):14–17.1922.

Stone, Robert G. "Why Collect Proofs and Essays?" *The Essay-Proof Journal* 26(1):13.1969.

Stott, Jay B. "Rate Usages of the Fourth Bureau Issue," *The United States Specialist* 60(4):183–186.1989; 60(5):239–242.1989; 60(6):309–312.1989; 60(7):333–339.1989; 60(9):469–474.1989; 60(10):525–532.1989; 60(12):653–657.1989; 61(1):19–26.1990; 61(2):93–97.1990; 61(3):148–152.1990; 61(4):211–216.1990; 61(6):309–313.1990; 61(7):411–417.1990.

—— "The Postal War Tax Rates of 1917–1919," *The United States Specialist* 64(5):218–219.1993.

Summerfield, Arthur E. *United States Mail: The Story of the United States Postal Service*. New York: Holt, Rinehart, and Winston, 1960.

Summers, Jerry. ed. *Catalog of the 20th Century Stamped Envelopes, Wrappers, Cut Square and Full Corners of the United States*. 2nd ed. Norfolk, Virginia: United Postal Stationary Society, 2004.

Swan, Walter M. *An Illustrated Guide to Meter Stamp Collecting with Valuations Quoted on Most Basic Types* 4th ed. Palmer, New York: W. Swan, 1967.

Tatelman, Edward. *Canal Zone Postage Stamps*. Balboa Heights, Canal Zone: Canal Zone Postal Service. 1961.

Thomas, William K. *History and Evolution of Metered Postage*. State College, Pennsylvania: American Philatelic Society,

Research and Literature Committee, c. 1962.

Thomson, Alan. "Hunting the Bison: Hunting for Answers," *The United States Specialist* 72(6):245–251.2001.

Toppan, George L., Hiram E. Deats, and Alexander Holland. *An Historical Reference List of the Revenue Stamps of the United States, Including the Private Die Proprietary Stamps*. Boston, Massachusetts: Boston Philatelic Society, c. 1899.

Treasury Department. *History of the Bureau of Engraving and Printing, 1862–1962*. New York, N.Y.: Sanford J. Durst Numismatic Publications, 1978.

Trumbull, Arthur J. "United States Stamps Overprinted for Use in Cuba, Guam, Puerto Rico and the Philippines," *U.S. Possessions Stamp Exhibition*. Philadelphia, Pennsylvania: National Philatelic Museum 1(11):53–67.1949.

Turner, George T. "What Comprises a Revenue Collection?" *American Philatelist* 54(6):391.1941.

—— ed. *Sloane's Column*. West Somerville, Massachusetts: Bureau Issues Association, 1961.

—— *Essays and Proofs of United States Internal Revenue Stamps*. West Somerville, Massachusetts: Bureau Issues Association, 1974.

Undersander, Dan. *Catalog of United States Stamped Envelope Essays and Proofs*. Norfolk, Virginia: United States Postal Stationery Society, 2003.

United States Post Office Department. "Railway Mail Service," *Post Office Department, Annual Reports for the fiscal year ended June 30, 1908*. Washington, D.C.: Government Printing Office, 1908. p. 55.

—— *Annual Report of the Postmaster General*. Washington D.C.: United States Post Office, 1910.

—— *Annual Reports for the Fiscal Year Ended June 30, 1911. Report of the*

Postmaster General. Miscellaneous Reports. Washington D.C.: United States Post Office, 1911.

—— *United States Domestic Postage Rates 1789–1956*. POD Publication 15. Washington D.C.: U.S. Post Office Department, 1956.

United States Postal Service. *The United States Postal Service: An American History 1775–2002*. Washington, D.C.: Government Relations, USPS, undated.

—— *Prominent American Series: Issues of 1965–1975*. Washington, D.C.: U.S. Government Printing Office, 1978.

—— *The Americana Series: Issues of 1975–1981*. Washington, D.C.: U.S. Government Printing Office, 1981.

—— *$1.00 Johns Hopkins Regular Stamp*. Postal Bulletin #21724. Washington, D.C.: United States Postal Service. May 11, 1989.

—— *DMM (Domestic Mail Manual) Notice, Free Mailing Privilege for Operation Desert Shield*. Postal Bulletin #21779. Washington, D.C.: United States Postal Service. December 27 1990.

—— *The Postal Service Guide to U. S. Stamps*. 30th ed. New York, New York: HarperCollins, 2003.

Unkrich, Steven R. *1954 Liberty Series Plate Activity & Precancel Checklists*. Bureau Issues Association Research Paper #12. Columbus, Ohio: Private Press. 1997.

—— "Test Stamps," *Krause Minkus Standard Catalogue of U.S. Stamps*. 7th ed. Iola, Wisconsin: Krause Publishing, 2004.

Ward Jr., Philip H. "Proposed Presidential Series," *Mekeel's Weekly Stamp News* 49(21):270.1935.

Warren, Arnold W. "The Forgotten Philippines," *American Philatelist* 61(4):266–268.1948.

Wasson, Stanley H. *Catalogue of U.S. and Canadian philatelic exhibition seals*. New York: Harvey Dolin & Company, c. 1946.

Waud, Morrison. "Problems of Continental Secret Marks," *Chronicle of the U.S. Classic Postal Issues* 25(3):171–175.1973.

Weiss, Larry. *The Washington-Franklin Heads: Simplified!* Belleville, Illinois: Bureau Issues Association, 1997.

—— "Designing and Engraving the Washington-Franklin Series," *The United States Specialist* 62(3):147–153.1991; 62(4):229–242.1991; 62(6):327–340.1991; 62(8):427–434.1991; 62(10):527–547.1991; 62(12):661–672.1991; 63(2):67–78.1992; 63(3):113–124.1992; 63(4):201–206.1992; 63(5):239–240.1992; 63(6):339–343.1992.

West, Christopher. *The Revenue Stamps of the United States.* Pacific Palisades, California: Castenholz and Sons, 1979.

Westerberg, Joshua F. *Plating the Hawaiian Numerals.* Honolulu, Hawaii: Mission Press, 1968.

White, R.H. *The Papers and Gums of United States Postage Stamps, 1847–1909.* Germantown, Maryland: Philatelic Research Ltd., 1983.

—— *Encyclopedia of the Colors of United States Postage Stamps.* 4 vols. Germantown, Maryland: Philatelic Research Ltd., 1986.

Willard, Edward L. *The United States Two Cent Red Brown of 1883–1887,* 2 vols. New York: H.L. Lindquist, Inc., 1970.

William, L.N. *Fundamental's of Philately.* rev. ed. State College, Pennsylvania: American Philatelic Society, 1990.

Winick, Les. "The Spotlight is on the Self-service Stamp Store," *Scott's Stamp Monthly* 14(1):39.1995.

Winter, Bob. *Prominent Americans Series Bureau Precancel 1965–1973.* Spring Valley, New York: B. Winter, 1974.

Wood, Kenneth A. "Perforation," *This is Philately* vol. 2 (G–P). Albany, Oregon: Van Dahl Publications, 1982.

Wylie, William W. ed. *Western Stamp Collector* p. 4. January 1, 1949.

Yeager, Charles. "U.S. Banknote Provides Love Sheet Stamp Details," *Linn's Stamp News* p. 1. April 30, 1990.

York, Norton D. "The Reason for the Two Types of the 1894 $1 Stamp," *American Philatelist* 79(1):39.1965.

Youngblood, Wayne L. "Service-inscribed-only Coil Call for USPS Clarification," *Linn's Stamp News* p. 1. June 20, 1988.

—— "United States 25¢ Self-adhesive Stamp Being Test-marketed in 15 Cities for 30 Days," *Linn's Stamp News*, p. 1. November 20, 1989.

—— *Stamps that Glow.* Sidney, Ohio: Linn's Stamp News, 1990.

—— "U.S. Stamps Below 8¢ Face Value Being Issued without Tagging," *Linn's Stamp News*, p. 1. March 11, 1991.

—— "Perforation Varieties on 1991 United States Banknote Issues," *The United States Specialist* 63(7):380–382.1992.

—— "Plate Varieties Give Challenge, Rewards," *Linn's Stamp News* p. 18. August 17, 1992.

—— "A New Section is Added for an Increasingly Popular Collecting Area," *1994 Scott Specialized Catalogue of United States Stamps.* Sidney, Ohio: Scott Publishing Co., 1993.

—— "Second Self-stick U.S. Test Coil Surfaces in Coil Rolls of 3,000," *Stamp Collector* p. 1. December 16, 1996.

Appendix C
Internet Resources

home.earthlink.net/~davinod/Initials.htm
Plate finisher and siderographer initials on
Washington-Franklins.

http://cscss.home.att.net Christmas Seal
and Charity Stamp Society.

http://marginal-markings.usstamps.org
Marginal markings.

members.aol.com/jlkcsa/index.htm
Confederate States of America Stamps and
Postal History.

www.1847usa.com U.S. Stamps 1847 USA.

www.7-1-71firstdaycovers.com First day
covers of *Scott* 1396.

www.afdcs.org American First Day Cover
Society.

www.askphil.org AskPhil, The Collectors
Club of Chicago.

www.asppp.org American Society for
Philatelic Pages and Panels.

www.csalliance.org The Confederate Stamp
Alliance.

www.efoers.org Errors, Freaks, and Oddities.

www.ericjackson.com Eric Jackson's website. Searchable listing of philatelic literature with an emphasis on U.S. and
Worldwide revenue. Includes links to
other informational sites on revenues.

www.eskimo.com/~rkunz/mposhome.html
Mobile Post Office Society.

www.hillcity-mall.com/SRS/ The State
Revenue Society.

www.jlkstamps.com United States of
America Modern Commemorative and
Regular Issue Stamps 1929–2000.

www.machinecancel.org The International
Machine Cancel Society.

www.pbbooks.com U.S. and worldwide
philatelic literature.

www.pennypost.org The Carriers and
Locals Society.

www.philbansner.com Phil Bansner's website. Allows a search by title, author, type
of book, auction company name, auction
number, sale date or "name" and a "wild-
card" search.

www.pnc3.org The Plate Number Coil
Collectors Club.

www.postal-markings.org The Auxiliary
Markings Club.

www.postalmuseum.si.edu The National
Postal Museum, The Smithsonian
Institution.

www.precancels.com The Precancel Stamp
Society.

www.rdhinstl.com/revs.htm A general reference to the *Scott* listed revenues.

www.revenuer.org The American Revenue
Association.

www.rigiastamps.com The source for alternative philately.

www.siegelauctions.com/enc/enc.htm
Robert A. Siegel Auction Galleries, Inc.,
Encyclopedia of Stamps.

www.sil.si.edu/libraries/npm-hp.htm The
National Postal Museum Library, The
Smithsonian Institution.

www.stamps.org The American Philatelic
Society (APS). Contains a link to the
American Philatelic Research Library,
where the library's card catalog, article
index and journal holdings can be
searched. Members of the APS may borrow most of the library's holdings through
the U.S. mail.

www.theswedishtiger.com/usstamps
United States Stamps, A Pictorial and
Price Guide.

www.us1909.com 1909 United States
Commemoratives.

www.uspcs.org U. S. Philatelic Classics
Society, Inc.

www.usstamps.org United States Stamp
Society.

www.webacps.org. The American
Ceremony Program, USPS First Day and
Philatelic-Related Event Programs.

Appendix D
Benefactors

Stanley S. Abel
Gilbert P. Ahrens
Albert Aldham
Steven A. Altman
American Plate Number Single Society
Charlie Austin
Roland Austin
George W. Baehr
David L. Bailey
Larry F. Ballantyne
John Ely Barkdoll
Lynn R. Batdorf
Dr. Rainard M. Beer
Steven R. Belasco
Dr. Jerome Beller
Mark A. Bennett
William Robert Benson, Jr.
Alan M. Berkun
James & Jerrie Berryhill
Phillip R. Beutel
John A Bizal
David Bize
McClellan G. Blair
John H. Bloor
Lyle C. Boardman
Frank Braithwaite
Brattleboro (VT) Stamp Club
John M. Bridges
British Virgin Islands Philatelic Society
Roger Brody
Douglas R. Brown
Judith Lynn Bruno
Lewis Burchett
Richard E. Burdsall
Maurice M. Bursey
Ralph J. Calabrese
Calumet Stamp Club
Alfred E. Cambridge, Jr.
Rosa M. Cardell
Charles E. Chambers, Jr.
Joseph S. Chervenyak
John Chunka
Dominick Cinti
Wallace Cleland
David M. Cobb

Alan E. Cohen
Stephen E. Cohen
Jeffery L. Cole
Harold B. Collins, Jr.
Collectors Club of Chicago
Columbian Stamp Company
Christopher J. Conlin, M.D.
Frank & Carol Covey
William T. Crowe
James W. Crumpacker
Ronald G. Damm
Doug D'Avino
Sheila J. D'Avino
J. William Davis
Des Moines Philatelic Society
James Leonard Diamond
DIB Enterprises
Gus Dimino
James F. Doetsch
Donald R. Dolan, Jr.
Wayne B. Dowdey
William F. Droessler
W. Douglas Drumheller
Wayne & Jennifer Duerkes
Lambert R. Dumask
Peter G DuPuy
Russ Dyer
David Eeles
Craig A. Eggleston
F. R. Ellwanger, Jr.
John G. Engle, Jr.
Merle Farrington
Jonathan Fein
Robert W. Finertie
Edward F. Fisher
Mark R. Forster
Sam Frank, in memory of Don Littlefield
John Leonard Frasca
Richard Friedberg
Herbert J. Friedman
Robin P. Friedman
Marshall Gates
Dr. Wallace Gaye
Melvin Gettlan
Charles R. Gherman
E. Gibson
Richard A. Giessler
David E. Gilchrist
Richard F. Glaze
Glen Ellyn Philatelic Club
Norman Jay Goldman
Hans Jakob Gram

Warren Granek, D.D.S.
Kenneth B. Grant
Eben W. Graves
James P. Griffin
Harry S. Griffith III
Charles G. Groneman
John R. Grosvenor
William A. Gulley
Harry Hagendorf
Michael D. Hancox
Lodge L. Hanlon
Robert J. Hansen
Charles A. Hanson
LTC John T. Hardy, Jr.
Edward K. Harr, Sr.
William R. Harris
Donald Hauenstein, Jr.
Chris Headley
Irv Heimburger
Robert A. Herman, M.D.
Charles W. Herren, Jr.
Douglas A. Hilton
Bob Hohertz
Jim & Friederike Holbrook
Douglas L. Horka
Houston Philatelic Society
Jonathan Humble
Thomas Iverson
Tom Jacks – Mountainside Stamps
Charles W. Jackson
Eric Jackson
Michael Jaffe
Richard A. Jeanor
Paul L. Jenkins
Barbara J. Johnson
Gregory A. Johnson
Kim D. Johnson
Johnson Space Center Stamp Club
James K. Joy (in memory)
Rodney Juell
Francis Jurkowski
Hikoharu Kagawa
Jerome & Jean Kasper
Jerry A. Katz
Patricia A. Kaufmann
Kennebec Valley Stamp and Collector's Club
Sean D. Kennedy
Kennedy's Stamps & Coins, Inc.
Carl M. Knudsen
James Larry Kobelt
John E. Kostinas, M.D.
Mutsuo Kozuka

George Jay Kramer
Don Kurki
Greg Lachowicz
J. Frank LaDue
Neal P. Lamb
Michael Lampson
Eliot A. Landau
Richard F. Larkin
John L. Larson
Alfred LaSala
Benjamin Y. Lee
Jeffery R. Lee
Earle Leeder
Joann & Kurt Lenz
Robert M. Levy
Keith Lichtman
W. Curtis Livingston
Eric J. Lobenfeld
Rob Loeffler
Nicholas A. Lombardi
Kevin G. Lowther
Edwin H. Lugowski, Jr.
Millard H. Mack
Tad Mackie
Ronald Maifeld
Stewart Mann
Raymond P. Mariella
Robert L. Markovits
Erroll Charles Marsh
Robert W. Martin
Theodore W. Maynard
Charles B. McClure
H. F. McDermott
Thomas McFarland
Chuck & Jan McFarlane
Bill McMurray
William F. Merlin, Jr.
Michael Meyer
Joel A. Miele, Sr.
Ward F. Milligan
Forrest C. Mischler, M.D.
Paul G. Moore
Barbara R. Mueller
John Murray
Richard F. Murray
Thomas P. Myers
Milton W. Nachman
Ralph H. Nafziger
Harold Nogle
Hon. Patrick L. O'Connor
Omaha Philatelic Society
Timothy O'Shea

Armando Paciello
Hennell S. Pack
Daniel S. Pagter
John M. Pancia, Jr.
Alan Parsons
James H. Patterson
Scott Pelcyger
George Perkins, Jr.
Michael O. Perry
Orville Peterson
Philatelic Club of Will County
John R. Phillips, DDS, MSD
Plate Number Coil Collectors Club (PNC3)
Bernard L. Pollack
Anne J. Porte
R. Craig Potter
John A. Pratt
Preston
Christopher Principe
Dr. W.A. Rader
Dr. & Mrs. Reuben A. Ramkissoon
Louis E. Reif
David A. Reyno
William and Peter Rice
Peter Rikard
John & Kathryn Robie
Adam & Renee Rod
Steven & Francine Rod
Gary M. Roush
John Ruocco
Quality Investors, Ltd.
Lawrence C. Salameno
Lawrence W. Salomon
Alexander Jerry Savakis
Henry B. Scheuer
Edwin C. Schneider
Jacques C. Schiff, Jr.
Theodore R. Schrock, M.D.
Mr. Kim R. Schroeder
Richard D. Schultz
William O. Schuman
Seth & Elana Rod Schwartz
Terry R. Scott
Lawrence N. Secchiaroli
Jorge M. Serpa
Frank Servas, Jr.
David Servies
Scott A. Shaulis
Lawrence Sherman, M.D.
Frank L. Shively, Jr. M.D.
William W. Sihler
Clark Smeltzer, Jr. M.D.

Michael D. Smith
Dr. Richard E. Smith
Charles E. Snee IV
Alan M. Solinger, M.D.
John D. Spangler
Paul Sparling
Arthur R. Spengler
Richard F. Spiek
Thomas A. Spina
Frederick A. Stahl
David P. Stiff
Seymour B. Stiss
David Sugar
Edward L. Suntrup
Robert C. Swed
Mark Taylor
Ron Tellier
Richard A. Thalheim, Jr.
Albert Thirkill
Robert B. Thompson
Wilfred L. Thornthwaite
Harvey G. Tilles
Verapon Towannasut, M.D.
James D. Trenchard
Frank Tritto
John M. Trusty
Michael S. Turrini
Itsuwo Uwoki
Norman W. Vachowiak
Charles Van Pelt
George Voltzow
George Waaser
Jeffrey Luckey Ward
Gregory Scott Ward
Alan Warren
Raymond E. Weber
Gary B. Weiss
David Wessely
The Westfield Stamp Club
West Suburban Stamp Club
Homer Whitacre
E. L. White, Jr.
Richard C. White
Rudolph W. Wittemann
Kirby E. Willems
Gary S. Wong
Michael Wrzesien
Tassilo Wunnike
James P. Yex
Nicholas Zevos
Ken Zierer
Max G. Zollner